教育部人文社科重点研究基地中山大学中国非物质
文化遗产研究中心非物质文化遗产保护研究丛书

Intangible Cultural Heritage Safeguarding Research Series
edited by the Institute of Chinese Intangible Cultural Heritage
at Sun Yat-sen University, one of the key research institutes
of humanities and social sciences in universities approved and
supported by the Ministry of Education of China

文化对话：中美非物质文化遗产论坛

Cultural Discourse:
China-US Intangible Cultural
Heritage Forums

宋俊华　[美]比尔·艾伟（Bill Ivey）　黄永林　编

中山大学出版社
·广州·

版权所有　翻印必究

图书在版编目（CIP）数据

文化对话：中美非物质文化遗产论坛／宋俊华，［美］比尔·艾伟（Bill Ivey），黄永林编.—广州：中山大学出版社，2017.11

（教育部人文社科重点研究基地中山大学中国非物质文化遗产研究中心非物质文化遗产保护研究丛书）

ISBN 978-7-306-06228-4

Ⅰ.①文… Ⅱ.①宋…②比…③黄… Ⅲ.①非物质文化遗产—保护—中国、美国—文集—汉、英 Ⅳ.①G122-53②G171.22-53

中国版本图书馆 CIP 数据核字（2017）第 281585 号

出 版 人：徐　劲
责任编辑：裴大泉　李海东
封面设计：曾　斌
责任校对：刘丽丽　赵　婷
责任技编：黄少伟
出版发行：中山大学出版社
电　　话：编辑部 020-84110771，84110283，84111997，84110779
　　　　　发行部 020-84111998，84111981，84111160
地　　址：广州市新港西路 135 号
邮　　编：510275　　传　真：020-84036565
网　　址：http://www.zsup.com.cn　E-mail:zdcbs@mail.sysu.edu.cn
印 刷 者：佛山市浩文彩色印刷有限公司
规　　格：787mm×1092mm　1/16　27.5 印张　655 千字
版次印次：2017 年 11 月第 1 版　2017 年 11 月第 1 次印刷
定　　价：168.00 元

如发现本书因印装质量影响阅读，请与出版社发行部联系调换

本书由中山大学中国非物质文化遗产研究中心、
美国亨利·鲁斯基金会、
华中师范大学国家文化产业研究中心共同资助出版。

The book is financially supported by the Institute of Chinese Intangible Cultural Heritage at Sun Yat-sen University, The Henry Luce Foundation, the National Research Center of Cultural Industries at Central China Normal University.

目 录 / CONTENTS

序 言 ·················· 比尔·艾伟 宋俊华 I

基础理论研究

中国非物质文化遗产保护政策与企业实践 ·················· 宋俊华（3）
美国历史保护运动和非物质文化遗产 ·················· 迈克尔·安·威廉姆斯（12）
中国城市化与非物质文化遗产保护 ·················· 高小康（18）
美国的音乐录制品版权：挑战、问题及对文化遗产政策的诉求 ·········· 丹尼尔·希伊（21）
非物质文化遗产的本真性问题 ·················· 刘晓春（24）
关于黄永林《从文化生态学角度看待非物质文化遗产的保护》的讨论
·················· 杰西卡·安德森·特讷（32）
谁在生产？怎样保护？
——透视中国非物质文化遗产的"生产性保护" ·················· 张士闪（35）
美国国家非物质文化遗产项目的特点、相互关系以及挑战 ·············· 罗伯特·巴龙（45）

案例分析、方法和技术

上中西部文化研究中心的民俗研究 ·················· 詹姆斯·P.利里（53）
民俗文化的遗产化、本真性和传承主体问题
——以浙江衢州"九华立春祭"为中心的考察 ·················· 王霄冰（56）
全国牧童诗会：关于文化真实性的个案研究 ·················· 查理·泽曼（70）

山野奇花的旷世魅力
　　——"撒叶儿嗬"简论 ………………………………………… 刘守华（72）
简论史密森尼民俗节的策展 ………………………………… 詹姆斯·I.道伊奇（75）
中国非物质文化遗产数字化技术运用研究 ……………… 黄永林　谈国新（78）
如何在遭受飓风"卡特里娜"和"丽塔"之后的休斯顿生存
　　——以幸存者为中心的灾难应对个案研究 ……… 卡尔·林达尔　帕特·嘉斯伯（88）
"熊龙"辨
　　——兼谈龙的起源与稻作文明 …………………………… 蒋明智（93）
美国的拼布
　　——在保存与保护传统文化遗产形式时的选择和挑战 ………… 玛莎·迈克道尔（100）
保护史诗吟唱传统的多形式实践：对于杜尔伯特部落格萨尔王史诗的个案
　　研究 ……………………………………………………………… 朝戈金（107）
虚拟展览《Dane Wajich – Dane-zaa原住民的故事与歌谣：梦想者与他们的
　　土地》：应用民族志与原住民生活展示 …………………… 安伯·瑞丁特（109）
非物质文化遗产传承人保护模式研究
　　——以中国湖北宜昌民间故事讲述家孙家香、刘德培和刘德方为例 …… 黄永林（117）
档案馆在保存和查询非物质文化遗产中的作用 …………… 尼克尔·塞勒（128）
非物质文化遗产项目"阿肯阿依特斯"的国际传播 ………………… 王霄冰（131）

持续关注的问题

关于"非遗"概念的再界定 ………………………………… 苑　利　顾　军（151）
认识幸福社区的传统实践
　　——打造可持续的非物质文化遗产保护模型 ……………… 艾米·基奇纳（157）
非物质文化遗产保护与族群冲突弥合 ………………………… 宋俊华（163）
与移民社区一起工作：民族志学最佳实践方式 ……… 德伯·兰坦兹·舒克（169）
非物质文化遗产生产性保护概念、原则及相关问题思考 ………… 萧　放（174）

后　记 …………………………………………………………………………（179）

Introduction ·· Song Junhua, Bill Ivey (181)

Major Themes and Overviews

Policy and Enterprise Practice of Intangible Cultural Heritage in China ······ Song Junhua (189)
The US Historic Preservation Movement and Intangible
    Cultural Heritage ·· Michael Ann Williams (202)
Chinese Urbanization and Intangible Cultural Heritage Protection ············ Gao Xiaokang (210)
Music Recording Copyright in the United States: Challenges, Issues,
    and the Need for Cultural Heritage Policy ···················· Daniel Sheehy (215)
Concerning the Authenticity of Intangible Cultural Heritage ···················· Liu Xiaochun (221)
Overview and Response to Huang Yonglin's "Intangible Cultural Heritage
    Safeguarding in the Vision of Cultural Ecology" ················ Jessica Anderson Turner (233)
Who is Producing? How to Protect?
    —In-depth Analysis of the "Productive Protection" of China's
        Intangible Cultural Heritage ·································· Zhang Shishan (237)
American State Intangible Cultural Heritage Programs: Characteristics,
    Interrelationships and Challenges ································ Robert Baron (251)

Case Studies, Techniques, Technology

The Center for the Study of Upper Midwestern Cultures ······················ James P. Leary (263)
Folkways as Intangible Cultural Heritage and the Question of Authenticity
    —A Study of "The Beginning of Spring" Festival in Jiuhua,
        Zhejiang Province, the People's Republic of China
        ·· Wang-Riese Xiaobing (266)
The National Cowboy Poetry Gathering: A Case Study in Authenticity
        ·· Charlie Seemann (285)
The Charm of a Wildflower
    —A Brief Survey Concerning "Saye'erhe" ························ Liu Shouhua (288)
Curating a Smithsonian Folklife Festival Program ························ James I. Deutsch (291)
Research on the Application of Digital Technology to Work in Chinese Intangible
    Cultural Heritage ·· Huang Yonglin, Tan Guoxin (295)

Surviving Katrina and Rita in Houston: A Case Study of A Survivor-Centered
　　Disaster Response ·········· Carl Lindahl, Pat Jasper (309)
Bear or Dragon?
　　——The Origin of the Dragon and China's Rice-Cultivating Civilization
　　·········· Jiang Mingzhi (316)
The "American" Quilt
　　——The Intersections and Challenges of Preserving and Safeguarding
　　a Traditional Cultural Heritage Form ·········· Marsha MacDowell (328)
Multiform Practices for Safeguarding Epic Singing Tradition: A Case Study of
　　King Gesar Epic in the Dur-bud Tribe ·········· Chao Gejin (337)
Applied Ethnography and Indigenous Representation in the Virtual Exhibit *Dane
　　Wajich – Dane-zaa Stories and Songs*: *Dreamers and the Land* ·········· Amber Ridington (339)
Research on the Mode of Protecting the Inheritors of Intangible Cultural Heritage
　　——Take the Folk Story Tellers Sun Jiaxiang, Liu Depei and Liu
　　Defang in Yichang, Hubei, China as An Example ·········· Huang Yonglin (349)
The Role of Archives in the Preservation of and Access to Intangible Cultural
　　Heritage ·········· Nicole Saylor (365)
Chinese "Kazakh Aqin Aytis" in Germany: The Intercultural Communication of
　　an ICH Item ·········· Xiaobing Wang-Riese (368)

Themes for Ongoing Consideration

Redefine the Concept of Intangible Cultural Heritage ·········· Yuan Li, Gu Jun (387)
Recognizing the Practice of Tradition in Community Well-Being
　　——Towards A Model of Sustainable Intangible Cultural Heritage
　　·········· Amy Kitchener (396)
ICH Protection and Bridging Ethnic Conflicts ·········· Song Junhua (403)
Working with Immigrant Communities: Best Ethnographic Practices
　　·········· Debra Lattanzi Shutika (413)
Considering the Concept, Principle, and Questions Related to the Productive
　　Protection of Intangible Cultural Heritage ·········· Xiao Fang (419)

Postscript ·········· (426)

序　言

比尔·艾伟　宋俊华

民俗是人际或代际之间通过口传心授传承的传统生活方式、艺术、知识和实践的总和。在联合国教科文组织的文化遗产保存、保护活动中，民俗（有时称为民俗生活）主要被划入非物质文化遗产（本书有时简称"非遗"）范畴。中国和美国都有丰富的传统文化，两国学者都对民俗和非物质文化遗产有深入的研究。本论文集就是中美两国民俗学和非物质文化遗产学者近十年相关研究成果的一个结晶。

2007年初，我们正式启动了中美民俗学会之间的学术交流。事实上，从上世纪80年代起，中美之间就已有关于民俗学的学术交流，当时已有中国学者、学生去美国一些高校和研究机构留学或做访问研究，也有许多著名的美国民俗学者来中国授课、交流。两国民俗学界有一个共同愿望：搭建一个合作交流平台，促进研究成果的相互分享，同时为青年学者提供互访学习的机会。

在中美民俗学会开启对话后的数年里，中美民俗学、非物质文化遗产学者通过共同举办研讨会和讲座、互派青年学者、联合开展学术调研等方式开展交流。在交流过程中，大家遵循一种共同理念：尊重不同经验和研究视角，发展理解、友谊和协作。除了中国民俗学会、美国民俗学会之外，中国教育部人文社科重点研究基地中山大学中国非物质文化遗产研究中心、华中师范大学国家文化产业研究中心、中国社会科学院少数民族研究所、美国范德堡大学、史密森尼学会都是这些交流活动的重要发起者和参与者。

或许由于中美两国在民俗、非物质文化遗产及其研究方面存在巨大差异，从首届中美非物质文化遗产论坛开始，所有参与者都意识到这种交流将是一个令人振奋的机遇。

中国是一个文明古国，有着十分悠久的农耕社会历史。许多中国古村落至今还保留着延续了数个世纪的传统习俗、表演和实践，这是中国学者能够对其进行长达数十年研究的重要原因。此外，在中国有50多个民族，每个民族都有自己不同的语言和文化传统，因此民族文化传统也是中国学术研究和政府制定政策所关注的重点内容之一。在中国，民俗和非物质文化遗产研究一直蕴含着学术和政策两个层面的意义。

美国是一个只有200多年历史的移民国家。在美国，只有土著美国人（印第安人）的文化才被认为是古老的，但连印第安人文化也常常被认为是从亚洲传入的。或许由于没有太多古老乡村及其多样的族群文化可供研究，美国学者多关注城市的族群传统文化和遗产，如对华裔美国人和意大利裔美国人的研究、对移居城市的乡村或农业人口的传统文化生存方式的研究等，这些研究多数是由大学的个体民俗学者所承担（尽管从19世纪70年代起，公共民俗学者在这个领域内已十分活跃），研究成果包括出版物、媒体记录、展览和节日等。美国政府虽然也曾鼓励建立研究机构对民歌、民间故事和其他民俗事项开展搜集、整理和保护工作，但相对于中国而言，美国政府对民间文化和传统社区保护的政策介入还远远不够。

那么，什么样的项目才有助于拓展我们的协作，使我们有能力表达这些或其他在中美民俗实践中的重要不同？我们是否可以把联合国教科文组织《保护非物质文化遗产公约》作为描述和对比两国民俗学者所处情景的一个参照？尽管美国到现在还没有加入这个公约，但美国民俗学者曾对公约起草做出过实际的贡献。中国是最早加入公约并建设非物质文化遗产新学科的国家之一。从《保护非物质文化遗产公约》视角考察中美民俗和非物质文化研究，我们可以发现一些通用原理对各自学术研究的影响，尤其要分析对非物质文化遗产保护政策的影响——中国在民俗、非物质文化遗产保护政策制定方面一直处于领先地位。

2010年秋，我们决定联合举办一系列研讨会来促进我们的合作，比较两国民俗和非物质文化遗产的研究和政策。在中美两国相关机构基金的大力支持下，我们共举办了四次论坛，分别在中国广东省佛山市、湖北省武汉市和美国田纳西州纳什维尔市、华盛顿哥伦比亚特区举行①。参会学者提交论文或发言提纲，用中英文打印。发言时用本国语言，讨论环节由参会研究生提供辅助翻译。本论文集的文章就是从四次"中美非物质文化遗产论坛"论文中选编而来。

鉴于联合国教科文组织倡导的保护非物质文化遗产是我们开展合作的基础，就有必要简要介绍一下联合国教科文组织的《保护非物质文化遗产公约》。

1972年，联合国教科文组织通过了一个历史性协议（《保护世界文化和自然遗产公约》，简称《世界遗产公约》），用来保护对人类具有普遍价值的历史遗址、文物和自然遗产。《世界遗产公约》中所指的世界遗产，都是指有物质形态、结构和特点的遗产，不包含非物质遗产。当时，联合国教科文组织有些成员国也表示了对诸如民间故事、歌谣、仪式、语言等非物质文化的关切，但他们的建议没有得到采纳。1989年，联合国教科文组织通过了一个保护传统文化与民间创作的建议案，但也只是强调对民间非物质文化遗产的调查、搜集和建

---

① 中国民俗学会与美国民俗学会等在2011—2013年共同主办的四次中美非物质文化遗产论坛，四次论坛的举办时间、地点、主办方如下：2011年11月6—7日，广东省佛山市，"首届中美非物质文化遗产论坛：政策比较"，中山大学中国非物质文化遗产研究中心主办；2012年4月29日—5月1日，田纳西州纳什维尔市，"第二届中美非物质文化遗产论坛：案例研究"，范德堡大学克博艺术、企业与公共政策研究所主办；2012年11月16—18日，湖北省武汉市，"第三届中美非物质文化遗产论坛：生产性保护"，华中师范大学国家文化产业研究中心主办；2013年5月23—24日，华盛顿，"第四届中美非物质文化遗产论坛：田野调查、档案、保存和访谈"，史密森尼学会主办。这些论坛是由亨利·鲁斯基金会、中国教育部人文社科基金、岭南基金会、美国人文基金、中山大学中国非物质文化遗产研究中心、华中师范大学国家文化产业研究中心、史密森尼学会等共同资助的。本论文集的论文要点已在这四次论坛上宣讲发表。

档工作，未能出台专门针对非物质文化遗产传承过程的保护政策，所以这个建议案没有得到各国政府的积极响应。

2003年秋，联合国教科文组织开始了一种新的尝试，即提供一种易于理解和便于操作的政策开展遗产保护。在一些成员国影响下，起草了一个全新的公约来拓展1972年《世界遗产公约》，把遗产保护范围从物质的、自然的对象拓展到如民俗、技艺、仪式、戏剧、舞蹈、故事讲述、语言和音乐等非物质领域。这个新公约（即《保护非物质文化遗产公约》）与此前的民间创作保护是截然不同的。1989年的建议案主要关注于对那些受到冲击的传统文化进行识别、建立清单、收集案例或者建立濒危非物质文化遗产的档案，常常用于档案馆或博物馆收藏。这种方法可以概括为观察法，即鼓励探索、搜集、研究和分析。如上所述，这是一种与西方民俗学者在通常情况下和美国学者在特殊情况下使用的方法。民俗观察研究关注民俗事项、物质、内容的保存，但很少尝试通过政府介入和私有企业参与等方式来履行对传统文化实践管理和保护的职责。

对非物质文化遗产的保护，联合国教科文组织把对民间创作观察研究改为对非物质文化遗产的有计划的行动保护——创造条件、维持传承。在20世纪后期，日本、韩国和中国已有了通过政府参与社区管理来影响民俗生活的经验，如尝试通过命名或奖励民间杰出艺术大师来鼓励对民俗和非物质文化遗产的保护和传承。可以这样说，联合国教科文组织对文化遗产从物质到非物质、从单纯档案记录向培育代际传承等的转变，标志了东方经验向西方的传播。

到2005年秋，已有23个国家批准了联合国教科文组织的《保护非物质文化遗产公约》，中国是最早加入《保护非物质文化遗产公约》的国家之一。美国却不同，尽管在《保护非物质文化遗产公约》起草阶段，美国一些民俗学者也曾积极参与其中，但这个公约却没有在美国获得批准；相反，由于美国议会法的种种限制，美国政府中止向联合国教科文组织缴纳2011年会费，此后美国对联合国教科文组织事务的参与程度也大大降低了。

公约是一种国际协议，对于缔约国而言，就要承担履约的责任。所以，随着《保护非物质文化遗产公约》的通过，联合国教科文组织保护民俗和非物质文化遗产的"新"方法就有了"抓手"。作为对这一重要国际文件的补充，该公约设置了许多独特的机构和程序安排——政府间委员会、选举程序以及有计划的激励机制，即鼓励社区保护非物质文化遗产传承人，通过保护非物质文化遗产的代际传承过程以确保其生命力。一般来说，按照公约的宗旨，要求学者和政策执行者通过三个步骤与社区、族群、民族、少数民族建立联系：首先要确定有代表性的和有价值的传统，接着确认这些传统的特征及其遭受冲击的程度，最后制定政策或设计激励机制来抵制冲击。

贯彻政府保护非物质文化遗产的政策，对中国民俗和非物质文化遗产学者而言，是十分重要的机遇和挑战。我们所组织的四场中美非物质文化遗产论坛，充分展示了中美民俗、非物质文化遗产研究中存在着广泛相关的历史性主题，它们首次把中美学者们吸引到了一起。当然联想到中国学者对政府各种非物质文化遗产保护政策的积极响应，看到他们中多数在发言中十分关注维护民俗政策及其效果，也就不足为奇了。

联合国教科文组织虽然对非物质文化遗产保护的许多原则性问题做了规定,但是一些具体、特殊的保护程序和政策却留给各缔约国自己来确定。作为最早批准公约的国家之一,中国在保护非物质文化遗产及其代际传承上积累了不少经验,也有许多有待探讨的问题。一些文章就集中讨论了在执行非物质文化遗产保护政策中所面临的种种挑战:非物质文化遗产传承人是否在获得政府褒奖的同时面临被孤立的风险?政府可否忽视传承人与他们所处社区的联系?什么是文化生态,如何存续?文化旅游和生产性保护能否在不影响非物质文化遗产本质特征的前提下提升它们的价值?这些或其他问题是否表达了根源于积极干预的核心观点?

联合国教科文组织《保护非物质文化遗产公约》和国家对非物质文化遗产保护方面的政策等,对美国学者而言,不像中国学者那样是作为当下迫切要解决的问题。继续延续西方民俗研究的观察者定位,强调搜集、整理、建档、保存以及通过展览、节日和声像资料汇编等方式,对民俗、非物质文化遗产及其从业者提供资料帮助等,是美国学者仍然沿用的主要研究方式。当然,也有人认为由于传统文化受到现代性的冲击,一些美国民俗学者已经注意到传统艺术和实践在城市的延续问题,正热衷于通过保护和传播提高社会对民俗和民间艺术的理解和尊重,以促使其持续存在。

尽管中美学者的论文所关注的领域有诸多不同,但民俗和非物质文化遗产保护比较却是大家共同关心的话题。非物质文化遗产的所有权和法律权益,非物质文化遗产保护中的虚拟现实与数字技术的运用,传统文化在处理族群冲突中的角色,社区关于自然灾难的故事讲述,作为非物质文化遗产重要特性——本真性的意义,都是中美专家共同关心的研究问题。

这本论文集是中美民俗与非物质文化遗产学界学术交流的重要见证,是理解中美民俗、非物质文化遗产学者当下所处状况、愿望和特殊机遇的重要窗口。当然,它也是一扇正在打开的文化对话之门,有助于两国民俗、非物质文化遗产学者的平等对话,增进理解,开展协作,共同推动民俗和非物质文化遗产研究的不断发展。

基础理论研究

中国非物质文化遗产保护政策与企业实践

宋俊华[*]

一、问题的提出

联合国教科文组织启动人类非物质文化遗产（后文简称"非遗"）保护，中国是积极参与国之一。2001 年联合国教科文组织公布首批"人类非物质文化遗产代表作名录"，中国昆曲就名列其中。联合国教科文组织随后公布的几批代表作名录都有中国的项目。截至 2013 年底，中国已有 30 个项目入选人类非物质文化遗产代表作名录，7 个项目入选急需保护的非物质文化遗产名录，1 个项目入选非物质文化遗产保护优秀实践名册，总数 38 项，数量居于世界各国之首。2003 年联合国教科文组织通过了《非物质文化遗产保护公约》；2004 年 8 月 28 日，中国第十届全国人大常委会第十一次会议表决通过并批准加入该公约，中国成为最早加入该公约的国家之一。

中国"非遗"保护工作从国家政府逐步扩展到基层，是自上而下的，国家政策主导的特点十分明显。国家"非遗"政策作为国家意志的体现，在实际工作中与"非遗"企业的实践存在一定程度的差异，这就带来了新的社会问题。因此，如何处理国家政策与企业实践的矛盾，发挥企业在"非遗"保护中的能动性，实现"非遗"保护与企业发展的良性互动，是中国目前面临的主要问题之一。

在联合国教科文组织启动"非遗"保护工作之前，中国就已有关于"非遗"保护的政策，分两种情况，一是如《宪法》《民族区域自治法》《刑法》《著作权法》《教育法》《义务教育法》《高等教育法》《民办教育促进法》《体育法》《药品管理法》《文物法》等法规中有涉及"非遗"保护的条款；二是针对某类"非遗"的专门法规，如 1993 年 1 月 1 日国务院颁布施行的《中医药品种保护条例》与 1997 年 5 月 20 日国务院第 217 号令发布的《传统工艺美术保护条例》。

---

[*] 宋俊华，中山大学中国非物质文化遗产研究中心教授。
[①] 教育部人文社会科学重点研究基地重大项目"非遗保护与国家文化生态保护区建设研究"（项目批准号：14JJD850002）阶段成果。

中国专门的"非遗"政策，多数是本世纪出台、实施的，与联合国教科文组织的步调基本一致。具体包括两种情况，一是国家各级政府及其部门针对"非遗"保护所颁布的通知、意见、办法等文件，如2000年2月文化部、国家民委印发的《关于进一步加强少数民族文化工作的意见》，2004年4月8日文化部、财政部联合印发的《关于实施中国民族民间文化保护工程的通知》及其附件《中国民族民间文化保护工程实施方案》，2005年3月国务院办公厅颁发的《关于加强我国非物质文化遗产保护工作的意见》及其附件《国家级非物质文化遗产代表作申报评定暂行办法》和《非物质文化遗产保护工作部际联席会议制度》，2006年7月财政部、文化部联合颁布的《国家非物质文化遗产保护专项资金管理暂行办法》，2006年11月文化部颁布的《国家级非物质文化遗产保护与管理暂行办法》，2007年2月商务部、文化部联合发布的《关于加强老字号非物质文化遗产保护工作的通知》，2007年7月文化部发布的《关于印发中国非物质文化遗产标识管理办法的通知》，2008年5月文化部颁布的《国家级非物质文化遗产项目代表性传承人认定与管理暂行办法》等。二是国家各级政府及其部门针对非物质文化遗产保护所颁布的法规、条例等，如2011年2月25日全国人大常委会通过的《中华人民共和国非物质文化遗产法》以及全国各地颁布的民族民间传统文化保护条例或非物质文化遗产保护条例。

上述政策从内容看，有的侧重宣传、引导非物质文化遗产的保护工作，如意见、通知类文件；有的侧重指导"非遗"保护工作，如办法类文件；还有的侧重规范"非遗"保护工作，如法规、条例等。从功能看，这些政策对各级政府及其部门提出要求，同时也对各企事业单位和个人的行为形成约束。部分"非遗"的传承、发展与企业有关，如传统手工技艺、传统艺术、传统医药等的项目保护单位多数是企业。早在联合国教科文组织启动"非遗"保护工作之前，这些企业就一直把"非遗"作为主要内容进行生产经营，受经济和行业法则、法规制约。当这些企业被认定为"非遗"保护单位以后，就必然要受联合国教科文组织及国家的"非遗"政策、法规的约束，这些政策、法规对这类企业而言，既是一种机遇，又是一个挑战。

二、"非遗"政策与"非遗"企业的发展机遇

第一，"非遗"名录的评审与公布，有利于"非遗"企业的品牌塑造。

国务院《关于加强我国非物质文化遗产保护工作的意见》"三、建立名录体系，逐步形成有中国特色的非物质文化遗产保护制度"中讲："要通过制定评审标准并经过科学认定，建立国家级和省、市、县级非物质文化遗产代表作名录体系。""对列入各级名录的非物质文化遗产代表作，可采取命名、授予称号、表彰奖励、资助扶持等方式，鼓励代表作传承人（团体）进行传习活动。"《国家级非物质文化遗产代表作申报评定暂行办法》第八条讲："公民、企事业单位、社会组织等，可向所在行政区域文化行政部门提出非物质文化遗产代表作项目的申请。"《国家级非物质文化遗产项目代表性传承人认定与管理暂行办法》第五

条："国家级非物质文化遗产项目保护单位可以向所在地县级以上文化行政部门推荐该项目代表性传承人"。《中华人民共和国非物质文化遗产法》第三章第十八条："国务院建立国家级非物质文化遗产代表性项目名录,将体现中华民族优秀传统文化,具有重大历史、文学、艺术、科学价值的非物质文化遗产项目列入名录予以保护。""省、自治区、直辖市人民政府建立地方非物质文化遗产代表性项目名录,将本行政区域内体现中华民族优秀传统文化,具有历史、文学、艺术、科学价值的非物质文化遗产项目列入名录予以保护。"第四章第二十九条："国务院文化主管部门和省、自治区、直辖市人民政府文化主管部门对本级人民政府批准公布的非物质文化遗产代表性项目,可以认定代表性传承人。"根据上述文件及法规,我国从2006年起,先后评审、公布了三批国家级非物质文化遗产代表作名录(1219个项目入选)、四批国家级非物质文化遗产项目代表性传承人名录(1986个传承人入选)、首批国家级非物质文化遗产生产性保护示范基地名录(41个企业入选)。同时,各省、市、县也评审、公布了非物质文化遗产代表作名录、项目代表性传承人名录及生产性保护示范基地名录。在这些名录中,有许多项目、传承人与企业有关,其中国家非物质文化遗产生产性保护示范基地就全是企业。

国家各级各类"非遗"名录评审、公布,对"非遗"企业产生了重要影响。在国家级非物质文化遗产代表作名录所划定的十大门类中,传统技艺、传统医药类项目多数与企业生产有关,传统音乐、民间美术、传统舞蹈、传统戏剧、曲艺、杂技与竞技、民俗也有相当一部分项目与企业生产有关。所以,"非遗"项目、传承人入选各级各类"非遗"名录,在一定程度上就赋予了这些项目、传承人及其所在企业一种社会性荣誉和合法性权利,"非遗"企业可以正当地运用项目、传承人名录的名义进行宣传、开展生产,寻求政府和社会各界的支持,强化企业已有品牌或树立新的企业品牌。

基于对国家各级各类"非遗"名录赋予"非遗"企业权利的认知,许多"非遗"企业十分重视对各级各类"非遗"名录的申请,传统技艺、民间美术、传统医药类"非遗"企业表现得尤为突出。如茅台、五粮液、剑南春、泸州老窖等酒类企业的传统酿酒技艺,苏绣、广绣、湘绣、蜀绣等刺绣类企业的刺绣工艺,同仁堂、胡庆余堂、鹤年堂、九芝堂、潘高寿、陈李济、同济堂等药企的中药文化都相继申报为国家级非物质文化遗产代表作,并用国家级非物质文化遗产代表作的名义进行产品宣传,大大提升了企业的品牌价值。

文化部在2012年1月为北京市珐琅厂有限责任公司(景泰蓝制作技艺)等41个"非遗"企业授予"国家非物质文化遗产生产性保护示范基地"牌匾,不仅肯定了这些企业的"非遗"保护实践,而且赋予了这些企业行业权威地位,使这些企业相对于其他企业更有竞争优势。

第二,"非遗"的展示、展览,有利于"非遗"企业参与市场竞争。

《关于加强我国非物质文化遗产保护工作的意见》"三、建立名录体系,逐步形成有中国特色的非物质文化遗产保护制度"讲："加强非物质文化遗产的研究、认定、保存和传播。……充分发挥各级图书馆、文化馆、博物馆、科技馆等公共文化机构的作用,有条件的地方可设立专题博物馆或展示中心"。《中华人民共和国非物质文化遗产法》第四章第三十条：

> 县级以上人民政府文化主管部门根据需要，采取下列措施，支持非物质文化遗产代表性项目的代表性传承人开展传承、传播活动：
> （一）提供必要的传承场所；
> （二）提供必要的经费资助其开展授徒、传艺、交流等活动；
> （三）支持其参与社会公益性活动；
> （四）支持其开展传承、传播活动的其他措施。

在上述政策、法规的指导下，从2006年起，各级文化部门、企事业单位组织了许多综合性或专题性的"非遗"展示展览活动。如中国（深圳）国际文化产业博览交易会（简称"文博会"）创始于2006年，每年一届，截至2013年底，共举办了八届。2010年（第五届）在2号馆创意生活馆首次设立了"非物质文化遗产展区"，到2011年起首次设立独立的非物质文化遗产馆，已经举办了四届"非遗"展，把展示、展览与文化产业交易相结合。中国成都国际非物质文化遗产节（简称"非遗节"）创始于2007年，每两年举办一次，截至2013年底共举办了四届，把"非遗"展示、"非遗"保护国际论坛、文化旅游相结合。2012年在北京举办中国非物质文化遗产生产性保护成果展是专门针对"非遗"企业的展览。上述展览活动都是由国家文化部主办的，对"非遗"企业在参展场地和经费上给予一定的扶持，并采取积极措施引导"非遗"企业把"非遗"保护与企业产品生产、销售、流通相结合，这些措施大大提升了"非遗"企业参与商业竞争、生产创新的能力。

第三，"非遗"保护资金的投入，有利于"非遗"企业的转型升级。

《关于加强我国非物质文化遗产保护工作的意见》"四、加强领导，落实责任，建立协调有效的工作机制"讲："各级政府要不断加大非物质文化遗产保护工作的经费投入。通过政策引导等措施，鼓励个人、企业和社会团体对非物质文化遗产保护工作进行资助。"《国家非物质文化遗产保护专项资金管理暂行办法》第五条："专项资金分为保护项目补助经费和组织管理经费两大类。"《国家级非物质文化遗产保护与管理暂行办法》第十条："国务院文化行政部门对国家级非物质文化遗产项目保护给予必要的经费资助。县级以上人民政府文化行政部门应当积极争取等地政府的财政支持，对本行政区域内的国家级非物质文化遗产项目的保护给予资助。"《中华人民共和国非物质文化遗产法》第四章第三十条也提出，县级以上人民政府文化主管部门根据需要，要为"非遗"项目代表性传承人开展传承、传播、交流等活动，"提供必要的经费资助"。以上政策、法规的规定，为"非遗"企业获得政府"非遗"保护经费提供了依据。

事实上，从2006年起，我国各级政府不断加大对"非遗"保护的财政支出。在2010年6月2日国务院新闻办公室举行的新闻发布会上，文化部副部长王文章讲："中央和省级财政已累计投入17.89亿元用于非物质文化遗产保护，确保了非物质文化遗产保护工作的顺利开展。"① 尽管国家"非遗"保护专项资金有十分严格的使用范围,保护项目补助如理论及技术研究费、传承人及传习活动补助费、民俗活动补助费、资料抢救整理及出版费、文化生态保护区补助费、普查经费、宣传费等,不能直接用于"非遗"企业的生产包括资金投入和场地和设备更新等,但这些宝贵的经费及使用要求,对"非遗"企业整理企业"非遗"资料、研究企业文化和技术、培养传承人、推进企业文化宣传有重要的作用,可以帮助"非遗"企业挖掘、利用自身的传统资源,从传统的物质产品生产向具有高附加值的文化产品生产转换,向文化创意产业转换,促进企业的转型升级。

三、"非遗"政策与"非遗"企业的新挑战

第一,传承传统技艺与发展现代科技之间的冲突。

《中华人民共和国非物质文化遗产法》第四条讲:"保护非物质文化遗产,应当注重其真实性、整体性和传承性,有利于增强中华民族的文化认同,有利于维护国家统一和民族团结,有利于促进社会和谐和可持续发展。"第五条讲:"使用非物质文化遗产,应当尊重其形式和内涵。禁止以歪曲、贬损等方式使用非物质文化遗产。"所以,保持"非遗"的真实性是"非遗"保护的基本原则。对传统技艺、民间美术与传统医药为主要经营内容的企业而言,传统的、独特的技艺等是企业存续与发展的根基,也是企业所承担的"非遗"保护的核心内容。如酿酒企业的传统酿造技艺、陶瓷企业的传统制瓷烧瓷技艺、刺绣企业的传统刺绣技艺、年画企业的传统年画雕版和印刷技艺、玉雕企业的传统玉雕技艺、凉茶企业的凉茶配制技艺等,有些是纯手工的,有些是半手工半机械的;有些是单个生产的,有些则是批量生产的。这些技艺往往与特定时代、特定区域、特定族群的人的民俗与文化生活息息相关,是他们精神生活的组成部分。

但随着时代和科技的发展,一些"非遗"企业的传统技艺正在部分或全部地被现代科技手段所替代。其一,工具的现代化。机械化、智能机器的运用,开始部分甚至全部取代了人工操作,如机器造纸取代手工造纸,现代酿酒设备取代人工酿酒,切割机器在雕刻中的运用,计算机在剪纸图案设计中的运用等。其二,现代科技在传统技艺传承中的运用。如计算机、录像、网络等部分取代了传统口传心授的传承方式,也使得传统技艺在传承过程中日益规范化、标准化。其三,生产过程的科技化。一些现代生产的流水线开始引入传统"非遗"企业,流水化的生产正在取代个性化的生产。确实,现代科技不可阻挡,成本低、效率高、符合现代市场需求,是"非遗"企业在现代社会竞争中必然的选择。

那么,"非遗"企业该如何处理传承传统技艺与发展现代科技的关系呢?这是"非遗"保护政策背景下,"非遗"企业面对的两难抉择。在前"非遗"时代,"非遗"企业的发展主要靠市场需要来调节,以适应市场发展的"创新"为基调,运用现代科技手段取代传统

---

① http://news.sohu.com/20100602/n272515635.shtml

技艺被认为是正当的、进步的标志。而在"非遗"时代,"非遗"企业不能完全按照市场需要去革新传统技艺,必须要承担保护"传统技艺"的责任,这就需要在二者之间寻求平衡点。有的企业采用半手工半机器的方式来处理二者的关系,如玉雕、石雕、牙雕等雕刻类企业,在处理粗料和打磨时往往用机器,而在雕刻的关键地方则用纯手工方式;有的企业采用分类生产的方式,如酿酒企业、刺绣企业对高端产品用手工制作,大众产品采用机器制作。但究竟哪种模式是最好的,还需要在实践中不断摸索才行。

第二,传承文化与满足现代消费需求之间的矛盾。

《关于加强我国非物质文化遗产保护工作的意见》指出,"非物质文化遗产既是历史发展的见证,又是珍贵的、具有重要价值的文化资源。我国各族人民在长期生产生活实践中创造的丰富多彩的非物质文化遗产,是中华民族智慧与文明的结晶,是联结民族情感的纽带和维系国家统一的基础。""非物质文化遗产与物质文化遗产共同承载着人类社会的文明,是世界文化多样性的体现。我国非物质文化遗产所蕴含的中华民族特有的精神价值、思维方式、想象力和文化意识,是维护我国文化身份和文化主权的基本依据。"所以,"非遗"最核心的价值是文化基因,是一个国家、民族、地区文化身份、文化认同的标志,"非遗"保护的本质是传承这种文化基因和精神,使其代代相传。这也是"非遗"企业传承"非遗"的基本内涵。

但是,无论是经营哪种"非遗","非遗"又不能不遵循企业运营的基本法则,即生产出的产品能否符合社会消费需求,能被消费者所认可。要达到这个要求,企业在产品内容和形式上就要因时因地而变,因消费者而变。与传统技艺相联系的传统文化的题材、内容、表现形式等就要因消费需求而变,从而使"非遗"历史、地域、民族的独特性被现代的和跨地域、跨民族的文化需求所消解。这虽然满足了企业的现代化发展要求,但却与国家的"非遗"政策要求大相径庭。一句话,国家"非遗"保护政策要求保持文化的个性,而商品流通却强调的是共性、普适性,这是"非遗"企业在国家政策与企业实践上面临的另一个难题。

第三,履行遗产保护义务与追求企业经济利益的冲突。

《国家级非物质文化遗产保护与管理暂行办法》第八条规定:"国家级非物质文化遗产项目保护单位应当履行以下职责:(一)全面收集该项目的实物、资料,并登记、整理、建档;(二)为该项目的传承及相关活动提供必要条件;(三)有效保护该项目相关的文化场所;(四)积极开展该项目的展示活动;(五)向负责该项目具体保护工作的当地人民政府文化行政部门报告项目保护实施情况,并接受监督。"第十三条规定:"国家级非物质文化遗产项目代表性传承人应当履行传承义务;丧失传承能力、无法履行传承义务的,应当按照程序另行认定该项目代表性传承人;怠于履行传承义务的,取消其代表性传承人的资格。"《中华人民共和国非物质文化遗产法》第三十一条也对非物质文化遗产代表性项目的代表性传承人的义务作了具体的规定。

以上政策、法规,对"非遗"企业及相关人员提出了保护"非遗"的义务要求:一方面,作为保护单位,企业有配合文化主管部门向公众展示、宣传"非遗"的责任,如参加奥运会、世博会、文博会、亚运会等国家大型活动的展示，参加各地政府及其部门举办的"非遗"展示会，建立"非遗"展示馆、资源库等；另一方面，作为"非遗"传承人，企业的技术人员或者管理人员也有配合文化主管部门开展"非遗"进校园、"非遗"进课堂的责任。但是这些责任与追求经济利益最大化难免发生冲突。保护"非遗"是国家要求的责任，利益的最大化则是企业的职责，"非遗"企业必须在二者之间找到平衡点。

四、"非遗"企业对国家政策的调适与存在问题

国家政策对企业实践不只是一种限制，也是一种权利和机遇。联合国教科文组织启动"非遗"保护工作十年来，"非遗"企业充分利用国家政策带来的机遇，对"非遗"保护经历了从消极被动到积极主动、从重申报到重利用的发展转变，取得了丰富的实践经验。

第一，"非遗"保护与企业品牌建设相结合，创新了企业品牌塑造方式。以王老吉凉茶企业为例。王老吉凉茶创于清道光年间，至今已有180多年历史，被誉为"凉茶始祖"。王老吉凉茶依据传统配方，采用上等本草材料配制，秉承传统的蒸煮工艺，经由现代科技提取本草精华、悉心调配而成，内含菊花、甘草、仙草、金银花等具有预防上火作用的本草植物，能预防上火，有益身体健康。加多宝集团正是充分整合了老字号"王老吉"和国家级"非遗"代表作"广东凉茶"的概念，运用现代品牌的运作方式（如慈善捐款等）树立起了"红罐王老吉"的品牌，既带动了广东凉茶产业的发展，又有利于广东凉茶遗产的传承。

第二，"非遗"保护与企业技术革新相结合，创新了企业技术革新模式。如顺德、深圳等地的香云纱企业在继承传统香云纱制作的基础上融入了现代技术手段，取得了很好的效果。也有的"非遗"企业因技术革新而得到政府在政策和资金方面的扶持，在一定程度上改善了企业经营的环境。

第三，"非遗"保护与企业经营相结合，创新了企业生产和营销模式。"九江双蒸"企业（广东省九江酒厂有限公司）把遗产保护与自身分类生产和经营相结合，形成金字塔式的企业经营模式，即传统手工技艺与现代科技、高端需求与普通需求相结合的经营模式，取得了良好的社会效益与经济效益，实现了遗产保护与企业经营的共赢。

第四，"非遗"保护与企业管理相结合，创新了企业或行业的管理模式。2011年7月13日，以红罐王老吉生产企业加多宝集团（从2014年12月19日起，红罐王老吉外包装装潢权归属广药集团）为首的50余家企业共同签署了《不动摇不懈怠不折腾，团结奋进，争当"创造中华文化新辉煌"排头兵——凉茶文化与产业发展公约》（简称《凉茶发展公约》），成为"非遗"企业在实践中坚持经济和文化、企业与行业等协调发展的典范。在质量技术监督部门的指导下，中山咀香园牵头制定了传统食品杏仁饼的联盟标准，规范了本地杏仁饼企业的生产行为。该联盟标准后经多次改进和完善后，从2005年1月1日起上升为广东省

地方标准。①

任何国家政策与任何企业实践都不是完美无缺的。无论是国家的"非遗"政策，还是企业的实践，都必须处理好过去、现实与未来的关系问题。如果说国家政策制定主要出于对"非遗"在现实和未来的文化价值的考虑的话，企业实践则更关注"非遗"在现实和未来的经济价值。对同一对象的不同的价值需求，国家政策与企业实践冲突的根源，又是企业实践与国家政策相调适的基础。国家政策与企业实践的冲突与调适，往往还潜伏着另外一些值得注意的问题。

第一，企业为了自身利益，滥用国家政策。如对申报各级"非遗"代表作、代表作项目传承人权利的滥用，尤其是对"非遗"生产性保护的误读与滥用，把生产性保护简单等同为产业化。"非遗"保护的目的是保护文化多样性，"文化差异性构成支持各民族社会生活和谐而持续展开的基本条件，是民族生存体系的核心价值"。然而，"大工业生产方式是拒绝差异性的。它割裂了空间和时间在人的劳动过程中的自然统一，消除了各自的局限性。其分裂的'时—空'结构排除了时间绵延和空间变化所造成的复杂性，免除了对付和处理这种复杂性的经济学负担。在现代生产过程中，'劳动'被作为一种具体的制造活动而预先以数学方式加以描述和设定，所有的东西都在理性规划中被明确化，所有的偶然因素都被这种理性的逻辑所排除。针对具体制造目标而展开的'劳动'，形成一个封闭而稳定的循环运动体系，'生产力'的运行情况尽在预先的掌握之中。这一切确保了资本投入的一次性和准确性，具有极大的生产效率和经济效益。'标准化'是大工业生产方式的核心技术力量，它根本排除并竭力消除所有'文化差异性'"。②"产业化要求有规模、有标准，但文化要求有个性、要求独特、差异。"③

第二，企业的多头领导与归属的混乱，使国家"非遗"政策赋予企业的权益难以落实。如传统工艺美术企业过去一直归口于国家经贸委管理，在管理和税收上套一般生产企业的模式和标准，使其难以享受到国家"非遗"和文化产业等方面的政策优惠。

第三，企业对"非遗"过度保护和资源垄断，一定程度上妨碍或剥夺了相关群体的共享权益。多数"非遗"是代际的、地域的、族群的创造物，是群体共享的文化资源。但是部分企业对"非遗"的知识产权申报或商标注册，在一定程度上会剥夺相关人群对该文化的享用权益，也与联合国教科文组织保护"非遗"的宗旨大相径庭。

五、结 论

"非遗"保护是个长期的系统工程，国家和企业必须明确各自的身份与角色。国家在制

---

① 参见《中山日报》2004年12月12日。
② 吕品田：《重振手工与非物质文化遗产生产性方式保护》，《中南民族大学学报》2009年第4期，第4页。
③ 徐艺乙：《非遗保护：重新发现"手"的价值》，《东方早报》2009年2月16日。

定"非遗"政策过程中,既要考虑国家的目的,又要考虑企业的诉求。中国的"非遗"政策是在联合国教科文组织《保护非物质文化遗产公约》的基础上形成的,既体现了该公约的精神,又有中国的特色。企业在执行国家政策的实践中,既面临着新问题,又会有新机遇,经历了从被动到主动、从他律到自律的过程。这既为世界"非遗"保护提供了经验,又提出了值得警惕的问题。

美国历史保护运动和非物质文化遗产

迈克尔·安·威廉姆斯[*]

在美国，历史保护运动、对历史研究的关注和对非物质文化遗产的保护通常并行存在，但各自独立进行。对国家、地区或民族认同的坚持引发了大量这种运动，对文化变迁影响的忧虑也由此而来。在19世纪，美国人试图通过创建民族文学和赞颂历史建立自己独立于欧洲的身份。最早对美国历史保护所做出的努力集中体现在保护与美国第一任总统乔治·华盛顿有关的建筑物上。1850年，华盛顿的前总部哈斯布鲁克宫殿成为美国第一栋获得保护的建筑，六年后成立了弗农山庄女士协会来保护华盛顿的私人住宅弗农山庄。在19世纪晚期，保护的注意力转向了国家独特的文化对象，重点关注土著居民文化（对非裔美国人文化的关注相对较少）。不像欧洲早期的民俗研究集中在欧洲农民阶级，美国民俗学会（成立于1888年）的研究对象包括在美国范围内更广泛的文化。

到19世纪晚期，美国联邦政府已开始用文献记录印第安人的非物质文化遗产，并采取措施保护文化古迹（即使其他政府分支机构有意破坏这种文化）。1906年通过了国家法律《古迹法》，该法案通过预留国家纪念地来保护联邦土地上的历史遗迹和自然景观，如考古遗址。怀俄明州的魔鬼塔成为美国第一处国家纪念地。近年来，被印第安族群视为圣地的魔鬼塔成为他们与来此攀登的非印第安人发生冲突的根源。

20世纪20年代至30年代早期，美国开始兴起保护和建构民俗文化的运动，产生了第一批民间节日（1928年到1932年之间在美国南部创建了三个阿巴拉契亚民间节日），在一些有意于保护其特色的城市创建了历史街区。1931年，美国南部城市查尔斯顿（位于南卡罗来纳州）建立了国家第一个历史街区；不久之后，诸如路易斯安那州的新奥尔良和德克萨斯州的圣安东尼奥等城市也建立了自己的历史街区。

美国第一个全国性的多元文化民间节日于1934年在密苏里州圣路易斯设立。国家民间节日由莎拉·格特鲁德·诺特创立，庆祝者包括印第安人、西班牙裔和非裔美国人（以及美国盎格鲁人），新近迁到美国的移民也加入其中。国家民间节日也是第一个以职业知识和为学龄儿童做规划为特色的节日。节日在不同的地方举行，在其早期几十年的大部分时间里主要由报纸赞助（尤其是《圣路易斯环球民主报》《华盛顿邮报》和《费城公报》），此外

---

[*] 迈克尔·安·威廉姆斯，西肯塔基大学民俗学与人类学系主任。

还有其他来源，但并非联邦政府赞助①。国家民间节日一直持续到今天，在美国不同城市仍然存在。

为了解决大萧条时期的经济困难，联邦救助工作始于20世纪30年代，尤其是公共事业振兴署（简称WPA），做了大量的项目记录非物质文化遗产和历史建筑。虽然这些项目的目的主要是缓解失业，但是他们为联邦政府该如何保护遗产提供了有价值的范例。为了实施美国历史建筑测绘（HABS）计划，WPA雇佣失业的建筑师，开始系统地记录民俗和时髦建筑。该计划最终转移到国家公园管理局，并与它的相关项目——美国历史工程记录和美国历史景观调查一直持续到今天。1935年美国政府通过了《历史古迹法》，宣布了一项国策：保护历史古迹和建筑作为公用。公共事业振兴署内的各种项目特别是联邦作家计划也记录了非物质文化遗产，著名的民俗学研究者如卓拉·尼尔·赫斯顿和阿伦·罗马克斯就曾服务于这些项目。"印第安新政"期间，美国政府对印第安人的政策发生变化，也使得内政部开展保护艺术和工艺传统的项目。

在大萧条后的20年间，联邦政府提出的保护物质或非物质文化资源的政策实施得相对很少。然而，20世纪50年代州际高速公路系统的建设和工业化以及60年代的"城市更新"等，促进了新的历史保护运动的兴起。20世纪60年代中期政府热情支持艺术文化遗产和建筑保护。1965年，《国家历史保护法》创建了我们今天所知的由政府经营的保护系统，包括《国家史迹名录》。四年后，《国家环境政策法》规定，文化资源和自然资源一样被写入联邦建设项目环境影响报告书。国家在60年代中期创建了艺术和人文学科基金，把民间艺术纳入立法计划，部分要归功于国家民间节日的创始人莎拉·格特鲁德·诺特的努力②。20世纪60年代末和70年代初，公共部门民俗项目有所革新，美国民俗学科也增多了。这包括创建第一个全州范围的民俗活动，以及1967年史密森尼学会（美国国家博物馆）创建美国年度民俗节日，1974年国家艺术基金会成立民间艺术项目，1976年国会图书馆（美国国家图书馆）依据《美国民俗保护法》建立国家民俗中心。

20世纪70年代末，人们越来越关心用联邦保护政策来保护非物质文化遗产。随着美国民俗研究运动的出现，越来越多的民俗学者对物质文化感兴趣。对乡土建筑特别感兴趣的民俗学者参与了政府资助的建筑调查和记录工作，他们很快意识到，联邦法律不像保护历史建筑和古迹那样保护无形文化。与此同时，关心他们所记录的古迹和建筑的文化背景的考古学家和保护主义者越来越意识到需要保护无形的文化。

到1979年，非物质文化遗产保护工作似乎前进了一大步，国家公园管理局的考古学家走进国家民俗中心，提出联邦政府授权的田纳西—汤比格比水道工程需考虑现有的文化因素。这样，人们在做联邦影响研究的时候就可能会习惯性地考虑到非物质文化资源。尽管提出保护物质和非物质文化遗产的项目并行发展，但整合这两方面的行动却踟蹰不前。《国家

---

① For a complete history of the National Folk Festival see: Michael Ann Williams, *Staging Tradition*: *John Lair and Sarah Gertrude Knott* (Urbana and Chicago: University of Illinois Press, 2006).

② Livingston Biddle, *Our Government and the Arts* (New York: ACAD Books, 1988), p. 30.

环境政策法》强制执行的《环境影响报告书》（*EIS*）可以用来保护非物质文化遗产，但现实中却很少这样去执行。美国陆军工兵部队建设连接田纳西河和汤比格比河的主水道成为一个在联邦缓解过程中考虑非物质文化遗产因素的测试案例。尽管美国民俗文化中心被要求记录因被新水道淹没而受影响地区的民众生活，但因为有影响力的民俗学者把"缓解"资金看作抚恤金，记录工作最终因政治和道德原因而中止了。因此，受影响区域的建筑因 HABS 得到记录，但是因这项工程而最终流离失所的住户们的生活大部分是没有记录的。

由于我是第一个为 HABS 工作的民俗学家，并参与记录田纳西—汤比格比水道受影响区域的建筑历史的暑期项目，我一直在思考这个水道工程中存在的问题。从一开始，我跟反对这个项目的外界人士的观点就不同。流离失所的人们看着我们仔细测量每一寸他们的家园，可能会觉得我们认为房子比他们更重要。在联邦保护和环境法律的背景下，如果保护主义者能够主张保存建筑，环保人士能够尽力拯救濒危物种，我们当然可以找到途径为人类做主张。难道我们真的希望所有的环境生物学家彻底闲下来，而不做任何尝试去确保建设项目符合联邦环境法律？

后来，一些著名的民俗学家重新决定退出田纳西—汤比格比项目。新近退休的美国民俗中心主任佩吉·布杰早在 2002 年在美国民俗学会的会长致辞中就对此提出批评（这事在她成为民俗中心主任很早之前就发生了）。她指出，水道附近几个选区的选民代表非裔美国活动家詹·萨浦回忆说，在决策过程中她听到"一些言论，而那些言论者从未到过该地区并且不了解事实真相"。布勒格博士总结道，"如果我们出于道德原因断然拒绝与变革者合作，我们也是在拒绝帮助传统的拥有者和社区去面对和减缓变化的影响。这样我们在文献记录中也留下一个空缺。我们需要更相信自己。"① 圈外的其他人认为民俗学者更像是拿道德做表面文章，而不是采取行动帮助人们保存文化。汤姆·金监督联邦法案第 106 节的复查工作（通过此次复查，建筑物和遗址均在工程建设项目中得到了保护），此后，汤姆·金撰文对民俗学者的立场进行了严厉的批评：

  虽然我觉得与民俗学者一起工作让人兴奋，但是在我看来他们似乎与我所处的混乱世界不相干——第 106 节相关的世界……民俗学者充满正义，但他们回避田纳西—汤比格比等项目，较少帮助因项目原因而使传统生活受到干扰的人们。我们应为后人记录他们的歌曲和故事，增加节日展示他们的技能，希望传统因此能以某种形式得以代代相传。这些都是有价值的事业，但是他们没有吸引变革者，他们不直接面对传统与现代之间的矛盾；他们不帮助我们审核第 106 节。他们不会帮助纳瓦霍人和霍皮人处理林务局的事情，也不会帮助波兰城的人民面对底特律市政府。②

---

① Peggy Bulger, "Looking Back, Moving Forward: The Development of Folklore as a Public Profession (AFS Presidential Plenary Address, 2002)," *Journal of American Folklore* 116 (2003): 384 – 388.

② Thomas F. King, *Places That Count: Traditional Cultural Properties in Cultural Resource Management* (Walnut Creek: Alta Mira Press, 2003), p. 32.

恕我直言，美国民俗中心确实继续提出将非物质文化遗产纳入联邦保护体系。由于中心主任谢丽·邦尼斯的影响，《国家文物保护法》1980年的修正案中502部分授权准备一份报告，该报告是关于保存和保护我们文化遗产中的无形部分，如艺术、技能、民俗和民风。生成的报告在1983年获得发表，主张"文化保护"。这是保护、支持物质和非物质文化遗产的一次综合性的努力。然而很大程度上，这份报告没有考虑到政府干预和其他鼓励基层的策略。报告特别指出"不建议联邦被动参与保护过程，即受到重大发展项目影响引发的行为"①，也因此对政府保护政策没有什么后续影响。现在回想起来，很难判断这份过于胆小和羞怯的建议报告在多大程度上受（左翼）民俗学学科内部的某种道德批判，又在多大程度上受（右翼）当时里根政府的政治气候影响。我想两者都是重要的原因。在这两种情况下，该报告对联邦文化和环境保护制度都没有任何持久的影响。正如汤姆·金提到的，在里根政府时期希望保护文化无形资产是"最飘渺的梦想，等到政府改变的时候，提议又淡出了文化资源管理者们的集体记忆"。②

美国民间生活研究（American Folklife Center）（注：这是一个研究机构）中心的报告在采用"文化保护"这一术语的时候做出了理智的选择，没有武断地区分物质和非物质的文化。选用"保护"这一术语部分原因是想与环境保护主义结合起来，暗示培养鲜活的文化，而不是把它们冻结在过去。然而，"文化保护"这一术语让我们疏于正视美国法律体系内保护法只承认物质文化这一问题。最近，随着圈内文化政策的讨论越来越国际化，我们发现我们在有关非物质文化遗产的国际协调会议的讨论中语言方面跟不上了。

不管怎样，文化保护报告发表后美国民间生活研究中心在20世纪80年代确实赞助了几个示范项目，包括综合了民俗学者和保护主义者方法的"格鲁斯·科瑞克城文化调查"和"一个空间，多处地点：新泽西松林地带自然保护区的民俗和土地利用"，这两个项目为民俗学家在土地利用规划的背景下工作提供了范例。③ 1990年，国家历史地名注册处进一步意识到文化遗产在定义传统文化财产方面的重要性，部分原因是受美国民间生活研究中心民俗学者工作的启发——地区与居民区的文化习俗和信仰相联系，这些根植于社区的历史，对于维护社区长久的文化形象很重要。④ 虽然提名文化遗产仍然必须有参照对象，但他们确实承认了地区非物质文化遗产的重要性。不幸的是，在实践中提名的对象几乎仅限于美国原住民的文化遗产。

2005年，民俗学者谢丽·邦尼斯把传统文化遗产的概念运用于美国大雾山国家公园北

---

① Ormond Loomis, *Cultural Conservation: The Protection of Cultural Heritage in the United States* (Washington D. C.: Library of Congress, 1983), p. 83.

② Thomas F. King, *Places That Count: Traditional Cultural Properties in Cultural Resource Management* (Walnut Creek: Alta Mira Press, 2003), p. 32.

③ Thomas Carter and Carl Fleischhauer, *The Grouse Creek Cultural Survey: Integrating Folklife and Historic Preservation Field Research* (Washington D. C.: Library of Congress, 1988), and Mary Hufford, *One Space, Many Places* (Washington D. C.: Library of Congress, 1986).

④ Patricia Parker and Thomas F. King, "Guidelines for Evaluating and Documenting Traditional Cultural Properties," *National Register Bulletin*, no. 38.

海岸环境影响报告书,论证了公墓扫墓传统的资格①。20世纪40年代建造丰塔纳大坝的时候,许多与公园接壤的社区以及去其他社区的通道被淹没。一部分社区随后被改造成了公园的一部分,流离失所的人们得到承诺:会为他们修建一条社区通往墓地的道路。迟迟未修的路开始动工不久,即表面上因为环境的原因而停工了。"未修通的路"让当地居民觉得联邦政府不守信用并产生了强烈的反环保情绪。②虽然国家名录提名未被写进环境影响报告中,但被认可资格也为文化实践本身提供了保护。诸如地上就餐、洗礼仪式等扫墓传统将同墓地一起得到认可。③北海岸的项目见证了民俗学者积极参与环境影响报告生成的过程,并成功将一个非印第安人居住区的文化提名为传统文化遗产。

国家公园管理局犯难的是确定提名文化财产写进国家名录的方式和原因,一些公众民俗学者试图找到更多草根方法来认定文化的重要场所。最成功的例子之一是由纽约城市民俗创设的"重要事件发生地"(Place Matters)④,比这个更乡土的例子是由纽约北部传统艺术(TAUNY)创造的"很特别的地方名录"⑤。两个例子中,提名系统都比国家名录要求的过程简单得多,并且理论上来说两例都来自当地公民,而不是保护专家。然而,尽管这些认定确实对文化财产(特别是那些处于危险状态的)起到宣传作用,他们不提供来自联邦政府资助建设工程的保护,或者像国家名录认定那样提供收益性财产税收优惠。

在过去的两年里,国家认定传统文化财产名录对象已扩大,尤其是对非美国原住民财产。美国民俗学会文物保护工作组,包括纽约城市民俗/重要事件发生地和纽约北部传统艺术的双方代表,与国家名录认定人员会面,正致力于一个由西部肯塔基大学资助的示范项目,试图把草根和国家名录认定项目做到最好(后者能为项目带来更大好处和税收优惠)。我们正在与国家名录认定人员合作提名重要事件发生地和纽约北部传统艺术已注册过的财产,想借此为如何提名非本土传统文化遗产提供范本。目前有一些我们在考虑的财产,我们发现其业主即使不反对登入草根名册所带来的宣传,也怀疑政府的参与。当前项目记录了纽约加勒比"小屋"(大多是建在荒地的小社区房屋)、纽约唐人街的中国茶馆和纽约州北部的村庄草地⑥。

在美国现有的历史保护系统之外,保护和支持非物质文化遗产的很多工作都已开展。然

---

① Alan Jabbour, Phillip E. Coyle, and Paul Webb, *North Shore Cemetery Decoration Project Report* (National Park Service, 2005).
② Michael Ann Williams, *Great Smoky Mountain Folklife* (Jackson: University Press of Mississippi, 1995), pp. 155 – 160.
③ See also Alan Jabbour and Karen Singer Jabbour, *Decoration Day in the Mountains: Traditions of Cemetery Decoration in the South Appalachians* (Chapel Hill: University of North Carolina Press, 2012).
④ Steven J. Zeitlin, "Conserving our Cities' Endangered Spaces," in *Conserving Culture: A New Discourse on Heritage*, edited by Mary Hufford (Urbana and Chicago: University of Illinois Press, 2006), pp. 215 – 228.
⑤ Varick Chittenden, "'Put Your Very Special Place on the North Country Map!'" Community Participation in Cultural Landmarking," *Journal of American Folklore* (2006) 119: 47 – 65.
⑥ 项目由西肯塔基大学的研究和创造性活动项目(RECAP)资助。迈克尔·安·威廉姆斯是项目总监,雷切尔·霍普金、莎拉·马卡特·杰克逊、凯特琳·科德和卡特里娜·韦恩是实地考察工作者。莫莉·加芬克尔代表纽约城市民俗/地方事件(Place Matters),瓦里克·奇滕登指导纽约北部的传统艺术(TAUNY)项目。

而，承诺说要制定一个完善的保护文化的政府政策体系还没实现。美国民俗学者和关注非物质文化遗产的其他人需要采取这些步骤：

·重新评估我们参与联邦政府授权的影响报告的方式，帮助保护当地社区和非物质文化遗产。
·倡导扩大现有的项目，如国家名录，以更好地识别和保护生活社区和文化遗产。
·联邦政府层面更新领导人员以制定更完善的联邦文化遗产保护政策。

中国城市化与非物质文化遗产保护

高小康[*]

一、当代中国城市化进程中非遗保护的历史趋势

"非物质文化遗产"（文中简称"非遗"）这个术语虽然是 2003 年联合国教科文组织颁布《保护非物质文化遗产公约》后才确定下来的，但在中国当代，与非遗保护概念相似或相关的活动如民俗民间文化和民间文艺的搜集、整理和保护工作早就在进行中。当然，在非遗保护观念产生之前的这些活动与非遗保护毕竟有所不同。非遗保护与以前的民俗民间文化保护的最大差异在于强调非遗在当今世界中的传承、振兴和发展，把传统文化的发展置于当代文化环境中，形成了非遗保护的特色，也由此产生了新的问题。

中国当代社会发展的最重要趋势就是城市化。经历了 20 世纪六七十年代城市的衰落之后，自 80 年代开始在全国迅猛发展的建设进程——大规模的城市改造带来社会生活和文化形态的巨大改变。这种改变对传统文化的保护和传承造成了重大影响。大致说来，80 年代城市化建设的主要目标是"现代化"，对城市的旧建筑、旧街区、旧环境进行大规模拆毁重建；生活方式也在"现代化"想象引导下追求从国外引来的时尚。这个时期对传统文化特别是乡土民俗文化的破坏很严重。到了 90 年代中期以后，城市建设的理念开始发生变化，一些城市对片面"现代化"建设造成的同质化和文化内涵缺失的问题开始反思和纠正。体现于城市文化建设，就是在城市建设和社会发展中逐渐重视传统文化（包括非物质文化遗产）的保护和传承。但许多传统文化遗产在此前的城市建设过程中已遭到破坏，同时保护传统文化遗产的理念往往是"文化搭台，经济唱戏"，把文化建设变成商业经营的手段。在这类"保护"理念指导下的行为往往是以假乱真或盲目改造，结果是造成了新一轮破坏。2000 年以来，特别是自昆曲、古琴列入世界非遗名录到中国签约加入《保护非物质文化遗产公约》和国家设立"文化遗产日"的这些年来，非遗保护迅速成为城市文化建设中的热门活动：首先是大规模的申遗热潮，而后在公共文化服务体系建设中加入非遗保护、展演、教育、传播的内容，以非遗为内容或卖点的文化产业开发也日益兴旺……

---

[*] 高小康，南京大学教授，中山大学中国非物质文化遗产研究中心兼职教授。

总之，近六七年来中国的城市发展进程与非遗保护活动正越来越密切地结合起来，城市文化建设中对传统文化的重视和保护使原生于乡民文化环境中的非遗有可能在当代城市文化生态环境中生存和传承发展，这可能使非遗保护获得新的生机。但与此同时也出现了新的问题：非遗的城市化、商业化是否会造成原有传统文化内涵的蜕变和消亡而变成仿真拟像（simulacrum）或商业品牌标签？进入城市的非遗脱离了原来的文化生态环境，是否也脱离了相关的文化群体，因而造成文化主体缺失的"无人非遗"？这些问题都是在城市化进程中非遗保护工作必须面对的现实。

二、从乡民社会向现代都市的转移

当代城市生活究竟能不能容纳传统的乡土文化？这是在非遗保护中一直有争论的问题。按照人们习惯的"现代化"思维，属于传统社会的文化形态会随着社会形态的变迁而消亡。事实上，尽管社会形态在变化，但作为"小传统"的文化群体的心理需要和认同感往往会跨越时代传承下来。广州市越秀公园的客家山歌墟就是这样一个例子。客家人在广州小北一带聚居。观音山（越秀山）东南面山脚一带俗称小北角，20世纪40年代开始，陆续有广东兴宁的客家人到此开布厂或作坊，从事染织业的生产。私人老板雇用的工人多是来自家乡的客家人。当这些工人在此立足后，又陆续吸引了乡里乡亲前来投亲靠友。这里的客家人群体不断壮大，成为这一带的主要居民，客家山歌也随之而来。50年代，小北一带的客家人开始在附近的越秀公园唱歌。传统客家山歌在"文革"期间被当作"四旧"而遭到禁锢，改革开放以后又重新兴盛起来。1996年组成了"洪桥客家山歌协会"，聚会唱歌的活动从自发走向有组织，影响也越来越大。1997年，"每月十二"山歌聚会被命名为"山歌墟"。

现在看来，这个山歌墟谈不上是广州城市文化的主流或时尚娱乐活动，却是当地客家人认同的一种表达方式。广州是个多元文化色彩比较浓厚的城市，不同地域、族群身份的文化群体杂居，不同群体的文化传统认同对于构造城市文化的多样性和人文内涵具有重要意义，也是城市居民的自觉需要。

三、城市休闲文化影响下的非遗开发

非遗保护与地方经济发展关系密切的形态之一是文化旅游的开发。从20世纪90年代后期起，随着经济发展，都市休闲文化也发展起来，休闲旅游产业迎来了繁荣时期。这个时期旅游开发的特点是从以前的单纯景观游览扩展到休闲文化活动，旅游内容中文化特色的重要性突出了。在具有较丰厚非遗资源的旅游休闲目的地，民俗民间文化的开发成为旅游产业形态的重要组成部分。以非遗为内容的文化休闲旅游对非遗保护的作用似乎是矛盾的。从积极意义上说，可能成为一种"生产性保护"的形态：通过旅游产业的发展带动地方经济和当地人民生活的改善，提高非遗的知名度，有助于提高相关文化群体对传统文化的热爱和保护的积极性。从消极意义上说，旅游产业的开发，尤其是几乎无法避免的过度开发，会破坏非遗的文化生态，比如贵州凯里地区的两个著名苗寨郎德和西江，就成为非遗保护与开发关系悖论的两个矛盾案例。以千户苗寨知名的西江在旅游开发方面十分积极，当地人因此而受惠，许多年轻人留在家乡从事服务业工作，整个村寨显得生机勃勃；但开发也造成了自然环境和文化生态的破坏。而郎德是另一种情况：这里被划为国家级文化生态保护区，环境和文化生态保护得比较完整；但由于缺少就业机会，居民收入低，很难留住年轻人，村寨里主要是老年人留守，文化的传承和环境的保护都成了问题。

这种两难状况是休闲旅游产业对非遗文化生态保护发生影响的典型现象，几乎成为不可破解的死结。

四、城市消费文化与非遗的"生产性保护"

非遗中的工艺美术类项目如广州的"三雕一彩一绣"等，传统上就是具有商业属性的消费类文化产品。对这样的非遗项目实行"生产性保护"应该说是比较合适的。但这类文化产品面临的问题是当代城市消费文化的发展与传统消费文化的距离越拉越大，工艺品制作的资源成本和劳动成本越来越高而市场日益狭小，加上大量粗制滥造商品的冲击，使得真正有价值的传统工艺在保护传承方面遇到不少困难。

尽管被列入各级名录的非遗项目会得到政府和各界的支持帮助，但离开了健康发育的市场，这种保护的效果就难以持续。就目前各地各类工艺美术类非遗项目的保护情况来看也是如此：凡保护传承状况比较好的地方，相关文化消费市场的发育情况也比较好。但从总体上看，传统工艺的美学、文化和历史价值在当代中国大多数城市消费文化理念中没有得到应有的认识和尊崇。培养对传统文化和手工劳作价值的认识，培养更具有文化品位和精神内涵的消费生活方式，可能是推进传统工艺保护传承的社会生态条件。

美国的音乐录制品版权：挑战、问题及对文化遗产政策的诉求

丹尼尔·希伊[*]

在美国，规范着音乐录制品的版权法，直接关系着其顺利进入音乐遗产名录，同时也影响着音乐创作的活力。版权法确保音乐遗产拥有所有权，但是不明晰的法律释义和细则可能会剥夺美国人，甚至世界各国人民进入音乐遗产重要场域的权利。我今天谈及这个话题，并非以文化遗产专家的身份，相反地，是以文化遗产的倡导者和受限于有缺陷的版权法的践行者的身份来谈。

在美国，版权法的目的是通过让创作者在一个合理的期限内享受与其作品有关的独家物质利益来鼓励创造性和创新性。尽管版权时间一直是个有争议的话题，但它最终仍由法律来规定。音乐录制品一般享有三类版权：机械版权、表演版权以及录制版权。至于通过合同准许第三方使用录音制品的问题，会另外再谈。

机械版权与作品的创作有关。尽管实际所付金额可能通过谈判降低，出售唱片所得的机械版税由相关法律条文规定。目前，法律规定每份售出作品的版税是9.1美分。对于录音制品来说，版税具有"强制性"，也就是说，只要支付某录音制品的法定版税，任何人都可以得到一张允许其使用该录音制品任何组成部分的许可证。这一"强制性"只适用于录音制品。对于电视、电影以及其他录像制品来说，任何人在没有得到版权持有者允许的情况下都没有使用作品任何组成部分的权利。对于电影、电视来说，每次购买使用某作品所需许可证要支付的版税要通过与版权所有者协商决定。

作曲家及其发行人享有表演版税，即每次作品在广播、电视或现场表演中"露面"，他们都可从中获利。作品表演者（而不是作曲家）所获的报酬由其与唱片公司所签的合同决定；如果某作品被重新灌制成唱片或以其他方式被表演和使用，唱片公司有权收取费用。举个例子来说，美国有一首很出名的乡村音乐民谣叫作《赌徒》（*The Gambler*）。其作曲者都·史丽兹（Don Schlitz）及其发行人享有机械版税和表演版税；而让这首歌"红"起来的歌手凯尼·罗杰斯（Kenny Rogers）的报酬则取决于他和他所在唱片公司所签的合同。

---

[*] 丹尼尔·希伊，美国史密森尼学会民俗音乐录音部主任。

最后，录制唱片的个人或公司，也就是通过录音设备将音频永久化在某种固定介质上的个人或公司——拥有对所录唱片的录制权。唱片录成的时间即为其版权开始的时间。

下面单独讲讲关于第三方使用许可证及由此获取的收入的分配问题。这些都由合同，而不是法律规定。第三方许可证持有者需要支付机械版权许可费用。与作曲及发行人被强制允许任何支付法定版税的人录制其作品不同，法律并没有强制录制权的拥有者将唱片的使用许可证出售给任何人。回到上面所举的例子：作曲家都·史丽兹无法阻止任何愿意付每张唱片9.1美分机械版税的人录制《赌徒》这首歌；但是歌手凯尼·罗杰斯所属的联美公司（United Artists）则可以对任何一个想在某电影、电视剧或者电玩里使用罗杰斯那支当红单曲的人说"不"。

在电视上播放唱片不仅要支付版税给唱片公司，也要支付版税给作曲者。而对同一作品的无线电广播则只需向作曲及其发行人支付版税，无需向唱片公司支付版税。互联网播放以及卫星广播需要向唱片公司、歌手以及作曲者支付一定费用，额度取决于预计使用者人数。

与音乐版权相关的重要问题和挑战：近100年来，美国围绕版权法的立法工作多为拼凑修补，尚不健全。这一零散性已经殃及音乐版权的公平对待及合理实施。我们需要通过公正和民主的协商来达到一个适度平衡：一方面让公众享有可录制的文化遗产，另一方面给予私人机构某些允许其限制使用这一文化遗产的权利。

唱片所有者不允许他人使用其所拥有的唱片，通常会造成文化遗产被其所有者"锁定"的局面，而该所有者持有的唱片越多，对我们接触和保存录制音乐遗产的限制就越大。这一所有权与文化遗产共享的矛盾在美国围绕老唱片、老电影的文化遗产政策的制定中异常突出。录音制品——包括用于商业和研究目的的录音——是传承音乐传统的一个重要途径。公众无法有效接触到这些唱片就意味着他们不能很好地享用这部分文化遗产。如《美国民间音乐选集》就是对美国文化传统继承至关重要的一张唱片。

同样，围绕"无名氏作品"即没有明确作者的作品，存在很多不确定性和不公平的法律漏洞。一个合理的"不利用，则浪费"的法律对上述两种情况都有好处。其作品被"锁定"而得不到有效利用的艺术家会受益于此，被剥夺了部分文化遗产的公众也将受益于此。我建议实施两年的"不利用，则浪费"法律，要求老唱片的所有者要么自行录制，要么允许他人录制和出售这些唱片。如果某一唱片已经绝版两年，法律应规定唱片所有者授权或以其他方式允许他人录制和出售该唱片。

美国目前没有将音乐录制品遗产定义为国家财产的健全的公共政策。这样的一个政策会为那些呼吁公众共享录制文化遗产的研究者提供有力的支持。

与录音制品有关的版权法在实施过程中有很多"模糊地带"。大多数情况下，诉讼是惯常的理清不确定性和解决纠纷的渠道。但是，整个诉讼过程可能会由于诉讼双方不对等的法律资源而产生新的不公平。在美国，合同谈判中的"弱肉强食"屡见不鲜，而这常常会影响政策的制定和开设先例。举例来说，一个请得起很多律师的有钱公司可能更敢于口出妄言、以大欺小，威胁对因法律资源或资金匮乏而不愿意打官司的小公司或个人采取法律行动。这样权力不对等下的政策制定甚至有可能违背相关法律。

最后，当前公众对于本来就很复杂的美国版权法体系如何运作所知甚为有限。高素质的公众能推动版权法律政策的发展和健全，特别是当政策涉及保存和共享文化遗产的时候。

非物质文化遗产的本真性问题

刘晓春*

一、问 题

在当下中国，众多历史悠久、影响广泛的地方文化被赋予政治、经济、文化价值，超越其原生语境的文化时空与传承享用群体，成为被展示、被消费的对象被重新发明出来，广为"传承母体"①之外的人们所享用、利用、再生产乃至消费，成为民族—国家甚至超越民族—国家界限的文化遗产。进入21世纪以来，随着非物质文化遗产保护运动的开展，文化多样性的观念在中国深入人心，极大地改变了中国人的文化观念，影响了人们对于地方文化的价值认定，那些之前被斥为"迷信""落后"的地方文化，被重新命名为民族—国家的"文化遗产"。在这一遗产化的过程中，各种政治、经济、文化力量也介入地方文化的发展，进而塑造了一种新型的文化生态，地方文化本身也被重新建构。这种关于地方文化的遗产化观念及其社会文化实践，笔者称之为地方文化的"遗产主义"。

在这样一个"遗产主义"的时代，地方文化从"生活文化"的语境中被抽取出来，被移植到"文化遗产"的语境之中，为不同的力量所重新建构，地方文化不可避免并且确确实实地发生了变化。在这一建构过程中发生了诸多社会文化变迁，似乎"一切坚固的东西都烟消云散了"。"真实"似乎成为一个虚假的命题。在当代中国，随着"遗产主义"的日

---

* 刘晓春，中山大学中国非物质文化遗产研究中心、中山大学中文系教授。

① "传承母体"是日本民俗学家福田亚细男为了批判柳田国男的"重出立证法"而提出的概念。他认为以重出立证法为唯一方法的民俗学研究成果是虚构的历史，必须放弃以资料的全国性搜集为前提的重出立证法，要在具体的传承母体中分析民俗现象之间的相互关联，从中得出变化、变迁，进而提出假设。他进而指出，那种认为重出立证法可以究明变迁过程的观点，只是一种幻想。在这个意义上，民俗学必须把民俗放在其传承地域进行调查分析，在其"传承母体"（即传承地域）究明民俗存在的意义及其历史性格（参见［日］福田亚细男《日本民俗学方法序说——柳田国男与民俗学》，於芳、王京、彭伟文译，学苑出版社2010年版，第100页，第160页）。基于此，笔者将"传承母体"的概念拓展为传承地域与传承群体，即包含特定的时空以及在这一特定时空中生活并传承文化传统的群体。在全球化与现代化过程中，本质主义意义上的"传承母体"面临被解体的可能，地方文化的遗产化过程，实际上表明将"传承母体"看作封闭的、具有稳定文化内核的观念，正面临着前所未有的合法性挑战。在这一意义上，"传承母体"概念可以被看作韦伯（Marx Weber）意义上的"理想类型"，只是一个分析性概念。

益盛行，参与这一文化建构过程的不同力量，无论是政府、学者、文化传承人还是普通大众，往往为"生活文化"与"文化遗产"的"真/伪"问题所深深困扰。

笔者认为，这一困扰与长期以来人们认为文化具有一种"本真性"的观念息息相关。文化本真性的观念认为，文化先验地存在，不证自明；具有久远的历史、稳定的内核和清晰的界限，可以与他者文化相区别；人们可以通过媒介客观、真实地予以表述（represent），并为他者所认识、理解乃至享用；本真的文化往往被看作已经消失或正在消失的、过去的文化，与被认为是非本真的现实文化形成强烈的对比而存在。文化本真性的观念在文化被发现、被表述之日起，就已根深蒂固地存在于人们的观念之中。这一观念建立在西方哲学有关现实、再现以及知识的认识论基础之上，现实被视为毫无疑问的存在，知识是关于现实的再现，而再现可以直达透明的现实。然而，随着文化研究的日渐深入，以及全球化、现代化进程的展开，围绕"本真性"这一观念，人们对文化的认识、理解及表述不断深化，逐渐认识到文化的本真性"具有多义性和不易把握的本质"[①]，处于不断的建构过程之中，无法定于一尊。本文试图通过分析人们的文化观念与对象之间相互建构的关系，进而梳理文化本真性的观念谱系，期望对当代知识界思考"遗产主义"时代文化传承与发展的关系有一定参考意义。

二、四个个案

1. 顺德广绣

传统广绣一直分散在千家万户进行。但是，1990年代以来，广东地区掌握广绣技艺、愿意从事广绣的绣工越来越少，无法实现集中生产，能安心刺绣的技工多在"老少边穷"地区。顺德富德工艺品有限公司在粤北、粤西以及广西、湖南、贵州、四川等全国共11个省100多个县，通过合营、自营、合作等多种方式开办广绣厂。公司配备了一支30人左右的技术队伍，常年分布在新绣区组织广绣培训、集中生产。迄今为止，经过广绣培训的人员超过3万，仍在从事刺绣的约有8000人，稳定的广绣厂有30家左右。现在一件广绣作品需要经过大约10道工序：调查市场、设计图案、刺针印花、制作样板、准备丝绸布料、染成所需颜色、配好各色针线、发送工坊人工刺绣、完工送回仔细验货、最后发货国外等，除了"人工刺绣"这一环节以外，其余全部在顺德总部完成。

2. 山西长子县响铜乐器制作

非遗传承引入现代技术，使传统手工技艺类非遗产品的制作从依靠手工经验积累的阶段进入到精确的规范操作阶段。虽然非遗产品的生产规模扩大，产量大幅提高，有了显著的经

---

① [德] 瑞吉娜·本迪克斯：《本真性》，李扬译，《民间文化论坛》2006年第4期。

济效益，但是，随着现代技术的运用，传统手工技艺的仪式性、严肃性逐渐消失，而代之以半机械化、机械化时代的机械性、重复性，精确化、标准化的生产使非遗产品的"独一无二性"①也随之消失。山西省长子县南漳镇西南呈村响铜乐器制作技艺的传承现状，是一个典型的案例。

在制作过程中引入半机械技术，响铜乐器制作技艺由传统的纯粹人力劳作走向了半机械化时代。闫××作为国家级代表性传承人，他既掌握了传统技艺，又善于进行技术革新，成为传承非物质文化遗产的中坚力量。他引进了切圆机、空气锤、成型机，既减轻了劳动强度，也从音量、音质、形状、光洁度等方面大大提高了响铜乐器的制作质量。无论是品种、产量，还是生产规模，都实现了突破性进展。

3. 顺德永春拳

非遗传承的地域性、群体性特征往往表现为非遗传承的家族传承、地域传承。如何处理好非遗传承的封闭性与发展的开放性之间的关系，非遗传承人应该审时度势，做出适合非遗传承发展的正确选择。在调查中我们发现，传承人坚持非遗传承的相对封闭性，一方面有利于保证非遗的传承与"传承母体"（地域、群体）之间的传统关联；另一方面，传承人如果过度坚持传统的、封闭的传承方式，则有可能使非遗传承无法应对现代社会变迁，直至面临濒危的绝境。顺德永春拳的传承现状，颇能说明非遗传承的封闭性与发展的开放性之间的关系。顺德永春与香港咏春、佛山咏春、广州咏春、古劳咏春同属于永春拳的一个支系，但顺德永春在外界的影响与声名却远不及佛山咏春。当前，顺德永春虽然已经形成了老中青三代的传承梯队，因其过度封闭，实际上潜藏着深刻的传承危机。

4. 广东吴川泥塑

广东吴川泥塑的发展变化，正是传承人、消费者（受众）、市场（传承空间）长期互动、相互作用影响的结果。

吴川泥塑从清末发展到今天，功能呈现出多样化的发展趋势，市场在其中起着关键的作用。根据消费者的不同需求，当前吴川泥塑市场可以分为传统信仰市场和新兴市场。传统信仰市场有年例泥塑、庙宇雕塑，新兴市场则有园林公园雕塑、城市雕塑等室外雕塑、房地产商要求的室内雕塑、小型雕塑礼品等。传统泥塑市场的年例泥塑因为有"送泥鬼"的原因，以娱神为主要功能，对艺术性的要求最低；庙宇雕塑作为庙宇建筑的一部分，要求较高。新兴市场的准入门槛最高，强调作品的艺术性，一般由受过专业训练的雕塑家承担。目前，吴川泥塑艺术的发展受到较大冲击，村民认为，泥塑浪费资源，年例一过还要处理被打烂的泥土，十分麻烦。相对而言，动态的飘色游行和粤剧远比静态的泥塑形象更为有趣，也更加吸引观众。

观众、投资方审美取向也在影响着吴川泥塑的发展。没有获得观众和投资方认同的泥塑

---

① [德] 瓦尔特·本雅明：《技术复制时代的艺术品》，胡不适译，杭州：浙江文艺出版社2005年版，第88—93页。

传承人会备感失落。泥塑传承人在本地的传统泥塑市场上逐渐地形成了以民间普通观众的眼光来构思的艺术创作方式,仙女必定是柳眉黛眼,武将一定是高大魁梧,用色则常用具有喜感的大红大绿;而在新兴的泥塑市场上则形成了以古典、自然、优雅为特点的制作风格,使它能符合现代人的审美趣味。① 从吴川泥塑的案例可以发现,适应社会变迁的传承人会根据受众、市场的要求,对非遗本身的内容、形式做出相应的改变,他们在非遗的现代转型过程中起着至关重要的作用;那些无法适应社会变迁之需求的传承人,往往为时代所淘汰。

三、讨 论

随着时代的变迁,作为"活态"传承的非物质文化遗产不断适应日益变迁的时代。随着非遗保护的不断开展,现实的境况却充满着悖论。一方面,作为保护者,坚持以"真实性"的原则,保护"原生态"的文化;另一方面,在急剧变化的时代面前,非遗传承人主动或被动地作出应对,以致非遗的传统内容与传统表现形式都在悄然发生变化。这一非遗保护实践中出现的、被人们称为"悖论"的现象,背后潜藏着保护者的"原生态"想象与非遗传承的"活态"真实之间的矛盾。

非遗传承面临的问题,不仅仅是现代化变迁对非遗传承的文化生态产生的深刻影响,而且,由于非遗保护运动的开展,官方、学者、商人、传媒等外在力量,介入在"传承母体"中历经世代传承的"活态"非遗之中,打破了非遗传承发展动力的固有平衡,重构了传承人与各种力量之间的结构与关系,非遗被赋予了超越"传承母体"的新的功能、意义与价值。传承人在面临新的结构与关系、已经发生变化的非遗传承空间的时候,肯定会对非遗的相关要素做出相应的调适,以适应社会与文化变迁。当非遗的意义、价值、功能发生改变的时候,非遗本身的内涵及其表现形式也会发生相应的改变,如果我们依然要求传承人按照所谓"原生态"的标准传承非遗的内涵与形式,难道不是漠视非物质文化遗产"活态"传承发展的规律?

因此,有必要对上述所谓"悖论"现象以及非遗保护存在的相关问题进行学理辨析,以期对非遗研究、保护有所助益。

1. authenticity ("本真性""真实性""原真性") 问题

当前非遗保护界普遍盛行的观点,认为非遗保护必须坚持"本真性"(或被表述为"真实性""原真性")原则②。至于什么是非遗的"本真性",没有一个确定的标准。一个似乎需要确切界定的概念,在非遗研究者、保护者的表述中却始终处于模糊混沌、争论不休的状

---

① 参见陈冬梅《吴川泥塑传承人调查研究》,中山大学 2010 届民俗学专业硕士学位论文,指导教师:刘晓春。
② 在汉语"文化遗产"文献中,"authenticity"被翻译为"本真性""真实性""原真性"等不同表述,本文引用相关文献时照录不同表述,其对应的英文表述即"authenticity"。

态。以何时何地何种形式承载的何种内容作为界定标准,以各级文化部门名录项目申报书的"基本内容"(通过文字及影像声音等媒介呈现)作为界定标准?还是以传承人口传身授的技艺、知识呈现的当下形态作为界定标准?非物质文化遗产本来是"活态"的,不断随时间、地点、情境发生变化,如果以某种看似科学的、客观的、"本真性"的标准予以固化,将扼杀非遗的生命力,从本质上违反文化多样性的本意。

(1) authenticity:"世界遗产"① 领域不断被修正、被深化的概念。

那么,"authenticity"的原则究竟来自哪里?实际上,"authenticity"概念是"世界遗产"领域不断被修正、被深化的概念。1964年5月,第二届历史古迹建造师及技师国际会议通过了《国际古迹保护与修复宪章》(International Charter for the Conservation and Restoration of Monuments and Sites),简称《威尼斯宪章》(The Venice Charter)。《威尼斯宪章》开宗明义地指出:"传递其原真性的全部信息是我们的职责。"虽然没有界定"原真性",但对"原真性"做了具体描述:绝不能改变该建筑的布局或装饰;绝不允许任何导致改变主体和颜色关系的新建、拆除或改动;不得全部或局部搬迁古迹;任何不可避免的添加都必须与该建筑的构成有所区别,并且必须能识别是当代的东西;任何添加均不允许,除非它们不至于贬低该建筑的有趣部分、传统环境、布局平衡及其与周围环境的关系。《威尼斯宪章》近乎严格苛刻地坚持物质文化遗产的原真性与完整性。

《威尼斯宪章》作为一种"普世"的标准,在东方国家却遭遇了与西方不同的文化遗产真实性观念之困境。对于中国、日本等东方国家,其文化和物质背景与西方全然不同,如何既考虑纪念物的美学价值和历史价值,又不违背《威尼斯宪章》的原则?有鉴于此,1994年12月12—17日,世界遗产委员会第18次会议通过了《关于原真性的奈良文件》(The Nara Document on Authenticity,简称《奈良文件》)。在奈良会议上,神户大学伸雄先生指出,在日本和其他亚洲国家没有"原真性"这个词,而且日本几乎所有的历史性建筑都是用易腐烂的植物材料构筑,需要定期修复、定期更换部件,不同于西方石材建筑的坚固,因此需要一种适合多样文化的"原真性"评估观念。于是,《奈良文件》倡导了一种宽泛意义上的"原真性",即不仅考虑纪念物的材料,而且考虑它的设计、形式、用途和功能、诠释和技术,以及衍生出来的"精神"和"影响"。从此,欧洲之外的地区执行《世界遗产公约》,可以不以欧洲的"原真性"概念为唯一标准。②

《奈良文件》具有里程碑式的意义。在文化多样性背景下,《奈良文件》对原真性的重新阐释,考虑到由于文化多样性而产生的不同的原真性判断标准。出于对文化多样性的尊重,对于文化遗产的价值和原真性的评价不再囿于一个固定的评价标准,而是充分考虑文化

---

① 在联合国教科文组织的文件中,"世界遗产"与"非物质文化遗产"分属两种不同的遗产类别,归属两种不同的体系(有独立的公约文本,有不同的遗产目录),执行两种不同的标准(遴选标准不同、类型标准不同、类型分枝不同)。——参见梁保尔、张朝枝《"世界遗产"与"非物质文化遗产"两种遗产类型的特征研究》,《旅游科学》2010年第12期。

② 联合国教科文组织编:《世界文化报告——文化的多样性、冲突与多元共存》,关世杰等译,北京大学出版社2002年版,第150页。

遗产的相关文化背景，尊重多样的背景信息来源，以此判断文化遗产的原真性。①《奈良文件》关于原真性标准的原则，在具体的实践过程中，直接影响了联合国教科文组织保护世界文化与自然遗产政府间委员会颁布的《实施保护世界文化与自然遗产公约的操作指南》。

（2）中国非物质文化遗产保护与研究领域对"原真性"的挪用。

综合考察联合国《保护非物质文化遗产公约》及其关联文件，我们发现，中国政府与学界将"世界遗产"领域的"原真性"概念挪用到"非物质文化遗产"保护与研究领域。

联合国教科文组织的《保护非物质文化遗产公约》在定义中明确指出："非物质文化遗产世代相传，在各社区和群体适应周围环境以及与自然和历史的互动中，被不断地再创造，为这些社区和群体提供认同感和持续感，从而增强对文化多样性和人类创造力的尊重。"公约强调了遗产的历史性以及随社会变迁的发展变化，强调非遗在与社会、历史、文化、自然的互动中，会被不断再创造。该公约并没有把非遗看作"活化石"，也没有将"本真性"作为非遗保护的原则。

根据《保护非物质文化遗产公约》的说明，该公约的关联文件如《世界人权宣言》（1948）等七个文件，均没有提及"原真性"。其中《保护民间创作建议案》强调完整保护民间创作，避免有任何歪曲，并且充分认识到，由于民间创作具有不断发展的特点而无法直接被保护，因此，以某种有形的形态确定下来的民间创作应该予以有效保护。②但并没有以某一确定的有形形态作为"原真性"的标准。此外，《保护世界文化和自然遗产公约》没有提及"原真性"；在《实施保护世界文化与自然遗产公约的操作指南》中对文化遗产的"原真性"进行了细致的描述和界定，并明确指出原真性的描述须与文化遗产突出的普遍价值相联系进行考察；《奈良文件》"为评估遗产的原真性提供了操作基础"。③

对于本真性概念，中国非物质文化遗产研究与保护领域未经认真梳理其来龙去脉及适用范围，便将"原真性"概念从"世界遗产"领域直接挪用到"非物质文化遗产"领域；"世界遗产"领域中一个不断深化、修正的概念，在"非物质文化遗产"领域演变成为"金科玉律"和僵化的教条。

（3）什么不是"原真性"？什么是"原真性"？

我们认为，任何通过媒介固化下来的某一特定时空的非物质文化遗产，不代表其唯一"原真性"；各级名录申报材料中描述、呈现的非物质文化遗产，不因为其所谓的官方"合法性"，而被认为代表非遗的唯一"原真性"。"活态的"，具有其自身功能、价值、意义的非物质文化遗产，随着时代的变化而变化，并持续地为人们所认同，即呈现其"原真性"。

2. 传承母体共享的非遗与脱离传承母体的非遗

在辨析"本真性"的基础上，有必要在传承母体共享的非遗与脱离传承母体的非遗之

---

① 同上页注②。

② 英文原文：While living folklore, owing to its evolving character, cannot always be directly protected, folklore that has been fixed in a tangible form should be effectively protected.

③ 参见中华人民共和国国家文物局网站：http://www.sach.gov.cn/tabid/312/InfoID/6973/Default.aspx。

间做出区分。

当下中国，由官方认定的传承人、传承群体及其传承的非物质文化遗产，开始作为"传承母体"之外的"想象的共同体"之符号及象征资源。非遗作为一种文化，从特定地域、特定群体共享的文化，到脱离"传承母体"而被移植、再利用，甚至被提升为地域的、民族—国家的文化遗产，承载着超越其"传承母体"的意义、功能与价值。于是，在特定的"传承母体"中传承的非物质文化遗产，被广泛地作为政治、经济、文化资源用于展示，并且为"传承母体"之外的人们所运用并获得利益，这是非遗保护过程中经常出现的文化现象。这些超越"传承母体"的"非遗"，被人们斥为"伪民俗"。人们更多地停留在"真"与"伪"的争辩之中，而没有考察分析这些作为"生活"的民俗之所以具有"文化资本"而进入"遗产"名录，以及被广泛地移植、利用、再创造，其背后蕴含的历史传统、当下社会结构以及文化变迁的动因。

我们认为，在具体的保护过程中，有必要对传承母体共享的非遗与脱离传承母体的非遗进行区分：前者是非遗保护的对象；后者是非遗作为文化元素，被移植、被利用到当代文化发展之中，而不是传承母体共享的非遗。被移植、被利用的非遗，因为脱离其传承母体，具有与传承母体不同的再创造者、文化时空、受众、传播渠道等，其内涵、表现形式自然会发生变化，有时甚至变得面目全非。这些脱离传承母体的非遗不是非遗保护的对象。在非遗保护的大背景下，其中一个突出而普遍的现象是，政府依托传统民俗节日打造的新兴节庆，如2011年2月17日，广州市越秀区在城隍庙忠佑广场举行首届"广府庙会"。这种由政府借助传统民俗文化资源创设的新兴节庆，可以看到国家力量对传统地方民俗文化的移植、利用以及再创造。如何使新兴节庆既保持来自民间的内在动力，具有可持续传承发展的社会结构基础，符合地方民众的文化心理需求，又契合传承传统民俗文化、创新传统民俗文化之现代价值、营造社会和谐氛围的国家意志，使其具有超越地方社会的政治、经济、文化功能，两者有机融合，是主办者需要认真考量的问题。

3. 体系外的文化与体制外的文化持有者

《中华人民共和国非物质文化遗产法》（2011）第二十一条规定："相同的非物质文化遗产项目，其形式和内涵在两个以上地区均保持完整的，可以同时列入国家级非物质文化遗产代表性项目名录。"但在实际的实施过程中，由于种种原因，许多相同的非物质文化遗产，其形式和内涵在两个以上地区均保持完整，却未能同时被纳入名录或扩展名录；形式、内涵相同的非遗，却因行政区划的不同，其文化价值被人为地划分为三六九等。此外，由于文化的多样，国家无法将所有的文化事项纳入保护体系，那些未被纳入保护体系的文化以及游离于体制外的文化持有者，有可能因为长期不为人们所关注，其存在的价值被忽视，这些文化持有者传承的文化面临濒危的绝境，直至最终消失。

闽粤赣地区客家山歌的不同遭遇即是典型案例。客家山歌是客家族群共同拥有的文化，在客家人聚居的区域具有广泛的传承，但目前只有梅州客家山歌、兴国山歌入选国家级非物质文化遗产名录体系。那些未被入选国家名录的客家地区传承的客家山歌，其价值、意义、功能是否不如梅州和兴国的客家山歌重要呢？其实未必如此。据调查，在福建长汀县，对于许多人来说，客家山歌依然具有重要的价值、意义与功能。2000年以来，随着农村人口大量进入城镇，客家山歌也从乡村进入到城镇，客家山歌的演唱空间从传统的山野（"山歌只能山上唱"）进入到如今的大庭广众（公园里面唱山歌）。涌入城镇的"乡下人"，脱离了原有的人际关系与文化网络，作为传统记忆的山歌被重新激活；借由传统的山歌，"乡下人"在城镇建立起新的人际关系和文化网络。1949年之后历经政治制度、生活方式的变迁而遭到破坏的山歌文化生态链条，又被重新接续起来。由于尚未被外界赋予超越传承母体的政治、经济、文化的功能，长汀客家山歌的功能依然保留着传统的娱乐和男女两性"风流"交际的功能。从某种意义上，"本真性"保护论者倒是可以在长汀发现客家山歌的"原生态"。现存歌手传承的长汀客家山歌类型多样，生活气息浓郁，保存了丰富的传统生活记忆，文化内涵深厚，在山歌的主题、套路、评价标准、演唱技巧等方面，形成了一套系统的山歌地方性知识。[①] 但是，这种无意识、完全自觉的文化传承，随着这群对山歌保有记忆的歌手群体的逐渐逝去，很有可能濒临断绝。而颇具讽刺意味的是，一直依靠外在力量赋予其政治、经济、文化价值的某地客家山歌，其真实的传承状态是：既传承大量传统山歌，又具有即兴编创能力的歌手如凤毛麟角，歌手的应时应景表演几乎依靠文化馆干部的创作，歌手只是照章背诵而已，但该地客家山歌却位列重要的名录体系。两相比较，究竟是谁的濒危程度更严重，谁更需要被纳入保护体系呢？

[①] 参见王维娜《从山野到大庭广众——长汀客家山歌的传承与地方知识》，中山大学2009届民俗学专业博士学位论文，指导教师：康保成。

关于黄永林《从文化生态学角度看待非物质文化遗产的保护》的讨论

杰西卡·安德森·特讷*

中国比其他国家有更多指定的非物质文化遗产（以下简称"非遗"）。这一点都不让人吃惊。其他国家将联合国教科文组织的这一项认证仅仅当成是国家建设的一部分；然而中国和其他国家不同，联合国教科文组织的政策变成了中国的国家文化政策，甚至是付诸实践。许多国家和非遗认证之间的交流只存在于文化决策者和公共领域的学者层面；不同的是，在中国，非遗这个概念在社会的各个阶层广泛传播。文化部甚至鼓励人们参与非遗的申报。在中国，非物质文化遗产的学术研究论文涉及各个方面，包括文化艺术，身份认同、遗产保护，以及阐述与非物质文化遗产相关的民俗学、音乐人类学等。本次会议所收到的文章表现得非常明显，其中也包括了黄永林教授的《从文化生态学的角度看待非物质文化遗产的保护》。

虽然我在会议进行的过程中已经发表了一些评论，这些评论是我对黄教授的文章的响应，因黄教授此次未能参会，由我代为做个综述。综述的内容包括中国与非遗的关系，令人震惊的中国非遗名录数量，以及一些常见于中国非遗理论和学术研究中的术语等。我认为这对于解释中国非物质文化遗产方面的一些观点和术语将起到作用，尤其能帮助到那些大体了解非遗，却不知道非遗的认证在中国是如何进行的人。

2001年，昆曲被联合国教科文组织列入"人类口头与非物质遗产代表作名录"，这是第一个享有此殊荣的中国非物质文化遗产项目。如今，在联合国教科文组织的《人类非物质文化遗产代表作名录》上已经有38项来自中国的非物质文化遗产项目，其中有一些项目更是被确认为亟须尽快保护。[①]

在2005年，中国政府发布了自己的"国家级非物质文化遗产代表作名录"。这是由文化部建立的内部认证系统。在2005年到2009年的四年之间，第一次摸查收集到了87万个文化项目作为代表名录的候选。文化部对这个国家名录的重视通过在这个项目上所做的努

---

* 杰西卡·安德森·特讷，弗吉尼亚州因特蒙特学院。
① http://www.unesco.org/culture/ich/en/lists.

力、资源的分配以及系统的调查和文化项目的分类都可以体现出来。在 2006 年到 2012 年之间，以这个初始调查为蓝本，一共有 1219 个文化项目被列入"国家级非物质文化遗产代表作名录"，范围涵盖了中国所有的省、直辖市和自治区。

中国与非物质文化遗产之间的关系为非遗的民族化提供了例证。它以联合国教科文组织的标准和政策为内核，并将其本土化。联合国教科文组织的标准和政策被融入中国的国家各个有关部门和各层级的认证系统当中，并且各层级的认证系统已经使得中国的非遗认定形成了一个系统性的工作体系和一门独立的学科。中国的非物质文化遗产保护开始于对联合国教科文组织的名录制度的采纳，并在社会生活中发挥了独特的作用。到目前为止，它已经影响到社会生活的方方面面，并作为一种新式的国家主义受到政府的强力支持。公民们意识到他们是文化传承中重要的角色；成都每年举办的国际非物质文化遗产节也成为一个国家性的节日。

2013 年 6 月，一位管理员金锁金（Sojin Kim）在第四届成都国际非物质文化遗产节上拍下了这张照片①。（见插图）

除了认定国家级非遗名录事项外，中国的非遗保护体系还包括保护民俗和非遗流派、创新和传承传统文化的技艺，以及具有突出群体信仰的文化实践等，并将传统文化的重要持有者认定为传承人，同时也命名非遗文化保护区。

为了支持这项新的国家产业，在 2011 年，全国人民代表大会通过了《中华人民共和国非物质文化遗产法》，旨在对非物质文化遗产的保护和保存进行认定与管理。这项法律细分为三大组成系统，分别是非遗的调查、代表性项目名录以及传承与传播。在文化部和学术界有一场十分重要的讨论：探讨研究（非遗的调查与传承）与发展（传承与传播）之间如何取得一个合理的平衡。

2013 年第四届成都国际非遗节上工作人员
服装上所印的口号　　　　　　（金锁金摄）

中国的学者们已经强烈地感受到在过去的一个世纪里，这个国家发生了怎样翻天覆地的变化，而且非遗的法律和名录无不是迎合保护与传承中国文化传统这一理念的。这一觉醒在民俗学、民族音乐学以及人类学领域过去二十年的研究所产生的文化表征当中体现得非常明显。相关研究首先集中在非遗的传播与变化，后来现代的研究焦点则主要集中在非遗的传承、保护与发展上。在非物质文化遗产的相关研究以及公共讨论当中，相关的概念如"原生态"（本土化，从字面上了解即是"original ecology"）以及文化生态（文化生态学，即文化系统必须在健康的生态系统之下才能繁荣发展的理念，文化系统必须受到保护）越来越

---

① 照片来源：史密森学会的民俗生活与文化遗产中心提供。

流行。有大量关于这些概念的理论知识，并且文化实践者广泛地应用这些术语来对他们的工作进行定位，同时，旅游业和工厂制造业的商品也从这些概念中获得认可。

文化部在它制定的政策当中体现出创造一个健康的文化生态系统的重要性。目前，已有15个非遗的文化生态保护区。在这些区域内，开发和工业受到管制，因为一切以保护传统文化实践为先；旅游业和制造业受到限制，同时，居民被鼓励积极参与到传统文化与艺术的实践中。除了这些文化生态保护区，还设立了14个"生产性保护基地"。这些基地是非遗商品化的制造中心，所有商品经过批准才可以进入市场。它们的传统制造工艺是经过认证的，用以投放市场并起到宣传作用。只有那些经过文化部审批通过的商品才可以用非遗名录上的方式或技术进行生产。这种做法的核心是努力规范新的与非遗相关的产品的生产，这些产品由技术精湛的工人使用传统的方法制作出来，并对其外在艺术表现形式进行了改进。但是，关于对生产性保护定义的理解也引发了许多争议，我们需要在提高生产力、提升产品利润和保护传统的文化形式、生产方式之间找到平衡。

黄教授的文章推进了许多今天在非遗研究领域广泛讨论的议题：发展是否可以成为保护"原生态"的一种方式？尽管人们会广泛讨论在这些情况下该如何适度发展的程度，那么适度发展的原则是不是保护"原生态"的关键和正确的途径？文化发展的目标不应该仅仅是用非物质文化遗产政策推动旅游业发展，而且是推动文化政策自身的研究和应用。中国学者对于非遗的最普遍看法正是发展比文化形式的保护更加重要。传统的转化会影响到新的社会功能，从而影响到文化传统的保护。

2011年在中国实施的《中华人民共和国非物质文化遗产法》以及这个项目所引发的一系列实践和产生的名录已经为这些非物质文化遗产带来了实实在在的成果：指定的文化传承人、非遗保护区（文化生态保护区）为传统文化实践的持续和创新不断绘制着宏图，在生产性保护区制造出来的产品也投放到市场。在黄教授的文章里，他提出：保护文化生态是保护非遗的重要组成部分，对保护非遗必须要平衡好"保护"和"发展"的关系，必须明确政府在这些举措中的责任。在分析非遗的实践中，他提出的这些问题受到许多中国学者的关注和赞同。这些学者也承认非物质文化遗产的实践必须是经过深思熟虑的，和在政策指导下的。贯穿在生产性保护中的保护和发展关系问题虽然富有争议性，但是也是必需的。随着法律和政策的执行和调整，乃至修订，非遗的保护将越来越向科学性和系统性靠近。

谁在生产？怎样保护？
——透视中国非物质文化遗产的"生产性保护"

张士闪[*]

一、非遗"生产性保护"：提出了早该提出的问题

21世纪初的中国，原本在民间生活中传承的民俗，被国家政府有选择地赋予荣誉和资助，有差别地置于非物质文化遗产（以下简称"非遗"）四级保护框架之内。随着国家非遗名录的审批、非遗传承人的评选、国家级文化生态保护区试点的确定，非遗运动声势渐壮，并初步呈现出政府、学者和民众合力推动的态势。与此同时，社会上对于非遗保护方式的讨论亦日益增多，并先后出现了"抢救性保护""整体性保护"及"生产性保护"[①]的说法，"生产性保护"更是在近年来由一般概念迅速上升为社会文化热点。如果说，非遗名录及传承人的评选制度代表的是某种"抢救性保护"的理念，那么国家级文化生态保护区试点工程则旨在实验一种对于非遗的"整体性保护"。

然而，不容忽视的社会现实是，当非遗保护已经成为我国的一项基本国策，各级政府对于非遗的拉网式普查宣告结束，其考虑更多的是如何运作已确立的非遗项目，"通过行政手段使之转化为实际生产力，达到经世致用的目的"[②]。"生产性保护"一说，大致以此为背景。特别是在2009年元宵节期间文化部举办的"非物质文化遗产生产性方式保护论坛"上，将"生产性保护"由传统技艺类项目延伸到整个非遗领域，成为与会专家的主流观点。在部分研究者和业界人士看来，"生产性保护"似乎已经成为非遗融入当代社会生活和生产实践的最直接、最现实的途径，凭此方式似可保证非遗传承的"长治久安"。

---

[*] 张士闪，山东大学文化遗产研究院教授。

[①] 关于非物质文化遗产"生产性保护"这一概念，最早出现在王文章主编的《非物质文化遗产概论》（文化艺术出版社2006年版）一书中。2009年文化部副部长周和平在"非物质文化遗产生产性方式保护论坛"开幕式上，对这一概念作了如下界定："它是指通过生产、流通、销售等方式，将非物质文化遗产及其资源转化为生产力和产品，产生经济效益，并促进相关产业发展，使非物质文化遗产在生产实践中得到积极有效的保护，实现非物质文化遗产保护与经济社会协调发展的良性互动。"

[②] 施爱东：《中国现代民俗学检讨》，社会科学文献出版社2010年，第194页。

非遗的"生产性保护",就其实现它自身所设定的目标"实现非物质文化遗产保护与经济社会协调发展的良性互动"而言,绝不是看上去那么乐观。"生产性保护"观念的提出,与"抢救性保护""整体性保护"相比,最重要的意义在于将社会现代性的最重要方面,即生产现代性,引入非物质文化遗产保护的视野。其实质是,它使得社会各个利益群体对非遗的诉求,在经历了国家政治诉求("抢救性保护")与学术群体诉求("整体性保护")后,当代产业群体借助"生产性保护"表达了自己的诉求。在上述多种诉求的叠合与冲突中,国家政策的经济中心倾向使政府决策部门不自觉地倾向于"生产性保护"。然而,"生产性保护"的观念并不会因为它附生在国家集体利益之上而更有说服力。与"抢救性保护""整体性保护"相比,"生产性保护"与其说提出了一种解决方案,毋宁说是使一个真正需要提出的问题在官方平台上被明确地提了出来:在一个产业化强势发展的时代,非遗保护与产业增益之间如何真正实现共赢?这一问题的真正解决方法无法凭借逻辑推导,而需要爬梳活生生的现实个案,在成功或失败的个案中找到解决上述问题的办法。

本文尝试从个案深度分析的角度对上述"如何"的问题进行探索,分析主要以山东省惠民县泥玩具和昌邑市"烧大牛"活动为个案,从商品交易与文化赋意、艺人与农民、传统与现代等层面,对民间手工技艺生产的功能、主体身份、语境等予以辨析,并对"生产性保护"在当下社会实践中的效度与限度予以评析。

二、商品交易与文化赋意:民间手工技艺类非遗的功能辨析

综观在非遗中蔚成大类的民间手工技艺活动,就不难发现,它们虽然都具有相当的功利色彩,但在功能预设方面,又有明显的商业性与自洽性的差异。商业性,是指制作者更加看重制品的经济交换价值,并期望通过商品交易活动来实现;自洽性,则是指制作者更加注重制品的精神满足功能,并期望通过社区活动中的文化赋意来实现。

河南张与火把李,是惠民县城西南部的皂户李乡的两个"对子村",相距约6公里。河南张村有300多年的泥玩具制作历史,所谓"河南张,朝南门,家家户户做泥人";每年一度于二月二定期举办的火把李庙会,不仅被本村村民视为"过第二遍年",而且名闻遐迩,每每引动鲁冀豫三省十几个县市民众前来赶会。造型古朴的泥娃娃是火把李庙会最具影响的"吉祥物",其影响之大,从河南张村俗称"娃娃张"、火把李庙会俗称"娃娃会"中可以想见。可以说,河南张村村民借助于火把李村的庙会销售自制的泥玩具,火把李村的庙会则因为有了河南张泥塑而享誉四方,两个村落之间的经济协作与文化分工由此实现,并在年复一年的延续中凝结为一种民俗传统。

可以设想一下当初"泥娃娃"进入火把李庙会的"准入问题"。现在已很难考察"泥娃娃"与火把李庙会的出现孰先孰后,但两者在当地乡民的功能认同上的确存在差异:"泥娃娃"无论如何谈不上是当地的农事"工具",火把李庙会就其普泛的功能定位而言,则是开春之前,当地乡民于此选购农事"工具"的市场。那么,"泥娃娃"为何会堂而皇之地出现

在火把李庙会上，而且成为众人热衷购买的对象呢？"泥娃娃"是凭借什么，解决了自己在"工具"市场上的"准入问题"？要想解答这一问题，必须深入追溯当地相关的民俗传统。

在惠民地区，"拴娃娃"习俗可谓由来已久。人们常常在集市上将做工精巧、细腻逼真的泥娃娃"请"到家中，作为家庭添丁的信祝之物。"拴娃娃"之俗，就其民俗祈愿而言，表征着对新生的祝望，因此又产生了其对时间节点的无意识倾向，即"拴娃娃"应当与自然人事的开始、新生的特定时刻相联系。在我国传统的时间制度中，一年四季始于春，"二月二，龙抬头"，"二月二"又是典型的春信时刻。因此，"二月二，拴娃娃"的时间点的约定俗成并非偶然。二月二火把李庙会，就其区域商集功能而言，是开春之际货卖春耕工具；"货卖工具"虽然是不折不扣的商贸行为，但因为和"一年之首"的神圣时间暗示杂糅在一起，这一"货卖"因之产生了"文化"的赋意，所谓"一年之计在于春"。这种"文化赋意"行为，氤氲在火把李庙会之上，自然而然成为具有同样文化意蕴的泥娃娃的进入通道。正是在"春首新生"的深度民俗意义上，泥娃娃与诸多农事"工具"便拥有了相同的身份；共处于庙会的神圣时空之中，二者是买卖也是仪式，是交易也是沟通，买卖行为发生的过程也是民俗意义的产生与民俗传统的再生产，而不同乡土社区之间的生产关系经此民俗认同而得以固化，获得长久传承的动力。这其实就是非遗"生产性保护"的活生生的形式。

然而，我们在昌邑市的东永安村，则看到了与惠民泥玩具在功能预设与意义产生方面差异极大的民间手工技艺活动。据东永安村村民口传，自建村以来的几百年间，每年一进腊月，村民就要拾掇出专门的场地，筹措备料，耗费相当的人力物力，扎一头牛角高约7米、牛身长约13米的"独角大牛"，然后在正月十四抬着大牛游行，最后在孙膑庙（俗称"老爷庙"）前烧掉。所需资金物资，由村里德高望重的老人出面张罗，大家自愿捐输，扎制者都是义务参与。这期间，每天都会有热心的村民前来围观，评头论足，整个村落沉浸在自由创造的社区欢乐氛围之中。

我们在调查中得知，类似"扎大牛"的活动在这一带并非东永安村所独有，而是比较普遍。东邻的远东庄，每年在正月十二庙会上要烧"牛"两头；与东永安村相距五华里的渔埠村，每年正月十六举行"演旨"活动，最后烧"牛"三头；西邻的西永安村，每年正月十五要烧掉"大轿"两台献祭老母娘娘；同在东永安村，除了以吕家、丛家为主举行"烧大牛"仪式外，齐姓人家近年来也会在正月初九这天烧掉一匹"大马"。具有产业经营头脑的人或许会觉得，东永安村人完全可以凭借其"扎大牛"的声望，借助这一带"焚烧圣物"信俗，将牛、马、轿等扎制做成一种利润可观的行业。我们甚至可以乐观地认为，已经进入市级非物质文化遗产名录的东永安村"烧大牛"，在得到更有力度的非遗保护制度支持及相应资助后，将通过牛、马、轿等扎制的成规模生产，获得真正的文化保护与传承、推广。

问题出来了：为什么要劳民伤财，花大量的金钱财帛与精力时间去扎制大牛，然后一炬燎之？在这种行为中，断言参与者心中没有钱财方面的计较是不可能的，但有什么东西比钱财计较更重要以至于不再计较了呢？

在"扎大牛"中，所产生的比钱财计较更重要的东西，是"社会资源"。"扎大牛"仪式的首要特点，在于它场面大，全村参与，人人有份。"扎大牛"耗资不菲，场面红火，是村里的"大事儿"，也是十里八村人人称羡的只有在过大年期间才会有的"要景"；"扎大牛"以其"大事儿"的身份，构成了当地乡土生活中的特殊时刻。唯其场面大，需要合村民众群策群力，因之成为神圣、隆重的"村际时刻"。其次，为村民合力举行的"扎大牛"活动，仪式意味极为浓厚。伴随"扎大牛""游大牛""烧大牛"系列仪式的次第展开，观演人数越来越多，形成了人群摩肩接踵争相观看的场面和氛围。而在"能看见"和"不能看见"的围观行为之间，自然形成了这一仪式的中心和边缘之分。尤其是"烧大牛"这一万众期待的最后时刻到来之际，火光冲天，雾匝四野，仪式意味氤氲而出。在此"仪式化"充分张扬的"村际时刻"，即使身处外圈，人们之间的交流也会平添某种神圣色彩；比较接近"圣物"的人群，他们观看并向外圈观者传递关于"圣物"的种种细节；再向里一层，是"圣物"操演的中心。上述三层人群形成了这一特定时空中的三重价值中心，这一格局与日常的村际政治有重合亦有疏离，其实是被充分展演与微妙调控的"社会资源"。花大价钱"扎大牛"，是为了巩固已有的"社会资源"，营造新的"社会资源"，而这些"社会资源"将是村内产业、村际产业与更加复杂的产业网络运行起来的前提。据此"社会资源"运行的产业，必将为此"社会资源"赋予意义，这一仪式的再生产机制由此建立。这是非遗保护"生产性保护"的又一个鲜活例子。

往更深一步说，大牛扎制过程本身，即意味着在年节期间为全村村民搭建了一个公共交流平台，意味着村落之中不同的人群可以借此来商榷事情。伴随着村民外出打工现象的普遍化与长期化，当下村落公共空间日益萎缩。从腊月十九开始"扎大牛"到"游大牛""烧大牛"，以大牛为话题，村民之间形成了一种高频度的情感交流与生活交际，村民心头期盼已久的热热闹闹的"年味"借此得到一定的营造。而且，对于东永安村村民而言，"扎大牛"其实还具有更深刻的文化意义。借助每年一度的"扎大牛"活动，村落生活明显地呈现出如下三层边界：①通过"扎大牛""游大牛""烧大牛"的组织运作、参与群体、巡游路线，以及潜在的消灾祛恶的功利设置，凸显出一村之内家族与家族之间的明确边界；②在这一带乡土社区之中普遍存在的"焚烧圣物"现象（如"烧牛""烧马""烧轿"等）凸显了不同的村落个性；③"圣物焚烧"现象共同构成了这一带乡土社区面向外部世界而呈现的"前台"，而其自身又成为"昌邑乡土风情"表演的后台。文化边界的多重设置，构成了乡土生活的多重层级结构。

可以说，大牛从开始扎制起，就注定是要被烧掉的。它是民众对于自身精神世界的文化设置，弥补由现代农村社会变迁所导致的安全感和归属感的缺失，进而安抚自己焦虑的灵魂，去除生活中的苦恼。作为乡土社会自治资源的自我培塑和实践再造，整个活动蕴含着乡民浓烈、纯朴的乡土情感的尽情抒发。每一次活动的组织，既是对区域社会中某种群体意志的不断彰显与强调，同时也是对人类个体情感的不断激发、重温与新的培育。它担负着联结周边村落、凝聚人心的社会功能，俨然已成为春节体系中的高潮点和乡民精神的情感寄托，也是各村落社区之间的一种别样的"拜年"形式。在这里，民间手工技艺的自洽性特征与社区公益性紧密联系在一起。

三、艺人与农民：民间手工技艺主体的身份辨认

"生产性保护"，显然倾向于将民间手工技艺的主体理解成艺人或行业经营者，或者期望通过一定的方式使这一部分人走向专业化、专营化道路。这其实是对于民间手工技艺的狭义理解所致。民间手工技艺，虽然也可以表现为作坊、行业的生产，但在更广泛的意义上是与民众生活世界交织在一起的。"生产性保护"的真正生产主体，应当是职业身份不明显或无职业身份的"所有民众"。

河南张村村民的泥塑工艺以及所制作的泥玩具，并不是每天每时都在进行，而表现为以年度为周期的季节性生产。玩具制作者并不是职业的"艺人"，同样，当他们操持起春种秋收、夏做冬藏等农业生计之时，我们也很难认定此时他们就是绝对的"农民"。民间手工技艺生产的节令性特点，使得制作者多是亦农亦艺的复合型人才。而民间手工技艺制品中浓郁的乡土色彩，正是他们在手工技艺与农事活动的双重劳作中涵育而成的。我们在对民间手工技艺进行制度性保护的时候，要特别注意创造一定条件，让民间手工技艺生产重新回归到一种与乡土日常生活相联结的、充溢着精神创造旨趣的"副业"活动。

在此，我们可对中国"前非遗时代"的相关保护状况简略追溯。一直到20世纪90年代中后期，中国社会有着非常发达的"副业"传统，就是忙时干"正经活"，闲时做点"营生儿"赚点零花钱贴补家用。这种"副业"传统，即涵括了"非遗"的大部分内容。这种"副业"行为，以充满张力的方式存身于民众的生活传统之中：一方面，"副业"没有任何的文化企图，只为做些东西贴补家用；另一方面，正是因为这些"副业"没有任何文化企图，却使之真正恢复到了民众日常生活的轨道上来，自然而然地承受着乡土民俗传统的温润。闲时为之，忙时而止，没有强烈的产业化冲动，所以并不苛求于数量和货卖金额，也不因伺服芸芸众生而自觉身价有跌，这自然保证了非遗产品的品质；因为没有谋求御赐皇封、一朝成名天下知的"文化野心"，所以在从事这类"副业"生产的过程中便更多是顺循"老辈儿教的"和个人兴之所至而操持，真是"做一个是一个"。总之，"副业"传统真正将"非遗"行为切实纳入日常生活之中，使"非遗"主体自觉保持着对其产业冲动的遏制，基本保持着对社区传统的尊重和个人兴趣的表达。时至今日，要想真正推行非遗的"生产性保护"，必须借鉴传统社会中所谓"副业"的产业结构，以此作为"生产性保护"的真正框架。

因此，仅仅选择一个或几个艺人，给予非遗传承人的名分与相应资助，寄望其在产业化生产中自然形成保护，未免过于乐观。事实上，在20世纪上半叶，河南张村全村男女老少几乎都能制作泥玩具。如今，靠这门手艺吃饭的人家越来越少。根据我们近年来的持续调查，2005年制作泥玩具的有近20户，2006年为10户，2007年、2008年均为9户，2009年为12户，2010年以后基本上是五六户的状态。虽然河南张泥玩具早在2006年便进入第一批省级非遗名录，2011年入选第三批国家级非遗名录，2010年村民张凯被评为省级非遗项

目代表性传承人,但这一民间手工技艺目前所面临的严重传承危机并未缓解。

正是在非遗保护运动急剧升温的大背景下,河南张泥玩具无论在技艺传承还是在制作规模上依然走向衰落,受制于非遗申报制度中对于民俗文化类别的精细分割,当地政府无论是在申报过程中对于保护方案的设计,还是后来对保护方案的实施,都难以将河南张泥玩具销售所依托的火把李庙会文化空间包括在内,难以实施整体、有效的保护,可能是重要因素之一。这也说明,非遗保护如果仅仅指向几类制品的开发工作,而未关注手工技艺的"活动"过程及所属的整体性文化空间,效果有限。①

相形之下,进入市级非遗名录的昌邑"烧大牛"活动,虽未产生由官方认定的非遗项目代表性传承人,却也因此没有因荣誉竞争而引发纷扰,这一活动目前仍处于良性的社区自治状态,未显疲态。在东永安村,因为丛、吕家族的"烧大牛"仪式的持续举办,反倒引发了村内齐氏家族的跟风,自2007年起每逢正月初九玉皇大帝生日之际,为其扎制一头红色大马举行烧祭仪式。我们在近年来的调查过程中,也见过邻村村民前来东永安村请教、试图"恢复"本村扎牛烧牛活动的现象。这或许说明,生产性保护并非民间手工技艺在当代社会中实现自救的唯一途径。

有一种民间手工技艺的产业化发展所走过的道路,也许并非偶然。在山西长治一带,布老虎艺人张健旺很早就致力于将这门民间手工技艺产业化,从大江南北搜集了大量布老虎造型,然后进行机器化生产的改造加工。他采用公司加农户的经营模式,基本上是两条腿走路:一条路是手工制作,价位高,走收藏品路线;另一条路是机器批量复制,价位低,市场化。实践证明,市场化的选择使得其中手工制作的比例已日渐缩微,通过市场化生产可以更好地保护非遗的想法,要想真正在实践中贯彻远非易事。制作者为了卖出产品,必然要让产品适应市场,而市场的引导导致制作者对本具有独特地方色彩的布老虎进行改造,使得大众喜爱的布老虎代替了独具地方特色的布老虎。最终,造型上"千虎一面",工艺上借用现代材料,最终丧失了传统布艺的韵味和技术含量。马知遥的基本判断是,"可以肯定地说,市场的冲击已经让他的布老虎失去了当地独特的风格……从保护的角度看,他的规模化生产已经破坏了传统。"②

大量田野调查表明,许多非遗传承人都期望在产业开发中获得利益。然而,如果将不适合产业化的非遗推向市场,不论国家支持的力度有多大,其最终结果也可能是对其自身的灾难性破坏。当非遗在所属社区中变了味甚或失去价值,其实就是对这一文化的变相扼杀。

四、传统与现代:民间手工技艺的语境认知

民间手工技艺发展的当代性问题,在文化全球化的时代显得日益重要。在世界范围内,

---

① 张士闪:《当代民间工艺的语境认知与生态保护——以山东惠民河南张泥玩具为个案》,《山东社会科学》2010年第1期。
② 马知遥:《非物质文化遗产保护的田野思考——中国北方民间布老虎现状反思》,《民俗研究》2012年第4期。

自 19 世纪西方工业革命以来，伴随资本主义经济的全球化扩张，文化与文明的输出逐步走向全球化。尤其是在 20 世纪五六十年代，伴随着资本主义经济的总体转型，跨国公司的全球蔓延不仅成为西方经济向全球扩散的载体，更成为西方文明全球化的强大推动力。民间手工技艺，作为典型的本土文化载体，在西方文明全球化的总体局势中，经历了先是被动整合、然后主动抗争的发展过程。

民间手工技艺的产业化应是现代社会的独特命题。在传统社会中，民间手工技艺活动与小农经济大致相适应。一方面，它与多种多样的经济与商贸活动相联系，如庙会、仪式活动中的商贸行为，但就其从属关系而言，这类经贸行为是民俗整体活动的重要部分。另一方面，民间手工技艺还承担了为社区仪式性活动提供道具或戏剧的任务，这使得它大大超出了传统文人所谓"奇技淫巧"的功能预期。民间手工技艺的产业化冲动，往往在传统民俗框架的整体导向之下，表现出适时适度的自我克制，使商贸行为自始至终在民间社会的价值格局中进行。换言之，民间手工技艺的商品性，始终在其对于这个民间社会的自洽性的制约之下，总是离不开人际交往的激活、社会关系的人文指向，其商品性与自洽性大致保持了良性关系。

新中国建立至"文革"结束，小农经济被彻底禁绝，民间手工技艺活动的萎缩同步发生。20 世纪 80 年代，随着农村小农经济的逐步恢复，传统民俗活动又有了活力。但与农村小农经济恢复相伴生的，是市场经济的勃兴以及官方作为经济主体的介入；进入 20 世纪 90 年代，包括民间手工技艺在内的民俗资源，在许多地方被尝试着"开发"成现代产业，民俗手工技艺对于社区的精神价值受到轻视，最终造成了民俗生态的败坏，引来众多批评。21 世纪以来，随着因"经济中心化"所引发的种种社会不公，自上而下发生了对当代中国经济发展的价值反思与文化深化，以及对传统文化、民俗文化对于中华文明当代复兴的根本性价值的追问与反思，同样影响到对民俗文化的产业价值与精神价值的重新定位。恰好，非物质文化遗产保护运动"忽如一夜春风来"，与上述需求深度契合，于是自国际而国内、自上而下地开展起来，形成热潮。社会上对于民俗文化的精神价值的评价渐高，民俗传统的定位正逐渐从"民俗资源"转向"公共文化"，这突出地表现在许多学者对于民俗文化产业化发展的持续质疑与批评方面。这种观点其实忽略了以民间手工技艺为代表的很大一部分民俗文化的商品性特征，即使在传统社会中，这一商品性特征其实也表现得相当明显，只不过在与其自洽性特征相冲突的社会格局中未显颓败而已。可以想见，这样一种批评因理论未臻圆融并未发挥出应有的力度。

其实，真正对民间手工技艺构成威胁的，不是当代社会的产业化冲动，而是以之为重要载体之一的乡土公共秩序的紊乱和民间文化精神的凋敝。当民间手工技艺因为被认为是烦琐的、劳累的、费力而不赚钱的而被扬弃，当大规模的机器生产被认为代表着科技进步和先进的生活方式，人们丢失的绝不仅仅是一种传统记忆，曾经借助民间手工技艺而存身的民俗文化，作为乡土社会中的生活惯性和文化根基，所具有的对于社会结构的温润与导引的作用也就削弱甚至消解了。① 可以说,自20世纪90年代中期以来民俗产业的畸形发展,已经使得民俗文化资源成为市场紧缺"物资"。在此前提下,大量伪民俗、仿民间手工技艺被制造出来,由此所造成的恶劣后果是真正的民俗文化被冲击乃至湮没,民间手工技艺的神圣性与对于社区生活的自洽性被削平,从而造成中国民俗知识建构在当代的整体失落。而这一切表明,"生产性保护"显然并非万能灵药,难以包治百病。

结语:中国当代非遗保护中的"应然"与"实然"

在过去十年中,中国社会结构变化之深、利益格局调整之大、遭遇的外部环境之复杂,实属罕见。市场经济的冲击余波未了,全球化、民主化、信息化的浪潮又不期叠加。中国正面临比经济转型更具挑战的社会转型。人民群众不仅要福利的拓展,也要公平的过程;不仅要权利的保障,也要权力的透明。满足"需求",回应"要求",不仅关系到发展能否实现"正义增长",关系到13亿人的政治信任,更关系到中国现代化的前途。在国家掌控庞大的社会资源,同时以此为依托致力于持续的渐进式的民主化改革进程中,随着公众参与意识、表达意识、监督意识的增强,来自公众的对于政府公信力的质疑将会持续存在并趋于具体化、明晰化。不言而喻,要"最大限度激发社会活力",关键之处在于尊重民意、民心,用好民智、民力,从倾听民众诉求中改善治理,在及时回应中引导公众参与,在良性互动中促成社会共识,让政府职能的转变促成社会的蓬勃发育,促进政府公信力的保值增值。②

具体到非遗保护,我们可以在中国社会历史的百年进程中,以民间手工技艺发展的起伏脉络予以观察。20世纪上半叶,中国处于农耕社会的"手工业时代",其经济生产与精神生产主要在家庭—村落的乡土框架中进行;20世纪50—70年代的"副业时代",民间手工技艺作为国营集体经济的补充而存在,主要在生产队—国家的政治框架中运作,其经济生产与精神生产被统摄在"全国一盘棋"的政治格局中;80年代以降,民间手工技艺的"现代工业体系"来临,在个人—企业—世界的既定框架中,在总体上处于凋敝状态的同时,其经济生产功能受到一定重视,因精神生产的弱化甚或缺失而导致整体生命力的偏枯。非遗保护运动,正是以此为背景而展开的。如果说,"抢救性保护"(以非遗名录和非遗传承人评选的启动为标志)的提出,是政府有感于非遗资源的大量流失而提出来的应急之策,这在21世纪初叶显然是及时而有力的;"抢救性保护"之缺失,在于理念层面对非遗活态性的理解不足与实践层面对非遗保护工作复杂性的预估不足,"整体性保护"的提出(以国家级文化生态保护区试点的评选为标志),旨在对此有所扩展;"生产性保护"的提出,则旨在促进关于非遗的"抢救性保护"在实践层面的落实,推进非遗"整体性保护"理想的真正实现。

---

① 刘星:《手艺传统与近现代乡土社会变迁》,山东大学2012届硕士学位论文,第42页。
② 陈琨:《激发中国前行的最大力量》,《人民日报》2012年11月3日;范正伟:《"回应":互动中筑牢信任的基石》,《人民日报》2012年11月5日。

非遗保护，牵涉到我国当前在政治改革、经济发展和文化复兴等方面的巨大需求。立足国情，当下这一"应然"向现实生活中的"实然"的落实，必然是以官方政策持续推动、全社会力量被广泛动员参与为特征的。非遗保护，涉及文化多样性、主体多元性、地域复杂性等，国家针对非遗保护所采取的施政措施，都是探索性的、预留弹性空间的实践工具，并非所谓"示范性样板"的简单推行。从三种保护方法的陆续提出及配套施政措施的及时出台可以看出，国家在非遗政策方面表现出很强的一贯性，我们有理由对"生产性保护"的理念及施政前景寄寓厚望，并应积极地建言献策，尽绵薄之力。

就笔者在田野调查中的观察来说，要想在当下现实生活实践中真正发挥"生产性保护"的效度，需要特别注意如下方面：

首先，政府应该在非遗工作中承担更加琐细的服务职能，兼顾特殊群体的需求与社区发展的均衡性。国家政府目前正致力于从管理职能向服务职能角色的积极转变中，各级决策部门必须知晓或倾听当事者、传承人的心声，并将非遗保护计划的制定和实施与社区生活的持续改善紧密结合在一起。文化传承人，是非物质文化遗产的传承主体。没有了传承人，非物质文化遗产也将随之消失，即所谓"人亡艺绝"。作为传承主体，"文化传承人更关心的是自己的生活如何能够'更舒适'，而不是如何能够'更有意义'，他们的文化就是现实生活。"[①]"我们必须坚持的是，政府在非物质文化遗产保护中绝不是一定文化的主人，而只是一定文化的外来启发者和建议者，不是一定文化的守护者。在非物质文化遗产保护中，政府的作用只能是通过经济的手段或者其他手段加以间接的引导、调节，为一定社群的人们提供更多样化的选择，而不是漠视他们的意愿，将保护非物质文化遗产的义务强加给他们，不公平地要求他们作非物质文化遗产的守望者。只有这样才能促使一定社群的人们自主选择符合非物质文化遗产保护的生产、生活方式，从而实现从经济自觉向文化自觉的逐步过渡。"[②]可谓深中肯綮。

其次，要充分重视非遗传承中人的因素，特别是民间手工技艺中人的创造精神，要将非遗的受益面充分扩展到具体的操作者那里。冯骥才强调，"非物质文化遗产的保护主要是活态保护，物质文化遗产的保护是静态保护。活态保护的关键是传承人。"[③] 刘魁立认为，民间技艺的手工制作过程本身就是一种非物质文化实践活动，民族性格、传统文化、制作者的个人文化创造和情感投入，最终会物化到这种实践活动的成品中，正因为如此，我们看到仿品、看到批量生产的工业产品，就觉得完全不是那么回事。[④] 二人角度不同，但都点到了问题的根本。然而，目前的现实是，作为真正的非遗传承主体，大多处于"被传承"的被动地位。有些名录项目的保护责任单位并非名录项目的传承主体（文化传承人、文化传承团体）。以山东省为例，前两批省级非物质文化遗产名录328项、418个项目保护责任单位，

---

① 施爱东：《中国现代民俗学检讨》，社会科学文献出版社2010年版。
② 何平：《非物质文化遗产保护中的政府责任》，http://www.mcprc.gov.cn/whzx/bnsjdt/zcfgs/201111/t20111128_341549.html。
③ 冯骥才：《灵魂不能下跪——冯骥才文化遗产思想学术论集》，宁夏人民出版社2007年版，第10页。
④ 韩冰：《"非遗"生产性保护之路》，《瞭望》2012年第8期。

有三分之二的是当地文化馆站和非物质文化遗产保护中心。这些单位承担管理任务尚可，再让其担负传承发展之责则明显心有余而力不足。

最后，重视农村建设，缩小城乡差距，对于以农村为主要阵地的非遗传承具有重要意义。城市对乡民有充分的诱惑，越来越多的青壮年村民离开村落，落户为城市一员，其在不确定的时间返回时势必带来或多或少的外来文化因素，而非遗主体的构成与变异状况日趋复杂。如果说，工业化的急速渗透与现代传媒的无孔不入，已经使得许多乡村在自然生态与人文生态方面严重受损，那么打工潮的普遍化与长期化，则使得乡土文明的传承陷入严重危机。我注意到，一些在乡土生活中传承已久的民间手工技艺被评为各级非遗项目的同时，一些并非"濒危"的大型国有企业里的如"茅台酒酿造技艺""泸州老窖酒酿造技艺""杏花村汾酒酿造技艺""同仁堂中医药文化"等也被列入（上述均为第一批国家级名录）。面对凋敝的乡村社区和金碧辉煌的庞大企业，我们在设计关于非遗的"生产性保护"工作框架时，细究"谁在生产？怎样保护？"的问题显然是必要的。

美国国家非物质文化遗产项目的
特点、相互关系以及挑战

罗伯特·巴龙[*]

在通常情况下，美国的文化政策是通过优先拨款、纲领性方案以及所开展的活动进行传达的，不是明确的策略性的由上至下。在这个模式当中最显著的一个例外就是美国国家艺术基金会（National Endowment for the Arts，以下简称 NEA）的政策。该基金会的政策通过各州民俗艺术项目促成了国家项目组织机构的建设，使记录、展示和保护非物质文化遗产的举措得到发展。这一政策根基于上世纪 70 年代，由"艺基金"民间艺术部（现为"民间传统艺术项目部"）主任贝丝·洛马克斯·霍斯确立。30 多年后，它完好无损，已包括遍布全美的 40 多个项目。

在霍斯（Hawes）的回忆录《唱得漂亮》中，她谈到了她对支持每个州的民俗艺术协调员的看法。她认为，"当我们试图在全国范围内为民俗艺术活动不断发展赞助者的时候，这些协调员被证实在其中扮演着关键角色"。各州艺术机构发现参与艺术活动和吸收艺术家的益处，因而参与到熟悉的艺术活动，并将那些散落各地的文化实践者纳入州立项目当中，再让州立项目进入社区，而不是指望那些芭蕾舞队或歌剧团。

由 NEA 支持并发起的州立民俗艺术项目已成为推动本地民俗生活不可或缺的手段。州立民俗艺术项目是国家基础建设的重要组成部分，在高度的网络协作下运行，并且与美国联邦政府和国家民俗生活项目保持紧密的联系。民俗艺术项目将更广泛的社区文化和艺术表现形式纳入自己的范围中，并反对用精英思维去解读它们，自然赢得了来自不同意识形态的竞选团队的政治支持。民俗艺术项目的一系列举措使得州政府各机构促进了文化的民主性发展。和其他国家不同，美国式的民俗艺术基础建设是多层次、广泛的网络运作和分散管理，其他国家非物质文化遗产则是由政府的文化机构进行集中管理。

一开始，国家民俗艺术项目只在国家的艺术机构中进行，而现在该项目立足于各种各样的机构、组织和协会当中，其中包括历史机构、非营利性民俗组织、国家人权委员会、文化研究组织、国家大学硕士生民俗学项目和一些独立的非营利性民俗组织。其中，数量最大的

---

[*] 罗伯特·巴龙，美国纽约州艺术委员会民间艺术部主任。

是国家的艺术机构。在美国，民俗艺术项目和其他艺术学科不同，它们更大程度地依赖于国家和联邦政府的资助，也更有可能设立于政府机构中。

创设于政府机构内的民俗艺术项目在体制内有着实质性的自治权利，比如说独立开展针对不同活动和资助标准的项目。同时，民俗艺术项目也会和其他的艺术项目合作，共同完成和其他艺术项目重叠和相互补充的任务，比如艺术展览、社区艺术和艺术教育项目。然而国家民俗艺术项目也不得不通过单独的项目来展示不同领域的艺术，从而证明它们的自治权是正当的。举个例子，人们希望证实为什么民俗音乐没有被一个音乐或艺术表演的项目所包括在内，而是被包括在一个单独的民俗艺术项目中；且有很多文化资助机构已经对其内部的机构组织和资金采取了功能性手段：机构服务于各种艺术活动和艺术组织的运行当中，而不仅仅奉献于某个特定的学科中。

在自治和一体化之间维持一个适度的平衡是非常具有挑战性的。这个挑战性和学术型民俗学项目所遇到的困境相似。学术型民俗学项目希望让民俗学成为一个独立的学科，而不仅仅是一个领域的学习，还需要通过其他更大型的学科来展示自己，即使许多机构已经将自己视为生产线上的一员，并且成为学科本位的项目。民俗艺术项目作为少数的例外，在维持自己的自治权方面上成功了。然而，由于资金方面的缩减，国家民俗艺术项目的总监不得不负起一些额外的责任。比如说，我在纽约州议会的艺术部门领导民俗艺术项目已有多年，现在我还管理着一些更加大型的音乐项目。

国家民俗艺术项目还不得不证实一些特别而且无私的 NEA 合作伙伴的支持是合法的。这些资金支持在以前被称为"组织机构"上的支持。为了回应 NEA 和国家艺术机构大会关于是否还需要继续资金支持的问题，国家和地区性民俗艺术项目成立了一个委员会，并在 2010 年做了一场 PPT 展示，名为"秘诀揭露：如何成功运作一场国家范围内的民俗传统艺术项目"。作为一个集合性的国家项目自我展示，这个展示清晰地将这些项目理想模式展现了出来。

作为委员会成员的我们同时也参与了一次对国家民俗艺术项目的调查，对该项目的成就、需求和挑战进行评定。这次对国家项目的一系列调查和讨论集结成一本白皮书：《国家民俗艺术项目：成就、需求和挑战》。这次调查得到了美国民俗学会的咨询公司和职业发展项目的资金支持，它们与美国民俗学会、NEA 和国艺大会联系紧密。这本白皮书和展示成功地取得了 NEA 接下来的支持。我从那场展示大会和白皮书中广泛摘录了一些片段。这些文字将用来描述国家民俗艺术项目的不同特点，以及它们取得的成就、现在和未来的挑战。白皮书是由一个专门的委员会写出来的，其中包括帕特·安克森（Pat Atkinson）、罗伯特·巴龙（Robert Baron）、维尼·马蒂（Wayne Martin）、威里·斯密斯（Willie Smith）和萨利·万·德沃特（Sally Van de Water）。帕特·安克森、罗伯特·巴龙、丽妮·马蒂·格兰特（Lynn Martin Graton）和阿米·斯肯曼（Amy Skillman）编写展示大会的内容并设计了整场大会。

当谈到如何定义国家民俗艺术项目时，"秘诀揭露：如何成功运作一场国家范围内的民俗传统艺术项目"承认每个子项目应迎合这个国家每个人的需求。对于主办机构或组织，每个项目都应该有合适的目标和宣传策略，并且应按照计划运行，同时还具有配套的服务。许多国家民俗艺术项目致力于特定领域的研究，还举办了不少公共项目（比如提供给青少年和儿童的演出、节日、展览以及公立学校项目）。这些项目立足于国家机构（特别是国家艺术委员会）并为一些独立艺术家或组织提供资助，帮助他们发展自己的民俗艺术项目。这些项目主要是资助项目，还有一些既是资助又是计划的项目。NEA 民俗传统艺术项目以及全国范围内的各种项目为以上项目提供了源源不断的支持，并成为它们稳固性和持续性必不可少的因素。NEA 民俗传统艺术项目以及全国范围内的各种项目还为这些民俗艺术项目的主管提供初期支持，并连续支持整个学术研究。

国家民俗艺术项目不断得到 NEA 合作伙伴的支持，虽然持续性不稳定，并且这些自治项目都是设立在机构当中。它们强调了自己在保护文化遗产方面的重要性，还致力于促进不同文化之间的互相理解，以为它们的机构取得更广泛的公共支持。即使由政府机构民俗艺术项目举办的活动和其他机构举办的活动很不一样，但它们依然具有共同点：它们需要经常证明田野调查的必要性以及长期的特别项目必须与不同族群和艺术家合作。

国家艺术委员会一直缺乏具有社会学和人类学方面专业知识的人才。因此民俗艺术项目还不得不向公众解释，经过专业训练的民俗学家对项目的专业性有着引导作用。它们强调专业训练对民俗学研究或相关学科的重要性，因为专业训练使得民俗学家能够辨别传统文化中的精华，在族群调查中具有文化敏感性，而且专业训练还使得民俗学家通过应用他们的专业知识对不同文化的传统进行分类和解读，并提供给不同类型的观众。

缺少民俗艺术项目是对民俗艺术支持的最大阻力。在 2011 年《国家民俗艺术项目：成就、挑战和需求》对国家民俗艺术项目的调查当中，有一个与会者的答案是这样的："历史告诉我们民俗生活事物并没有退出和其他艺术形式竞争的舞台，并不是因为这些事物没有价值，而是因为这个领域之外的人们不知道如何去判断它们的价值。对能够产出艺术作品的族群民俗的环境、发展过程以及意义缺乏关注使得传统艺术家渐渐失去竞争力。这往往意味着他们将不再得到任何支持。"

国家民俗项目在文化发源地关注保护和维持传统，并把这些传统展示给新的观众。那些和族群合作的项目承认传统总是在当地被忽略，但是文化机构不会忽略这些传统。和族群合作的民俗艺术项目始终遵循着这样的方向：这些合作项目应使社区用他们自己的方式对传统文化进行整理、展示和解读。为多重文化背景的人设计的民俗项目对新观众和这些传统所代表的族群有着多重的好处，同时艺术家也能得到对他们传统更广泛的肯定，并引起人们对他们族群更多的关注。为新观众设计的项目通过体验不同的文化，为不同文化背景的人们搭建起尊重和互相理解的桥梁，因为在他们的日常生活中，往往没有机会去接触其他文化。

大部分的国家民俗艺术项目支持学徒制。通过一个传统艺术家教授其族群里的人，首要的是那些没有继承者的民俗艺术，以此来保证民俗艺术的传承。国家民俗艺术项目还举办一些公共项目，比如说展览、节日活动或者是讲座、展示、演奏会，同时还发行一些传统艺术家的视频、电影产品，甚至介绍传统艺术家的居住地。这些项目将这个国家的所有传统文化视为一个整体进行宣传和介绍，其中包括次区域文化或是一些特别主题，比如说儿童民间传说、牧场文化、纺织品传统。国家民俗艺术项目还致力于将民俗艺术融入教育项目中。这使得学生可以通过调查或当地艺术家的展示来发现他们邻居、族群成员、家庭成员的活的文化传统。这些项目通常牵涉到那些关注本地文化资源的学校选修课的发展，而这些选修课又往往和教育指标、标准检测程序联系紧密。

田野调查在国家民俗艺术项目中起到关键的作用。在过去的三十年里，国家民俗艺术项目已经在某一程度上使得记录传统族群这项浩大工程在美国历史上史无前例。田野调查不仅仅是国家民俗艺术项目发展的基石，它所记录的真实的地方传统还为下一代提供了持久且独一无二的研究资源。田野记录还产生图片、视频以及录音，这些资源可以广泛地应用于展览、多媒体产物或是其他公共项目。

在过去，即使"民俗学家"并不是一个官方称谓，国家民俗艺术项目的主管依然被贴上这样的标签。这事实上的头衔反映了他们的重要地位。即使在现在，国家民俗艺术项目的主管依然是所有传统艺术家、艺术族群和普罗大众最主要的信息和服务来源。他们扮演着文化经纪人的角色，为艺术家和族群搭建起桥梁，并为资助项目、新观众以及媒体、教育系统提供资源。这些主管通过和国内的民俗艺术家或是提供资助的组织的直接接触来帮助艺术家们找到演出的场地、市场，为他们提供工作机会，同时帮助艺术家们充实他们的简历，使他们有机会成为艺术教育项目的参与者。

国家民俗艺术项目的主管是沟通和合作的大师。民俗艺术项目的国家结构是高度的网状化运作，同国家或本地机构、组织一起与联邦、国家民俗项目展开广泛合作。民俗项目的国家机构和其他项目的合作使得它们成功地稳固那些正在进展中的项目的地位。国家民俗艺术项目还和各种各样的国家机构合作，帮助合作机构增强影响，增加资源。国家民俗艺术项目同时还和公园、娱乐机构、卫生和人权服务中的国家机构、旅游机构以及国家教育部门紧密地合作。文化旅游项目和经济发展牢牢地联系在一起，并且在近几年已经成为国家民俗艺术项目的主要关注对象。比如说，北卡罗来纳州艺术委员会的民俗艺术项目和北卡罗来纳学院一起开展的非裔美国人音乐项目，是一个由北卡罗来纳州东部的八个郡县的文化遗产旅游机构发起的，该项目的发展包括了东部乐队切诺基的传统文化，因为此文化是"蓝色屋脊国家遗产区域"的产物。

民俗艺术国家基金会和传统艺术国家基金会之间相互支持，立足于高等院校。NEA 的资助使得国家项目每年通过国家艺术机构召集所有民俗艺术群体，举办全国性集会。国家民俗艺术项目的主管们是 NEA 合作项目审核小组的主要组成成员，他们参与同业审核那些申请资助或推荐的国际项目，通过专业性参与管理国家项目和公共民俗学的经验保证了审核资助申请的高标准。这些成员对其所在州的民俗艺术项目使用同样的标准来审核。除了审核小组的成员外，一些民俗学家、人种音乐学家、传统艺术家、本地文化领袖，也为审核提供专业指导。

国家民俗艺术项目组织开展田野调查，确认参与者，并提供给他们参与史密森尼民俗生活节日的机会（史密森尼学院即美国国家博物馆）或是由 NGO 传统艺术国家委员会组织的国家性或地区性的节日。国会图书馆的美国民俗生活中心举办了各式各样的演奏会，邀请由国家民俗艺术项目的主管们推荐的来自各州的传统艺术家。这个中心还和国家民俗艺术项目正在开展的项目或其他特别活动密切合作。最近发起的研究关于民俗艺术项目的需求得到 NEA 合作伙伴的继续支持。

和本地或者州立的机构合作使得国家民俗艺术项目的资源得到利用，并为这些机构提供了广泛的政治支持。在他们自己的机构里，民俗艺术项目总是被认为没有政治价值。因为民俗艺术项目展示的是和一个国家的全部人口有关的艺术，而不是那些精英阶层或受过高等教育的人的艺术。这些合作使得艺术机构有更多的支持者，范围扩大至农村地区、有色人种的社区、工人阶级、外来移民、避难者、年长者以及其他因为历史原因而受到不公平待遇的人群。并且这些合作向人们展示了一个现象：范围广泛的文化族群都有着优异的艺术细胞。来自不同政治意识形态的国家立法者和统治者支持民俗艺术。民俗艺术是人民的艺术，也是传统文化价值的宝库。同时，国家民俗艺术项目还担当着为普罗大众传播和解读传统价值的责任。民俗艺术是活的传统，是不断进步的创新精神，是传统族群中艺术陈俗的革新。

在美国，民俗学的职业在学术性和政治性一体化上比其他国家更加成熟。有一些国家民俗艺术项目的主管在学院或大学里教学或授课，有一些在硕士生的实习项目里工作。越来越多的国家民俗生活项目在州立大学里迅速发展，同时还有相对应的民俗学硕士生项目。亚利桑那州、印第安纳州、密苏里州、俄勒冈州和西肯塔基州的大学都有该项目。密歇根州的民俗艺术项目在密歇根州立大学由来已久。在 2011 年，国家民俗艺术项目主管调研和召集过程中，主管们早已达成一致：国家民俗艺术项目和民俗学硕士生项目之间的关系应该更加紧密。具体操作应通过经验丰富的民俗学家来指导硕士生，提供更多的实习机会，由已工作的公共民俗学家返回课堂提供短期的民俗学硕士生项目。主管们还呼吁民俗学硕士生项目参与到公共民俗学家的实践中，比如，为硕士生介绍公共民俗学的工作，参加论坛、教学与科研实践基地和学术研讨会，教授公众民俗学相关的课程。

在国家民俗艺术项目的基础机构刚刚创立的上世纪 70 年代末期，当时只为一个民俗学硕士生项目提供培训，而现在几乎所有的硕士项目都强调公众民俗学。当国家机构的民俗艺术项目面临巨大挑战的时候，立足于大学和非营利组织的国家民俗艺术项目往往被视为特别可行的。它们有更大的灵活性，并且可以将注意力集中在民俗学相关的活动上。

在近期的衰退中，几乎所有国家机构的项目都展现了强大的顺应力，它们一直在面对着新的挑战。压在国家民俗艺术项目总监身上的额外的和非民俗艺术的责任在不断增加，并且他们不得不去适应结构内部的重新调整。艺术机构已经和国家机构相结合，共同致力于经济发展和旅游业的开发，伴随的结果则是艺术要随着机构的任务进行调整，并达到一致。资金的缩减使得艺术家的旅行、田野调查和服务受到限制。

国家民俗艺术项目面对的这些挑战正使新一代的项目主管正在不断涌现，而成功的主管们已经在位几十年。国家民俗艺术项目目前的挑战正是开发新的组织模式和资金上的合作伙伴与来源。整个项目结构基础从三十年前建立以后到现在依然强大，这都是 NEA 源源不断的支持和国家项目之间广泛的、多方面的、资源丰富交流的结果。

但是，从长远来讲，当一个项目的组织结构非常依赖于政府的支持时，这个项目的可持续性是不确定的。民俗艺术和其他形式的艺术有着巨大的反差。在美国,民俗艺术项目异乎寻常地依赖于政府的资助。无论是国家项目还是其他机构,几乎没有非营利组织毫无保留地奉献于民俗艺术。作为2011年国家民俗艺术调查的响应者,我在《国家民俗艺术项目:成就、挑战和需求》一文当中是这么主张的:

> 我们所运作的项目并没有一个指导性的机构,也没有能够接触其他艺术领域的结构的途径……(这些项目)总是在文化上、经济上、制度上被部分忽视,只因为它们需要不断地向外扩展。除非这个向外扩展是广泛的、深层次的、不间断进行的,否则国家和艺术中重要的那部分就没法体现出来,也会因为一系列的原因无法被包括进去。艺术教育有着高度发达的结构,交响乐有着高度发达的结构,本地的艺术机构有着良好的结构。事实上,这个国家的民俗艺术基础结构正是基于NEA民俗艺术合作伙伴的拨款。这个拨款囊括了整个国家所有州的民俗艺术项目。

NEA是持续支持民俗艺术项目的机构。支持的成效是非常显著的,如果失去了它的支持,国家民俗艺术项目将会面临重大损失,NEA的支持就是国家民俗艺术项目的顶梁柱。但是,联邦政府的艺术基金会在过去的二十年里一直受到威胁,即使它现在看起来很稳定。一个如此依赖政府资助的组织机构本质上是脆弱的。在一些机构中,退休的员工因为资金限制和机构优先权的调整并没有被取代,从而导致的结果就是国家民俗艺术项目的流失。

国家民俗艺术项目的灵活性组织模式不断发展,是非常令人鼓舞的,也是非常必要的。在最近的几十年里,立足于政府的国家项目不断增加。这些项目能够更加专注地关注它们自己的民俗艺术任务,从不同渠道筹集资金,而且它们的运作比政府项目更具有灵活性。在一些州,立足于政府之外的国家民俗艺术项目和国家艺术机构联系紧密,共同评估资金需求和申报项目。在其他州,比如马里兰州、纽约州和北卡罗来纳州,建立在国家艺术机构之上的民俗艺术项目依然保持强壮的生命力。当地成立了许多国家民俗艺术组织,对州立民俗艺术组织形成了支持,使得那些游离于国家艺术机构的民俗艺术活动充满生气。国家民俗艺术项目这种智慧性、灵活性及由特别的合作所带来的成功将在未来几十年里为国家民俗艺术机构建设提供源源不断的希望和力量。

案例分析、方法和技术

上中西部文化研究中心的民俗研究

詹姆斯·P. 利里*

上中西部文化研究中心①（The Center for the Study of Upper Midwestern Cultures，简称CSUMC），位于美国威斯康星州的首府麦迪逊市，在威斯康星大学和美国国家人文基金会（一个联邦机构）的支持下于2001年成立，设于威斯康星大学的文理学院。由于民俗学者和语言学者侧重于运用平民化视角的人文方法，所以我们致力于上中西部地区多元民族的语言、民俗的研究、馆藏建设、相关研究的出版、协作项目和教育计划的推行。我们的研究范围包括明尼苏达州、威斯康星州和密歇根州上半岛（与密歇根州下半岛，加拿大安大略省和马尼托巴省，南、北达科他州，爱荷华州，伊利诺伊州有重叠，并延伸到密苏里州圣路易斯等河口城市）。上中西部地区境内有森林、水域、田地、小城镇和工业城市，是文化中间地带，数个世纪以来是加拿大林地印第安人和美国平原印第安人的聚会地，是拥有最稳定和最多元欧美人口的美国地区，最近还是非裔、亚裔和拉美裔美国人社区的所在地。由于有威斯康星大学的支持、各种捐赠、产品收入，还有通过各种渠道（如威斯康星大学、州政府、联邦政府机构、美洲印第安部落和私人基金会）竞争得来的基金资助以及与许多组织的合作关系，我们已经与前文提到的所有文化团体建立合作关系。我们与威斯康星大学民俗项目②合作紧密，事实上，CSUMC的几位关键成员也是该校民俗项目的成员，我们还经常让项目的研究生参与我们的活动。我们的努力着重于以下三个主要领域：①资料的保存和机构互访；②教育和拓展；③相关研究成果的出版和制作。

资料的保存和互访。我们在整个地区积极地展开新的田野调查，使用数字音频录音机、数码相机和数码摄像机归档记录各种语言的使用者和多样文化传统的实践者。通过与威斯康星大学图书馆系统的数字馆藏中心③和大学档案馆④合作，我们正在创建新的民俗学和民族志的数字田野档案库。我们还与威斯康星大学米尔斯音乐图书馆（Mills Music Library）有定期的合作，从传统音乐家那里获得藏品，例如数字和模拟格式的田野录音与商业录音、活页

---

* 詹姆斯·P. 利里，威斯康星大学民俗学教授，上中西部文化研究中心创立人之一。
① http://csumc.wisc.edu.
② http://folklore.wisc.edu.
③ http://uwdc.library.wisc.edu/.
④ http://archives.library.wisc.edu/.

乐谱、歌曲集、音乐活动的海报和日程安排、照片等。这些藏品属于威斯康星大学图书馆的威斯康星音乐档案①中的区域性"民间和民族"藏品。

我们与马克斯·卡德研究所②共同承担的威斯康星州英语项目③关注以下几个方面的问题：①本州和上中西部英语的区域性和族群性的变化和差异；②在我们地区所说语言的全貌，包括过去的和现在的；③通过居民选择使用的语言所反映的地域文化和身份认同。我们目前正与德语、苗语、挪威语、瑞典语和西班牙语的使用者在合作。我们还与《美国区域英语词典》④合作。在本地建立有关土著语言的档案资料资源中心的同时，我们"保护和促进土著语言"的倡议项目⑤与威斯康星大学麦迪逊分校和其他几个分校的部落语言项目有所合作。

我们为民俗归档所做的主要工作，即上西部公共民间艺术和民俗项目⑥，是一系列的项目采集指南，突出了20世纪70年代以来产生的丰富的民俗志文档和公开发表的书籍。项目经费一般来源于美国国家艺术基金会、美国国家人文基金会和州、县、地方人文艺术委员会的资助。这个在线的数字化信息交换中心提供项目描述并介绍项目历史，引领研究者获得该地区乃至国家的各种信息库。这些信息库藏有项目档案，例如田野报告、田野录音、田野视频、商业录制品、摄影、展览和临时性的出版物。项目关注该地区独特的表述文化，调查各土著和移民的人口，并记录了大量的传统表演者和实践活动——从艺术的到音乐的、从职业的到休闲的、从宗教的到精神的，无所不包，展现了在威斯康星州、伊利诺伊州、爱荷华州、明尼苏达州、密苏里州和密歇根州上半岛西部的研究成果。

教育和拓展。我们与威斯康星州艺术委员会的民间艺术项目⑦合作的"威斯康星州地方文化教师"倡议项目⑧是深谙地方文化和地方教育的民俗学者和教育者的联盟。根据州政府要求，该项目让教师能够创建具有学术标准的综合性课程，并且由这些教师把具体知识运用到更广泛的语境中。补充的网络资源，包括课程指南以及应对当地社区不断变化的人口统计数据而带来的机遇和挑战。并且，该项目开创性地利用暑期文化旅游，让教师可以直接与当地的文化传统从业者联系⑨。此外，还有一个相关的文化地图/文化旅游项目，此项目⑩是一个数字档案馆，专为教师打造。他们可以将各种文化群体的图像、书面资料、传统音乐的录音和录像、饮食方式、民间艺术和其他物质文化作为一种刺激源，与学生共同记录他们自己的社区。

---

① http://music.library.wisc.edu/wma/.
② http://mki.wisc.edu/.
③ http://csumc.wisc.edu/wep/.
④ http://dare.wisc.edu/.
⑤ http://csumc.wisc.edu/?q = node/110.
⑥ http://digicoll.library.wisc.edu/w/wiarchives/csumc.html.
⑦ http://artsboard.wisconsin.gov/category.asp?linkcatid = 3658&linkid = 1652&locid = 171.
⑧ http://csumc.wisc.edu/wtlc/.
⑨ http://csumc.wisc.edu/wtlc/?q = tours.
⑩ http://csumc.wisc.edu/?q = node/19.

CSUMC 员工经常给上中西部的社区团体讲述地方语言和民俗的各个方面。我们常常接受广播记者关于各类主题的采访。我们会定期向作家和制片人咨询,给不同社会组织和普通公民提供技术援助并回答他们的问题。

出版和制作。我们已经出版了一系列的书籍,制作了相关的纪录片,保存了一些录音。[1] 我们与威斯康星大学出版社合作,最近出版了"上中西部地区的语言和民俗"[2] 系列丛书,其中包括原始的专著、翻译、再版/新版本、编辑选集和纪录片光盘,它们记录该地区不同民族的生活、语言和文化传统,包括历史的和当代的。另外,我们已经制作了播客和纪录片,主题包括奇特的威斯康星州话和从事钢结构建设的钢铁工人的劳动知识等。

最后,补充一些我们在资料保存和机构互访方面所取得的成果——建立在我们威斯康星大学收藏的基础上,然而又集中了几乎遍布整个地区的收藏——我们制作了六个在线展览[3],还有更多的在线展览正在开发。此外,我们创办了挪威美国民间音乐门户网站[4],这是我们想象中的第一个系列门户网站,它联合与本地区民族音乐传统有关的表演者,组织实施相关音乐档案的收藏。

---

[1] http://csumc.wisc.edu/?q = node/4.
[2] http://uwpress.wisc.edu/languagesandfolklore.html.
[3] http://csumc.wisc.edu/?q = node/44.
[4] http://vanhise.lss.wisc.edu/nafmp/.

民俗文化的遗产化、本真性和
传承主体问题

——以浙江衢州"九华立春祭"为中心的考察

王霄冰[*]

民俗，是在民众当中流行的生活范式、礼仪习俗和价值观念，带有集体性、地方性、传承性和口头性等特点；它自发形成，形式自由自在，可不受文字文本、教条教义、政治制度等等条条框框的约束。[①] 一般来说，传统的小型社会，如村落，是滋生民俗文化的最佳土壤，虽然一项民俗的发生也往往有赖于外界因素的影响。[②] 20 世纪以来，随着中国社会的彻底变革，传统农村社会的宗族、村社等组织走向解体，各类民间民俗活动受到了主流文化的轻视和打压。尤其是在实行改革开放政策的最近 30 多年中，中国加剧了现代化的进程，乡土社会的版图日益缩小，作为农村社会栋梁的青壮年农民成群结队地涌向城市，乡村人口稀少化和老龄化现象日趋严重，地方民俗所赖以生存的文化生态渐趋消亡。在这种情形下，如何能将祖先创造的、世世代代流传下来的民间文化保存起来、传承下去，使之成为现代社会的有机组成部分，以保持中华文明的本土特色？这是社会各界所共同关心的问题，也是中国

---

[*] 王霄冰，中山大学中国非物质文化遗产研究中心教授。

[①] 这当然并不排除民俗在乡土社会中所担负的类似于礼法的社会制约功能。美国社会学家萨姆纳（William Graham Sumner, 1940—1910）在《民俗：论惯例、风度、风俗、德范和精神的社会学意义》（*Folkways: A study of the sociological importance of usages, manners, customs, mores, and morals*, Boston: Ginn and Co. 1906）中认为，民俗虽然"并非人的有目的的、理智的创造"，是"通过偶发事件形成的"，但"当关于真实与是非的初步观念发展成关于福利的教义时，民俗就被提高到另一个层次上来了。它们就能够产生推理、发展成新的模式，并把它们的建设性影响扩及每个人和整个社会。这时，我们就称它们为德范了。德范是包含了关于社会福利的普遍的哲学和伦理内容的民俗，其哲学和伦理思想本来就蕴藏在其中，民俗的发展使它们从暗到明确"。引自高丙中《民俗文化与民俗生活》，中国社会科学出版社 1994 年版，第 175、182 和 185 页。书名中的 Folkway 一词，意为"民间方式"，这里译为"民俗"。

[②] 关于民俗的发生，学术界曾有过多种理论，萨姆纳的民俗自发形成于民间生活的观点只是其中的一种。与此完全唱反调的则是瑞士人霍夫曼 - 科拉耶尔（Eduard Hoffmann-Krayer, 1864—1936），他认为"民众不生产什么，而只是再生产"。德国学者诺曼（Hans Naumann, 1886—1951）则提出了"沉降的文化物"（gesunkenes Kulturgut）的概念，指的是由上层社会流向民间而在民间得到传承的那部分文化，与天然成长起来的"原始的整体物"（primitives Gemeinschaftsgut）相区别。参见简涛《德国民俗学的回顾与展望》，载周星主编《民俗学的历史、理论与方法》（下册），商务印书馆 2006 年版，第 808—858 页，其中"汉斯·诺曼和'沉降文化物理论'"一节，见于第 828—330 页。

政府发起非物质文化遗产保护运动的旨意所在。

然而，由于民间文化本身带有一些与官方正统文化不相融合的特征，各类民俗事项在被认可为非物质文化遗产并受到保护的过程中，往往会经过一个被改造、被包装甚至被重新打造的过程。由此出现的一系列问题也是近年来社会各界有目共睹的，如：（1）民俗民间文化的官方化/政治化，即将非物质文化遗产的申报和展演与地方官员的政绩挂钩，民间的事情变成由政府包办，当地民众失去了对于自身文化的自主权；（2）民俗民间文化的博物馆化/物质化，原本活生生的民间活动变成展示馆中静态的图片和实物；（3）民俗民间文化的市场化/商品化，非物质文化遗产变为商家逐利的工具和大众消费品。

非物质文化遗产的保护如何才能在尊重民间、保存文化的前提下进行？入围民俗事项的本真性、活态性与承续性如何能够得到充分保证？笔者以为，一个实实在在、名副其实的传承主体的确立和当事人文化自觉意识的提高，正是解决以上问题的关键所在。以下将以浙江衢州的国家级"非遗"项目"九华立春祭"为例，根据本人2012年2月在当地收集到的田野调查资料，来论证这一观点。

一、中国古代的句芒神话与立春礼俗

2011年5月，国务院颁布了《第三批国家级非物质文化遗产名录》（共计191项）和《国家级非物质文化遗产名录扩展项目名录》（共计164项）。由浙江省衢州市柯城区申报的"九华立春祭"和浙江省遂昌县的"班春劝农"、贵州省石阡县的"石阡说春"一起，以"农历二十四节气"为总体名称，被纳入国家级非遗名录的扩展项目名录中（项目编号 X-68）。① 九华立春祭所祭祀的，是古代神话中的木神和春神句芒，祭祀日期设在农历二十四节气之首的立春日（公历2月4日或5日）。

农历二十四节气是古代中国人的伟大发明之一。华夏民族对于由太阳运行带来的节气转换的认知到底源于何时？显然这是一个容易引发争议的问题。② 胡厚宣、杨树达等老一辈的甲骨学者，曾研究过一片记录有"四方风名"的商代甲骨（《甲骨文合集》14294）③，考释出与《山海经》等后代文献记载基本一致的四个方位的名称和所属的神灵之名：④ "东方曰析，凤（风）曰劦（协）。南方曰因，凤（风）曰微。西方曰□，凤（风）曰彝。□〔北〕

---

① 参见 http://www.gov.cn/zwgk/2011-06/09/content_1880635.htm（2012/2/12）。
② 迄今为止，学者们在对从地下出土的殷商甲骨文的研究中，尚未发现有与节气相关的时间概念。参见常玉芝《百年来的殷商历法研究》，载王宇信、宋镇豪（主编）《纪念殷墟甲骨文发现一百周年国际学术研讨会论文集》，社会科学文献出版社2003年版，第38—54页。
③ 郭沫若主编：《甲骨文合集》第五册，中华书局1979年版。
④ 参见胡厚宣《甲骨文四方风名考证》，《甲骨学商史论丛初集》第二册，成都齐鲁大学国学研究所石印本，1944年。杨树达《甲骨文中之四方风名与神名》，载《中国现代学术经典·余锡嘉·杨树达卷》之《杨树达卷·积微居甲文说》，河北教育出版社，1996年，第800—807页。

□〔方〕□〔曰〕夗，凤（风）曰□。"①

周代的四方神灵观念，见于《周礼·春官·大宗伯》。其中提到应以各种不同的玉石制成六样不同的礼器，以供奉各方神灵："以玉作六器，以礼天地四方。以苍璧礼天，以黄琮礼地，以青圭礼东方，以赤璋礼南方，以白琥礼西方，以玄璜礼北方。"②《左传·昭公二十九年》中也有关于四方神灵的记载："木正曰句芒，火正曰祝融，金正曰蓐收，水正曰玄冥，土正曰后土。"③ 这里已经把句芒和东方联系在了一起。对此，郑玄注曰："礼东方以立春，谓仓精之帝，而太昊、句芒食焉。"④ 战国末年的《吕氏春秋·孟春纪》亦载："其帝太皞，其神句芒。"高诱注曰："太皞，伏羲氏。以木德王天下之号，死，祀于东方，为木德之帝。句芒，少皞氏之裔子曰重，佐木德之帝，死为木官之神。"⑤ 关于句芒的神话，则最早见于《墨子·明鬼下》，说他曾替"帝"传话、为有德之郑穆公添寿十九年。他的形象乃是"鸟身，素服三绝，面状正方"⑥。

成书于汉代的《礼记》在"月令"篇中将一年四季的主宰神明加以体系化，其中提到春三月的"帝"为太皞，"神"为句芒；夏三月的"帝"为炎帝，"神"为祝融；秋三月的"帝"为少皞，"神"为蓐收；冬三月的"帝"为颛顼，"神"为玄冥。⑦ 这里的"句芒"，郑玄注释为："少皞氏之子，曰重，为木官。"⑧

民俗学者简涛曾指出，句芒在古代神话体系中是"神"，而不是"帝"；他"身为春神、木神、东方之神，又为青帝的助手，它作为一个理想的媒介把季节中的春天、五行中的木、方位中的东方和五帝中的青帝连接了起来，构成了立春迎气礼仪中的完整的象征系统。"（见表1）⑨ 虽然其中的某些元素出自上古，但这一理想化的系统的形成不可能在汉代之前，而是在两汉时期所盛行的天人相应和阴阳五行观念影响下才得以完备起来。不仅如此，就是立春祭祀的礼仪习俗，起源也应在汉代，其礼仪设计所依据的主要是《礼记·月令》中的有关设想，并基于西汉时期的郊祀礼。⑩ 汉代的立春礼俗虽然吸收了民间的"出土牛"习

---

① 前人对这片甲骨的转写用字略有不同，这里采用的是今人王晖的释文。该作者在总结前人研究的基础上，认为商代卜辞中虽然"只有春、秋二季的划分，还没有用作季节的夏、冬之称"，"但从四方及四方风的蕴义看，四季的观念应该是产生了"，并引用于省吾的观点认为，这为"由两季向四季的发展准备了一定的条件"。在他看来，由于"季节的变换可根据季风的变化来推定，于是四方季风便被古人视作上帝改换时令的使者"。参见王晖《论殷墟卜辞中方位神与风神的蕴义》，夏商周文明研究之六《2004年安阳殷商文明国际学术研讨会论文集》，社会科学文献出版社2004年版，第321—322页和第326页。
② 《十三经注疏》（附校勘记）之《周礼注疏》卷十八，中华书局2003年版，第762页。
③ 《十三经注疏》（附校勘记）之《春秋左传正义》卷五十三，中华书局2003年版，第2123页。
④ 《十三经注疏》（附校勘记）之《周礼注疏》卷十八，中华书局2003年版，第762页。
⑤ 王利器著：《吕氏春秋注疏》，巴蜀书社2002年版，第9—10页。
⑥ 《墨子》，李小龙译注，中华书局2007年版，第116—117页。
⑦ 《十三经注疏》（附校勘记）之《礼记正义》卷十四，中华书局2003年版，第1352—1360页。
⑧ 同上书，第1353页。
⑨ 简涛著：《立春风俗考》，上海文艺出版社1998年版，第41页。
⑩ 简涛著：《立春风俗考》，第23页以下。恰如作者所言，像《礼记》这样的著作不能被当成史书看待，其中的种种描绘多属理想性质的设想，而非对于事实的记录。

俗，但和官礼的迎气礼属于互不相关的两个部分。立春迎气礼在东郊进行，参加者的服饰以青色为主，句芒以青帝的助手身份出现，也是祭祀对象之一。同时，京城和各地要在城门之外设置土牛和耕人，向广大百姓报春，以示劝农之意。

表1 东汉立春迎气礼仪的象征系统

季 节	五 行	颜 色	五 帝	方 位	神 明
春	木	青	青帝	东方	句芒
夏	火	赤	赤帝	南方	祝融
立秋前十八日	土	黄	黄帝	中央	黄灵
秋	金	白	白帝	西方	蓐收
冬	水	黑	黑帝	北方	玄冥

东汉以后，一直到清代，立春礼俗在各代都有延续，但每个时期的表现形态有所不同。例如，唐代的立春礼仪不再像汉代那么庄严肃穆，而是多了些欢乐色调，增加了像皇帝赏赐大臣春花这样的节庆内容。① "出土牛"的习俗也有所改变，耕人变成了策牛人，他和土牛的相互位置被用来象征立春节候的早晚，而且出现了官员杖打土牛的仪式性行为。这些都应是后世"扮芒神""鞭春"等立春习俗的源头。由人扮演的"芒神"取代耕人或策牛人进入"出土牛"礼仪，应是在南宋时期才出现，且"很可能是由于迎气礼衰微或者废止的缘故"。② 到了明代，朝廷制定了相应的礼规，从礼制上确立了芒神的地位。

到了民国时期，政府取缔传统夏历（农历、阴历），改用西历（公历、阳历），立春不再是一个官方认可的节日，立春的官方礼俗也从此彻底消失。但在一些地区的民间，却依然流行着在立春日迎春、鞭（打）春、吃春饼/春卷等习俗。到了1949年以后，由于意识形态的原因，这些习俗也不流行了。作为二十四节气之一的立春虽然还常常被感知，但它作为一个古老的农事节日的属性却已被逐渐淡忘。中国人有关青帝、句芒、春牛的记忆和情感已十分淡薄，扮芒神、鞭春牛、吃春饼/春卷/生菜等立春习俗真正变成了历史的"残留物"，仅见于一些偏远的乡村和特殊的人群当中。③ 位于浙西山区的九华乡外陈村，因拥有一座供奉句芒的梧

---

① 简涛著：《立春风俗考》，第67页。
② 同上，第87页。
③ 上个世纪90年代，简涛曾就立春习俗的传承情况做过调查。他得出的结论是，"即使在民间，大陆许多地区也不再把立春作为节日，不再举行节庆活动，而只是把立春作为一个节令。各级政府只是把立春作为农业节令，作为春耕生产的开始而予以重视。"因此，当代的立春民俗"只是一些零星的民俗事象，并且只限于某些地区，无论是事象的规模还是流行的范围都不能与清代立春民俗相比。它们只是清代立春文化的残留"。在探讨立春习俗式微的原因时，作者认为并不能完全归咎于外界原因，而且也与节日功能本身的转换有关："今天立春不再作为一个节日，人们甚至失去了立春迎春的观念，却不是由于立春文化变迁的突变造成的，而是由于它的渐变造成的。这里一个重要的原因是立春节日功能转移。立春不再作为一个节日庆祝，它的功能已经被另外一个重要节日所取代，这个节日就是春节，也就是中国的传统新年。立春的民间习俗也部分地转移到了春节的习俗之中。"参见简涛：《略论近代立春节日文化的演变》，载《民俗研究》1998年第2期，第58—72页，引文出自第68、69页。

桐祖殿并保留有一些立春古俗，可谓是国内现有保留立春民俗文化最为完整的一处。

二、梧桐祖殿及其立春祭祀

九华乡位于浙江省衢州地区的西北部，距离城区大约9.5公里。此地有山有水，风景秀丽，古属浮石乡，民国九年（1920）改称毓秀乡，民国28年才改名九华乡，大约因临近当地的九华山而得名。① 该乡行政上归属衢州市柯城区，面积82.32平方公里，现有乡民2万多人，分35个行政村。外陈村是其中之一，有212户、632人，近年来由于青壮年外出打工较多，村里常住人口只有280多人。村民多属苏、傅、王、龚四大姓，前两姓居多，迁来时间也较早，据说来自福建。四姓都拥有自己的族谱，村中尚有苏氏和傅氏两个宗厅，供宗族活动之用。

位于村口的梧桐祖殿是村中唯一的庙宇，里面供奉的主神就是中国古代神话中的春神和木神句芒。现有一个偏殿，供奉的是佛祖的雕像。该建筑在民国22年（1933）曾经大修，1949年后遭到较为严重的毁坏，一度被用作村里的锯板厂和碾米厂。2001年，一位名叫汪筱联（1943年生）②的当地人士在帮助柯城区旅游局进行旅游资源普查时，偶然发现了这幢老房子，见它有三扇门，不像是一般的民居，就猜是座古庙。当他刮去覆盖在老屋门额上的黄泥时，便看到了"梧桐祖殿"四个大字。后听村里老人讲，这是"梧桐老佛殿"，"文革"时里面的神像已被毁弃，他们只记得小时候村里每年都要在此举行立春祭和中秋祭，里面供奉的佛像长着一对翅膀。根据这一线索，汪氏便推断村民们相传的"梧桐老佛"就是春神句芒。③

此后，在汪筱联等人的呼吁下，锯板厂和碾米厂终于在2004年从庙内搬走。村民们自发捐款，凑了三四万元钱对"梧桐老佛殿"进行修缮。当时负责这项工程的，就是现任外陈村党支部书记龚元龙的弟弟龚卸龙（1965—2008）。在复原春神像时，他们参考了各类古代文献中有关句芒的记载并加以汇集，如前面提到的《墨子》中的描述和《山海经·海外东经》中的"鸟身人面，乘两龙"的说法，④ 从而把他塑造成了一个长方形脸、身穿白衣、脚驭两龙、背上有两扇翅膀、右手举着圆规、左手握着装有五谷的布包的人物形象。

主殿采用这一带典型的民间建筑格局，当地称"三间六"，即分为上、中、下三堂，两边各可隔出三间（普通人家用门板隔开，在宗祠、庙宇中则不隔），共得六间房。中间部分为上堂、中堂（天井）和下堂。梧桐祖殿上堂中部的神坛供奉句芒塑像，主神左手边的祭

---

① 有人称这里的九华山为小九华，以区别于安徽的大九华山。
② 原为衢州市建筑器材公司总经理，从早年开始就喜爱研究当地的地理、民俗与传统文化，已出版《峥嵘山志》（与叶裕龙合著，中国文史出版社2010年）、《毓秀九华（中国衢州）》（衢州日报社2011年）等著作。
③ 李啸、姚宏东、江毅丹：《春天来了，梧桐祖殿立春祭》，《衢州日报》2012年2月6日，第7版。
④ 参见袁珂《山海经校注》，上海古籍出版社1980年版，第265页。

台上摆放着三尊大小不一的关公像,右手边则是尉(迟)、晏、杨、蔡四位"灵公"的雕像。① 在他们背后的墙上,分别描绘着"风""雨""雷""电"四位神灵以及"富""贵"和另外两位天王的形象。大殿左右两边的墙壁上,绘有二十四节气主题的壁画做装饰。天井的井边照例放着一盛满水的水缸,表示钵满盆满。下堂是两层的戏台,正门就开在台后。因为台不高,所以大人进门后都必须躬身穿过台下的走廊。对于村民们来说,这个设计正好用来强制人们在神灵面前低头,以示恭敬之意。

位于外陈村村头的梧桐祖庙背面靠山,前面也望山。隔着街道和田地,山脚下流淌着一条名叫"庙源"的小溪。顺着小溪沿路而上,途经与外陈村毗邻的三皇殿村,② 就会走进一个名叫"石娲"的山谷,半道上可以找到梧桐祖殿的原址。原址已无建筑,只在树木草丛间隐约可以辨识出一个用石头垒成的平台。人站在这里,面对着一座郁郁葱葱的名为梧桐峰的山峰,和山脚下一条清澈、奔流的山涧,初春的太阳正好从山坡的斜角探出头来,暖洋洋地照在当头,丝丝回暖的地气氤氲在脚跟,草木间一股春的气息将你团团围住,真有一种如沐春风般的美妙之感。"风水"如此之好,无怪乎古人会在此选址建造春神殿了。

然而当地人对于梧桐祖殿的来历,却有着自己的说法。据汪筱联解释,当地人之所以称春神殿为"梧桐祖殿",是因为古谚有云:"家有梧桐树,引得凤凰来"。凤凰非梧桐不栖。句芒鸟身,原是凤鸟氏族,凤鸟就是凤凰。相传古时外陈村境内的山岭主峰上多梧桐树,被句芒看上了,他便在这里居住下来。从此山上梧桐树以及其他树木都长得愈发茂盛。山民感恩,便在梧桐峰上盖起了一座庙宇,用一根巨大的梧桐树根雕了一个神像供起来,称之为"梧桐老佛"。后来为何搬迁到了山下呢?原来,在梧桐峰对面的天台峰上还居住着一对修炼成仙的兄弟:赤松子和赤须子,他们是神农氏的雨师。赤松子小时放羊出身,成仙后仍在天台上养了一群羊,而且任其繁育而不食用,最后变得像天上的云朵那么多,把原本长满百草的山坡吃成了个秃头山。木神句芒看了十分心痛,就和赤松子暗中斗法,让天台山上只长乔木和毛竹,不长百草。赤松子赶着羊群想到别处去,句芒就让在移动的羊群前突然长出一片密密的乔木,好像木栅似的挡住了羊的去路。但赤松子在晚上还是偷偷地把羊群赶到了石梁方向的治岭山坡。谁知句芒又让这里不长羊吃的草。赤松子只好命令羊群进入"冬眠"状态,都变成白石头,等山上长草后再还原成白羊。赤松子的哥哥赤须子,不想让他们斗下去伤了和气,以致连累到百姓,就出面调解。他劝弟弟不要再养羊,让那些白羊永远成为石头。而农家可以养些羊供人食用,这样数量不会多起来,平时又可听到羊羔的悦耳叫声。赤

---

① 据"九华立春祭"国家级传承人汪筱联介绍,四位灵公(又称令公)都是历史上与衢州有直接关系的伟大人物。尉灵公即唐代大将尉迟恭,历史上被衢州府城守军奉为守护神。晏灵公是宋代一位衢州府知府(疑为晏敦复,但其死因与传说中不同),传说他为了警示百姓井中已被瘟神下毒,跳入井中,结果尸体被打捞上来后因中毒而变成黑色,所以这位灵公的形象是黑脸的。杨灵公是唐代诗人杨炯,和当地的干系不详。过去在衢州有座"杨公祠",被称为"第三城隍"。蔡灵公则是汉代发明造纸术的蔡伦,因为这一带出产毛竹,过去山中有许多造纸的小工场。关于四位灵公的姓名和身份,衢州市博物馆副馆长占剑的说法有所不同。他认为这四位灵公原本是在当地民间备受崇拜的西周徐国国君徐偃王的从神。

② 该村村头原有一座"三皇殿",过去(具体时间不详)供奉的是上古传说中钻木取火的"燧人氏"、"轩辕氏"(黄帝)和"神农氏"(炎帝),当地人称"三朝天子"。这一庙宇已遭毁坏。

松子顺从了哥哥，他的羊就永远成了满山的石群。赤须子又劝说木神句芒不要再一个人住在梧桐峰了，不如搬到在山下水口那片平地上，造所大殿，将"三皇""五官"都请来，大家居住在一起。句芒依允了。可怎么搬呢？赤松子是雨师，一天他让梧桐峰上突然下起暴雨，将山中的梧桐庙冲倒了，"梧桐老佛"也顺着山洪漂流到山下，只在水口的波涛中打着旋转。正当许多村人在围观这一奇怪现象时，一位过路人劝他们赶快下水打捞，并说这是"梧桐老佛"的意思，因山庙太小，要大家在此为他盖所大殿居住，就叫"梧桐祖殿"。原来这个人就是赤松子所化。当地人听了他的话，就地建造了这座"梧桐祖殿"。①

这虽是神话故事，却也能透露出一些接近事实的信息：一是梧桐祖殿确是为春神句芒而建，原为一座山间小庙，后来因洪水冲垮了这座庙宇，将句芒塑像冲到外陈村村口，所以当地人才为他就地建造了新的庙宇。二是在迁址后的梧桐祖殿中，原本或许还有"三皇""五官"（疑为"三皇五帝"）等神位，但这些在近年新修的殿堂中，已被关公和四大"灵公"的塑像所取代。

为恢复梧桐祖庙的立春祭，汪筱联等人还整理出了一些有关当地立春习俗的资料：②

立春日，俗称"接春日""开春"，这天人们起床后的第一件事就是翻看历书，查明交春的时刻。人们用一株新鲜的黄芽菜植在盛满细砂的大碗里。碗里插有一面长条形的红纸小旗，旗上写着"迎春接福"四个字，碗的后面放着一杯清茶。然后把桌子搬到天井里，插香点烛。等红烛燃完后，再把将黄芽菜移植于菜地或花盆中，表示春天到了，生气勃勃、万象回春。③ 这一日，"报春人"要挨家挨户上门送《春牛图》，即一种木刻印刷的民间版画。家家将《春牛图》贴于中堂，上面印着"风调雨顺""国泰民安"等吉语。《春牛图》一般以红纸黑线版为主，也有套色彩印的。它的图式象征着节气的早晚。如果有牛倌手提绳子牵着耕牛，意为当年农时节气迟，耕牛较空闲；有牛倌手提竹鞭在耕牛后面赶的，意为当年农时节气紧，耕牛特别忙；有牛倌骑在牛背上横笛的，意为当年风调雨顺，年成特好；等等。《春牛图》除了预卜一年的农业丰歉外，还要标出年中的生产节气和潮水涨落的时辰。

过去立春日，在衢州府城要由地方官率僚属迎春于东部，"出土牛"行"鞭春礼"，称"打春"。鞭打完毕后，老百姓一拥而上抢夺牛身上的土，谓之"抢春"，以抢得牛头为吉利。俗信抢到牛身上的"肉"，养蚕必丰收；抢到牛角上的土，庄稼必丰收；抢到牛肚子里的粮食，就预示着这一年五谷丰登，粮食仓满囤流。民间还流传，牛身上的土是天赐的灵丹妙药，只要用布包上它在病患处磨磨擦擦，病马上就好。所以每年都会发生为"抢春"而在拥挤踩踏中有人受伤的事件。立春日在梧桐祖殿也举办庙会，有迎春（敲锣打鼓迎接春神）、探春（外出踏青）、插春（采集松枝翠柏等插在门上）、戴春（儿童将柳枝编成环状戴到头上）、尝春（"咬春"、"吃春盘"、食用新鲜蔬菜）、"迎春牛"等习俗。所谓"迎春

---

① 参见汪筱联、邹耀华撰稿，于红萍整理《衢州梧桐祖殿立春祭祀——立春祭祀申报"人类传说及无形遗产著作"的依据和理由》（内部资料，由衢州市文化广电新闻出版局提供）。

② 同上。

③ 一说天刚破晓，家家就要拿香、纸、肉、豆腐干等到各自田里去祭拜。见李啸、姚宏东、江毅丹《春天来了，梧桐祖殿立春祭》，《衢州日报》2012年2月6日，第7版。

牛"，就是用竹篾扎成牛形，糊上彩纸，脚下装小轮，身上披红挂彩，由一乞丐扮成"牧牛太岁"，在迎春祭毕后牵着牛沿街游行。队伍打着旗子，敲锣打鼓。小孩子用七粒（或六粒）豆子系在牛角以避痘灾。庙会期间还进行投壶、击鼓传梅、踩高跷、竹马灯等游戏娱乐活动。祖殿的戏台上要连演三天三夜的大戏。其他节日如春节、元宵、二月二、清明、端午、中秋、重阳、冬至等也要在殿内演戏，并邀请亲朋好友来做客助兴。节日小吃则有春饼、春卷、米粿、米糊等。

三、"壬辰年梧桐祖庙立春祭"实录

外陈村从2004年起开始恢复立春祭祀的仪式，主要由村里自行组织。2012年的立春祭是"九华立春日"被列为国家级非物质文化遗产之后的头一次，当地各级领导格外重视，由柯城区教育体育局（文化局）一位主管副局长亲自把关。媒体也给予了高度关注，除电视台、报纸进行现场采访报道之外，"衢州新闻网"还对祭祀仪式进行网络直播。①

为迎接祭典，村民们提前好几天便开始忙碌。梧桐祖殿被打扫一新，门口贴上了新的春联："黄道轮回，四时节令从今始；春神下界，千树梅花报喜来。"殿门口则挂上了一排排红色的大灯笼，里面堂上挂起了24个代表二十四节气的小灯笼。勾芒的祭台前贴着"迎春接福"的红色标语，旁边摆着一只竹制的、身裹绿绸和红巾、头戴大红花的"春牛"。厨房里准备了好几百斤的大米和成箩成筐的白菜、萝卜、豆腐等，以备招待工作人员和来宾香客之用。为保仪式顺利进行，2月3日村委会还专门把老老少少的村民召集起来"彩排"，里里外外忙得不亦乐乎。

2月4日9时，祭祀开始之前，先在梧桐祖殿大门外举行了授牌仪式，由柯城区委宣传部部长致辞，浙江省文化厅"非遗"处处长和衢州市文广新局局长为"国家级非物质文化遗产·九华立春祭"授牌，柯城区副区长接牌。之后全体进入大殿，9点18分左右，祭祀开始。担任司仪的是村委会主任傅亦武，主祭为村支书龚元龙，陪祭的是两位年轻村民傅洪民和吴海根。由于场地狭窄，村委会对入场人数进行了严格控制，只有几十名村民代表在场，分老中青三拨，从老到幼且男女对称地分列在上堂和天井的两边。老年人都穿着平常的服装，青壮年要参加抬佛巡游活动的，则穿黄色绸服，戴黄巾；儿童（共八男八女）都穿着绿衣绿裤，头戴竹枝编成的花环，脸上化了妆。

仪式开始时先在户外燃放鞭炮，奏乐。然后分成三大拨向春神献礼：第一拨为公共的祭品，有20多样，分别装在漆成红色的木盘里或直接摆在案前，内容包括：饭甑（即在木制的饭桶里将蒸好的米饭擦成高高的小山的模样，表面压入一排排红枣，上盖红色剪纸，并插上一枝翠柏做装饰）；牛头（当日用猪头代替）；猪头；羊头；清茶；苹果；香蕉；桔子；桂圆；金桔；蛋糕；红糕；芙蓉糕；油爪（江米条）；麻球；年糕；粽子；青粿；青菜；五

---

① http://news.qz828.com/system/2012/02/03/010435143.shtml.

谷种子；甘蔗；还有梅花、松柏枝和一对大蜡烛等。第二拨是由领导和来宾敬献给春神的花篮，都已提前摆在了大门口，届时只象征性地把其中两个抬到祭台上。第三拨是村民们自发准备的祭品。当日有40多名老人排着队、有序地献上了自家的装有祭品的竹篮或木盆，其内容和摆设大同小异：一条肉、一株青菜、两个粽子、一杯开水、一碗米饭（也要压成山形，嵌上红枣）、两条年糕、青白米粿、水果、糕点等，上面同样用红色的剪纸和翠柏枝条装饰起来。因当日的交春时刻是在黄昏的18点22分，所以祭品一直要摆放到交春仪式结束之后才能收回。（见图1）

祭品、鲜花献完后，由主祭、陪祭和群众代表到天井的香炉前焚香祭拜。之后主祭宣读《迎春接福祭词》。词曰："四时复始，万象更新。金龙报喜，岁序壬辰。木神下界，大地回春。调风度雨，惠泽民生。自然和谐，天道遵循。十龙治水，七牛躬耕。天泰地泰，寿臻福臻。三衢大地，物阜风淳。国强民富，五谷丰登。"仪式的最后一项，是由陪祭导唱《祭春喝彩谣》。其形式是陪祭喊一句话，在场所有人就接一声"好啊"。共有八句：

图1　春神句芒和献给他的祭品

（王霄冰摄）

　　壬辰立春，金龙报喜普天庆。——好啊！
　　春回大地，周而复始万象新。——好啊！
　　迎春接福，天泰地泰三阳泰。——好啊！
　　春神护佑，世荫福祉惠万民。——好啊！
　　春色满园，沃野千里江山好。——好啊！
　　春风浩荡，国泰民安遍地金。——好啊！
　　春华秋实，风调雨顺粮仓满。——好啊！
　　春赐万福，人寿年丰万家欣。——好啊！

殿内仪式在大约9时40分结束，其后众人移至殿外的一块地头，观看"鞭春牛"仪式。"春牛"是跟一位名叫王六古的村民借的，因此也就由他本人驾驭。老人穿着蓑衣，戴着斗笠，扮演着人们印象中的"老农"形象。而鞭打春牛的"芒神"，却不像古礼所规定的那样由男童扮演，而是由一位12岁少女来装扮。她头扎发髻，披一件白色斗篷，装束并未完全依据用红纸张贴在殿前的《壬辰年立春交春、芒神、春牛图》。① "芒神"一边象征性地鞭打牛的头部、左身、右身、尾部和背部,口中一边念诵道:"一鞭春牛,风调雨顺;二鞭春牛,幸福安康;三鞭春牛,三阳开泰;四鞭春牛,万事顺利;五鞭春牛,五谷丰登。"

古俗中的"抢春"仪式没有进行,取而代之的将糖果、花生等分撒给观望的人群。前任老支书傅生耀提了两篮祭品,代表村民们在田头焚香烧纸,祭拜天地。王六古开始来回犁地,之后傅亦武和傅生耀一个在前平地,一个在后播种,并将几株小青菜整齐地种到地里。此时,有人在地头放起了鞭炮。在一片硝烟弥漫之中,穿着黄色绸衣的村民们抬着纸糊的春牛、关公和四大"灵公"的坐像来到殿外,后面跟着一条绿色的长"龙"。他们在广场上转了几圈之后,就开始浩浩荡荡地沿村巡游。(见图2)在事先约好的一些人家门口,他们停下来,让神灵们接受祭拜。村民们把盛有整套祭品的篮子摆出来供奉,并将事先准备好的红包放在牛头上和神灵们脚跟的"功德箱"里,② 然后焚香烧纸,为家人祈福。等祭拜结束,他们会把祭品拿回家去给小孩们吃,因为相信这样孩子们会长得"蛮气"(壮实)一点。

跑在巡游队伍最前面的,还有一位"报春人"。他手中拿着一叠红纸,每到捐过钱、做过奉献的人家,就贴一张在门口或墙上,或直接交到主人手里。红纸上的文字为"九华乡外陈村梧桐祖殿祭祀",下有两幅图,一幅是春神像,上方写着"新春大吉",左右分别写着"风调雨顺""国泰民安"的条幅;另一幅是儿童在日光下、田地里鞭打春牛的图像。文字部分主要介绍梧桐祖殿及其"立春大典",并告知"今年的'立春祭祀'将于农历正月十三上午九时在外陈村隆重举行。届时将有知名婺剧团来梧桐祖殿连演四天大戏。欢迎社会各界人士即时前来同庆,共同祈福"。最后还有乘车路线和下车地点。显然这是本次活动的宣传传单,在巡游时则被用来"报春"了。

巡游队伍在本村转完一圈之后,吃过午饭,又到临近的各村去继续巡游,直到下午三点多钟才回到庙里。这边庙里中午摆满了饭桌,香客们可以免费用餐。饭桌上坐不下的就领了盒饭到外面找地方吃。饭是白饭,菜以白菜、萝卜为主,都是素食。当天来拜神和看热闹的估计有上千人。庙里摆放的功德箱也因此收入了几千元的捐款。加上一路巡游的"收入",估计总共有上万元。

以上这些仅仅只是"迎春"的前奏,因为当天交春的时刻是在黄昏。这时,来宾都已离开,香客也大都散去,只剩下了外陈村的村民和他们的亲朋好友。时辰到来之前,殿门紧闭。时辰一到,殿门即被打开,在一群打着灯笼的儿童引领下,手拿香烛的村民们一涌而出,纷纷在殿门口点上蜡烛,焚香烧纸,迎接春神降临。一时间,鞭炮大作,烟花四起,几位村民代表捧着两枝象征"春天"的树枝回到庙中,将它们摆到祭台前。又在庙中祭拜之

---

① 纸上写道:"二〇一二年二月四日,正月十三18:22分为交春时刻,鸣放鞭炮,焚香行祭迎春。壬辰年春牛:二〇一二年(壬辰)春牛,身高四尺,长八尺,尾长一尺二寸,头黑、身黄、腹黑、角、耳、尾青,膝胫黄、蹄白,青牛口开,牛尾左激,牛笼头用丝。壬辰年芒神服式:芒神下界,二〇一二年(壬辰):芒神孩童像。身高三尺六寸五分,系行缠鞋挎全,平梳两髻在耳前,本年是农晚闲,芒神于春牛并立左边也。"

② 据一位老村民介绍,他和老伴给五位神灵各捐了10元,共50元,他女儿多给了10元(也许是给春牛的),共60元。

图2　巡游的队伍　　　　　　　　　　　　　　　（王霄冰摄）

后，仪式才告结束。之后戏台上好戏开场，以飨春神等各位神灵。

四、对"九华立春祭"本真性的探讨

外陈村梧桐祖庙立春祭祀与相关习俗原本是一种地方性的民间文化，但在上个世纪中国社会大变革的冲击之下，已被当地民众抛弃和忘却，只剩下了一些零星的记忆。2004年修复祖殿时，由于当地人只记得里面供奉的是"长着一对翅膀"的神，所以现在的句芒塑像所根据的完全是汪筱联等人的推测和考证；包括当代的许多立春节俗，显然也参考了古书的记载和来自其他地方的民俗志，而并非完全以村民的回忆或当地的民俗文献为依据。在前往考察梧桐祖殿遗址的路上，我特意向两位陪同的村民打听了"梧桐老佛"迁址的故事。其中一位尚能较为完整地讲出，不过版本和汪筱联等人撰写的文本相当接近，所以很可能是从他们那里学来的。另一方面，由于立春礼俗和相关的神灵信仰在全国各地都已基本消亡。目前只在偏僻的外陈村，还留有这么一座春神殿及与立春相关的习俗，所以它能成为国家级非物质文化遗产也是理所当然的事情。

进入"非遗"名录也使得外陈村梧桐祖殿的立春祭祀和习俗发生了一些根本的变化。首先是它被冠以一个原本没有的正式名称——"九华立春祭"。地方性的民俗文化在迈向公共化和遗产化的过程中，"更名"往往是必经的步骤。梧桐祖殿立春祭之所以不用"外陈"而用"九华"命名，大约是为了照顾到九华乡对于外陈村的行政管理关系。正所谓"县官不如现管"，笔者在调查中也注意到，村里在做各项决策时对于九华乡政府这一直接领导十分尊重，事事都要请示，不敢有所逾越。而在外陈村与柯城区文化部门的沟通方面，九华乡也确实能起到穿针引线的作用。

其次，祭祀仪式的官方色彩有所增强，民间信仰的宗教色彩相对减弱。因为各级官员的参加和授牌仪式的举行，村民们意识到了官方的在场，所以在操办祭典时会自动地去模仿当代官礼的一些形式，比如发放专门制作的参祭牌，增加"敬献花篮"这样的礼节，并由村中少女担任礼仪小姐引领嘉宾，让儿童们化上妆、集体朗诵《春晓》等诗歌作品，等等。这些在近年来公祭典礼上常见的套路，都被搬用到了祭典当中。与此相反，一些被认为是"宗教迷信"的行为则被去除或遮掩了起来。2月4日下午，庙门口突然悄悄地张贴出了一张红纸，上书一大大的"忌"字，并写道："正月十三下午祭台。生肖属鼠、牛、狗三生肖回避。孩童适时回避。祭台时间：16:00—18:00，特此告知"。从落款时间为二〇一二年二月一日来看，这是一个早就计划好的除秽仪式，但之前却没有通知，想必是不想引起外人注意。听村支书介绍，他本人想阻止这个行为，但老人们坚持说，老戏台多年不唱戏，不除晦气不行。我听到这个消息自然非常兴奋，连忙跑到殿中守候，但支书亲自来劝我离开，要我跟他去用晚餐。我想辩驳，说自己不属鼠、牛、狗，看看没关系，而且我从来没看过"祭台"，很想一睹为快。支书还是不让，说我的生肖虽然没问题，但还没有达到可以参观的年龄（只有老人才可观看），所以最好还是离开。出于礼貌，我只好顺从他。后来从村民口中听到一些祭祀的情况，好像是类似于袚除一类的仪式：表演鬼神者要到乱坟堆里化妆，戴上面具，然后在戏台上舞蹈，并用鸡血祭台。之后有追赶仪式，即让村民把鬼神驱逐出村外，后者在没人的地方卸妆，把鞋子扔掉，换上别的鞋子回来就算是阴魂消散、万事大吉了。因为有鬼魂出没，小孩（包括青壮年）和上述三个生肖的人容易为其所害，所以才有此禁忌。尽管如此，我还是怀疑支书不让我在场的原因多半是出于他的顾虑，而不是因为我的年龄。也许在他的心目中，这样的"迷信"仪式与非物质文化遗产的名号格格不入，所以最好不要公开，以便产生不良影响。可见，当民俗成为公共的文化遗产之后，即便行政部门不直接干预，承载它的民众群体也会进行自我监控，尽量让仪式及其背后的信仰意义能与现时代的主流意识形态相符。

最后，仪式的表演性增强，民间活动的随意性减弱。2月3日，村中老人们都提着空篮子，在殿里一遍又一遍地排练怎样入场，怎样把祭品整齐地摆放到祭台前，然后怎样有序地退场。儿童们都化了妆，穿上统一的服装。敬献祭品和抬佛巡游的男人们也穿上了统一制作的绸衣绸裤。扮演"芒神"的男童由少女顶替，大概是因为女孩相貌俊秀、声音清亮的缘故。仪式行为也相对地集中到了梧桐祖殿周围，每家每户的活动明显减少。大家整天都在庙里帮忙，三餐也在庙里吃，原来以家庭为单位举行的"插春""咬春"和到自家田头祭拜等习俗也就自然而然地遭到了冷落。

德国学者汉斯·莫泽（Hans Moser）在上个世纪 60 年代曾提出"民俗主义"（Folklorismus）的概念，批评的是"在旅游业的影响下和由于大众传媒的需求、习俗由经常是非常简单的表演形式而转向夸张的色彩斑斓的表演形式的改变"。① 其后发生的德国民俗学界的相关讨论主要聚焦于四个问题:"1)过去的民俗之面向观众和当前的民俗主义之作秀效果之间的区别;2)恰恰经常被民俗主义的当事人所征用的'真实'这一范畴的可疑性,以及与此相应的对不真实的伪民俗加以排斥的问题;3)民俗学对民俗主义——在多数情况下属非自愿——的贡献;4)在对美好的古老的过去进行安抚性展现的民俗主义在政治上的可被利用性。"② 由此可见,原始意义上的民俗自身也带有表演的特征,具有服务于地方政治和经济的功能。但相比之下,"民俗主义"行为的表演性和功利性更为强烈,也更加明显,几已从仪式性的表演转化成了迎合游客和媒体的炒作与作秀;民俗主义者借助民俗学的研究成果,打着"真实"的旗号,贩卖着最不真实的"二手民俗",使其为政治、商业、旅游等其他目的服务。③

"九华立春祭"的最初发现,也与当地开发旅游业的动机有关。在立春祭祀与习俗的恢复过程中,当地的文化人像汪筱联、衢州民间文艺家协会主席崔成志(已故)、衢州市诗词协会副会长叶裕龙等都发挥了极大的推动作用。他们为村民们重新"发明"仪式提供了专业咨询。但在由他们整理的"申遗"资料中,历史的和现代的、全国的和地方的、神话的和真实的信息全部融汇在一起,且都被作为"历史的真实"对待,让人一时难辨真假。最后,"九华立春祭"被当地政府的文化部门看中,并推荐申报成为省级和国家级的非物质文化遗产,祭祀由此也染上了官方色彩,或多或少地为地方政治所利用,比如乡政府的官员们就难免会把这场仪式当成是自我展示和引起领导和媒体关注的机会。那么,我们由此是否就可以给它戴上一顶"民俗主义"的帽子,而对其本真性产生怀疑呢?

笔者根据自己的参与观察,认为今天的"九华立春祭"与德国学者所批评的"民俗主义"现象还不能同日而语,这是因为到目前为止,它所受到的外力干预与影响还是比较有限的。其中最关键的一点,就是它的传承主体并未发生转移。在整个活动中,外陈村的村民始终担任主角,其中直接在活动中负有职责的主动参与者有近 200 人,包括不少平时在外地打工的青壮年。④ 再者,村民们祭祀春神、"迎春接福",为自己、为家人也为国家祈福、祈寿、祈财、祈年的中心主题也没有改变。人们在准备祭品、参加排练和祭祀时都带着虔诚和敬意,包括被化妆起来朗诵诗歌和喧嚷"春来了"的儿童们,也是一腔真诚,不带丝毫做作的成分。当然,为了给外人留下一个美好的印象,村民们也会以他们自身的理解尽量把仪式举办得体面一些,把自己认为阴暗的部分遮盖起来,把儿童们乔装打扮后推到前台来表演,等等,但这些都还在适度的范围之内,尚属民俗本身所带有的面向观众的仪式表演性使

---

① 引自鲍辛格《民俗主义》(Hermann Bausinger *Folklorismus*),载《童话百科全书》第四集(*Enzyklopaedie des Maerchen*: Handwoerterbuch zur historischen und vergleichenden Erzaehlforschung Ⅳ),1984,第1406—1407页。
② 同上,第1407页。
③ 语出莫泽。参见王霄冰《民俗主义论与德国民俗学》,《民间文化论坛》2006年第3期,第100—105页。
④ 其中最远的一位来自卡塔尔。他告诉笔者,自己出国已有6年,早就听说村里恢复了立春祭,这次回家过年正好赶上,感觉非常幸福、自豪。为了出份力,他自愿报名,替村委会用私家车接送往来客人,并在祭祀日担任维持秩序的工作。

然，不能被指责为是炒作和作秀。

由此，笔者得出结论认为，只要有一个实实在在的传承主体存在，其中成员的文化主体意识并未丧失，非物质文化遗产的本真和活态传承就可以得到保证。所谓的传承主体，指的是传承人背后的那个集体，它和传承人的关系，应是民众群体及其代言人的关系。

以外陈村为例，国家级代表性传承人目前只挂着汪筱联一个人的名字。当地的文化部门正准备将龚元龙这样的本村主事者也报批为传承人。还有傅洪民、吴海根等年轻一代的村民，也将作为后备人才得到培养。乡政府和村委员也在筹备建立一个非宗教性的民间组织（协会），专门负责管理和推动梧桐祖庙和立春祭的运营。这些生于斯长于斯、习惯于穿西装和牛仔裤的当代农民，一方面依然扎根农村，另一方面又具备现代人的眼光和管理能力，一旦他们认识到自身所拥有的乡土文化的价值，的确可以在传承家乡文化方面发挥出巨大的能量。

但是，光有这些还不够。在树立与培养传承人的同时，我们也不应忘记在个别的传承人之后的那个作为传承主体存在的民众群体。在"九华立春祭"中，他们就是外陈村的600多名村民和临近各村的九华乡民众。立春日当晚，迎春完毕，一支名为"九九红"的婺剧团的男女演员们舞着一条鳞光闪闪的"龙"，登上梧桐祖庙的戏台亮相。照例先要"闹花台"，然后"摆八仙"。台下人头攒动，老老少少，有的坐有的站。当台上所有的神仙一一登场，汇聚一堂，由"天官"发令将他们派往民间送福送财、护佑百姓时，一位村民代表按例给剧团领队送上了一个红包和四条香烟，"天官"则及时地亮出了"风调雨顺""国泰民安"的锦旗，以示降福，并把一个硕大的塑胶"金元宝"交到村民代表的手上，顿时群情欢腾，一片欢喜。当看到这一幕时，我对于民俗遗产化后的本真性问题的担忧和疑虑全都烟消云散了。因为我相信，只要有这片土地在，有这座古庙在，有这些农民在，有这种生活的欢乐在，民俗就一定可以以它本土、本色、本真的面目永久地生存和发展下去。

全国牧童诗会：关于文化真实性的个案研究

查理·泽曼[*]

  本文主要介绍笔者所在的西部民俗中心及其每年举办的最大型的活动——全国牧童诗会。今年（2011年）这一活动已经走进第二十八个年头了。特别令人感兴趣的是由该活动参与者们（包括牧童诗诗人、音乐家及其他艺术家）提出的文化真实性问题。

  西部民俗中心是一个私立的、非营利的民间组织，其使命是通过体验、理解和欣赏美国西部的多样的文化遗产，以加强美式生活的活力。这一使命是通过一年一度的全国牧童诗歌聚会实现的，同时也通过以下方式得以贯彻：演出、展览、教育活动、媒体宣传（广播和电视）、研究、文件编制以及宣扬美国西部民俗的智慧、艺术性和创造性的文化保护项目。

  为了继续完善我们的工作，我们关注了美国西部大量多样性文化的民族身份。虽然民俗中心历来重视有关牧业文化的小说、诗歌、音乐和工艺品，但我们更深远的任务是尊重并保存我们所发现的美国西部不同职业、种族、民族和历代传承的精神传统中表现的生命力。今天，我要特别介绍的是我们关于牧业文化和牛仔的工作。

  我所说的美国牛仔，并不是使牛仔的形象神话般地闻名世界的电影中所塑造的不朽的牛仔形象。我们并不是在谈论约翰·维恩和克林特·伊斯特伍德，也不是对所谓早期"旧西部"的怀旧游戏。我们在西部民俗中心是和现实中的牛仔打交道，他们的工作和马、牛等其他牲畜密切相关。牛仔的职业一点也不浪漫，他们的工作危险、困难、肮脏，却只拿低微的薪水。选择这个职业不是为了金钱而是出于对它单纯的热爱。追求牛仔这个职业的人很珍惜这种在户外工作，栖居于开放的国度，在马背上驰骋的生活方式。真正的牛仔为他们自身的特殊技能和马术感到非常的自豪，他们憎恨那些试图代表他们的牛仔文化却没有真正体验过牛仔生活、从事过牛仔工作的人。这一点对于我们的组织非常重要，因为我们现在要付出巨大的努力去展现真正的牧业和牛仔文化的代表者。这项"真正的事业"并非盛装的演员或那些通常被称为"模仿者""药房牛仔"或者称为"只有帽子，却没有牛"（只有风格却没有实质）。

  牧童诗歌和音乐起源于牛仔从美国南部赶着牲畜北上，跋涉千里去有铁路能运送牲口的城市时的口头传统吟唱。像许多职业如水手、伐木工人、矿工的无形口头文学一样，牛仔们

---

[*] 查理·泽曼，曾任（美国）西部民俗中心主任。

创作的职业韵律诗歌和音乐反映了职业牛仔的日常生活和艰辛的工作。这些诗歌和音乐创作都是关于他们最喜欢的马、恶劣天气中的长途跋涉以及放牧生活和可怕的牲畜践踏。一些牧童诗歌和音乐非常幽默，另外一些则是在讲述牛仔工作中的悲剧和死亡。当今，尽管很多牧童诗歌和音乐都已经有了印刷品，但是几乎所有的牧童诗歌和音乐总是存在于记忆和口头传诵中而不是从书页上读到的。

这是前蒙大拿州民俗学家迈克·科恩对牧童诗人和牧童诗歌所作的定义："牧童诗是由将人生的重要部分融合在美国西北部畜牧文化中的人写的押韵、字数固定的诗歌。诗歌反映了对这种生活方式最亲密的认知，这个社会团体本身就包含了自身的传统。牧童诗也许作者不详，但一定是质量高、内容丰富、风格独特的，这样才能被文化团体所接纳；同时，在风格、形式和内容方面能体现该文化团体的美学意义。牧童诗的结构风格传承自英格兰和阿巴拉契亚山脉南部的民谣，与作家罗伯特·W. 瑟维斯和拉迪亚德·吉卜林的知名作品类似。"我们的创始人霍·加农补充说："今天的许多诗人是农场的家庭主妇、牧场主、拍卖行老板、竞技牛仔、牧人伙计以及日常工作八小时饲养牲畜的人。"

全国牧童诗会始建于28年前，当时在美国西部工作的民俗学家做出记录和识别这项非物质文化遗产的重要决定，否则这一传统可能随着老牛仔们的逝去而消亡。这些民俗学家进行了实地调查工作，在各自的州查找和确认还在工作的并能背诵或写下来牧童诗和牧童音乐的牛仔。他们组织成立了"牧童诗会"，将这些人聚集在一起，相互传诵并和大众分享他们各自的诗歌和音乐。尽管当时他们只是想举办一次，但这项活动却非常轰动并成为每年举办的活动。

作为畜牧和牛仔文化的展示者，我们所面临的挑战一直都是如何把"真正的"牛仔文化代表引入集会这项工作做到最好，绝不只是简单地穿上牛仔的服装，学习表演一些牧童诗、音乐，却少有或几乎没有和牲畜一起工作的生活经历。我们想要强调的是从生活体验中诉说心声的人，体现诗歌和歌曲中生活的人。真正的牛仔对真实性和矫揉造作非常敏感。1922年，诗人柏格·克拉克在最早出版的牧童诗诗集的前言中写道："牛仔是对那些试图代表西部文化人的最严厉的批判者。他们不虚伪、不欺骗，有着不逃避的姿态。"了解到这些后，我们决定应该让牛仔们自己选择他们最尊敬的参会者。

想要在集会中表演的人需要申请参与权，必须提交他们音乐或诗歌朗诵的音频资料和作品样本，而且要有一个简要自述，讲述他们与畜牧文化相关的经历，如作为牧场主人、工作的牛仔、农妇、兽医或从事其他相关的工作。为了审查这些申请表，我们创建了一个年度评审小组，包括牛仔诗人、牛仔歌手和音乐家，以及熟悉这些传统又非西部民俗中心工作人员的特邀民俗学家。这个同行委员会的人员都是匿名的而且每年人员都会有变动，他们在春天会面，花两天或三天来倾听意见、讨论所有的文件。然后他们对申请表进行投票，我们的工作人员并不参与投票。在200至300名候选人中，我们将邀请50至60名参与集会表演。这个允许牛仔们自己选择他们最尊敬、作品最能充分反映牛仔生活和文化的候选人的流程取得了巨大成功，并且使我们成功地将真正的牧童诗、音乐持续推行了28年。因为是传统活动的承载者自己做决定，结果总是反映了这一群体不断变化的审美观念以及当代对于本真性的定义。

山野奇花的旷世魅力
——"撒叶儿嗬"简论

刘守华*

中国强劲实施的非物质文化遗产保护工程,从2005年开始,截至2016年底,已评审公布了四批国家级非物质文化遗产代表性项目共1372项,其中列入首批名录的民间舞蹈——湖北长阳土家族的"撒叶儿嗬",源于土家族先民——古代巴人的"军阵舞",具有深厚的文化传统,它是显现旷世魅力的一朵山野奇花,深受国人喜爱及文化界关注,也是中国非遗保护工作的亮点之一。笔者不仅作为湖北省非遗保护工作中心的专家委员会成员参与过评审活动,还在长阳、五峰、房县、神农架等处亲临现场,乃至通宵达旦亲身体验了这项跳丧歌舞的原生态情景,现特作简要评述。

文化部非遗保护中心评介"撒叶儿嗬"如下:

> "撒叶儿嗬"是一种传统祭祀歌舞,乡亲们聚在孝家堂屋里的亡者灵柩前,男人载歌载舞,女人们穿戴着鲜亮服装围观助兴,这种活动往往通宵达旦地举行。土家族认为人的生死有如四季变化,是自然而然的,享尽天年的老人辞世是顺应自然规律,值得庆贺。土家人就这样用绝妙的歌腔舞态表达自己旷达的生死观。跳舞时先由歌师击鼓叫歌,舞者随鼓声应节起舞。
>
> "撒叶儿嗬"是歌、舞、乐浑然一体的艺术,它的声腔和歌调仅存于兴山一带,其曲体结构与楚辞体式多有相似,从中尚能看到古代巴楚之地祭神乐歌的影子。歌舞中显示出难能可贵的积极人生态度,贯穿着豁达通脱的生死观念。

这里说它是一种"传统祭祀歌舞",更简明的说法是"跳丧"或"跳丧歌舞"。在鄂西清江中游土家族居住地区及其周边,老人寿终正寝离世,居民称为"白喜事",办理丧事时须以歌舞相伴,聚众高歌狂舞一个通宵乃至两三夜,俗称"打丧鼓"或"跳丧"。"撒叶儿嗬"是土家语,来自土家族民间舞蹈音乐中出现频率较高的一个号子,久而久之,人们便把这种

---

* 刘守华,华中师范大学文学院教授。

舞蹈叫作"撒叶儿嗬"了。

一

"撒叶儿嗬"的独特形态与感人魅力何在？按笔者多年考察体验所得，试从以下三方面给以解说。

首先是聚众治丧，将丧事作为喜事来办。特别的生死观造就了土家人对死亡的坦然与豁达，很自然地形成以聚众歌舞的方式来办理丧事的奇特民俗。

其次是歌、舞、乐的浑然一体。这项跳丧歌舞活动，在停放灵柩的孝家（丧家）厅堂举行，有锣鼓伴奏。场上一人站在棺左侧掌鼓领唱，众人即跟唱起舞。整个场面由掌鼓歌师通过鼓点和唱腔控制，随时变换节奏与曲牌。而且掌鼓歌师、舞者和围观者的身份可以自由变换。

最后，土家族跳丧活动还有既高歌狂舞、热烈奔放，又严守丧礼规范、井然有序的审美特质。掌鼓的歌师按歌词内容配腔，歌词十分丰富，既可以唱祖先功业，也可以唱亡人生平德行，还可以唱地方风土人情及男女性爱。其中，叙说古人古事的长篇叙事歌，如《黑暗传》，最适宜在跳丧时演唱；人们喜爱的情歌也是丧场上最为流行的品种。

这一民俗文化传统并非孤立地自动延伸而来，它是在土家族地区因发挥着积极的社会功能而贯通古今传承至今的。

二

土家族跳丧活动长盛不衰的原因归纳为三点：

高山深谷，人户稀疏，住地分散的生活环境，使得跳丧适应了料理丧事这种乡村民俗群体活动的需要，具有广泛的大众参与性。

土葬习俗，需要邻里乡亲的协助，因而"一跳丧鼓二帮忙"就成为世代沿袭不变的乡俗了。

此外，淳朴善良的土家儿女为了表达对逝去父母的哀悼思念，众亲友以高歌狂舞、欢声笑语来陪伴孝家并互相取乐，以驱除冷清哀伤。该习俗由此深得民心而世代相承下来。

湖北长阳土家族自治县对"撒叶儿嗬"这项非物质文化遗产代表作从普查申报到保护、利用都取得了突出成绩，是为中国非遗保护的成功典型之一。

三

  就非遗保护须尊重其本真性和整体性而言，以跳丧、哭嫁为例，其整体显然不适宜进行商业性开发。但谭学聪等将其歌舞拆分开来，以土家"撒叶儿嗬"原生态民歌组合形式参加全国青歌赛并获得金奖，受到全国观众喜爱赞赏，则是一个文化产业开发的成功事例；但它已属于对这项民间传统歌舞的改编与再创造，不是原生态的跳丧表演了。

  不少地方的文化部门对已入名录的非遗项目的历史源流与生存背景、文化内涵与形态特征，所知相当浮浅，却急功近利地去搞经济开发，结果往往难以收到满意效果。因而著名文化人冯骥才近期提出，"开发这个概念绝对不能使用在文化遗产上"，想利用遗产赚大钱的想法和做法，常常造成对遗产的扭曲和破坏。就湖北长阳土家族"撒叶儿嗬"这非遗项目而言，虽然在申报评审利用过程中出现过一些波折和争议，总体来看却是成功的。

简论史密森尼民俗节的策展

詹姆斯·I. 道伊奇[*]

通常被称为"没有围墙的博物馆"或"生动的户外博物馆"的史密森尼民俗节始于1967年，用以纪念一些最好的非物质文化遗产实践者和传承者。早在联合国教科文组织提出保护非物质文化遗产之前，每年举办的这个美国民俗节（直到1998年才被世人所知）就与成千上万的参观者分享着那些与非物质文化遗产相同的文化形式，即"社区、群体，有时是个人视为其文化遗产组成部分的习俗、表现形式、表达方式、知识、技能，以及与之相关的工具、实物、手工艺品和文化场所"。在史密森尼学会（即美国国家博物馆，成立于1846年）的支持下，其旗下的史密森尼民俗节从开始至今，通过举行庆祝活动来帮助保护了100多个不同国家以及美国各州、各种行业群体和宗教团体的传统文化（包括音乐、舞蹈、表演、手工艺、饮食方式等等）。

史密森尼民俗节无疑是每年发生在华盛顿特区国家广场上的最突出和最流行的活动。国家广场是由美国国家公园管理局管理。除了国家广场外，美国国家公园管理局还管理大峡谷国家公园、黄石国家公园、自由女神像国家纪念碑以及其他近400个特殊场所。国家广场不仅是马丁·路德·金发表《我有一个梦想》演讲的地方，抗议游行和示威经常发生的地方，而且是2009年1月数百万人不顾严寒观看美国总统奥巴马就职典礼的地方。由于它的东端是国会大厦，西端是林肯纪念堂，中间矗立着华盛顿纪念碑和美国国家"二战"纪念碑，南端和北端分布着史密森尼学会的几个博物馆，国家广场可以说是美国最重要的公众空间。史密森尼民俗节一般在7月4日即美国全民最重要的节日美国独立日前后举行，持续10天左右。活动完全在户外的帐篷和临时建筑里举行，这些帐篷和临时建筑面积为200～11000平方英尺（或约19～1000平方米）。

据狄龙·里普利（史密森尼学会1964年至1984年的负责人）在1966年告诉民俗节的创始理事拉尔夫·林兹勒说，"让他们从陈列柜里拿出乐器并歌唱"，这意味着民俗节不仅要展现史密森尼学会的大量乐器（其中大部分锁在博物馆的陈列柜和橱窗里）的实用性和生命力，也要呈现多样化的音乐家和表演者的活力，从而呈现文化遗产的生命力（包括旧的和新的）。自那时起，史密森尼民俗节一直围绕两个主要目标进行：①用在国家广场恭

---

[*] 詹姆斯·I. 道伊奇，史密森尼学会民俗与文化遗产研究中心策展人、编辑。

敬、详细地展示这一措施来强化和保护文化遗产；②通过"文化对话"这一方式促进民俗节参与者和参观者之间的相互了解，"文化对话"是一种文化交流，民俗节的参与者和参观者直接向对方表达自己的想法。

自1967年以来，民俗节的活动主题已经非常多元化，包括：以美国各州为主题，如俄亥俄州（1971）、新泽西州（1983）和新墨西哥州（1992）；以城市为主题，如费城（1984）、华盛顿特区（2000）和纽约市（2001）；国际主题，如韩国（1982）、塞内加尔（1990）和苏格兰（2003）；包含几个州或国家的区域性主题，如密西西比三角洲（1997）、格兰德河（2000）以及湄公河（2007）；职业文化主题，如美国出庭律师（1987）、白宫工作人员（1992）和建筑艺术大师（2001）；美国政府机构主题，如美国林业局（2005）、美国国家航空和航天局（2008）、和平队（2011）；还有与跨国文化遗产相关的广泛主题，如美洲栗色文化（1992）和弗吉尼亚州的非洲、英国和印第安人传统（2007）。1967年以来，代表他们的文化遗产和传统参加民俗节的人数虽然没有精确的统计数据，但粗略估计已达到30000人次。

在典型的史密森尼民俗节上，人们会看到在国家广场同时上演的三个不同主题的活动。（唯一的一个例外发生在2002年，当年只有一个主题，即"丝绸之路：连接文化，创造信任"，呈现了古代丝绸之路上22个不同国家人们的生活传统，古代丝绸之路从东方的中国、日本和韩国一路到达西方的意大利威尼斯。）例如，2013年的三个主题分别是：①"匈牙利文化遗产：起源到复兴"，这凸显了匈牙利的音乐、舞蹈、服装、工艺品、烹饪等方面文化遗产的生命力；②"同一个世界，多种声音：濒危语言和文化遗产"，通过来自世界各地的社区文化专家展示他们的文化知识、特性（identity）、价值观、技术和艺术，说明语言多样性是我们人类遗产的重要组成部分；③"装扮的意愿：非裔美国人的多样性、风格和特性"，通过服装和装饰品的多样性传达出来的文化传统、艺术性和身份特征展示非裔美国人的独特性。由于史密森尼学会和中国文化部之间的合作关系，2014年民俗节将展现中国的文化遗产，有大约150位代表十类中国非物质文化遗产的传承人参加。

每个史密森尼民俗节活动方案都是在一两个史密森尼民俗节策展人（通常是全年在民俗和文化遗产中心工作的员工）的带领下起草的，他们与由主题专家组成的策展团队紧密合作，有时与为主题和议题提供专业知识的联合策展人紧密配合。所有的民俗节活动，特别是像"匈牙利文化遗产：濒危语言""非裔美国人的饰品"那样多样化的主题活动，都可能会有不同的理念、目标和策展视野，更何况他们还面临着各自特定的挑战。然而，无论参与者是来自布达佩斯、波哥大还是巴尔的摩，所有的活动都有一个共同的目标，这就是帮助参观者更好地了解和欣赏文化传统，尤其是国家广场上那些传统文化传承人本身。实现这一目标的最佳途径之一，如前所述，是促进"文化对话"，即民俗节的参与者和参观者直接交流，表达自己的看法，而不受史密森尼学会任何的干扰或审查。

因此，策划过程中几乎每一个步骤都旨在使参加者和参观者走得更近：基于田野调查和研究挑选参与者；不断与参与者进行对话以了解他们的传统、习俗和技能；场地和参观路线的设计，指示牌和其他视觉标牌的书写和摆放；内外空间的布置；发言人和主持人的角色；

等等。

毫无疑问，策展人也与史密森尼民俗节团队的其他成员非常密切地合作，这些成员包括活动协调员、艺术总监和设计师、技术人员（包括电工，木匠和水管工）、管理员和预算专家、交通运输协调员、节目市场销售助理、物资供应者、参与人员（负责住、行的安排）以及许多其他相关人员。

民俗节策展人还必须定期向他们的策展团队、活动赞助商、社区成员以及潜在的参观者咨询。例如，2013年匈牙利文化遗产活动的策展团队包括来自巴拉斯研究所（总部设在布达佩斯，向世界各地介绍匈牙利文化）、匈牙利民间艺术家协会（打造布达佩斯民间艺术年度盛典）、捷尔吉·马丁民间舞蹈协会、匈牙利传统之家、匈牙利露天博物馆以及位于布达佩斯的国家民族博物馆的专家。民俗节是高度协作的结果，史密森尼的工作人员根据多年在国家广场上举办大型公共活动的经验提供专业知识，也利用了且受益于那些在民俗节上起重要作用的国家和地区的合作伙伴的文化遗产研究成果，其目的是促进合作学习，而不是完全依赖于史密森尼的专业知识，专业知识更适合更加规范的史密森尼室内博物馆展览。

根据对参观者进行的年度调查，结果表明史密森尼民俗节正在做一些有意义的事。2012年民俗节调查发现，65%的参观者认为在民俗节的体验是极好的，27%的参观者评为良好，只有8%的人认为一般。2011年民俗节的调查结果更好，78%的调查对象认为在民俗节的体验是极好的，29%的参观者评为良好，只有3%的人认为一般。当然，总是有改进的空间。

如果一切按计划进行，2016年第50届民俗节将如期举行，为筹划这次50周年纪念，史密森尼的工作人员将继续重新审视过去的实践及未来的工作重点。很显然，今天的民俗节参观者，特别是那些30岁以下的参观者，其教育和娱乐更加依赖于数字媒体而较少进行面对面互动（以及"文化对话"）。同样明显的是国家广场似乎一年比一年暖和，可能是全球气候变化的缘故。例如2012年民俗节期间创下有史以来最热的记录：平均气温高达99华氏度（37摄氏度），还由于狂风的破坏而减少了一天。鉴于此，史密森尼民俗节是否应该继续努力吸引尽可能多的现场参观者，让他们在6月下旬和7月初这10天闷热的日子里来到令人汗流浃背的国家广场呢？或者说，民俗节是否应该试着提供更多的线上活动和参与机会来吸引21世纪的观众呢？

中国非物质文化遗产数字化技术运用研究

黄永林　谈国新[*]

上世纪90年代以来，以信息技术、网络手段为代表的的数字化技术得到了长足的发展。数字化技术不仅在各种工业领域得以广泛应用，而且给文化遗产保护事业开辟了新的途径。对于物质文化遗产的数字化保护，世界各国以及联合国教科文组织已经做了大量的工作，然而对于非物质文化遗产的数字化保护，很多国家，尤其是中国，才刚刚起步。究其原因，主要是由于非物质文化遗产大多是长期经验的积累，主要靠口传心记、言传身教传承，具有活态性、生态性、传承性、变异性等特殊性质，保护难度较大。本文在研究数字化技术在非物质文化遗产保护与传承中重要作用的基础上，进一步研究数字化技术在非物质文化遗产保护与传承中的深度开发与运用问题，以期为促进我国非物质文化遗产数字化技术的发展与运用提供思路。

一、数字化技术在非物质文化遗产保护与传承中的重要作用

非物质文化遗产数字化就是采用数字采集、数字储存、数字处理、数字展示、数字传播等技术将非物质文化遗产转换、再现、复原成可共享、可再生的数字形态，并以新的视角加以解读，以新的方式加以保存，以新的需求加以利用。[1]现代数字化技术的发展，为非物质文化遗产的采集、保存、展示与传播提供了更为广阔的空间。

1. 数字化采集和存储技术为非物质文化遗产完整保护提供了保障

我国现在的非物质文化遗产的保护还基本上停留在拍照、采访、记录、物品收藏等简单的工作层面上，这种文字、录音、摄影、录像等传统的非物质文化遗产技术保护手段，曾保存了大批珍贵的非物质文化遗产。但是书籍的生霉、录像带的老化、录像色彩的蜕变、录音带的失真等，都会使所记录的非物质文化遗产的信息不同程度地出现失真，加上拍摄角度的限制，影响了长期保存和利用。数字化技术为非物质文化遗产的保护提供了许多全新的采集

---

[*] 黄永林，华中师范大学国家文化产业研究中心主任、教授；谈国新，华中师范大学国家文化产业研究中心教授。

记录手段,包括图文扫描、立体扫描、全息拍摄、数字摄影、运动捕捉等。数字化存储技术也为非物质文化遗产的保护提供了许多新的保护手段,包括通过数据库、磁盘阵列、光盘塔、光纤和网络连接以及一系列相关规定、协议,实现对非物质文化遗产资源的有效保护。通过这些现代数字化采集和储存信息技术,不仅可以把一些非物质文化遗产的档案资料(如手稿、音乐、照片、影像、艺术图片等)编辑转化为数字化格式,保存于数字磁带、光盘等物质介质中,而且还可以利用多媒体网络数据库来存储和管理,使它们完整有序、便于检索,这能够整体提升对非物质文化遗产保护的水平。

目前,运用数字化多媒体等现代化科技手段对珍贵、濒危并具有历史价值的非物质文化遗产进行真实、系统和全面的记录、建立档案和数据库已成为中国非物质文化遗产保护工程的主要实施内容之一。然而,非物质文化遗产包括传统文化表现形式及其赖以生存的文化空间,单一的数字化存储通常忽视了其赖以生存的文化空间特性,很难将非物质文化遗产作为一个完整的整体给予保存。以舞蹈动作的数字化为例,在传统的记录保存工作中,演员的舞蹈动作多通过文字、照片、视频进行记录。然而,上述手段难以对舞蹈表演,特别是演员的表演动作进行准确全面的记录。拍摄录像或 DV 只能从几个有限的角度以二维图像的方式进行录制,记录的数据虽然可以方便地存贮在录像带、电脑硬盘等媒体中,但数据的可重用性和可编辑性较差。在重现时,还需要舞蹈艺术家和演员的参与。获取的数据难以被进一步地开发利用(如直接用于影视、动画制作等)。若希望对获取的数据进行修改,则需要演员全部重新表演,产生较大的工作量。现代数字信息获取与处理技术能更好地整理、收集、记录非物质文化遗产的信息,可以突破传统意义上的保护方式所不能达到的展示要求与保真效果,更为安全和长久地保存这些弥足珍贵的非物质文化遗产。

2. 数字化复原和再现技术为非物质文化遗产有效传承提供了支撑

非物质文化遗产传承之难,归根结底均由于生产方式、生活环境的变化,而维持原有的生产方式、生活方式,乃至生存环境,是与全人类的现代化奋斗目标相抵触的。这就是我们在非物质文化遗产保护问题上最根本的两难选择。现代计算机图形学、数字图像处理与虚拟现实等数字复原和再现技术以及设备日趋成熟,为非物质文化遗产的传承提供了更先进的手段与方法。对非物质文化遗产进行传承,可以将传统的非物质文化遗产资源进行数字化后,制作成可视化虚拟产品,供人们学习、交流与创新。比如采取 2D、3D 数字动画技术,恢复、再现和解读非物质文化遗产现象、场景、事件或过程,通过图片、视频、三维动画等形式实现非物质文化遗产可视化,实现与原物或原事项完全一样的恢复和再现;应用真实感角色生成、场景搭建、动作绑定、人机交互、知识建模等技术,快速生成非物质文化遗产中的情景和行为,实现非物质文化遗产的虚拟再现、知识可视化及互动操作,以便尽可能多的人通过观看而了解这些非物质文化遗产,包括濒临消失的非物质文化遗产的原貌。此外,还可通过互联网或数据光盘将数据上传到系统的高级端,从而实现非物质文化遗产信息化更为广泛的交流,让更多的人对我们的民族文化增加了解,增强艺术兴趣,激发民族文化发展的活力。

比如在世界上久负盛名的南通板鹞风筝，它融雕、扎、书、画、绣等多种工艺于一体，其中哨口的雕刻工艺最为精湛。板鹞风筝上的哨口，随大小、形状、材料各异，以及哨面进风口的位置、角度、长短、宽窄的改变，发出的音量、音质、音调千变万化，加之人们巧妙地将各种音调哨口立体组合，可产生各种美妙的空中交响曲。对于哨口的大小、形状以及哨面进风口的位置、大小、角度、长短、宽窄等等这些技术参数，都可以通过计算机进行数字化归纳，设计出一套相应的软件程序，这样能让设计出来的哨口的音质、音调等更为精准；再结合虚拟场景建模、计算机辅助设计等技术将哨口雕刻的过程进行数字化编程，通过三维动画对哨口的制作进行展示，这样人们就可以通过计算机欣赏到哨口制作的全过程。板鹞风筝的鹞布上的绘画也颇有讲究，画面精细，重人物，大多是采自民间故事，代表着人们放飞的理想与愿望。数字化保护开发可以对其画面题材内容、风格样式等特征进行数字化的归纳，开发相应的软件及图形库，形成板鹞风筝特色的图形语言系统，并将其运用到现代设计中去，将这种民间传统文化的观念基因传承下去。[2]

3. 数字化展示与传播技术为非物质文化遗产广泛共享提供了平台

随着数字化虚拟展示技术的发展，这种虚拟展示集虚拟现实、图文声像等多媒体表现手段于一体，将非物质文化遗产在计算机虚拟世界中进行展示，以平面显示、全景显示或立体空间成像的方式，将声、光、电产生的效果全方位、多视角、直观地向大众展示。非物质文化遗产的数字化展示与传播主要包括以下方面：第一，利用三维场景建模、特效渲染、虚拟场景协调展示等动画技术，对非物质文化遗产特别是传统手工艺的生产方式、使用方式、消费方式、流通方式、传播传承方式等进行真实再现；第二，借助多媒体集成、数字摄影、知识建模等技术，建立包括文字、声音、图像、视频、知识在内的非物质文化遗产数字博物馆；第三，基于数字媒介统一平台建立数字博物馆，将多种媒介形式的非物质文化遗产信息整合在一起，借助电信、无线通信、互联网、有线电视以及各种数字电视网络进行传播，打破特定时间、场所的限制，使之成为现代技术条件下适合于大众传播的一种新的应用平台，让非物质文化遗产的展示、传播与利用更为便利和充分，使海量存储的非物质文化遗产资源得到最大限度的共享利用。

例如，数字博物馆就是一种适合于民族民间非物质文化遗产大众传播的数字化展示平台，它与普通博物馆不同，不仅仅是静态藏品的展示，更是将一些民间工艺制作过程的历史流变、工艺存在的文化状态、民间艺人档案、民间艺术传播方式、制作工艺、原材料以及民间生活方式等成千上万种文化艺术的全过程进行数字化转换后存入数据库网络。因此，在虚拟的数字博物馆里，是以活态文化的方式展示各种民族民间非物质文化的具体内容和艺术精髓。比如民间蓝印花布是我国传统的印染工艺品，它以手纺、手织、手染的民间工艺，纯真而又朴素、鲜明而又和谐的蓝白之美闻名于世。当我们进入数字博物馆后，只需轻轻点击鼠标，就可以看到蓝印花布制作技艺从种植兰草、制作颜料、雕刻花版到染色、晾晒的全过程。数字博物馆的发展与普及，必将使大众更为方便地了解我们中华民族各种优秀的非物质文化遗产。

4. 虚拟现实技术为非物质文化遗产开发利用提供了空间

在新的历史时期,我们要进一步提高对非物质文化遗产的认识,创新思维,拓展非物质文化遗产的保护思路。非物质文化遗产真正的价值在于其所蕴含的丰富的文化因子,这些文化因子可以通过生产、流通、销售等方式转化成为体现独特的民族风格和地方特色的优秀文化产品,使之重新融入现实社会,走进人们的日常生活。这种对非物质文化遗产的生产性保护是最具文化延续性和创造力的保护。[3] 虚拟现实技术为非物质文化遗产的开发利用提供了广阔的空间,通过数字化技术可以将非物质文化遗产进行产业化经营,并转化为文化生产力,形成规模经济效益,可以调动民众保护和发展非物质文化遗产的积极性。

数字化虚拟非物质文化遗产是指运用先进的虚拟现实技术对非物质文化遗产进行数字重建,虚拟现实的人机交互技术是其应用发展过程中的关键技术,与虚拟现实技术相应的高性能硬件设备是其产业化的重要的条件,随着科学技术的进步,数字化、信息化的发展,这些关键技术将被攻克,高端设备也将被制造出来,这将大大提高非物质文化遗产生产性保护的能力。非物质文化遗产资源数字化最大的益处是不仅可以保存和记录非物质文化遗产的各方面的信息,而且可以在不改变非物质文化遗产原貌的情况下利用这些信息进行数字生产(数字复制、数字出版、数字再现)和数字传播,发挥非物质文化遗产独有的文化价值、经济价值。因此,利用数字化虚拟现实技术实现对非物质文化遗产的开发和利用,进行产业化生产与经营,有利于形成新的行业及衍生产品,延长产业链,使文化产业的比重得到提高,这对当今文化产业发展具有不可估量的经济价值和意义。比如通过数字化技术加快非物质文化遗产的产业化步伐,促使各民族的服饰文化、民间技艺文化、民间文学、民间舞蹈、民间音乐、消费习惯、交际礼节、节日庆典、娱乐游戏、艺术技能以及饮食文化等知识和技能的价值不断得到增值。

二、数字化技术在非物质文化遗产保护与传承中的深度开发

数字技术在非物质文化遗产的保护和传承领域功不可没,但是它的效用却仍然没有完全被开发出来。随着信息化技术的发展,数字化技术在非物质文化遗产保护、传承与开发方面的作用将更大。鉴于非物质文化遗产具有活态性(传承、演变情况)、传统性(特定的文化渊源与所处地方、环境有内在联系)、整体性(包括生态、文化)等特殊性质,简单的数字化存储通常忽视了其赖以生存的文化空间特性。因此,我们应该对非物质文化遗产领域资源重新审视、重新评价、重新挖掘其潜在价值,从知识表达及可视化的深度开发再认识,通过知识工程及语法粒度角度建立非物质文化遗产资源的多层次类型分类体系;建立非物质文化遗产的数据采集技术标准;构建国家非物质文化遗产保护与传承技术体系的方式和路径。在对情景建模和行为交互技术、知识可视化技术、动作绑定技术、Web技术等进行综合分析研究的基础上,建立一套适合不同类型非物质文化遗产的数据记录、保存、保护、传承工作的综合应用技术方案,构建非物质文化遗产多媒体交互体系平台,从而推动我国文化产业及

相关上下游产业的发展,提升我国文化产业的科技含量、促进原创性文化产品的设计开发和应用。这对于促进我国非物质文化遗产的保护、传承与产业开发均具有重要的意义。

1. 建立非物质文化遗产资源数字化分类体系

我国非物质文化遗产品种丰富、形式多样,既有多姿多彩的民俗文化,如风土人情、传统礼仪、宗教及节庆活动等,又有口头流传的各种民间文学,如传说、史诗、民间故事、寓言、民谣、谚语等;既有淳朴生动的各类表演艺术,如音乐、舞蹈、民间戏剧、曲艺杂技等,又有技艺精湛、美轮美奂的工艺美术,如面人、糖人、剪纸、编织、刺绣、彩绘、蜡染等。由于各类非物质文化遗产的表现形式不同、创造方式有别,对其数字化既要遵循普适性的保护原则与方法,又要采取因类制宜、适合各自特点的方法和措施。基于非物质文化遗产的活态性、传统性和整体性,在对其知识的系统性、复杂性和内隐性等特征进行详细分析研究的基础上,从民俗学、社会学、人类学、美学、历史学、心理学等多重角度探索非物质文化遗产知识的构成要素,提取知识的特征并对其进行归纳总结;从 When、How、What、Where、Why 五个方面分别表示非物质文化遗产的时间演变、表现方法、形式、相应地域及其内涵,并对分类后的知识从语法粒度角度建立其间的关系,建立非物质文化遗产资源的多层次类型分类体系。即利用数字化技术对非物质文化遗产资源进行学术分类、信息化存储,以便科学地建立非物质文化遗产资料性的符号库和素材数据库。

2. 创建非物质文化遗产资源数据采集技术标准

针对目前全国各地非物质文化遗产资源数据库建设中存在的技术目标不一致、技术标准不统一、技术管理不规范的情况,立足于现代信息技术的发展趋势,与国家数字化图书馆、数字化博物馆和国家文化信息资源共享工程建设相配套协调,围绕非物质文化遗产资源的创建、描述、组织、检索、服务和长期保存的需求,深入研究符合我国非物质文化遗产特点的资源建设相关技术标准,包括资源数字化采集、资源描述(元数据)、资源组织、资源管理、资源长期保存等技术标准;制定关于我国非物质文化遗产资源管理的统一、科学和规范的技术管理规程。并应用资源管理与分发技术对非物质文化遗产资源进行统一有效的整合,以促进非物质文化遗产资源采集、资源统一表示、资源权利信息描述、资源目录服务、注册服务、资源检索和发布等功能的实现。

3. 探讨非物质文化遗产知识可视化表达

非物质文化遗产可视化技术与物质文化遗产可视化技术有着本质的区别。物质文化遗产的可视化可以通过图片、视频、三维动画等形式实现,非物质文化遗产除了使用传统数字化技术进行可视化外,更多的是属于知识可视化的范畴。非物质文化遗产的知识可视化还是一个崭新的领域,这方面的研究还不多,离应用还有距离,但知识可视化是解决非物质文化遗产保护与传承的有效手段。非物质文化遗产知识可视化表达主要包括知识源层、知识描述层、可视化表达层和知识应用层。非物质文化遗产中包括了不同的知识源,如史料记载文档、民俗活动、民间技艺、戏曲、舞蹈等,这些知识源在语义上具有异构性。知识描述层描述文化空间知识的特征及其构成分类,如地域类、时间类、表现方式类、表现形式类、原因含义类。可视化表达层阐述根据知识的特征及其构成分类,选择恰当的模型进行表达,以便于不同用户进行知识的学习、共享与创新。知识应用层可以让用户根据自身的文化背景、知识构成等情况选择最适合自己实际情况的知识可视化表达方式来学习、构建文化空间知识等。用户通过对非物质文化遗产中相关文化空间知识的学习与交流,自身的用户类型信息就会随之得到更新,并且文化空间知识经过学习与交流将会得到发展与创新,从而更新文化空间知识源。

4. 构建非物质文化遗产新技术综合运用体系

非物质文化遗产是经过长期实践检验传承下来的,可以代表一个地方的文化,它包括与群众生活密切相关的各种传统文化表现形式和文化空间。其文化空间具有活态性、传统性、整体性等特殊性质,仅通过文本、图像、视频或动画等表示的说、唱、舞蹈等形式难以将其错综复杂的关系完整地表达出来。因此,单一的数字化存储通常忽视了其赖以生存的文化空间特性,需要研究将多种新技术手段综合运用到非物质文化遗产的保护和传承中,构建国家非物质文化遗产保护与传承技术体系。该技术体系主要包括非物质文化遗产的数字化技术、情景建模及行为控制技术、资源管理与服务技术、可视化技术的融合构成,如图1所示。

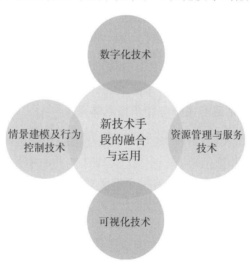

图1　新技术手段的融合与运用

(1)非物质文化遗产数字化技术:建立一套针对不同类别非物质文化遗产数字化的数据采集方法,包括综合运用动作捕捉技术获取运动对象三维数据,研究从这些测量数据中计算和推演动作数据的方法,建立运动物体三维动作;利用三维扫描技术,探索新的适合遗产对象特点的,简单、可靠的三维建模方法,以及几何与纹理一体化数据模型技术,建立三维物体对象的模型库与纹理库等。

（2）情景建模及行为控制技术：综合利用真实感角色生成技术、动作绑定技术、多Agent的群体控制技术、场景生成技术等快速生成非物质文化遗产中三维场景、角色以及动作；应用 Agent 模型表示虚拟环境中所有的角色，重点解决非物质文化遗产内容制作中的三维表达及互动技术实现等难题。

（3）资源管理与服务技术：综合应用分布式数据库技术、海量数据存储技术、非物质文化遗产本体技术、语义检索技术等实现非物质文化遗产资源统一表示、知识存储、资源权利信息描述、资源目录服务、注册服务、资源检索和发布等功能。

（4）非物质文化遗产可视化技术：综合利用三维动画技术、虚拟现实技术、语义 Web 技术、知识可视化技术等构建基于本体的非物质文化遗产知识可视化模型系统，实现基于知识点语义的查询、自然语言的知识点分解和语义理解、不同本体之间的知识共享和补充知识库等功能；通过知识可视化技术，基于本体的概念参考模型 CIDOC CRM（Conceptual Reference Model）对具体非物质文化遗产项目的文化空间知识表示进行研究。

5. 搭建非物质文化遗产多媒体交互体系平台

面向非物质文化遗产数字化产品开发中的瓶颈问题，针对文化活动中三维场景和角色动画交互式制作中存在的技术难点，利用非物质文化遗产资源库模型数据，引入高精度地形构建及文化元素交互式搭建等方法，为三维场景的快速生成提供新的思路和途径。同时，利用真实感人脸角色模型创建技术为非物质文化遗产传承人角色动画的制作提供真实感人物模型，利用资源库中动作数据，高效生成角色动作动画。最后利用知识建模、行为建模与交互等可视化技术对非物质文化遗产资源进行可视化制作，通过多媒体交互体系平台实现非物质文化遗产可视化产品的传播。其平台框架如图 2 所示。

6. 构建国家非物质文化遗产保护与传承技术体系

非物质文化遗产是各族人民世代相承、与群众生活密切相关的各种传统文化表现形式和文化空间，与物质文化遗产相比，它具有一定的特殊性，如不易保存，保存的方式也不同。由于其独有的特殊性质，加上国家还没有一个有关非物质文化遗产保护与传承方面的技术规范，非物质文化遗产保护与传承工作一直难以开展。因此，研究构建国家非物质文化遗产保护与传承技术体系就显得尤为重要。

国家非物质文化遗产保护与传承技术体系应该包括非物质文化遗产从数字化技术（文本、音视频、图片、动作、模型数字化的技术流程规范）、资源入库技术（资源的分类体系、元数据标准、存储的技术规范、版权保护技术）、资源管理技术（资源发布技术、检索技术、资源注册及目录服务技术等）、情景构建技术（角色、场景、动作生成技术等，以及多 Agent 的群体控制技术）、可视化技术（三维动画技术、虚拟现实技术、语义 Web 技术、知识可视化技术）到最后的传播和服务技术等方面。通过对非物质文化遗产的技术体系进行构建，使我国优秀的民族文化资源得到"整体性保护"，即连同它生存的文化土壤一起保护下来。该技术体系框架如图 3 所示。

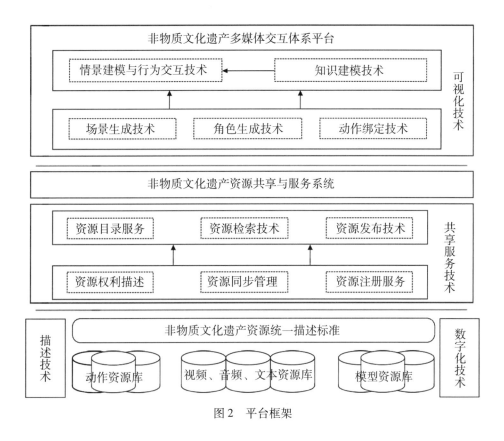

图 2　平台框架

图 3　技术体系框架

三、数字化技术在非物质文化遗产保护与开发应用中的问题思考

数字化技术是当今最为前沿的信息科学技术,特别是虚拟现实技术的出现,使21世纪成为"虚拟时代"。将最前沿的科学技术应用到对非物质文化遗产的保护与开发中来,这将为非物质文化遗产保护提供更加深层的高科技技术支持,使非物质文化遗产的保护与开发的途径得到进一步拓展与衍生。但数字化技术在非物质文化遗产保护与开发应用中仍有以下四个方面的问题需认真思考。

1. 数字化技术与文化生态平衡

数字化技术虽然对非物质文化遗产的保护与复原、虚拟与重建具有重大的意义,但过度依赖数字化技术也容易造成文化的数据化和遗产化,在一定程度上也会损害文化多样性和文化生态的平衡。因此,对数字化技术在非物质文化遗产中的应用要有一定的"人文把握",使技术富有方向性和一定的文化立场。因此,数字化技术的运用必须从重视"静态遗产"的保护,向同时重视"动态遗产"和"活态遗产"保护的方向发展。因为非物质文化遗产并不是静止不变的,而是动态、发展、变化的。数字化技术的运用还必须从重视"物质要素"的文化遗产保护,向同时重视由"物质要素"与"非物质要素"结合而形成的文化遗产保护的方向发展。因为物质与非物质文化遗产所反映的文化元素是统一的,相互融合、互为表里、不可分割的。另外,尤其要注意保护非物质文化遗产的生态性,让它们具有原生意义,让它们在属于自己的领域中生存和发展。总之,对于非物质文化遗产来说,运用数字化技术仅仅只是一种新型手段,而保护文化的多样性、鲜活性和生态平衡才是最根本的目的。

2. 数字化技术与多学科交叉融合

非物质文化遗产数字化是在虚拟空间呈现文化,与传统的文化表现在形态上有本质的区别,它不是一个物理存在的实体,而是一个跨地区、跨国家的信息空间和信息系统,它们汇集了人文社会科学、自然科学、技术科学学科,带有明显的跨多学科性质。比如对非物质文化遗产特征的抽取、加工规则的拟定则需要人类学、民族学、社会学、影视学、传播学以及人文艺术等领域专家的共同参与才能完成。非物质文化遗产数字化研究对象、涉及领域、技术特点是一个大跨度交叉和高度综合的集成体。数字化技术已开始应用于非物质文化遗产保护与利用,我们应该以开放的学科视野,打破学科界限,融合各学科知识,开展跨学科研究和创新,发展出综合的、交叉的、比较新的领域,逐步建立非物质文化遗产数字化的新学科;加强跨行业战略研究,探索适合一套非物质文化遗产数字化保护与利用规律的管理体制及运行机制。

3. 数字化技术与复合型人才培养

非物质文化遗产的数字化保护与利用工作是一项系统性、持续性和技术性很强的工作，然而，由于文化领域缺乏在 IT 业方面的有经验的数字化技术专家，导致优势技术的应用和深层次文化内涵的结合成为数字化过程中存在的突出的薄弱环节。因此，人才队伍培养成为非物质文化遗产数字化发展的关键。非物质文化遗产数字化人才除了具备传统科学研究所要求的较高专业科学素质外，还要有跨学科研究的严格训练。我们必须加强各大高校、科研机构对遗产保护数字化技术的研究和专业人才队伍的培养，融合民族、人文、艺术、信息、工程等学科资源，将培养复合型高层次人才作为一项重要工作内容，纳入文化产业经济发展与人才队伍建设规划。探索建立多渠道培养、多元化评价、多层次使用、多方式激励、多方位服务的复合型人才培养机制，逐步建立一支懂文化、通管理、精技术的复合型文化人才队伍。

4. 数字化技术与文化产业发展

文化产业和信息产业是现代社会的两个"互为表里的超级产业"，信息技术从根本上改变了文化产品的生产、传播和消费方式，利用信息技术可以提高文化产品的原创力，开发新的文化产品，增强文化产业的竞争力和生命力。然而从产业发展的逻辑上说，信息技术只是手段，内容服务才是目的和核心。因此，我们应将重点放在内容的建设上，数字文化内容越丰富，信息的共享度就越高，人们从中捕捉的商机就越多。我国的信息技术产业正在蓬勃发展，非物质文化资源的优势通过采用数字化技术手段合理开发与利用的前景更广泛，从而形成文化与传媒、信息交融的特色产业。非物质文化遗产数字化作为高科技与高文化价值结合的产业交汇点，在加以有效保护的同时，使之上升为具有知识产权和资源资本属性的文化产品，可以更好地促进文化资源优势转变为经济优势，创造出巨大的经济与社会效益，推动经济社会更好、更快地向前发展。

（原刊于《华中师范大学学报》2012 年第 2 期，《新华文摘》2012 年第 11 期）

参考文献：

[1] 王耀希主编：《民族文化遗产数字化》，北京：人民出版社 2009 年版。
[2] 《非物质文化遗产的数字化保护》，来源：文化传播网，发布时间：2006 年 9 月 11 日。
[3] 黄永林：《非物质文化遗产生产是最好的保护》，《光明日报》2011 年 10 月 7 日。

如何在遭受飓风"卡特里娜"和"丽塔"之后的休斯顿生存
——以幸存者为中心的灾难应对个案研究

卡尔·林达尔 帕特·嘉斯伯[*]

"如何在遭受飓风'卡特里娜'和'丽塔'之后的休斯顿生存"（Surviving Katrina and Rita in Houston, SKRH）是民俗学家利用灾区地方知识创建的一个以幸存者为中心的记录项目（documentation project）。这个项目的核心是由幸存者讲述、其他幸存者记录故事，通过这个过程，幸存者成为他们自我治愈的活性剂。下面的讨论将首先简要介绍项目的缘起，然后描述用来训练幸存者成为采访者的方法，最后评估项目的结论和效果。

2005年8月下旬，"卡特里娜"飓风横扫美国墨西哥湾沿岸各州。约150万人在8月29日风暴来临前成功撤离。然而仍有数十万人未能撤离，其中大部分是来自新奥尔良和路易斯安那州贫穷的黑人。他们被困在城里长达一个星期，大多数人只有很少的或根本没有食物或水。这次飓风造成了1836人死亡，摧毁了至少45万个家园。到了9月初，新奥尔良被水淹没，20万受困市民从灾区获救并被送往安全区域。这是美国历史上最严重的自然灾害：约120万人被迫离开自己的家园，有的暂时离开几个月或几年，其他则永远离开了自己的家园。

2005年9月初，数百辆公交车将飓风幸存者从新奥尔良运送到休斯顿大量的庇护所里。休斯顿的人口增长了多达25万，而新奥尔良的人口则减少到几千人。市政府、援助机构、教会团体和普通民众自愿加班加点募集大量物资，分发给幸存者，以满足他们的需求。

该项目负责人之一卡尔·林达尔参加了休斯顿的乔治·布朗会议中心的志愿活动，帮助分发必需品给在那里避难的数千幸存者。慷慨的市民捐赠了大量的衣物、毛毯和个人物品。物质援助是巨大的，但避难所里的需求超出志愿者能力。幸存者的物质需求不可否认是巨大的，他们也都表达了对志愿者们的感激之情。然而，在听这些男人和女人们诉说的过程中，林达尔立刻发现他们需要的东西远不只是一些有形的二手衬衫或牙膏，而是更有价值的东

---

[*] 卡尔·林达尔，休斯顿大学教授；帕特·嘉斯伯，休斯顿艺术联盟民俗和传统艺术中心主任。

西。他们需要的是诉说他们的故事，休斯顿的人们则需要倾听。诉说的过程中，当他们从志愿者们脸上看到终于有人开始理解他们所经历的痛苦时，他们的状况有所改观。

此外，SHRH 项目也是一次满足幸存者倾诉需求和外界倾听需求的尝试。该项目是由卡尔·林达构思并与帕特·嘉斯伯共同指导的，旨在应对媒体的炒作报道，记录幸存者的故事，并将它们详尽地传播到世界各地。项目设计的明确目的是用幸存者自己的语言和方式进行陈述。如果依赖幸存者自己，给他们机会呈现自己的历史，在经济需求和生活改变的情况下让他们开创自己的"职业"，该项目将最有效地和创造性地实现其目标。

在美国国会图书馆的美国国家民俗中心的帮助下，我们设计了"田野学院"，让幸存者接受采访者培训。我们开发了一套密集课程，以适应学员的需要，并提供相应的报酬。大多数受训者并不具备人种学研究的教育背景，不过我们强调的是共同体验而不是学术准备。每位学员与其受访者共享一条重要的纽带：他们的生命都遭受过飓风的打击。该项目最终创建了一份包含 433 份录音采访的档案，存放于休斯顿大学。目前，美国国家民俗中心也有 100 多份了。

由于以前在记录灾难时没有以灾难幸存者为中心的先例，我们的田野学院没有参考模式，因此，我们首先确定了一个基本原则，即幸存者对自己的故事享有主导权。有些人的故事是他们珍贵的财产，也就是他们所拥有的经历本身是最有价值的。失去家园、经历与家人和朋友分离的痛苦使得"卡特里娜"飓风幸存者常常抓住自己那些故事不放。能够诉说自己的故事对他们来说非常重要，因为那些参加我们培训的人会深深感受到媒体报道对事实的歪曲，他们想找回自己的故事，他们不希望被我们打断或预先干预。

因此，我们寻求"自然叙述者"：故事由受访者和其他幸存者自然流露，而不是由采访者进行塑造。实际上，正是在这个社区中，也正是通过这种方式，我们发现了"自然叙述者"。我们希望这个项目中故事的叙述都很自然，足以让全世界旁听幸存者的对话，这样的记录不仅对民俗研究者有价值，而且对幸存者自己也是最好的：那是他们最想要的以及康复初期最需要的。

由于幸存者所陈述的亲身经历深受社区环境的影响，因此他们远比信息本身重要。我们要求采访者记录 3 个独立的却又以社区理念为中心、有着紧密联系的故事。

首先，每个受访者被要求描述在飓风袭来之前他居住的社区。这部分访谈有着重要的纪实作用，因为大部分社区受到很大改变，或者完全被飓风摧毁。这对很多受访者（特别是年纪较大的幸存者）来说也是有益健康的，他们可以详细地说出他们在那些特别的却再也回不去的地方的经历。

其次，采访者要求幸存者叙述飓风来袭时的经历。在项目开始最初的几个月里，"飓风故事"在他们的叙述中占绝对主导地位；随着岁月的推移，对于飓风袭来之前和之后的生活的记录变得更长。而"飓风故事"更像是一个很长故事中的一个章节，而不是幸存者想要表达的整个故事。

第三，为了记录幸存者如何努力重建社交网络和创建新的社区，采访者询问了幸存者飓风之后在休斯顿的生活情况。对很多人来说，努力适应休斯顿的生活成为叙述的焦点，这为叙述者们提供了一个机会，借此机会，他们开始对过去的生活认真地思考。

田野学院培训包括分享管理公告以及同意书的技术信息和说明，但大多数培训是强调特别照顾受访者的方法和准则。田野学院采用以下规则指导培训工作：

·确保幸存者口述的动机。培训刚开始时，我们要求参与者分享他们签约的原因，很少有人提到金钱，尽管一份临时工作和微薄的收入都将在很大程度上改善他们的生活。不约而同地，他们都提到了幸存者的心声需要被倾听；不约而同地，他们都认为采访幸存者最好的人选是其他幸存者。大多数人跟我们说过类似这样的话："我们希望人们知道我们是谁。很多人都非常慷慨，但即使最慷慨的人也无法明白我们经历了什么。我们不是罪犯、傻瓜、落魄者，我们尊重别人也尊重自己，我们为别人也为自己感到骄傲。我们不希望人们轻视或者同情我们，只要了解我们是谁就好。"这一实践进一步说明该项目的目标实际上恰恰是幸存者需要的。

·认可幸存者的专业知识。我们告诉幸存者他们是专家，事实上，每个人都是她（大多数受训者是女性）自己个人经历的主要专家；我们也告诉他们，在"卡特里娜"飓风中，他们每个人都有着我们这些老师所不能完全分享的经历，他们在日常生活中就诉说也倾听着那些故事，他们知道这些故事在日常生活中是如何展开的，他们不需要提醒就知道这些故事对其叙述者有多重要。这种姿态是为了认可受训者的知识和经验；他们最常见的反应就是会意而自信地点点头。他们像是松了一口气，终于来到一个自己的经验被重视的地方。

·以自愿为原则。如果你还没有准备好诉说自己的故事，那么你还没准备好记录别人的故事。培训期间，参与双方轮流发言，这对于采访者保持客观中立的立场是非常重要的。

·绝不强迫对方诉说故事。双方自由叙述是受训者应该遵循的一个原则，这也是我们稍后要明确的一个中心原则，即受访者必须是已准备好且乐意叙述。不能诱导、劝诱或以其他方式迫使对方诉说自己的飓风故事。让叙述者自愿呈现出来对其康复的可能性至关重要。一些心理健康专家警示我们，让幸存者诉说自己的飓风故事有可能是有害的。然而，给我们建议最多的创伤专家强调叙述者有自我选择的自由，他们知道什么时候可以说出来。只要我们不使用强迫手段，征求故事可能带来的危害是极其微小的。

·创建餐桌环境。尊重叙述者并感同身受，让他们自然而然来到受训者面前；但是引导他们叙说是最大的挑战，我们学院的一句话"讲述故事比记录容易得多"反复得到证实。期望的结果是能够有一半的记录是"餐桌环境"得到的故事，优先考虑叙述者的表现而不是信息，记录他们的主观想法，且在这一过程中总结幸存者社区传统的口头交际和治愈策略。受训者本能地意识到并重视我们正在寻找的，但由于访谈需要录音，跟自然语境相比存在许多障碍，我们用如下的话进行解释：

在餐桌对面将坐着一个你将与之分享深刻改变你人生的经历的人，你立刻感到与他有了联系，他也立刻感到与你有了联系，但是这张特殊的餐桌堆满了阻碍那种联系的东西：有一个录音机、一个麦克风，你还需要戴耳机。当你安放麦克风、测试音量、监测房间周围的噪音时，你和故事讲述者都可能有点紧张；接着，在你开始访谈之前，你必须向对方读一篇长长的用法律术语写成的"同意书",然后让他们签字。对于最近同样有着许多痛苦经历,并签署几乎对他们没有好处的政府文件的幸存者来说,文书工作可能不仅仅是不方便,还有可能使人不安。

而那还仅仅只是开始,因为当你弄乱桌子的同时你又试着去整理,将一个不随和的、人为的环境变成一个容易亲近的环境。当你鼓励叙述者放松并找到最自然的声音时,你还要监控录音的声音质量。你要做一切你能做的让叙述者感到自在,你必须充当三种角色:桌子对面的朋友、跟踪声音的技术员、读心记事并想出故事结束后要问的问题的评估员。

当叙述者和采访者打破技术和法理的束缚后,成功地营造出餐桌环境的访谈氛围,这样他们就能听到更多的幸存者的经历分享,而这些是在文献记载中所不能获取的。

· 训练热心倾听。培训班的重点在于采访者如何通过将叙述主动权转移给对方,将自己转变成听众,其基本理念是"热心倾听但不强势询问"。口述历史研究方法通常喜欢结构化访谈,由采访者设定叙述话题;我们这个理念是让采访者通过专心倾听,传达出愿意跟随叙述者的思路走的信号。口述历史研究方法也指导采访者诱导受访者对任何有可能不够清晰的叙述进行解释,与此相反,我们的采访者从不打断。当她非常想打断以便填满缺失信息时,她必须让叙述者按照自己的方式进行。在一次较早的田野学院访谈练习中,叙述者正生动地描述她在"卡特里娜"飓风袭来的那天早上是如何突然醒来、感受到水流汹涌而来,然后她用手指向自己的身体说:"在救援人员到达之前,水已经到这了。"采访者为了让不在场的听众明白,于是打断她问道:"你的意思是高过你的腰部,对吗?"在这个例子中,叙述者顺利冲过问题并回到她的叙述,但我们提醒她以及她的受训同伴们不要为了恢复一个事实而毁掉一个故事,而是要将手势的含义变成书面记录与录音一起递交。在访谈最后,采访者可以要求叙述者做一些澄清说明,或者填补一些缺失细节;但由于"故事比信息难于获取",她应该永远将发言权交给叙述者。

· 坚持关注具体事实。即使叙述者已经开始叙述他们的故事,采访者也必须允许他们自己选取他们最舒服的方式。采访者请对方叙述可以说"然后发生什么呢?",但要避免询问情感及要求解释。"那时你感觉如何?"或者"那对你意味着什么?"这样的问题都是一种预先干预。叙述者有权用自己的方式,在恰当的时候表达情感、做出解释。

· 受访者永远是对的。这是我们以上讨论过的所有准则的指导原则。

幸存者充当采访者和叙述者的工作创建了人们对"卡特里娜"飓风破坏的短期反应和长期反应。首先,参与者很快就能发现这个项目不仅记录了新的"卡特里娜"灾后社区的形成,它也创建了新的社区。仅仅只是聚集到一起这一过程就让流散的幸存者相互成为朋友,互相支持,他们创造了一种社区意识,让他们可以更快、更容易地适应一座新的陌生城市的生活;通过分享自己的故事以及帮助别人说出他们的故事,幸存者们其实参与的是一个群体自我康复项目。因此,SKRH 项目开始作为一个行为健康项目而得到资金支持。

通过与休斯顿人分享自己的故事,幸存者们能够面对媒体的陈词滥调了。通过公众节目,包括广播节目和现场坐席轮讲,幸存者们利用自己的故事向休斯顿人介绍了自己。由于SKRH是世界上第一个由幸存者主导并记录其同伴们受灾经历的项目,访谈记录是特别的文件。SKRH项目省去了外在的研究议程,能够让外界人士直接进入幸存者们的视角。卡尔·林达尔建立了一个数据库,确定了幸存者们经历的最普遍的问题以及幸存者们灾后克服困难的策略。通过研究这个数据库,研究者们可以发现亲历者对灾难的看法,并呼吁受灾社区的传统治愈策略者们制定更有效的灾难应对策略。

在像"卡特里娜"飓风这样大规模的自然灾害中,最大的未开发的反应资源是幸存者社区本身。幸存者们觉得需要帮助他们的同伴们,他们经常随时可以承担新的工作,因为他们已经无家可归或者处于失业状态,而且他们通常比外界人士、专业急救员更了解他们的社区。通过富于同情心的倾听和社区建设,以及由民俗学研究者提出并经幸存者们完善的有效工具,SKRH项目已经为以后的灾难幸存者们叙述自己的故事并通过这些故事得到康复创建了一个典范。我们希望世界各灾区的人种学者们能够与幸存者们形成类似的合作伙伴关系,以便让幸存者们成为自我治愈过程中的活性剂。

参考文献:

[1] Carl Lindahl: "Storms of Memory: New Orleanians Surviving Katrina and Rita in Houston," *Callaloo* 29, 4 (2007): 1526 – 1538.

[2] Carl Lindahl: "Legends of Hurricane Katrina: The Right to Be Wrong, Survivor-to-Survivor Storytelling, and Healing," *Journal of American Folklore* 125 (2012): 139 – 176.

"熊龙"辨

——兼谈龙的起源与稻作文明

蒋明智[*]

"玉雕龙"是红山文化玉器群中最具代表性的一种器类。考古学家最先把它定为"猪龙"。后来,祖籍辽阳的台湾人李实根据红山文化遗址中有几起完整的熊下颚骨,联系北方民族从古至今有关熊崇拜的材料,力主红山文化有熊崇拜,并将此与古史所记黄帝"号曰有熊氏"相联系。[①]

受此启发,考古学家郭大顺对红山文化玉器群重新进行定位,认为"以猪或鹿为原形的是'C'字形龙,而玦形龙是以熊为原型的,可直称之为'熊龙'"[②]。为此,他努力在红山文化及有关遗存中寻找熊的线索作为旁证,并正式提出,"神奇的玉雕熊龙,也许是解开长期以来扑朔迷离的五帝传说的一把钥匙"[③]。

在这一学术背景之下,叶舒宪先生结合欧亚大陆曾经普遍存在的将熊作为死而复活象征的信仰历史,对"玉雕龙"作了更深入的阐发。他先后写下《我们是龙的传人还是熊的传人——关于中华祖先图腾的辨析与反思》等文,并于 2007 年出版《熊图腾——中华祖先神话探源》一书,把熊图腾提高到了一个前所未有的高度。他指出:"华夏第一图腾动物——龙,从发生学意义看,与熊有直接关系。新石器时代红山文化女神庙的发现给龙的起源研究带来崭新局面。从熊女神崇拜到熊龙,隐隐勾勒出在后代父权制的中原文明中失落的女神神话传统。"[④] 他甚至推断:"熊图腾的再发现,使我们再次意识到'龙的传人'这样的流行说辞背后,潜伏着更加深远而广阔的'熊的传人'的信仰,使我们得以在欧业大陆的宏观背景中,重新理解中国文化之根。"[⑤]

不曾想,叶舒宪的观点随后引发了韩国学者和网友的抗议。这本是一册在中国神话中寻

---

[*] 蒋明智,中山大学中国非物质文化遗产研究中心教授。
[①] 郭大顺:《龙出辽河源》,百花文艺出版社 2001 年,第 117 页。
[②] 郭大顺:《龙出辽河源》,第 126 页。
[③] 郭大顺:《龙出辽河源》,第 126 页。
[④] 叶舒宪:《熊图腾——中华祖先神话探源》,上海锦绣文章出版社 2007 年,第 90 页。
[⑤] 叶舒宪:《熊图腾——中华祖先神话探源》,第 99 页。

找"熊图腾"痕迹的书，但在韩国却被解读成"中国连檀君神话都要抢走"。叶舒宪自己也承认，自己的"熊图腾学说"在中国不受待见。

对于上述观点，已有学者提出了不同意见。中国社会科学院考古研究所所长刘庆柱研究员就认为，有些部落确实以熊为图腾，但那还不能作为中华民族的图腾。尽管龙的意象是虚构的，但如果华夏文明真是熊图腾崇拜，就不会有龙的意象，后来出土的大量文物中也不会有龙这一造型。如果以熊为图腾，熊是最高尚的，那怎么解释龙的地位呢？① 但刘庆柱先生未作具体论证。本文拟在此基础上，试作深入分析。

一、红山文化彩陶龙纹及其意义

据研究，辽河流域考古发现的早期龙，可分出八个类型，它们按年代早晚排列，大致为摆塑型、浮雕型、木雕型、刻画型、彩陶型、泥塑型、玉雕型和彩绘型。② 发现于红山文化遗址上的龙以玉雕型最为多见，可以分为两种亚型。亚型Ⅰ以三星他拉龙为代表，为墨绿色玉，高26厘米，长吻，端面截平，有双鼻子，细梭形目，有长鬣，上举飘扬，端部起尖，龙体细而弯曲如"C"字形，因头部特征近于猪，曾被视为猪头龙。此型龙被视为红山文化玉龙中的典型标本，但至今尚无正式发掘出土实例。有正式出土地点的两件都在赤峰以北地区，那里同时有较多赵宝沟文化遗址分布。此类龙首部形象有与鹿接近处，而赵宝沟文化又多鹿头龙，从而以为这类"C"字形龙有可能属赵宝沟文化，而其原型可能与鹿有关。

亚型Ⅱ共有16件，其中两件见于牛河梁积石冢中，其他见于红山文化分布区内的辽宁省建平县、河北省围场县和内蒙古巴林左旗、巴林右旗和敖汉旗等地。它们的共同特征是：头部硕大，环体肥厚，双短立耳，大圆睛，吻部刻画多道皱纹。最初将这类龙鉴定为红山文化时，也曾从猪首形象产生联想。后来，因牛河梁积石冢还多次出土过完整的熊下颚骨，人们将其与熊联想在一起，称其为熊龙。

然而，红山文化遗址除了玉雕龙以外，还有年代更早的泥塑龙和彩陶龙。泥塑龙见于牛河梁女神庙内，似熊非猪，有人认为是泥塑熊龙。彩陶龙则见于红山文化的彩陶器上，可分为两个亚型。亚型Ⅰ为在彩陶瓮的腹部盘绕的龙纹，红地黑彩，两道或三道，龙体上饰成排黑彩红地相间的龙鳞。从龙鳞形状的固定、线条的规整和黑白单元相间的等距以及与商代青铜器上表现龙鳞纹的相同手法等几方面看，红山文化时期的龙鳞纹已经定型化。亚型Ⅱ为无龙体而只有放大的龙鳞纹，见于红山文化特有的两种彩陶器卵腹罐和无底筒形器上。所以，即便是在同样的红山文化遗址中，就有不同的龙型。这说明在红山文化带，龙的造型已出现了多元性，具有地域文化互相融合的倾向。

事实上，玉雕龙的出现，是石器时代向青铜时代过渡时期，即铜石时代的标志。突出以

---

① 李健亚：《"熊图腾说"证据不充分》，《江南时报》2006年8月15日第8版。
② 郭大顺：《龙出辽河源》，第56页。

玉为葬，以玉为祭，是红山文化上层建筑的重要组成部分。这一时期氏族成员已经等级化，出现了氏族显贵。依等级而使用、随葬玉器的制度已在形成中，原始氏族公社正走向解体之中。其龙的造型应该是较晚才出现的。

相对而言，彩陶龙的地位更为重要。这不仅因为它在时间上比玉雕龙早，而且其质地和造型都与中原仰韶文化有共同特征。这些陶器上的纹饰是"以直线条组成的几何图案为主，如三角形纹、菱形纹、平行宽带纹等；其次为一种多道同心圆条纹和三角勾连纹的组合"[①]。所谓的三角纹实际上是连续的横S图案，跟半坡型的连续纹样大致相同。这说明，红山文化中的彩陶受到了仰韶文化的影响。仰韶文化彩陶主要分布在陕西、河南、河北和山西，其陶器可分为半坡类型和庙底沟类型等。半坡类型的彩陶多为盆、罐、瓶、钵等生活器皿，口沿、上腹、瓶颈或盆的内壁等位置多绘制花纹。花纹图案有几何纹样，也有比较具象的动物、人面、渔网等。庙底沟类型典型器物有敛口曲腹钵、卷沿曲腹盆、尖底瓶、平底瓶等，以黑彩为主，少量有红彩，甚至出现了带白衣的彩陶。彩陶纹饰多为几何图形，少见动物纹饰。

彩陶是母系氏族社会的产物。在新石器时代中期盛行彩陶制作，氏族社会是处在母系阶段；只是在彩陶艺术衰微的后阶段，氏族社会开始向父系过渡。彩陶的兴盛是母权制强大的一个标记，它记载着那一个时代女性的辉煌。[②] 同时，彩陶纹饰也是一定的人们共同体的标志，它在绝大多数场合下是作为氏族图腾或其他崇拜的标志而存在的。[③] 在区分不同文化类型时，纹饰是居于核心地位的标志，一定的陶纹就是一种文化的代表。因此，红山文化彩陶上类S的纹饰，与中原仰韶文化一样，是母系氏族的图腾象征物。

比彩陶要早的是印纹陶，可以溯源于新石器时代早期。印纹陶的纹饰主要可以归类为编织纹、曲折纹、格形纹、圆形纹、波形纹、条纹、云雷纹、叶脉纹、齿形纹、绳纹、爪形纹等[④]。印纹陶主要有七个分布区域，即赣江鄱阳湖区、太湖区、南京—镇江区、湖南区、岭南区、福建区、粤东闽南区等七区。"人们公认，几何印纹陶遗存与古代越族有密切关系，也可以说它就是古越人创造的陶器文化。"[⑤]

那么，这些类S纹饰象征的到底是熊，还是别的什么呢？

二、"S"纹与虹崇拜

甲金文的"龙"字，实际上是在"S"纹上加了一个王冠；金文则特别在"S"纹下加了一双手，以示膜拜。以甲金文的"神"字形象对比，"龙"字不过是在"神"的基础上

[①] 《辽宁省喀左县东山嘴红山文化建筑群址发掘简报》，《文物》1984年第11期。
[②] 参见郑为《中国彩陶艺术》，上海人民出版社1985年版，第68页。
[③] 石兴邦：《有关马家窑文化的一些问题》，《考古》1962年第6期。
[④] 叶茂林：《陶器鉴赏》，漓江出版社1995年版，第153页。
[⑤] 叶茂林：《陶器鉴赏》，第151页。

的加工而已；或者说，"龙"字就是比照"神"字而造出来的。"神"字是首先被创造出来的，它不仅是后来创造其他具有神性物的文字的基础，还为神灵形象的创造立下规范。商周青铜器为祭祖祀神的神器，上镌龙纹，也照例以"S"状呈现之，龙的这种刻意追求"S"形的图形创作正是在神的形象规范驱使下的结果。正如日本学者海野弘在《装饰空间论》所指出的："雷纹与龙纹都能简化分解为 C 或 S 型，这正说明龙纹与雷纹具有共同的基本纹或称基调。"①

从世界各国的神话可知，原始宗教信仰的核心是自然力，因此最为原始的神既不是动物神，也不是植物神，而是以宇宙、天象为主的各种自然力和自然现象本身。以中国汉民族为例，"神"字，就是从"申"字发展而来的。"申"，即"神"的古字。"神"字最早出现在金文中，左边的偏旁当为周人所加。"申"，虽然在古籍中主要用于干支义，但《说文》解释为"神也"，而"神"则解释为"天神，引出万物者也"。最早的神是天神，地上万物源于天神所造，当为后来才有的。

丁山在《中国古代宗教与神话考》中较早提出龙的原型是"虹"这一观点。②何星亮也认为："龙蛇是最早的虹神形象。"③早在 3000 多年前，甲骨文中就已出现"虹"字，弓形半圆弧，两端有首，似为蛇（或龙）头。周代青铜器中的虹霓纹更加逼真，身作弓形，两端向下，呈对称的两个龙首。《说文》说："虹，螮蝀也，状似虫。从虫，工声。"段玉裁注："虫者，它也。虹似它，故字从虫。"这个像"虫"的"它"实际就是蛇。段氏所说的"虫"也并非泛指爬行小动物的"虫"，而是虺，即是两头蛇。

龙的原型是虹，就可以很好地解释龙与雨水的关系。彩虹多出现在雷雨之后，雷电交加，狂风大作，暴雨倾盆而下。随后雨过天晴，出现彩虹。这令原始先民产生无比敬畏的心理。人们以为都是悬在天空的巨大彩虹左右着这一切，于是将彩虹神化，对虹的崇拜便应运而生。

从历代的文献记载中也可找到有关的依据。如《管子·水地篇》说："龙生于水，被五色而游，故神。欲小则化为蚕蠋，欲大则藏于天下，欲上则凌于云气，欲下则入于深渊。"《说文》则说："龙，春分而登天，秋分而潜渊。"凡此等等，说明龙与水有密切关系，而且变幻莫测。

虹既然是龙的原型，也就构成了原始母系氏族社会的图腾象征。这在中国上古的感生神话中有着生动的再现。《河图稽命征》载，黄帝之母附宝"见大电光绕北斗"而生黄帝。"大电光"也就是雷电。由于雷电的细长蜿蜒和威力，古人常将它们与龙联系在一起。东汉王充在《论衡·龙虚篇》说："见雷电发时，龙随而起；当雷电击树木之时，龙适与雷电俱在树木之侧，雷电去，龙随而上，故谓从树木之中升天也。实者，云龙同类，感气相致，故易曰'云从龙，风从虎'。"在《帝王世纪》中说到少昊的出生："少昊帝名挚，字青阳，

---

① 转引自（日）中野美代子著，何彬译《中国的妖怪》，黄河文艺出版社 1989 年版，第 36 页。
② 参见丁山《中国古代宗教与神话考》，上海文艺出版社 1988 年，第 261 页。
③ 何星亮：《中国自然神与自然崇拜》，上海三联书店 1992 年版，第 299 页。

姬姓也，母曰女节，黄帝时有大星如虹，下流华渚，女节梦接意感，生少昊。""虹"亦即"龙"，它"五彩、硕长、沟通天地的形态及其与雨水的密切关系，使先民将其与龙联系了起来"。① 看来少昊氏也是感龙而生的。《路史后纪》第七卷也说，少昊"其父曰清，黄帝之第五子"。清马骕《绎史》卷七引《诗含神雾》说："瑶光如蜺，贯月正白，感女枢，生颛顼。""蜺"即"虹"，颛顼和少昊的感生神话如出一辙。

尧、舜、禹也是感龙而生的。《春秋合诚图》载："尧母庆都……常在三河之南，天大雷电，有血流润大石之中，生庆都……赤龙与庆都合婚，有娠，龙消不见，生尧。"《诗含神雾》说："握登见大虹意感生帝舜。"《帝王世纪》说："禹父鲧，妻修己，见流星贯昴，梦接意感，又吞神珠薏苡，胸坼而生禹。"

为什么会将虹说成是自己的祖先呢？这来源于生命诞生于太阳的最古老的信仰。虹是阳光照射到变幻的云彩上所致，它的出现和太阳有关；又由于虫状条的虹和男性的生殖器相似，所以原始先民把始祖的诞生和虹联系在一起。更重要的是，始祖感天而生，由此获得了神性。因此，在神话传说中，始祖都是半人半神的形象。

由此可见，构成中华民族共同人文始祖象征的，不是熊龙，而是虹龙。

三、龙的起源与稻作文明

考古学家孙守道和郭大顺认为："促成文明到来的因素很多，如农业和水利灌溉的发展、城堡和城市的形成、文字的出现，以及阶级和国家的产生等。而龙的起源，既以原始农业的发展为前提，同与农事联系的天象有关，又是原始宗教信仰、原始意识形态、原始文化艺术发达的产物，可以说是诸文明因素的一个结晶。"② 这一意见是中肯的。但孙守道、郭大顺探讨的是辽河流域的原始农业文明与龙的起源问题，虽然从局部上看，有一定的道理，但是放眼整个中华大地，其理论是站不住脚的。

目前，农业考古学家业已达成共识，上古时期我国有两个农业起源中心：一个是以长江中下游为主的稻作农业起源中心，后来逐步发展为以稻作为主的水田农业体系；另一个是以黄河中游为主的粟作农业起源中心，后来逐步发展为以粟、黍种植为主的旱地农业体系。辽河流域对于粟作农业来说，只是第一传播区。虽然，对于黍的栽培，它可能也是一个创造发明者，不过即使这样，它也不是一个独立于黄河中游之外的另外一个农业起源中心，而不过是同一中心的边缘部分。③ 学者们指出："东北亚农业的发生和传播先后依赖于两个农业起源中心。首先是黄河中游旱地粟作农业起源中心经辽河流域传入辽东和朝鲜半岛，然后又经吉林、黑龙江传入俄罗斯远东区。接着是长江中下游水田稻作农业起源中心经山东半岛与旱

---

① 刘志雄等：《龙与中国文化》，人民出版社1992年版，第111页。
② 孙守道、郭大顺：《论辽河流域的原始文明与龙的起源》，《文物》1984年第6期。
③ 严文明：《农业发生与文明起源》，科学出版社2000年版，第37页。

地农业合流，再经过辽东半岛和朝鲜传入日本。"①

在靠天吃饭的上古时期，对于稻作农业而言，水是命脉。换言之，原始农业的丰收在很大程度上是建立在风调雨顺的基础之上的。因而，祈雨成了稻作文明最主要的祭祀活动。龙便在原始稻作农业的祭祀活动中应运而生。

中国最早记载神话的《山海经》说，应龙被黄帝从天上派到南方追杀蚩尤和夸父，后来不知怎么回事，没有上到天上去行云播雨，于是天下大旱。由于应龙长期待在南方，所以南方多雨。因此，根据顺势巫术的原理，原始先民要求雨时，就仿造一条应龙来对付。《山海经》同时也说，干旱时，用土做成应龙的样子，抬着它到处巡游，就可以求来大雨。这是上古中国舞龙求雨的最早记载，开了中国民间舞龙求雨的先河，也是后世源远流长的舞龙习俗的起源。

造龙求雨在中国汉代的画像石中有所反映。画像石中的"祈龙求雨图"顶部画的是一条弧形的双龙头（即虹），龙头向下张开作喷雨状，下面有长跪之人头顶盆皿接雨。龙下有凤鸟、羽人和巫师作乐的图案，反映了古代以龙求雨的真实图景。

中国造土龙以求雨的习俗，在弗雷泽的《金枝》里也有记载："中国人擅长于袭击天庭的法术。当需要下雨时，他们用纸或木头制作一条巨龙来象征雨神，并列队带它到处转游。"②

1993年下半年，在京九铁路施工过程中，在长江以北25公里的湖北黄梅县焦墩，在屈家岭文化前身的大溪文化遗址中，发掘出了卵石摆塑原龙：龙全长4.46米，高2.28米，宽0.3至0.65米，昂首直身，曲颈卷尾，背部有三鳍，腹下伸三足，长须曲折弯卷，独角上扬，恰似一条正在腾飞的巨龙。这是一条距今6000年的卵石摆塑原龙。研究者们对这条龙属于何种原型争论不休，却忽视了对它的意义的挖掘。笔者认为，这条龙也和前述的土龙一样，用于稻作农业的求雨。

西汉经学大师董仲舒在《春秋繁露》中记载了汉代祈雨巫术：

> 春旱求雨，令县邑以水日，令民祷社稷山川，家人祀户。……以甲乙日为大苍龙一，长八丈，居中央。为小龙七，各长四丈，于东方。皆东乡，其间相去八尺。小童八人，皆斋三日，服青衣而舞之；田啬夫亦斋三日，服青衣而立之。
>
> 夏求雨，……以丙丁日为大赤龙一，长七丈，居中央。又为小龙六，各长三丈五尺，于南方。皆南乡，其间相去七尺。壮者七人，皆斋三日，服赤衣而舞之；司空啬夫亦斋三日，服赤衣而立之。……
>
> 以戊巳日为大黄龙一，长五丈，居中央。又为小龙四，各长二丈五尺，于南方。皆南乡，其间相去五尺。丈夫五人，皆斋三日，服黄衣而舞之；老者五人，亦斋三日，衣黄衣而立之。……

---

① 严文明：《中国稻作的起源和向日本的传播》，《文物天地》1991年5、6期。
② 弗雷泽：《金枝》，徐育新等译，中国民间文艺出版社1987年版，第112页。

秋暴巫尪至九日，无举火事，无煎金器……以庚辛日为大白龙一，长九丈，居中央。为小龙八，各长四丈五尺，于西方，皆西向，其间相去九尺。鳏者九人，皆斋三日，服白衣而舞之。司马亦斋三日，衣白衣而立之。

冬舞龙六日，祷于名山以助之。……以壬癸日为大黑龙一，长六丈，居中央。又为小龙五，各长三丈，于北方。皆北乡，其间相去六尺。老者六人，皆斋三日，衣黑衣而舞之。尉亦斋三日，服黑衣而立之。……

四时皆以水日，为龙，必取洁土为之，结盖，龙成而发之。①

汉代祈雨巫术虽沿用了远古祈雨巫术的主要礼仪，但已经将祈雨巫术纳入阴阳五行学说的框架之内。龙成与五行相配的苍、赤、黄、白、黑五色，参与者的衣服颜色也必须与之相应。汉人以土龙祈雨的观念，东汉桓谭《新论》中有所阐述："刘歆致雨，具作土龙，吹律，及诸方术无不备设。谭问：'求雨所以为土龙何也？'曰：'龙见者，辄有风雨兴起，以迎送之，故缘其象类而为之。'"东汉王充也说："董仲舒申《春秋》之雩，设土龙以招雨，其意以云龙相致。《易》曰：'云从龙，风从虎。'以类求之，故设土龙，阴阳从类，云雨自至。"（《论衡·乱龙篇》）由此可知，汉人设土龙是利用它具有的与云雨相同的水属性来招雨，这与商人用龙通神乞雨的观念有着质的不同。

弗雷泽在《金枝》中曾精辟地指出："在公众巫师为部落利益所做的各种事情中，最首要的是控制气候，特别是保证有适当的降雨量。"② 因而，巫师通过神龙来控制雨水，便成为古代中国最重要的一种巫术活动。

巫师与巫术最早产生于原始部落之中，是通神、事神、降神、娱神的使者。当作为个体巫术执行者的巫师一旦上升到作为公众巫术的执行者时，便取得了与众不同的地位。弗雷泽说："当部落的福利被认为是有赖于这些巫术仪式的履行时，巫师就上升到一种更有影响和声望的地位，而且可能很容易地取得一个首领或国王的身份和权利。"③ 可见，原始部落的首领，往往履行着巫师的神职，其最重要的工作就是控制雨水。

从这个意义上说，中国神话传说的"乘龙"故事便可以有一个新的解释。《大戴礼·五帝德》说："颛顼乘龙而至四海。"《山海经》里的四方神东方句芒、南方祝融、西方蓐收、北方禺彊，都是乘二龙的。禹的儿子夏后启也"乘两龙"。把"乘两龙"与其解释为凭借龙沟通于天地、人神之间，还不如说是为了求雨更契合稻作文明的实际。

由于中华民族农业文明的源远流长，以龙求雨的巫术信仰构成了龙文化最基础的部分。只有从龙的司雨属性及其与稻作文明的密切关系出发，来理解龙的原型及其文化内涵，才能把握中华龙文化的精髓。

---

① （清）苏舆撰《春秋繁露义证》，中华书局1992年版，第426—436页。
② 弗雷泽：《金枝》，第95页。
③ 弗雷泽：《金枝》，第70页。

美国的拼布
——在保存与保护传统文化遗产形式时的选择和挑战

玛莎·迈克道尔[*]

在本次演讲中,我将依据物质、非物质的不同纬度,通过拼布这一富有表现力的艺术形式,就文化遗产的保存与保护问题进行讨论。拼布这种纺织品得以被人们熟知是因为它有不同的缝制方法,如拼布;有不同的用途,如毛毯和壁挂。在构思本篇论文时,我调用了自己作为民俗学家和美术史学家的经验。我曾做过田野考察,翻阅过大量博物馆、档案室和图书馆的资料,长期担任着我校博物馆的管理者和教授等职务并经常与学术界和大众接触。此外,之前我在密歇根传统艺术项目中担任项目经理的经历也进一步充实了本场演讲的内容。该项目为传统艺术家们和不同的艺术形式提供存档、保存、展示和支持服务,不仅服务于本州的艺术事业,还服务于我之前在南非、泰国和现在在中国参与的文化遗产工作。[①]

在美国,拼布这种艺术形式的起源可以追溯到世界各地的纺织传统。先是对布匹进行拼接、修补和贴花,接着用针线把各层布匹缝制在一起,这样就组成拼布最基本的元素。这种技术在不同地区、不同文化中已经存在了数千年之久。像拼布这样的纺织品通常用作床罩、壁挂甚至是裹尸布。在一些古迹中也能发现它们的身影,比如在中国,通过考古发现了公元

---

[*] 玛莎·迈克道尔,美国密歇根州立大学博物馆教授。

[①] 在此我想声明,本文中的许多活动由我和密歇根州立大学博物馆的同事们合作完成。他们针对拼布的历史、生产和意义等方面建言献策。我想特别感谢库尔特·杜赫斯特、玛丽·沃洛、贝丝·唐纳森、琳妮·斯旺森和王珠仪等学者,他们在我准备这篇演讲时提供了莫大的帮助。我还想感谢我的同事比尔·艾伟、库尔特·杜赫斯特、张举文和迪姆·罗仪德,他们的研究方向是物质与非物质文化遗产,并通过美国民俗社区致力于搭建中美两国之间沟通交流的桥梁。我同样十分感激密歇根州立大学的悉达多·钱德拉和赵魏军,中国国家博物馆的馆长吕章申,还有中国文化部非物质文化遗产中心检查组成员屈盛瑞,他们均给予了我莫大的支持与帮助。特别感谢陈熙,她对美国拼布制作的学习充满热情,并且加深我对不同语言中拼布制作术语的理解。此外,我对中国拼布的研究涉及了中美两国多个博物馆,我们对许多方面有着共同的兴趣,比如展览的研究和发展、数字资源,还有拼布的相关出版物。其中一个美国拼布项目已经在中国巡回展览,还有一本相关的展示名录叫《化零为整——21 世纪 25 位美国拼布制作者》(*The Sum of Many Parts*:25 *Quiltmakers in 21st Century America*),麦道维尔和沃洛合作组织和撰写了这本名录。

前770年东周时代丝绸质地的装饰性拼布。①

美国的拼布最早出现在200多年前的殖民时代。拼布的制作工艺很可能是随着西欧人民定居美国东海岸的浪潮传播到了北美大陆，受西欧文化的影响开始在当地流行起来。久而久之，这种拼布的制作工艺同时受到了原住民的本土文化和美国移民的移民文化影响。由于拼布制作者选择的图案、样式、构造技术、颜色、材质和功能千差万别，所以人们可以清楚地辨别出他们的种族、地区、信仰、职业和所属部落的特点，甚至找出制作者居住的社区，绝不会让人产生混淆。

在21世纪初期，有数百万人对这种艺术有着浓厚的兴趣。根据一份2010年美国工艺品行业的报告，目前在美国有2100万人以个人形式参与到拼布制作的相关行业中，而在世界范围内则有更多的从业人员。② 这个人数不仅包括了拼布的制作者、使用者、收藏者和销售者，还有那些制作、推广和收藏与拼布相关的工具、图案和织物的人。这些工具、图案和织物用于拼布相关的主题节日、收藏展示、线上线下的俱乐部、信息交流市场、档案学习等领域。在1978年，女权主义学者、艺术评论家帕特丽夏·麦纳迪（Patricia Mainardi）把拼布称为"伟大的美国文化"③。因为拼布这种纺织品大多由女性制作，所以对于拼布的历史和传统的研究由女权主义学者、民俗学家、艺术历史学家、收藏家、博物馆馆长等人进行。从20世纪80年代早期至今，数千人参与到了国家和地区基本文档的组建工作中，其中大部分人都是志愿者。他们记录了上万条有关拼布的信息，这些信息占了美国制造的拼布中的一小部分。④ 我们逐渐可以通过"拼布指数网"⑤查询到这部分数据，从制作者和使用者那里找到与拼布相关的故事。到2013年7月为止，在"拼布指数网"上已经可以找到超过7万篇与拼布历史和现状有关的文章。⑥

如今，拼布通常被认定为美国艺术形式的典范、国家价值的象征，体现了人们对手工制作和传统文化的尊敬。不管是在大量纪实文学作品，比如日记、口述史和信件中，还是在美

---

① 参见 Patsy Orlofsky and Myron Orlofsky, *Quilts in America*, New York: Abbeville Press, 2005, p. 17, citing Mary Symonds (Mrs. Guy Antrobus) and Louisa Preece, *Needlework Through the Ages*, London: Hodder and Stoughton, London, 1928, p. 82; Shelagh J. Vainker, *Chinese Silk: A Cultural History*, London: British Museum Press, 2004, p. 36. For an especially good resource on Chinese textiles, including examples of quilts made by Chinese minority artists, see *Writing with Thread: Traditional Textiles of Southwest Chinese Minorities* (exhibition catalogue), Honolulu: University of Hawaii Art Gallery, 2009.

② *Quilting in America*. 2010. Presented by Quilters Newsletter, a Creative Crafts Group publication, in cooperation with International Quilt Market & Festival, divisions of Quilts, Inc. http://www.quilts.com/announcements/y2010/QIA2010_OneSheet.pdf.

③ Patricia Mainardi, *Quilts: The Great American Art*, San Pedro, CA: Miles & Weir, Ltd., 1978, p. 2.

④ Kathlyn F. Sullivan, *Gatherings: American's Quilt Heritage*, Paducah, Kentucky: American Quilter's Society, 1995.

⑤ www.quiltindex.org.

⑥ "拼布指数网"是一个持续增长的数据网，可以搜索储存的数字格式的照片、文字，包括录音、录像和笔迹。还有与拼布、制作者和相关活动的文档。这个研究实验平台搜集了世界范围内博物馆、图书馆、档案馆、研究项目和私人收藏的主题文化资料的电子文件。"拼布指数网"是由密歇根州立大学博物馆、人类艺术中心、密歇根州立大学社会科学在线和美国拼布联盟领导的合作项目，此外项目也包括了很多捐赠者。

国知名作家的科幻作品中,我们都可以找到与拼布有关的故事、习俗和信仰等内容。[①] "拼布"这个单词已经渗透到了美国的语言和对话当中,人们用它们来象征从零散碎片整合成统一整体的事物,也用它们表达一些概念,诸如家庭生活、爱国精神、照顾、培养、多样性和整体性。[②] 一些学者甚至认为拼布和拼布制作作为一种文化概念已经超越了它们的物质性质。

在美国这幅制作和使用拼布的壮丽景象中,我们可以找到与传统文化遗产相关的问题。这些问题是最基本却又棘手的问题,包括本真性、文化错位、对传统的定义、市场化影响等。在一些情况下,用适当的策略来保存和保护与拼布制作相关的物质与非物质文化遗产大有必要。

在本次演讲中,我首先将简要描述拼布的构成,之后从宏观和微观两个方面研究相关例子,例子包括了拼布,以及传统物质和非物质文化遗产的保存问题。

首先,什么是拼布?在世界上很多地区,当然也包括美国在内,对拼布最严谨的定义是:用缝纫技术把两到三层的布匹缝制在一起做成的矩形纺织品。但制作拼布基础样式的过程千差万别。它们的形状可能并非矩形,大小也有很大的差别。小的长宽只有几英寸,大的比一整个橄榄球场都大,像"艾滋病纪念被"长约100米,宽约50米[③]。拼布的表层和背面可能是由一种、两种甚至多种类型的织物制成,这些织物有片状的、块状的,有些图案还有特定的名字。有些缝制拼布的针法还可以通过商业盈利。拼布制作者发明了新的针法后,其他制作者也会借鉴、改良和学习。如果拼布有填充物或者中间层的话,这部分可能由天然纤维、人工布料、回收的旧拼布或者其他纺织品制成。制作者会用刺绣、绘画和其他手工制作的作品点缀拼布。通常全部或者部分拼布的制作是由纯手工或者高度计算机化的机器完成。制作者由一至多人组成,他们有着类似的文化、宗教和职业背景,相互了解。有时各司其职,有时团队协作。从历史角度看,拼布制作的知识和技术、与此相关的审美偏好大多数是通过非正式的渠道口口相传。拼布的知识则是通过更为正式的形式分享,比如课堂、工作坊、协会、基础读物,还有最近流行起来的网络研讨会、网络研讨班、YouTube 视频和博客。

有关为何制作拼布和如何使用拼布的回答也千差万别。拼布通常用来当床上用品,但在日常生活中还有其他用法,如遮阳罩、婴儿摇篮、隔热层、坐垫。拼布也可以用来纪念重要

[①] Among the most well known is Alice Walker's "Everyday Use" in *In Love and Trouble: Stories of Black Women*, New York: Harcourt Brace, 1973.

[②] Although many scholars have recognized the use of quilt-related terms in American language, two have paid particular attention. See Judy Elsley, *Quilts as Textiles: The Semiotics of Quilting*, New York: Peter Lang Publishing, 1996 and Elaine Showalter, *Sister's Choice: Tradition and Change in American Women's Writing*, Oxford: Clarendon Press, 1991. See also Marsha MacDowell and Wolfgang Mieder. 2010. "When Life Hands Your Scraps, Make a Quilt": Quiltmakers and the Tradition of Proverbial Inscriptions, *Proverbium: Yearbook of International Proverb Scholarship* 27, 2010, pp. 113–172.

[③] 艾滋病纪念被,http://www.aidsquilt.org/about/the-aids-memorial-quilt;"拼布",作者:Mickey Weems,玛莎·麦道维尔和 Mike Smith,发布于 2011 年 10 月,http://www.qualiafolk.com/2011/12/08/the-quilt;"创造与危机:解读艾滋病纪念被",2012 年史密森尼民俗文化节,http://www.festival.si.edu/2012/creativity_and_crisis/。

的人物、家庭、社区和国家。拼布可以当作礼物，可以用于贸易，可以促进社会变化、辅助教育，也可以用来作为谋生工具或增加收入。一些拼布可以体现制作者的个性，展现她对颜色、结构、图案、形状的思考。也有用来展示的拼布，有的作为收藏品挂在集市和美术博物馆的墙上，或者作为艺术品放在公共场所。每一个拼布制作社区不仅仅评估拼布的材质，还有评估的特征和标准。不同特性的社区，如家庭的、民族的、职业的、宗教的等等，他们对拼布评估的特征和标准也各不相同。[①]

美国拼布制作的传统千变万化，我们可以肯定地说这个领域为非物质文化遗产的保护提供了诸多试验的机会。请让我来说明以下七个例子，它们解释了社区内外的活动如何影响了美国的拼布传统，还有另外一个例子则解释了新兴传统是如何兴旺起来的。

（1）所谓的"史密森尼拼布争论"。在1991年，史密森尼学会授权中国制造商复制和销售四条该学会收藏的拼布。数千在美的拼布制作者致电并写信抗议学会此举，他们认为这些复制品造价低廉，售价也远远低于美国制作者的劳动价值。一群反抗者称自己是"美国拼布防卫基金"的人，并且雇佣了一位说客与史密森尼学会协商。结果是该学会不再与中国签订新的复制品制作合同，转而和美国本土的一家合作商生产自己设计的三条拼布。"美国拼布防卫基金"与史密森尼学会共建了一个特别的拼布遗产项目，包括了拼布相关的展示、保存和教育活动，还包括一个美国国家历史博物馆正在展示的案例。[②]

（2）Gee's Bend 拼布。Gee's Bend 是美国南部亚拉巴马州的一个郊区，当地的非洲裔美国妇女长久以来一直制作着拼布。20 世纪晚期，在纽约市的大部分百货商店均可买到他们的作品，记者和民俗学家们也一直研究着他们的设计。当一位民俗艺术收藏家在纽约市的博物馆中推广展示他们的作品时，文化评论界和媒体都感到惊奇并且给出了极高的评价，《纽约时报》的艺术评论家也把这场展示选为年度十佳。[③] 经由这些展示和评论后，这些郊区艺术家们的拼布很快成为畅销商品，这些拼布的复制品也开始大量生产。[④]

---

① This description of the elements of a quilt in adapted from Marsha MacDowell "Folk Art," in Yvonne Lockwood and Marsha MacDowell, eds. 1999 *Michigan Folklife Annual*, East Lansing: Michigan State University Museum, 1999, pp. 30 – 35.

② For a good overview of the controversy, see July Elsley, "The Smithsonian Quilt Controversy: Cultural Dislocation," pp. 199 – 136 in Laurel Horton, ed., *Uncoverings* 1993, Volume 14 of the *Research Papers of the American Quilt Study Group*, San Francisco: American Quilt Study Group, 1993.

③ Michael Kimmelman, "Art/Architecture: The Year in Review—The Critics/10 Moments; Richter, And Cloth, Were Abundant," *The New York Times*, December 29, 2002.

④ The two books accompanying the exhibition were John Bearsley, William Arnett, Paul Arnett, and Jane Livingston, *The Quilts of Gee's Bend*, Atlanta, GA: Tinwood Books, 2002 and John Bearsley, William Arnett, Paul Arnett, and Jane Livingston, *Gee's Bend: The Women and Their Quilts*, Atlanta, GA: Tinwood Books, 2002. Patricia A. Turner examined the evolution of the attention to and the impact on Gee's Bend quilters in her *Crafted Lives: Stories and Studies of African American Quilters* (University of Mississippi Press, 2009). Andrew Dietz examined the role of an outsider in cultivatingattention to the quilters in his *The Last Folk Hero: A True Story of Race and Art*, *Power and Profit* (Atlanta, GA: Ellis Lane Press, 2006). Victoria P. Phillips also provides an insightful look at the commodification issues regarding the Gee's Bend quiltmakers in "Symposium: Commodification, Intellectual Property and the Quilters of Gee's Bend." *American University Journal of Gender*, Social Policy & the Law. 15, no. 2 (2007): 359 – 377.

(3)"密歇根传统艺术学徒项目"和"密歇根遗产奖"。在密歇根州底特律市,非洲裔美籍拼布制作者卢拉·威廉姆斯很早便开始学习制作拼布,之后也一直在学习和教授相关知识。鉴于她出色的艺术作品和她对拼布制作知识孜孜不倦的学习与传授,她荣获了密歇根遗产奖。密歇根传统艺术项目是一个全国性的艺术合作项目,由密歇根州立大学博物馆和密歇根州艺术文化事务委员会管理并颁奖,通过这个项目和密歇根传统艺术学徒项目,全州的传统艺术家们可以直接得到认可与支持。①

(4)赫蒙族与阿米什拼布。阿米什人是美国一支保守的基督教信徒,他们设计制作手工拼布。拼布的色彩展示了他们的宗教信仰以及宗教社区独特的地理位置特征。他们还制作不同款式的拼布卖给非阿米什人,为手工艺品打开了一个巨大的市场。在20世纪70年代末,赫蒙族难民开始在美国定居,同时也把自己出众的纺织品技术和传统带到了这片土地。在定居的地区,他们和阿米什人相互交流,双方的纺织品艺术家也开始合作。赫蒙族艺术家们开始制作床铺大小的纺织品,双方也将合作完成的作品放在市场上兜售。作品名曰"阿米什拼布",其实绝大部分甚至整条拼布都是赫蒙族的纺织品工人制作的。②

(5)工厂制造的夏威夷拼布。在19世纪早期,来自美国的传教士向夏威夷本地居民介绍了拼布制作的工艺,但他们随后发展出了自己独特的拼布样式和传统。经过样式拥有者的授权后,其他制作者才可以使用相同的款式。在夏威夷当地的社区,拼布有很多用途,也可以卖给社区外的居民,包括游客。这么多年来,游客都可以到夏威夷当地的手工艺品商店买到夏威夷的本土拼布。如今,夏威夷的拼布连锁商店里买到的产品大部分只是在模仿夏威夷的风格,事实上它们的产地都不是夏威夷,也不是当地人制作的,只是非法盗用了夏威夷本土设计师们的图案罢了。③

(6)拼布搜索网及其制作人保存的故事网。经由数千名志愿者的努力,拼布的数字照片和相关的故事都收集、保存和展示在了这两个平台上——"拼布搜索网"和"拼布制作

---

① Michigan Traditional Arts Apprenticeship Program, http://museum.msu.edu/s-program/mtap/mtaap/mtaap.html and Michigan Heritage Awards, http://museum.msu.edu/s-program/mh_awards/mha.html. Accessed July 25, 2013.

② Two of the first published studies of this cultural exchange were Marsha MacDowell, "Old Techniques of Paj Ntaub, New Patterns of Expression," in Ruth Fitzgerald and Yvonne Lockwood, eds. 1993 *Festival of Michigan Folklife*, East Lansing: Michigan State University Museum, 1993, pp. 42 – 45 and Trish Faubion, "The Amish and the Hmong: Two Cultures and One Quilt," *Piecework* 1 (1993), pp. 26 – 35. More recently, Janneken Smucker devoted deep attention to the continuation of the interaction of Hmong and Amish in producing and marketing quilts in her dissertation *From rags to riches: Amish quilts and the crafting of value* (University of Delaware, August 2010) and Amish Quilts: Crafting an American Icon (Johns Hopkins University Press, forthcoming 2013).

③ Marsha MacDowell and C. Kurt Dewhurst, field notes. *To Honor and Comfort: Native Quilting Traditions project*. Two businesses, in particular, each of which has several retail stores in Honolulu and also sell online are Royal Hawaiian Quilt (http://www.thehawaiianquilt.com/) and Hawaiian Quilt Collection (http://www.hawaiian-quilts.com/). Marsha MacDowell, field notes, 2012.

人保存的故事网（QSOS）"①。通过这两个平台，人们能够接触到有关材料的文化、物品和设计师背后的故事都是空前的，不管是科研还是教育从业者都可以借此得到诸多机会。个人拥有图片和故事的所有权，那些向"拼布搜索网"贡献信息的组织可以使用拼布相关的图片和故事，但必须经过作者的同意，提交的信息也不可重复。"拼布搜索网"一开始只是收集美国的拼布信息，现在正走向国际化。在2013年，该平台增加了南非和加拿大的收藏品信息，澳大利亚和中国的拼布信息也正在添加中。②

（7）地下通道拼布密码故事。在1999年，《目不可及》(Hidden in Plain View) 一书出版。这本书讲述了一个未经证实的故事，在美国独立战争开始之前到战争打响，一群生活在南部的非洲裔美国奴隶通过拼布上找到的密码逃到了北方，重获自由。许多官方机构都十分认可和推崇这本书，如今仍然有很多人相信这个广为流传的故事。自1999年以来，成百上千展现《目不可及》一书中所描绘街道的拼布被制作了出来。博物馆也举行了地下通道拼布的展览会，教育工作者用这个故事告诉孩子们非洲裔美国人的历史。之后人们又制作了很多有关这本书的纺织品、读物和录像带。③

（8）设计推广"传统"和"民俗"的艺术风格。在1983年，时尚设计师拉夫·劳伦介绍了一种用拼布制成的衣物和家庭装饰品，广告中声称"一个新的传统就此开始"④。劳伦和其他许多人一样，认为把传统艺术的设计稍稍改动一下就可以做出新产品，然后大量生产

---

① See note 5 for information about the Quilt Index. The Quilters Save Our Stories project (http://www.allianceforamericanquilts.org/qsos/) is led by the Quilt Alliance. Stories can be accessed through the QSOS website or through the Quilt Index. QSOS interviews are archived at the American Folklife Center, Library of Congress.

② The addition of Chinese quilts to the Quilt Index is being led by Michigan State University Museum and facilitated through support from several sources, including the Luce Foundation and the Asia Cultural Council which have supported museum staff exchanges. As of 2013, Chinese partners include the Yunnan Nationalities Museum (Kunming, China), Guizhou Nationalities Museum (Guiyang, China); Guangxi Museum of Nationalities (Nanning, China); and the Department of Intangible Cultural Heritage, Ministry of Culture, China. American partners include the American Folklore Society, Arts Midwest, International Quilt Study Center and Museum, University of Nebraska-Lincoln (Lincoln, Nebraska), Mather Museum of World Culture, Indiana University (Bloomington, Indiana), Museum of International Folk Art (Santa Fe, New Mexico) and a private collector.

③ Jacqueline L. Tobin and Raymond G. Dobard, *Hidden in Plain View*: *The Secret Story of Quilts and the Underground Railroad*. New York, N. Y.: Doubleday, 1999 quickly became a subject for public and scholarly debate. One of the first scholarly refutes of the story was Marsha MacDowell, "Quilts and Their Stories: Revealing a Hidden History", *Uncoverings*: *Journal of the American Quilt Study Group*, 21, 2000, pp. 155 – 166. An analysis of the authoritative agencies that have contributed to credentialing the story has been conducted and reported by Marsha MacDowell "Quilts, Primary Sources, and Authenticity". Unpublished paper from invited Presidential Panel, American Historical Association, San Diego, California. January 9, 2010. Folklorist Laurel Horton's inquiry into the beliefs surrounding the story can be seen in an online podcast, "The Underground Railroad Quilt Controversy: Looking for the 'Truth'" at http://www.quiltstudy.org/education/public_programs.html. Patricia A. Turner has also examined the secret quilt code story in *Crafted Lives*: *Stories and Studies of African American Quilters* (University of Mississippi Press, 2009). Leigh Fellner, "Betsy Ross Redux: The Underground Railroad 'Quilt Code'", 2006. Downloadable at http://www.ugrrquilt.hartcottagequilts.com/. Another excellent analysis of the contestation surrounding the quilt code story can be seen in Shelley Zegart, "Myth and methodology: Shelley Zegart Unpicks African American Quilt Scholarship," Selvedge, Issue 21 (Jan/February 2008) pp. 48 – 56.

④ C. Kurt Dewhurst and Marsha MacDowell, "The Marketing of Objects in the Folk Art Style", *New York Folklore*, Vol. 12, Nos. 1 – 2, 1986, pp. 49 – 55.

以满足全球市场。这样的情况多数发生在好心的领导人希望通过经济建设项目帮助社区团体解决就业、传统文化消亡和背井离乡等问题。任何人都可以将见到的市场上在售的产品进行仿造,虽然这些产品是他人的文化遗产。

以上这些内容涉及了拼布的生产、保存和展示情况,也分析了相关诸多重要的问题,比如传统的真实性、网络的影响、全球以及本土市场对非物质文化遗产的影响,还有博物馆和其他官方组织在维护传统文化中产生的积极与消极影响。

现在有如下这些全国性的项目:史密森尼民俗文化节,国家遗产团队奖,州立民俗文化节,民俗生活遗产奖传统艺术学徒项目(如由密歇根州立大学博物馆的密歇根传统艺术项目运营的项目),博物馆组织的民俗艺术展览,"拼布搜索网"在线储存的数字文档。民俗学家和其他文化遗产工作者都在使用这些方法让人们认同和维护传统非物质文化遗产,这些遗产让整个国家和社区都与众不同。① 以上这些例子展示了本土拼布制作传统的相互交融、相互影响。其中文化保护的观念十分复杂,每一项传统活动都应该仔细审查,然后决定哪些传统需要保护、如何保护、谁来保护,还有谁是保护的受益人,接着再评估保护活动的影响。民俗学家和其他文化工作者有义务在非物质文化遗产的保护活动中保持积极和批判的态度。关于非物质文化遗产的保存与保护问题十分复杂,作为民俗学家,我们不仅要参与到对传统文化的归档与研究中,更要积极探讨传统与保护项目之间相互影响,发表自己的见解。

---

① For more information on the Smithsonian Folklife Festival, which offers a companion marketplace for not only the work of artists presented in the festival but from other traditional artists around the world, see http://www.festival.si.edu. For more information on the Great Lakes Folk Festival, which also includes marketing opportunities for traditional artists, see www.greatlakesfolkfest.net. For more information on the National Heritage Fellowships, go to http://www.nea.gov/honors/heritage/. A special issue of *New York Folklore* Vol. 12, Nos. 1 – 2, 1986 contained a number of articles examining facets of marketing folk art. Two articles are of special interest for the ways in which folklorists could serve as advocates and activists in preserving traditions while at the same time helping them become stronger and more economically viable. See Mary Arnold Twining, "Marketing the Art of Migrant Workers", pp. 25 – 41; Rosemary O. Joyce, "To Market, To Market, to Sell Some Folk Art," pp. 43-47; Alf H. Walle, "Mitigating Marketing: A Window of Opportunity for Applied Folklorists," pp. 91 – 112; Robert T. Teske, "Crafts Assistance Programs and Traditional Crafts", pp. 75 – 85; Egle Victoria Zygas, "Who Will Market the Folk Arts?", pp. 69 – 74; Elaine Eff, "Traditions for Sale: Marketing Mechanisms for Baltimore's Screen Art, 1913 – 1983", pp. 57 – 68; Geraldine Johnson, "Commentary", p. 85, and John Michael Vlach, "Commentary", pp. 88 – 89. For engagement by a folklorist in surveying areas of folk arts in one state for which targeted efforts could assist in preserving and strengthening them, including in the marketplace and in tourism, see Marsha MacDowell and Julie Avery, *Craftworks in Michigan: A Report on Traditional Crafts and Economic Development in Michigan*. East Lansing, MI: Michigan State University Museum in collaboration with Office of Economic Development, Department of History, Arts, and Libraries, State of Michigan, 2006.

保护史诗吟唱传统的多形式实践：
对于杜尔伯特部落格萨尔王史诗的个案研究

朝戈金*

杜尔伯特部落位于青藏高原东南部果洛藏族自治州甘德县的柯曲乡，比邻阿尼玛卿雪山及黄河源头。杜尔伯特不断扩大的影响力正在延伸至位于北纬29°48′和36°17′之间，东经91°59′和102°01′之间的安多和康巴两个藏族方言区，涵盖了青海省果洛、玉树，以及海南州的藏族社区，甘肃省甘南州的玛曲县，四川省甘孜州的德格、色达、石渠等县，以及西藏自治区的那曲和昌都地区。

格萨尔王口述史诗是人类语言艺术的卓越典范，讲述古代英雄格萨尔王神圣事迹的"格萨尔系列诗歌"，主要流传于中国的藏族和蒙古族。

20世纪80年代以来，现代化、全球化、城市化和信息技术发展先后给当地居民生活带来了巨大的变化。即使在当地社区，史诗吟唱和故事讲述也渐渐乏人问津，一个自救方案由此开始形成。比如，自2003年以来，学术机构，民间协会和政府机关之间的密切合作已经催生了一系列的保障措施以及一个长期的、旨在保持史诗活力和知名度的自我管治计划。

得益于杜尔伯特部落以社区为基础的实践，拟议的项目已经经历了几个关键阶段，并采取了以下一系列措施，以保护格萨尔史诗传统：①氏族、家庭、表演者、喇嘛，以及佛教寺院的广泛参与；②在民间节庆期间积极推广史诗吟唱；③成立"杜尔伯特格萨尔文化史诗村"及其"村委会"；④给德高望重的长老支付财物酬劳以培训年轻人；⑤学术机构和政府机构合作建立"岭·格萨尔表演团"。

为维护文化生态系统，当地政府已采取多种扶持手段重振吟唱传统，包括：①举办"玛域格萨尔文化艺术节"；②为吟唱大师举办荣誉大会；③把"格萨尔文化"列入中小学课程；④拟定保护果洛州格萨尔文化的发展计划；⑤在黄河沿岸修建果洛玛域格萨尔文化长廊；⑥建设格萨尔史诗传统专题博物馆及果洛格萨尔文化生态保护区。

本案将为在中国其他社会文化条件类似的地区保护格萨尔史诗提供一个有效的工作模式。

---

* 朝戈金，中国社会科学院民族文学研究所研究员。

作为世界上最大的口述史诗传统之一，《格萨尔》在中国周边众多国家和地区中以不同语言流传，包括不丹、尼泊尔、巴基斯坦、印度、蒙古，以及俄罗斯的布里亚特和卡尔梅克地区。因此，这一工作模式也适用于中国以外的传统。

虚拟展览《Dane Wajich–Dane-zaa原住民的故事与歌谣：梦想者与他们的土地》：应用民族志与原住民生活展示

安伯·瑞丁特[*]

这个案例主要研究[①]多依格河第一民族所指导的展览 *Dane Wajich–Dane-zaa Stories and Songs: Dreamers and the Land*。本展览于2007年开始在加拿大虚拟博物馆的门户网站展出，可以点击以下网址进行观看：http://www.museevirtuel-virtualmuseum.ca/sgc-cms/expositions-exhibitions/danewajich/。

多依格河第一民族是加拿大不列颠哥伦比亚省东北部四个Dane-zaa（在以前又被称为海狸印第安人）原住民社区之一。Dane-zaa人居住在属于北冰洋集水区的皮斯河流域。在欧洲人对加拿大进行殖民统治之前，他们在近北极地区打猎，并将一些小部落以亲属关系为基础聚集起来。他们的族群通过打猎逐渐繁荣起来，并以半游牧和等级关系的形式不断聚集在一起。他们的传统语言是Dane-zaa语。这门语言同时还被称为海狸语，它属于北美西北部的土著所讲的阿萨巴斯卡语系。

从18世纪晚期开始，Dane-zaa人就已经开始和先期到达他们土地的欧洲人进行文化交流和原材料的交换，并作为供应商参与到皮草贸易中。但是，他们并没有放弃自己的半游牧生活方式：他们在夏天的时候收集食物资源，并以亲属关系分散成一个个小群体进行狩猎活动；到了秋天和冬天，他们哪里也去不了。直到第二次世界大战时期，美洲殖民地最重要的象征之一——阿拉斯加到加拿大的高速公路建成，才打开了Dane-zaa人赖以生存的土地。

自从上世纪50年代开始，加拿大政府开始强迫Dane-zaa人迁到印第安人保留地，并要求他们将孩子送去学校接受教育。因为政府对他们传统生活的强行干预，殖民化进程、"文化同化"政策再加上欧洲定居者的文化大大改变了Dane-zaa人的生活和学习方式。多依格河第一民族在近二十年开始努力赋予文化遗产新的生命力，比如说举办一些文化夏令营和传统语言项目，为的是让年轻一代重新开始学习他们祖辈的传统知识和语言。

---

[*] 安伯·瑞丁特，加拿大纽芬兰纪念大学博士候选人，民俗学者，遗产顾问。
[①] 本讨论PPT可参见 http://prezi.com/rqhfb1t57jaq/?utm_campaign=share&utm_medium=copy&rc=ex0share。

从 21 世纪初开始，多依格河第一民族就将他们重振文化遗产的努力付诸数字平台，他们开始和一系列的数字传媒项目合作，主要集中在：

- 档案的保存
- 通过在线访问的形式对文化遗产的材料进行虚拟传输
- 合作并参与到民族志文档的编制和整理
- 以网络为平台用多媒体展示 Dane-zaa 人的文化和传统

我和多依格河第一民族之间的合作始于 2002 年。我以一名拨款申请撰稿人、项目主持人、几个新数字媒体文化遗产项目的民族志学指导者的多重身份参与和多依格河第一民族的合作。我一辈子都和 Dane-zaa 紧密联系着，1969 年我的父母亲在 Dane-zaa 做人类学的研究时，我出生在 Dane-zaa 人的领土上。我的父母亲——Antonia Mills 和 Robin Ridington 从 1964 年开始以哈佛大学硕士研究生的身份整理关于 Dane-zaa 文化的文件。他们直到现在还在为这项事业贡献着自己的力量。（R. Ridington，1978，1981，1988，1990；Mills，1982，1988，2004；R. Ridington，J. Ridington，2003，2006，2013）

我与多依格河第一民族的工作关系是建立在我与这个族群之间的联系之上，还包括我对 Dane-zaa 文化和历史的熟悉程度，以及我和这些人的互相信任。即使我与这个族群之间的关系成为我启动这个合作性数字多媒体项目的有利之处，我依然采取非常谨慎的态度来维持这个族群对我的信任。尤其是，我通过协调传统的 Dane-zaa 交流习俗来努力维持开放的对话途径，只有这样我们才能一起面对挑战，共同从事文化遗产管理工作，并发起面向公众的文化遗产展览。

我已经简要地介绍了 Dane-zaa 文化以及我为何和多依格河第一民族进行合作。以此为开端，我现在将把话题转向本次论坛的案例研究——以《Dane Wajich–Dane-zaa 的故事与歌谣：梦想者和他们的土地》为题的线上多媒体展览。多依格河第一民族的文化遗产通过新型的数字平台与全世界的观众在网上多媒体展览当中进行分享。在这次展示当中，我将和大家分享一些我们使用的方法以及这种展览对传统带来的影响。

这场展览以应用民族志为原则，主题展现了 Dane-zaa 人的故事和歌谣，以及这两者与 Dane-zaa 梦想者和传统土地之间的关系。整个展览的过程都是经过设计的，只有这样才能由多依格河第一民族为主导。但是专业的民族志专家、语言学家、教育工作者、策展人以及网站设计者也同样贡献了自己的力量，来帮助第一民族传达他们的信息，同时也提供一个机会使他们能学习到其中一些专业技能。这场展览是构建在口头叙述（非物质文化遗产）的基础上的。Dane-zaa 的年轻人在这个项目进行的过程中都接受了培训来负责整理所有的数字视频。整理口头故事和歌曲（非物质文化遗产）其实就是将它们变成有形的媒体产物。这些产物还增补了现代的档案照片和专门为其他观众所准备的带有语境文本解读的歌曲录音。这个展览展示了大量的加拿大多伊格河第一民族 Dane-zaa 语言时期的物品。为了使更多的观众能够理解这个展览，展览中所有的 Dane-zaa 语材料都加上了文本解释，并且所有材料都被翻译成了加拿大的两门官方语言——英语和法语。因为口头交流是 Dane-zaa 人感到最舒服的交流方式，因此将他们根深蒂固的口语传统（故事和歌谣）推广到数码时代对于多依格河第一民族是非常重要的。通过将视频记录分享到网上，多依格河第一民族的人们已经可以将他们的故事讲给当地人以及来自全世界的观众。这种通过口头交流的自我展示比文字交流更加原汁原味，而且可以避免许多由非原住民文化带来的不利影响。（Brody，1981；Roe，2003）

　　因为整个族群主导这个项目，这个展览展示了许多人四年以来的工作成果。这个项目刚开始是由多依格河第一民族的首领加里·奥克发起并设计的，同时加入的还有一小组的族群长辈和我。我是团队中提供咨询的独立民俗学家。这个团队人数迅速地扩张，因而给多依格河第一民族带来广泛的影响。团队不仅仅包括了族群的长辈和领导人（三位在项目期间由多依格河第一民族的群众们选出来的首领和代表），还包括了成年人、年轻人以及一些族群的成员，因为他们在文化实践方面具有专长和广泛的知识储备，所以在项目进行的过程当中我们需要时不时地请教他们。除了我以及作为项目的合作策展人和合作协调员的凯特·轩尼诗，这个团队还包括了来自各个学科的专业人士，他们带来一套自己的专业知识和技术，并与项目团队分享。与我们合作的专业人士有：民俗学家和遗产顾问安伯·瑞丁特（加拿大纽芬兰纪念大学的博士研究生，即本文作者），媒体人类学家凯特·轩尼诗博士（目前已经是西蒙·弗雷泽大学的教授），语言人类学家帕特里克·穆尔博士（加拿大不列颠哥伦比亚大学教授）和朱利亚·米勒博士（华盛顿大学的博士生），视觉人类学家彼得·比尔拉博士（旧金山州立大学教授），文化人类学家罗宾·瑞丁特博士和吉莉安·瑞丁特（瑞丁特是加拿大不列颠哥伦比亚大学的退休荣誉教授，他和他的同事以及妻子吉莉安·瑞丁特与 Dane-zaa 族群保持长期联系），来自"无限数字通信"的网站设计者，来自北皮斯学区第一民族资源中心的课程开发团队，以及独立课程顾问安吉拉·惠洛克。所有的专业人士为该族群的展览投入了大量精力，将重心放在使更多的年轻人和长者参与到活动中，并且实现了语言和传统文化的整合与复兴，以及文化遗存的保护、技术发展和培训，使多依格河第一民族的自我展示最终成真。

　　Dane Wajich 展览最终能实现得益于大量拨款和财政支持。我以多依格河第一民族的名义申请了加拿大虚拟博物馆合作基金，并得到批准。这个项目的财政合作伙伴包括：作为加拿大文化遗产部门发起者之一的加拿大虚拟博物馆（主要的项目资助者和网站出版者）、多依格第一民族（为项目管理以及长老委员会的参与提供支持）、大众汽车基金会濒危语言项目（为 Dane-zaa 和海狸语的翻译与视频材料转写提供资金支持）、东北本地促进会（为 Dane-zaa 年轻人的培训与工作提供视频材料）以及北皮斯学区#60 第一民族教育项目（根据学区的课程要求，协助并支持配套的教师资源准备）。展览团队广泛利用多渠道的财政支持，根据每个赞助商的不同要求，使得该项目的影响范围大大拓展，以及在设计该公共展览的过程中，将更多的族群目标融合在其中。

　　该项目是以一个相对广义的应用方法进行有组织的发展。在事后的分析中，发现该项目有个显而易见的特点：这个项目采用合作型行动导向的研究模型的，并且有着明确的目标，那就是授权给族群，让他们对研究的日程进行调整，并选出他们的公共代表。这些方法包括：①参与式行动研究；②参与式影像；③合作型民族志；④后殖民主义的理论和言语。通俗地讲，这些方法论的各个层面相互结合，因此这个项目还实现了一些这个族群优先考虑的事情：年轻一代的技术培训，文化和语言复兴，记录和整理多依格河第一民族使用土地的传统方式以及工业对其土地的影响，多依格河第一民族的一些条约和原住民权利声明。

参与式行动研究（PAR）是一种研究模式，研究者用这种研究模式来帮助被研究对象解决他们所认定的社会问题。在1948年，索尔·塔克斯与美国爱荷华州的麦斯格瓦奇大（又被称为福克斯印第安人）合作过程中采用了这种工作方式，然后提出这一术语。从此，PAR广泛地应用在不同的学科研究中。（Ervin，2005：222；Kindon, Pain, Kesby, 2007）参与式影像的应用是由兼任视觉人类学家和电影制作人的让·鲁奇发起的。早在20世纪40年代，他在非洲工作时，最早提出"实录电影"——早期的一群民族志学者将照相机交给了研究对象，让他们自行选择要记录的内容（让·鲁奇正是这群民族志学者的其中一员）。并且，这些研究者还提出"共享人类学"的概念，在得到成果的过程当中，运用反思性媒体（还包括研究对象的反馈）进行实践活动（Henley，2009，Hennessy，2010：165-170）。虽然鲁什的成果受到他所工作的环境——殖民时期的"气候"所影响，但是并不妨碍他为合作型/参与型电影制作与多媒体展览提供一个广阔的舞台（Henley，2009：357-58）。从20世纪70年代晚期开始，在不断反思中成长起来的合作型民族志发展成为民族志田野调查。民族志田野调查将关注点从野外研究员的日常工作转向了被调查人或是族群，同时承认研究员者对田野调查的影响。这一成果已经由卢克·埃里克·拉斯特在自己关于合作性民族志的作品中展现出来（2001，2005）。几位贡献者登青、林肯以及图海华·史密斯也在他们编著的关于批判性本地方法论的书中展现了这一观点（2008）。这些后殖民时期的方法论和实践已经被问题化，在期刊《合作性人类学》（2008）中，还有研究者对此做了一个详细的汇报。

因为受到以上提到的方法论的影响，整个Dane Wajich项目前期召开了一系列的策划会议以及脚本设计练习。团队的所有成员都参与其中，并且Dane-zaa的年轻人及其视频制作的导师还将整个过程都拍摄下来。当授权的应用程序上已经列满了故事和歌曲作为展览的候选内容，实际的选择权才交予Dane-zaa族群，让他们来选择展览的材料以及情景化的风俗习惯。作为制作过程当中一个重要的组成部分，族群代表不断地对脚本和展览草案进行审核与修订。比如说，在口述史视频的后期制作中，一些视频片段被布展者挑选出来进行展览，并且整个族群的人们都可以看到展览草案并提供反馈意见。草案以LCD投影的形式被展现在屏幕上，因此，他们可以看到详细的视频剪辑、图片、歌曲以及从网页中挑选出来的文本，由此完成对展览内容的审核。翻译文本被大声地朗诵出来，因为Dane-zaa族群偏好用口头形式来审核文本，而不是在纸上编辑书面语。

在一次前期筹备会中，奥克首领带来了一面鼓，上面有梦想者的涂鸦。奥克解释说，他对这面鼓的历史知道得并不多，但是他的祖父艾伯特·阿斯克提一直小心翼翼地呵护着这面鼓。他的祖父是多依格河第一民族的一位重要的作曲家。同样是一名作曲家的汤米·阿塔奇很快地就认出了这面鼓。阿塔奇开始口述相关的故事,不仅仅将这面鼓和鼓面上的涂鸦与Dane-zaa人的家族史联系在一起,还有Dane-zaa人在特定地点的经历以及Dane-zaa人的世界观和处世态度(即精神生活)。他说道,这面鼓是由梦想家Gaayęą制作的。Gaayęą,1923年在Gat Tah Kwâ(蒙特尼)去世。阿塔奇解释说Gaayęą在鼓面上画的是一幅地图,是通往天堂的道路。Gaayęą描绘的是他在梦中见到的。阿塔奇还说,Gaayęą利用这面鼓分享了他的看法,因此Dane-zaa人可以记住这条通往天堂的道路,在人们死了以后,可以经由这条道路的引导通往精神世界。这面鼓成为了引导故事情节和内容的中心象征,最终被选入展览项目中。它通过口述史也成了Dane-zaa文化复兴的象征。因为这面鼓将Dane-zaa的年轻人与Dane-zaa梦想家这条长线在这片土地上的历史联系在一起。

第二天,在接下来的脚本会议中,汤米·阿塔奇使用了Dane-zaaZáágé?(Dane-zaa/Beaver)语,进一步将梦想家Gaayęą的鼓和Dane-zaa的历史、回忆、土地利用以及精神世界联系在一起。他遵循着这些原则来引导他的族群,并告诉族人们这些重要的故事,同时也引导着整个项目团队来整理所有的视频材料。所有视频材料在Dane Wajich的网站上都可以看到。其中有一段视频剪辑是阿塔奇在筹备会当中的讲话。它被放到了展览当中,也可以在线观看。这段视频播放的过程中还有双语转录文本滚动播出。族群和专业语言学家在一起工作,不仅利用Dane-zaa的正字法认真地将这段用Dane-zaa语叙述的视频翻译并转录出来,还将展览中其他叙述片段也进行了处理。以下摘录的就是筹备会中的一段视频转录:

02:58
你应该把你能记住的事情告诉他们
03:09
一代又一代,孩子们被抚育长大
03:13
我们的祖母告诉我们
03:16
如何生存
03:18
在很久的过去以及现在
04:08
你所记住的事情都来自你的长辈们
04:12
(告诉他们)那些事情
04:14
当我们走遍大地
04:18
你要告诉他们那些重要的故事

（这个选段是汤米·阿塔奇 2005 年在 Dane Wajich 脚本会议上的讲话。由比莉·阿塔奇、玛德琳·奥克以及 Eddie Apsassin 于 2006 年 7 月翻译。同月，博士帕特里克·穆尔、朱利亚·科琳·米勒、比莉·阿塔奇以及玛德琳·奥克对翻译版本进行 Dane-zaa 语正字。您可以在以下网站观看：http://www.museevirtuel-virtualmuseum.ca/sgc-cms/expositions-exhibitions/danewajich/english/stories/video.php?action=fla/tommyatcomplex。)

项目团队首先召开了一个会议，制定了故事发展框架。在 2005 年的夏季，项目团队参观了多依格河领土的八个地方，只有这样老一辈才能分享和这片土地紧密联系的知识，包括重要的故事、歌曲、名人以及经验。族群成员利用这次机会详细地描述了他们和这片土地的关系，以及对当代问题的关心——石油和天然气工业化将如何影响 Dane-zaa 人数世纪以来赖以生存的这些土地和植物、动物。

The Places 主页在 Dane-zaa 语的复兴和大众宣传上也满足了族群的优先权——在该地区的政府官方地图上使用 Dane-zaa 语的地名而不是英文名。除此之外，主页还有一个交互式听觉元素：当使用者移动鼠标，将光标放在地图上的地名时，由 Dane-zaa 长者录制的音频材料会被播放，说出该地方的名字。参观者点击八个地名的任意一个都会进入一个新的单元。新单元将播放关于该地方的多媒体材料（包括视频故事、音频歌曲、文本以及图片）。我诚挚地邀请读者们来探索 the Places 的主页以及子页面。在这场展览中，你将通过不同的网页链接看到原始材料是如何被文字化的。这使得操作者有机会在视频中找出不同说话者的介绍。你将看到这个项目的信息以及整个设计过程，以及多依格河第一民族的历史、广阔的文化、语言和梦想家年表。

整个族群选择的泛化过程以及三年来对展览的回顾使得这个族群越来越意识到他们有机会通过互联网向本地和全世界的观众们展示自己。与这个机会相伴随的是他们意识到互联网也带来了风险——展览中的图片、故事、歌曲会被盗版或随意使用。这些风险总是和数字移动和传播联系在一起，因此多依格河第一民族选择他们的一些文化遗产资料进行保护，使其免受未经审核的使用，向公众关上了大门，只留作自用。实际上，这正好在实现文化分享的目标以及保护他们的数字文化遗产资料之间达到了平衡。

族群的审核进程还促进了一项以文化为基础的协议顺利进行。该文化财产协议控制了数字文化遗产的访问和不同的分配方式，使得这些遗产的机动性比传统形式上的物质遗产更强。通过处理的带有文化敏感性的材料，并处理为歌曲和图像之类的数码文化材料而设定的 IP 协议，多依格河第一民族平衡了开放的访问形式与闭合的访问形式，并制定了一份协议。该协议为文化遗产的保护设定了许多内容，比如说有关内部/本地的传统使用和控制形式，以及外部/西方现代的财产概念。对于整个族群来说，这个过程和最终产出结果是同样重要的。

在整个脚本会议以及族群审核过程中，族群掌握了选择展览内容的主动权，这其中包括审核布展者与网站设计者提交的草稿。我们承担着反思、对话及利益相关者的问题调解工作，他们为我们更改和校对布展内容指明了方向。因为他们引导布展者对展览内容进行变化和编辑。整个过程一直持续到族群对网络展览的内容感到满意才结束。

我认为，维持开放的意见交换渠道是整个项目中必要的组成部分，并且要运用各种各样的意见交换形式更是至关重要，特别是展览中包括了 Dane-zaa 人的民俗习惯。展览的内容应避免直接的冲突，同时还需人们不考虑成果中的既得利益。如此，不同的意见才能在各个族群中传递。意见分歧与误解往往出现在整个项目的创作过程、布展和非物质文化遗产项目档案处理的后期。比如说，为了更好地调解意见分歧与误解，我的同事凯特·轩尼诗（项目的合作布展人和协调人）和我一起让不同的利益相关者参与到了个人与小组讨论中。

在展览进行的这些天里，为了达到表现自我和起到社会活动的目的，多依格河族群已经运用了辐射面遍布全球的公共数字论坛。通过使用新媒体表现原住民生活，他们有能力为西方文化占优势的大叙事形式提供替代品，并且有能力记录下现代加拿大社会背景下的 Dane-zaa 文化与传统复兴。这个项目就是一个典型的例子，表现了多依格河第一民族的人民，与许多其他原住民和人数稀少的族群一样，正在使用数字在线媒体作为一种社会活动的形式，通过在网上讲故事，让自己的声音和力量让更多的人感受到。

参考文献

1. Research Methodologies

Henley, Paul. 2009. *The Adventure of the Real：Jean Rouch and the Craft of Ethnographic Cinema*. Chicago and London：University of Chicago Press.

Kindon, Sara, Rachel Pain and Mike Kesby. 2007. *Participatory Action Research Approaches and Methods：Connecting People, Participation and Place*. New York：Routledge.

Lassiter, Luke E. 2005. *The Chicago Guide to Collaborative Ethnography, Chicago Guides to Writing, Editing, and Publishing*. Chicago：University of Chicago Press.

Rouch, Jean. 1981. La mise en scene de la realite et le point de vue documentaire sur l'imaginaire. In P. E. Gallet (ed.) *Jean Rouch, une rétrospective*. Paris：Ministère de relations exterieures/Centre National de Recherches Scientifigues.

Seeger, Anthony. 2008. Theories Forged in the Crucible of Action：The Joys, Dangers, and Potentials of Advocacy and Fieldwork. In Gregory Barz and Timothy J. Cooley (eds) *Shadows in the Field：New Perspectives for Fieldwork in Ethnomusicology. Second Edition*, pp. 271-288. New York：Oxford University Press.

2. The Dane-zaa

Brody, Hugh. 1981. *Maps and Dreams：Indians and the British Columbia Frontier*. Vancouver：Douglas and McIntyre.

Doig River First Nation. 2004. *Hadaa ka naadzet：The Dane-zaa Moose Hunt* [Virtual Multimedia Exhibit]. Doig River First Nation; Canada's Digital Collection/Industry Canada. Currently offline. Previously available from http://www.moosehunt.doigriverfn.com, accessed December 11, 2006.

——2007. *Dane Wajich–Dane-zaa Stories and Songs：Dreamers and the Land* [Virtual Multimedia Exhibit]. Doig River First Nation; Virtual Museum of Canada. Available from http://www.museevirtuel-virtualmuseum.ca/sgc-cms/expositions-exhibitions/danewajich/, accessed December 10, 2011.

Hennessy, Kate. 2010. Repatriation, Digital Technology, and Culture in a Northern Athapaskan Community.

PhD. Thesis, Anthropology, University of British Columbia, Vancouver.

Mills, Antonia C. 1982. The Beaver Indian Prophet Dance and Related Movements Among North American Indians. PhD. Thesis, Anthropology, Harvard University.

—1988. A Preliminary Investigation of Cases of Reincarnation among the Beaver and Gitksan Indians. *Anthropologica* 30 (1): 23-59.

—2004. The Ghost Dance and Prophet Dance. In *Shamanism: An Encyclopedia of World Beliefs, Practices, and Culture*, ed. Maria Walter and Eva Friedman, pp. 287-292. Santa Barbara: ABC-CLIO Press.

Ridington, Amber. 2012. Continuity and Innovation in the Dane-zaa Dreamers' Song and Dance Tradition: A Forty-Year Perspective. In Anna Hoefnagels and Beverly Diamond (eds.) *Aboriginal Music in Contemporary Canada: Echoes and Exchanges*, pp. 31–60. Kingston: McGill-Queens University Press.

—In Press. After Digital Repatriation: Reflecting on Collaborative Projects, Processes, and Products with a Northwestern Athapascan Community. *Journal of American Folklore*.

Ridington, Amber, and Kate Hennessy. 2008. Building Indigenous Agency Through Web-Based Exhibition: Dane-Wajich - Dane-zaa Stories and Songs: Dreamers and the Land. In J. Trant and D. Bearman (eds.) *Museums and the Web* 2008: *Proceedings* (CD-ROM), Toronto: Archives & Museum Informatics. Published March 31, 2008. Available from: http://www.archimuse.com/mw2008/papers/ridington/ridington.html, accessed January 12, 2012.

Ridington, Robin. 1978. Swan People: *A Study of the Dunne-za Prophet Dance*. Vol. No. 38, Mercury Series. Ottawa: National Museum of Man.

—1981. Beaver Indians. In June Helm (ed.) *Handbook of North American Indians*, Vol 6: 350–360, Washington, DC: Smithsonian Institution.

—1988. *Trail to Heaven: Knowledge and Narrative in a Northern Native Community*. Vancouver: Douglas and McIntyre.

—1990. *Little Bit Know Something: Stories in a Language of Anthropology*. Iowa City: University of Iowa Press.

Ridington, Robin, and Jillian Ridington. 2003. Archiving Actualities: Sharing Authority with Dane-zaa First Nations. *Comma: International Journal on Archives* 2003. 1: 61–68.

—2006. *When You Sing It Now Just Like New: First Nations Poetics Voices and Representations*. Lincoln: University of Nebraska Press.

Ridington, Robin, Jillian Ridington and Doig River First Nation. 2003. *The Ridington/Dane-zaa Digital Archive-Dane-zaa Archive Catalogue* [Password-Secured Online Database]. Doig River First Nation. Available from http://fishability.biz/Doig, accessed January 12, 2012.

Ridington, Robin, Jillian Ridington and Elders of the Dane-zaa First Nations. 2013. *Where Happiness Dwells: A History of the Dane-zaa First Nations*. Vancouver: University of British Columbia Press.

Ridington, Robin, and J. Ridington, P. Moore, K. Hennessy and A. Ridington. 2011. Ethnopoetic Translation in Relation to Audio, Video, and New Media Representations. In Brian Swann (ed.) *Born in the Blood: On Native American Translation*, 211-241. Lincoln: University of Nebraska Press.

Roe, Steve. 2003. "If The Story Could Be Heard:" Colonial Discourse and the Surrender of Indian Reserve 172. *BC Studies* 138/139 (Summer/Autumn): 115-136.

非物质文化遗产传承人保护模式研究[①]
——以中国湖北宜昌民间故事讲述家孙家香、刘德培和刘德方为例

黄永林[*]

冯骥才先生指出:"历朝历代,除了一大批彪炳史册的军事家、哲学家、政治家、文学家、艺术家以外,各民族还有一大批杰出的民间文化传承人,掌握着祖先创造的精湛技艺和文化传统,他们是中华伟大文明的象征和重要组成部分。当代杰出的民间文化传承人是我国各民族民间文化的活宝库,他们身上承载着祖先创造的文化精华,具有天才的个性创造力。……中国民间文化遗产就存活在这些杰出传承人的记忆和技艺里。代代相传是文化乃至文明传承的最重要的渠道,传承人是民间文化代代薪火相传的关键,天才的杰出的民间文化传承人往往还把一个民族和时代的文化推向历史的高峰。"[②] 非物质文化遗产保护的重点在于根据其固有特点建立和健全一个适合时代需要和可持续发展的传承机制,从而使通过传统的口传心授的方式传承的非物质文化遗产,在现代条件下仍然能够得以继续传承,而居于这个机制核心的是传承人。因此,对传承人的保护是非物质文化遗产保护的重中之重。

一、非物质文化遗产传承人保护模式

我国政府十分重视对非物质文化遗产传承人的保护,在政治上给予他们较高的社会地位和声望评价,在经济上给予他们一定的生活补贴和文化传承与利用的资金资助,其目的是更好发挥他们保护和传承非物质文化遗产的积极性。湖北省宜昌市长阳土家族自治县的孙家香、五峰土家族自治县的刘德培和夷陵区的刘德方这三位民间故事家是中国民间文化传承人

---

[*] 黄永林,湖北仙桃人,华中师范大学副校长、博士生导师,国家文化产业研究中心主任,中国新文学学会会长,中国民俗学会副会长,主要研究方向文化资源与文化产业。

[①] 基金项目:国家文化科技提升计划项目"国家非物质文化遗产保护与传承技术体系的构建"(文科技函〔2011〕821号)

[②] 中国民间文艺家协会编:《中国民间文化杰出传承人调查、认定、命名工作手册》,2005年8月印行,第11页。转引自刘锡诚著:《非物质文化遗产:理论与实践》,学苑出版社2009年版,第140—141页。

的典型代表,这三位民间故事传承人生活的年代大体相同,活动的范围基本上都在湖北宜昌地区,讲故事的能力都十分强,农民故事家的身份完全一致,都是在国内外有一定影响的民间故事家,而且故事家的身份在一定程度上改变了他们的命运。然而,对这三位民间故事传承人,不同地方政府却采取了不尽相同的保护模式,即对孙家香采取的是在文化基本隔离中安度晚年的静态保护模式,对刘德培采取的是在文化自然生态中继续传承的活态保护模式,对刘德方采取的是在文化产业发展中利用创新的生产性保护模式。

(一) 静态保护模式

静态保护主要是指通过各种保护性措施延续非物质文化遗产传承人的传承生命,以抢救性策略,用现代高科技工具和科学的方法,通过录像、录音、照片拍摄、文字语言记录等方式和声像、图书、网络、信息库、数字化多媒体等手段,对传承人所传承的非物质文化遗产资料进行持续的、完整的、真实的、系统的跟踪记录,在保持其真实面貌的基础上,制作成文件,建立起完整的档案,便于人们广泛使用,信息共享,从而起到学习、研究、传承、发展、弘扬的作用。其目的主要包括以下两个方面:

延续传承人的传承生命

非物质文化遗产最大的特征是以人的个体或群体世代相承的活动而传承,一旦人的个体或群体活动终止,它也就消失了。在现代化的巨大冲击下,现在许多宝贵的非物质文化遗产正在随着时间的流逝而消失,随着传承人的死亡而失传。因此,对于非物质文化遗产的抢救性保护与对传承人生命的保护是同步的。传承人维系着非物质文化遗产的兴衰,保护传承人在某种程度上就是保护非物质文化遗产。按照这一思路,我国十分重视对一些年事已高、身体处于高危状态的非物质文化遗产代表性传承人的保护,在生活和健康方面给予特别关照。各级政府纷纷出台非物质文化遗产代表性传承人生活待遇政策,力所能及地解决他们的生活困难,让他们没有后顾之忧,全神贯注地从事非物质文化遗产的传承工作。有的还建立了传承人医疗保障制度,为他们购买医疗保险,安排他们定期进行身体检查,无病早防,有病早治,保证传承人良好的身体传承条件,从而控制、降低因为代表性传承人身体健康原因给非物质文化遗产传承带来的风险和损失。

抢救传承人的文化遗产

传承人是非物质文化遗产的重要创造者和传承者,他们掌握并承载着比常人更多、更丰富、更全面、更系统的非物质文化遗产的知识和技艺,他们既是非物质文化遗产"活"的宝库,又是非物质文化遗产代代相传的代表性人物。对传承人传承的非物质文化遗产进行抢救与保护是当前非物质文化遗产保护工作的重点。2008年5月14日颁发的《国家级非物质文化遗产项目代表性传承人认定与管理暂行办法》,进一步规定并细化了对代表性传承人的保护与管理。第十一条明确规定:"国家级非物质文化遗产项目保护单位应采取文字、图片、录音、录像等方式,全面记录该项目代表性传承人掌握的非物质文化遗产表现形式、技艺和知识等,有计划地征集并保管代表性传承人的代表作品,建立有关档案。"这一规定包括两个方面内容,一是全面记录代表性传承人所掌握的项目的表现形式、技艺和知识等;二是有计划地征集并保管代表性传承人的代表作品,建立有关档案。这项规定是对国家认定的项目代表性传承人的基础性保护措施。

长阳土家族自治县对民间故事讲述家孙家香的保护就是采取"静态保护"模式。孙家香,女,土家族,农民。1919年11月30日(农历十月初九)出生,长阳土家族自治县都镇湾镇杜家冲人。她没上过学校,连自己的名字都不认识,但她自幼聪明过人,记忆力特强,天性乐观,从不屈服于命运,在她所生活的长阳都镇湾杜家冲这样的特殊环境、特殊历史和特殊文化的作用下练就了一套讲述故事的特殊本领。① 孙家香能讲600多个故事,是第一位被中国民间文艺家协会命名为"中国民间文化杰出传承人"的土家族女故事家,是第三批国家级非遗项目代表性传承人。1998年长江文艺出版社公开出版了她的故事专集《孙家香故事集》。《人民日报》、《光明日报》、新华社等媒体先后对她的事迹进行过专题采访报道。孙家香口头讲述的民间故事结构完整、语言通俗流畅、故事曲折动人、含义深刻,具有引人入胜的艺术魅力和十分鲜明的口头讲唱风格,反映了她对民间艺术的广泛兴趣和得心应手的驾驭能力。她讲述的故事以童话故事居多,在用幻想编织的艺术世界里,洋溢着浓郁的土家族乡土风情,洋溢着乐观开朗、积极向上的精神。我国著名的民间故事研究专家刘守华教授指出:孙家香讲述的故事"许多篇都不是土生土长之作,而是在中国乃至世界范围内流行的著名故事类型……孙家香能够讲出这么多属于中国和世界民间故事宝库中闪光耀眼的精品,这正是她作为大故事家的重要标志"②。

孙家香在成为民间故事讲述家前一直生活在都镇湾,无论是生产劳动之中,还是休闲之时,她在哪故事就能讲到哪。孙家香讲故事与别人不同之处在于,她是"只要有人听就愿意讲",而且听故事的人越认真,她讲得就越好、越带劲。孙家香被命名为故事讲述家之后,因她所居住的地方条件较差,经济困难,加之年事已高,身患胃病、眼病,身体状况较差,政府对她实行了特殊保护,为她提供良好的生活和医疗条件,解决其生活后顾之忧。在各级政府的关怀下,2003年8月21日,政府将孙家香从穷乡僻壤的杜家冲接到都镇湾福利院,从此,孙家香由政府全面供养,成为该县第一位享受政府特别待遇的农民婆婆。为了进一步提高孙家香的生活质量和医疗保障水平,2005年3月16日,当地政府又将时年86岁的孙家香接到该县第一福利院,使之得到更好的照顾。同时,当地政府还设立了民间文化高龄传承人救助基金,专门资助像孙家香这样的高龄民间文化传承人。时任中共湖北省委书记俞正声还亲自过问民间文化高龄传承人的生活情况,为基金捐款。③ 长阳县政府尽量给老人创造一个舒适幸福的生活环境,让老人能安享晚年,其目的是让她能够继续进行故事传承。尽

---

① 林继富:《土家村寨盛产故事能手 都镇湾民间故事多广奇趣》,《中国文化报》2010年9月2日。
② 刘守华:《土家族故事讲述家孙家香故事集序》,《土家族故事讲述家孙家香故事集》,萧国松整理,长江文艺出版社1998年版,第7页。
③ 林继富:《宜昌民间故事家孙家香》,宁夏人民出版社2009年1月版,第77—80页。

管孙家香入住福利院后生活条件有了很大改善,然而她离开原来的乡土生活后,整日与鳏寡残疾老人相处,熟悉的听众不见了,过去你一言我一语的故事场面不复存在了,她讲述的故事活动大大减少了,往日那些散发泥土芳香的故事逐渐消失了。从事民间故事传承研究的林继富教授从1997年开始一直"跟踪"研究孙家香,收集了她前后讲过的几百个故事。他通过比较发现,离开乡土情境和邻里社会的孙家香,口中那些散发着泥土芳香的故事渐渐少了,过去激情讲述故事的场面不再出现。①

非物质文化遗产的最大特点是依托于人本身而存在。以声音、形象和技艺为表现手段,以身口相传作为文化链而得以延续,是"活"的文化及其传统中最脆弱的部分。因此,对于非物质文化遗产传承的过程来说,人的传承就显得尤为重要。尽可能延续传承人的生命,并把他们掌握的非物质文化遗产表现形式、技艺和知识整理出来,编印成书、刻成光盘、制作成数据库,放在图书馆和档案馆里,这种静态保护是非常必要的,但这样还很不够。我们还应该采取积极措施让他们能够将这些非物质文化遗产继续传承下去,传承给后代。"只有活水才能养活鱼",孙家香进入福利院前后讲述故事状态的变化告诉我们,对传承人的保护要特别注意维持"文化生态",让传承者、传承对象处于一个相对稳定的原生态文化系统内,使他们在一个适宜的环境里传承创新。很多非物质文化遗产是群体性拥有的,所以应该将着眼点放在社群环境的维护上,而不是让他们脱离这种群体文化生态。保护现有传承人最好的办法是让传承人生活在他们所熟悉的特定环境中,只有这样,非物质文化遗产的传承才不至于走样、不会绝种,文化的传统也就不会中断。

(二) 活态保护模式

芬兰著名学者劳里·航柯说:"把活生生的民间文学保持在它的某一自然状态使之不发生变化的企图从一开始便注定要失败。可能被滥用或被适当地加以保存和保护的,不是民间文学说唱表演,而是说唱表演的记录。……民间文学财产的'第二次生命'的标志是人们想利用它们……也许可以这样说,只有对做成文件的民间文学,即'从民间文学衍生出的作品',才能够实施有效的保护,而活生生的民间文学,传承人心目中的、在演唱过程中以千变万化的方式表现出来的主题和思想是无法直接保护的。因为它随着个人的社会生活而存在、变化和消亡,而其方式又不能从外界加以控制。"② 非物质文化遗产保护必须是活态的保护,而活态保护的关键是文化传承的生态环境的保护。因此,保护非物质文化遗产传承人还必须特别注意按照文化生态的要求,让他们能在适宜的文化环境中进行传承。在老百姓中被称为手艺人或讲故事、唱山歌的能手,他(她)在群体中就必定是一个知识丰富、受人尊敬、给人以欢乐和知识的人,在繁重的体力劳动之余,他(她)要带头或积极参加群体的(族群的、社区的、村落的)民间文化活动,推动族群的或社区的或村落的非物质文化

---

① 林继富:《民间叙述传统与故事传承》,北京:中国社会科学出版社2007年版,第70—128页。
② 刘守华:《故事村与民间故事保护》,《民间文化论坛》2006年第5期。

遗产的传播、普及、传承，活跃民众的业余文化生活，提高他们的精神境界和道德风尚，增加族群的、社区的、村落的团结、稳定与和谐。因此，政府文化主管部门对于非物质文化遗产杰出传承人保护的责任，除了尽量为传承者的传承活动提供良好的社会的、物质的条件外，更重要的还是要使他们能在原有的文化生态中继续发挥传承作用。

宜昌市五峰土家族自治县政府对民间故事讲述家刘德培的保护就属于"活态保护"模式。刘德培，男，1912年出生于五峰土家族自治县白鹿庄珍珠山村。他一生阅历丰富，读过两年私塾，当过长工、短工、背夫、邮差；进斋铺当过学徒，帮人捡过屋瓦；农忙时务农，农闲时跟戏班唱过皮影；学过算命、看病；乡里红白喜事、大小会头，常请他去当支客使或都管。他生活的足迹遍及湖北省的五峰、松滋、宜都、长阳、枝江、秭归、鹤峰等鄂西诸县，对社会底层的各类人物，他多有接触。从小开始讲故事说笑话，成为他娱人自娱的方式。他能讲故事笑话512则、唱山歌1000余首、讲俗谚2000余条、谜语800余则等。上海文艺出版社自1989年以来一版再版的48万字的故事集《新笑府》，为他的传世之作。国内外20多家报刊、出版社和大学文科教材发表、采用了他传承的民间文艺作品400余篇。刘德培讲述的故事，内容从开天辟地到当代生活，各色人物生动传神，技巧娴熟，说唱兼用，语言既平实又含蓄，极具感染力。1982年他口述的故事《杜老幺》被收入民间故事集《杜老幺》，由长江文艺出版社出版。1983年9月他被接纳为中国民间文艺研究会湖北省分会会员，同年12月湖北省群众艺术馆和湖北省民间文艺家研究会授予他"民间故事家"称号。1998年联合国教科文组织表彰"中国十大民间故事家"，他名列榜首。2000年3月"中国民间文艺山花奖"首届成就奖颁布，他是全国民间故事家中唯一入选者，与学术泰斗钟敬文、贾芝等一起获此殊荣。

五峰土家族自治县政府对本地土生土长的杰出民间故事讲述家刘德培关爱有加。无论是刘德培生前，还是刘德培辞世以后，都采取了一系列特殊的保护措施。早在1983年刘德培获得"湖北省民间故事家"称号后，县政府就决定从1984年起对他的晚年生活实施特殊照顾，每个月给刘德培生活补贴。其后，还给他供应商品粮；逢年过节县和乡镇村负责人还上门慰问；民政部门在冬天还送去御寒的棉衣棉被；县人民保险公司还从1994年起对刘德培实行平安、医疗"双保险"，一直持续到他病故。县政府还拨专款出版刘德培的故事集和资料集，成立刘德培研究会，建立刘德培资料馆，资料馆共收藏、展览刘德培生活用品实物20余件、有关文字音像资料共计1万多件。

县政府从1984年起从各方面给予刘德培生活照顾，但他从没有离开过家乡白鹿庄珍珠山，至死一直活跃于乡邻之间，传承着他的民间故事。从1938年他讲述民间故事开始出名算起，到2000年底老人作古，长达62年。他相濡以沫48载的遗孀梅祖佑婆婆这样解说刘德培："人家在坡里搞事（做农活），他在坡里讲。路上碰到哪个哒，他边走边讲。今日跟这些人讲，明日跟那些人讲，只要有人听，哪里不讲？哪里有红白喜事呢，讲经（即讲故事——笔者注）他为主。老哒他帮人家捡屋（捡瓦补漏），今日讲这些子，明日讲那些子，总有讲的笑的。没得旁人的时候，他就跟孙伢子们讲几个。若是孙伢子们睡哒、出门了呀，他就跟我讲。他又不分你是在剁猪草，还是在洗衣服、弄饭。后来病了呢，只要病得不重，他都要说说笑笑的。若是三天不讲经，那就是害了大病。"① 笔者曾多次参加过刘德培讲述民间故事的活动，对他进行过专门的追踪调研，特别注意观察他在不同场合，面对不同对象以及听众各种不同反应的情况下所作出的种种反应。从观察中发现，在民间故事演述现场，民间故事讲述人与听众的双向互动十分明显。没有听众的参与，故事演述很难完成，即使讲出来，也是断片残简，更谈不上对故事传统的丰富和补充。由于有了听众参与，演述现场听众的类型、性别、人数、神情、反应和插话以及与讲述人之间的交流、竞争，都会影响讲述人，激发讲述人的情绪，对讲述人选择故事、精炼故事、提升故事的演述技巧产生作用。②因此，在给予非物质文化遗产传承人生活关照的同时，我们更应尊重传承人的传承习惯，保护传承文化的生态环境，让他们生活在他们所熟悉的传承环境中，与听众打成一片。

非物质文化遗产是以人为本的活态文化遗产，它强调的是以人为核心的技艺、经验、精神，其特点是活态流变，它是不脱离民族特殊的生活生产方式，是民族个性、民族审美习惯的"活"的显现。因此，对于那些身体健康的非物质文化遗产传承人的保护不能搞"圈养性""温室型"的保护，而应该在给予非物质文化遗产传承人生活关照和身体关怀的同时，尊重传承人的传承习惯，保护好传承的文化生态环境，让他们生活在他们所熟悉的传承环境中，与民众打成一片，采取回归自然文化生态环境的活态的保护，使其在不断变化着的社会文化环境中进一步传承，从而在传承中发展，在发展中传承。

（三）生产性保护模式

非物质文化遗产生产性保护是指在具有生产性质的实践过程中，以保持非遗的真实性、整体性和传承性为核心，以有效传承非物质文化遗产为前提，借助生产、流通、销售等手段，将非物质文化遗产资源转化为文化产品的保护方式。③ 对于非物质文化遗产传承人来说，主要是沿袭传统，保守家法，将过去留下来的文化财富传承下去，这是传承人的根本的义务。然而，一种文化现象如果失去了生命力，就算予以特殊保护，其前景也是可悲的。非物质文化遗产产生和存在于特定的自然和社会文化环境，并随之演化而被传承或绝灭。许多非遗的濒危和灭绝，要么由于其不适应自然和社会文化环境的变化，要么由于其赖以存活的特定社会文化环境已经巨变乃至消失。客观地看，非物质文化遗产总是在变化发展中传承的。现在我们保护的许多所谓"原生态"项目，其中不少并不是本真意义上的"原生态"，而是我们在今天的历史横断面上认定的"原生态"，因为我们不可能阻止现代生活的改变，也很难大规模保留非物质文化遗产的原生语境。我们应当看到，不是社会文化环境要去适应非物质文化遗产，使其得以传承，而是非物质文化遗产保护要适应不断变化着的社会文化环境而得以传承。对非物质文化遗产来说一成不变的保护只是一种理想，它既不切实际，也不

---

① 王作栋：《他是一座珍珠山——追忆五峰民间故事家刘德培》，《湖北日报》2003年12月5日。
② 黄永林：《从信息论看民间故事的讲述活动》，《中国民间文化》1991年第4集。
③ 黄永林：《非物质文化遗产　生产是最好的保护》，《光明日报》2011年10月7日。

符合文化演化的规律,文化创新才是保护非遗的根本出路。杰出的非物质文化遗产传承人应是在继承传统中有能力作出文化选择和文化创新的人物,他们在非物质文化遗产的传承、保护、延续、发展中,起着超乎常人的重大作用。传承人应该根据时代的变化(包括工作条件与民众心理需求),在尊重传统文化根本价值与意义的基础上,沿着传统文化的路径进行积极的演化,以体现非物质文化遗产的精神活力及其在现代社会延展的生命力量。在抢救濒危、扶持保护的基础上,应大力提倡生产性保护,合理利用非物质文化遗产代表性项目,开发具有地方特色、民族特色和市场潜力的文化产品和文化项目。这种生产性保护是一个很好的保护模式,如果一个非物质文化遗产的项目能够通过生产变成产品,带来很好的社会影响和经济效益,它就会有生命力,就能够持续发展下去。

散布于广大农村的"民间艺术家"们生在农村,长在农村,其艺术养分直接来自农村,和农民有着天然的相通性,在民间文化的传承中,起骨干和桥梁作用。发挥民间艺人在活跃农村文化生活、传承民族民间文化方面的积极作用,激发农村自身的文化活力,在新农村文化建设中尤为重要。① 湖北省宜昌市夷陵区政府对著名的民间故事讲述家刘德方的保护就属于"生产性保护"模式。刘德方,1938年出生,宜昌市夷陵区下堡坪乡谭家坪村人,出身地主家庭,小时候只读过两年半书,因病休学之后就迷上了故事。成年后,刘德方先后远离家乡筑河堤、修铁路,长期在外与五湖四海的人接触,听天南地北的人讲故事。刘德方具有惊人的记忆和表述能力,各种故事他只要听过一遍,就能绘声绘色地讲出来。他能讲400多个故事,能演唱几十首山歌民调,他掌握的民间故事、山歌歌词、皮影戏唱词和丧鼓唱词共约1000万字。近几年来,宜昌有关部门先后整理出版了刘德方民间故事集《野山笑林》、刘德方民歌集《郎啊姐》、长篇刘德方传《奇遇人生》和DVD光碟《刘德方笑话馆》。刘德方讲述故事由于"兼收并蓄"了大量的古代和现代民间故事,再加上自己独特的创造,故事内容丰富、风趣生动、富于艺术感染力,具有民间文学、语言学、社会学、伦理学、民俗学、美学等多学科研究价值,备受学界和媒体关注。2004年12月8日中国民间文艺家协会授予刘德方"中国民间故事家"称号,2007年6月,中国文学艺术界联合会、中国民间文艺家协会授予刘德方中国民间文化杰出传承人称号。

在当地政府的关心下,成名后的刘德方"出山"了,他从下堡坪的深山密林中迁到了夷陵城区,被安排在文化馆工作和生活;当地一位民营企业家把他当"名人"看待,免费送他一套三居室的房子;他的生活费和医疗费纳入财政预算;政府还多次为他的专著和音像出版拨出专款。为了充分发挥这位民间艺人的潜能,当地政府成立了"刘德方民间艺术团",依托三峡旅游景观,开展商业性的民间文学演唱活动。刘德方现在忙着到各地演出,到车溪、晓峰古兵寨等旅游景点为游客讲故事。他还积极培养农民文化骨干,培养新一代传承人,在下堡坪乡招收了20多名弟子,年纪最大的56岁,最小的还不到30岁。他除讲述传统的民间故事外,还进一步吸取各地民间故事精华,创作了许多新故事。正是他对前人讲述作品的大量接收、储存、传递、创新,为民间文学的保存与发展做出了重要贡献,才被有

---

① 黄永林《充分发挥传统民间文化在新农村文化建设中的作用》,《光明日报》2006年5月15日。

关专家评价为"目前三峡地区最具活力的民间故事家和民间艺术家"。[①]

刘德方作为"非遗"项目代表性传承人被政府命名，享受政府提供的各种物质和精神待遇，特别是经组织安排，离开了他土生土长的村落下堡坪，离开了其故事传播传承的土壤，从农村到城市，从阶级身份重压下的痛苦挣扎到作为各级政府和民众关注的"明星"，个人身份的变化、生活环境的变化、生活方式的改变和思想观念的转变直接影响着他的故事讲述。[②] 民间故事家刘德方进城前所生活的湖北宜昌夷陵区下堡坪乡属于典型的山区乡镇，地形地貌复杂，境内山峰林立，交通不便，信息闭塞。特殊的地理环境造就了当地闲暇之时讲故事的主要文化娱乐方式。刘德方就是在这个有着浓厚讲述传统的故事乡中成长起来的突出人物。成名之后，刘德方在夷陵区政府的重视下移居到夷陵区小溪塔，这是地处宜昌市近郊的一个新近发展起来的小城镇。身处城市以故事讲述家身份出现的刘德方的讲述环境、讲述行为、讲述内容发生了很大的变化，在这里刘德方已经完全感受不到闲暇之余乡邻围坐一圈，你一言我一语争相逗乐的讲述氛围，在这里其讲故事的环境或是文艺演出中的带有表演性质的讲述，或是面对领导和专家学者考察有选择性的讲述，或是在旅游区面对游客带有迎合性质的讲述。在这里他更多是把民间故事讲述推向市场，进行商业化运作，为获得一定经济效益而讲述。

笔者认为，对于非物质文化遗产传承人来说，坚守传统是第一位的，同时也可作符合逻辑的渐进式演化的尝试，也可以根据不同情况适当进行生产性开发利用。然而如果不顾非物质文化遗产的特点，盲目把非物质文化遗产推向市场，很容易把原生态的非物质文化遗产撕成碎片，势必会糟蹋其本质，从而有可能加快珍贵文化遗产的消亡速度。事实上，近些年，我国许多地方在保护非物质文化遗产时，将其作为旅游资源来开发是较普遍的方式，如把大量民族民间艺术表演形式开发成旅游项目和产品，确实取得了很好的社会和经济效益。但是由于非物质文化遗产的实际情况非常复杂，其中只有某一些才可以进行生产性保护，一定要区别清楚，更不要让非遗项目为了迎合市场而"变味"，陷入"商业化""产业化"的误区。以民歌为例，许多文化工作者花大力气去寻找民间歌手，记录他们原生态的歌曲和唱腔，结果凡是唱得好的民歌手都进了旅游区，几年以后不断异化，这些源自生活的艺术形式最后与实际生活距离越来越远。在保护工作还不够完善时，就将其盲目推向市场进行开发利用，实际上等于把原生态的非物质文化遗产撕成碎片，这无疑违背了保护的初衷。非物质文化遗产生产性保护一定要坚持正确的方向，要在坚守《非遗法》确定的保护原则，坚持真实性、整体性、传承性的基础上，进行开发利用，积极地推动它走向社会，为当代人服务，为社会做更多的贡献。

[①] 刘守华：《野山笑林：长江三峡民间故事家刘德方传讲故事选集序》，《野山笑林：长江三峡民间故事家刘德方传讲故事选集》，余贵富采录，黄世堂整理，北京：大众文艺出版社1999年版，第4页。

[②] 王丹：《从乡村到城市的文化转型——刘德方进城前后故事讲述变化研究》，《民族文学研究》2009年第2期。

二、对非物质文化遗产传承人保护的思考

通过对上述三个民间故事家保护的三种模式的分析,我们可以总结出加强非物质文化遗产传承人保护的一些基本经验和规律。

1. 发挥不同保护主体的积极作用是传承人保护的关键

非物质文化遗产保护的实施主体主要有各级政府、学术界、新闻媒体、社会团体以及商界人士。宜昌市在对这三位民间故事传承人实施保护的过程中,政府和民间的保护主体都起到了积极作用。政府的高度重视和行政权力的运用使这些民间故事传承人被发现,使他们从普通农民转变为有政府固定补贴、受人尊重的文化名人;专家学者的介入使他们作为民间故事传承人的身份能够得到认可,改变了他们的命运;新闻媒体的宣传造势加快了他们故事家身份的认可进程和提升了他们的影响力;社会团体和商界人士的大力支持,使他们的社会地位得到进一步提高,经济生活上获得更好的照顾。由此可见,只有各级政府、学术界、新闻媒体、社会团体以及商界人士发挥各自的作用,以其所具有的强大行政优势、学术优势、资金优势以及舆论优势,在政策、法律、学术以及资金等各个层面,对非物质文化遗产传承人保护工作给予高度重视、积极扶持、热情鼓励和真心推动,非物质文化遗产传承人的保护才能落到实处。

2. 重视关照传承主体的身体生活是传承人保护的基础

对非物质文化遗产保护来说,关键还是对传承主体——传承人的保护,尤其是对重点传承人的保护,这既是保护主体实施的对象,更是非物质文化遗产保护的重点。因为即使政府的权力再大,商界的资金再多,学界的水平再高,新闻媒体的影响再大,都不可能取代非物质文化遗产传承人作为传承主体的作用。因此,保护主体对传承主体实施保护的过程中,首先必须坚持以传承人保护为本,通过主动关心他们的生活,照顾他们的身体,达到保障他们的健康、延续他们的生命,进而延续他们文化传承生命的目的。无论是长阳县政府对孙家香实行的将她送到县第一福利院、为她提供良好的生活和医疗条件的全面供养保护,还是五峰县政府对刘德培每个月发放生活补贴、供应商品粮,实行平安、医疗"双保险"等特殊照顾,以及夷陵区政府将刘德方从偏僻的山村迁到了城区,安排到文化馆工作,提供住房、将他的生活费和医疗费纳入财政预算等特殊措施,都体现了各级政府对传承人本体生命与生活的高度重视。重视对传承人生活的关照、健康的保障,尽量为传承人解决生活后顾之忧,提供较好的医疗条件,使他们能够健康长寿,延续他们文化传承的生命,这是对重点传承人保护的首要的最基本的措施。

3. 针对传承主体状况实施不同模式是传承人保护的重点

本文在以湖北省宜昌市民间故事讲述家孙家香、刘德培和刘德方为例的非物质文化遗产传承人保护措施研究中，提出了在现代社会和经济背景下对非物质文化遗产重点传承人保护的三种模式——静态保护、活态保护和生产性保护模式，而这三种模式分别适应不同状况和特征的非物质文化遗产传承人保护。

第一，"静态保护模式"有利于年迈体弱型传承人的文化生命延续。

对于那些老无所依、生活困难、健康状况不佳、年龄较大的传承人来说，为其生存、生活提供保障，改善他们的生活条件，提供良好的医疗保障，给予其一定的经济补助，并且将其安置于敬老院（福利院），让传承人能安度晚年，尽可能延续他们的人体生命和艺术生命，这种保护是一条很好的途径。然而这种"圈养性""温室型"的静态保护模式，往往是把传承人隔绝于现实民众的生存土壤，使他们脱离传承的文化生态，割裂了非物质文化遗产传承的文化传统与空间，容易导致其艺术生命的枯竭。长阳县利用行政力量将孙家香从偏僻的山村接到城镇福利院，虽然其初衷是为了更好地照顾传承人生活，然而生活在福利院后，民间故事传承人孙家香曾经熟悉的那种村民围坐一圈你一言我一语竞相讲故事的情景不复存在，她讲的故事渐渐少了，过去激情讲述故事的场面不再出现了。因此，这种"养起来"的静态保护模式，对像孙家香这样一类年迈体衰、风烛残年的传承人的抢救性保护是适合和有效的，但是不适用于那些成百上千健康活跃的非物质文化遗产传承人。

第二，"活态保护模式"有利于身体健康型传承人的文化生态保护。

汤普逊指出："我们把当事人的行为归位到他们的生活史中，再把他们的行为归位到他们所属的那个社会场景下的历史中。个人生活的叙述，是相互关联的一组叙述的一部分，它被镶嵌在个人从中获得身份的那些群体的故事中。"① 每一位非物质文化遗产传承者个人的才能与创造，都无一例外地与他所处的社会场景、生活的群体密切相关，体现着他们对民众集体智慧和审美取向的综合与归纳。非物质文化遗产主要是以口传心授为主的传承，只有将其放在活态中进行保护，才有可能将非物质文化遗产尽可能原汁原味地保存下来和传承下去。五峰县对刘德培的保护与孙家香的保护不同，他们没有让他离开原来的乡土生活，而是让他继续生活在他所熟悉的特定的环境中，在原有的文化生态中继续发挥传承作用。传承人是社区文化的积极弘扬者、保护者，社区文化活动、社区民众生活是传承人故事素材的重要来源，社区传统的伦理观念和道德准则成为传承人故事世界的审美原则，社区的民俗环境和自然环境构成了传承人故事活动的文化背景。② 因此，在给予他们身体和生活关心和照顾的基础上，活态保护对于那些身体健康的非物质文化遗产传承人来说是保护最重要和最好的保护模式之一。

---

① ［英］保尔·汤普逊：《过去的声音——口述史》，辽宁教育出版社2000年3月版。
② 林继富：《传承人保护策略研究——以湖北省民间故事传承人保护为例》，载文化部民族民间文艺发展中心编《中国非物质文化遗产保护研究》（下），北京师范大学出版社2007年版。

第三,"生产性保护模式"有利于健康活跃型传承人的文化品牌开发。

联合国教科文组织《保护非物质文化遗产公约》第二条指出:"各个群体和团体随着其所处环境、与自然界的相互关系和历史条件的变化不断使这种代代相传的非物质文化遗产得到创新,同时使他们自己具有一种认同感和历史感,从而促进了文化多样性和人类的创造力。"当今,在努力改善非物质文化遗产传承人的生活处境,提高他们社会地位的同时,更应该发挥他们的创新精神和创造性作用,通过生产性保护措施,将他们传承的可转化为生产资源的非物质文化遗产转化为经济效益。与刘德培和孙家香的保护不同,成名后的刘德方"出山"了,为了充分发挥这位民间艺人的潜能,当地政府成立了"刘德方民间艺术团",依托三峡旅游景观,开展商业性的民间文艺表演活动。这种生产性保护模式就是给传承人以社会表达的机会,给他们扩大社会影响,传承文化遗产的社会空间,使非物质文化遗产的传播和传承活动融入社会、融入生活、适应时代。比如为他们提供专门面向公众的讲述与表演机会,在大型文化演出活动中邀请传承人参与;努力将他们传承的文化艺术楔入传统节日活动、群众文化活动及旅游活动之中等等,激励他们积极主动地开展非物质文化遗产的传承和开发活动,使非物质文化遗产传承具有较好的社会效益和经济效益。

第四,从静态到活态再到生产性保护是传承人保护的发展趋势。

中国政府十分重视非物质文化遗产的保护、传承和开发利用,大力支持非物质文化遗产代表性项目的代表性传承人开展传承、传播活动。《中华人民共和国非物质文化遗产法》第三十条规定"县级以上人民政府文化主管部门根据需要,采取下列措施,支持非物质文化遗产代表性项目的代表性传承人开展传承、传播活动:(一)提供必要的传承场所;(二)提供必要的经费资助其开展授徒、传艺、交流等活动;(三)支持其参与社会公益性活动;(四)支持其开展传承、传播活动的其他措施。"非物质文化遗产传承人在静态的"非遗"信息储存、活态的口传技艺的传播以及生产性的开发利用方面,都负有神圣的使命。目前在抢救濒危、扶持保护的基础上,应大力提倡活态保护和生产性保护。现在我们对这些濒危非物质文化遗产项目的保护,要在抢救的基础上,千方百计为其找到市场、营造市场、找到销路,让其在市场中重新找回自己的生存价值。这就要求我们对非物质文化遗产项目传承人的保护走从静态保护,到活态保护,进而到生产性保护之路,既要照顾好传承人的身体生活、又要保护好传承人的文化生态,更要利用好传承人的文化品牌,为传承文化、发展文化产业服务。当然,生产性保护就是要走市场之路,然而市场以追求最大经济效益为宗旨,有其弊端,所以我们反对非遗保护的市场化,反对将所有非遗项目都推入市场,更反对一些经营者将非物质文化遗产项目任意"恶搞",我们要及时掌控、正确引导市场。

总之,我们探讨非物质文化遗产传承人的保护必须立足于中国实际,在对我们自己的经验和教训给予科学总结的基础上,探索出一条合理有效的中国化的保护新路子,使非物质文化遗产传承人能够得到切实保护。

(本文是2012年4月29日至5月1日在美国纳什维尔市举办的"第二届中美非物质文化遗产论坛:案例研究"国际学术研讨会作的主题报告)

档案馆在保存和查询非物质文化遗产中的作用

尼克尔·塞勒[*]

  1890年,当杰西·沃尔特·费克斯完成他的第一次野外实地记录时,他意识到爱迪生发明的蜡筒留声机可以让民族志学者将在民间采集到的音乐和故事带回图书馆,以供后人研究。非物质文化遗产的研究、保存需求与已生成档案的访问形式之间强有力的联系在此之后的一个多世纪里一直延续着。

  非物质文化遗产的存档可以采取很多种形式,本文将着重探讨以实时记录的方式采集的民族志学档案如何保存以及如何查询的问题,正是这种实时记录的民族志学档案构成了美国民俗生活研究中心(The American Folklife Center, AFC)档案馆的基础。美国民俗生活研究中心位于华盛顿的国会图书馆(即美国国家图书馆)内,中心档案馆收藏着300多万件来自世界各地的有关传统文化的各类照片、手稿、录音和动态影像资料,这些资料包括来自世界各地的传统文化,19世纪90年代最早一批在蜡筒上运用数码技术实地录制的档案也保存于此。该档案馆是美国第一所国家民俗档案馆,也是世界上最古老、规模最大的民俗档案馆之一。

  时至今日,档案馆在进行非物质文化遗产保存工作中面临巨大的挑战,主要原因就是原生数字文件的泛滥和形式的退化,与此同时,支付大型文档文献项目所需的资金支持变得日益困难。为了迎接这些挑战,非物质文化遗产档案馆将致力于跨学科和利用新技术来找到创新的解决方案。

  在这里,我想首先讨论美国最大的非物质文化遗产档案馆——美国民俗生活研究中心档案馆的起源。该档案馆位于全世界最大的图书馆——美国国会图书馆之内。现将档案馆的价值、所藏资源,以及面临的挑战做个简要的介绍。档案馆的首任管理者是罗伯特·W. 戈登,他是在1928年被美国国会图书馆馆长所聘,主要进行美国民间音乐大合集的收集和整理工作。这是美国民间音乐开始进行记录和保存的象征,从此便开启了一段数十年努力工作的岁月。与此同时,这也标志着图书馆在进行收集由他人创建的出版资料和档案馆藏这样的传统工作之外,第一次踏上了开展自身收藏的征途。

  让我们将目光跳转到1976年,档案馆的起源和民间音乐紧密相关,档案馆已经悄然成

---

[*] 尼克尔·塞勒,美国民间生活研究中心档案馆主任。

为美国民俗生活研究中心的一部分了。美国国会在意识到地区和民族文化对美国文化的重要性之后，批准并创建了民俗中心。巧合的是，民俗中心的建立与美国大革命两百周年纪念在同一年；不过从某种程度上来说这也不算巧合，因为这仿佛是承上启下一样，标志着美国多元化生活的转变以及政府和社会开始更加强调国家多元化文化的发展。民俗中心的任务既包括馆藏，也包括展示和推广美国的民俗文化，这就意味着伴随着档案馆的创立，另外的一些公共项目也将随之上马，比如邀请传统艺术家开办音乐会，请一些非物质文化遗产学者来做讲座，到各地学校进行人类学文档技术的传授，以及与传统文化的传承人和学者进行一系列的合作计划。该中心的工作重点是直接与传统文化传承人合作，而展现和延续传统文化也是档案馆的一种合作方式和反馈方式。

保存。作为非物质文化遗产档案馆的一项重要工作，档案的保存始终都面临着很大的挑战，不过庆幸的是美国民俗生活研究中心档案馆是位于美国国会图书馆之内的，而美国国会图书馆则是业界采用数字防腐和音视频保护存储的领先者。图书馆在设施和系统方面进行了大量的投入，以便支持可扩展的和可持续的保存方案。

位于华盛顿以西75英里的帕卡德园区中，有一个视听资料保存中心。这个坐落在大山坡上的设施号称是全美最先进的仓储设施，这里拥有630万件藏品，其中就有许多是我们的音频和视频馆藏品。它同时还拥有一个PB级（100万GB）水平的数字档案馆，主要用于保存数字信息和内容。除了这些基本的馆藏和保存工作，档案馆还与图书馆的声音存储记录部合作，来尝试一些新兴的保存技术。在接下来的一年里档案馆还计划进行一些新项目，比如使用数字技术从无法播放的蜡筒资料中抓取图像槽，再通过抓取的图像槽来重建音频信息。

在图书馆的主藏区，我们管理的数字档案馆大约有25万个数字对象，包括Story Corps的录音资料等。为了就档案馆的规模给你一个直观的感觉，我给你下面的一条信息：从2012年的3月1日到2013年的4月1日，我们共获取了60720份独特的原生数字原始信息。同时，为了就我们所面临的各种挑战给大家一个概念，我在这里简要地介绍一下Story Corps。Story Corps提供给各种不同背景和信仰的人们一个平台，让他们有机会来记录、保存和分享他们的故事。自从2003年起，Story Corps一共收集和储藏了差不多90,000名参与者的超过45000份采访资料。每一个对话都被记录和收藏在美国民俗生活研究中心。在数字化藏品方面，统计到目前为止，我们收到的资料中，手稿占了大部分，共有约202274件，还有139480份图片资料、47173份音频资料以及单个的视频资料。如果按照所占存储空间的大小这个角度来看这些资料的话，音频资料占了绝大部分的存储空间，差不多有16TB，与之相比，管理手稿资料（10.48GB）、图片资料（397.74GB）和视频资料（0.35GB）的工作简直就是小巫见大巫。

存档。美国民俗生活研究中心的核心任务是开启、鼓励、支持、组织和推动美国的非物质文化遗产的科研、学术和培训。美国民间生活研究中心在美国全境内与各社区组织和田野调查人员一起工作，为大家提供培训，鼓励大家进行文献编集活动，并在美国民俗生活研究中心和各社区之间创造沟通对话的机会。在美国民间音乐方面，从1928年美国民俗生活研究中心档案馆的前身——国会图书馆音乐分部创立之日开始，已有不计其数的文献项目得到了这个组织的协调和支持。

　　档案馆最近的一些成就启动于2010年，主要是提供了一个关于美国民俗生活研究中心档案馆传统文献项目的新方法。这个职业的民俗项目的目标主要是通过对全美各地工人的采访，来描绘一幅经济转型期的美国各阶层劳动力的画像（在获得批准之后，采访者将基于美国民间生活研究中心网络存储的口述历史采访资料的数字记录上传，并同时通过在线分类管理工具提交采访的相关信息）。这使得美国民俗生活研究中心可以在既符合成本效益，又符合劳动力效益的情况下，协调全国范围内的收集项目。反过来，分散在全国各地的现场工作人员也可以获得口述历史技术和21世纪数字档案技术的处理经验。

　　数据库管理系统。无论是面对面，还是通过数字接入，我们都需要考虑本土文化产品的必要保护和传统知识细致入微的思考等两个数据库之间的平衡。当你试着达到数字化规模的要求后，你会发现很多有趣的对立关系。不过，一些非物质文化遗产档案馆正在进行一些软件和系统的开发实验，这些软件和系统主要是能提供档案的注解、重放以及让用户可以更容易访问查询具有有个性化的人类学文献等相关功能。

　　对于拥有超过75年综合经验的美国民俗生活研究中心来说，在引用和参考员工收集资料的知识方面是不可撼动的。中心的工作人员在关于人类学和研究图书馆学方面接受过非常专业的学术训练，这使得他们能很好地为那些寻找有关收藏和存储方面信息的人提供深入的援助。最后，我们有责任向社会进行书面告知，我们的工作人员把所收集的材料以数据库的方式提供出来。如果说田野工作者是第一档案员，那么文献记录者就是最后的档案员。只有将档案材料植入数据库中，档案馆的价值才真正得到了完整的体现。

非物质文化遗产项目"阿肯阿依特斯"的国际传播

王霄冰*

"2009/2010 德中科学教育年"期间,与两国数所大学的多位学者一道,笔者参与策划并开展了一项有关"哈萨克阿肯阿依特斯:仪式、文本与表演"的研究。① 来自德国方面的学者,除了少数中亚民族学专家之外,大部分都和本人一样,既没有研究哈萨克文学的学术背景,也不懂得哈萨克语。我们的动机,一则是为了填补德国学界的一项空白,② 二则是为了做了一个跨文化交流的实验,想看看阿依特斯这一来自中国天山深处的哈萨克文化瑰宝,在遭遇到一群生活在德意志文化环境中的、没有任何哈萨克学知识的学者以及普通人时,将会发生怎样的文化碰撞,并做出怎样的自我调适与文化选择。本次活动共由两大部分构成:一是哈萨克的阿肯歌手和学者访问德国(2010 年 5 月,为期 10 天),并在不同的场合表演阿肯阿依特斯;二是德国的学者团队访问新疆(2010 年 6 月,为期 12 天),考察当地的阿依特斯文化及其传承状况。以下的研究,主要基于第一部分活动的内容以及当时所搜集到的资料。

---

* 王霄冰,中山大学中国非物质文化遗产研究中心教授。
① 当时参与的德方学者除本人之外还有:波恩大学的民族学家 Berthold Riese(中文名:白瑞斯,项目负责人)、汉学和伊朗学专家 Ralph Kauz(中文名:廉亚明),洪堡大学的土耳其语专家 Ingeborg Baldauf,慕尼黑大学的汉学和民族学家 Thomas O. Höllmann(中文名:贺东励),班贝格大学的中亚学专家 Ömer François Akakça,科隆大学民族学专业博士生 Martin Böke,《人类》杂志编辑 Harald Grauer。中方参加者有:新疆塔城地区的阿肯歌手纳戈曼·许汉,新疆阿勒泰地区的阿肯歌手贾米哈·达吾来提,新疆师范大学的学者地木拉提·奥迈尔,曼拜特·吐尔地,巴格达提·叶斯特买提,莱再提·克里木别克,努尔巴哈提·土尔逊等,以及中央民族大学教授王建民,和中国社会科学院文学研究所副研究员邹明华。
② 在德国,专门以中国哈萨克为研究对象的学者少之又少,过去只有一些项目涉及新疆哈萨克的游牧文化。洪堡大学的中亚研究所和马普社会人类学研究所等机构中,有部分学者从事哈萨克斯坦的社会、历史及语言文化的研究。

一、作为口头艺术的阿肯阿依特斯

阿肯阿依特斯，是一种源于哈萨克民族民俗生活的民间艺术形式，据推测起源于15至18世纪间。它在文学上被认为植根于在各种民间仪式上演唱的传统民歌，如婚礼歌和挽歌等。① 阿依特斯（aytis）在哈萨克语中，包含"索求、竞争、争论、较量、轮唱、对唱"等多种意义，后来被引申为"用诗歌进行智慧的较量"。② 阿肯（aqin）则是对阿依特斯诗人／歌手的专用名称，哈萨克学者哈拜认为，把"阿肯"翻译为"即兴诗人"、"游唱诗人"或"民间歌手"，都不足以确切地表达它的含义。③ 但我们可以从中了解到，阿肯是一种集诗人、说唱者、歌手、乐师于一身的、多才多艺的即兴创作者与表演者。在演唱阿依特斯时，阿肯一般都成对地出现，相互展开言语的竞技。由于是现场编诗、自弹自唱，所以他们所用的乐曲大多并不复杂，且经常重复。曲调多来自民歌，在风格特征上带有一定的区域性和部落性。④

阿肯阿依特斯的难度，在于即兴创作与演唱。一位出色的阿肯，不仅要有动人的歌喉，会娴熟地弹奏冬不拉，背会一些常用的乐段，而且最为重要的，是要掌握临场作诗的本领。为了做到这一点，阿肯们在平时就注意积累，除了日常的生活知识之外，也要学习书本知识。作为民间的天才诗人，他们吸收和消化各种信息的能力极强，能够把所见所闻很快地转换成诗句，并即刻融入演唱当中。在德国期间，两位阿肯有时会一边走在街上一边独自吟唱编词。据其中的一位阿肯纳戈曼介绍，在每次前往自治州或自治区参加阿肯大会之前，他都要提前好几个月做准备，有时候想词想得晚上都睡不着觉，感觉自己老得很快，年纪轻轻的头发已很稀少。可见得即兴弹唱是一种需要精神高度集中的相当辛苦的脑力劳动。

我们也可以说，阿肯阿依特斯是一种典型的表演性口头艺术，即理查德·鲍曼（Richard Bauman）所谓的"情境性的行为（situated behavior）"。它"在相关的语境（contexts）中发生，并传达着与该语境有关的意义。这些语境可以从不同的层面来确认，比如场景（settings），它是由文化所界定的表演发生的场所。再比如制度（institutions，如宗教、教育、政治等）"⑤。传统形式的阿依特斯的情境性十分明显，特别是民俗阿依特斯，即在婚礼、丧礼、婴儿出生和其他节庆娱乐场合上进行的对唱，有时以集体的形式（一群小

---

① 阿布都玛纳夫·艾比夫：《论阿肯阿依特斯》，新疆维吾尔自治区文化厅编：《哈萨克族阿依特斯论文集》，新疆人民出版社2010年版，第170—182页；贾合甫·米尔扎汗：《论哈萨克族阿依特斯艺术的历史根源和艺术形式》，同书第162—169页。

② 阎建国：《哈萨克族阿依特斯类型划分》，新疆维吾尔自治区文化厅编《哈萨克族阿依特斯论文集》，新疆人民出版社2010年版，第152页。

③ 哈拜：《哈萨克阿肯》，民族出版社2006年版，第3页。

④ 巴格达提·叶斯特买斯：《哈萨克族阿依特斯曲调的区域性与部落性》，新疆维吾尔自治区文化厅编《哈萨克族阿依特斯论文集》，第54—70页，新疆人民出版社2010年版。

⑤ 引自理查德·鲍曼《作为表演的口头艺术》，杨利慧、安德明译，广西师范大学出版社2008年版，第31页。

伙对一群姑娘）展开。其中婚礼中哭嫁的部分称为"萨仁"，由新郎方和新娘方组成两个团体，曲调较为忧郁舒缓，女方抒发离别家乡的忧伤情感，男方则极力安慰新娘。在婚礼仪式结束后、姑娘行将出门之前，所唱的是送别的阿依特斯，由坐在帐篷中的新娘及其嫂子们、女友们，和帐篷外的小伙子们对唱，前者继续表达依依不舍之情，后者告诉新娘已经嫁人、成了一名家庭主妇。这种阿依特斯曲调较为轻松活泼，被称为"阿吾—加尔"，又因为每句唱词后面大都要加一个"加尔—加尔"的短句，所以也被称为"加尔—加尔"。①

这种情境性表演的本质，正如理查德·鲍曼所言，在于现场的交流。② 它首先发生在对唱的两位歌手之间，二者通过你一段我一段的口才竞技，仪式性地展开相互的"攻击"。另一方面，即便二者之间的竞争再激烈，他们也从来不会忘记眼前的受众。阿肯们在阿依特斯开场时往往会面面俱到，把眼前的"情境"与"事件"（event）直接转化为诗行。以纳戈曼和贾米哈在柏林洪堡大学的第一场对唱为例，由年长一些的男阿肯纳戈曼开头，他唱道：

  作为男人不支持自己的民族
  这是民族的耻辱
  辜负了民族的期望是男人的错
  召唤我像白骏马的灵感
  我会成为滋润柏林的雨
  带着诗歌进军欧洲
  感觉像阿特拉爷爷一般
  哺育了像阿拜、乔汗、克勒士等的民族
  是我的哈萨克族
  有着辽阔的阿勒泰、塔尔巴合台、伊犁
  我携带着祝福来到这里
  朋友愿神明的光芒照耀着你
  望我们被幸福围绕
  在柏林加把劲来
  像叶德圪（部落）的金骏马一样

  祈祷着真主保佑得到了唱的轮次

---

① 民俗阿依特斯之外还有宗教阿依特斯，即在萨满驱邪仪式上所唱的"巴迪克"，其功能在于为人、畜治病，且多在晚间举行，称"巴迪克之夜"。参见加尔肯·阿布力孜《论阿依特斯的种类》，新疆维吾尔自治区文化厅编《哈萨克族阿依特斯论文集》，新疆人民出版社2010年版，第132—151页。
② 该作者认为，"以表演为中心（performance-centered）的理念，要求通过表演自身来研究口头艺术。在这一方法中，对语言特征在形式上的巧妙操纵让位于表演的本质，而表演在本质上可被视为和界定为一种交流的方式（a mode of communication）"。引自理查德·鲍曼《作为表演的口头艺术》，杨利慧、安德明译，广西师范大学出版社2008年版，第8页。

我的诗歌在寓意上不会出错
在我身边的是我的对手贾米哈
你是位有鹰眼的猎手
曾战胜哈里哈和哈那提别克
对自己的艺术天赋充满自信
你是位阿巴克（部落）的姑娘
大家尊重你让你坐上尊位
我总是娇惯可爱的你
怎么突然长大
像只獾一样，像水壶（又圆又胖）
我给你这样的评价
你是不是很迫不及待
别着急，我会把轮次给你
那现在尽情地开始阿依特斯吧
就像龙卷风的咆哮一般，哎吔吔吔①

在这里纳戈曼唱出了他和贾米哈二人前来欧洲弹唱的语境与心境：他们肩负着民族的期望而来，就像曾经进军欧洲的先辈阿特拉那样，希望能不负众望，让自己的歌声变成"滋润柏林的雨"。他也介绍了自己和对手贾米哈出身的部落，以及他们共同归属的民族——哈萨克。同时他把祝福送给了眼前陌生的异国听众，鼓励同伴"加把劲"，并马上开始了第一轮的调侃，取笑她矮胖的身体特征和"迫不及待"想要出场的情形，为她的出场做好准备。

当然这样的开头不会是千篇一律的，而是根据每一次的场景都会发生变化。几天后，我们离开柏林，到了莱茵河畔的波恩，在波恩大学俱乐部举行"哈萨克阿肯阿依特斯与中亚口头传统"的学术研讨会，晚上请两位阿肯为出席会议的学者们做现场表演。同样是纳戈曼开头，这回他唱道：

以安拉的名义开始梳理语词
我们是以精辟的语言来开拓前方道路的青年
特意感谢你们
因为你们宣传了哈萨克的阿依特斯
从历史上说起
我们是赛人、匈奴和突厥的后代
跟卫拉特打仗二百多年

---

① 齐纳尔、达尔恩别克、卡力克波力根据演唱的录像带转写、翻译，努尔巴哈提·吐尔逊、叶丽努尔·朱马拜校对。下同。

也有过像野鹿受猎人的惊吓般恐慌
在阿布赉汗时期恢复士气
在白宫（毡房）前竖起一面面旗子
哈班巴依、波跟巴依等英雄们带领军队
全力打垮了准噶尔
我们带来了这个民族的问候
我们是勇敢青年
不断复述长辈们的话
贾米哈，祝你的阿依特斯顺利
安拉又让我们碰面
为了编诗我会更加努力
像平时一样别失去你的耐心
在莱茵河边唱好
我们可能不会再有这种机会
该把轮次给贾米哈了
像奶奶们的黑肥皂的美丽女孩，哎呗呗呗

这段唱词中只有开首一句"以安拉的名义开始梳理语词"和最后的感叹词"哎呗呗呗"属程式性的套话，其他全都是针对当时的特殊情境即兴编唱的诗行。面对前来参加会议和倾听演唱的各国学者们，纳戈曼先是表示了感谢，然后一连用八句歌词，精辟地叙述了哈萨克的历史。接着，他强调了自己和贾米哈今天是作为这个民族的儿女和代表出现在这里，并鼓励对方唱好，提醒她不要失去耐心，这样的机会一生也许只有一次！最后一句则是对贾米哈的调侃，为她的弹唱提供话头，并让听众们把注意力转向她那一边。

那么贾米哈是怎样回应的呢？在柏林，她接口唱道：

啊，朋友你说什么我们都高兴
希望阿依特斯永驻人间
不知柯尔克孜朋友在议论什么
得出了这样一个结论
柯尔克孜、哈萨克自古以来是一个家族
我们会沉浸在见到亲人们的喜悦中

……

你让我唱我就尽情地唱
阿肯是不会止步在赛马跟前的

自古以来就是突厥根源、哈萨克血统
我来讲述、翻阅我的历史
几百年以来保留着阿依特斯
是神圣的哈萨克古老智者的功劳
为了研究哈萨克族的阿依特斯
外国的学者们积极参与
我对这个国家的学习精神十分佩服
我高兴得心花怒放
研究完自己国家的历史
背诵完了另一民族的史诗
诗词如绸缎般绚丽多彩
在绸缎之神旁翩翩起舞
女儿的诗歌如同马奶子一样
让他们如痴如醉
柏林的所有人都来倾听
小巧可爱的姑娘弹唱吧
家乡将我抚养成为一个心灵手巧的姑娘
别想用讽刺的话语打败我的信心
母亲曾引导你做个真诚的人
你的讽刺会使我越战越勇，
狗獾是越打越肥胖
大家多次让我们两人对比较量
我们要为去往梦想的巅峰而不懈努力
在新疆大名鼎鼎的阿肯
拥有英雄的优秀血统

今天我们满心欢喜
人们惊讶于阿依特斯的神奇
让我们的盛会响彻德国首都的天空
在柏林进行了阿依特斯我们还有什么愿望

贾米哈在这里也是首先抒发了自己激动和欢喜的心情。接应纳戈曼刚才的话语，她更进一步完善了对发生这次对唱的情境与事件的描述："为了研究哈萨克族的阿依特斯，外国的科学家们积极参与"。因为现场的听众多是洪堡大学的学者，一批研究柯尔克孜语言文化的专家，所以她把哈萨克和柯尔克孜的友谊放到开始来歌颂，并因有人在交头接耳（现场翻译）而开他们的玩笑。她也针对纳戈曼要自己加把劲的勉励，立志为实现梦想而"不懈努力"，唱出了"柏林的所有人都来倾听"、"让我们的盛会响彻德国首都的天空"等豪言壮语。为了造成有趣的氛围，她又幽默地夸自己是"小巧可爱的姑娘"，宣称自己的"诗词如绸缎般绚丽多彩"、"诗歌如同马奶子一样，让他们如痴如醉"。

不仅开场白如此，在演唱的过程中，阿肯们也会不断地把周围发生的事件，即刻编入唱词当中。像贾米哈故意批评有些听众"在议论什么"。在波恩大学对唱时，她也使用了类似的手法：

> 哎，我愿意对唱到天亮
> 宁静的夜、宁静的世界会颤抖
> 我们对这当地的亲戚特别满意
> 都有着热情好客的美德
> 而跟我们一起来的
> 大姐大哥怎么会窃窃私语
> 在这种场合应该用心倾听
> 骏马没人精心照顾，也不会驰骋万里，哎呗呗呗

和老成持重、擅长用典、诗味浓重的纳戈曼相比，贾米哈似乎更善于用平白的话语来表达自己的所思所感。如当纳戈曼把她比喻成被捕猎的狗獾时，她马上机敏而幽默地回应道：

> 哎，贾米哈来称赞好哥哥
> 你肩负着民族的希望
> 你说狗獾从山涧也抓得到
> 你向我炫耀自己的能力
> 但德国有着严谨的法律
> 你却没有掌握一条
> 不仅保护狗獾甚至保护蚂蚁
> 这个国家的法律你还不懂
> 所以贾米哈备受保护
> 想碰我要小心会被抓住

不断地把对手和听众考虑进来，唱出现场的情境与事件，并编出风趣的话语来引逗对手，以博得听众们的会心一笑，这就是阿依特斯作为表演的口头艺术的魅力所在。由于这种交流都是即时的、随机的，而不是程式化的、事先准备好的，所以特别需要阿肯和听众之间能够达成良性的互动与交流。否则一旦失去回应，阿肯们的情绪就可能低落，创作欲望与现场编诗能力也会大大下降；他们的艺术就会变成贾米哈所言的"没人精心照顾的骏马"，"不会驰骋万里"。

二、交流的困境

　　阿肯之间、阿肯与听众之间达成默契的最佳条件，当然是大家都来自同一语言环境，且都相互熟悉。我们在新疆考察时曾听阿肯们介绍，近年来有人尝试着把新疆的阿肯和哈萨克斯坦的阿肯安排在一起对唱，结果由于文化背景不同，常常出现交流不畅的情形。这样的情况我们在新疆特克斯县访问时也有遇到。当时是在一个民俗风情园中，当地政府临时找了几对阿肯来为我们演唱，也许是县领导事先对他们提了些要求，但也可能是因为他们与我们素不相识的缘故，阿肯们比较拘谨，只是例行公事地表演了几段，内容也是礼节性，显然没能表现出他们应有的水平。

　　对于表演中的阿肯们来说，听众的回应如简单的喝彩声、掌声和笑声等，都是至关重要的。在德国访问期间，两位阿肯在柏林、波恩等地共表演了四场。在柏林举行的第一场演唱是在洪堡大学的中亚研究所，其中一些学者能听懂哈萨克语，并不时地报以掌声和欢笑声，这使得两位年轻人大受鼓舞。但第二天在中国文化中心，来了二十多个德国人或旅德华人，大家都不懂哈萨克语。席间，听众们出于对歌手的尊重，就像在音乐厅欣赏古典音乐那样，一直绷着脸孔静静地倾听，中途既不鼓掌也不喝彩。唱完这场之后，贾米哈似乎非常泄气。我们来听听她在第三场时是怎么"抱怨"的吧：

>哎，阿肯们有阿拉希（群众）时更有生命力
>为了梦想之地飞翔不会疲倦
>哈萨克神奇的阿依特斯
>是为后代传下来的
>德国之行已经是五天了
>我们的心情像花儿怒放般开心
>第一天观众多、心情也好
>他们也非常珍惜阿肯对唱
>第二天来了将近二十个德国人
>因为听不懂内容他们摇头
>第三天来了不到十个研究者
>他们也要衡量我们的才能
>这样下去谁知会怎么样
>听众比阿肯少了很多，哎呸呸呸

　　当交流遇到困境时，阿肯们只有通过互相激励来打气了。年长些的纳戈曼一边思索着该怎样来取悦眼前这些陌生人，一边还在安慰着同伴贾米哈：

怎么唱才能符合你们的心意
有你们做听众我的诗歌才会更加精彩
约翰森奶奶①也来到现场
是为了欣赏盛会
手上有了像冬不拉的遗产
诗会给我们无穷的力量
地木拉提、曼拜特、王教授在
遇到了像巴格达提这样的知音
这里受到了很多专家的造访
不要发愁没有人听弹唱
我认为这些人
能顶一千个人的倾听哦，哎吔吔吔

他的这一招固然灵验，似乎说服了贾米哈。后者回唱道：

哎，妹妹会按你说的做
会唱关于你的幽默的诗
有哥哥的人会有出路
有哥哥在我还会为我的路发愁吗
那是真正的研究者们在倾听
有哈萨克在阿依特斯就不会消失
如果研究者们研究我们的阿依特斯
全世界就会了解哈萨克族

哎，你将理想的鸟儿放飞向了天空
珍贵的哥哥希望你一切顺利
为后代留下你的诗做他们的榜样
俗话说：有能力的时候做力所能及的事
将幽默诙谐融入生活的哈萨克族
有什么能比得上已放飞的灵感之鸟
哥哥你那辉煌的事迹
似乎已向全世界发出五彩光芒
德国的男人都是脱了顶的
基因也不像穆斯林

---

① 指科隆大学民族学研究所荣休教授 Ulla Johansen。

哎，在新疆年轻人中只有你是谢顶
请你找出合适的理由来作答
假如说为人民编诗而脱发
这只是你在尴尬时为自己找的借口
你的头发稀少的原因
是否是化学物品所致
还是这原本稀少的头发
在嫂子的抚摸下一扫而光了吗

于是两个人开始就"谢顶"的问题展开了口角，以下的几段唱词十分精彩：

纳戈曼：
……
仔细思考一下这个世界
会存在各种各样的头
有着大耳朵的，有油腻鼻子的，有智慧的头
也有人人见而躲之的
双手被手铐铐上
犯过罪的头
而我的这个头
日益稀少的头发
是因为为人民（编诗）多发愁
是有智慧、有价值的头
但你会懂得么
贾米哈你这傻子头

贾米哈：
哎，不要在陌生人前说不合适的话
这不像是我哥能说的话
那为了能超过我哥
我就不得不找一个谢顶子
哎吔吔吔

你像羚羊似的奔跑
我加入了阿肯的队伍里
我从不花时间去想什么男人

只想着天天往馕上抹黄油
在此跟纳戈曼哥进行对唱
命运之神安排我们来到德国
是谢顶子还是别的，我不得而知
也不知会遇到怎样的男人
我的命运掌握在安拉手中
何须在途中挑选别人
哥哥还未到而立之年
尽管头发稀少像老人一般
从外表看似乎非常彪悍
是不是一部分头发被嫂子摸光
另一部分头发也已经掉光
是因为你从年少开始为人民（编诗）发愁
因为头发的脱落
也像和尚一般
头的大部分都成了前额，哎吔吔吔

纳戈曼：
你不停地说着漂亮的话
希望你不要唱出随意的诗歌
拿出哈萨克女孩的修养来
注意你的言行举止
但是你嘲笑了你的大哥
在那里信口开河
哈萨克有句名言"聪明的头上不长毛"
在盛开的生命之花中
如果我有属于哈萨克的灵性
希望这个灵性能降临在我一生的某一天
贾米哈，希望你懂得这个
为了阿依特斯我从不放弃
在亚洲时已稀少的头发
来到德国你把剩余的都拔掉了，哎吔吔吔
……
我们是突厥联盟的一支
是生活中充满了歌声的民族
贾米哈祝福你幸福

可爱漂亮的你
希望你永远陪在我的身边
尽管还没摆脱你的麻烦
我们是伟大哈萨克的儿女
母亲将歌曲的精华灌输于我
如果你是真正的阿肯
就把这种传统继续下去
从生活中要学得的还有很多
给这些人留下一个好的印象
让他们体会一下哈萨克族多彩的世界，哎咃咃咃

贾米哈：
哎，你的付出怎么会没有回报
大哥你将传统一一列清
朋友是真心为你着想
我只是开个玩笑你就发火
我是故意让你灵感的火花不断涌现
看起来你挺憔悴的
我觉得做谢顶子也挺好的
有些事不要不懂装懂
在经济危机时就占了便宜
能节约香皂和梳子吧，哎咃咃咃
……

  两位阿肯就这么自娱自乐地编唱出了一连串美妙的诗行，完成了这场精彩的对唱。这一方面在于他们过人的表演能力，另一方面或许也因为他们心里非常清楚：这样的困难只是暂时的，几天后回到家乡，一切就会回归正常。所以他们开始情不自禁地用对家乡的回忆和想象，来弥补眼前的空虚，就像纳戈曼在波恩对贾米哈唱的那样：

你要像小马驹一样快乐地玩耍
这样你哥才时刻心满意足
为了让我宣传介绍哈萨克的阿依特斯
家乡人给予我真心的祝愿
……

这里五彩缤纷的生活

> 这种生活就是充满歌声的日子
> 幽默诙谐已融入哈萨克族的生活
> 贾米哈我不会介意你的玩笑
> 我会找机会返还于你
> 千万别以为我会放在心里
> 把朋友们请到家乡
> 唱出了哈萨克阿依特斯的天籁之音
> 伊犁、阿勒泰、塔城、叶米里河等
> 如画一般的美景都让他们去欣赏欣赏
> 在哈萨克的大草原欢迎他们
> 让他们品尝我们的马奶子（酒）

初次来到欧洲的两位阿肯，不仅要面对语言交流的困境，而且也要面对种种的"文化冲击"（culture shock），其中的部分经历也被贾米哈用调侃的口吻编进了诗歌当中。比如在贾米哈眼中，德国人总是一脸严肃，一点也不热情，还总是给他们吃比萨饼、汉堡包、生蔬菜（沙拉），并且总是步行而没有车接车送。这一切都和她家乡的习俗完全不同：要是有尊贵的客人来到哈萨克的毡房中，主人们不都是要杀马宰羊的吗？于是，这种鲜明的对比也出现在她的歌词中：

> 走在德国的首都
> 找不到奶茶和面食
> 观察首都的每个餐厅
> 那啤酒享誉全世界
> 尝一口就会头晕成醉
> 给你提供蔬菜和汉堡
> 如果不吃就会饥肠辘辘[①]

> 哎，大哥你肩负着民族的希望
> 希望你的光荣事迹在哈萨克中传颂
> 你要真将亲戚请到家乡
> 可以说我们能够款待他们
> 我是个很大方的克列依部落的女孩
> 从不会因招待客人而说累
> 在那边不会找到叫比萨（饼）的东西

---

① 选自2011年5月7日在洪堡大学的对唱。

>   你们去了给你们宰羊和小马
>   会看到哈萨克的宽容面貌
>   我们会非常欢迎你们的到来，哎吡吡吡
>
>   哎，我们一直尊敬的大哥
>   秋风吹散了想念的梦
>   非常感谢地木拉提领导
>   这一次的路途很顺利
>   未来我们还会去更多大陆造访
>   希望您能创造出更多丰功伟绩
>   想向亲友开一个小小玩笑
>   希望您露出温暖的笑容
>   到这里以来一直都是徒步
>   尽管周围都是交通工具
>   整天走着去逛街
>   我们的鞋也快烂掉了
>   害怕地木拉提领导（不敢说）
>   两脚都不管动了
>   虽然大限没从安拉那里下来
>   但却受到了人间的惩罚，哎吡吡吡[1]

这些话语通过现场其他专家的翻译，都一一传到了我们的耳中。从那以后，负责接待的我们再也不敢让他们徒步行走了，出门时尽量坐公共汽车或叫出租车。从这个细节中我们也可以了解到，哈萨克阿肯是一群多么聪明且善于交流的人。据说在古代，有的哈萨克歌手可以凭靠三寸不烂之舌，去说服统治者做一些符合人民利益的事情。就是在今天，他们也常常通过善意的玩笑，在轻松愉快的气氛中讽谏领导或批评时政。例如领队的新疆师范大学历史学与民族学院院长地木拉提教授，因为怕两位阿肯掉队，一路上都让他们跟着自己。所以在柏林对唱时，贾米哈就讽刺他说：

>   我们到柏林已经两天了
>   行为举止都是合法的
>   逛逛街我们会迷路
>   不知道而盘桓
>   领导想平安无事（把我们）带回去

---

[1] 选自 2011 年 5 月 11 日在波恩大学的对唱。

晚上都不能安心睡觉
再三点我们这些人的名
就像我们会丢失
在新疆他要清点教学课时
在柏林则为每天点名而疲倦了，哎呸呸呸①

三、民族的怎样才能成为世界的

　　哈萨克阿肯纳戈曼和贾米哈在跨文化语境中所遇到的交流困境，对他们来说或许只是偶发事件，可以凭借个人能力加以克服。但我们可以想象，当这样的困境不是偶然而成为必然时，即便再有智慧再有勇气的阿肯，一定也无法超越。有一句流行的话："越是民族的，就越是世界的。"② 鲁迅先生也说过，"有地方色彩的，倒容易成为世界的"。③ 两种说法都是指向一种世界性的文学和艺术。但它们所说的只是一种可能性，可能并不等于必然，所以无论如何都不能被简单化为"民族的就是世界的"。尤其是在各国民族主义高涨的今天，民族的要成为世界的，实非易事。正如刘大先所言："'世界主义'的思潮早在18世纪就盛行一时。1827年，歌德通过若干文章、信件和谈话，普及了'世界文学'这一概念。但是，20世纪的民族自觉自立运动在世界范围内的普及和民族国家的建立，却使得'世界主义'只是一种美好的理想。"④

　　即便没有民族意识在背后推波助澜，世界化也非易事。中国的古典名著《红楼梦》，一旦出了国门、到了欧洲，就不能为大多数人所赏识。在德国，直到2007年才出现了一个完整的德译本⑤；之前所流行的只是一个删节版的译本，而其中被删去的，恰恰就包括被汉语母语者视作最精彩部分的诗词⑥。令中国的文学爱好者感到难以理解的，还有像高行健获得2000年诺贝尔文学奖这样的事件。高氏的文学真的有那么好么？除了评委会的政治偏向之外，是否还有其他因素在作怪？考虑到高行健具有法语科班出身的背景和他对于这门外语的精湛掌握，或许我们会联想起德国汉学家顾彬对于中国当代作家"不懂外语"现象的批评。精通一门母语之外的语言，所解决的或许并非只是语言本身的问题，而是能赋予作者一种超越自身文化的国际视野，让他们在创作时顾及世界性的价值观念和审美趣味。

　　或许有人认为，只要有好的传译就可以解决一切。然而，凡有翻译经验的人都知道，语

---

① 选自2011年5月7日在柏林洪堡大学的对唱。
② 此语出处不详。有人认为是歌德所言，但歌德的原话似乎并非如此。
③ 《致陈烟桥》，1934年4月19日，见《鲁迅全集》第13卷，人民文学出版社2005年版，第81页。
④ 刘大先：《地方色彩、世界主义与中介》，载《中国民族报》2010年4月9日。
⑤ *Der Traum der Roten Kammer oder Die Geschichte vom Stein*, übersetzt von Rainer Schwarz & Martin Wösler, Bochum: Europäischer Universitätsverlag, 2007–2009.
⑥ *Der Traum der Roten Kammer*, übersetzt von Frank Kuhn, Insel Verlag, 1932.

言的转换又是一件多么艰难和多么不可靠的事情。即便语言能力再高、责任心再强的译者，也难免因这样那样的原因导致误读。一部好的文学作品经过翻译，所传达的美学趣味与文化内涵也一定会大打折扣。有时候即便语言的转写（直译）不成问题，但由于文化背景的不同，在阅读理解上也会出现偏差。对此我们在事后整理对唱文本时深有体会。比如在洪堡大学的第一段唱词，转写和直译后的文本是这样的：

Er　tuip　holdamasa　eline　min
男　生　不支持　民族　错

　el　umietien　ahtamaw　erine　min
民族　希望　辜负　男　错

xaqirsam　xabitimning　xalhuyrigin
　叫　　灵感　　白骏马

Berlynning　jangbiri　bop　togilemin
柏林的　　雨　成　下（我）

Olengmen　jorih　tarthan　evropaga
　诗歌　　进军　　欧洲

Attyla　babama　uhsap　sezilemin
阿特拉　爷爷　像　觉得

Abay　xohan　khilxtay　ghalim　tughan
阿拜　乔汗　克勒士　学者　出生

khazakh　deytin　el　edi　mening　elim
哈萨克族　叫　民族　是　我的　民族

arda　altay　tarbaghatay　khart　ileden
辽阔　阿勒泰　塔尔巴合台　老　伊犁

Sizderge　salem　aytip　kelgen　edim
您们　问好　说　来　是的（我）

Assalaw　maghalykum　aghayingha
　　你们好　　　朋友

tek　tolsin　jakhsilikhpen　aynalamiz
只有　满　　好事　　　周围

Berlyinde　bel　bosatpay　bir　calayin
在柏林　腰　松　一会　摔到

Altin　jal　tulparinday　edigening
金　马鬃　骏马一样　叶德圪的

Alghan　song　alla　jarlap　soz　kezegin
得到　后　真主　保佑　词　轮次

aryne	khate	ketpes	mengzegenim
当然	错	过去	我的意思

Jamygha	ariptesim	khasimdaghi	
贾米哈	我的对手	在我身边	

huralaydi	kozge	atkhan	mergen	eding
雀鸟	眼睛	击中	射击手	是

khatirip	halyha	men	khanatbekti
整	哈里哈	和	哈那提别克

Ozingning	oneringe	sengen	eding
自己的	艺术天分	相信	是

Abahha	tartip	tuwghan	bir	khiz	eding
阿巴克（部落）	像	出生的	一个	姑娘	是

El	khurmettep	beretin	torden	orin
大家	尊重	给	尊位	位置

Torsihtay	dep	jurwxiem	erkeletip
水壶	以为	在想	娇惯

Neboldi	munxalih	tez	ozgerering
怎了么	这么	快	变化

Borsihtay	hiz	bop	endi	xiga	kelding
像獾的	姑娘	成	现在	出	来了

Osilay	bir	bagangdi	men	beremin
这样	一个	评价	我	给你

Tihirxip	alasatip	otirmising
焦急	慌	坐着

Asihpa	soz	kezegin	men	beremin
别急	词	轮次	我	给你

Al	endi	arindatip	aytis	basta
那	现在	喧哗地	阿依特斯	开始

Jeti	bal	jel	sohsin	jelbezeging
七	级	风	刮风	鱼鳃

对于不懂哈萨克语的人来说，对这样的文本根本无从着手，其中的一些专名和象征性表达，比如"阿拉希""卫特拉""白宫""白旗""白骏马""白味""白色的祝福""金骏马""红舌头"等，只有通过母语研究者的"二次翻译"才能读懂。整个翻译的过程就必须经过以下四个环节：（1）从把阿肯歌手的口头文本转化为哈萨克语（阿拉伯字母或拉丁字母）的书写文本；（2）将歌词按照原本的语序一字一句地转换为汉语文本；（3）经过哈萨克语母语学者的"二次翻译"，重新调整语法、解释单词；（4）由汉语母语学者或精通汉语的哈萨克学者梳理润色全文，完成翻译。

经过这样的四次转换，现场表演所具有的审美与文化内涵，究竟丧失掉了多少？当我们通过现场的语言学家那只言片语的翻译，或是在事后通过阅读翻译的文本，来体味阿依特斯的艺术魅力时，我们所能获得的乐趣，能有一位哈萨克本地人所享受到的十分之一吗？于是便出现了这样一种悖论：越是民族的，就越有可能成为世界的，但也越不容易成为世界的。我们今天处在一个文化全球化的时代，中外交流越来越频繁，民族艺术走出国门也变得越来越容易了。但是，只要仔细观察就会发现，能够率先打入国际艺术市场的，往往是一些经过改装的、肤浅单一的艺术形式。戏剧学家傅谨曾一针见血地指出："当我们似乎获得了世界的视野，我们的艺术欣赏范围和审美趣味迅速超越国家与民族的界限时，这种超越的指向却惊人地单调。我们会沮丧地发现，拂去那个日渐丰富的表层，我们所看到的情况与理想相去甚远，我们这个时代的文化娱乐在丰富的背后潜藏着无比的单调，因为这个世界的美学正在被少数几家跨国公司用十分显著的刻意手段所模塑；……"①

正因为此，当今不少国家和民族都对"全球化"和"世界化"怀有一种抵御心理。一些国家试图通过加入联合国教科文组织的《保护非物质文化遗产国际公约》（2003），以确保人类文化的多样化，使得自身的民族文化能逃脱单一化的命运。对于这种心理，中国民俗学家刘魁立先生曾做过如下的表述："在全球化和经济一体化、社会生活现代化的大潮中，我们的民族文化受到外来文化的强势撞击。强势的外来文化会被一些人视为时尚，而时尚久而久之会改变越来越多的人的价值观。面对这种趋向单一的文化模式，人们感到极有必要挖掘和发扬中华民族文化的优秀传统。"② 但保护非物质文化遗产，是否就可以抵御全球化的负面影响？事实上并非所有民族都对此持积极看法。例如欧洲很多国家目前都还不是该公约的缔约国，德国也属其中之一。2010 年年底，笔者在走访巴伐利亚州家乡文化保护协会总理事沃尔兹穆勒（Martin Wölzmüller）时了解到，德国也正在考虑是否加入该公约，这对于发展地方文化或许有益。但包括沃尔兹穆勒本人在内的很多有关人士都担心，在挑选文化事项申报进入联合国教科文组织的"非遗"代表作名录时，是不是真的能够贯彻本项活动的初衷？他诙谐地说：人们或许会把（为旅游者而举办的）慕尼黑十月（啤酒）节，当成德国的非物质文化遗产代表来"保护"，同时却将许多真正值得保护的民俗事项置之度外。的确，"十月（啤酒）节"虽然是为吸引游客而打造的节日，但在国内外都很著名，几已成为德意志民族文化的"标志"。和它相比，那些名不见经传的地方性民间文化，则恐难以进入世界的视野，不会得到外界的充分认可。

调查和清理非物质文化遗产，将其列入名录，对其历史和现状进行研究，并对其传承人给予关注和支持，政府和学术界目前所能做的，似乎也只有这些了。但若要让这些民族的文化遗产最终变为"世界的""人类共享的"，是否还得依靠跨国公司、张艺谋或萨顶顶等流行艺术家呢？民族的文学与艺术如何才能在全球化的语境中求得自身的生存与发展？这是本文在最后所要提出的问题。它的答案还有待于在今后的研究中去寻找。

---

① 傅谨：《全球化时代的中国戏剧》，《艺术百家》2008 年第 6 期，第 7 页。
② 刘魁立：《论全球化背景下的中国非物质文化遗产保护》，《河南社会科学》2007 年第 1 期，第 27—28 页。

持续关注的问题

关于"非遗"概念的再界定

苑 利 顾 军[*]

户县农民画、金山农民画算不算非物质文化遗产？历史上的"泰山封禅"算不算非物质文化遗产？政府组织的大型公祭活动、张艺谋编导的大型实景演出《印象刘三姐》算不算非物质文化遗产？缠足、典妻抑或人人都会的传统手艺算不算非物质文化遗产？四合院、古村落算不算非物质文化遗产？雷锋精神、毛泽东思想算不算非物质文化遗产？这里，我想明确告诉大家的是，上述事例都算不上非物质文化遗产。但在现实生活中，甚至在申报过程中，为什么会有此类问题出现呢？很简单，是我们的非物质文化遗产观出了问题；再具体点儿说，是我们对非物质文化遗产的理解出现了问题。

就像材料学一定要弄清楚"什么是材料"，历史学一定要搞明白"什么是历史"一样，非物质文化遗产学在展开它的学术论战之前，也应该把"什么是非物质文化遗产"讲得清清楚楚，明明白白。这是这门学科的逻辑起点。如果我们在"什么是非物质文化遗产"这个问题上出了错，在这门学科的逻辑起点上出了错，我们在今后的非遗认定过程中，就会出现种种偏差——这就像我们小时候自己给自己系扣子——第一个扣子系错了，以后所有的扣子都会一错到底。那么，为什么说上述事例不是非遗呢？下面，我们就集中笔墨，谈谈这个问题。

一、为什么说户县农民画、金山农民画不是非遗？

从传承时间的角度看，非物质文化遗产应具有悠久的历史（至少要有100年以上的历史）。所以产生于20世纪50年代的户县农民画以及产生于20世纪70年代的金山农民画，因时间不足百年，故现在都还不能被认定为非物质文化遗产。

活态传承是非物质文化遗产的重要特征。但这并不意味着所有能以活态形式原汁原味流传至今的文化事项都能成为非物质文化遗产。譬如我们经常谈及的户县农民画、金山农民画等，都因在传承时限上，尚没有达到非物质文化遗产的准入门槛——必须具有100年以上的

---

[*] 苑利，中国艺术研究院研究员；顾军，北京联合大学教授。

历史，故无法认定为非物质文化遗产。

将我国非物质文化遗产准入门槛限定在100年以上，一是秉承世界上许多国家认定物质文化遗产的传统，二是因为清末民初是我国传统手工技术、传统表演艺术以及传统节日仪式等发展过程中的最后一个高峰期。将这一时期（包括这一时期之前）产生并流传至今的优秀遗产钩沉出来，对于非物质文化遗产保护而言，无疑会起到事半功倍的作用。当然，百年历史只是我们对非物质文化遗产在时限上设下的一个最为基本的准入门槛。其实，像中国这样一个具有五千年文明史的文明古国，一般的非物质文化遗产事项通常也都会有数百年乃至上千年历史——昆曲、京剧等表演艺术至少有数百年的历史，木版年画至少有近千年的历史，风筝制作有近两千年的历史，而像钻木取火这样的古老技术等，至少也有几十万年的历史。因此，我们将时间下限限定在百年以上，更多的是将"百年"理解为非遗申报的一个准入性门槛。这是因为我们所说的"遗产"，应该是指财富创造者亡故后留给我们的一笔文化财富。如果该文化财富的创造者尚健在人世，我们怎么会将他赠予给我们的文化财富称为"文化遗产"呢？

其实，在非物质文化遗产遴选过程中，各国对非物质文化遗产都有一定的时限上的限定。以日韩等国为例，这些国家虽然对非物质文化遗产的准入门槛不曾有过明确的时间上的限定，但历史最短者，通常也都控制在百年以上。可见，这一标准的制定，对于绝大多数国家来说显然是比较合适的。

需要说明的是，我们所说的百年，并非特指某一事物，而是泛指某类事物。只要某类事物已经具有百年以上的历史，其他条件也已具备，该项目便有了评选非物质文化遗产的资格。

二、为什么说历史上的"泰山封禅"不是非遗？

从传承形态看，非物质文化遗产都应以活态形式传承至今。所以历史上确实存在，但现在已经消失了的类似"泰山封禅"一类的项目，都不能申报非物质文化遗产。

有人认为非物质文化遗产不一定是活态的，即使已经消失，只要具有历史认识价值，或是通过文献、实物可以复原者，均可申报非物质文化遗产。对于这种说法我们并不认同。

非物质文化遗产与物质文化遗产的最大区别，就是它的"活态"性。也就是说，所谓的非物质文化遗产，必须是以活态的形式原汁原味传承至今的。那些历史上确实存在，但后来消失了的传统文化事项，哪怕具有非常重要的历史价值、文化价值、艺术价值、社会价值和科学价值，也不能申报非物质文化遗产。譬如，泰山封禅始自秦朝，是典型的传统文化。自秦始皇登泰山祭天开始，之后许多朝代的帝王一旦登基，都会率群臣赴泰山祭天以示神威，仪式相当隆重。但即或如此，这类项目也不能申报非物质文化遗产。因为尽管泰山封禅历史上确有其事，但该仪式早在宋代就已经绝迹（最后一次泰山封禅是在宋真宗赵恒大中祥符元年——公元1008年），像这样已经绝迹了1000多年的传统文化事项，即或再优秀也无法申报非物质文化遗产。

三、为什么说政府组织的大型公祭活动不是非遗？

从生存状态看，非物质文化遗产应以"原汁原味"的面貌传承至今。所以人为改造、打造的各种大型公祭活动不是非物质文化遗产。

为弘扬地方文化，打造地方名片，许多地方都在挖掘历史上的地方名人，并为之举行大型公祭活动（所谓公祭特指由当地政府举办的各种大型祭祀活动）。从某种角度来说，这些大型公祭活动尽管不乏正面意义，但与非物质文化遗产无关。

判断一个公祭活动是不是非物质文化遗产，首先要看这些活动历史上是否真实存在，其次还要看它们是否以活态的形式原汁原味传承至今。如果这些公祭活动历史上就有，且以活态形式原汁原味传承至今，那么，这些祭祀活动很有可能就是非物质文化遗产。如果历史上没有，仪式是当地政府自己"打造"出来的，或是历史上确有其事，但后因各种原因早已中断而今又重新恢复起来者，通常都不能视之为非物质文化遗产。

判断一个公祭活动的真伪，最简单的办法就是看传承人。如果找不到当年主持仪式的祭司（理论上的非物质文化遗产传承人），说该仪式为活态传承就是一句空话。实地调查告诉我们，中原历史上的公祭活动，绝大多数已经断流，更没有哪位传承人能将古代公祭的所有程式原汁原味地传承下来。今天我们所看到的"公祭"活动除"名分"外，几乎与历史上的公祭活动无任何关系——他们所用舞蹈是今天的编导们演绎出来的"古代舞蹈"，他们所用音乐是今天的音乐家们创作出来的"古代音乐"，他们所用服饰是今天的服装设计师设计出来的"古代服饰"，他们所用祭品也多是今天的策划大师们从古书中抄袭过来的"古代祭品"。如此面目全非的"公祭"活动，会有什么历史价值？还有什么资格参评非物质文化遗产！我们并非一味反对公祭活动的参评，而是说参评项目必须要像历史上遗留至今的一块"活化石"一样，将远古信息尽可能多地保存下来。我们之所以反复强调申报项目的"原汁原味"，是因为只有原汁原味保留下来的当时的舞蹈，才能使我们知道几千年前祭祀大典中祭舞的样子；只有原汁原味保留下来的当时的音乐，才能使我们知道几千年前祭祀大典中祭乐的样子；只有原汁原味保留下来的当时的祭服，才能使我们知道几千年前祭祀大典中祭服的样子；只有原汁原味保留下来的当时的祭品，才能使我们知道几千年前祭祀大典中祭品的样子。这样的公祭仪式才有历史价值。如果这所有的一切都是假的，都是当代人"创造"出来的赝品，我们当然没有必要将其视为祖先留给我们的遗产并加以继承。

当然，考虑到这些公祭活动所具有的独特的历史价值，我们并非不可以在评审标准上做出些让步。譬如这些公祭活动仅因"文革"等政治运动发生断流，断流的时间并不长，主持仪式的祭司或是当时参与过这些公祭活动的人还在，那些仪式的亲历者基本上还能将这些公祭仪式原汁原味地呈现出来，我想这些项目仍可申报非物质文化遗产。但如果那些亲历者已经故去，仅凭当时的文字记录来恢复的所谓公祭活动，则是万万不能申报非物质文化遗产的。

四、为什么说缠足、典妻不是非遗？

　　从传承品质看，非物质文化遗产应具备重要价值和优秀基因。所以，不仅缠足、典妻等陋风陋俗不能申报非物质文化遗产，就是人人都会的传统手工技艺也不能申报非物质文化遗产。

　　在许多人眼中，所谓"非物质文化遗产"，就是"传统文化"，也就是我们平常所说的"民俗"。所以有些人认为抽大烟、裹小脚、典妻、纳妾这些"传统文化"事项都可申报"非物质文化遗产"。其实，这些说法不仅大错特错，而且也从根本上误读了非物质文化遗产保护的初衷。

　　毫不讳言，"非物质文化遗产"与"传统文化"确实有其相似的一面。如两者都是历史的产物，都是人类在历史上创造并以各不相同的形式传承至今的，都是历史的一部分，都具有历史认识价值。但两者又确有明显的不同。其中最大的不同，就是非物质文化遗产不是普通的传统文化，而是经过价值衡量之后的传统文化。也就是说，它是从一个民族传统文化中挑选出来的最能代表一个民族优秀传统的传统文化。这与未经价值判断的传统文化是有着本质的区别的。

　　那么，将非物质文化遗产从传统文化中筛选出来的价值衡量标准是什么呢？标准有五：（1）是否具有重要的历史价值；（2）是否具有重要的文化价值；（3）是否具有重要的艺术价值；（4）是否具有重要的科学价值；（5）是否具有重要的社会价值。这五大价值非常突出者就是非物质文化遗产，没有这五大价值或是这五大价值并不特别突出者就不是非物质文化遗产。譬如老奶奶做的猪肉炖粉条、泥鳅钻豆腐、鱼香肉丝、摊煎饼、炸果子并非没有历史价值、科学价值，但与满汉全席、洛阳水席在认识中国烹调艺术发展方面所体现出来的历史价值、科学价值相比，程度肯定不同。非物质文化遗产是一个民族最优秀的传统文化精华，是一个民族优秀的民族传统的重要见证。如红河梯田、龙脊梯田，代表着中国历史上梯田开发技术的最高水平，荣宝斋水印木版年画代表着中国木版年画的最高水平。而这远非一块块技术含量并不是很高的普通梯田、一张张艺术价值并不是很高的普通年画能望其项背的。这就是非物质文化遗产与传统文化的不同之处。但在现实生活中，很多人并没有意识到非物质文化遗产与传统文化的区别，把许多不具有遗产价值的普通传统文化甚至是陋风陋俗的传统，都当成了非物质文化遗产。这种好坏不分、良莠不辨的乱保护，到头来只能给非物质文化遗产保护运动带来不必要的伤害。

　　如果说一定要用一句话将非物质文化遗产与传统文化区别开来，那么，我们是否可以这样说：所谓的"非物质文化遗产"，就是经过价值衡量之后的传统文化。

五、为什么说"道具""实物""制成品"及 "相关场所"不是非遗?

从传承本质看,非物质文化遗产的最大特性就是它的"非物质"性。所以"道具""实物""制成品"及"相关场所"无论对非物质文化遗产保护有多重要,都不是非物质文化遗产。

在2003年联合国教科文组织颁布的《保护非物质文化遗产公约》中有这样一句话:"所谓非物质文化遗产,是指那些被各地人民群众或某些个人视为其文化财富重要组成部分的各种社会活动、讲述艺术、表演艺术、生产生活经验、各种手工艺技能"。如果这个定义说到这儿,问题也许还不会太多。但该定义也许是出于对非遗衍生环境的重视或是别的什么原因,又紧接着补充了一句,说:非物质文化遗产除上述诸项外,还包括"在讲述、表演、实施这些技艺与技能的过程中所使用的各种工具、实物、制成品以及相关场所"。按《公约》解读,我们似乎可以做如下推演——如"徽州传统建筑营造技艺"是非物质文化遗产,那么,与徽州传统建筑营造技艺息息相关的传统建筑工具——庞大的吊车、绞车,与徽州传统建筑营造技艺息息相关的实物——如砖瓦、木材,与徽州传统建筑营造技艺息息相关的制成品——如那些气势恢宏白墙黛瓦的徽州古民居,甚至与徽州传统建筑营造技艺息息相关的各种场所——如西递古村、宏村等等,也都是非物质文化遗产。如果连这些"看得见""摸得着"的物质遗存都变成了"非物质"遗存,还有什么是物质文化遗产呢?如果按此逻辑推演下去,中国的《非物质文化遗产名录》很容易在不远的将来变成《中国名村名录》《中国名宅名录》《中国名酒名录》《中国名画名录》《中国名品名录》……

我们想在此再重申一遍:所谓非物质文化遗产,是指深藏于传承人头脑中的那些知识与经验、技术与技艺,有些工具、实物、制成品甚至某些场所,尽管对我们认识、传承、保护非物质文化遗产有重要帮助,我们也需要通过博物馆的方式加以收藏,但这些工具、实物、制成品以及相关场所的本身并不是非物质文化遗产。

六、为什么说文学作品、道德理念、政治主张不是非遗?

从传承范畴看,非物质文化遗产主要分布在表演艺术(民间文学、表演艺术)、传统工艺技术(传统工艺美术、传统生产知识、传统生活知识)和传统节日仪式(传统节日、传统仪式)三大领域。不在此范畴内的文学作品、道德理念、政治主张都不能视为非物质文化遗产。

非物质文化遗产概念的设定,除应考虑到时限、形态、生态、品质、本质等方面的限定外,还应考虑到范畴方面的限定。非物质文化遗产分布是有规律性的。与许多传统文化不同，非物质文化遗产通常只分布在传统表演艺术、传统工艺技术以及传统节日仪式等三大领域。三大领域之外的传统文化，通常都不是非物质文化遗产。如近年来有人准备申报的"非物质文化遗产"项目——如中国古典四大名著、名人家谱、传统孝道思想，甚至包括某些政治名人的思想精髓与政治主张（如马克思主义、孙中山思想、毛泽东思想）等，尽管也都是历史的产物，也具有重要的历史价值、文化价值、艺术价值、社会价值甚至科学价值，但由于不在非遗三大领域之内，所以，都不能申报非物质文化遗产，更不能进入《非物质文化遗产名录》。

综上所述，一个正确的非物质文化遗产定义，应该对非物质文化遗产进行如下限定：

其一，从传承时限看，非物质文化遗产必须是人类在历史上创造的。时间不足百年者，不能称其为非物质文化遗产。

其次，从传承形态看，非物质文化遗产必须是以活态形式传承至今的。历史上有，但在现实中已经消失了的，或是仅以文字或实物遗存的方式保存至今者，都不能视之为非物质文化遗产。

其三，从传承生态看，非物质文化遗产必须是原汁原味传承至今者，那些已经经过人为改造，特别是已经经过政府、学界、商界甚至包括传承人刻意改造过的"传统文化事项"，都不能视之为非物质文化遗产。

其四，从传承品质看，非物质文化遗产必须具有重要的历史价值、文化价值、艺术价值、科学价值和社会价值，没有上述重要价值者，也不能视之为非物质文化遗产。

其五，从传承本质上看，非物质文化遗产特指那些人类在历史上创造并以活态形式传承至今的传统知识与经验、传统技艺与技能。所以，即或用这些知识与经验、技艺与技能创造出来的实物、工具与制成品，或是与之相关文化场所对保护非物质文化遗产意义重大，也不能视之为非物质文化遗产。因为它们都是物质的存在，这是一个起码的事实。

其六，从传承范畴看，非物质文化遗产特指一个民族传统文化中表演艺术类、工艺技术类与节日仪式类传统文化事项，除此之外的传统文化——如杰出的作家文学作品、著名政治家的政治主张，甚至包括一些传统的优秀的道德思想，都不是非物质文化遗产，都不在非物质文化遗产保护之列。

认识幸福社区的传统实践

——打造可持续的非物质文化遗产保护模型

艾米·基奇纳*

在本篇论文中,我将提出一个在保护非物质文化遗产中使用的"生产性保护"模型的替代方案。通过参与自己文化中的传统艺术形式,人们培养了社区观念、文化自豪感和个人成就感,人们的幸福感因此得到提升,且对个人和社区成员的健康有益。传统行业的从业者们都深刻意识到了传承文化的意义与影响。当问及参与传承的动机时,他们明确表示是受健康和幸福因素的影响。通过参与非物质文化遗产的实践并付诸积极的行动,文化引领者们维持着社区的健康。而我们可以认识并为加深社区幸福范围提供支持,避免由门外汉操作并引入的外部市场来扰乱社区的流程和审美。

通过建立联盟帮助社区维护非物质文化遗产时,以小额贷款、召开会议和个性化援助等形式来认识文化的领导权并提供直接帮助十分有效。加利福尼亚州(以下简称加州)传统艺术联盟的工作方式可以被定义为积极主动,并以从业者和社区为主导,以此来维持文化的价值和实践。该联盟是非政府组织,由我合伙创办并且领导,也被政府指定为全加州民间和传统的艺术、艺术家们提供支持。(见图1)

加州的370万人口呈多元化结构,其中37%为拉美裔,13%为亚裔,6.2%为非洲裔。此外,还有17%的非白种人。超过25%的总人口起源于美国之外。我们已帮助加州保护历史文化元素,让这些传统的表现形式

图1 每年新年和圣诞,人们跳着Wanaragua舞纪念自己的加里福纳祖先,歌颂着祖先抗击殖民者的故事。加州传统艺术联盟资助了南加州的美国加里福纳遗产基金联合会,用以发展加里福纳语和开办文化学院。

(陈思摄)

---

* 艾米·基奇纳,加利福尼亚州传统艺术联盟执行理事。

在动态发展的过程中得以繁荣昌盛、适应各种各样的环境，从而生生不息。加州传统艺术联盟对传统传承者进行认证，与他们做直接交流，并响应他们的需求，为其中的从业者和参与者提供资源，诸如与传统艺术形式相关的实践机会、分享平台、参与渠道和证明文件。

加州传统艺术联盟的诸多项目旨在与社区进程相结合。通过观察我们了解到，驱动非物质文化遗产得以保留并不断兴盛的主要因素根植于社区实践。我们努力推广各种形式，让人们可以实践、欣赏和交流。虽然我们认可对传统形式进行存档、分类、归纳的价值，但还是把主要精力放在了识别传统形式的传输过程、保存方式（保存方式的传承性比它的形式更为重要）和关注它对社区的影响上。这让我们与大众有了更多接触，而不是只关注非物质文化遗产的类型和形式。作为民俗学研究者我们意识到，基于人类的活动、社区的跨文化交流，还有人类在不断情境重置的空间和时间层面的实践，导致了传统形式产生大量连续变化。这些变化过程折射出美国在这短暂历史中的演变，从而塑造了人口多元化的加州，并使之创造自己独特的非物质文化遗产。

图 2　来自加州传统艺术联盟"学徒项目"的艺术大师奥菲利亚·埃斯帕萨（右）和她的女儿罗珊娜·阿伦斯·埃斯帕萨制作了这个"逝者之日"祭坛。在洛杉矶每年 11 月 2 日的万灵节上，用祭坛来纪念已故亲友是墨西哥人的传统。

加州传统艺术联盟有两个招牌项目——"学徒项目"和"生活文化补助金项目"。它们为个人、非正式组织和非政府组织提供小额补助金，让传统艺术在加州一系列文化社区中得以实践。"学徒项目"也像其他 30 个州那样采用类似这样的模式：加州传统艺术联盟为大师级的传统艺术家提供一份含 3000 美元（约合 1.9 万元人民币）的合同，他可以带着一位经验丰富的学徒在半年至一年的课程中进行紧密合作。在竞争激烈的申请流程中，经由学者和从业者组成的评审委员会评选出入围的艺术家。一旦通过，加州传统艺术联盟的工作人员将与每年选出的 17 ～ 20 对师徒密切合作，给他们提供支持，并且监督和记录每一对师徒的进度。（见图 2、图 3、图 4）

图 3　在加州格林菲尔，由加州传统艺术联盟资助、本土文化运动联盟组织的"特里基梦想"项目中，教授学员特里基传统的背带编织技术。

（拉尔·哈拉齐摄）

在"生活文化补助金项目"中，我们为小型非政府组织或社区组织提供了多达 7500 美金（约合 4.7 万元人民币）的补助金，供他们举行大范围的活动，支持文化实践和文化参与，最终目标是保护加州丰富多彩和独特的文化遗产。尽管这笔资金相对还比较少，但我们为每个项目提供了大量有形资源与金融回报。我们把这些参与者当成"投资伙伴"，而非项目的"承担者"。这种关系更像是小额贷款，只是不需要偿还这笔款项。在社区主导型的保护项目中，这些相对较小的投资取得了瞩目成就，其中包括五个主要支持策略。

图 4　乔恩·梅萨·谷埃罗（左）和他的学徒斯坦·罗德里格斯演唱传统库米亚歌曲。谷埃罗是少数几个知道库米亚"野猫"歌唱圈的人。如今，经过多年练习，斯坦·罗德里格斯也开始自己带学生。

（克利思·西蒙摄）

（1）我们工作的核心是传播富有表现力的文化，联盟很大一部分项目也致力于推动此进程。许多学员在参与传统艺术形式时有着强烈动机，希望能和自己的文化遗产维持联系或是产生关联，由此获得重要的认同感与幸福感。与文化遗产的关联基于以下几点：认同感的维持或重建，幸福感的建立，一个通过参与传统文化实践构成的知识库。对一部分人来说，他们可以重新获得曾经失去的认同感。这种认同感可能是自己或父辈在移民过程中、与美国文化同化中丢失的，也有因文化断层遗失的，譬如殖民或像加州原住民那样遭受文化灭绝。

不管是在紧密的一对一学徒制学习还是在小组式学习中，关于传统艺术的学习不仅包括了对艺术形式中技能、技巧方面的训练，还要求对该艺术文化在知识、价值、礼仪和精神上有深层次的理解。通过传统模式的学习，学员可以逐渐理解自己的艺术形式

图 5　意第绪语文化节上的舞者。意第绪语文化节是加州旧金山海湾地区 Klez 的区域节日。在那天人们可以沉浸于犹太音乐和舞蹈中，并且能够学习意第绪的语言和文化。加州传统艺术联盟资助了艺术大师们，让他们和不同年龄段的人积极沟通、密切合作。

（迪·珀尔曼摄）

如何与其他文化的价值、实践相互交融。巴里·托尔肯（Barre Toelken）是一名杰出的民俗学研究者，曾记录过自己和艺术大师艾尔维拉·马特女士（Mrs. Elvira Matt）在加州胡帕原住民区组织制作篮筐。她先教学生唱了几首本土歌曲，这些歌曲是关于人们采集当地作物，努力准备编织材料的场景的。直到最后才她开始教授他们如何编织篮筐。当一个学生问为何

花这么多时间学习唱歌而不是编织篮筐时,她答道:"你们要知道,篮筐便是歌曲的具体表现。"我们只有理解并体验了相关的文化概念,在实践和传统的交融中,才能理解它更深层次的表达。

(2) 第二种策略是通过节日、音乐会和展览来展示和传承非物质文化遗产。通过这些形式繁多的展示,有可能会把相同传统的人联系起来。譬如那些在庆祝意第绪语文化节时演奏犹太音乐和表演传统舞蹈的人们,或者是把非物质文化遗产继承者之外的观众与活动桥接起来。有时候这样的"联系"和"桥接"会在同一情境中发生。(见图5、图6、图7)

(3) 第三种策略是把非物质文化遗产的参与者们召集起来。经证实,该策略颇有成效。它为非物质文化遗产的传承者们提供了大量机会,让他们得以会面、学习、讨论关键问

(4) 在民俗与非物质文化遗产的实践中加快空间的创造和物资的获取,这个策略也很有帮助。加州传统艺术联盟资助了蓝河

图6 2003年,加州传统艺术联盟全国的师徒小组在旧金山美国亚洲艺术博物馆前的台阶上合影。

图7 小维拉德·卡尔顿站在新建的"刷子舞"舞池旁。舞池所在的蓝溪尤罗克村,当地人致力于修复耕地、森林和河流,恢复鲑鱼的生长环境,保护生态资源和动物栖息地,重新发掘本土文化的传统价值和精神价值。村庄的部分建设由加州传统艺术联盟的"生活文化补助金项目"资助。

(艾米·基奇纳摄)

图8 拉姆森奥龙尼的篮筐制作者琳达·亚马内正在大英博物馆做调查。她希望能让族人重拾篮筐制作的传统。她本人已经参加了三次加州传统艺术联盟的"学徒项目"。

(照片由林达·雅马尼提供)

Yorok 原住民，帮他们用红杉树建起了仪式用的舞池。

（5）我们的最后一项支持策略把重点放在了记录、调查和归档上，这其中包含了一系列活动。例如，奥龙尼当地的篮筐制作者琳达·亚马内，通过向隔壁部落学习并且调查了博物馆的篮筐后，重新了解了自己祖先篮筐编织的传统。可以看到，她正在伦敦大英博物馆记录关于拉姆森奥龙尼文化中羽毛和贝壳篮筐的数据。（见图8）

我们接收的社区补助金申请的主要类别由以上这五种支持策略组成，它们都在保存加州文化社区的非物质文化遗产过程中起到了有效作用。在那些成功孕育了保护策略的情况中，民俗和非物质文化遗产继承者们的主要动机来自健康社区的影响。（见图9、图10、图11）

图9 人们在"海地舞蹈锣鼓居所"参加舞蹈工作坊。每年在旧金山海湾地区，这项活动培养着下一代的舞者和音乐家。 （拉尔·哈拉齐摄）

参与传统的程度和个人健康、社区健康、幸福程度之间大有关联。在2006年，为识别这种关联的频率和连贯性，加州传统艺术联盟在加州大学戴维斯分校开展了为期多年的健康调查研究，正式评估了该联盟"学徒项目"和"生活文化补助金项目"参与者的健康状况和其他情况。这项调查研究揭示了以下主题的相关内容——生长，健康，关

图10 泰伊斯瑞哈·艾伦（中）、多利·麦克维（左）和奥蕾莉亚·罗宾斯（右），摄于2006年Ihuk 庆典。

图11 在加州塞尔玛，当地的墨西哥农场工人社区每年都庆祝法蒂玛圣母典礼，表演队伍延绵数英里。 （艾米·基奇纳摄）

于个人、家庭、社区和社会整体的幸福观。

这些主题引人注目,因为其中有个人深刻的见解,涉及艺术事业、多元文化、多种语言、不同年龄群体等领域。从事传统艺术的老师、学习者和展示者作为调查的参与者,以不同的身份形象地展示了参与到民俗传统中的种种益处。他们提到了传统艺术对自己个人层面的提升,诸如增强了自尊心、加强了与传统社区的联系、增进了身心健康。

在家庭层面,参与者们分享了在数代人共同参与的活动中收获到的快乐和意义。他们更加尊敬长者和传统文化,更加关心文化遗产的传承,对一些历史问题带给自己的创伤更加释然。

在邻里或社区层面,所有年龄层的参与者齐聚一堂,相互交流自己的收获。这样就自然而然地产生了更深刻的影响。像艺术家们领悟到自己应该作为社区的引领者和组织者,在单一的文化或种族中,用民俗艺术弥合社区和代际间的鸿沟。

要牢牢记住,个人和社区的幸福感有着重要的影响力,它可以刺激社区、外部政策制定者、政府资助机构和私人慈善事业去保护民俗和非物质文化遗产。自从我们的健康研究报告在 2011 年 10 月发布以来,人们表现了极大的兴趣。联邦艺术和健康机构也启动了新的资助计划来研究文化和健康的交互影响。在参与民俗学和非物质文化遗产项目时健康会发生变化,社区也对自身有了进一步认识,并通过价值和资源的产生来维持文化发展。人们对这点有了更深刻的理解。因为外部市场会潜在扰乱民俗学和非物质文化遗产的活动进程、审美系统和社会背景,所以我相信这个方案优于"生产性保护"。

图 12 艺术大师卢瓦纳·奎特奎特在和她的侄女一同工作。学徒伊莱恩·奎特奎特正在编织一个波曼婴儿摇篮。摇篮由柳木、山茱萸或榛木制成,用来携带和保护孩子。　　　　　(陈思摄)

波莫当地的篮筐编织工卢瓦纳·奎特奎特(Luwana Quitiquit)说过的一句话放在这里十分合适,"讲故事很健康。因为通过讲故事,我的孩子们重新开始接触我的祖母,并且去拜访那些他们之前从不看望的人。让孩子们重拾起了自己的文化,这样子很健康。"(见图 12)

非物质文化遗产保护与族群冲突弥合[①]

宋俊华[*]

一、问题的提出

非遗[②]保护与族群冲突弥合是一对相互关联的社会难题。

以文化差异和碰撞为特征的族群冲突，随着城市化与全球化发展而变得日益突出，尤其是在像中国这样短时间内高速城市化、全球化的国家，族群冲突已经成为社会发展过程的重要问题之一。

最近几年，在中国一些地方爆发了不同族群间的冲突事件。如2011年6月10日至14日广州增城新塘镇大郭村四川籍外来工因摆摊一事与本地人发生冲突，2011年6月1日至6日潮州市古巷镇四川籍外来工因讨薪与本地人发生冲突，2012年6月25日至26日广东中山市沙溪镇因两名少年冲突引发外来人员聚集，2012年6月28日深圳龙岗外来工与警方对峙，等等。这些冲突产生原因各有不同，但无不涉及族群关系问题，族群冲突已经成为影响国家稳定的一个重要因素。

与族群冲突相似，非遗保护也是在人类发展过程中凸显出的问题。其一，城市化和全球化正在迅猛地侵蚀、消解那些基于传统乡土、族群生活的非遗，许多非遗面临被遗忘、被破坏、被改变的危险。其二，人类在社会发展中遇到的许多问题如资源浪费、生态破坏、创新衰退等，可以从非遗保护中找到解决的思路和方法。非遗是可持续发展的保证，已经成为人类的共识。其三，从2001年联合国教科文组织公布首批"人类非物质文化遗产代表作名录"和2003年通过《保护非物质文化遗产公约》至今，非遗保护已经进行了十多年了，取得许多成功的经验，非遗保护已经被大多数国家所认可并参与。

当然，非遗与族群本身也有密切关系。每个族群都有自己的非遗，非遗是族群自我认

---

[*] 宋俊华，教育部人文社会科学重点研究基地中山大学中国非物质文化遗产研究中心、文化遗产传承与数字化保护协同创新中心教授。

[①] 本文为广东省委宣传部"党的十八大精神与广东实践研究"重大课题"非物质文化遗产与社会管理创新研究"（2013SBDZB09）阶段成果。

[②] 为简便起见，文中"非物质文化遗产"一律简称"非遗"。

同、自我发展的文化基础，也是区别于其他族群的重要标志。因此，非遗保护对族群间关系的两个方面——族群冲突和族群融合都会产生影响。近几年来，关于非遗代表作项目、代表性传承人等的申报、评审，曾在一些国家或地区间引发了一些文化争议。如在中韩之间，围绕端午节、汉字、中医等文化归属问题曾引起了一些争议；国内厦门与泉州围绕南音申报非遗代表作问题也产生过争议。国家、地区之间的非遗争论或冲突，本质上是族群之间文化冲突的体现。

那么，如何认识非遗保护与族群冲突的关系，能否从非遗保护中找到解决弥合族群裂痕的良方，能否从族群关系处理中找到非遗保护的对策，以及如何处理族群的个性诉求与非遗保护的普遍目标之间的矛盾，如何处理族群认同与现代社会发展需求的关系，都是我们要思考的问题。

二、非遗与族群认同

联合国教科文组织在《保护非物质文化遗产公约》中这样界定非遗："指被各社区、群体，有时是个人，视为其文化遗产的各种社会实践、观念表述、表现形式、知识、技能及相关的工具、实物、手工艺品和文化场所。这种非物质文化遗产世代相传，在各社区和群体适应周围环境以及与自然和历史的互动中，被不断地再创造，为这些社区和群体提供持续的认同感，从而增强对文化多样性和人类创造力的尊重。在本公约中，只考虑符合现有的国际人权文件，各社区、群体和个人之间相互尊重的需要和顺应可持续发展的非物质文化遗产。"[①] 简而言之，非遗就是人类社区、群体或个体所创造而被后代所认可并以口传心授等精神交流方式传承的文化财富。非遗具有传承性、活态性、实践性、群体性和精神性等特点。

族群（英文 ethnic）一词来自希腊文 ethnos，原意是部落与种族。后来族群意义不断变化。据马戎的统计，在英文文献中有二十几种族群的定义[②]，其中马克思·韦伯（Max Weber）的定义对中国影响较大。他这样定义族群："某种群体由于体质类型、文化的相似，或者由于迁移中的共同记忆，而对他们共同的世系抱有一种主观的信念，这种信念对非亲属社区关系的延续相当重要，这个群体就被称为族群。"[③] 一般而言，族群就是指一个较大的社会和文化体系中，由于客观上具有相同或相似的渊源（世袭、血统、体质）和文化（语言、宗教、信仰、习俗），因此主观上自我认同并被其他群体所区分的一群人。[④] 族群可以按照出生地、居住地和祖籍地来分，如海外华人、陕西人、台湾人等；也可以按照宗教信仰

---

① 这个界定有意义，但也有缺陷，参见拙作《非物质文化遗产概念的诠释与重构》，《学术研究》2006 年第 9 期。
② 马戎：《民族关系的社会学研究》，周星、王铭铭主编《社会文化人类学讲演集》，天津人民出版社 1996 年，第 501 页。
③ Max Weber, *The Ethnic Group*, In: Parsons and Shills, et al (eds.). *Theories of Society*, Vol. 1, Gleercol Illinois, The Free Press, 1961, p. 306.
④ 孙九霞：《试论族群与族群认同》，《中山大学学报》1998 年第 2 期，第 25 页。

来分,如信奉伊斯兰教的穆斯林;还可以按照生活方式来分,如现代的相亲族、SOHO族、丁克族等。

在概念上,非遗与族群具有相关性。非遗的传承性、活态性、群体性、精神性等特点,也是族群的特点。非遗是其所属群体的自我确认和他者确认共同作用的结果,与族群的自我认同和他者确认十分相似。此外,非遗往往与特定的族群相联系,是特定族群自我认同的基础和标志。族群是非遗创造与传承的主体,也是非遗意义实现的主体。

"认同"一词源于心理学,本义指一个个体对另一个个体的接纳。后来因哲学、社会学、人类学的运用,转为揭示个体与群体,甚至群体与群体的归属。① 族群认同就是指"社会成员对自己族群归属的认知和感情依附"②。共同或相似的渊源(世系、血统、体质)和文化(语言、宗教、信仰、习俗),是族群产生的基础,也是族群认同的基本要素。共同的祖先、共同的来源和共同的生长环境,是族群认同达到一致性。相同或相似的方言、信仰、习俗、艺术、生活方式等,是族群区分的标识,也是族群在交往中强化我群(self-group)与他群(others-group)的区分力量。

非遗既体现在族群世系、血统和体质等渊源要素中,也体现在族群语言、信仰、习俗、艺术和生活方式等文化要素中。非遗是族群认同的重要符号,有关族群自身的史诗、传说、信仰、语言、习俗、艺术等非遗,是族群自我标识的符号,也是与他群识别的标志。更重要的是,非遗还是族群认同的实践,它通过对共同祖先曾经创造、实践文化的再创造、再实践过程,与祖先达到精神沟通的同时,在族群内部达成一种默契和认同。这种既基于非遗外在符号又基于非遗内在实践的族群认同是深刻的、持久的。

三、非遗与族群冲突

族群认同是在族群差异基础上进行的,只有与他族群的比较、区别中才会产生对本族群的认同。反之亦然,族群的差别,也是在各个族群的自我认同基础上形成并被强化的,这种差别也往往成为族群对立或冲突发生的原因。

联合国教科文组织《保护非物质文化遗产公约》明确指出,非遗保护以《教科文组织世界文化多样性宣言》为基础,"强调非物质文化遗产的重要性,它是文化多样性的熔炉,又是可持续发展的保证"③。非遗是文化多样性的体现,保护非遗就是要保护文化多样性存在,包括保护族群的多样性存在。而这种保护,是以文化、族群之间的平等、尊重和相互理解为基本原则的,如果这个原则能够得到很好的理解和执行,那么族群之间的冲突就会避免。

当然,文化多样性存在是以肯定文化及其所属族群之间的差异性为前提的。这种差异,

---

① 孙九霞:《试论族群与族群认同》,《中山大学学报》1998年第2期,第27页。
② 王希恩:《民族认同与民族意识》,《民族研究》1995年第6期,第17页。
③ 联合国教科文组织《保护非物质文化遗产公约》,参见宋俊华、王开桃《非物质文化遗产保护研究》"附录1",中山大学出版社2013年,第180页。

会为人类文化生态和文化可持续发展提供基因资源，但会给族群之间的沟通和理解造成一定的障碍。如语言、民俗、宗教、生活方式等的差异，会导致误解或偏见，引发对立和冲突。尤其当一个族群试图把自己的语言、民俗、宗教和生活方式凌驾于其他族群之上、甚至取而代之时，就必然会带来严重的族群冲突问题。"在多民族国家内部，各个族群在社会地位、经济收入等方面，存在着以族群为基本分野的社会阶层划分。族群身份决定了一个人在社会利益和机会分配中享有特权或遭受歧视，其中的族群差别越大，族群之间的歧视程度越严重，优势族群捍卫自身特权和弱势族群力图改变现状的动力也就越强烈。"①

非遗在维护文化多样性的同时，强化了族群的地域、宗教、语言和文化的特殊性，这种强化会导致族群间的对立和冲突。就以地域为例来说，"认为自己是民族的族群渴望拥有自己的地域国家（例如库尔德人、巴勒斯坦人、泰米尔人、魁北克人、巴斯克人等），甚至当这种地域国家不存在的时候，认同某一地方是自己族群的地域，对于判断族群认同和族群延续就变得非常重要"②。所以，土著斐济人反对印度斐济人，科索沃的塞尔维亚人与阿尔巴尼亚人的冲突，美国土著美洲人与墨西哥裔、美国黑人之间的冲突，都是源于地域性冲突。如果对不同族群的地域非遗形式，如音乐、舞蹈、戏剧、民俗等进行宣传、保护，那势必会强化它们之间固有的地域差异，从而加大了族群发生冲突的概率。

一般而言，一种非遗在族群内部发挥的认同作用越强，在族群之间造成的差异性就越大，族群之间的理解难度就越大，发生对立和冲突的可能性就越大。当然，族群对立和冲突的原因复杂多样，族群文化的差异是其最深刻的原因之一。

四、非遗保护对族群冲突弥合的意义

作为代际传承的活态文化实践，非遗在处理族群内部代际之间、内部各成员之间以及本族群与他族群等关系上发挥着重要的作用，具有丰富的经验。

首先，非遗是弥合族群内部代际、同代之间冲突的重要手段。如后代通过对源于共同祖宗、图腾、宗教、信仰、理想等的仪式、民俗、歌舞等非遗的再实践，可以使实践者在代际、同代之间达到观念上的统一和认同，有助于消弭代际之间、个体之间、个体与族群之间的分歧或对立。这种以某种共同的文化认知和实践来弥合族群内部分歧或对立的方式，在增强传统族群内部凝聚力方面一直发挥着重要的作用，当然，也可以延伸到不同族群之间关系的处理上。

渡河神话是瑶族的非遗，也是瑶族通过奉祀共同祖先以凝聚族群的重要方式。瑶族文献《过山榜》和盘瑶村落传说中都有这样一个故事，说瑶人因躲避灾难，渡海迁徙，在海上遭遇风暴，他们跪求盘王，盘王施法力救了瑶人。瑶人于是许诺："无人救得瑶人子孙，三庙

---

① 罗惠翾：《族群认同与国家认同：和谐何以可能》，《理论视野》2009年第8期，第45页。
② 王剑峰：《族群性的陷阱与族群冲突》，《思想战线》2004年第4期，第61页。

圣王救得瑶人子孙;无人伏伺连州三庙圣王,瑶人子孙则永远敬奉,人财兴旺,万代荣昌"①。瑶人用这个神话,与盘王建立了一个契约,成了整个瑶族社会各种礼仪和非物质文化遗产的基础,瑶族的姓氏、祭祀和婚姻等都是在此基础上发展起来的。瑶族的还盘王愿,就是渡海以后瑶族发展起来的一种宗教活动,一般每三五年一小祭,十年一大祭。人们穿上传统服饰,唱盘王歌,跳长鼓舞,传颂盘王和祖先的功德。这种操同一种语言、着统一的服饰、祭祀共同神灵的礼仪活动,使参加仪式的每一个人从中获得了明确的瑶族身份认同,同时拉近了祖先传说与现实生活的距离,达到了凝聚族群的效果。②

东莞市麻涌镇大步村的"菩萨过坊"习俗,是大步村七个坊即张、郭、王、宁、赵、蔡、彭七个小族群间消弭间隙、和谐共处的文化基础。每年农历正月十八、十九,由七坊轮流主办菩萨巡游活动,保境安民,驱邪纳吉。大步村的七坊是由明代屯军发展而来,为屯军七姓兵头的后裔。他们在大步村屯田垦土,发展出了以某种姓氏为标志的小族群,同时,又通过菩萨过坊这种每年举行的祭祀活动建构共同信仰的实践如祭祀、歌舞、巡游等实现了小族群之间的融合。像这样以某种相同或相似的民俗信仰活动以促使不同族群之间的和谐共处的例子非常普遍。③

与大步村"菩萨过坊"十分相似,每年元宵节之前,广东省徐闻县前山镇各村都要择日举行游神活动,往往是邻近的两三个村子一起举行。当日,各村游神队请出各村的神,汇集到事先约定的神庙前,先举行一系列的见面寒暄、饮茶、祭祀等仪式后,大家汇成一个大的游神队,一起到各村巡游,为人们驱邪纳吉。这天,主办游神活动的村子家家户户要大摆宴席,邀请邻村亲朋好友来聚餐。整个仪式既有村落神灵之间的交往,又有人与人之间的交往,对不同族群之间的交流和融合发挥了重要的作用。④

其次,基于人类文化多样性存在与可持续发展需要的非遗保护,在理念上为族群之间的相互理解与消弭分歧创造了条件。尊重并保护相互之间的差异性,是人类可持续发展的需要,是非遗保护的基本要求,当然也是不同族群的共同诉求。在这样的基础上,求同存异,和谐共处才具有了可能。

联合国教科文组织关于非遗保护的理念,体现了人类对发展的渴望,也体现了对人权、文化权的尊重,强调了不同国家、地区、民族或阶层的人都有权利拥有和传承自己的文化遗产,不同族群的文化在本质上是平等的。这对经济社会发展处于弱势的国家、地区和民族的文化传承发展来说是一种十分有力的支持,对那些强势国家的文化殖民则是一种限制。这种

---

① 渡河神话是各地瑶族普遍存在的一个神话,在各地有不同的传说版本,内容大同小异。此处依据《过山榜》的记载。《过山榜》是瑶族民间文献,又称《评皇券牒》、《评王券牒》、《盘王券牒》。

② 罗宗志、陈桂:《神话传说与族群认同——立足于盘瑶渡海神话的考察》,《贵州民族学院学报》2009年第6期,第43—46页。

③ 2012年春节期间,笔者到东莞市麻涌镇大步村调查"菩萨过坊"活动,亲身感受到了这个非遗活动对不同族群协调发展的作用。

④ 2000年春节期间,笔者曾专门到徐闻县前山镇调查游神民俗。参见拙作《广东省徐闻县前山镇元宵节游神仪式》,《民俗曲艺》(台北)2001年总第134辑。

在国际法规层面的规定，有利于推动世界各族群在文化上的相互交流和理解，有利于消弭因文化差异、文化误解而导致的对立和冲突。

最后，非遗保护是一种基于自知与他评的实践过程。族群对非遗保护的自知与他人的评价是相互联系的。所以，非遗保护有利于推动族群文化内部与外部的交流，有助于针对同一对象的自知与他评的互动。这种互动，对于不同族群之间的相互理解，具有重要的意义。

联合国教科文组织倡导、各缔约国积极推动的非遗保护运动，虽然是自上而下、自外而内的，但非遗保护的任何一个环节，从申报名录、到制定措施到实施保护等，都必须是建立在自知、自主与他评、外助相结合的基础上的。这种内、外结合保护机制的建立，既体现了对非遗特殊价值和普遍价值的规律的认识，又体现了不同人包括不同族群在非遗保护上的协作。这种认识和协作，对于弥合族群冲突、建立和谐族群关系至关重要。

当然，城市化、全球化而带来的移民与族群互动，对非遗及其所属族群的独特性存在带来了冲击；但若能从非遗保护的视角重新认识和实践城市化、全球化，不仅有助于减缓这种冲击，而且对建构一种基于非遗及其所属族群独特性的新型和可持续的族群关系具有十分重要的意义。

五、结 论

非遗保护与族群弥合是现代社会必然面临的两大难题。

非遗保护的困难，不仅仅在于它要保护一种无形、活态和易逝的文化传统，也不仅在于它要克服代际之间观念、需求与实践方式的巨大差异，而且在于它要面对如何协调非遗及其所属族群的独特性与城市化、现代化和全球化所要求的文化普遍性的矛盾。

族群弥合的困难，一方面在于随城市化、全球化带来的移民与族群互动，不断强化了族群的自觉，强化了本族群与他族群的差异性，并把这种差异性作为族群内部凝聚和对外争取资源、权利的标志；另一方面在于民族国家和城市化、全球化的发展，需要消解或搁置族群的差异性和自利性，建构一种兼顾不同族群传统和权益的新型族群关系。这两种相互对立的诉求，共存于现代社会的族群互动中，是每个族群都必须面对的难题。

族群内部用非遗处理内部关系的经验、非遗保护所倡导的文化平等和现代社会发展理念，以及非遗保护中的自知与他评、自主与外助的关系处理，无论对非遗保护本身，还是对族群弥合而言都是十分重要的。它们不仅仅在理念、法理上为族群和谐相处提供了依据，而且在实践上为族群内部、族群之间的和谐相处提供了可借鉴的经验和方法，所以，从族群、族群关系的角度认识非遗、非遗保护，从非遗、非遗保护的角度认识族群及族群关系，是非遗保护与族群冲突弥合课题研究提供给我们最重要的启示。

与移民社区一起工作：
民族志学最佳实践方式

德伯·兰坦兹·舒克[*]

民族志学是一个古怪的研究学科，它允诺提供关于一个社区或团体的第一手资料，但是这种资料的获得却在很大程度上取决于个体研究员及其与实地的关系。尽管民族志的变化（即无法有效复制民族志信息的采集工作）常被引用来批判民族志学（Messsy，2000），但是这种变化也正是民族志学的活力之源。民族志的进程如渐进的关系般展开，它紧密地记录着研究客体的日常生活，描述着用定量的方法不可能收集到的细微差别。虽然也有其局限性，但民族志的研究仍是移民社区研究的一个十分有用的途径。

我最早和拉美人一起工作的经历可以追溯到1991年，远早于我考虑成为一名民俗研究者之时。那时候，我还是一名在华盛顿哥伦比亚女子医院工作的注册护士，我注意到在我们医院生产的拉美人越来越多。我可以趁着午餐时间去拜访他们，表面上看是为了练习我的西班牙语，其实我从高中二年级之后就没怎么好好学过西班牙语了。我确实希望我的西班牙语更加流利，但是事实上，我去的真正目的只是出于好奇。我很好奇为什么这些大部分来自萨瓦尔多的家庭会不远万里来到华盛顿？他们是如何在美国生活的？他们和自己的社区间有什么关系？

从在医院工作开始，我就在附近的亚当斯·摩根街区的一家诊所做义工。后来，我去了费城的宾夕法尼亚大学学习民俗学，我发现在当地一个移民诊所做义工护士是一种融入社区、赢得信任的有效方式，而且后来我以这种方式开始了我的民族志研究项目，并最终完成了于2011年出版的《超越边界：美国与墨西哥的迁移与归属》一书。从那时起，我便一直与来自拉美尼加拉瓜、危地马拉和洪都拉斯的住在北弗吉尼亚州偏远郊区的拉美人一起工作，现在我又与在弗吉尼亚阿灵顿县的玻利维亚人一起工作。

我以一名非学者的身份与移民们一起工作，让我有机会可以制作一张最佳实践方法表，我常常在乔治·梅森（George Mason）大学的民族志方法论课堂上使用这张表。本文如下所述的是在我正式开始研究前，在移民社区开展民族志工作的探索阶段总结出的方法。

---

[*] 德伯·兰坦兹·舒克，美国乔治梅森大学民俗学副教授。

如果要我找出一个与前述民族志实践方式相同的问题，我认为是大多数研究生项目在教导民族志的方法上缺乏一个一致的结构体系。当然所有的研究生项目都有教授方法论的课程，研究生会读民族志报告，做小规模的项目，与自己的同学和教授讨论实地考察；但这些课程很少要求学生在教员的监督下完成一个全面的民族志项目。在向学生讲授民族志学的基础知识的同时，这些实践对于那些要完成长期的民族志研究的学生而言是远远不够的。最重要的是，他们没有掌握如何管理数百页的实地考察报告、数字录音采访、照片、录像和非正式文献，而这些正是民族志信息采集的基础。

遵循好的方法能让民族志研究者更好地收集数据，以便在研究报告中呈现一个更全面准确的移民社区。

了解社区。我的研究有别于其他民族志学者的地方是我更加关注移民的接收社区。在大部分拉美人移民研究中，研究者几乎都只关注拉美人种族。而我所说的了解社区是指长住居民，也就是在移民到达之前就已经在社区居住的人们。这十分重要，因为这些长住居民对移民的生活和经历的影响更大。将他们纳入移民研究对于细致地理解你所记录的社区必不可少。（Lattanzi Shutika，2011）

对于这种拥有长住居民的社区，你需要找出利益相关者及其对新邻居的看法。他们对于移民和移民对社区的改变怎么看？他们是否愿意帮助建立新来者的支持系统？他们是否准备好与他人一起生活在一个社区？长住居民如何坚持传承自有文化？他们的社区是否为新来者适应、变化留出了位置？这种地方性的变化对于理解移民经历必不可少，包括左邻右舍、当地商人以及政客在内的长住居民会塑造移民社区的日常生活体验。

了解移民种族。一旦你了解了当地的环境，下一步你需要全面地检查你对移民种族了解多少。从人口数据开始，评估构成这一种族的人。他们来自哪里？社区是由家庭还是未婚的工人组成？他们的职业是什么？什么原因（如当地产业还是强劲的经济）促使他们移民至该地区？

大多数民俗学家认为拉美人是一个广义的概念，是对来自墨西哥、中美州和南美洲的人的总称。了解你所研究的某一特定的种族的文化传承和他们的故乡十分重要。比如说，许多玻利维亚人认为自己是玻利维亚人，而不是拉美人。

了解故乡（及其与社区成员之间的联系）。一个群体移居的原因是纷繁复杂、多种多样的，这其中通常与其故乡和迁入国均有关系。了解移民群体来自何处后，考察他们自己的故乡的历史以及促成其移民的大事件也同样重要。多数情况下，移民的原因无外乎与经济或教育机会有关，但是并不是所有的案例都是以摆脱贫困为目的。有些移民则是由政局的不稳定导致的（Massey，et al.，1987；Massey，2008）。

绝大多数的移民仍保持着与其出生社区之间的联系，这对移民与其故乡的联系有多重要？他们采用了何种策略实现这种联系？移民会在节假日回家探亲吗，或参加婚礼、洗礼等家族活动吗？移民如何使用现代科技（电话、邮件、视频聊天软件和网络电话）维持其和亲人、朋友的联系？（Smith，2006）

了解学术环境。想要全面了解移民社区，那么对于移民的学术大环境的调查是必不可少的。尽管有的民俗学家只想记录一个移民社区的职业的民俗文化，重要的是研究项目需要以人口内迁或外迁的文献为基础。民俗传统不是存在于真空中的，移民习俗的社会政治背景也不只是比当地较大的区域（Shuman，1993），社会学家、人口学家和政治家等深入研究的全球经济发展也同样塑造着移民习俗。

我提出这点，究其原因，是因为了解大环境并将其用于我们的移民研究中将极大地扩展对我们研究项目感兴趣的读者群。作为一项职业，我们可以向研究移民特别是使用定量分析研究的学者们，提供更多的信息。他们的工作是提供一幅广阔的移民地图，而不是移民个体的故事。将我们民俗学家的工作置于这个学术传统中加深了民族志研究的进程，也为更为广大的学术领域提供了有用且易得的信息。

了解移民社区的文化习俗，但是不要理所当然地认为所有的习俗都来自移民的故乡。罗伯特·雷德菲尔德（Robert Redfield）（1947）认为，学者们常常假定移民团体来自同一个民俗社会或小团体，抑或移民们将自己特别的才能（如民间工艺、民间音乐）从自己的故乡带到新社区。大多数情况下，移民美国的拉美人来自偏远的地区，而来自偏远山区的人在移民至美国以前往往先迁往本国的城市居住。到达美国以后，他们会先在一个地方住一段时间，然后他们再选择在别的地方永久定居。这种经历过多次迁徙的移民会改变迁入社区的文化习俗，同时也会促成新习俗的产生。

位于北维吉尼亚州的玻利维亚社区就是一个很好的例子。移民美国的玻利维亚人大多来自城市，并接受过良好的教育；很多人在移民美国之前就已经有自己的专业职业。这里居住的玻利维亚人人数仅次于拉巴斯（玻利维亚的行政首都及最大城市），他们以活力四射的民间舞蹈闻名。但是仅有居住在美国的玻利维亚人才有这一文化习俗；在他们玻利维亚的家乡，他们并没有这一传统。相反，这个社区于19世纪80年代成立时，舞蹈是作为玻利维亚移民为维持其身份认同的一种方式产生的。

了解他们的信仰。人们往往认为大部分拉美人都信奉罗马天主教，但是也需要认识到在中美洲和南美洲有很多新教福音派教徒，而且也存在像萨泰里阿教和坎东布雷教这一类融合的宗教传统。

信奉罗马天主教的拉美移民或许和制度化的教会的联系并不强烈，他们更多地与当地教区，特别是来自他们自己村庄的圣人联系紧密。由于信仰是为数不多的可以跟随移民们一起迁往美国的传统之一，因此了解移民和他们信仰之间的联系也非常重要。在很多情况下，教会社区是移民互帮互助的关系网的基础。（Lattanzi Shutika，2011）

了解相关语言。毋庸置疑，大部分来自拉丁美洲的移民讲西班牙语，但是也不尽然，比如说来自拉丁美洲的土著人。土著移民的母语是当地语，西班牙语对他们而言是第二语言。同样，来自巴西的移民则使用葡萄牙语。

了解法律。国家的移民法律对移民行为的影响是最广泛的，联邦法律对日常生活的影响可能会被当地或州的法令所掩盖。比如说，如果当地认同移民的家庭为社区的一部分，那么一个非法移民就有可能在该地区找到工作，买房、赚钱养家。

很多时候，州与州之间的移民法的不同也会体现在县、市一级的法律上。2007年至

2008 年间，一些县区将居住在弗吉尼亚州马纳萨斯的移民作为其驱逐拉美移民条例的首批目标，这导致了近一年内移民数量的急剧下降。许多拉美人将家安在邻近的费尔法克斯和阿灵顿县，这些地方的司法律令对于移民更为宽容。由于不确定地方当局是否会拘捕滞留移民，留在马纳萨斯的拉美移民们普遍注意到生活已经十分艰难，很多人甚至表示对一些普通的日常活动——让小孩子到户外活动，接送小孩上下学，或者去杂货店购物——感到担忧和恐惧。（Cleaveland and Pierson，2009；Singer，Wlison and DeRenzis，2009）

许多移民社区都同时拥有备案（法律）移民和未备案移民。在多数情况下，不管其是否备案，移民社区都会对其家庭和朋友提供支持和帮助。地方法律将会决定移民们如何建立自己的社区以及他们将在何种程度上与同社区的其他居民接触。

有计划地对你采集的信息进行组织分类。当大多数民族志学家提到他们的研究计划，他们往往会想到受试者的批准、申请书的编写、购买实地考察设备。的确，这些对于研究项目的结果十分重要。但是，民族志信息收集更长远的成就还应包括项目计划、组织收集好的资料和上交所有资料到档案馆以便后人将其用于别的研究。记住，实地考察的民族志学者是第一个文件档案保管者。

有很多资源可以用于组织分类最为复杂的民族志信息。在国会图书馆的美国民俗中心为研究项目计划提供了一系列免费的资源（http://www.loc.gov/folklife/edresources/ed-trainingdocuments.html）。采集的每一项信息都应按照都柏林核心标准使用正确的元数据记录在电子表格中。（http://dublincore.org/）

尽管将实地考察收集的民族志资料进行分类存档是一项十分普通的工作，但是许多研究人员却将其视为职业终了的最后一项工作。实习时，我坚持让我的学生在完成研究项目、研究报告或论文时上交他们的研究资料。将这些资料捐献给当地的档案机构，可以确保它们有效地归还至移民社区以及供将来的研究使用。在乔治·梅森大学，学生们通过全国民俗档案馆（http://folklorecollections.org/）或开展实地考察所在社区的当地图书馆档案处归档他们的项目成果。

民族志研究方法为移民社区的研究提供了一个全面的途径。通过采用最佳实践方法，研究人员能够收集到有关移民社区更全面准确的资料信息。研究人员应该利用许多可用的资源以实施自己的研究计划，也应该将自己采集整理的最终资料捐献给档案馆。

参考文献：

（1）Cleaveland, Carol, and Leo Pierson. 2009. "Parking Lots and Police: Undocumented Latinos' Tactics for Finding Day Labor Jobs." Ethnography 10 (4) (December 1): 515 – 533. doi: 10. 1177/1466138109346987.

（2）Lattanzi Shutika, Debra. 2011. Beyond the Borderlands: Migration and Belonging in the United States and Mexico. Berkeley: University of California Press.

（3）Massey, D. S. 2000. "A Validation of the Ethnosurvey: The Case of Mexico-US Migration." International Migration Review 34 (3): 766 – 793.

（4）Massey, Douglas S, Rafael Alarcon, Jorge Durand, and González Huberto. 1987. Return to Aztlan: The Social Process of International Migration from Western Mexico. Berkeley: University of California Press.

(5) Redfield, Robert. 1947. "The Folk Society." American Journal of Sociology 52 (4) (January 1): 293 – 308.

(6) Shuman, Amy. 1993. "Dismantling Local Culture." Western Folklore 52 (2/4) (April 1): 345 – 364. doi: 10. 2307/1500094.

(7) Singer, Audrey, Jill H. Wilson, and Brooke DeRenzis. 2009. "Immigrants, Politics, and Local Response in Suburban Washington". Metropolitan Policy Program. Brookings Institution.

(8) Smith, Robert C. 2006. Mexican New York: Transnational Lives of New Immigrants. Berkeley: University of California Press.

非物质文化遗产生产性保护概念、原则及相关问题思考

萧 放[*]

非物质文化遗产相对于物质文化遗产其精神性特征明显，它强调人的主体认知、情感体验、精神创造与智慧表达。非物质文化遗产保护就是要保护和传承人类情感、精神与知识智慧的多样性文化传统。在全球化的今天，我们如何保护非物质文化遗产，有多种选择与实践。中国政府建立的非物质文化遗产三级名录体系、文化生态保护区的划定、非物质文化遗产传承人制度的确立等都是行之有效的保护方式，这些保护方式对于多数非物质文化遗产来说，是非常重要的方式。当然，这些保护方式都是由政府主导的外部力量来推动实现的，因此，它总是有一些被动、消极。如何激活非物质文化遗产自身的文化能量，让它在政府提供的良好环境下健康传承发展，是我们应该思考的问题。非物质文化遗产生产性保护概念的提出，无疑为非物质文化遗产保护工作开辟了广阔天地。非物质文化遗产的性质决定了它在生产性保护方面有着独特的优势。对非物质文化遗产的生产性保护是在当前社会环境下非物质文化遗产活态传承的有益实践。

一、非物质文化遗产生产性保护的概念、范围与对象

非物质文化遗产是对特定群体文化传统中具有积极性认知价值与生活服务意义的精神性遗产及其相关活动、实物与场所的认定，联合国教科文组织《保护非物质文化遗产公约》中对此概括为五大类别：口头传说与表述，包括作为非物质文化遗产媒介的语言；表演艺术；社会风俗、礼仪、节庆；有关自然界和宇宙的知识和实践；传统的手工技能等。这五大类别囊括了非物质文化遗产的全部内容，对于内容如此丰富而形态十分复杂的非物质文化遗产的保护，就决定了我们的保护方式应根据对象不同采取不同的保护方式。非物质文化遗产的生产性保护是其中的方式之一。

---

[*] 萧放，北京师范大学文学院民俗学与社会发展研究所教授。

所谓非遗的生产性保护,"是指在具有生产性质的实践过程中,以保持非物质文化遗产的真实性、整体性和传承性为核心,以有效传承非物质文化遗产技艺为前提,借助生产、流通、销售等手段,将非物质文化遗产及其资源转化为文化产品的保护方式"[1]。文化部的这一定义,强调是以生产技艺为主的物质性生产的保护,所以它说:"目前,这一保护方式主要是在传统技艺、传统美术和传统医药药物炮制类非物质文化遗产领域实施。"即是说非物质文化遗产中的绝大多数部分是不适用生产性保护的,生产性保护只限定在技艺、美术、医药等显见的部分,这种狭义的生产性保护的界定,体现了政府部门在非遗保护工作中的审慎态度。

但作为学者来说,我们可以对这一政策进行讨论,发表我们对非遗生产性保护工作的意见,以供相关部门参考。我觉得非物质文化遗产的生产性保护应该作为非物质文化遗产的主要保护方式,可以将一般抢救保护的方式与生产性保护方式并举。我们在理解生产性保护的概念的时候,应该突破技艺等狭义的物化生产保护方式范围,将文化的再生产纳入广义的生产性保护范围。非物质文化遗产的口头传统、艺术表演、风俗、节庆、礼仪等的保护与传承都需要强调广义的生产性保护方式。但我所说的生产性保护不是让这些项目参与一般概念的生产性竞争,而是强调它们通过文化再生产的方式,使传统文化样式重新回到日常生活之中。如口头传统中的史诗、故事、歌谣、谚语除了在原初环境中传承外,在今天的时代,我们也应该采取多种新媒体手段进行传播,这种传播与传统的口耳相传在形态上会有差异,但我们只要充分重视遗产的文化内涵,尽量减少它的变形与损耗,我想其社会影响不仅不会降低,而且其传播范围会更广,也会收到更好的传播效果。又如传统戏剧,我们创造演出条件,通过演出的宣传吸引观众,并通过戏剧的魅力培养观众,这同样属于广义的生产性保护。还有城市节庆庙会,也可进入生产性保护概念。我们通过城市历史传统的研究,选择时间节点,复兴城市节会,通过文化、市政、公益等部门的共同规划与协力,定期主办城市节会,以节会带动城市非物质文化遗产的其他项目,如表演、城市记忆、城市工商传统、城市技艺等,都可在节会中找到展示的空间。这样的方式也是非物质文化遗产的生产性保护。

非物质文化遗产生产性保护的动态方式让我们今天的国民能够亲近、感受、体验并享受非物质文化遗产,进而培养我们对非物质文化遗产的亲密情感,唤起整个社会对非物质文化遗产保护、传承的自觉意识。在扩大社会影响的同时,同样会增强非物质文化遗产自身的活力。在社会生活中进行活态传承,是非物质文化遗产最有效的保护传承方式,同时也符合《中华人民共和国非物质文化遗产法》第四章第37条的规定:"国家鼓励和支持发挥非物质文化遗产资源的特殊优势,在有效保护的基础上,合理利用非物质文化遗产代表性项目开发具有地方、民族特色和市场潜力的文化产品和文化服务。"

---

[1] 《文化部关于加强非物质文化遗产生产性保护的指导意见》,文非遗发〔2012〕4号。

二、非物质文化遗产生产性保护的基本原则

自从 2011 年 6 月 1 日《中华人民共和国非物质文化遗产法》颁布后，非遗保护就成为每个公民的法定义务，该法第一章总则第 4 条对非遗保护工作有明确的原则规定："保护非物质文化遗产，应当注重其真实性、整体性和传承性，有利于增强中华民族的文化认同，有利于维护国家统一和民族团结，有利于促进社会和谐和可持续发展。"真实性、整体性和传承性是非物质文化遗产保护的基本原则。非物质文化遗产生产性保护是当代中国社会非遗保护的新方向，也是一个新课题。非物质文化遗产在生产性保护过程中，尤其要坚持真实性、整体性和传承性这三大原则。对于非遗的生产性保护在真实性原则上更需强调。

大家知道，将非物质文化遗产中某些适宜于生产物质成品与开展文化活动的项目列为生产性保护对象的时候，就会让人自然联想到这会不会影响到非物质文化遗产的真实性问题。因为作为非遗对象的物质生产与文化生产在传统社会是自然发生的，今天我们所说的生产性保护是在这种自然性生产过程变成遗产之后的人为的恢复与重现，所以就有真实性原则的提出。非遗生产性保护的真实性问题，我觉得作为首要原则强调是必要的，它必须在成品的文化内涵与核心技艺上完全真实，在成品形式上尽量符合传统。但文化是流动的，非物质文化遗产也要随着时代变化而做出适应性的调整，非物质文化遗产在生产性保护过程中会在因应社会环境或非遗传承人的代际差异等因素影响下自然发生变化。比如民间工艺技术类的非物质文化遗产，它既要继承传统题材，制作完全真实的传统作品，同时既然它不是文物古董的复制，它就可以以传统技艺生产新的题材的工艺品，适应民众的欣赏习惯的变化，满足社会需求。比较起来工艺技术上的真实性应该严格，也容易把握。

我们在开展群体性节庆非遗活动时，其真实性原则也必须坚持，但更加困难。它不像工艺产品制作有核心技艺与较为固定的载体形式，人只要将自己的精神对象化，让物来表达即完成了自己的工作。节庆类非遗是人的群体互动，是特定时空下的人们的情感、精神、欲望、利益的交汇。它的真实性把握就应该在注意节庆庙会的基本形式，如时间、空间、参与方式外，偏重文化内涵的理解。在节庆庙会的生产性保护中，应充分重视它在调节特定地区民众生产生活节奏与精神需要方面的文化核心意义。节庆庙会的外在形式可能有多种变化，但其内在核心意义必须坚持。这就是我们强调的非物质文化遗产生产性保护中需要坚持的真实性原则。非遗保护的真实性原则是有历史限定的，需要根据社会与民众的心理需要进行局部调整，相对灵活地理解真实性原则可能才是真正科学的真实。

整体性原则是非物质文化遗产保护的另一重要原则。非物质文化遗产不仅自身是一个形式、内涵完整的有机构成，同时它与外部环境也有着密切关系。非物质文化遗产的整体性的保持在现代社会面临较大困难，社会环境的巨大改变，让生活于其中的人们在承载非物质文化遗产的过程中思考如何对非遗进行整体性保护，特别是对非物质文化遗产机体之外的环境保护成为更大的难题。因此，我们在看待非遗保护的整体性原则的时候同样应该有变通与区

分性理解，总体上，我们对非物质文化遗产自身的完整性应该高度强调，对于非遗与环境的完整性尽量强调。在具体非遗项目中根据各自特性予以考虑。因此在非遗的生产性保护过程中，应对民间美术、手工制品、药物采集、炮制的工艺流程及其背后的文化理念作整体性保护，对口头传统、表演、节庆等的展演场景、主要情节与要素、程序、体裁样式及附属的道具物件等进行整体保护，对其中的主要环节与关键要素不可随意更改。在群体活动的文化遗产生产保护过程中，重视传统性的时间、空间、组织、物与活动过程等关键要素之间协调的整体性。因此非物质文化遗产生产性保护的外部环境，在今天的社会条件下只能是参考的要求。我们关注的是非遗自身的整体性。当然，非物质文化遗产与当代社会环境的关系，以及它如何与现代社会机体的协调，是一个新的整体性问题。

传承性是非物质文化遗产保护的根本性原则，非遗保护的目的就是通过特定手段实现文化传承，传承性是非遗的内在特性。非遗的传承与一般物质财富的形态继承不同，它重在精神内涵与技艺手段的非物质性要素的传承，非遗传承对接受者与环境都有特定要求。因此我们在进行生产性保护时应明白我们是在为传承非遗才进行的生产活动，这种生产的目的是为了让社会大众能够感知我们的非物质文化遗产，同时非物质文化遗产也丰富了我们的日常生活，非物质文化遗产的物质消费与经济收益是生产过程中的自然结果，它有助于非物质文化遗产的自我维护与发展。

当然，我们在非物质文化遗产的生产性保护中要时刻记住生产是传承的手段与传承的方式，这样就可避免在非物质文化遗产生产性保护名义下对非物质文化遗产资源的滥用与过度开发。如在节庆庙会类的非物质文化遗产的生产中，如果我们有文化传承意识，我们就会在非遗展示、非遗保护活动的参与等方面面向社会大众设计节会主题，围绕主题进行程序安排，调动民间组织与相关个人参与其中，在形式与内涵上体现节会的社会影响力，从而实现非物质文化遗产在社会生活中的动态传承。如果将具有非物质文化遗产性质的节会当作一次简单的大众物质消费活动，一切以商业利益为追求目标，那就是对非遗生产性保护初衷的背离，即使它的商业运作再成功，社会影响再大，也毫无文化传承的意义。

三、非物质文化遗产生产性保护应注意的几个问题

非物质文化遗产的生产性保护是文化遗产保护的新的实践，它与传统的遗产保护的不同是它将以前的被动保护置于积极的生产过程中。遗产一旦进入生产，它要保持自己的文化特性，就会面临许多实际问题。因此我们对非遗的生产性保护的确应该慎重，要作细密周全的考虑，然后才可能避免生产性保护变为生产性破坏的后果。以下几个问题值得关注：

第一，非物质文化遗产的生产性保护有特定的对象，不是所有的非物质文化遗产都可以进行生产性保护。根据非物质文化遗产的不同性质，我们确定它是否能够进行生产性保护。文化部通知中将生产性保护限定在传统技艺、传统美术和传统医药药物炮制类非物质文化遗产领域，这是生产性保护初步阶段的严格限定，防止人们一窝蜂地滥用遗产资源，它在目前

有积极意义。但我们也可尝试在节庆庙会等群体文化领域进行非物质文化遗产的生产性保护。节会文化再生产与工艺技术等物质再生产的形式不同，但其文化保护与文化传承的宗旨是同一的。

第二，非物质文化遗产生产性保护应根据不同对象实行不同的生产性保护方式。技艺性的遗产领域与文化性的遗产领域应该采取不同的生产性保护方式。前者以技艺传承与产品销售为主，后者以群体活动、社会参与与认知为主，二者有各自的评价指标与评估方法。

第三，非物质文化遗产生产性保护应合理、适度。非遗的保护性生产与普通商品生产不同，经济效益的追求不是第一位的，我们开展生产的目的是实现技艺的动态传承，服务与丰富民众的社会生活。当然，如果有些非遗产品具有广阔市场，能够获取丰厚的利益回报，也可适度利用。多数非遗产品的市场受限于特定消费群体，保护性的生产一定要考虑它的销售与流通。并且我们在生产性保护过程中，要坚守原有的材料、技艺与造型风格，允许局部更新，但一定要适度，且不影响非遗的基本特性。如昆剧《牡丹亭》的演出，在坚持传统唱腔、戏曲故事情节、基本扮相风格的前提下，适当加快演出节奏，对服饰的色彩作适应性微调，增强灯光舞美效果，这样的局部更新是合理、适度的。相反，如果我们在认定某一非遗项目有生产价值后，只以非遗名号进行产品的广告宣传，对非遗产品生产的工艺流程缺乏保护或者任意更动，那就是非遗生产性保护旗号下的破坏性生产。所以非遗的生产性保护工作应该纳入政府非遗保护部门的监管范围。

非物质文化遗产的生产性保护工作是我们面临的新课题，我们并无实践经验，理论探讨更加不足，还有许多实际的工作问题需要进一步研究。本文只是就此提出一些不成熟的看法，仅供各位参考。

（原文发表在《学习与研究》2013年第1期）

后　记

　　为了推动中美非物质文化遗产研究的学术交流，从 2011 年到 2013 年，中国民俗学会、美国民俗学会、中山大学中国非物质文化遗产研究中心、范德堡大学克博艺术、企业与公共政策研究所、华中师范大学国家文化产业研究中心、史密森尼学会共同主办了四次中美非物质文化遗产论坛，大大推动了中美学者在非物质文化遗产保护的政策、案例、生产性保护和田野调查、建档等研究方面的对话和合作。

　　本书就是上述中美非遗学者对话与合作的成果。

　　本书是中山大学中国非物质文化遗产研究中心宋俊华、美国民俗学会前任主席 Bill Ivey、华中师范大学国家文化产业研究中心黄永林等共同主编的，美国民俗学会执行主席 Tim 等参与了英文审校工作，中山大学中国非物质文化遗产研究中心陈熙以及中山大学翻译学院在读研究生、毕业生共同承担了本书的翻译工作。博士生何研、黄皓参与本书的校对工作。由于种种条件限制，本书的翻译难以做到"信、达、雅"，望作者和读者能够体谅。

Introduction

Song Junhua, Bill Ivey

"Folklore" is composed of the traditional art, knowledge, and practices passed from person to person and generation to generation through oral communication and face-to-face examples. Within the preservation and protection programs organized by UNESCO, folklore (sometimes called *folklife*) is defined as "Intangible Cultural Heritage". Both China and the United States are rich in traditional culture, and scholars in each country have conducted extensive folklore research. This collection of articles is the result of a 10-year collaboration between folklorists and Intangible Cultural Heritage specialists in China and the United States.

Early in 2007, the China Folklore Society initiated conversations with its US counterpart, the American Folklore Society. From the 1980s forward, scholars and graduate students from China had studied, conducted research, and served as visiting faculty at US institutions, and at the same time a number of prominent American folklorists lectured in China. Both Chinese and American folklore specialists expressed interest in sharing research and theory more deeply, and in offering graduate students opportunities for international study, but there existed no shared framework for interaction that would enable ongoing communication and possible collaboration.

For years after dialogue began in 2007, China and US scholars met at conferences, delivered guest lectures at universities, and conducted informal meetings assessing many aspects of folklore activity in China and the US. These conversations were conducted in a spirit of respect for differing experiences and perspectives, building friendships and establishing the foundation for cooperation and understanding. In additional to the CFS and AFS, the Institute of Chinese Intangible Cultural Heritage at Sun Yat-sen University, the Department of Folklore at Central China Normal University, the Chinese Academy of Social Sciences and Smithsonian Institution became key partners in the collaboration.

Because the situation of folklore and folklore studies in China and the US are quite different, from the first meeting all participants recognized an exciting opportunity.

China is a very old civilization, and China scholars had for decades been able to study ancient villages where traditional performances and practices had existed for centuries, unaffected by the forces of modern life. Chinese society also contained more than fifty officially-recognized "nationality" cultures, each with a distinct language and unique cultural practices. These nationality communities had long been the subject of both research and government policy, and folklore in China had for decades included both a scholarly component and a system of government regulation designed to protect minority cultures.

In the US only Native American ("Indian") cultures could be considered "ancient," and even Indian tribes were acknowledged to be of Asian origin. Without isolated peasant villages or multiple ethnic nationalities to study, US folklorists had become expert in the traditional culture and heritage of ethnic groups in cities. They conducted research on "Chinese-American" and "Italian-American" neighborhoods, and studied the way traditional culture survived when rural, agrarian populations moved to the city. Most of this work was conducted by individual scholars based in universities (although since the 1970s public folklorists have become active in our field), and the products of research included publications, media presentations, exhibitions, and festivals. Although the US government had developed institutions dedicated to the collection and preservation of folksongs, folk tales and other aspects of folklife, government policy intervening in folk traditions and folk communities was not highly developed.

What project would encourage the expansion of our collaboration and enable us to address these and other important differences between folklore practice in China and the US? Perhaps we could use the *Convention for the Safeguarding of the Intangible Cultural Heritage* as a framework in which to describe and contrast the situation for folklorists in our two countries? Though the US has not signed the Convention, US folklorists had actually assisted in developing basic principles of the convention, while China was one of the first countries to implement new ICH methodology. By examining folklore in China and the US through *the Convention for the Safeguarding of the Intcengible Cultural Heritage*, colleagues could compare and contrast general themes influencing research in each country while specifically addressing the impact of ICH policy—the arena of folklore activity in which China has been a pioneer.

By the fall of 2010, it was decided that a series of conferences in China and the US would offer the best opportunity to advance our cooperoution and compare examination of folklore research and policy. With funds provided by organizations in both China and the US (they are listed on the second page of this volume), four conferences— "Forums" —were planned, two in each country. Invited scholars prepared detailed abstracts of presentations which were printed in Forum programs in both Chinese and English. Presenters read papers in their native language and bilingual graduate students provided interpretation for discussion sessions. Forums were held in Foshan, Guangdong Province, in Nashville, Tennessee, in Wuhan, Hubei Province, and in Washington, DC.

Articles included in this volume are edited and expanded versions of many of the papers presented at each "Comparative Forum on Intangible Cultural Heritage: China-US."

* * * * *

Because the UNESCO approach to the preservation of traditional culture and folklore transmission provided the framework for our China-US collaboration, it is important to outline the main features of the 2003 Convention.

In 1972, UNESCO issued a historic agreement designed to preserve buildings, monuments, and natural reserves of universal value. *The World Heritage Convention* addressed the protection and preservation of cultural items that had a physical presence—structures and features of the natural environment. Almost immediately, some UNESCO members expressed concern with threats to *immaterial culture*—stories, songs, rituals, language—around the world. In 1989 the organization issued "recommendations" for the safeguarding of folklore. However, the recommendations did not include policies specifically aimed at preserving the essential process of oral tradition, instead emphasizing surveys, collecting, and archival work. Few governments participated.

In the fall of 2003 UNESCO took a new approach by presenting a comprehensive policy-driven preservation regime. In effect member states extended that 1972 Convention by drafting an entirely new convention that expanded the scope of heritage policy from objects and environmental features into the realm of "intangible" aspects of culture like folklore, craftsmanship, rituals, dramas, dance, storytelling, language, and music.

This new, 2003 Convention represented a distinct departure from earlier efforts to protect folklore. The 1989 Recommendations were primarily concerned with identifying threatened traditions, creating lists, and collecting examples or documentation of endangered intangible assets, frequently placing them in archives or museum collections. This approach can be characterized as *observational*, encouraging research, collection, study and analysis. As noted above, this is an approach familiar to Western folklorists in general and US scholars in particular. Observational folklore studies pay attention to the preservation of folklore items, materials, and contexts, but rarely attempt stewardship of traditional practice through interventions by government or private industry.

In modifying its approach to folklife preservation, UNESCO shifted away from the *observation* of intangible heritage toward *action* designed to preserve a process—the enabling conditions—that sustain transmission. By the late 20th century, Japan, Korea, and China had experience with government action in communities intended to influence folk expression. And because Asian countries had already experimented with government policies that encouraged preservation and transmission by celebrating the work and lives of master folk artists, the UNESCO shift from documentation toward the nurturing of intergenerational transmission also represented a shift from East to West.

By the fall of 2005, 23 states had ratified UNESCO's *Convention for the Safeguarding of the*

Intangible Cultural Heritage, and China was one of the first countries to become a party to the new agreement. The situation in the US was different: even though American folklorists had been active participants in planning the new convention, the US did not ratify the convention. Further, because of legal constraints enacted by Congress, the US ceased payment of UNESCO annual dues in 2011. Although the US retained UNESCO membership, after 2011 its level of participation in UNESCO affairs was greatly reduced.

Because a "convention" is an international agreement, for participating countries, carries the obligations of a treaty, this new UNESCO approach to folklore preservation policy had "teeth." In addition to its high standing as an international document, the Convention also outlined a number of specific procedures and structures—intergovernmental committees, selection processes, and incentives designed to encourage communities to protect intangible heritage and master artists while also securing the underlying intergenerational process of oral tradition that keeps heritage alive. In general, pursuing the objectives of the Convention required that scholars or policy actors engage communities, ethnic groups, nationalities, or minorities in a three-step process—first to identify representative and valued traditions, then determine the character and strength of threats to those traditions, and then develop policies or interventions designed to offset those threats.

* * * * *

The implementation of Intangible Cultural Heritage preservation policies created many opportunities and a number of challenges for folklore specialists in China. The four Forums on Intangible Cultural Heritage did address the broad contextual and historical themes that distinguish folklore studies in China and the US—the themes that first brought China and US scholars together. However, given the rapid implementation of various government ICH programs, it is not surprising that many presentations by Chinese specialists addressed the effects of policies designed to sustain folklore and folklore transmission.

UNESCO specified many elements of ICH protection under the 2003 Convention, but many procedures and the nature of specific preservation policies were left to scholars and officials within signatory countries. As one of the first nations to ratify the convention, it is natural that China has been a pioneer in experimenting with different approaches to intangible heritage and intergenerational transmission. Articles in this volume address the challenges faced by folklorists in the implementation of ICH policies. Can Inheritors of traditions be singled out for special acclaim and government attention without altering their connection with community? What is "cultural ecology," and how can it be sustained? Can cultural tourism and "productive protection" increase the value of ICH treasures without disturbing their essential character as elements of sustainable tradition? Can these and other questions address the central issues that arise in the context of active intervention?

The UNESCO convention and government ICH policy are not immediate, pressing concerns facing US contributors. In keeping with the observational orientation of Western folklife research, US authors emphasize collecting, preservation through archival work, and providing increased access to collected materials and folklore practitioners through exhibitions, festivals, and the compilation of sound recordings. While there exists a sentiment that traditional culture is threatened by forces of modernity, folklorists in the US have observed the resilience of traditional art and practice in big-city settings, and have remained content to encourage continuity by preserving folk culture and by expanding societal respect for folklore and folk artists.

Although articles by the US and China scholars emphasize distinct areas of concern, *Comparative Perspectives on Folklore and Intangible Cultural Heritage* also addresses overarching questions facing folklorists in both China and the US. Ownership and legal rights affecting traditional material, the use of virtual reality and other digital techniques, the role of traditional culture in ethnic conflict, storytelling as a community response to natural disaster, and the meaning of "authenticity" as an essential attribute of Intangible Cultural Heritage are questions of research and policy that resonate with specialists in China and the United States.

This volume is a celebration of a collegial process of exchange that has produced a new understanding of the situation, perspectives, and special opportunities facing folklorists in the US and China. It is also an open door to expanded communication that will allow the best practices of folklorists in two great societies to improve the quality and intensity of their work.

Short versions of the papers in this volume were presented at one of four 2011-2013 "China-US Forums on Intangible Cultural Heritage" co-sponsored by the China Folklore Society and the American Folklore Society.

The dates, locations, themes, and hosts for each forum were as follows:

November 6-7, 2011 (Fontainebleau Resort, Foshan, Guangdong Province): The First China-US Forum on Intangible Cultural Heritage: Comparative Policies (Institute for Chinese Intangible Cultural Heritage, Sun Yat-Sen University)

April 29-May 1, 2012 (Vanderbilt University, Nashville, Tennessee): The Second China-US Forum on Intangible Cultural Heritage: Case Studies (Curb Center for Arts, Enterprise, and Public Policy, Vanderbilt University)

November 16-18, 2012 (Central China Normal University, Wuhan, Hubei Province): The Third China-US Forum on Intangible Cultural Heritage: Productive Safeguarding (National Research Center of Cultural Industries, Central China Normal University)

May 23-24, 2013 (National Museum of the American Indian, Smithsonian Institution, Washington, DC): The Fourth China-US Forum on Intangible Cultural Heritage: Fieldwork, Documentation, Preservation, and Access (Office of the Under Secretary for History, Art, and Culture, Smithsonian Institution)

These forums were made possible by a major grant from the Henry Luce Foundation and through the support of the Ministry of Education of the People's Republic of China, the Lingnan Foundation, the National Endowment for the Humanities, the Institute of Chinese Intangible Cultural Heritage at Sun Yat-sen University, the Department of Folklore at Central China Normal University, and Smithsonian Institution.

Major Themes and Overviews

Policy and Enterprise Practice of Intangible Cultural Heritage in China

Song Junhua*

1. Introduction: The Problem

China is one of the most-active participants in the UNESCO-launched program of protection for intangible cultural heritage ("ICH" for short). *The Convention for the Safeguarding of the Intangible Cultural Heritage* was passed by the UNESCO in 2003, and China's ratification of the convention was approved by the eleventh meeting of the Standing Committee of the Tenth National People's Congress on August 28, 2004, thus China became one of the earliest countries to join the convention. In 2001, the first list of masterpieces of oral and intangible masterpieces of human cultural heritage was published by UNESCO; China's Kunqu opera was included. Chinese items have been included in all subsequent lists of masterpieces published by UNESCO. By the end of 2013, thirty items from China have been listed as masterpieces of oral and intangible heritage, seven items on the list of intangible cultural heritage items requiring urgent attention, one item on the list of good practices for ICH protection, thirty-eight items in total, placing China first among countries of the world.

China's protection program for intangible cultural heritage has expanded gradually, from the national government to the grassroots— "top-down" —showing very obvious characteristics of a program led by national policies. As a reflection of state willpower, national policies for intangible cultural heritage are distinct from entrepreneurial activities affecting intangible cultural heritage in authentic or traditional work settings, creating tension and new social problems. Therefore, one of the main problems facing modern China is how to manage the contradiction between national policies and entrepreneurial practice so as to provide opportunity to business initiatives in the protection of

---

* Song Junhua, Professor and Director of the Institute of Chinese Intangible Cultural Heritage, Sun Yat-sen University.

ICH in a manner that achieves positive interaction between official protection of intangible heritage and development of commercial enterprises.

Before the launch of UNESCO's protection convention, relevant policies had already been established in China. Here are two examples: 1. Clauses concerning protection of intangible cultural heritage can be found in laws and regulations such as *the Constitution*, *Law of Regional Ethnic Autonomy*, *Criminal Law*, *Copyright Law*, *the Education Act*, *the Law on Compulsory Education*, *Higher Education Act*, *Non-governmental Education Promotion Law*, *Sport Law*, *Drug Administration Law* and *the Law of Cultural Relics*. 2. There are Laws and regulations that address specific kinds of intangible cultural heritage, such as Regulations on *the Protection of Varieties of Traditional Chinese Medicine* enacted by the state council on January 1, 1993, and *Regulations on the Protection of Traditional Crafts and Fine Arts*, issued as the 217th order of the state council on May 20, 1997.

Most special policies addressing intangible cultural heritage in China were created and implemented in this century, keeping in step with UNESCO. Here are two cases in detail: 1. Documents such as notices, opinions and procedures especially for protection of intangible cultural heritage issued by governments and their departments at all levels, such as, *Opinions on Further Strengthening Cultural Work of Ethnic Minorities*, printed and distributed by the Ministry of Culture and the State Ethnic Affairs Commission in February, 2000; *Notice on Implementation of Protection Project for Chinese Ethnic Folk Culture* and its attachment, *Implementation Plan for the Protection Project for Chinese Ethnic Folk Culture*, jointly issued by the Ministry of Culture and Ministry of Finance on April 8, 2004; *Opinions on Strengthening Protection of Intangible Cultural Heritage in China* and its attachments, *Interim Measures for Application and Evaluation of Masterpieces of State-level Intangible Cultural Heritage*, and *Joint Inter-ministerial Meeting System for Protection of Intangible Cultural Heritage*, issued by the General Office of the State Council in March, 2005; *Interim Measures for the Management of Special Funds for Protection of National Intangible Cultural Heritage*, jointly issued by the Ministry of Finance and Ministry of Culture in July, 2006. *Interim Measures for Protection and Management of State-level Intangible Cultural Heritage*, issued by the Ministry of Culture in November, 2006; *Notice on Strengthening Protection of Chinese Time-honored Intangible Cultural Heritage*, jointly issued by the Ministry of Commerce and Ministry of Culture in February, 2007; *Notice on Printing and Distribution of Administrative Measures using the Logo of "Intangible Cultural Heritage"*, issued by the Ministry of Culture in July, 2007; *Interim Measures for Identification and Management of Representative Successors of State-level Intangible Cultural Heritage Items*, issued by the Ministry of Culture in May 2008. 2. Laws, regulations and rules targeting the protection of intangible cultural heritage issued by governments at all levels, such as *Law of the People's Republic of China on Intangible Cultural Heritage*, passed by the Standing Committee of the Eleventh National People's Congress on February 25, 2011, and rules for the protection of traditional ethnic folk Culture or intangible cultural heritage issued throughout the country.

According to the content of policies mentioned above, some of which provides information and guidance for the protection of ICH, such as documents like ideas and notices; some of which emphasizes how to protect intangible cultural heritage, such as documents outlining procedures; some of which defines specifications for the protection of intangible cultural heritage, such as laws and regulations. According to their purpose, these policy statements present requirements affecting governments and departments at all levels, while at the same time constraining the behavior of enterprises and individuals. Transmission and development of specific aspects of intangible cultural heritage are connected with commercial activity, like enterprises that serve as the primary protection contexts for items like traditional handicraft, traditional art and traditional medicine. Long before the development of ICH protection by UNESCO, these enterprises had been engaging intangible cultural heritage as the principle object of both production and management, not restricted by ICH policy but by economic and industrial rules, laws and regulations. Once these enterprises have been identified as units of protection for intangible cultural heritage, they are inevitably regulated by ICH policies, laws and regulations of both UNESCO and the nation. For such enterprises, such numerous policies, laws and regulations have multiple effects, bring both opportunities and challenges while, of course, creating new problems.

2. ICH Policies and Development Opportunities for ICH Enterprises

First, let us review published of policies regarding ICH traditions that may be beneficial to brand-building within ICH enterprises.

In Opinions on Strengthening Safeguarding of Intangible Cultural Heritage in China, it is stated in the third point ("establish directory system and gradually develop a protection system of intangible cultural heritage with Chinese characteristics") : "establish a directory system for national, provincial, municipal and county-level intangible cultural heritage masterpieces by setting standards of review with scientific confirmation," "encourage successors of intangible cultural heritage masterpieces to conduct publicity campaign and learning activities for masterpieces enlisted in the directory system in ways of naming, conferring titles, commendation and reward, funding and support, etc." Article 8 of *Interim Measures for Application and Evaluation of Masterpieces of State-level Intangible Cultural Heritage*, states that "citizens, enterprises and institutions, social organizations, etc., can apply to the culture administrative department in its administrative region for items of intangible cultural heritage masterpieces." Article 5 of *Interim Measures for Identification and Management of Representative Successors of State-level Intangible Cultural Heritage Items* indicates that: "protection units of state-level intangible cultural heritage items can introduce representative successor to the local culture administrative department that above county levels for a certain project." Article 18 of the 3rd Chapter of *Law of the People's Republic of China on Intangible Cultural Heritage* states that: "state-level representative intangible cultural heritage items established by the State Council will enlist and protect items reflecting traditional culture of Chinese nation and having significant historical, literary, artistic or scientific value." "Local representative intangible cultural heritage items established by people's governments of province, autonomous region or municipality will enlist and protect items reflecting traditional culture of Chinese nation and having significant historical, literary, artistic or scientific value." It also says in article 19 of the 4th chapter that:" "The appropriate culture department of the State Council and people's governments of province, autonomous region or municipality can decide representative successors for representative intangible cultural heritage items approved by the people's governments at the corresponding levels."

In conformance with documents, laws and regulations mentioned above, three batches of masterpieces of state-level intangible cultural heritage (1,219 items have been selected), four batches of representative successors of state-level intangible cultural heritage items (1,986 successors have been selected), and the first batch of productive protection demonstration bases of state-level intangible cultural heritage (41 enterprises have been selected) have been successively reviewed and published in China since 2006. Meanwhile, masterpieces, project-representative successors and productive protection demonstration bases of state-level intangible cultural heritage have also been reviewed and published in provinces, cities and counties. Many ICH items, demonstration projects and successors have connected with enterprises, including productive protection demonstration bases (of which are all enterprises).

National review and publication of lists of intangible cultural heritage representing different levels and types have had significant influence on ICH enterprises. Among the 10 categories classified for masterpieces of state-level intangible cultural heritage, most examples of traditional techniques and traditional medicines are involved in production of enterprises; a number of items of traditional music, folk arts, traditional dances, traditional drama, folk opera, acrobatics & athletics and folklore are also involved in production enterprises. To some extent, selection and placement on lists of intangible cultural heritage of different levels and types provides an element of social honor and legal right to these items, the successors, and the activities concerned. Thus ICH enterprises can properly conduct publicity campaigns, carry out production and seek support from the government and all sectors of society using names of listed items and successors, strengthening an existing brand or building a new one.

Aware of opportunities provided by inclusion on national lists of intangible cultural heritage of different levels and types, many ICH enterprises attach great importance to the utilization of lists of intangible cultural heritage, particularly enterprises of traditional crafts, folk arts and traditional medicine. For example, traditional techniques of liquor-manufacturing enterprises like Moutai, Wuliangye, Jiannanchun, Luzhou Old Cellar, etc. ; embroidery technology of enterprises of Shu embroidery, Guang embroidery, Xiang embroidery, Shu embroidery, and others; traditional Chinese herb culture of drug companies like Tongrentang, Huqingyutang, Heniantang, Jiuzhitang, Pangaoshou, Chenliji, and Tongjitang have all been declared masterpieces of state-level intangible cultural heritage, and publicity campaigns for their products have been conducted in name of masterpieces of intangible cultural heritage, greatly enhancing their brand image.

In January 2012, 41 ICH enterprises including Beijing Enamel Factory Co. , Ltd, were awarded honorary plaques by the ministry of culture recognizing " productive protection demonstration bases of state-level intangible cultural heritage," which not only affirmed the practices of these enterprises in the protection of intangible cultural heritage, but also gave them a position of authority in the field, making recognized enterprises more competitive in comparison to others.

Second, the display and exhibition of intangible cultural heritage will help ICH enterprises to participate in market competition.

"The third point, establish directory system and gradually develop a protection system of intangible cultural heritage with Chinese characteristics," presented in *Opinions on Strengthening Safeguarding of Intangible Cultural Heritage in China* continues: "enhance research, identification, preservation and spreading of intangible cultural heritage ... give full play to functions of public cultural institutions such as libraries, cultural centers, museums and science and technology museums at all levels, and topic museums and Exhibit Centers can be established in places where conditions permit."

Article 30 in the 4th chapter of *Law of the People's Republic of China on Intangible Cultural Heritage* states that:

> Appropriate departments of culture of the people's government at all above the county level shall take the following measures to support inheriting and transmitting activities conducted by the representative successor for intangible cultural heritage as required:
> 1. provide necessary places for inheriting;
> 2. provide necessary funding support for activities of training apprentices, passing down art and communication;
> 3. support representative successors for their participation in social public welfare activities;
> 4. other measures taken to support inheriting and spreading activities conducted by the representative successor.

Since 2006, guided by the policies, laws and regulations, many comprehensive and special exhibitions of intangible cultural heritage have been held by culture departments and enterprises at all levels. For example, the China (Shenzhen) International Cultural Industry Fair (Cultural Fair for short) was founded in 2006, which has been held annually eight times by the end of 2013. An "Exhibition area for intangible cultural heritage" was first included in the No. 2 hall of creative life in 2010 (the 5th Cultural Fair). Before the first designation of an independent hall for intangible cultural heritage in 2011, the fair of intangible cultural heritage had already been held four times, combining display, exhibition and trade in cultural industries.

The International Festival of Intangible Cultural Heritage (IFICH for short), Chengdu, China was founded in 2007. It was held every two years and by the end of 2013 has taken place four times. It combines the display of intangible cultural heritage with an international forum on both the protection of intangible heritage and cultural tourism. The Exhibition of Achievements on the Productive Protection of China's Intangible Cultural Heritage, held in Beijing in 2012, was especially for ICH enterprises. The above-mentioned exhibition activities were all held by the Ministry of Culture, which greatly enhanced the business competence, competitive capabilities and production innovation of ICH enterprises by offering support for exhibition venues and funding and in-kind support for activities combining protection of intangible cultural heritage with production, marketing and distribution of enterprise products.

Third, the input of funds for the protection of intangible cultural heritage helps transform and upgrade enterprises involving intangible cultural heritage.

Opinions on Strengthening Safeguarding of Intangible Cultural Heritage in China states, "The fourth point: strengthen leadership, implement responsibility and set up coordinated and effective working mechanism," continuing that: "governments at all levels should continuously increase input of funds for protection work of intangible cultural heritage. Encourage individuals, enterprises and social groups to provide fund support for protection work of intangible cultural heritage by measures such as policy guidance." Article 5 of *Interim Measures for Management of Special Funds for Protection of National Intangible Cultural Heritage* states: "the special funds is divided into two categories: subsidies for protection projects and expenses for organization and management." Article 10 of *Interim Measures for Protection and Management of State-level Intangible Cultural Heritage* states: "cultural administrative department of the State Council will provide necessary fund support to protection projects of national intangible cultural heritage. Culture administrative departments of the people's government at or above the county level should try actively to get financial support from the local governments and provide fund support to protection projects of national intangible cultural heritage within their respective administrative regions". Article 30 of the 4th chapter of *Law of the People's Republic of China on Intangible Cultural Heritage* also requires that appropriate departments of culture of the people's government at or above the county level shall "provide necessary funding support for activities of training apprentices, passing down art and communication," to support inheritance and spread activities conducted by the representative successor for intangible cultural heritage as required. Provisions of the above policies, laws and regulations provide the basis on which enterprises can obtain funds from the government for the protection of intangible cultural heritage.

In fact, since 2006, all levels of government in China continuously increased fiscal expenditures in protecting intangible cultural heritage. According to statements by vice-minister of Ministry of Culture Wang Wenzhang in a news conference held by the State Council Information Office on June 2, 2010, "Central and provincial financial departments have invested a total of 1.789 billion in the protection of intangible cultural heritage, by which smooth running of protection work of intangible cultural heritage is ensured."[1]

Although the use of national special funds for the protection of intangible cultural heritage is strictly limited to subsidies for projects such as theory and technology research, successors and their teaching and learning activities, folk activities, materials' saving, sorting and publication, cultural ecology protective zone, general survey and publicity, and not directly available for production, including capital investments, updating plants and equipment of ICH enterprises, these precious funds and requirements for their use play an important role in enabling enterprises to sort out materials, research corporate culture and technology, cultivate successors and promoting publicity about cooperate culture. This process helps enterprises develop and take advantage of their own resources, promoting the transformation of enterprises from the traditional production of products to the manufacture of cultural products possessing high added value capable of transforming the cultural and creative industries.

3. ICH Policies and New Challenges Surrounding ICH Enterprises

First, the conflict between inherited traditional techniques and the developments in modern science and technology.

Article 4 of *Law of the People's Republic of China on Intangible Cultural Heritage* states that: "the protection of intangible cultural heritage should pay attention to its authenticity, integrity and continuity, helping to enhance the cultural identity of the Chinese nation, maintain country unification and national unity and promote social harmony and sustainable development." Article 5 indicates that: "both forms and connotations of intangible cultural heritage shall be respected in their usage. Intangible cultural heritage shall not be used in the form of distortion, derogation, etc." Therefore, maintaining authenticity is the basic principle in the protection of intangible cultural heritage. As for enterprises whose main operational content are traditional techniques, folk arts and traditional medicine, such traditional and unique skills are fundamental to their existence and development, and are also core content of the intangible cultural heritage whose protection has been undertaken by them. ICH such as traditional liquor-making techniques of liquor-making enterprises, traditional porcelain making techniques of ceramic enterprises, traditional jade-carving techniques, and herbal tea preparation techniques of tea enterprises, etc., have a special character: some are purely manual and some are half-mechanical and half-manual; some are individually produced and some produced through mechanical processes. Production techniques are often closely linked to people's folk customs and to the cultural life of particular times, areas and ethnic groups—actually becoming part of spiritual life.

However, given current developments and technological progress, traditional techniques that characterize some ICH enterprises are being partly or wholly replaced by modern manufacturing practices. First, the modernization of tools, and the mechanization and application of intelligent machines, begin to partly or even wholly replace manual operations. Methods of making paper by hand are replaced by mechanized papermaking, artificial wine-making techniques are replaced by modern wine-making equipment, cutting machines are used in sculpture, computers are used in design of paper-cut images, and so on. Second, modern science and technology now play a role in the transmission of traditional techniques, such as the partial replacement of oral instruction and rote memory in the process of transmission by computers, videotapes and online networks, an inheriting process that makes traditional techniques more standardized. Third, "hi-tech" manufacturing process play a role. Modern production lines are introduced to traditional ICH enterprises and individualized production is replaced by streamlined production techniques. Indeed, modern technologies are irresistible, offering low cost, high effectiveness and adaptability to market demands, and thus become the inevitable choice of ICH enterprises in the competitive environment of modern society.

How do we deal with the relationship between inheriting traditional techniques and development of modern technology? It is the dilemma intangible cultural heritage enterprises framed against the background of policies for protection of intangible cultural heritage. In pre-ICH times, the development of ICH enterprises was adjusted by market demand, honoring the key idea of "innovation" that adapted to market development, an approach in which the replacement of traditional skills by means of modern science and technology was considered to be a valid sign of progress. But in ICH times, ICH enterprises cannot apply innovation to traditional skills simply in accordance with market demand, as these enterprises should bear the responsibility of protecting traditional techniques. A balance should be found between the two extremes. Some enterprises try to deal with the conflict by employing a half-manual and half-mechanical processing method, such as jade carving, stone caving and ivory carving enterprises, in which machines are used for processing raw materials and polishing while pure manual sculpture remains in certain key parts of a carving. Some enterprises adopt a two-tiered model of classified production, such as liquor-making enterprises and embroidery enterprises in which high-end products are made by hand and mass-market products are made by machines. But which mode is the best one? The alternatives need to be explored in practice.

Second, the conflict between inheriting culture and meeting modern consumer demand.

Opinions on Strengthening Protection of Intangible Cultural Heritage in China states that: "intangible cultural heritage is not only witness of historical development, but also cultural resource of important value. Rich and colorful intangible cultural heritage created by people of all ethnic groups in China during their long process of living and production practice is crystallization of wisdom and civilization of the Chinese nation, is the bond to link national sentiments and foundation to maintain national unity." "Intangible cultural heritage and tangible cultural heritage jointly carry forward the civilization of human society, reflecting diversity of the world culture. The unique spiritual value, way of thinking, imagination and cultural consciousness of the Chinese nation contained in China's intangible cultural heritage are the fundamental basis to maintain our cultural identity and cultural sovereignty." Therefore, the most-central value of ICH is the "cultural gene," which is the sign of cultural identity and cultural unity of a country, a nation and a region. The essential importance of ICH protection is to enable inheritance this kind of cultural gene and spirit, allowing it to be passed down from generation to generation. This is also the basic context in which ICH enterprises inherit and expand the role of intangible cultural heritage.

However, enterprises of whatever kind have to follow the fundamental rules of enterprise operation: that is, can products meet social demand, will they be accepted by consumers. To meet this requirement, enterprises should change the content and form of their products depending on time and place, as well as desires of consumers. Theme, content, and form of traditional culture that are tied to traditional techniques will change depending on consumer demand. Thus the unique historical, regional and ethnic character of intangible cultural heritage will be overwhelmed by modern China's culture and by cultures that cut across regions and nations. Although this adaptability meets the requirements of modern enterprise development, it is far removed from ICH policy requirements. In a word, policy on ICH protection requires the maintenance of culture individuality while commodity circulation focuses on general characteristics and universality. This situation stands as another challenge faced by ICH enterprises balancing between national policy and enterprise practice.

Third, the conflict between fulfillment of obligations to protect and the pursuit of economic interests.

Article 8 of *Interim Measures for Protection and Management of State-level Intangible Cultural Heritage* prescribes that: "Protection units of national intangible cultural heritage project should perform the following duties: 1. comprehensively collect material object, data of the project, register, sort out and file them; 2. provide necessary conditions for inheriting and related activities of the project; 3. provide effective protection for the project-related cultural sites; 4. actively carry out exhibition activities for the project; 5. report implementation of the protection to the culture administrative department of the local people's government that in charge of specific protection of the project and accept their oversight." Article 13 prescribes that: "A representative successor of national intangible cultural heritage items should fulfill the obligation of inheritance; in case the successor loses the capacity to inherit or be unable to perform the obligations, another representative successor shall be separately determined in accordance with the procedures; in case the successor fail to comply with the duty of inheritance, the successor shall be disqualified." Article 31 of the 4th of *Law of the People's Republic of China on Intangible Cultural Heritage* also includesclear regulations specifying the obligations of representative successors of representative intangible cultural heritage items.

Obligations put forward in these policies, laws and regulations of ICH enterprises and people involved hold the potential for conflict: On the one hand, as protection units, enterprises have a responsibility to cooperate with appropriate culture departments to show and publicize intangible cultural heritage to the public, participating in such national activities as The Olympic Games, World Exposition, China (Shenzhen) International Cultural Industry Fair and intangible cultural heritage exhibitions held by local governments and their departments, establishing ICH exhibition halls and repositories, and so on. On the other hand, as successors of intangible cultural heritage, technicians and managers of the enterprises also have the responsibility cooperate with competent culture departments to carry out campus and class activities of intangible cultural heritage. However, it is hard to avoid conflict between these preservation and presentation responsibilities and the pursuit of maximum economic benefit. Protection of intangible cultural heritage is the responsibility that our nation requires, while maximization of economic benefits is the responsibility of enterprises, thus ICH enterprises must find the balance between the two.

4. Adjusting the Issues of ICH Enterprises to National Policy

National policy is not only a kind of limitation, but also both a right and an opportunity for ICH enterprise practice. And over decade since launch of ICH protection by UNESCO, ICH enterprises have taken full advantage of opportunities afforded by national policies, experiencing a transformation from passivity to being active, from worrying about application to focusing on utilizing ICH during protection, all the while gaining rich practical experience.

First, innovative approaches to enterprise have been achieved through a combination of ICH protection and enterprise branding. Consider herbal tea maker Wanglaoji as an example. *Wanglaoji*

Herbal Tea was invented in the period of Emperor Daoguang in the Qing Dynasty; boasting a history of more than 180 years, it has been praised as "Ancestor of Herbal Tea." According to traditional formulas of adopting ingredients of first-class herbaceous materials and adhering to traditional cooking techniques, *Wanglaoji* Herbal Tea is carefully prepared, its herbal essence extracted using modern science and technology. Containing herbaceous plants which have effect of preventing excessive internal heat in body, such as chrysanthemum, liquorice, mesona (a kind of plant used as a medicinal herb in ancient times), honeysuckle, *Wanglaoji* can prevent excessive internal body heat and is beneficial to health. The JDB group sets up its red-can Wanglaoji brand by fully integrating the time-honored brand "Wanglaoji" with a masterpiece of national intangible cultural heritage—the concept of "Guangdong herbal tea"—while using operating practices of modern brand (such as charitable donations, etc.), which not only promotes the development of Guangdong herbal tea industries but at the same time helps its inheritance and transmission.

Second, the development of enterprises' technical innovation model has been reached through combination of ICH protection and technical innovation of enterprises. For example, enterprises of the gambiered Guangdong gauze in places like Shunde, Shenzhen, and other sites integrate modern technological methods into the manufacture of gambiered Guangdong gauze while using as its basis the inherited traditional manufacturing process, with fairly good effect. Some ICH enterprises get policy and financial support from the government as a result of such technical innovation, which, to some extent improves the management environment of the enterprise.

Third, some innovation of modes of production and marketing have been achieved through a combination of ICH protection and business practices. Guangdong Jiujiang Distillery Co., Ltd., formed a vertical business model through a combination of ICH protection and its own classified production and management (the business model featuring a combination of traditional handicraft and modern science and technology, simultaneously targeting both high-end demand and popular demand), which obtained favorable social and economic benefits, achieving a "win-win" outcome for both ICH protection and business operations.

Fourth, innovation of management pattern for enterprises or industries has been reached by connecting enterprise management with government ICH protection regulation process. More than 50 enterprises led by the manufacturer of red-can Wanglaoji, the JDB Group, Since Dec. 19, 2014, the Red Can Wanglaoji's external packing decoration right has been escheated to Guangzhou Pharmacy Holdings. jointly signed *The Convention on Herbal Tea Development* on July 13, 2011, which became a model for the participation of ICH enterprises in the harmonious development of the economy and culture, of enterprises and industries. Under guidance of Department of Quality and Technical Supervision, Zhongshan Juxiangyuan Food Company Limited (a local enterprise that mainly produce bakery foods) took the lead to set a unified standard for the traditional food—almond cake: a standard which regulated production practices of local cake-producing enterprises.

After many steps to improve and perfect it, the unified standard has been set as the local standard of Guangdong Province since January 1, 2005. [2]

Neither all of the national policies nor every one of the enterprise practices are perfect. Whether national ICH policy or enterprise practice, both should take into account relationships linking the past, present and the future. If national policies are primarily established in consideration of the present and future cultural value of intangible cultural heritage, it is its present and future economic value that is mostly attended to by enterprise practice. These different value demands—often for the same object—are the source of conflict between national policy and enterprise practice, and are also the basis for the two to adjust to each other.

There are some other notable problems residing in the conflict and necessary adjustment between national policy and enterprise practice.

First, national policies have been abused by enterprises for their own benefit, such as abuse of rights for application of ICH masterpieces and successors of representative projects at all levels. Especially, there has been misunderstanding and abuse of ICH productive protection, in which enterprises simply equate productive protection with industrialization. ICH protection is aimed to protect cultural diversity, that, "cultural difference constitutes the basic condition of supporting harmonious social life of all nationalities so to achieve its continued development, being the core value in system of national existence." However, "industrialized mass production rejects difference. It severs the natural unification between space and time that developed in the laboring process and removes their own limitations. Its disseverance of the 'time-space' structure excludes complexity caused by stretching of time and change of space, exempts the economic burden to deal with this kind of complexity. In productive process of modern times, 'labor' has been regarded as a kind of concrete manufacturing activity to be described and set mathematically in advance, that is all things are made explicit during rational planning and all accidental factors are eliminated by this kind of rational logic. 'Labor' with specific manufacturing goal forms a closed and stable circulation system, in which running of 'productivity' is entirely under the predefined control. All these have ensured the one-off and accurate capital input, with huge production efficiency and economic benefit. 'Standardization' is the core technical strength of industrialized mass production, which fundamentally excludes and strives to eliminate 'cultural difference.'"[3] "Industrialization requires scale and standard, while culture requires individuality, uniqueness and difference."[4]

Second, overlapping areas of authority and chaotic management of enterprises have made it difficult to implement the rights and interests given to enterprises by ICH policies. For example, enterprises of traditional arts and crafts which have been being managed by the State Economic and Trade Commission, which applies the pattern and standard of general production enterprises in areas of management and taxation, which made it difficult for these enterprises to enjoy the national preferential policies aimed at intangible cultural heritage and cultural industry.

Third, the overprotection and resource monopoly of intangible cultural heritage enjoyed by some enterprises has, to some extent, hampered or deprived the rights and interests also shared by related groups. Most of the intangible cultural heritages are intergenerational, territorial and ethnic creations—cultural resources shared by all groups. But to some extent, the application for ICH intellectual property protection and the trademark registration by some enterprises undermines the rights of related groups to share the culture, an outcome that strays far from the UNESCO's purpose of protecting intangible cultural heritage.

5. Conclusion

Protection for intangible cultural heritage is a long-term systemic project, So both our nation and enterprises have to proceed with clear identities and explicit roles. The goals of the nation and demands of enterprises should both be considered when establishing ICH policies. ICH policies of China are formed on the basis of the *Convention for the Safeguarding of the Intangible Cultural Heritage*, which reflect the spirit of the convention while honoring "Chinese characteristics." When engaged in the practice of implementing national policies, enterprises are faced with new problems as well as new opportunities, experiencing the transition from passivity to being active participants, from autonomy to self-discipline. Attention to these questions not only provides valuable experience for all those engaged in the world-wide protection of intangible cultural heritage, but also puts forward problems deserving of continual vigilance.

Bibliography

[1] http://news.sohu.com/20100602/n272515635.shtml。

[2]《中山日报》2004 年 12 月 12 日。

[3] 吕品田《重振手工与非物质文化遗产生产性方式保护》,《中南民族大学学报》2009 年第 4 期, 第 4 页。

[4] 徐艺乙《非遗保护:重新发现"手"的价值》,《东方早报》2009 年 2 月 16 日。

The US Historic Preservation Movement and Intangible Cultural Heritage

Michael Ann Williams[*]

In the United States, historic preservation movements and concerns for the study and preservation of intangible cultural heritage have typically developed in parallel, but separate, movements. Assertions of national, regional, or ethnic identity spawn such movements, as do anxieties about the impact of cultural change. In the 19th century, Americans sought to establish their own identity separate from that of Europe through the creation of a national literature and the glorification of its history. The earliest American historic preservation efforts centered on the preservation of buildings associated with George Washington, the first president of the US. In 1850, Washington's former headquarters, the Hasbrouck House, became the first building in the United States acquired for preservation purposes; six years later the Mount Vernon Ladies Association formed to preserve Mount Vernon, Washington's private home. In the late 19th century, attention also turned to the unique cultural make-up of the country and a focus on its native population (and to a lesser extent, the culture of African Americans). Unlike early folklore studies in Europe, which focused on the European peasant class, the American Folklore Society (founded in 1888) included the wide range of cultures in the United States within its purview.

By the late 19th century, the federal government had taken steps to preserve ancient sites as well as to document the intangible heritage of Native Americans (even as other branches of the government were intent on destroying this culture). In 1906 *the Antiquities Act*, a national law, set aside federal lands containing significant tangible cultural resources, such as archaeology sites. Devil's Tower in Wyoming was the first site so designated. In recent years this site has been a source of conflict between Native American groups, who consider that site to be sacred, and non-Native recreational climbers.

---

[*] Michael Ann Williams, Professor and Head of Department of Folk Stualies and Arothoopology at the Western Kentucky University.

During 1920s and early 1930s, local and regional efforts to preserve folk culture and the builtenvironment began to flourish. The first generation of folk festivals was born (three Appalachian folk festivals were created between 1928 and 1932 in the southern US) and a few cities, concerned with preserving their distinctive character, created historic districts. In 1931, the southern US city of Charleston, South Carolina, established the first historic district in the country; soon after, cities such as New Orleans, Louisiana, and San Antonio, Texas, established districts of their own.

The first folk festival in the United States that was both national and multi-cultural was created in 1934 in St. Louis, Missouri. Founded by Sarah Gertrude Knott, the National Folk Festival included Native American, Hispanic and African American performers (as well as Anglo-American) and soon also included the recent immigrants to the United States. The National Folk Festival was also the first to feature both occupational lore and programming for school children. The festival travelled to different locations and for most of its early decades was funded primarily by newspapers (most notably the *St. Louis Globe-Democrat*, *the Washington Post* and *the Philadelphia Bulletin*) and other sources rather than the federal government.① The National Folk Festival continues today and still travels to different cities across the US.

Federal relief efforts created in the 1930s to address the economic hardships of the Great Depression, especially the Works Progress Administration (WPA), spawned programs that documented both intangible cultural heritage and historic buildings. While the intent of these programs was primarily to relieve unemployment, they provided valuable models for how the federal government could work to preserve heritage. The Historic American Buildings Survey (HABS), started under the WPA to employ unemployed architects, began systematic documentation of buildings, both folk and high style, and was eventually transferred to the National Park Service, where it continues today with its sister programs, the Historic American Engineering Record and the Historic American Landscapes Survey. In 1935 the US national government passed *the Historic Sites Act*, declaring it national policy to preserve historic sites buildings and objects for public use. Various programs within WPA also documented intangible cultural heritage, especially the Federal Writers Project. Notable folklorists, such as Zora Neale Hurston and Alan Lomax, were employed in these efforts. Changes in US national government policy toward Native Americans, under the "Indian New Deal," also lead to programs within the Department of Interior to preserve art and craft traditions.

In the two decades after the Depression years, relatively little was accomplished in federal policy addressing the preservation of tangible or intangible cultural resources. However, the

---

① For a complete history of the National Folk Festival see: Michael Ann Williams, *Staging Tradition: John Lair and Sarah Gertrude Knott* (Urbana and Chicago: University of Illinois Press, 2006).

building of the interstate highway system and industrialization that took place in the 1950s and the "urban renewal" projects of the 1960s would ultimately encourage the insurgence of a new historic preservation movement. The mid-1960s saw also a renewed enthusiasm for national government support of the arts and protection of the built environment. In 1965 *the National Historic Preservation Act* created the national government-run preservation system as we know it today, including the refashioned *National Register of Historic Places*. Four years later, *the National Environmental Policy Act* mandated that cultural as well as natural resources be included in environmental impact statements accompanying federal construction projects. The National Endowments for the Arts and the Humanities were created in the mid-1960s, with folk arts specifically included in the enabling legislation, thanks in part to the efforts of Sarah Gertrude Knott, founder of the National Folk Festival. [1] The late 1960s and early 1970s saw the growth of the academic discipline of folklore in the United States as well as the reinvention of folklore programs in the public sector. This included the creation of the first statewide folklife programs, as well as the birth of an annual Festival of American Folklife at the Smithsonian Institution (the US national museum) in 1967, the establishment of the Folk Arts Program within the National Endowment for the Arts in 1974, and the establishment of the American Folklife Center at the Library of Congress (the US national Library) by *the American Folklife Preservation Act* in 1976.

During the late 1970s, concerns grew for protecting cultural intangibles as part of federal preservation policy. With the advent of the folklife studies movement in the United States, more and more folklorists became interested in material culture. Folklorists with special interests in vernacular architecture, who found employment in government funded architectural survey and documentation programs, soon realized that federal law did not protect cultural intangibles as they did historic buildings and archaeological sites. At the same time, archaeologists and preservationists concerned with the cultural context of the sites and buildings they documented became increasingly aware of the need to preserve the intangible aspects of culture.

A major step forward seemed to come in 1979 when the archaeologists of the National Park Service approached the American Folklife Center at the Library of Congress to propose adding a living culture element to the federally mandated Tennessee-Tombigbee Waterway project: a collaboration that could have made the consideration of intangible cultural resources a routine part of federal impact studies. While programs addressing the preservation of tangible and intangible cultural heritage had developed on parallel tracks, efforts to integrate the two faltered. *The Environmental Impact Statement (EIS)* process mandated by *the National Environmental Policy Act* could be used to protect intangible cultural heritage but infrequently had done so. The construction of a major waterway connecting the Tennessee and Tombigbee rivers by the Army Corps of Engineers

---

[1] Livingston Biddle, *Our Government and the Arts* (New York: ACAD Books, 1988), p. 30.

became a test case for the inclusion of intangible cultural heritage in a federal mitigation process. Although the American Folklife Center had been asked to document folklife in the impact area, which would be flooded by the new waterway, it ultimately withdrew for political and ethical reasons when influential folklorists however chose to see the funding for "mitigation" as a form of blood money. Consequently, the architecture of the impact area was documented by the Historic American Buildings Survey, but the lives of the people who occupied the architecture and were ultimately displaced by the construction went largely unrecorded.

The "Tenn-Tom" dilemma has been an issue that has weighed upon my mind, as I was the first folklorist ever employed by HABS and I worked on the summer project documenting the histories of the structures in the impact area of the Tennessee-Tombigbee Waterway. From the ground up, I saw the project very differently than those who opposed the project from the outside. People who were being displaced sat and watched on as we carefully measured every inch of their homes and the message they probably received was that the structures were more important than they were. If preservationists can argue to save buildings and environmentalists to save endangered species within the context of federal preservation and environmental law, surely we can find a way to act as advocates for human beings. Would we really want all our environmental biologists to chastely sit back and refuse to dirty their hands rather than ensure that construction projects comply with federal environmental law?

Some prominent folklorists have since reassessed the decision to withdraw from the Tennessee-Tombigbee project. Recently retired American Folklife Center Director Peggy Bulger, in her 2002 presidential address before the American Folklore Society, criticized the decision to withdraw (which took place long before she became AFC director). She noted that African American activist Jane Sapp, who represented several constituencies along the proposed waterway, recalled that in the decision-making process, she heard "arguments from people who had never been in the area and did not know the real issues." Dr. Bulger concluded, "If we refuse categorically to work with agents of change for ethical reasons, we also are refusing to assist tradition bearers and communities to confront and mitigate the effects of that change—and we leave a hole in the documentary record. We need to have more faith in ourselves."[①] Others outside the discipline concluded that folklorists were more interested in splitting ethical hairs than in taking action to help people and preserve culture. Tom King, who oversaw the federal Section 106 review process (the process by which buildings and sites are protected in federal construction projects), later wrote scathingly about the folklorists' stance:

---

① Peggy Bulger, "Looking Back, Moving Forward: The Development of Folklore as a Public Profession (AFS Presidential Plenary Address, 2002)," *Journal of American Folklore* 116 (2003): 384-388.

Although I found it stimulating to work with the folklife people, they never seemed to me to relate to the rough-and-tumble world I was involved in—the world of Section 106 ... The folklife people shied away from projects like the Tenn-Tom with righteous morality but did little to help the people whose traditional lives were upset by such projects—except to record their songs and stories for posterity, and to put on festivals to showcase their skills in the hope that they would thus be transmitted down the generations in some form or other. These are worthy enterprises, but they didn't engage the agents of change; they didn't confront the conflicts between tradition and modernity directly; they didn't help us with the Section 106 review. They wouldn't help the Navajo and Hopi with the Forest Service or the people of Poletown with the Detroit city government. ①

With due respect, the American Folklife Center did continue to address the issue of the inclusion of intangible cultural heritage within the federal preservation framework. Through the influence of the AFC's director Alan Jabbour, Section 502 of the 1980 amendments to *the National Historic Preservation Act* mandated the preparation of a report on preserving and conserving the intangible elements of our cultural heritage such as arts, skills, folklife, and folkways. The resulting report, published in 1983, advocated for "cultural conservation," an integrated effort to preserve and encourage both tangible and intangible cultural heritage. To a large extent, however, the report backed away from national government mitigation and enumerative strategies in favor of grassroots programs of "encouragement." The report specifically recommended against "reactive Federal involvement in the preservation process, that is, on actions triggered by the impact of major development projects"② and consequently had little subsequent effect on national government preservation policy. It is difficult to judge in retrospect how much the overly timid and modest recommendations of the report were shaped (on the left) by the moral critique of some within the discipline of folklore or (on the right) by the political climate of the Reagan administration. I suspect a good bit of both. In either case, the report failed to have any lasting impact on the federal system of cultural and environmental protection. As Tom King noted the hope to include cultural intangibles during the Reagan administration was "the most ethereal of dreams and by the time the administration changed, the recommendation had dropped out of [Cultural Resource Management's] collective memory."③

---

① Thomas F. King, *Places That Count: Traditional Cultural Properties in Cultural Resource Management* (Walnut Creek: Alta Mira Press, 2003), p. 32.

② Ormond Loomis, *Cultural Conservation: The Protection of Cultural Heritage in the United States* (Washington D. C.: Library of Congress, 1983), p. 83.

③ King, *Places that Count*, p. 32.

In adopting the term "cultural conservation," the American Folklife Center's report made the intellectually justifiable choice not to distinguish arbitrarily between intangible and tangible culture. The term conservation was chosen partially to ally the concept with environmentalism and to suggest the nurturing of living cultures, rather than freezing them in the past. However, the term "cultural conservation" moved us away from confronting the problem that within the American legal system, preservation law only recognizes the tangible. More recently, as our discipline has moved in the direction of greater international dialog about cultural policy, we have found ourselves linguistically out of step in discussions of intangible cultural heritage or "ICH."

After the publication of the Cultural Conservation report, the American Folklife Center however did sponsor several model projects in the 1980s, including *"The Grouse Creek Cultural Survey"*, which integrated the methods of folklorists and preservationists, and *"One Space, Many Places: Folklife and Land Use in New Jersey's Pinelands National Reserve"*, which provided a model for folklorists working in the context of land use planning. [1] In 1990, inspired in part by the work of the folklorists affiliated with the American Folklife Center, *the National Register of Historic Places* took a step forward in recognizing the importance of cultural heritage in creating the designation of "traditional cultural properties," places associated with cultural practices or beliefs of a living community that are rooted in that community's history and are important in maintaining the continuing cultural identity of the community. [2] Although properties nominated under this designation must still have place referents, they do acknowledge the significance of intangible cultural heritage associated with place. Unfortunately, in practice, this designation has been used almost solely to nominate Native American properties.

In 2005, folklorist Alan Jabbour used the concept of Traditional Cultural Property in the North Shore Environmental Impact Statement in the Great Smoky Mountains National Park, arguing for the eligibility of cemetery decoration traditions. [3] In the 1940s, the construction of the Fontana Dam inundated a number of communities bordering the park and flooded access roads to others. The latter communities were then made part of the park and the displaced were promised that an access road to their cemeteries would be constructed. The long-delayed road was begun, and then stopped, due ostensibly for environmental reasons. The "road to nowhere" became emblematic to the local community of the bad faith of the federal government and festered into a much local anti-

---

[1] Thomas Carter and Carl Fleischhauer, *The Grouse Creek Cultural Survey: Integrating Folklife and Historic Preservation Field Research* (Washington D. C.: Library of Congress, 1988), and Mary Hufford, *One Space, Many Places* (Washington D. C.: Library of Congress, 1986).

[2] Patricia Parker and Thomas F. King, "Guidelines for Evaluating and Documenting Traditional Cultural Properties," *National Register Bulletin*, no. 38.

[3] Alan Jabbour, Phillip E. Coyle, and Paul Webb, *North Shore Cemetery Decoration Project Report* (National Park Service, 2005).

environmental sentiment.① Although a *National Register* nomination was not prepared as part of the Environmental Impact Statement, acceptance of eligibility alone offered protection for the cultural practices. Decoration traditions such as dinner on the ground and the baptism would be recognized along with the cemeteries themselves.② The North Shore project exemplifies both the constructive involvement of a folklorist within an Environmental Impact Statement process and also the successful use of the traditional cultural properties designation for a non-Native American affiliated place.

While the National Park Service struggled with how and why to designate traditional cultural properties under the National Register system, some public folklorists sought to find more grassroots approaches to recognize cultural significant places. Among the most successful is Place Matters, created by City Lore in New York City.③ A more rural example, based on Place Matters, is the Register of Very Special Places, created by Traditional Arts of Upstate New York (TAUNY).④ In both cases, the nomination system is considerably simpler than the process required by the National Register of Historic Places and ideally comes from local citizens, rather than preservation professionals. However, these designations, while they do provide publicity for the property (especially in cases where they are endangered), do not provide protection from federally funded construction, or tax incentives for income producing properties, as the National Register designation does.

Within the past two years, the National Register has become open to a broadening of the application of the Traditional Cultural Property designation, especially its application to non-Native American properties. The American Folklore Society's Task Force on Historic Preservation, which includes representatives from both City Lore/Place Matters and TAUNY, have met with National Register personnel and are working on a model project, funded by Western Kentucky University, to bring the best of both the grassroots and National Register programs (adding the benefits of greater projection and tax incentives from the latter). We are working with the National Register staff to nominate properties already registered by Place Matters and TAUNY, in order to provide models on how to nominate non-Native Traditional Cultural Properties. So far we have discovered that some owners of considered properties are suspicious of the involvement of the national government, even though they did not object to the publicity connected to being on the grassroots register. Current projects are documenting Caribbean "casitas" (small community houses built mostly on abandoned

---

① Michael Ann Williams, *Great Smoky Mountain Folklife* (Jackson: University Press of Mississippi, 1995), pp. 155-160.

② See also Alan Jabbour and Karen Singer Jabbour, *Decoration Day in the Mountains: Traditions of Cemetery Decoration in the South Appalachians* (Chapel Hill: University of North Carolina Press, 2012).

③ Steven J. Zeitlin, "Conserving our Cities' Endangered Spaces," in *Conserving Culture: A New Discourse on Heritage*, edited by Mary Hufford (Urbana and Chicago: University of Illinois Press, 2006), pp. 215-228.

④ Varick Chittenden, "'Put Your Very Special Place on the North Country Map!'" Community Participation in Cultural Landmarking," *Journal of American Folklore* (2006) 119: 47-65.

lots) in New York City, a Chinese tea house in New York's Chinatown, and a village green in upstate New York. ①

Much work has been carried out in the United States to preserve and encourage intangible cultural heritage outside of the existing historic preservation system. However, cultural conservation's promise of an integrated national government policy has not been realized. American folklorists and others concerned with intangible cultural heritage need to take these steps:

· Reassessing how we can be involved with federally mandated impact statements to help advocate for local communities and intangible cultural heritage.
· Advocating for the expansion of existing programs, such as the National Register, in order to better recognize and protect living communities and cultural heritage.
· Renewing leadership at the federal level to move toward a more integrated federal policy on cultural heritage.

---

① The project is funded by a Research and Creative Activities Program (RECAP) grant from Western Kentucky University. Michael Ann Williams is Project Director and Rachel Hopkin, Sarah McCartt Jackson, Caitlin Coad, and Katrina Wynn are fieldworkers. Molly Garfinkel represented City Lore/Place Matters and Varick Chittenden guided the Traditional Arts of Upstate New York (TAUNY) project.

Chinese Urbanization and Intangible Cultural Heritage Protection

Gao Xiaokang[*]

1. Historical Trends in Intangible Cultural Heritage Protection during Chinese Urbanization

Although the phrase "Intangible Cultural Heritage Protection" came into use after UNESCO introduced *the Convention for the Safeguarding of Intangible Cultural Heritage*, in contemporary China there had already been many activities similar to intangible cultural heritage (ICH) protection long before the Convention was launched, including collecting, filing and protecting folk culture, literature and art. Undoubtedly, before the UNESCO concept of ICH Protection was brought forth, the mechanisms for protecting heritage were obviously different from what we now understand as ICH Protection. The most obvious difference is that ICH Protection today emphasizes the inheritance, revitalization and development of ICH in the modern world. Integrating the development of traditional culture into our present-day cultural environment has shaped the character of ICH protection, but this focus also brings new problems.

Urbanization is one of the most important trends in modern-day China. Following a decline in urban centers during the 1970s, since the 1980s there has been large-scale reconstruction and expansion of cities all over our country. This trend has, to some extent, brought huge changes to China's social life and cultural forms. In fact, these changes had a significant impact on the inheritance and protection of traditional culture.

Broadly speaking, during the 1980s the primary goal of urbanization was "modernization," a concept that was implemented by tearing down old buildings, removing old city blocks, getting rid of the old environment, then constructing a new one. In keeping with the "modernizing" concept,

---

[*] Gao Xiaokang, Professor at the Institute of Chinese Intangible Cultural Heritage.

people's lifestyles changed, tilting toward fashion imported from abroad. During this period, "modernization" seriously damaged traditional culture—folk culture in particular. Since the middle of 1990s, different concepts about city construction began to emerge. People started to rethink and correct problems of homogenization and the loss of the real culture caused by the implementation of all-encompassing modernization. As to the management of a city's culture, emphasis was now given to traditional culture, including protecting and carrying forward ICH during the development and construction of a city. However, much traditional cultural heritage had already been destroyed during the construction of cities. And although people had thoughts about protecting traditional culture heritage, what they actually did was to build the economy under the banner of protecting culture, using culture simply as a means to develop the economy. Given this approach to protection, what people accomplished was something that looks right, but in effect was blind. As a consequence, a new round of destruction occurred.

Since 2000, especially since the Kun Opera and Qin were included on the world intangible cultural heritage list, China ratified *the Convention for the Safeguarding of Intangible Cultural Heritage*, and our national government set up the "Cultural Heritage Day," the popularity of ICH protection in city construction has been increasing. First, the ICH application boom occurred, then ICH protection, exhibition and performance, education and transmission were added to the development of the public cultural service system. Since then, cultural industries centered on ICH have thrived.

In brief, over the past six or seven years, activity in the fields of urban development and ICH protection have been increasingly connected. Because of this emphasis on protection of traditional culture, there exists the possibility of a new chance for intangible cultural heritage to both survive and be transmitted in an era of modernization. However, even though there exist opportunities, a new problem has arisen: ICH has become modernized and commercialized. Will this reality change the real meaning of traditional culture, causing its decline? And can ICH become a simulacrum or commercial brand? Can ICH heritage separate itself from its underlying cultural group, lose its own character when it leaves behind its cultural ecology and relocates in a modern city? These issues were the facts-on-the-ground we had to face during China's urbanization.

2. Leaving the Village for the Modern City

Can modern life in the city accommodate folk culture? This is a controversial question within the frame of ICH Protection. According to conventional wisdom about modernization, traditional cultural forms and old social structures may die out together as city live evolves. However, as a matter of fact, even as social structure is transformed, the psychological benefits and the sense of identity maintained by the "Little Tradition" groups can still be transmitted down through the ages.

The Hakka Folk Song Fair from Yuexiu Park in Guangzhou was a good example for this phenomenon. The Hakka people lived in the southeast foot of Hwun Yam Shan (Yuexiu Hill), a district known as Xiaobei. In the early 1940s, Hakka from Xingning of Guangdong opened a cloth factory or workshop, and began to develop a cloth-dyeing industry. Private businessmen hired many workers from the Hakka hometown. When these workers settled down in Xiabei, they attracted more and more relatives and friends from their hometown. As a result, the Hakka community grew, Hakka became the most-numerous residents of the area, and Hakka folk songs naturally followed.

In 1950s, Hakka people from Xiaobei began to sing near Yuexiu Park. Back then, during the "Cultural Revolution", traditional Hakka folk songs were seen as one of the 4-old things (old thoughts, old customs, old habits, and old traditions), so the music was suppressed. But after Reform and Opening-up, Hakka folk songs flourished again. In 1996, the Hongqiao Hakka Folk Song Association was set up. People had gathered to sing songs spontaneously, but now their activities became organized and their influence spread. In 1997, the gathering of 'Monthly Twelve' was renamed Folk Song Fair.

As we can see, the folk song fair is not actually in the mainstream of fashion or entertainment in Guangzhou, but instead is a specific kind of expression that local Hakka support. This phenomenon has wide significance, for Guangzhou is a city possessing a fruitful multi-culture, in which people from different regions and different ethnic groups live together, in which identities of different traditional cultures play a major role in constructing the city's cultural diversity and its cultural reputation, while providing benefits consciously desired by city people.

3. Intangible Cultural Heritage and the Influence of Urban Leisure Culture

The development of cultural tourism is one phenomenon that demonstrates the close relationship between intangible cultural heritage and local economic development. Beginning in the late 1990s, an urban leisure culture developed in tandem with growth of the Chinese economy, as did the tourism industry. In this period, tourism shifted from its emphasis on visiting nature to using leisure time to visit cultural activities. As a result, culture became a highlighted feature within tourism. In travel destinations rich with ICH assets, the development of folk culture turned out to be an important component of tourism products.

But leisure travel based on ICH collections and events seems to have had contradictory effects on ICH. On the positive side, leisure travel can be a form of "Productive Protection" —the development of tourism industry may improve local economies, give people a better life, and improve the visibility of ICH. Such outcomes increase the enthusiasm of relevant cultural groups for traditional culture, and for its protection as well. On the other hand, development of the tourism industry, especially the irresistible attraction of over-development, can actually destroy the cultural ecology of ICH. For example, two well-known Miao Villages—Langde and Xijiang in Kaili of Guizhou Province—became studies in the contentious relationship between ICH protection and development. Xijiang, which is well-known for its big population of Miao residents, is actively developing a tourism industry. Local people have benefited, and today many young people prefer to stay home and work in tourism service businesses. Because of this, the village is full of vigor. But at the same time, unchecked economic development destroyed both the natural environment and the cultural ecology. The village of Langde represents the alternative. This region was designated as a national ecological reservation, and the environment and ecology were protected quite well. But because of the absence of employment opportunities, local people have a little income and young people are seldom willing to stay, the whole village is filled mostly with old people; as a consequence cultural heritage protection and environmental protection both created problems.

This confounding situation is a typical outcome of leisure-industry influence on ICH protection, a conflict which almost can sometimes appear as an unbreakable deadlock.

4. City Culture Consumption and the "Productive Protection" of Intangible Cultural Heritage

Within the world of ICH, arts and crafts such as "Three Carvings, One Colored Porcelain and One Embroidery" were traditional cultural products that also contained commercial elements. It was therefore relatively appropriate to apply "Productive Protection" to this kind of intangible cultural heritage. But the distance between the demands of contemporary consumption in the city and the culture of traditional consumption has widened; this is the problem that traditionally-marketable ICH has had to face. Material resources and labor costs rose, while the historical traditional market was actually becoming smaller. Even worse, a large number of shoddy goods entered and had an impact on the market. Thus, it has become a big challenge for truly worthy crafts to both receive sufficient protection and be transmitted to future generations.

Although ICH items included in lists of intangible cultural heritage at all levels received support from the government and other segments of society, without a healthy market the effects of protection will not last for long. Currently, the situation of protecting intangible cultural heritage—such as arts and crafts protection—seems to succeed in this balance: where the character of protection is quite good, and where the cultural-consumption market is developing relatively well. Generally speaking, the aesthetic, cultural and historical value of traditional crafts cannot receive appropriate recognition and respect within the atmosphere consumption values found in most of cities. In this regard, it may be that the cultivation of knowledge about traditional culture and the value of manual labor, as well as the nourishment of cultural taste and an understanding of the spiritual implications of the consuming lifestyle, may be required if we are to create necessary conditions within modern social ecology that will enable us to advance the protection and transmission of traditional arts and crafts.

Music Recording Copyright in the United States: Challenges, Issues, and the Need for Cultural Heritage Policy

Daniel Sheehy[*]

Copyright laws and practices in the United States that govern music recordings have a direct bearing on the accessibility of our recorded music heritage and the vitality of musical creation. Laws favoring ownership over accessibility, a patchwork of inconsistent laws enacted over nearly a century, uncertainties of legal interpretation, and lack of public awareness of theprinciples and particulars of copyright law may deprive Americans and people around the world of access to important reservoirs of our musical heritage. I come to this topic not so much from the perspective of a cultural heritage policy specialist, but rather as a promoter of cultural heritage and a practitioner often caught in the web of heritage-unfriendly laws and practices.

I base my remarks mainly on my 11 years of experience as Director of Smithsonian Folkways Recordings, the nonprofit record label of the Smithsonian Institution, the national museum of the United States. Both policy and practice in the realm of music recording copyright in the United States can be very complex, so given the limited time available here today, I will streamline my approach and be targeted in my scope. I first will give a compact, selective, and simple overview of US recorded music copyright law for audio and video as it pertains to the issues I will highlight. Then, I will point to several current issues and challenges that could benefit from cultural heritage policy development and laws that reflect it.

First, it is important to keep in mind the rationale for copyright. The purpose of copyright in the United States is to encourage creativity and innovation by allowing the creator to receive exclusive material benefits from his or her work for a reasonable period of time. This goes back to the beginnings of our nation: Article 8, Section 8 of *the United States Constitution* says, "the Congress

---

[*] Daniel Sheehy, Director and Curasor of Smithsonian Folkways Recordings.

shall have Power... To promote the Progress of Science and useful Arts, by securing for limited Times to Authors and Inventors the exclusive Right to their respective Writings and Discoveries." Building on this, our Congress established the length of copyright as a matter of law, and, as in the making of many laws, it is the subject of ongoing debate, and the length has changed over time. Currently in the United States, the basic length of copyright is the lifetime of the creator plus 70 years. The intent of this period of time is to allow both the creator and his or her heirs to benefit from the work. After that time period, the creation passes into the public domain for the benefit of all. This balance between the rights of the copyright ownerand use by the public is a key point of copyright law debate that pertains to cultural heritage.

Music recordings, audio or video, have their own peculiarities among the many areas of copyright law. For example, there may several categories of copyright in a single work. The four categories of relevance here are 1) mechanical rights, 2) synchronization rights, 3) sound recording rights, and 4) performance rights. The first three—mechanical rights, synchronization rights, and sound recording rights—are forms of what are known as reproduction rights; the fourth—performance rights—is a category of public performing rights. These rights may be delegated to others through legal contract, usually called a license. The laws and practices surrounding the contractual licensing of rights to a third party for the use of a pre-existing sound recording are directly related to the accessibility of our recorded musical heritage.

Mechanical rights have to do with the composition of a work. A composer creates a piece of music, and when it is recorded and sold, the composer receives a mechanical royalty from those sales. [As an aside, the term "mechanical" derives from the reference to the mechanical piano rolls of the early 20th century when this right was created.] In the United States, the US Congress determines by law the mechanical royalty rate for the sale of audio recordings. Currently, the statutory amount paid to authors is 9.1 cents per unit sold of that composition. If my record label publishes a CD with your composition on one of the tracks, I must pay you 9.1 cents for every copy sold of that CD, unless I can negotiate a lower price from you. For audio recordings, mechanical rights are compulsory, that is, anyone can get a license to use a composition in an audio recording they make, as long as they pay the statutory rate to the author, or more often, to the publishing company that manages that author's works.

In contrast, for video recordings (or moving image recordings in general), the artist or producer of a video does not have the right to use the composition without the expressed permission of the rights holder granting what are known as synchronization rights. Synchronization rights to use a composition are not compulsory. The royalty paid the author or publishing company must be negotiated in order to get a license to use it, and there is no fixed statutory rate.

Next, the person or company making the recording, that is, making the sound of the performance permanent through a fixed medium—such as a recording device fixing the sound of the performance to an audiotape or a hard drive—has sound recording rights to the recording made.

Typically in the music industry setting, a recording company contracts with an artist to make a recording and consequently owns the master recording, entitling it to receive payment from the sale or other exploitation of that recording. The artist is then paid a royalty from the record company as established by that contract. Artists typically receive 10-15% of the suggested retail price of the recording, after the recording company deducts various expenses for making, marketing, and distributing the recording. Owners of sound recording rights are not required to license their works to anyone, and the amount paid for the license is negotiated, not statutory.

Performance rights require that a royalty be paid for the public transmission of a sound recording. In the United States, there are inconsistencies in the application of this right, just as there were in the applicant of reproduction rights I just described. When a composer's work is played on the radio, a royalty is paid to that composer, but no royalty is paid to the owner of the sound recording, also meaning that no royalty is paid to the performing artist on that recording. When played in a film or video, both composer and sound recording owner receive a royalty. In recent years, a law established a new right, the Digital Performance Right in Sound Recordings, requiring that a royalty be paid to the owner of a sound recording for its streaming on the Internet.

To illustrate, a simple example would be the famous American country song "The Gambler." The composer, Don Shlitz, is paid mechanical royalties for the recording made through the publishing company that manages his work and collects the fee. The record company that made the recording of country singer Kenny Rogers performing "The Gambler" is paid both for the recording and for the performance rights that it owns, and Kenny Rogers is paid in turn for the performance rights through his contract with the record company.

In general, from the perspective of public access to cultural heritage, a main advantage of a compulsory, statutory rate system is that music is made more readily accessible to the public, and the costs of its use are known in advance. From the point of view of the rights holder, an advantage of a non-compulsory, negotiated rate is that it allows for free market principles to determine the amount charged. Consequently, in addition to the length of copyright, the tension between statutory rates and negotiated rates is another important point of the music recording copyright debate.

So, in sum, these are the four basic rights associated with an original audio recording: mechanical rights, synchronization rights, sound recording rights, and performance rights.

Licensing of sound recordings to third parties also has a direct bearing on access to our musical heritage and merits its own explanation. Licensing arrangements are determined contractually among interested parties, not by overarching law. Typically, a record label that owns a recording negotiates a fee to a user for the use of that recording, and often shares the income 50/50 with the artist performing on that recording. Such licensing of a recording is not compulsory, and the amount paid is negotiated, not set forth in law. The producer of a mainstream television commercial, for example, may be asked to pay tens or hundreds of thousands of dollars for the use of a single excerpt of a track of music, while a record label licensing the same track for a compilation CD may have to pay 5 cents for every track sold, amounting to 50 dollars per thousand copies sold. The third-party licensee also must negotiate fees for the synchronization rights to use the composition in the television advertisement, or pay the mechanical rights statutory amount in the case of the record label publishing the audio compilation. An important point here is that the owner of the sound recording is not required to share the sound recording with anyone and is not required to keep it in circulation.

Now, how might cultural heritage policy come to bear on this situation? First, since owners of recordings are not legally required to allow sound recordings they own to be used by others, this at times creates a situation in which a significant source of cultural heritage is "locked up" by its owner. From my own experience, the cause of this is likely to be financial efficiency, rather than ill intent. Companies may be reluctant to invest their human resources in financial deals that will not generate a significant profit. For example, I recall a case in which a large company stated it generally would not respond to a request to license a track of music unless it could be guaranteed a minimum upfront payment covering the sales of 25,000 units of that recording, quite a large number by most standards outside the realm of commercial pop music. When recordings of traditional music are withheld from public circulation, it limits access to an important source of our musical heritage.

As an aside, it is worth mentioning that in the United States, recordings have become a key resource in the transmission of musical tradition. We have very few intact, isolated, rural villages in which musical or spoken word traditions are preserved, and both commercial and field recordings of regional music traditions have provided a vital link to the past and played a key role in the preservation of musical style and repertoire. A great example of this is Smithsonian Folkways Recordings' Anthology of American Folk Music, originally a six-LP compilation of early commercial recordings of folk music from rural America edited by Harry Smith and published in 1952. The Anthology immediately attracted the interest of many devotees of folk music performance, who enthusiastically learned the repertoire and absorbed the style they heard on those recordings. Some musicians even searched for and found the surviving performers on the Anthology and brought them to perform in US cities and college campuses, where an entire new generation of musicians embraced their values and life style as well as their music, feeding the major American folk music revival of the 1950s and 1960s. When Smithsonian Folkways Recordings reissued the Anthology in 1997, it once again renewed broad public interest in these traditions, as hundreds of thousands of copies of the reissued recording were sold. The next year, the National Academy of Recording Arts and Sciences recognized the importance of the Anthology with two Grammy awards. If UNESCO were to recognize influential treasures of American intangible cultural heritage, the set of recordings known as the Anthology of American Folk Music might well be one of them.

Now, returning to our main thread—related to the "locking up" of musical heritage is the category of sound recordings known as "orphan works": recordings of unknown ownership. When it is not clear what record label or person owns an historical sound recording or the mechanical rights in the work recorded, it is clouded in legal uncertainty, discouraging its use. The recording may languish and not be circulated, in effect "locking it up" too.

To address these two problematic situations, I suggest creating "use it or lose it" legislation that would "unlock" sound recordings that have gone out of public circulation for two years. If a recording company does not allow, for whatever reason, the use of its recordings, then others should be allowed to exploit it for their purposes. For the moment, I would limit this legislation to the publication of new or reissued audio recordings, as opposed to moving image use, since the financial stakes for the latter are potentially much higher. A reasonable "use it or lose it" law could be of great benefit, both to the artist whose work is locked up and not being exploited, and to the culture that is deprived of part of its heritage. Under this scenario, financial benefits would be shared with the rights holders in the fashion of a compulsory license. All stakeholders—artists, authors, recording companies, and the public—would stand to benefit, as music would be integrated into society in a more free-flowing, dynamic way.

Next issue: The "patchwork" of copyright legislation created piecemeal over nearly a century has distorted the equitable, coherent application of music copyright. This is a question of practice as well as policy. There are many ambiguities in the application of copyright law as it pertains to audio recordings. Litigation—taking a lawsuit to the courts for resolution—is the usual way to resolve uncertainties and disagreements. Unfortunately, the overall process of litigation may be distorted because contending parties have access to legal services of unequal strength. For example, a wealthy company with many lawyers may be more inclined to make unwarranted claims or threaten legal action against a smaller company or individual who is unable to afford an expensive legal response or a costly trial. Corporate power ends up producing policy that may not match the law. Also, in the United States setting, strident assertions of rights, or arguments made in the process of contractual negotiation, often end up determining policy or setting precedent.

A comprehensive public policy based on framing our recorded musical heritage as the property of our nation, developed through equitable and democratic negotiation of the appropriate balance between public access to recorded cultural heritage and the privileges of private entities to restrict its use, could create a more equitable and understandable environment. To achieve this, public awareness of how the complex United States copyright system currently works must be raised through better public education. An educated public would be empowered to shape copyright law and the policy shaping their own heritage. (Another potential benefit of greater public awareness is the reduction of music piracy, since experience has shown that the majority of the American public is inclined to pay for music, as long as the price is reasonable and the service is convenient.) It is the responsibility of all stakeholders—authors, artists, recording companies, and publishers—to elevate these issues in the public discourse and to create sound, equitable, and democratic cultural heritage policy.

Concerning the Authenticity of Intangible Cultural Heritage

Liu Xiaochun[*]

1. The Question

Today in China, many local cultures that have a long history and broad influence have been embellished with the addition of political, economic and cultural value. Transcending the culturalspace-time of the original context and the community that owns traditional inheritance, cultures have been reconfigured to be displayed, owned, utilized, reproduced and even consumed broadly by people from outside the range of "the parents of inheritance,"[①] becoming cultural heritage of the entire nation and evenbeyond. Ever since the beginning of the 21st century, as the concept of cultural diversity works its way deeper into the heart of the Chinese people through

---

[*] Liu Xiaochun, Professor at the Institute of Chinese Intangible Cultural Heritage, Sun Yat-sen University.

[①] "The parent of inheritance" is a concept proposed by FUKUTA AJIO, a Japanese folklorist, against "the Method of Determining the Repetition" raised by Kunio Yanagita. Considering that the history shaped by the research conclusion in folklore exclusively drawn from Determination of Repetition is just mythological, he insists on abandoning the method of Determining the Repetition based on national search and replacing it with analysis of "the parents of inheritance" for the correlation among phenomena of folklore, from which the transformation can thus be found and hypothesis be raised. It is further pointed out that it is an illusion that the method of Determining the Repetition can figure out the process of transformation. In the light of this, the folklore should base its research on the parent of inheritance, i. e. the location of inheritance so as to find out the meaning of existence of folklore and its historical character.

参见［日］福田亚细男《日本民俗学方法序说——柳田国男与民俗学》，於芳、王京、彭伟文译，学苑出版社2010年版，第100、160页。

On the basis of above, the writer expand the concept of "the parent of inheritance" to the reference of the location of inheritance and the community of inheritance, which include the specific time and space and the community living within that inherits the cultural traditions. In the course of globalization and modernization, the entity of the meaning of "the parent of inheritance" is faced with the probability of disintegration. Turning the local cultures into heritage actually shows that considering "the parent of inheritance" exclusive with a stable core of culture is likely to be invalid. Consequently, "the parent of inheritance" can be taken as "an ideal type" in Marx Weber's sense, which is a concept for analysis.

protection activities addressing intangible cultural heritage, transforming old cultural values and assessments of rural life, those local cultures that used to be criticized as superstitious and lagging-behind have been renamed as "cultural heritage" of the nation. During the process of turning local cultures into heritage, political, economic and cultural forces enter into the development of villages and districts, building up a new type of cultural ecology that also reconfigures local cultures. In considering this concept of turning the local cultures into heritage and its related social cultural practice, we call it "Heritagism."

In the era of Heritagism, local culture, removed from the context of "life cultures", are reconfigured by diverse forces and replanted into the context of "cultural heritage." Inevitably, the local cultures are really changed. In the process of this construction, various social cultural transformations have taken place; it seems that all the stable things are bound to "vanish" while "authenticity" becomes a false proposition. In the contemporary China, given the prevalence of Heritagism, the various forces participating in cultural construction tend to be deeply confused by the authenticity of "life cultures" and "cultural heritage," be they governments, scholars, cultural inheritors or common people.

In my opinion, such confusion is closely related to the perception of cultural "authenticity," an idea long held by people. The perception of the authenticity of culture assumes the prior existence of culture—self-evident; having a long history, a stable core and distinct boundaries, each distinguished from one another; free for objective and reliable representation through media and acquaintance, understanding and utilization by others. This authentic culture, believed to be culture of the past, disappeared or disappearing, is considered to be functioning in extreme contrast to our modern, realistic but inauthentic one. Such a perception of the authenticity of culture has been deeply rooted in people's minds ever since the idea of culture was discovered and represented. Perceptions of culture are grounded in epistemology within Western philosophy, dependent on such concepts as Reality, the undoubted existence; Knowledge, the reoccurrence of reality; and Recurrence, which leads to a transparent reality. However, given ever-deepening cultural research and ongoing globalization and modernization, our knowledge, understanding and representation of culture have become deeper and deeper. Observers gradually realized that "authenticity"—in the sense of having "multiple meanings and the essence of uncertainty"[①]—is constantly under construction so that it cannot be settled by any single authority. In this paper, I will analyze the mutual construction connecting people's cultural values and specific objects so as to determine historical concepts of cultural authenticity—a determination which is should be of referential value to the intellectual's search to understand the relationship between cultural continuity and development in the era of "Heritagism."

---

① ［德］瑞吉娜·本迪克斯：《本真性》，李扬译，《民间文化论坛》2006 年第 4 期。

2. Four Cases

2.1 Shunde Cantonese Embroidery

Traditional Cantonese embroidery has long been widely dispersed and carried on in thousands of households. However, since 1990s, fewer and fewer people in the Canton area where the technique of Cantonese embroidery is centered are willing to take up the job; most artisans who concentrate on embroidery are located in the "Lao – Shao – Bian – Qiong" regions (Former revolutionary base areas, areas inhabited by minority nationalities, remote and border areas, and poverby – stricken areas), which prevents embroidery from achieving intensive production. Beginning in the 1990s, the Shunde Fude Art Work Co. Ltd. opened mills of Cantonese embroidery in over 100 counties of 11 provinces throughout the nation, including those from the north and the west of Guangdong, such as Guangxi, Hu'nan, Guizhou, and Sichuan. Organized as joint operation, self-operation, cooperatives, etc., the company is equipped with a technical group of about 30 members who carry out training and centralized production of Cantonese embroidery in the new regions of embroidery throughout the year. To the present day, 30 thousand workers have been trained, with about 8000 still engaged in embroidery and about 30 mills of embroidery operating with stability. Today approximately 10 processes have to be completed before a piece of embroidery work is finished, including market surveys, pattern design, embroidering and printing, model making, preparation of silk, dyeing, preparation of various needles and threads, delivery and manual embroidery in workshops, and finally return and careful checking after completion, and delivery. Except the procedure of manual embroidery in workshops, all other steps are carried out at the headquarters in Shunde.

2.2 The Making of Copper Percussion Musical Instruments in Zhangzi County, Shanxi

The introduction of modern techniques has carried the making of intangible cultural products with traditional craftsmanship from a stage dependent on manual practices to the stage of accurate and standardized operation. Despite the expansion of manufacturing scale, the enhancement of production and the related boost in economic impact, the ceremony and seriousness in traditional craftsmanship has gradually vanish, replaced by mechanical, repeated, accurate and standardized production of the era of mechanization or semi-mechanization which deprive the products of the unique character of intangible cultural heritage①. A typical case is the present situation surrounding the inheritance of techniques of copper percussion musical instrument production in Xi'nancheng Village, Nanzhang Town, Zhangzi County, Shanxi.

Having introduced semi-mechanized techniques into the process, the making of copper percussion musical instruments enters a new era of semi-mechanization that has replaced the period of traditional manual labor. Yan ××, the national representative inheritor, has not only mastered the traditional technique, but is also adept in technical innovation, which makes him the crucial force in the inheritance of intangible cultural heritage. With circle cutter, air hammer and forming machine employed by Yan ××, not only is the intensity of labor reduced, but the quality of the copper percussion musical instrument is far enhanced in terms of volume, quality of sound, shape, fineness, etc. Breakthroughs have been achieved in many aspects of the process, no matter the organization, the pace of productivity or the scale of production.

2.3 Shunde Yongchun Quan

When considering intangible cultural heritage, its regional and communal character is usually embodied in the tradition of continuation within the family and within the region. In order to effectively manage the relationship between the exclusiveness of inheritance and the inclusiveness of development, the inheritors should themselves carefully asses the opportunity and the context so as to make an appropriate decision favorable to both the inheritance and development of intangible cultural heritage. It has been determined through research that on one hand, the comparative exclusiveness of inheritance is good for retaining traditional relationships between the inheritance and "the parent of inheritance" (the region and the community); but on the other hand, if the inheritor overemphasizes traditional and exclusive approaches to continuation, the intangible cultural heritage may fail to keep pace with modern social transformation to the point at which it finally becomes endangered.

The current status of the inheritance of Shunde Yongchun Quan clearly illustrates the relationship between the exclusiveness of continuity and the inclusiveness of development in the field of intangible cultural heritage. As a category of the Yongchun Quan, along with Hong Kong Yongchun, Foshang and Guangzhou Yongchun, Gulao Yongchun, Shunde Yongchun cannot compare to Foshan Yongchun in either its influence or reputation. Currently, Shunde Yongchun has formed its hierarchy of inheritance made up of three generations, senior, middle and junior, but its inheritance is actually under a profound threat.

---

① [德] 瓦尔特·本雅明：《技术复制时代的艺术品》，胡不适 译，杭州：浙江文艺出版社 2005 年版，第 88—93 页。

2.4 Wuchuan Clay Sculpture in Guangdong

The development and changes affecting Wuchuan Clay Sculpture in Guangdong are a result of long-term interaction among the inheritors, the consumer (the receiver) and the market (the space of inheritance).

Originating in the late Qing Dynasty, Wuchuan clay sculpture has been developed and its functions diversified, primarily influenced by the market. In response to the demands of different consumers, the market for Wuchuan clay sculpture today can be divided into the traditional religious market and the newly-developed market. The former features annual ceremonial sculptures and temple sculptures; the latter produces outdoor pieces such as garden sculptures and urban sculptures, indoor sculptures, small sculptural gifts demanded by real estate developers, and so on. In the traditional market, the annual ceremonial sculptures are made primarily to entertain gods, carrying out the custom of "sacrificing clay sculptures to the god of clay", so this work has the lowest artistic requirements; temple sculptures are also traditional, but as components of temple construction, maintain a higher standard. In its emphasis on artistry, the newly-developed market exhibits the highest standards, requiring specially-trained sculptors to do the job. Currently, the development of Wuchuan clay sculpture has both favorable and unfavorable aspects. For one thing, the traditional market of clay sculpture is faced with great impact challenges in that villagers consider the clay sculpture a waste of resources because broken clay has to be dealt with once the annual ceremony ends, which is quite troublesome. In addition, during the annual ceremony, the dynamic Piaose and Cantonese operas by comparison are far more interesting and attractive than the static clay sculpture.

Aesthetic preferences of audiences and investors have also shaped the development of Wuchuan clay sculpture. Without recognition from the audience and investors, inheritors of clay sculpture would feel very frustrated, so in the traditional market inheritors have gradually developed a style of artisanship that they conceive represents the perspective of common people. As a result, fairies are made with arch eyebrows and made-up eyes, military officers must be tall and well-built, and the amusing colors of bright red and bright green are frequently chosen. However, in the newly-developed market, the classical, natural and graceful craft style emerges, catering to the aesthetic interests of modern people.① From the case of Wuchuan clay sculpture, it can be seen that the inheritors, in adapting themselves to social transformation, will make adjustment of the content and form of intangible cultural heritage they inherit according to the needs of the audience and the market, so that inheritors are themselves playing significant roles in the modern transition of intangible cultural heritage. Those inheritors who fail to adapt their inheritance to the demands of

---

① 参见陈冬梅:《吴川泥塑传承人调查研究》,中山大学2010届民俗学专业硕士学位论文,指导教师:刘晓春。

social transformation tend to be discarded by the era in which they live.

3. Discussion

As the times change, intangible cultural heritage that is actively inherited adapts accordingly. While the preservation of intangible cultural heritage is carried on endlessly, the reality of the situation is full of paradoxes. On the one hand, the protector insists on the principle of "authenticity" in order to retain "the original state" of culture. On the other hand, the traditional content and manner of presentation quietly undergo changes as inheritors actively or passively respond to the dramatic changes of the times. Such paradoxical phenomena taking place in the practical preservation of intangible cultural heritage actually reveal the contradiction between the protectors' imagination of "the original state" and the reality of activeness that characterizes the inheritance.

Apart from the profound influence of the general changes in cultural ecology brought about by modernization, intangible cultural heritage is also faced with the reality that due to work in heritage preservation, external forces from governments, scholars, businessmen, and media directly interfere in the continuity of intangible cultural heritage actively carried on over generations, breaking the previous balance of motivation for development and then reconfiguring the relationship between inheritors and these diverse forces. New functions, meanings and values are attached to intangible cultural heritage. Confronting new structures, relationships, and the altered context of inheritance, inheritors will definitely make adjustments to multiple interrelated elements so as to adapt to changing society and culture. As the meaning, value, and function of intangible cultural heritage change, the content and the manner of representation vary accordingly. If we insist that inheritors carry heritage forward according to the standard of "authenticity" for both its content and form, aren't we neglecting the rule of active continuation and development of intangible cultural heritage?

Therefore, it is necessary to advance a theoretical analysis of the above-mentioned "paradoxes" and related problems that exist in the protection of intangible cultural heritage in the hope of contributing to both research and protection efforts.

3.1 The Question of Authenticity

At present, it is a prevailing viewpoint in the circle of intangible cultural heritage protection that the protection process must insist on the principle of "authenticity". ① As to the definition of "authenticity", no single, specific criterion has emerged. Awaiting confirmation, the concept remains vague, blurred and controversial in the representation of researchers and the protectors alike. What content, in what time, what place and in what form should authenticity be based on? Should it depend on the "basic content" (presented by text, video audio, etc.) presented in the application forms for the List of Intangible Cuttural Heritage at all levels of cultural departments, or on the current state of techniques or the knowledge that is transmitted in person? It is a problem, for using any seemingly-scientific, objective and "authentic" standard to confine the definition would pose a threat to the vitality of the heritage, which is originally active and changing with the time, place and the situation.

3.1.1 Authenticity: a concept now being modified and deepened in the field of "World Heritage" ②

So where does the principle of "authenticity" come from? Actually, it is a concept that has been constantly modified and deepened within the field of "World Heritage". The *International Charter for the Conservation and Restoration of Monuments and Sites* (also *The Venice Charter*) adopted by the Second International Congress of Architects and Technicians of Historic Monuments held in May 1964 makes clear from the very beginning that "It is our duty to hand them [monuments and sites] on in the full richness of their authenticity." Although authenticity is not defined, it is specifically described as follows: " ... it must not change the lay-out or decoration of the building ... No new construction, demolition or modification which would alter the relations of mass and colour must be allowed ... The moving of all or part of a monument cannot be allowed ... in this case moreover any extra work which is indispensable must be distinct from the architectural composition and must bear a contemporary stamp ... Additions cannot be allowed except in so far as they do not detract from the interesting parts of the building, its traditional setting, the balance of its composition and its relation with its surroundings." *The Venice Chapter* is, almost rigorously, insisting on the authenticity and integrity of intangible cultural heritage.

As a standard generally acknowledged, *The Venice Chapter* encountered a dilemma in eastern countries where the concept of authenticity within cultural heritage in general differs from that of the West. To such eastern countries as China and Japan, where the cultural and material background is

---

① In the Chinese literature *Cultural Heritage*, the word "authenticity" is translated into such diverse terms as "本真性" "真实性" and "原真性". In the Chinese version of this essay, quotations from related literature is in accordance with the original representation, which are all translated into "authenticity" in the English version.

② In the documents of UNESCO, "world heritage" and "Intangible cultural heritage" belong to two different categories and two different systems (having dependent text of convention and different list of heritage) and use two different standards (distinct in the criteria for selection, for types and for divisions of types). —see 梁保尔、张朝枝:《"世界遗产"与"非物质文化遗产"两种遗产类型的特征研究》,《旅游科学》2010 年第 12 期.

totally different from that of the West, how do they find the balance between the consideration of aesthetic and historical value in the heritage and the principle of *The Venice Chapter*? Engaging such considerations, *The Nara Document on Authenticity* was passed on the 18th Session of World Heritage Committee from 12th to 17th Dec. In the conference, it was pointed by a professor at Kobe University that the word "authenticity" does not exist in Asian countries, including Japan. Furthermore, unlike the durable stone architecture in the West, most historic architecture in the East is made of plant material that decays easily, requiring regular restoration and replacement of components. In response to demand for an "authoritative" assessing mechanism suitable for diverse cultures, a broader sense of "authenticity" is put forward in *The Nara Document on Authenticity*—a definition which takes into consideration not only the materials of monument construction, but the design, form, use and function, the representation and the techniques, and the resulting "spirit" and "influence" as well. From that point forward, it has not been necessary for districts outside Europe that implement *The Convention of World Heritage* to accept the European concept of "authenticity" as the only standard. ①

The Nara Document on Authenticity serves as a milestone because it has modified the concept of "authenticity" against the backdrop of cultural diversity, which is considered to be a source of multiple standards for judging "authenticity". Out of respect for cultural diversity, assessment of value and authenticity of cultural heritage is no longer based on one specific standard. Instead, authenticity is assessed based on consideration of cultural background related to specific cultural heritage and to respect for diverse sources of background information.② In its practical implementation, the standard of "authenticity" memorialized in *The Nara Document on Authenticity* has had direct influence on the content of *Operational Guidelines for the Implementation of World Cultural and Natural Heritage Convention* by the Intergovernmental Committee for the Protection of World Cultural and Natural Heritage Committee of UNESCO.

3.1.2 The employment of "Authenticity" in the field of China Intangible Cultural Heritage Safeguarding and Research

Completing a general review of the *Convention for the Safeguarding of the Intangible Cultural Heritage*, it is clear that both the Chinese government and China's academic circle have transferred the narrow concept of "authenticity" from the field of "world heritage" to activities in safeguarding and research that address "intangible cultural heritage."

As is clearly pointed out in *Convention for the Safeguarding of the Intangible Cultural Heritage* by UNESCO, "This intangible cultural heritage, transmitted from generation to generation, is

---

① 联合国教科文组织编:《世界文化报告——文化的多样性、冲突与多元共存》, 关世杰等译, 北京大学出版社 2002 年 10 月第 1 版, 第 150 页。

② Ibidem.

constantly recreated by communities and groups in response to their environment, their interaction with nature and their history, and provides them with a sense of identity and continuity, thus promoting respect for cultural diversity and human creativity." Apart from its historical significance and the development and changes accompanying social transformation, the convention also emphasizes the fact that intangible cultural heritage is constantly recreated in response to interaction with society, history, culture and nature. The convention does not regard intangible cultural heritage as "living fossil", nor does it accept "authenticity" as the underlying principle influencing safeguarding of intangible cultural heritage.

As *Convention for the Safeguarding of the Intangible Cultural Heritage* makes clear, "authenticity" is not mentioned in any of the convention's seven related documents such as *Universal Declaration of Human Rights* (1948). Among them, *Recommendation on the Safeguarding of Traditional Culture and Folklore* puts emphasis on the protection of folklore in order to avoid distortion. The *Recommendation* does state that, "while living folklore, owing to its evolving character, cannot always be directly protected, folklore that has been fixed in a tangible form should be effectively protected." But it is important to note that even this document does not accept a single tangible form as a standard determining "authenticity". Apart from this example, *Convention Concerning the Protection of the World Cultural and Natural Heritage* does not refer to "authenticity" at all. In *Operational Guidelines for the Implementation of World Cultural and Natural Heritage Convention*, while "authenticity" is described and defined in detail, it is clearly written that the description of authenticity should be viewed in relation to the more general values prominently exemplified within cultural heritage. In fact, it is *The Nara Document of Authenticity* that has provided a practical basis for the activity of assessing the authenticity of heritage. [1]

In considering the concept of authenticity, it is clear that the field of China intangible cultural heritage research and protection has directly transported the concept of "authenticity" from the field of "world heritage" to "intangible cultural heritage" without careful research on authenticity's source or on its range of applicability. A concept that has been continuously deepened and modified in the field of "world heritage" has now been enshrined as a fixed, undoubted "golden rule" in the field of "intangible cultural heritage."

3.1.3 What is "authenticity" and What is not?

We believe any intangible cultural heritage of a certain time and space fixed by media cannot by itself secure its "authenticity"; nor does intangible cultural heritage described and presented in the material of application for the List of Intangible Cultural Heritage at all levels exclusively reflect the "authenticity" of heritage simply because of its "legitimacy" in the application process.

---

[1] See website of China State Administration of Cultural Heritage: http://www.sach.gov.cn/tabid/312/InfoID/6973/Default.aspx.

"Authenticity" is represented when "active" intangible cultural heritage that has its own function, value and meaning varies over time but is still continually recognized.

3.2 The Intangible Cultural Heritage Shared by the Parent of Inheritance and the Intangible Cultural Heritage Broken Away from the Parent of Inheritance

In determining "authenticity", it is necessary to make a distinction between the intangible cultural heritage shared by the parent of inheritance and the intangible cultural heritage broken away from the parent of inheritance.

In China today, the officially-recognized inheritors, inheriting communities and the intangible cultural heritage they inherit become a source of signs and symbols delineating "the imaginative community" separate from "the parent of inheritance." More and more meanings, functions and values beyond "the parent of inheritance" are attached to intangible cultural heritage, which evolves away from a culture shared within certain regions and communities into one removed from "the parent of inheritance," transplanted and reused and even elevated to serve as the cultural heritage of a region or the entire nation. Therefore, it is a common phenomenon in safeguarding that intangible cultural heritage carried on within certain "parents of inheritance" is more broadly used for representation as political, economic or cultural assets, employed for the benefit of people outside "the parents of inheritance." In criticizing as "false folklore" intangible cultural heritage that has transcended "the parents of inheritance," people focus on the debate of "true and false" instead of making observations on or analysis of the background causes in historical tradition, current social structure and cultural transformation that give the folklore in everyday life "the cultural capital" required for admission to the List of Heritage.

It is believed that in the practical course of safeguarding, it is necessary to distinguish between the intangible cultural heritage shared by the parent of inheritance and the intangible cultural heritage that has broken away from the parent of inheritance. The former is targeted intangible cultural heritage to be safeguarded, while the latter is intangible cultural heritage that has, as a cultural element, been transplanted to the developing contemporary culture and exploited. Separated from its parent of inheritance, transplanted and utilized, the latter has re-creators, cultural time and space, audience and sources of transmission distinct from those of the parent of inheritance so that both its content and techniques of representation will, naturally, experience changes—even unrecognizable ones. However, intangible cultural heritage of this kind—separated from the parent of inheritance is not the object of safeguarding.

Under the general umbrella of intangible cultural heritage safeguarding, one of the prominent and common phenomena is the diverse newly-arisen celebrations based on traditional folk festivals put on by governments, such as the first Canton Temple Fair held in Zhongyou Plaza, Ch'eng Huang Temple, Yuexiu District, Guangzhou on 17th Feb, 2011. From these newly-arisen celebrations in which governments take advantage of traditional folk culture resources, we can witness the national effort contributed to the transplantation, utilization and recreation of traditional local folk culture. Not only is the newly-arisen celebration supposed to retain an inner motivation from the masses to solidify its social structural foundation for sustainable development while remaining desirable to mass cultural psychology, but it is also expected to carry out a political, economic, and cultural function transcending local society by conveying the modern value of continuing traditional folk cultures with innovation as well as the national objective of creating a harmonious society. It deserves the consideration of presenters to craft an organic combination of both functions.

3.3 Inheritors of Cultures outside the Catalogue

As Article 21 in *Law of People's Republic of China on Intangible Cultural Heritage* says, "the same items of intangible cultural heritage with its form and content fully preserved in more than two regions may simultaneously be included in the catalogue of the representative items of intangible cultural heritage at the national level." However, within the realities of implementation, for various reasons, many items of intangible cultural heritage that are the same and fully preserved in more than two regions fail to be simultaneously included in the catalogue. The cultural value of those items that are the same in form and content is artificially categorized into diverse levels because of different division within regions. In addition, due to cultural diversity, not all of these cultural items manage to be included in the catalogue of protection, so after being out of the spotlight for a long time, the inheritors of those cultures may then fail to value both the very existence of the inheritance as well the underlying culture itself. As a result, these cultures are in endangered and hopeless situations, which can lead to disappearance in the end.

A typical case is the Hakka folksongs in Fujian, Guangdong and Jiangxi, which have been treated differently. As a culture owned in common by the Hakka, Hakka folksongs have been broadly transmitted in Hakka resident regions, but to the present, only Meizhou Hakka folksongs and Xingguo folksongs have been incorporated into the system of the List of National Intangible Cultural Heritage. As for those Hakka folksongs in other Hakka regions not included in the National List, are their value, meaning and function less significant than those of Meizhou folksongs and Xingguo folksongs? Not necessary. Based on the survey, for most people in Changting County, Fujian, Hakka folksongs still have great value, meaning and function. Since 2000, Hakka folksongs have entered the urban area with a large rural population. As a result, the area in which singing takes place has expanded, from the traditional range in mountains into general public areas such as parks. Separated from original interpersonal relationships and cultural connections, countrymen relocated to urban areas begin to build up new connections with the help of traditional folksongs, which have been activated as traditional memories. The ecological chain of folksong culture damaged by transformation in political institutions and lifestyle since 1949 is now reconnected. Changting Hakka folksongs, to which political, economic or cultural function transcending the parent of inheritance has not yet been established by the outside world, retain their traditional function as entertainment and romantic communication between men and women. To some extent, holders insisting on "authenticity" in protection can find, if any exists, "the original stage" of Hakka folksongs in Changting. The existing Changting folksongs inherited by singers are diverse in types, rich in aspects of life, abundantly conveying memories of traditional life, profound in cultural implication and boasting a system of knowledge concerning local folksong themes, patterns, criteria of assessment and singing techniques.① Nevertheless, such unconscious and totally-spontaneous cultural continuation is threatened with extinction as these groups of singers with memories of folksongs gradually pass away.

In meaningful contrast, the real situation of the continuation of folksongs in another places, where the folksongs are constantly given political, economic and cultural value by exterior forces, is that singers who not only inherit the numerous traditional folksongs but can also improvise are hardly found. Nearly all of their performances are actually creations of officers from the culture center, but it is the folksongs in this place that have been included in a key List of Heritage. If we consider a comparison, over the entire earth which of them is facing a more severe threat of extinction and which is more in need of participation in the system of safeguarding?

---

① See 王维娜:《从山野到大庭广众——长汀客家山歌的传承与地方知识》,中山大学 2009 届民俗学专业博士学位论文,指导教师:康保成.

Overview and Response to Huang Yonglin's "Intangible Cultural Heritage Safeguarding in the Vision of Cultural Ecology"

Jessica Anderson Turner*

It should come as no surprise that China has more designations of intangible cultural heritage (ICH) than any other nation. Not unlike other countries that use UNESCO's recognition as nation-building, in China the policies of UNESCO are models for national cultural policy, rhetoric, and practice. But whereas most nations' interactions with ICH recognition come from cultural policy makers and scholars working in the public sector, in China ICH concepts are found in all levels of society, and the Ministry of Culture encourages an engagement with and ownership of ICH. A scholarly engagement with ICH issues in China permeates writings on culture and the arts, and discourses on identifying, safeguarding, and developing intangible cultural heritage surround disciplines of folklore or ethnomusicology. This is evident through the papers delivered at this conference, including Prof. Huang Yonglin's paper on "Intangible Cultural Heritage Safeguarding in the Vision of Cultural Ecology."

Though my initial remarks at this conference were intended to provide a response to Huang Yonglin's paper, in his absence due to circumstances that kept him from traveling I have decided to provide an overview of China's relationship with ICH, some staggering numbers of ICH designations within China, and an introduction to a few of the terms common in Chinese ICH theory and scholarship. I thought it useful to unpack the ideas and terms common in discourses of Chinese ICH particularly for those familiar with ICH scholarship in general but perhaps not as practiced in China.

In 2001, Kunqu Opera was the first Chinese cultural form to be recognized by UNESCO as Intangible Cultural Heritage. Presently there are 38 Chinese items listed on UNESCO's *Representative List of the Intangible Cultural Heritage of Humanity*, some of which are recognized as

---

* Jessica Anderson Turner, Ph. D. , teaching at Virginia Intermont College.

being in need of urgent safeguarding (http://www.unesco.org/culture/ich/en/lists).

In 2005, China launched its own National Representative List of Intangible Cultural Heritage, an internal system of designation facilitated by the Ministry of Culture. From 2005 to 2009, the first survey collected 870,000 cultural items to consider for ICH listing. The effort given to this project, the allocation of resources, and the systematic research and classification of items all indicate the weight and significance given by the Ministry of Culture to this national list. Based on this initial survey, 1,219 items were listed in the National Representative List of Intangible Cultural Heritage from provinces, municipalities and autonomous regions throughout China between 2006 and 2012.

China's relationship with intangible cultural heritage illustrates a particular nationalization of ICH, one that took the UNESCO designations and policies and localized them, fitting them into national institutions and levels of recognition that have emerged as an enormous enterprise and discipline of its own. Chinese ICH, which began as a proud adoption of UNESCO designations, has taken a social life of its own, affecting all areas of society and being promoted heavily by the government as new nationalism. Citizens are reminded that they are important cultural transmitters themselves; a new national holiday centers around the International Festival of Intangible Cultural Heritage, held in Chengdu annually.

Curator Sojin Kim took this photograph at the Fourth International Festival of Intangible Cultural Heritage, held in Chengdu, China, June 2013. Photo courtesy of Center for Folklife and Cultural Heritage, Smithsonian Institution

In addition to the recognition of items on the national list—including folklore and ICH genres, techniques for creating or passing down traditional forms, and cultural practices significant to a group of belief—the Chinese ICH system recognizes people who serve as important bearers of tradition as well as designates places as special zones for the protection of ICH. These designations are recognized for the purpose of continuing the cultural traditions honored by the national system. At present, the Ministry of Culture has named 1,986 people from across China as ICH "representative inheritors." These people are chosen through a nomination process that recognizes their knowledge and continuation of cultural practices, and inheritors are expected to give public performances and work with apprentices as a means of passing on traditions. Inheritors receive an annual stipend as an award for their service. Adding to the National Representative List of Intangible Cultural Heritage is the Provincial Representative list, where currently there are 8,556 designated items of ICH and 9,564 designated inheritors.

To aid this new national industry, in 2011 the National People's Congress passed *Law of the People's Republic of China Intangible Cultural Heritage*, which identifies and regulates the protection and preservation of ICH. The law details three systems: investigation, representative lists, and inheritance and dissemination. One of the key debates in both the Ministry of Culture and in scholarly discourses is the appropriate balance between research (investigation and inheritance) and development (inheritance and dissemination).

Scholars in China are keenly aware of the changes the country has seen in the past century, and the ICH laws and lists embrace the notion of protecting and carrying on Chinese cultural practices. This awareness is evident in the scholarship on cultural expression produced during the past two decades in fields such as folklore, ethnomusicology, and anthropology. Scholarship focused on issues of transmission and change has shifted the current focus on ICH to issues of inheritance, protection, and development. Concepts such as yuan shengtai (indigenity, literally "original ecology") and wenhua shengtai (cultural ecology and the notion that cultural systems must flourish in a healthy ecosystem and must be conserved) are prevalent in ICH scholarship and public discourse. Theoretical scholarship on these concepts is abundant, practitioners use these terms to situate their work, and the tourism and manufacturing industries market items identified by these terms.

The Ministry of Culture recognizes the need for healthy cultural ecosystems in its policies and designations. Currently, there are 15 "cultural ecology protection zones" for ICH, where development and industry are regulated in favor of protecting traditional cultural practices. In these zones, tourism and manufacturing are limited, while citizens are encouraged to participate in traditional methods and art forms. In addition to the cultural ecology protection zones, there are 14 "productive protection bases." These bases are centers for the manufacturing of approved items to penetrate the market, using recognized traditional methods for creating pieces to disseminate to the public. Only those items approved by the Ministry can be manufactured using a form or technique on the list of ICH. Central to this practice is the effort to regulate the production of new ICH-related materials, using trained workers and traditional methodologies while also promoting these art forms. Considerable debate has emerged around various definitions of "productive protection," and about the balance needed to develop productive and lucrative products while at the same time protecting the cultural forms and traditional practices used to make these products.

Prof. Huang's paper carries forward many of the arguments common in ICH scholarship today: development can be used as a means of safeguarding "original ecology," and the principle of moderate development is key to doing this correctly, though many will argue the parameters of moderate development in these cases. Goals of cultural development are not only effects of ICH policies or tourism development, but are frequent goals in research and application of cultural policy. A common viewpoint among Chinese scholars discussing ICH issues is that development is important to the survival of cultural forms; the transformation of tradition reflects new social uses and therefore preservation of cultural practices.

The 2011 ICH law in China, and the lists and practices that have developed around this project, have created tangible products of the intangible: people are designated as inheritors, ICH safeguarding zones (cultural ecology zones) are mapped spaces for the continuity and creativity of traditional cultural practices, and products are created in protective production zones for the marketplace. Huang's paper argues that safeguarding cultural ecology is an essential component of safeguarding ICH, that the need to balance "safeguarding" and "developing" is crucial to ICH protection, and that the government's responsibility in these initiatives should be clarified. These arguments are shared by many scholars in China in analyses of ICH practices, who acknowledge that these practices must be deliberate and policy-driven. Preservation and development, as carried out through productive protection, are seen as conflicting but necessary. As laws and policies are enforced and adapted, and perhaps revised, ICH protection is approached as scientific and systematic.

Who is Producing? How to Protect?
—In-depth Analysis of the "Productive Protection" of China's Intangible Cultural Heritage

Zhang Shishan[*]

1. "Productive protection" of intangible heritage
—An issue that should have been addressed earlier

In early 21st century of China, folk-customs originally preserved and inherited in civil society were selectively given honors and subsidies by the national government, and were brought into the 4-level protection framework of intangible cultural heritage (hereafter referred to as ICH). With the examination and approval of the national ICH list and the selection of the inheritors of ICH and the confirmation of the pilot national eco-cultural protection areas, the protection of ICH has been more and more influential, buoyed by a rising trend of cooperation linking government, scholars and the public. At the same time, discussions about how to protect ICH have been raised frequently in society—ideas of "rescuing conservation", "integrated conservation" and "productive protection"[①] have been put forward one after another. Among these, "productive protection" has advanced rapidly from general concept to a hot cultural/social issue. If the ICH list and the selection of inheritors represent the idea of "rescuing conservation", then the pilot program of national eco-cultural protection area should be considered as an example of "productive protection" of ICH.

---

[*] Zhang Shishan, Vice-president, Professor and Doctoral Supervisor of Institute of Cultural Heritage, Shandong University.

[①] The idea of "productive protection" of ICH was first brought up in the book *An Introduction of the Intangible Cultural Heritage* (Culture and Art Publishing House, 2006) edited by Wang Wenzhang. In 2009, the deputy culture minister Zhou Heping made a definition of it in the opening ceremony of the forum of productive protection of ICH: by means of manufacturing, circulation, sales, etc, turning ICH and its resources into productivity and production to generate economic benefits and accelerate the development of related industries, thus ICH can be effectively protected in the production practice and a positive interaction between ICH protection and economic development can be achieved.

However, one issue should not be ignored: as the protection of ICH has become a basic state policy and the government's general survey of ICH has been completed, we should now focus more on how to manage these resources, "to turn them into real products and toward practical uses through administrative measures."① This change in focus is the primary background of "productive protection". In conjunction with 2009's Lantern Festival, a forum addressing the productive protection of ICH was held by the Ministry of Culture; from this meeting the idea of extending productive protection beyond "traditional artistry" to encompass all ICH entered the mainstream. In the view of some researchers and industry insiders, productive protection appeared to be the most immediate and practical way for ICH to maintain lasting stability while fitting into society and manufacturing.

The outcome promised by productive protection is a state of balance between ICH protection and economic development. However, the real situation is not as promising as it might appear. When compared to "rescuing conservation" and "integrated conservation," the most important effect of productive protection is to introduce the idea of productive modernity—the essential component of the entirety of [Chinese] social modernity—into the field of ICH protection. Essentially, this change adds the involvement of modern industrial sectors in ICH to the already-achieved national political outreach (rescuing conservation), and outreach by academic groups (integrated conservation). In the overlap and conflict produced by these multiple engagements, the government is naturally drawn to productive protection because it fits with the economically-oriented policy of the country.

However, the idea of productive protection doesn't become more compelling or true just because it is linked to national interests. Instead, when compared to rescuing conservation and integrated conservation, productive protection is less a solution than a vital question, a question that should had been officially asked long ago: how to achieve a win-win situation for both ICH protection and industrial growth in today's industrialized age? There is no way to simply use logic to deduce this question; only by studying real cases, whether successes or failures, can we extract knowledge and reach a conclusion.

This essay will study two real cases: the clay toys in Huiming County, Shandong, and the "paper-cow-burning" in Changyi. Through these cases, this essay will analyze the functional significance, subject identity and context of folk craft production from the perspectives of commodity transaction, cultural meaning, the craftsmen's characters as artists and as farmers, viewing production from both the "traditional" and "modern" perspective. The current function and limitations of productive protection will also be addressed.

---

① 施爱东:《中国现代民俗学检讨》,社会科学文献出版社 2010 年,第 194 页。

2. Commodity transaction versus cultural meaning: functions of folk handcrafts within ICH

As we examine major categories of folk handcrafts, it is not difficult to discover that despite their common utilitarian motives, they exhibit many differences in how they are valued. Some of them are commercial; the producer thinks highly of the products' economic value and expects to gain profit through commodity transaction. The other kind of value function is more self-contained; the producer values the spiritual satisfaction of handcraft and wishes to fulfill its cultural meaning through social activities.

Henanzhang and Huobali are two villages in the southwest of Huimin County, 6 kilometers away from each other. Henanzhang has a three-century history of producing clay toys; there is even an old proverb that describes the way every family in Henanzhang is involved in making them. On the lunar February second every year, a temple fair is held in Huobali village. The temple fair enjoys tremendous fame; it is considered a second New Year Festival by the villagers, and also attracts a large number of visitors from many cities in Shandong, Hebei and Henan Province. Primitive and classic-looking clay dolls are the most important mascots in the temple fair. They are so influential that even Henanzhang village itself and the temple fair have acquired the nicknames "Dolls' Zhang" and "Dolls' fair." The nicknames convey a truth; it can be said that the temple fair in Huobali village has provided a platform for villagers in Henanzhang to sell their hand-made clay toys, while at the same time the clay toys have enabled the temple fair to gain a more-prominent reputation. In this way, economic cooperation and cultural specialization evolved between these two villages, and year after year such collaboration was itself sustained as a traditional custom.

We should look back and consider just how the clay toys became central to the fair. Today, it is very difficult to investigate the question of whether it was the clay toys or the temple fair that existed first. In the local people's view, these two functions are valued differently. In terms of general function, the temple fair has played a role in agricultural activity, providing local people with an opportunity to purchase farming tools in early spring. But clay toys are totally unrelated to this essentially-agricultural event. So, how have clay toys gained access to the village's temple fair, even becoming a defining phenomenon? What gave clay toys the right to enter a fair of farming tools? To answer this question, we must dig deep into local folkloric customs.

"Bonding dolls" have been a time-honored birth custom in the Huimin area. Couples would select and purchase a pair of delicate and vivid clay dolls, bringing them home in the hope they would help in the conception of new babies, especially boys. This "bonding dolls" custom symbolizes a wish for newborns, therefore it has been gradually and unconsciously linked to some specific point of time. That is, "bonding dolls" connect with the onset of some natural process, and to a special time of beginning or birth. In the traditional Chinese calendar, spring is the beginning of the year. As one old Chinese saying goes, "February the second, awakening of the dragon." February the second is considered a significant moment marking the beginning of the spring season; this is why "bonding dolls" should be acquired on that day.

The Fair is also about beginnings. In its commercial function, Huobali's temple fair is a bazaar selling farming tools just as the planting season arrives. Although bazaar transactions would appear to constitute mere business activity, the fair has somehow been acquired deeper cultural significance through its connection with the sacred start of the year. The cultural significance attached to the temple fair provided an entry point for clay toys, since they possess a compatible cultural connotation: It is the folkloric meaning of "newborn spring" that allows clay toys to share the same room with farm tools. In the same sacred room of the temple fair, there is both commerce and ceremony, business transaction and cultural communication. The procedure of selling and buying are also producing and reproducing folkloric meaning. As as farm tools and dolls merge in cultural identity, the productive relations between different villages and communities are reinforced and made permanent. This process presents a vivid and positive model of the productive protection of ICH.

In Dongyongan village in Changyi we observed another folkloric activity which offers distinctively dissimilar functions and implications when compared to Huimin's clay toys. According to the local story, in the hundreds of year since the foundation of this village, a tradition of "paper-cow-burning" would be celebrated during lunar December. A special space is set up and materials carefully prepared, and great effort expended to build a one-horned paper cow which is nearly 7 meters tall and 13 meters long. On lunar January fourteenth, this cow was first paraded and then set afire in front of the Sunbin Temple (commonly known as "Laoye Temple"). Funds and materials required for the parade were raised by highly respected elders in the village; monetary donations and contributed labor are totally voluntary. During preparations, enthusiastic onlookers would gather around every day, making comments and gossiping about the event; the whole community immersed itself in the joy of the creative activity.

We know that "paper-cow" is not an exclusive custom in Dongyongan village, but a common one in the surrounding region. Yuandong, a village east to Dongyongan, has a custom of burning two paper cows in their temple fair on lunar January twelfth. Yubu village, which is

2. 5 kilometers away from Dongyongan, maintains a tradition of parading the local god and burning paper cattle and two sedan chairs as a sacrifice to the local goddess. (Actually, in Dongyongan village, besides "paper-cow-burning" which is mostly arranged by the Lv family and the Cong family, there has been a similar custom, "paper-horse-burning," which in recent years has been arranged by the Qi family.)

Anyone possessing good business sense will realize that this custom can be exploited commercially—that the fame of this sacred burning ceremony, paper cattle, horse and sedan chair could be turned into a profitable industry. To dream more ambitiously, as an ICH of the city, it is possible that "paper-cattle-burning" would be well-protected—inherited and popularized through full scale production of the paper craft with the assistance of a government ICH protection system and additional funds.

The question is, why waste all this labor, money and time to make a giant cow, only to burn it to ashes? Is it possible that financial concerns are left out of consideration in such event? If this is the case, what factors make money irrelevant?

Within this custom, the importance of money is surpassed by the tradition's social value. The primary feature of this ceremony is its large scale and the participation of the whole village. Despite the expensive cost, paper-cattle-burning is a momentous event, a joyful spectacle that makes neighboring villages jealous. As a significant custom, paper-cow-burning has turned into a special moment within local life. Because of its grand scale, cooperation of different villages is required, thus it has also become a sacred "inter-village" occasion. In addition, such an activity generates a dense ritualistic atmosphere. As the process of cow-making, cow-parading and cow-burning goes on, the scene becomes more and more crowded as a growing number of spectators try to see the show. However, only some of the viewers can actually see what's going on. Therefore, between those who can see and those who can't, a natural division separating the ceremony's center and margin is created, especially at the final moment when the cow is burned. In the long-anticipated burning, flashing flames and swirling smoke produce an intense feeling of sacred rite, and in such a holy moment, even casual conversations around the event perimeter are endowed with a certain sacred character. People close to the center watch and pass along details of the ceremony to the outer viewers, while within the nearest group of spectators is the ceremony itself. Thus three layers of participants form a triple layer of value in this specific moment and place.

Although this structure of participation doesn't precisely coincide with existing political patterns in the villages, it is in fact a "social resource map" which is relevant to politics yet subtly adjusted. The large sum of money spent on the paper cattle is a mechanism for consolidating existing social resources while creating new ones—resources expected to produce future industry networks in and among the villages. In this fashion volunteer industry triggered by social resources in return give the resources new significance, and a system for reproducing the custom is established.

Further, the cow-making process itself provides a communication platform for the whole village; local people can gather and carry out discussions of all kinds. Today, available spaces for this kind of public interactions have been shrinking, as more and more people have left their hometowns as migrant workers. In this circumstance, the village engagement around paper cattle becomes a highly-frequented channel for effective social contacts beginning lunar December 19th. In this way, the meaningful New Year atmosphere anticipated by villagers can somehow be achieved.

Beyond this general effect, the paper cow process provides an even more profound cultural meaning for villagers in Dongyongan. Here, by observing this annual custom, we clearly see the three "borders" of the local area. First, in the organization and operation of the ceremony and its participation groups, parade route and positioning for good fortune, internal boundaries separating family from family are revealed. Second, because burning of sacred objects (cattle, horses, sedan chairs, etc.) is a common custom in neighboring villages and communities, these events display the varied characters of different villages. Third, when viewed as a whole these burning customs constitute a stage on which to local culture performs for the outside world; in this sense, villages themselves serve as backdrop for ritual performances. Such multiple indicators of cultural borders conform to the multiple structural layers structure of village life.

The giant cow is destined to be burned from the day it is created. As a symbol of the spiritual world of the masses, it is created to compensate for loss caused by transitions affecting rural society, providing a sense of security and belonging. Souls can be comforted and sorrows removed. The ritual ceremony, as a self-shaping production drawing on indigenous rural resources, is brimming with an intense but simple affection exhibited by the villages. Every event of this kind is a demonstration of a regional collective as well as a continual review and reshaping of human affection. It serves as a bridge to connect neighboring villages and public feelings, and has undoubtedly become both the climax of the Spring Festival system as well as an emotional comfort to villagers. And, along the way, it has also become an icon justifying a New Year's visit to the local area. In all these ways, in this example, the self-consistency of a folk craft is closely interrelated to the commonweal of the community.

3. Craftsman or farmer: Identifying the character of the folk artist

Productive protection tends to assume that craftsmen or merchants are the main agents of folk craftsmanship, as it appears they can easily transform themselves professionalized businessmen. But in fact this is too narrow a view of folk craftsmanship, for while folk crafts may have something of the character of industrial products manufactured in workshops, crafts are frequently mingled with the daily life of the masses in a much broader sense. The real subject of productive protection should encompass all of the folk: those with indistinct professional identity or even those without any professional identity at all.

Observe that the manufacture of clay toys in the Henanzhang village is seasonal, not a regular job. Producers of clay toys are not strictly professional craftsmen, but on the other hand, cannot be strictly identified as farmers either (although they do have farm work to deal with). This seasonal character of folk toys gives their producers competence and identity in both agriculture and craftsmanship. And this dual engagement in both crafts and farming endows their products with an especially strong flavor of the countryside. So when we are trying to systematically protect folk crafts, we should create specific conditions so that craft production can retain this character of "sideline," which maintains both creative spirit and ties to village life.

This concept of craft protecting can be found in the conservation approach to China's ICH crafts in earlier times. Until the late 1990s, Chinese society exhibited a well-developed "sideline tradition." Within this craft tradition, people were accustomed to doing their "serious job" when work is busy, and participating in the "sideline" for extra money during leisure time. (These "sideline" traditions actually include most of the ICH practices discussed here.) These sideline jobs attached to everyday life in a flexible way: on the one hand, these sidelines are just part time jobs for extra income without any cultural intention; on the other hand, the absence of cultural intention is exactly why they fit comfortably with both folkloric customs and the daily life of the masses. Taken up in leisure and set aside in busy times, lacking strong industrial intention, sidelines do not demand the aggressive pursuit of sales volume and profits, which enables them to retain a high status, distinct from mere worldly business. Pursued for their own sake, not for money, the quality of these products tends to be well maintained. Likewise, the culture of sideline crafts exhibits no ambition for fame and celebrity, so their manufacture mostly honors standards of the older generations joined to the personal objectives of artists: every product is unique. In brief, the tradition of "sideline" has truly kept ICH within the daily life of the masses. It has also kept the ambitions of industrialization within limits, so crafts can remain personal expressions that respect tradition. In order to carry out the productive protection of ICH, the traditional "sideline" structure must be used as a framework.

Therefore, the expectation that industrialization can establish a kind of natural protection for ICH crafts is overly optimistic. Real productive protection won't occur by simply giving subsidization and the title "ICH inheritor" to a few selected craftsmen. In fact, during the first half of the 20th century, almost every villager in Henanzhang village was skilled in making clay toys. But today that number has been decreasing. According to our recent research, the number of households that produce clay toys in 2005 was nearly 20, in 2006 it decreased to 10, in 2007, 2008 the number was 9, and 2009 it was 12, since 2010 the number has remained either 5 or 6. Although the clay toys were included on the first list of Provincial ICH in 2006, and the third list of the National ICH, and even though the villager Zhang Kai was selected as the representative inheritor of the Provincial ICH in 2011, the inheritance and sustainability of this folk craft remains in serious crisis.

Despite the background of increasing public support for ICH, the clay toys tradition in Henanzhang village is still in decline, in both artistic inheritance and scale of production. According to the descriptive system of ICH recognition, folkloric cultures are carefully classified into different categories. Given this classification system, neither the design nor the implementation of the protection project could include the temple fair in Huobali village—the event that is critically important in the selling of clay toys. In truth, our ICH descriptive frame might itself be one of the key causes behind the limited success of preservation efforts, for it is difficult for any integrated and effective protection to be carried out under this system. Clearly, this case provides the lesson that ICH protection cannot achieve a satisfactory result if it focuses solely on a few artistic products instead of the whole cultural space and the traditional activities attached to it. [①]

Compared to clay toys, the civic ICH "paper-cow-burning" in Changyi is another story. There are no official inheritors of this ICH item, a situation that sidesteps the competitive arguments and disputes surrounding such an honor. At present, this custom is in a vigorous and well-preserved condition. In Dongyongan village, the custom of paper-cow-burning arranged by the Cong and the Lv families has been so popular that the Qi family in the village decided to follow suit. Since 2007, the Qi family has made a red paper horse for the burning ceremony on every lunar January ninth, birthday of the Jade Emperor (the supreme deity of Taoism). During our recent research, we have also seen people from other villages visit Dongyongan for consultation to help revive paper-cow-burning ceremonies in their own villages. This real-life example could be an indication that productive protection might not be the only way for folk crafts to save themselves.

---

① 张士闪：《当代民间工艺的语境认知与生态保护——以山东惠民河南张泥玩具为个案》，《山东社会科学》2010年第1期。

Perhaps the path of folk craft industrialization is not coincidental, but planned. For example, in the Changzhi area in Shanxi Province, there is a craftsman who makes cloth tigers named Zhang Jianwang who has been attempting to industrialize his products for a long time. He sought and collected large numbers of cloth tiger models from all over China, then had them adapted to enable manufacturing by machines. Zhang's corporation works in two ways: a "high-end" in which tigers are produced in expensive hand-made collections, and the "industrialized" way in which products are low-priced machine-made copies to meet the needs of a mass market.

The experience of Zhang and others has proven that marketization tends to shrink the proportion of total production that is handmade. Therefore, the idea of protecting ICH simply by market-oriented production alone might be easier said than done. And, in this situation, craftsmen would certainly adapt their products to the market to increase sales volume, which would lead to the transformation of localized cloth tigers; the cloth tigers with special local characteristics would be replaced by the most popular versions. Eventually, modern materials will be employed in production and all cloth tigers will be tediously alike; as a result, the charm of traditional fabric and artistic technique of art will in the end vanish. In the opinion of Ma Zhiyao, "it can be said with certainty that the marketization has taken away the unique characteristics of his cloth tigers...From the perspective of preservation, his scale production has caused damage to the tradition."[①]

Extensive field research has shown that almost every ICH inheritor is expecting financial benefits from product development. However, if the ICH products themselves are not suitable for industrialization, then putting them in the market would only cause devastation, no matter how much support they receive from the government. After all, once an ICH loses its nature or value in the place it belongs, it is equivalent to saying its culture has been murdered.

4. "The traditional" and "the modern:" the cognitive context of folk crafts

The contemporary issue of folk craft development is becoming increasingly significant in the era of cultural globalization. Since the industrial revolution of the 19th century, exports of culture and civilization have gradually become worldwide with the expansion of a capitalistic economy. In the 1950s and 1960s, the globalization of international corporations not only

---

① 马知遥:《非物质文化遗产保护的田野思考——中国北方民间布老虎现状反思》,《民俗研究》2012 年第 4 期。

became a platform for economic expansion, but also served as a powerful engine advancing the globalization of western civilization. In the overall environment of an overwhelming western culture, folk craftsmanship, as a characteristic component of local culture, has been through two stages in global developments. In the first stage, traditional craftsmanship was passively altered and commingled; in the second stage, it began to find a way to fight against its rivals.

The industrialization of folk craftsmanship is an issue unique to modern times. In the past, folk craft activities were quite compatible with markets of small, peasant economies. For one thing, folk crafts were linked to all kinds of local economic and commercial events, such as business associated with temple fairs and ritual ceremonies. (In fact, this kind of transaction has been an important part of the entire fabric of folkloric customs.) In addition, folk crafts have frequently serve to supply things stage sets for traditional operas or materials supporting community ceremonies. Thus, folk crafts are more than the mere "funny wicked tricks" observed by the eyes of some traditional literati.

Within the pre-1990s traditional environment, the process of industrializing folk crafts proceeded with a certain degree of self-restraint, so that commercial behavior would be modified to fit within the structure of folk society. In other words, even as commodities, the exploitation of folk crafts still took place under certain restrictions imposed by folk society. For example, crafts were never severed from interpersonal communication and social relations.

From the foundation of PRC to the end of the Cultural Revolution, small-peasant economic activity was totally banned in China, shrinking folkloric artistry. Then, with the gradual recovery of the small-peasant economy in the 1980s, declining folk crafts began to regain lost vigor. But this recovery has been accompanied by an expansion of our national market economy, in which the government has involved itself as the primary actor. In the 1990s, there were many attempts to develop folkloric resources, including folk crafts, as modern industries. However, such commercial efforts undermined respect for core spiritual values that are part of tradition and were severely criticized for inflicting damage on folk culture. In the 21st century, market-oriented policies have again caused many injustices, giving rise to self-examination in both the economic and cultural sphere. In addition, people have begun to reconsider the meaning of traditional and folk cultures in the modern rejuvenation of China, a process which has also realigned both the industrial and spiritual meaning of traditional cultures.

Coincidentally, the campaign for ICH protection experienced vigorous growth during the same period, intersecting with China's new spirit of national introspection. As a result, a passionate interest in traditional and folk cultures emerged all over the country. Understanding of the spiritual value of folk cultures has been increasing in the eye of the public, and the status of folkloric customs is shifting from "folkloric resources" to "public cultures," a transformation which can be observed in questions and criticism directed toward the industrialization of folk culture by many scholars. But it must be understood that such critical opinion neglects the truth that most folkloric practices, such as craft production, exhibit the character of commodity—a commoditized character that was very obvious even in traditional society. The difference is that in the past, this commercial aspect could blend into the surrounding social structure without conflict. Lacking a complete understanding of how commerce works within traditional society, this line of criticism is not yet sufficiently mature to bring significant influence to the ICH policy process.

Frankly speaking, the real threat to folkloric artistry is not the drive toward industrialization, but the disorder of village public order and the decline of the "folkloric spirit," both of which are vital to craftsmanship. When crafts are abandoned because they are tedious, arduous and unprofitable, and when large scale production is admired for serving a progressive lifestyle, what we will lose is more than just a memory of the past. As habits of village life and the roots of culture vanish, folkloric culture which has been attached to folk craftsmanship will gradually decline and even disappear, as will their guiding influence on our larger society. ①

In fact, the abnormal development of folkloric industries since the mid-1990s has actually made cultural resources scarce. In this environment, a massive quantity of fake folkloric culture and phony crafts were fabricated, which had such a dramatic impact on real traditions that they almost disappeared. The sacredness of folkloric craftsmanship and its ability to self-sustain were severely damaged, producing confusion within China's entire folkloric culture sector in the contemporary era. If nothing else, these examples and anecdotes have demonstrated that productive protection is by no means a magic cure for all disease.

Conclusion: the "reality" and "obligations" of China's ICH protection

During the last decade, China has experienced tremendous change in its social structure, interest groups and position within the complicated outside world. On the heels of the impact of the market economy and globalization, democratization and the information revolution have also come onto the stage. At present, the social transformation faced by China is far more challenging than an economic one. Not only do the masses demand more welfare, but also

---

① 刘星:《手艺传统与近现代乡土社会变迁》,山东大学2012届硕士学位论文,第42页。

greater fairness in the welfare process; not only do people demand more rights, they also want clean government. How to meet the masses' demands and requirements is not only about the political trust of 1.3 billion people, but also depends on the future character of China's modernization. In the on-going democratic reform in China, the government still control enormous social resources. With increasing public sentiment favoring participation, open expression and citizen authority, widespread doubts about the government's credibility will become increasingly specific and clear. There is no question that the key to motivating social energy is respect for the popular will and utilization of the intelligence and force of the public. Let the voices of the public provide guidance for governing; let government respond to public participation. In this form of benign interaction, shared understanding can be developed. Such an evolution of government function will accelerate the development of society, and in return increase public trust in government itself. ①

To further explore the protection of ICH, we must understand the development of folk craftsmanship in China over the last century. During the first half the 20th century, China was in the handcraft stage as an agricultural society, a stage in which its economic production and spiritual culture were mainly sustained in a household-to-village framework. In the "sideline era" discussed above—between the 1950s and 1970s—folk crafts mostly functioned in a political pattern of team-to-nation production as a supplement to China's state operated economy. In this pattern, economic production and spiritual values were combined within a national united front. With the development of the modern industrial system in the 1980s, folk crafts have been in a general decline despite an expanded function within the larger economy. In this person-to-enterprise pattern, the general vigor of folk crafts has been withering due to weakening of the spiritual significance of folk culture. These developments form the background of China's current campaign of ICH protection. Even if "rescuing conservation" (characterized by the ICH list and election of ICH inheritors) was a quick fix by the government to deal with the loss of ICH resources, the policy did achieve its aim in the early 21st century. However, rescuing conservation lacked a full understanding of the living nature of ICH, and also failed to anticipate the complexity of the protection project. There was an expectation that "integrated conservation" (marked by the pilot national eco-cultural protection areas) would extend the earlier concept, while the policy of "productive protection" was intended to carry out a practical rescue of ICH while truly achieving its integrated conservation.

ICH protection is linked to the needs of China from the perspectives of political reform,

---

① 陈琨:《激发中国前行的最大力量》,《人民日报》2012年11月3日;范正伟:《"回应":互动中筑牢信任的基石》,《人民日报》2012年11月5日。

economic development, and the revitalization of culture. If ICH policy is to help make these "obligations" come true, the movement must have both public participation and the full support of government. The protection of ICH is connected to many issues affecting Chinese society, such as cultural diversity, subject diversity and regional complexity. Measures of ICH protection taken by the government should not be developed as ideal projects, but rather as a series of exploratory practices awaiting future adjustment. The three evolved concepts regarding policy and folk culture have demonstrated that the government has a lasting interest in ICH protection. As scholars, we have reasons to believe in the idea and policies of productive protection, and reasons to offer our advice and suggestions policy makers.

Based on my field research, to bring productive protection into effective practice, the flowing things should be noted:

First, government should be a collaborative actor in the protection of ICH, balancing the needs of special groups and community development. The national government is going through a transformation from "administrator" to "server." In "serving," official departments should get to know and understand the voices of ICH inheritors and other involved individuals. In addition, protection projects should be linked to the improvement of community life.

Cultural inheritors are considered the central figures in ICH inheritance; without them ICH would no longer exist. As the main beneficiaries of inheritance, "the inheritors care more about how to get a comfortable life than a meaningful one; their culture is the real life itself."[①] "What we must insist is that the government is never the owner or a watchman of a culture, but a helper and an advocate. In ICH protection, the government is only a middleman offering indirect guidance and regulations through economic or other means, and offering more choices to the public. The government should never neglect the will of the community, nor is it fair to force the community to be a watchman and take the duty of ICH protection. Only in this environment can people in certain communities choose their way of working and living compatible with ICH protection, so that ICH can be gradually transformed from a commercial entity to a cultural one."[②] These quotations convey the deepest significance of the issue.

Second, the importance of ICH inheritors should be taken account of, especially the creativity of folk craftsmen; It should be made certain that those who handle and the advance ICH receive benefits. Feng Jicai has once emphasized, "The protection of ICH is to preserve traditions as living culture, while the protection of tangible cultural heritages is to preserve them

---

① 施爱东:《中国现代民俗学检讨》,社会科学文献出版社,2010 年。
② 何平:《非物质文化遗产保护中的政府责任》,http://www.mcprc.gov.cn/whzx/bnsjdt/zcfgs/201111/t20111128_341549.html。

as static ones, the essence of living cultures are their inheritors."① Liu Kuili argues that the very process of producing the folk crafts is itself an activity of ICH protection. For Liu, national character, traditional culture, and the creativity and emotional impact of producers will somehow be combined and made real in the act of production itself. It is for this reason that, when we see a knockoff or a mass-produced craft, the product does not inspire any deep emotional response.② These two opinions have each approached the root of the issue, but reality makes it difficult for ICH work to preserve and advance process. For example, the truth is that as the main bearers of ICH inheritance, most inheritors play a passive role. And some of the organizations responsible for ICH items do not actually have inheritance (cultural inheritors, cultural heritage groups) as their subject. Take Shandong Province as an example, out of 328 items and the 418 responsible organizations in the first two groups of the Provincial ICH list, two thirds of them are local houses of culture or protection centers for ICH. These organizations are capable of managing or coordination, but taking care of cultural inheritance and its future development is far beyond their capability.

Third, because ICH mostly exists in rural areas, it is very important to the inheritance of ICH to pay increased attention to rural construction, decreasing disparities between urban and rural districts. Cities hold great appeal for people living in villages; more and more young people leave their hometowns to become a migrant workers in the city. Their periodic visits home will inevitably bring back the some sort of culture from outside the villages, making ICH subjects increasingly complex. If the rapid penetration of industrialization and modern media have damaged the natural and cultural environment of many villages, then the growing phenomenon of migrant work has put rural culture into a serious crisis. I have observed that when certain long-lost folk crafts included on ICH lists at different levels, some so-called "crafts" of some large state-owned enterprises have also gained entry, such the brewing technology of Maotai, the brewing technology of Luzhoulaojiao, the brewing technology of Xinghuacun wine, and the Tongrentang Chinese medicine (all the items above are of the first national ICH list).

It is clear that, in dealing with withering rural communities and powerful luxury enterprises at the same time, we really should, in the design of any ICH protection project, focus ever more-closely on the key questions of "who is producing" and "how to protect".

---

① 冯骥才:《灵魂不能下跪——冯骥才文化遗产思想学术论集》,宁夏人民出版社2007年,第10页。
② 韩冰:《"非遗"生产性保护之路》,《瞭望》2012年2月20日。

American State Intangible Cultural Heritage Programs: Characteristics, Interrelationships and Challenges

Robert Baron[*]

Far more often than not, cultural policies in the United States are expressed through programmatic and funding priorities, initiatives and ongoing activities rather than through the explicit, strategic articulation of policy. An outstanding exception to this pattern is the policy of the Folk Arts Program of the National Endowment for the Arts (NEA), which developed a national infrastructure for documenting, presenting and safeguarding intangible cultural heritage through state folk arts programs. This infrastructure was established by Bess Lomax Hawes, Director of NEA's Folk Arts Program (now known as the Folk and Traditional Arts Program) in the late 1970s. Over thirty years later, this infrastructure remains intact, consisting of over 40 programs throughout the United States.

In her *Sing It Pretty: A Memoir*, Hawes discussed her vision of supporting folk arts coordinators in every state, which "proved to be a linchpin in our attempts to develop sponsors for folk arts activities around the country." State arts agencies saw that it was advantageous for them to become involved with "familiar and friendly-sounding art forms," involving practitioners "scattered all over the scenery," giving "state programs apresence in communities that couldn't hope to house or support a ballet or opera company" (2008: 151 – 52).

State folk arts programs, initiated through NEA support, have continued to be indispensable vehicles for the development of local folklife programs. As a national infrastructure, they are highly networked among each other and work closely with American federal and national folklife programs. They have enabled state agencies to be more culturally democratic through including a broader spectrum of cultural communities and artistic expressions

---

[*] Robert Baron, Director of the Folk Arts Program at the New York State Council on the Arts.

in their compass, countering perceptions of the arts as inherently elitist and attracting political support from elected officials of diverse ideologies. In contrast to other countries, where intangible cultural heritage programs are dominated centrally by government cultural agencies, the American model of folk arts infrastructure is multilayered, extensively networked, and decentralized.

Initially established only in state arts agencies, state folk arts programs are now situated in a variety of kinds of agencies, organizations, and institutions. These include historical agencies, non-profit folklife organizations, a state humanities council, a cultural research organization, state university graduate folklore programs, and independent non-profit folklife organizations. The largest number, however, are programs within state arts agencies. In contrast with other arts disciplines in the United States, folk arts programs are far more extensively dependent upon state and federal government funding and more likely to be situated within government agencies.

Folk arts programs based in government agencies have substantial autonomy within their agencies, as discrete programs with distinctive activities and funding criteria. They also collaborate with programs representing other arts disciplines, including performing arts presenting, community arts, and arts education programs, which have missions that are both overlapping and complementary. However, state folk arts programs have had to justify maintaining their autonomy as separate programs representing a distinct field of the arts. For example, there may be the expectation to justify why folk music isn't covered by a music or performing arts program rather than a separate folk arts program. And many cultural funding agencies have adopted a "functional" approach to internal agency organization and funding, with the agency as a whole devoted generally to arts activities and organizations rather than to specific disciplines.

Maintaining an appropriate balance between autonomy and integration can be challenging. This challenge is similar to the case academic folklore programs need to make for folklore as an independent discipline rather than a field of study adequately represented by one or more larger academic disciplines. Folk arts programs have, with a few exceptions, succeeded in maintaining their autonomy, even as many agencies have reorganized along functional lines, remaining as discipline based programs. However, due to funding cutbacks, state folk arts directors have been obliged to take on additional responsibilities. For example, while for many years I was only responsible for directing the folk arts program at the New York State Council on the Arts (NYSCA), now I also direct the much larger music program.

State folk arts programs have also had to justify their support through special, dedicated "partnership" funding from the NEA, formerly known as "infrastructure" support.

Responding to questions from NEA and the National Assembly of State Arts Agencies (NASAA) about the need for continuing funding, a committee of state and regional folk arts folk arts programs developed a PowerPoint presentation in 2010 for NEA and NASAA, "Keys to a Successful Statewide Folk and Traditional Arts Program." The PowerPoint served as a collective self-representation of state programs which articulated the characteristics of an ideal type of these programs.

Several of us on this committee also engaged in a survey of state folk arts programs to assess their achievements, needs and challenges. This survey and discussions at a convening of a number of state programs resulted in a white paper, "State Folk Arts Programs: Achievements, Needs, Challenges," undertaken through funding from the American Folklore Society's Consultancy and Professional Development Program, in association with AFS, NEA, and NASAA. (http://c. ymcdn. com/sites/www. afsnet. org/resource/resmgr/Best_ Practices_ Reports/State_ Folk_ Arts_ Programs_ - _ A. pdf). The white paper and presentation successfully made the case for continued NEA support. I draw extensively here from the PowerPoint presentation and white paper in describing the distinctive features of state folk arts programs, their achievements and their current and future challenges. A committee consisting of Pat Atkinson, Robert Baron, Wayne Martin, Willie Smyth and Sally Van de Water wrote the white paper. Pat Atkinson, Robert Baron, Lynn Martin Graton and Amy Skillman wrote and designed the PowerPoint presentation.

In characterizing state folk arts programs, "Keys to a Successful Statewide Folk and Traditional Arts Program" recognized that each program must be "configured to meet the needs of the population of the state," have "goals and strategies appropriate to the host agency or organization" and can involve programming, grantmaking and/or services. Many state folk arts programs engage in field research and produce public programs (such as performances, festivals, exhibitions, and public school programs for children and youth). The programs situated in state agencies, (especially in state arts councils) provide funding to individual artists and to organizations developing their own folk arts programs, with several of these programs primarily functioning as funding programs and others engaged in both funding and programming. Continuing support by the NEA Folk and Traditional Arts Program to statewide programs of all kinds has been indispensable to the stability and continuity of these programs, providing initial support for folk arts program director positions and ongoing support for field research programming.

As state folk arts programs make their case for continuing NEA Partnership support and their continuation as discrete, autonomous programs within their agencies, they emphasize their importance for sustaining cultural heritage, fostering mutual understanding among cultures, and enhancing broad based public support for their agencies. Since the kinds of activities carried out by folk arts programs in government agencies are often quite different from the kinds of activities carried out by other programs in their agencies, they must often also justify the need for fieldwork and special projects undertaken over long periods in collaboration with communities and artists.

In state arts councils, which generally lack staff with advanced degrees in the social sciences or humanities, folk arts programs have also had to explain the importance of professional direction by academically trained folklorists. They emphasize that training in folklore studies or a related discipline enables them to discern excellence within a tradition, engage with communities with cultural sensitivity, and appropriately document and interpret traditions of diverse cultures for various audiences through application of their professional expertise.

Support for folk arts has suffered in states that lack folk arts programs. One of the respondents to the 2011 survey of state folk arts programs cited in "State Folk Arts Programs: Achievements, Challenges and Needs" stated that "we know from the past that folklife projects do not fare well in competition with other art forms. This is not because they are not as valuable, but those outside the field do not know how to judge their worth or value. The lack of focus on context, process, and meaning to the folk group that produces the art work prevents traditional artists from being competitive and most likely would mean that they would no longer receive support." (2011: 12)

State folk arts programs are concerned with both safeguarding and sustaining traditions within the communities where they originate, and with presenting them to new audiences. Projects undertaken in collaboration with communities recognize traditions which are often overlooked locally and unrecognized by cultural institutions. These partnerships are often directed towards enabling communities to document, present and interpret traditions in their own ways. Programming directed towards participants of multiple cultural backgrounds has multiple benefits for both these new audiences and the communities whose traditions are represented, with artists gaining wider recognition for their traditions and spurring renewed interest in their own communities. Programming for new audiences also builds respect and mutual understanding among different cultural groups experiencing each other's cultures, who might not ordinarily encounter one another in their everyday lives.

Most state programs support apprenticeships, which foster the perpetuation of traditions within communities through enabling a master traditional artist to teach another member of his or her own community, with priority given to folk arts no longer widely practiced. State programs also produce such public programs as exhibitions, festivals, lecture/demonstrations, concerts, recordings, film and video productions, and residencies by traditional artists. These programs may deal with the traditions of the state as a whole, the cultures of sub-regions, or particular themes like children's folklore, ranching culture, or textile traditions. State folk arts programs are also engaged in folk arts in education programs, which enable students to discover the living cultural heritage of neighbors, community members, and family members through their own research and by experiencing presentations by local artists. These programs may involve the development of school curricula focused upon local cultural resources, which are often tied to state educational standards and benchmarks.

Field research is a key feature of state folk arts programs. Over the past three decades, state folk arts programs have made possible documentation of traditional communities to an extent unprecedented in the history of the United States. In addition to serving as a foundation for the development of programming, field research also provides enduring and unique documentary records of local traditions that can serve as a resource for future generations. Field research also generates photography, video, and sound recordings, which are incorporated in exhibitions, media productions, and other public programs.

In the past, state folk arts program directors were labeled "state folklorists," although it was rarely an official title. This de facto title reflectstheir focal positions, which continues today, as primary resources for information and services relating to folk arts for traditional artists, the arts community and the public at large. Acting as cultural brokers, they connect artists and communities to resources for funding, new audiences, the media and educational systems. Through direct involvement with artists or funding of organizations in their state, they assist artists in finding performance venues and markets for their work, help them develop portfolios and promotional materials, and prepare them for participation in arts education programs.

State folk arts program directors are master networkers and collaborators. The national infrastructure of folk arts programs is highly reticulated on every level, involving extensive collaboration with federal and national folklife programs, along with state and local agencies and organizations. Their collaborations with other programs within their agencies have helped them become successfully entrenched as ongoing programs. State programs also collaborate with a wide variety of other state agencies, which enables them to expand their reach and resources. They have worked closely with parks and recreation agencies, government programs in health and human services, tourism agencies, and state education departments. Cultural tourism projects are tied to economic development, which has become a major concern of state arts agencies in recent years. For example, the North Carolina Arts Council's Folklife Program and North Carolina Folklife Institute produced the African American Music Project, an eight county heritage tourism initiative in eastern North Carolina, and developed programming involving the traditional culture of the Eastern Band of Cherokee that resulted in the creation of the Blue Ridge National Heritage Area.

Relationships with the National Endowment for the Arts Folk and Traditional Arts Program are mutually supportive and collegial. NEA funding enables state programs to convene as a folk arts peer group at the National Assembly of State Arts Agencies assembly, held every other year. State folkarts programs directors constitute a majority of the panelists on peer review panels of the NEA partnership program reviewing applications by state program for funding and recommending policy. Their presence on the panels ensures that professionals with expertise and experience in public folklore and the management of state programs maintain high standards for the review of proposals for funding. In their own states, folk arts programs utilize peer review panels to evaluate applications from local programs, with panel members who may include, in addition to folklorists, ethnomusicologists, traditional artists and local cultural leaders, thus providing both professional expertise and community perspectives.

State programs have conducted field research, identified participants and provided presenters for the Smithsonian Folklife Festival (the Smithsonian Institution is the national museum of the US) as well as the national and regional festivals organized by the National Council on the Traditional Arts, an NGO. The American Folklife Center of the Library of Congress (our national library) produces concerts featuring traditional artists from each state recommended by state folk arts program directors, and it has worked closely with state folk arts programs on other ongoing programs and special activities. The recent initiative to research the needs of folk arts programs and develop a case for continued NEA partnership support engaged the state folk arts programs with the American Folklore Society and National Assembly of State Arts Agencies.

Collaborations with local, state and federal agencies leverage the resources of state folk arts programs and help build broad political support for them. Within their own agencies, folk arts programs are frequently recognized as politically invaluable for demonstrating that the arts relate to all of a state's population rather than to only the elite and better educated. They have expanded the constituencies of their agencies, reaching rural areas, communities of color, working class populations, immigrants, refugees, the elderly, and other historically underserved groups, while demonstrating that artistic excellence is possessed by a broad spectrum of cultural communities. State legislators and governors of widely diverse political ideologies support the folk arts, which can be viewed as the art of the people as well as a repository of traditional cultural values. While state folk arts programs, of course, value traditionality, they are also obliged to explain to colleagues and the general public that the folk arts are living traditions, involving creativity and innovation within the artistic conventions of traditional communities.

The folklore profession in the United State enjoys a higher degree of integration of the academic and public sectors than is the case in other countries. Many state folk arts program directors teach or lecture at college and universities, and some work with graduate student interns. A growing number of state folklife programs are well situated in state universities, in association with their graduate folklore programs. They include programs at the universities of Arizona, Indiana, Missouri and Oregon as well as Western Kentucky University. The program in Michigan has long been situated at Michigan State University. During the 2011 survey and convening of state folk arts program directors, there was consensus that the relationship between state folk arts programs and folklore graduate programs should become even stronger, through the mentoring of graduate students by experienced public folklorists, more internships, and courses for working public folklorists returning for brief periods to graduate folklore programs. They also called for graduate folklore programs to engage practicing public folklorists to introduce public folklore work to graduate students; to participate in seminars, field schools and colloquia; and to teach courses relating to public folklore.

While only one graduate folklore program provided training for public folklore when the national infrastructure of state programs was created in the late 1970s, now public folklore is addressed by all graduate programs. State folk arts programs situated in universities and non-profit organizations are often seen as especially viable at a time of substantial challenges to programs based at state agencies. They are able to have greater flexibility and can focus exclusively on folklife related activities.

While nearly all state programs in government agencies demonstrated great resilience during the recent recession, they have been facing new challenges. State folk arts program directors increasingly have additional, non-folk arts responsibilities, and they have had to adapt to internal reorganizations of their agencies. Arts agencies have merged with state agencies devoted to economic development and tourism, which results in adaptations to reconcile the arts with changes in agency missions. Reductions in funding have limited travel, field research, and services to artists.

State programs are facing these challenges at a time when a new generation of state folk arts program directors has begun to emerge, succeeding directors who have been in their positions for decades. State programs are confronting current challenges through exploring new organizational models, partnerships and resources for funding. The foundations of the infrastructure established over thirty years ago remains strong, thanks to continued dedicated NEA support and the extensive, multi-faceted and resourceful networking of state programs.

Nevertheless, the sustainability of an infrastructure so dependent on government support is uncertain over the long term. In sharp contrast to other sectors of the arts, folk arts programming in the United States is unusually dependent on government funding, and there are few non-profit organizations primarily or exclusively devoted to folk arts, whether state programs or otherwise. As a respondent to the 2011 survey of state folk arts programs contended in "State Folk Arts Programs: Achievements, Challenges and Needs."

The constituents that we work with do NOT have an institutional infrastructure or access to such infrastructure as other areas of the arts ... [They] often are culturally, economically and institutionally marginalized partly because lots of outreach is required. Unless that outreach is extensive, deep and ongoing, a significant part of the country and of the arts will not be represented nor included for a variety of reasons ... Arts education has a well developed infrastructure ... Symphonies have a well-developed infrastructure. Local arts agencies have a well infrastructure ... In reality, the country's infrastructure for folk arts is the NEA's Folk Arts Partnership grant, which reaches out through the states that have a folk arts program.

The case for the continuation of ongoing folk arts infrastructure support by the NEA is compelling, and the loss of such support would cause significant damage to the state programs that are the pillars of this infrastructure. Nevertheless, federal government arts funding has been threatened during the past two decades, and even though it seems secure at the present time, an infrastructure so dependent on government funding is intrinsically vulnerable. In several agencies, retiring staff members have not been replaced due to funding constraints or shifting agency priorities, resulting in the loss of the state folk arts program.

The development of alternative models for state programs is encouraging and imperative. In recent decades, the number of state programs situated outside of state government agencies has increased. These programs are able to concentrate more exclusively upon their folk arts mission, fundraise from multiple sources, and operate with greater flexibility than government programs. In some states, the state folk arts program, while housed outside of a government agency, works closely with the state arts agency to evaluate funding requests and generate projects. In other states, like Maryland, New York and North Carolina, while the state arts agency based folk arts program remains strong, its support for regional and statewide folk arts organizations has created a state folk arts infrastructure which helps insure vibrant state folk arts activity in addition to and apart from the state arts agency folk arts program. The resourcefulness, resiliency, and exceptional collaborative successes of state programs should give us hope for the continuation of a national folk arts infrastructure for decades to come.

References

Hawes, Bess Lomax. *Sing it Pretty: A Memoir*. Champaign: University of Illinois Press. 2008.

"Keys to a Successful Statewide Folk and Traditional Arts Program." PowerPoint Presentation. [Pat Atkinson, Robert Baron, Lynn Martin Graton and Amy Skillman.] [2010]

State Arts Agencies Folk Arts Peer Group Planning Committee. [Patricia Atkinson, Robert Baron, Wayne Martin, Willie Smyth, Sally Van de Water]. "State Folk Arts Programs: Achievements, Challenges and Needs." State Folk Arts Peer Group Planning Committee, in association with the American Folklore Society, National Assembly of State Arts Agencies and National Endowment for the Arts, Folk and Traditional Arts Program. http://c.ymcdn.com/sites/www.afsnet.org/resource/resmgr/Best_Practices_Reports/State_Folk_Arts_Programs_-_A.pdf. 2011. Accessed May 24, 2013.

Case Studies, Techniques, Technology

The Center for the Study of Upper Midwestern Cultures

James P. Leary[*]

The Center for the Study of Upper Midwestern Cultures (http://csumc. wisc. edu), or CSUMC, is situated in Madison, the capitol city of Wisconsin. Based in the College of Letters and Science at the University of Wisconsin (UW), CSUMC was created in 2001 with support from the UW and from the National Endowment for the Humanities, a federal agency. As folklorists and linguists collectively embracing a populist approach to the humanities, we are committed to research, collections development, publications, collaborative projects, and educational programs concerning the languages and folklore of diverse peoples in the Upper Midwest. Our region includes Minnesota, Wisconsin, and the Upper Peninsula of Michigan (with overlap into Lower Michigan, Ontario, Manitoba, the Dakotas, Iowa, Illinois, and extends to river towns like St. Louis, Missouri). A territory of woods, waters, fields, small towns, and industrial cities, the Upper Midwest is a cultural middle ground: the meeting place for centuries of Woodland and Plains Indians, the American region with the most entrenched and varied European-American population, and recent home to communities of African, Asian, and Hispanic Americans. Thanks to UW support, donations, earned income from productions, competitive grants from many sources (e. g. UW, state and federal government agencies, American Indian nations, private foundations), and partnerships with many organizations, we have worked with all of the aforementioned cultural groups. We collaborate closely with the Folklore Program at UW (http:// folklore. wisc. edu); indeed several key CSUMC staff members are members of the Folklore Program, and we often involve graduate students from the Program in our activities. Our efforts emphasize three major areas: 1) Preservation and Access; 2) Education and Outreach; and 3) Publications and Productions.

---

[*] James P. Leary, Professor of Scandinavian Studies at University of Wisconsin, CO-founder of the Center for the Study of Upper Midwestern Cultures at UW-Madison.

Preservation and Access: We actively conduct new field research throughout the region, using digital audio recorders, as well as digital still and video cameras to create documentation regarding speakers of various languages and practitioners of diverse cultural traditions. Collaborating with the UW library system's Digital Collections Center (http://uwdc.library.wisc.edu/) and University Archives (http://archives.library.wisc.edu/), we are in the process of creating digital repositories for new folkloristic/ethnographic field documentation. We also work regularly with UW's Mills Music Library to acquire collections (field and commercial sound recordings in analog and digital formats, sheet music, song books, programs and posters for musical events, photographs, etc.) from traditional musicians that form part of the regional "Folk and Ethnic" component of the Library's Wisconsin Music Archives (http://music.library.wisc.edu/wma/).

Our Wisconsin Englishes Project (http://csumc.wisc.edu/wep/), undertaken with the Max Kade Institute (http://mki.wisc.edu/), concerns: 1) regional and ethnic changes and differences in English across the state and the Upper Midwest; 2) the full range of languages spoken in our region, past and present; and 3) the reflection of regional culture and identity through language choices residents make. We currently work with German, Hmong, Norwegian, Swedish, and Spanish speakers. We also partner with *the Dictionary of American Regional English* (http://dare.wisc.edu/). And our initiative for Indigenous Language Preservation and Promotion (http://csumc.wisc.edu/?q = node/110) connects tribal language programs with UW-Madison and other UW campuses, while establishing a resource center for archival materials on the indigenous languages in the region.

Our major folklore archiving effort—Public Folk Arts and Folklife Projects of the Upper Midwest (http://digicoll.library.wisc.edu/w/wiarchives/csumc.html) —is a series of project collection guides highlighting a wealth of ethnographic documentation and public productions generated since the 1970s, often with funding from the National Endowment for the Arts, the National Endowment for the Humanities, and state, county, and local arts and humanities councils. This digital on-line clearinghouse provides project descriptions and history, and leads researchers to the varied repositories across the region and nation that house project documentation such as field reports, sound, video, and commercial recordings, photography, exhibits, and ephemeral publications. Representing research in Wisconsin, Illinois, Iowa, Minnesota, Missouri, and the western Upper Peninsula of Michigan, projects focus on the region's distinctive expressive cultures, survey diverse indigenous and immigrant populations, and record an incredible range of traditional performers and practices, from the artistic and musical, occupational and recreational, to the religious and spiritual.

Education and Outreach: Our Wisconsin Teachers of Local Culture initiative (http://csumc.wisc.edu/wtlc/), undertaken in partnership with the Wisconsin Arts Board's Folk Arts Program (http://artsboard.wisconsin.gov/category.asp?linkcatid = 3658&linkid = 1652&locid = 171), is a coalition of folklorists and educators deeply involved with local culture and curricula. WTLC enables teachers to create integrated lessons linked with academic standards required by the state and to place specific knowledge in broad context. Supplemental online resources, including curriculum guides, address tensions and opportunities arising from changing demographics in local communities (http://csumc.wisc.edu/?q=node/21). And WTLC makes innovative use of summer cultural tours connecting teachers directly with practitioners of local cultural traditions (http://csumc.wisc.edu/wtlc/?q=tours). The related Cultural Maps/Cultural Tours project (http://csumc.wisc.edu/?q=node/19) is a digital archive created especially for teachers who may use images, written information, audio recordings and video recordings of traditional music, foodways, folk art and other material culture from a variety of cultural groups as a stimulus to working with their students in documenting their own local communities.

CSUMC staff members frequently give talks on various aspects of regional languages and folklore to community groups around the Upper Midwest. We are often interviewed by print and broadcast journalists on a broad range of topics. We consult regularly with writers and filmmakers, and we offer technical assistance to and field questions from diverse community organizations and ordinary citizens.

Publications and Productions: We have published a series of books and documentary sound recordings (http://csumc.wisc.edu/?q=node/4). In cooperation with the University of Wisconsin Press, we have recently established a series, "Languages and Folklore of the Upper Midwest" (http://uwpress.wisc.edu/languagesandfolklore.html), which will include original monographs, translations, reprints/new editions, edited anthologies, and documentary compact discs that focus on the lives, languages, and cultural traditions of the region's diverse peoples, both historical and contemporary. In addition we have produced podcasts and documentary films on topics ranging from peculiar Wisconsin words to the "laborlore" of ironworkers engaged in structural steel construction.

Finally, complementing our preservation and access efforts—which build upon our UW collections, while virtually organizing collections scattered throughout the region—we have produced six online exhibits (http://csumc.wisc.edu/?q=node/44), with more being developed, as well as a Norwegian American Folk Music Portal (http://vanhise.lss.wisc.edu/nafmp/), the first of what we imagine as a series of portals uniting performers, organizations, and archival collections related to ethnic musical traditions in our region.

Folkways as Intangible Cultural Heritage and the Question of Authenticity
—A Study of "The Beginning of Spring" Festival in Jiuhua, Zhejiang Province, the People's Republic of China

Xiaobing Wang-Riese*

    Folkways, as pointed out by the American sociologist William Graham Sumner (1906: 3 – 4), "are not creations of human purpose" but "are made unconsciously."[①] They are present in folklife in a free and self-determined way, although their development might have been influenced by outside powers as politics and elite culture. Generally speaking, traditional small societies, such as village communities, are the best soil for folk culture, though the occurrence of a folk custom tends to depend on external factors also.[②] In the 20th century, with the radical changes it brought to Chinese society, many traditional rural organizations like clans and village communities disintegrated, and all kinds of folk activities were often despised and suppressed by the mainstream culture. Especially in the last 30 years, after the reform and opening-up policy, as China intensified the process of modernization, the number and size of rural territories shrank, the backbone of the rural society (young and mid-aged farmers) migrated to the cities, the rural population has become increasingly depleted and aging, and cultural ecology in which local folk custom lives is often dying. How can traditional folk culture be passed down from generation to

---

    * Xiaobing Wang-Riese, Professor at the Institute of Chinese Intangible Cultural Heritage, Sun Yat-Sen University.

    ① William Graham Sumner, *Folkways: A study of the sociological importance of usages, manners, customs, mores, and morals*, Boston: Ginn and Co. 1906, p. 3 – 4.

    ② Folklorists have put forward many theories about the occurrence of folk customs. Sumner's viewpoint that folk customs are spontaneously formed in folk life is just one of them. The complete naysayer is a Swiss, Eduard Hoffmann-Krayer (1864 – 1936), thinking that "people do not produce, but simply reproduce". The German scholar Hans Naumann (1886 – 1951) put forward the concept of "gesunkenes Kulturgut", referring to cultural items invented and developed by the upper classes of society and slowly spreading to the folk, in opposition to his concept of the naturally grown "primitives Gemeinschaftsgut" among the lower classes of societies. See Hans Naumann, *Grundzuege der deutschen Volkskunde*, Leipzig: Verlag Wissenschaft und Bildung, 1922.

generation under these circumstances and become an organic part of modern society, so as to keep the indigenous features and roots of Chinese civilization alive? This is a common concern of people from all segments of society, and it is the reason why the Chinese government launched the intangible cultural heritage protection movement.

However, folk culture itself has some characteristics that conflict with official orthodox culture, and it tends to be transformed, packaged, or even reconstructed during the process of being recognized as intangible cultural heritage and protected. For example, folk culture can become (1) official/politicized, (2) materialized, and (3) commercialized. (1) means relating the declaration and exhibit of the intangible cultural heritage with the achievements of local officials, private things becoming arranged by the government and local people lose their cultural autonomy; (2) originally lively folk activities become static pictures and objects in the exhibition hall; (3) intangible cultural heritage is transformed into businessmen's profit-making tools and public consumer goods.

How can folkways be respected and preserved through the government leading projects of safeguarding of the intangible cultural heritage? How can the authenticity of folk culture in their living state and inheritress be fully guaranteed? In May 2011, the State Council issued the third batch of national intangible cultural heritage list (191 in total) and the extension list (164 in total). "Sacrifice for Beginning of Spring in Jiuhua" reported by Kecheng district, Quzhou city, Zhejiang Province; "Spring Declaration to Advise Farming" in Suichang County, Zhejiang Province; together with "Singing Spring in Shiqian" in Shiqian County, Guizhou Province were included in the extension lists of Chinese national intangible cultural heritage under the general heading of "lunar 24 solar terms" (item number X – 68).[①] Sacrifice for Beginning of Spring in Jiuhua is performed for the wood and spring god Gou Mang in ancient myth. The sacrificial date is set in the spring day, the first of the 24 periods of the year (according to the solar calendar on February 4 or 5). Since Quzhou lies close to my hometown of Jiangshan, I undertook a one-week fieldwork project in the village of Waichen in February 2012 to investigate the first sacrificing ritual held after its nomination as national ICH. My intention was to observe which impact the nomination of ICH would have on the people in Waichen and how they would respond to it, in order to find out what should be the key to the authentic inheritance of the Sacrificing Festival of Beginning of Spring in its living form.

---

① See http://www.gov.cn/zwgk/2011-06/09/content_ 1880635.htm (accessed on 2012/2/12).

1. The Gou Mang Myth and the Festival of Beginning of Spring in Ancient China

The system of 24 solar year periods representing the sun's movement is one of the great inventions of the ancient Chinese. When this calendar system started to be used remains controversial. In the earliest written documents of Chinese history, the oracle bone inscriptions of the Shang Dynasty (17. – 11. Century B. C.), there is a oracle bone recording "names of four directions and their winds": The east is called Xi; its wind is Xie. The south is Yin; its wind is Wei. The west is ...①; its wind is Yi. The north is Yuan, its wind is ...②"③ The concept of four directions gods in the Zhou Dynasty (1046 – 256 B. C.) is documented in *Zhou Li* (*Rites of Zhou*). The chapter of "Spring Officer" writes: "Making six vessels with jade to worship heaven, earth and the four directions. Using blue Bi to worship the heaven, yellow Cong for the earth, green Gui for the east, red Zhang for the south, white Hu for the west, black Huang for the north."④

Later, Gou Mang as a deity was related to the element wood and the direction of the east. In *Zuozhuan* (*Master Zuo's The Spring and Autumn Annals*) under the entries for the 29 years of Zhao Gong's regime it is said: "The deity of wood is Gou Mang, the deity of fire Zhu Rong, the deity of metal Ru Shou, the deity of water Xuan Ming, the deity of earth Hou Tu."⑤ In *Lüshi chunqiu* (*Lü's Spring and Autumn Annals*) from the late Warring States it is recorded under the category "mid-spring" (mengchun): "Its emperor is called Tai Hao and its deity is Gou Mang."⑥

Liji (*The Book of Rites*), written during the Western Han Dynasty (202 B. C. –9 A. D.) put the deities in charge of the four seasons systematically in the chapter *Yueling* (*The order of Lunar Months*). It names the spring emperor Taihao, and the spring deity is called Gou Mang. The summer emperor is Yan Di, and the summer deity is Zhu Rong; the autumn emperor is Shao Hao, and the autumn deity Ru Shou; the winter emperor is Zhuan Xu, and the winter deity Xuan Ming. The commentator Zheng Xuan annotated "Gou Mang" with the following words: "the son of Shao Hao, named Zhong, is the officer of wood."⑦ As for his image, it was described by Mo Zi during

---

① Not available in original text.
② Not available in original text.
③ Oracle Bone Inscription Collection No. 14294. See 郭沫若编:《甲骨文合集》第五册,中华书局 1979 年版.
④ 《十三经注疏》(附校勘记)之《周礼注疏》卷十八,中华书局 2003 年版,第 762 页.
⑤ 《十三经注疏》(附校勘记)之《春秋左传正义》卷五十三,中华书局 2003 年版,第 2123 页.
⑥ 王利器著:《吕氏春秋注疏》,巴蜀书社 2002 年版,第 9—10 页.
⑦ 《十三经注疏》(附校勘记)之《礼记正义》卷十四,中华书局 2003 年版,第 1352—1360 页.

the Warring State as "a bird body, white clothing and square face."①

Folklorist Jian Tao has pointed out that in ancient mythology Gou Mang was a deity linking spring, wood, and the east, and a complete system of symbols in the state rites (see Table 1) was established during the Eastern Han Dynasty (25 – 220 A. D.). Although some of the elements included originate in more ancient times, the formation of this idealized system cannot have taken place before the Han Dynasty, since the influence of the concepts of the correspondence between human beings and the universe, yin-yang and five elements prevailing in this period, is clearly visible. Moreover, the origin of the custom of the sacrifice for the Beginning of Spring should also be ascribed to the Eastern Han Dynasty. The design of the rite was mainly based on the relevant proposals in the *Liji*.② Although the custom of Beginning of Spring in the Han Dynasty absorbed the folk custom of "making clay oxen," it belongs to an irrelevant part different from the official rite of greeting the seasons. The rite of beginning spring to greet the seasons was held in the eastern suburb of the capital and the participants' dress was mainly green. Gou Mang was also one of the ritual targets as the assistant of the "Green emperor". At the same time, the capital and other cities should set up a clay oxen and a clay peasant idol outside the city gate as a harbinger of spring symbolizing beginning farming activities.

Table 1   The symbolic system of the "greet the seasons" rites during the Eastern Han Dynasty③

Season	Five Elements	Color	Five Emperors	Direction	Deity
spring	wood	green	Green Emperor	east	Gou Mang
summer	fire	red	Red Emperor	south	Zhu Rong
18 days before autumn	clay	yellow	Yellow Emperor	center	Huang Ling
autumn	metal	white	White Emperor	west	Ru Shou
winter	water	black	Black Emperor	north	Xuan Ming

The rites of Beginning of Spring were inherited from the Eastern Han Dynasty and survived into the Qing Dynasty (1644-1911), but the forms of expression changed to a certain degree. During the Tang Dynasty, for example, the rite was no longer as solemn as in the Eastern Han Dynasty, but more joyful. Rewarding ministers by the emperor with flowers made from jewelry-made to

---

① 《墨子》,李小龙译注,中华书局2007年版,第116—117页。
② 简涛著:《立春风俗考》,上海文艺出版社1980年版,第23页以下。恰如作者所言,像《礼记》这样的著作不能被当成史书看待,其中的种种描绘多属理想性质的设想,而非对于事实的记录。
③ 简涛著:《立春风俗考》,第41页。

celebrate the festival was added.① The custom of "making clay oxen" was also changed somewhat, and the name of the clay peasant idol was changed from the original "ploughman" to "a man whipping the oxen." Their positions were used to symbolizing the time for Beginning of Spring, and it had the ritual behavior of officials hitting the clay oxen with rods. This could be the origin of the later customs of Beginning of Spring like "play the part of Gou Mang" and "whipping the clay oxen." That the deity of Gou Mang replaced the clay peasant idol in the rite of "making clay oxen" was an innovation during the Southern Song Dynasty (1127-1279) and "was probably a result of the decline or abolishment of the rite of greeting the seasons."② During the Ming Dynasty (1368-1644), the government formulated the corresponding ritual establishing the status of Gou Mang in the set of etiquette.

During the first half of the 20th century, the government of the Republic of China abolished the traditional Chinese calendar and introduced the western Gregorian calendar. The beginning of Spring was no longer an official holiday, and the corresponding official rites also completely disappeared. Traditional customs like greeting the Spring, whipping the clay oxen, and eating Spring pancake/Spring rolls on the first day of Spring nevertheless remained popular among in some areas. After 1949, these customs have not been popular any more because of ideological reasons. While the beginning of Spring is often perceived as one of the seasonal feasts of the 24 solar periods, its attribute as an ancient farming festival was gradually forgotten. The Chinese memories and emotions attached to the "Green emperor," Gou Mange and clay oxen were very weak. Related customs, like playing the part of Gou Mang, whipping the clay oxen, and eating Spring pancake/Spring rolls/lettuce, declined to become just historical reminiscences that existed only in some remote villages and among special people.③ The village of Waichen, located in Jiuhua Township, in the western mountain areas of Zhejiang Province, is such a place. It is the most complete domestic existing place that still retains Spring folk culture, due to the Wutong Temple, the worship of Gou Mang, and other ancient Spring customs that remained.

2. Wutong Temple and Its Sacrifice for Beginning of Spring

Jiuhua Township is located in the northwest of Quzhou district, Zhejiang Province, about 9.5 km from the city of Quzhou. Administratively it belongs to the Kecheng District. It covers an area

---

① 简涛著:《立春风俗考》, 第67页。
② 简涛著:《立春风俗考》, 第87页。
③ Jian Tao has made investigation about the inheritance of spring customs in the 1990s. According to him the customs centering on the Beginning of Spring has been supplanted by the Spring Festival in modern China with similar implications. 简涛:《略论近代立春节日文化的演变》, 载《民俗研究》1998年第2期, 第58—72页。

of 82. 32 square kilometers with more than 20,000 inhabitants in 35 villages. Waichen, one of these villages, has 632 registered residents distributed in 212 families. The population of permanent residents in recent years has been only somewhat above 280, due to the fact that young and middle-aged villagers mainly work outside. Most villagers carry one of the four surnames Su, Fu, Wang, and Gong, representing clans or extended families. Su and Fu members are the majority and are said to have moved there earlier than the others, from neighboring Fujian Province. All four clans have their own family genealogical books. There still exist clan halls of Fu and Su in the village, which are used for clan activities.

Wutong Temple, located at the village entrance, is the only remaining religious site in the village. The main deity worshiped inside is the spring and wood deity Gou Mang known from ancient Chinese myths. Nowadays, in a side hall of the temple a statue of Buddha is also worshipped. According to local information, the original building of the temple was seriously damaged after 1949, and was formerly used as a rice milling factory. In 2001, Wang Xiaolian, a culturally interested man from Quzhou born in 1943,[①] happened to see this old house while helping the Tourism Bureau of Kecheng District with a census of touristic resources. He believed it to be an ancient temple because of its three doors, untypical for a normal dwelling. When scraping off the yellow mud on the wooden board of the old house, he saw the four Chinese characters "Wutong Temple (梧桐神殿)." After that, he heard from aged villagers that the Buddha statue inside had been discarded during the Cultural Revolution. They only remembered that the sacrifice for Beginning of Spring and the Mid-Autumn were held in the temple every year in their childhood, and that the Buddha worshipped inside had had a pair of wings. According to this clue, Mr. Wang concluded that what the villagers called "Wutong Buddha" was indeed the mythical spring deity Gou Mang.

Since then, under the appeals of Wang Xiaolian and others, the sawmill and rice milling factory were moved out of the temple in 2004. The villagers repaired the "Wutong Temple" with thirty or forty thousand Yuan of voluntary contributions. At that time, Gong Xielong (1965-2008) was in charge of the project. His older brother was the current Party branch secretary in Waichen. In restoring the statue of spring gods, they referred to the relevant accounts about Gou Mang in the previously mentioned ancient documents, *Mozi* and the description in the *Classic of Mountains and Rivers* as "bird body, human face, riding two dragons."[②] So they made him into a figure with rectangular face, white garments, riding two dragons/snakes with feet, with two wings on his back, holding the compasses in the right hands and the left hands grasping a cloth bale with five

---

① Wang was the general manager of a construction company in Quzhou before. He was fond of studying the local geography, folk and traditional culture from his early age and has published several books on the local landscape and culture.

② 袁珂:《山海经校注》,第265页。

cereals.

The main temple follows the typical folk building pattern in this area, called "three big and six small houses (三间六)" by local people. It is divided into the upper, middle, and lower halls. Each side can be divided into three partitions. The common houses are closed by door planks while not in the ancestral hall or temple. Altogether there are a total of six rooms. The middle section has upper hall, central hall (patio) and lower hall. The altar in the middle of the upper hall of the Wutong Temple worships the statue of the main deity Gou Mang. The sacrificial altar on the left side of main deity has three statues of Guang Yu of different sizes and on the right side the statues of four "Spirit Dukes (灵公)" with their surnames of Yu, Yan, Yang, and Cai.① Figures of four deities representing "wind," "rain," "thunder," and "lightning" and two heavenly kings with the name "richness" and "dignity," respectively, are painted on the wall behind them. On the two side walls of the hall, there are decorative paintings with the theme of 24 solar periods. A vat filled with water is placed beside the patio as usual; its symbolic meaning is "abundance." The lower hall is a two-layered theatre stage. The entrance is on the back. Adults must go through the corridor with their bodies bending as a result of the low stage. For the villagers, this design is has the purpose to force people to bow in front of the gods and thus to express their respect.

Although the Wutong Temple stands at the entrance of the Waichen village, the villagers told me that it had once stood in the valley behind the village. Across the streets and fields, a brook called "temple source" flows at the foot of the mountain. When going down the road along the stream, after passing through the village of the destroyed Three Emperor Temple②adjacent to Waichen Village, one enters a canyon. The original location of Wutong Temple is halfway up in this canyon. Nowadays, no building remains there and one can only vaguely identify a former stone platform between trees and grass. Standing here, facing the lush Wutong Mountain and a clear, flowing stream at the foot of the mountain, the early spring sun just poking its head in an oblique angle from behind the mountain slope and shining warmly, the warming air enshrouding the heel, a

---

① According to the introduction of Wang Xiaolian, all four Spirit Dukes were legendary figures having a direct historic relationship with Quzhou. Spirit Duke Yu was General Yuchi Gong of the Tang dynasty, who was called patron saint by the city defenders in Quzhou. Spirit Duke Yan was a Song dynasty magistrate in Quzhou (perhaps Yan Dunfu, but with a different death compared to the legend). The legend said that he jumped into the well and died from poisoning by drinking the water poisoned by the Deity of Plague in order to warn the people. The salvaged body turned black for poisoning, so the duke's image is represented in dark color. Spirit Duke Yang was the Tang dynasty poet Yang Jiong, whose relation with the locality is unknown. There was a "Duke Yang Temple" in Quzhou in the past, known as "the third city god". Spirit Duke Cai was Cai Lun from the Han Dynasty who invented papermaking. There were many small papermaking workshops in the mountains growing fair amounts of moso bamboos which could be used as material of papermaking. Yet, Deputy Curator of the Museum of Quzhou Zhan Jian had another saying about the names and identites of the four dukes. He thinks these four dukes were originally the accompanying gods of the local king during the Western Zhou dynasty, Xu Yan, who had gained much worship in the locality.

② It worshiped the legendary three founders of the Chinese nation: "Suiren" who made fire by rubbing sticks, "Xuanyuan" (the Yellow Emperor) and "Shennong" (the Yan Emperor).

flavor of spring between vegetation surrounds you completely, and one can indeed sense a beautiful feeling like the spring breeze. The "wind and water" is so good, no wonder the ancients built a spring deity temple here.

However, local people have their own explanation of the origin of Wutong Temple. According to Wang Xiaolian, they call the temple "Wutong" because of the old proverb: "The Chinese parasols at home attract the phoenix." The phoenix lives only where the Chinese parasols grow. Since Gou Mang has a bird body, he belongs to the phoenix clan. According to a local legend, the abundance of Chinese parasols on the peaks of mountains surrounding Waichen Village attracted Gou Mang so that he settled down here. From then on the Chinese parasols and other trees in the mountain grew even more luxuriant. The mountain men felt thankful for it and therefore built a temple in the Wutong Mountain using a huge parasol root to carve a statue called "Wutong Buddha" for worship. Why was this statue later moved to the temple at the foot of the mountain? The legend says that on the peak of Tiantai Mountain opposite to Wutong Mountain lived a pair of brothers who were masters of rain of the ancient emperor Shennong. They became immortals by exercising and gained the name of Chisongzi and Chixuzi. Chisongzi was born a shepherd and kept a flock of sheep on the Tiantai Mountain after being immortalized. He gave them freedom to graze and breed and never slaughtered them for food, so finally they were as numerous as clouds in the sky and turned the slope originally overgrown with all kinds of herbs into a bald hill. The deity of wood and plants, Gou Mang, felt a heartache at seeing this, and secretly plotted against Chisongzi by making the Tiantai Mountain grow only arbors and moso bamboos instead of herbs and grasses. Chisongzi drove the sheep, wanting to go somewhere else, while Gou Mang grew a thick stretch of arbors suddenly in front of the moving herd of sheep to block their way. Nonetheless Chisongzi still drove the sheep secretly in the evening to the Zhiling slopes towards Shiliang, Gou Mang saw to it that no grass would grow there for the sheep to eat. Chisongzi had no choice but to order the sheep to hibernate and thus to become white stones; he hoped to turn them back into sheep when herbs and grass grew on the mountains again. The elder brother of Chisongzi, Chixuzi, didn't want them to continue to fight hurting the harmony and trouble the people, so he mediated advising his younger brother not to raise sheep anymore and accept that they remain stones forever. The peasants could keep some sheep for eating, so the number of sheep wouldn't be too large and people can hear the pleasant sound of sheep again at ordinary times. Chisongzi listened to his brother and his sheep remained a mountain full of rocks. Chixuzi suggested to the deity of wood to move to the flat land downhill instead of living solitarily on the peak of Wutong Mountain. Gou Mang agreed, but wondered how he could move. Since Chisongzi was the Master of Rain, one day he let down a heavy rain on Wutong Mountain, which destroyed the old Wutong Temple. The statue of "Wutong Buddha" drifted with the mountain torrent downhill and remained spinning around in a whirl at the entrance of Waichen village. While many villagers looked at this strange phenomenon, an old man passing by asked them to salvage the statue from the water and said, "Look, the Wutong Buddha wants you to build a new hall for him where he can live. It should carry the name of 'Wutong Temple' because the old one on the mountain was too small for him." At that time, the villagers did not know that the passer-by actually was the immortal Chisongzi in disguise. Nonetheless they followed his advice and built a "Wutong Temple" there which is preserved up to the present.

To restore the sacrifice for the Beginning of Spring in Wutong temple, Wang Xiaolian and other people sorted out some information about local customs.①

On the first day of Spring, commonly known as "greeting Spring day" or "starting Spring," the first thing to do after awakening is to read the almanac to find out the exact moment when Spring begins. People plant a fresh soybean sprout in a large bowl full of fine sand. A small elongated red paper flag is stuck into the bowl with the four characters "greeting spring and receiving blessing（迎春接福）" written on it. A cup of green tea is put behind the bowl. Then people carry the table to the courtyard, planting incense sticks into the offering bowl and lighting red candles. When the candles have burned down, the soybean sprouts will be transplanted into a vegetable patch or flowerpot. This conveys the meaning "Spring is coming, full of vitality and fresh breeze." On this day the "harbinger" will give a picture of an ox to every household, that is, a kind of folk printed woodcut. Every family will paste the picture of the oxen in the middle hall with blessing words like "good crop weather" or "peace and prosperity" printed on it. Most pictures of oxen are printed on red paper with black outlines, though some are fashioned in color printing. The pictures represent the early or late beginning of Spring. A cowboy carrying a rope and leading an ox means that the farming season starts late and the cattle can enjoy a leisurely time. A cowboy walking behind an ox and driving it with a bamboo twig means that the farming season will begin early and the cattle will have to work hard this year. A cowboy riding on the back of a cow playing flute means weather for a good crop. The picture of oxen can not only foretell whether the agricultural year will be good or not, but also marks the working schedule according to solar periods.

In the past, the local officials of Quzhou let subordinates greet Spring in the eastern part of the region on the day of Beginning of Spring. The "clay ox" practicing "whip spring ritual" was called "whip spring." After that, people rushed forward to rob the soil covering on the cattle; this was called "rob spring," and it was believed that grabbing the cow's head brought good luck. People believed that those who got "meat" from the cattle's body would harvest silkworms, those who got soil from the horn would harvest crops, and those who got food from the stomach would have an abundant harvest of all crops with full store houses. The people believed that the soil from the "clay-oxen" was good medicine, as long as one rubbed the infected body part with a cloth bag

---

① 参见汪筱联、邹耀华撰稿，于红萍整理《衢州梧桐祖殿立春祭祀——立春祭祀申报"人类传说及无形遗产著作"的依据和理由》（内部资料，由衢州市文化广电新闻出版局提供）。

containing this soil. So, every year there were accidents of damaging the body for "rob spring" during a stampede in the crowd pushing and squeezing.

Temple fairs were also held in Wutong Temple on the Beginning of Spring day with customs like *yingchun* (beat gongs and drums to greet the Spring god), *tanchun* (go out for an outing), *chachun* (collect pine and cypress branches and insert them into proper spaces of the door), *daichun* (children make rings from willow branches to put them on their heads like crowns), *changchun* ("bite Spring," eat Spring food, eat fresh vegetables) and greet the clay oxen. To "greet the clay oxen," people formed bamboo sticks into an ox-like shape, covered it with colored paper, attached small wheels to the feet of the ox, and dressed him with red or other colorful cloth. A beggar dressed as the leading cowboy (*muniu taisui*) would lead the clay oxen to parade on the street after the sacrifice for the Beginning of Spring, and his team raised flags and beat gongs and drums. Children tie seven (or six) beans to the oxen's horns to avoid acne. The temple fair also offered amusements such as the games of pitch-pot, drum-and-pass, walking on stilts, and trotting-horse lamp. Full-scale dramas are played on the theatre stage of the temple for three days and nights.① People invite friends and relatives to join in the merry-making on these days, and to consume holiday snacks, including spring cakes, spring rolls, rice cakes, and rice mash.

3. Sacrifice for the Beginning of Spring in Wutong Temple as Observed in 2012

In 2004, Waichen Village begun to revive the ceremony of Sacrifice for the Beginning of Spring, which is mainly organized by villagers. 2012 was the first year for the revived ceremony after the "Beginning of Spring Day in Jiuhua" had been listed as a state-level intangible cultural heritage expression. Local leaders at all levels attached special importance to it, and a deputy director of the Education Sports Bureau (Cultural Bureau) was personally responsible for it. Local media also paid high attention: television and newspapers reported on the ceremony and interviewed people on site, and the Quzhou News Network webcast the sacrificial ceremony live.②

Villagers busily began the preparation several days in advance to welcome the ceremony. They cleaned the Wutong Temple, and pasted a new Spring Festival couplet at the door. They also hung rows of big red lanterns in front of the temple gate and 24 small lanterns, representing the 24 solar periods, inside the temple. Hanging from Gou Mang's altar a red banner read "greet spring and

---

① Dramas were also played during other festivals, such as the Spring Festival, the Lantern festival, on February 2, the Tomb-sweeping Day, the Dragon-boat Festival, the Mid-Autumn Festival, the Double Ninth Festival, and the Winter Solstice, etc.

② http://news.qz828.com/system/2012/02/03/010435143.shtml (2012/2/16).

receive blessings" and a spring ox made of bamboo was put on display, wrapped in green silk, adorned with a red scarf, and wearing a large red silk flower on his neck. Hundreds of pounds of rice, and baskets of cabbages, radishes, and bean curd, were prepared in the kitchen to serve staff, guests, and pilgrims. To ensure a smooth ceremony, the village committee specially called together young and old villagers to rehearse on February 3 and everyone was extremely busy inside and outside of the temple.

At 9 a. m. on February 4 before the sacrifice, the award ceremony was held outside the gate of Wutong Temple. The director of the Department of Propaganda of CCP Committee of Kecheng District delivered a speech. The director of the Office for Safeguarding Intangible Cultural Heritage in the Cultural Department of Zhejiang province and the director of the Bureau for Culture, Broadcasting and News in Quzhou City inaugurated a tablet bearing the inscriptions "State-Level Intangible Cultural Heritage/Sacrifice for the Beginning of Spring in Jiuhua." The deputy director of Kecheng District Administration received this tablet in representation of the local people. Thereafter all entered the hall. The sacrifice began at about 9:15. Master of ceremonies was the village head Y. Fu. Chief sacrificer was the leader of the local communist party Y. Gong, and assistant sacrificers were two young villagers H. Fu and H. Wu. Due to limited space, the village committee strictly controlled the number of people who were allowed to enter the temple, and only a few dozen village representatives were present. They were divided into the old, middle-aged and young, and men and women, and stood symmetrically on two sides of the upper hall and courtyard in descending order from the old to the young. The old dressed as usual, and the young adults who carrying Buddha to parade wore yellow silk clothing and yellow headbands. Children (a total of eight boys and eight girls) were wearing green dresses, trousers and bamboo woven garlands with make up on their faces.

At the beginning of the ceremony, people set off firecrackers outside and played music. Then three big gifts were presented to the Spring god. First, over 20 kinds of public offerings were respectively put on painted red wooden plates or directly in front, including rice steamer (i. e. piling steamed rice into high hills in the wooden rice bucket, pressing rows of

Spring God and offerings to him

(Photo: Wang Xiaobing)

red jujube on the surface, covering it with red paper-cut and plugging in a cypress as decoration); cow head (a pig head was substituted on that day); pig head; sheep head; green tea; apple; banana; orange; longan; kumquat; cake; red cake; lotus cake; oil claws (polished glutinous rice strips); sesame balls; rice cakes; rice dumplings; herb cakes; green vegetables; five-cereal seeds; sugar cane; plum blossoms; pine braches and a pair of large candles, etc. The second were flower baskets, offered respectfully by leaders and guests to the Spring god, which were put in front of the gate in advance and two of them were later carried symbolically to the altar. The third was offerings spontaneously prepared by villagers. On that day nearly 40 old men and women from the village lined up presenting their own bamboo baskets or wooden basins with offerings inside. The food and arrangement was very much the same: a strip of meat, a vegetable, two rice dumplings, a glass of water, a bowl of rice (also pressed like a hill and embedded in red jujubes), two rice cakes, green and white rice cakes, fruits, pastries, etc. They were decorated with red paper cutting and cypress branches on top as well. Since the beginning of spring was set on 6: 22 p. m. of this day and year, the offerings remained displayed until evening and were taken back by the families who offered them after the ceremony was over.

After presenting the offerings and flowers, the sacrificers and several representatives of the villagers burnt incense and worshiped in front of the censer in the patio. After that the chief sacrificer read "prayers for greeting spring and receiving blessings." The wording was: "The four seasons renew and everything takes on a completely new look. In the year of *renchen* the golden dragon reports good news. The wood god comes down to earth and spring returns. The God adjusts wind and rain to help people's livelihood. Be harmonious and follow the natural law. The tenth day of the first month is the fifth of the Twelve Earthly Branches 'chen' and the seventh day is the second, which means there will be floods and autumn drought this year and the farmland will be a little stiff. Everything will be lucky according to the divinatory symbols. People will enjoy a long life and good fortune. In Qu County, Zhejiang Province, supplies will be abundant and people simple, honest and unspoiled. The people will be rich and the country strong. This year produces good harvests." The last in the ceremony were the assistant sacrificers leading "the cheer song for sacrifice of the Beginning of Spring." One of them shouted a sentence and all people present answered "good." A total of eight sentences were pronounced, they are:

In the Beginning of Spring of *renchen* year, the golden dragon reports good news. —Good!

Spring returns and moves in cycles. Everything takes on a completely new look. —Good!
People greet spring and receive blessings, everything will be lucky. —Good!
Protection from the spring god benefits all the people. —Good!
So good is the land: the gardens are full of the beauty of spring, vast expanse of fertile

plains. —Good!

The spring wind is vast and mighty: peaceful country, safe people and gold everywhere. —Good!

Trees bloom in spring and bear fruits in autumn. The weather is good for crops, so the granary is bursting with grain. —Good!

Spring gives happiness to all: the land yields good harvests and the people enjoy good health, so all families are joyful. —Good!

The ceremony in the hall ended around 9:40 a. m. Than the people moved to a field outside the house to watch the ceremony "wiping the clay oxen." The "clay ox" was borrowed from a villager L. Wang, and therefore driven by him. He wore a palm-bark rain cape and a bamboo hat as to represent a "farmer" according to people's impression, while the deity Gou Mang was played by a 12-year-old girl instead of a boy as required by the ancient rites. She wore her hair in a bun and was clad in a white cloak, symbolically whipping the head, left side of the body, the right side of the body, the tail and the back of the oxen, and recited: "The first whip brings goodweather for crops; the second, happiness and health; the third, luck; the fourth, everything goes well; the fifth, abundant harvest of all crops." Candies and peanuts were scattered to the watching crowd instead of the ancient ceremony of robbing the decoration of the oxen.

The elderly former branch secretary S. Fu carried two baskets of offerings, and on behalf of the villagers he burned incense and paper and worshiped heaven and earth at the edge of the field. L. Wang began plowing back and forth, then Y. Fu leveled the plowed land and S. Fu, following behind him, sowed and planted different small green vegetables neatly into the ground. At this time, somebody set off firecrackers at the edge of the field.

Penetrating the pervasive smoke, the villagers, wearing yellow silk garments, carried the sitting statues of the paper spring oxen, Guan Gong, and the four Sprit Dukes to the outside of the temple, followed by a long green "dragon." They ran several rounds of the square and then began the procession through the village. They stopped at the door of some prearranged families letting the gods receive worship. The villagers brought out baskets filled with a complete set of offerings for enshrinement and worship, and put the prepared red envelopes on the head of the cow and in the "merit box" at the heels of deity statues,① and then burnt incense and paper to pray for the family.

There was also a "harbinger of Spring" running in front of the parade. He held a pile of red paper in his hands and posted one on the door or on the wall of every dwelling of those families who had donated money or offered something, or directly handed one to the host. The words on the red

---

① An old villager told me that he and his wife donated 10 yuan to the five deities each, which amounts to a total of 50 yuan. His daughter donated 60 yuan which included 10 yuan to the spring oxen.

papers were "Sacrifice of Wutong Temple in Waichen Village, Jiuhua Township." Below there were two pictures: one was the picture of the spring god, with the words "good luck in the New Year" on top and with banners "good weather for crops" and "the country is prosperous and the people are at peace," respectively, on his left and right sides. Another described children whipping clay oxen in the field under a shinning sun. The text mainly introduced Wutong Temple and the "Ceremony for the Beginning of Spring" in it. It also told people: "This year's sacrifice for the Beginning of Spring was going to be held solemnly at 9 a.m. on January 13 of the lunar calendar. There will be full-scale dramas played by the famous Wu-opera troupe in Wutong Temple for four days continuously. We welcome all people to celebrate forthwith and pray together." Finally there were routes getting there and places to get off. Obviously this was the propaganda sheet for this activity, while used as "harbinger of Spring" during the cruise.

After finishing the parade in the village, they ate lunch, and went to the nearby villages to continue their cruise. They didn't return to the temple until three o'clock in the afternoon. The temple was filled with tables at noon. Pilgrims could have lunch for free and those who couldn't find a table at which to sit down took their box lunch along looking outside to find a place to eat. The rice offered was plain white rice. Dishes were mainly Chinese cabbage and radishes, and all were vegetarian. The number of people coming for worship and pleasure-seeking during the day was estimated over one thousand. The "merit box" put in the temple therefore gained a donation of several thousand Yuan. Adding to this the "income" during the cruise, it was estimated that the total income amounted to several tens of thousands of Yuan.

Procession through the village　　　　　　　　　　　　（photo: Wang Xiaobing）

The above was only the prelude to "greeting Spring" because the moment for Spring to set in was in the evening. At this moment, all guests and most pilgrims had already left, and only the villagers, along with their relatives and friends, were still present. Before the ceremony began, the door was closed. As soon as the right time arrived, the door of the temple was opened. Led by a group of children carrying lanterns, villagers with incense sticks in their hand swarmed out. They lit candles and burned incense and paper one after another at the gate of the temple to welcome the Spring god. For a moment, firecrackers and rockets were set off everywhere. A few villagers held two pine branches representing "Spring" in both hands, brought them back to the temple, and placed them in front of the altar. Further rituals with incense, candles, and prayers followed in the temple. Thereafter, dramas were played on the stage to entertain the gods including the Spring deity.

4. On the Authenticity of "The Sacrifice to the Beginning of Spring in Jiuhua"

The Sacrifice to the Beginning of Spring at Wutong Temple in Waichen Village and its related customs were originally part of local folk culture. Under the impact of China's social change in the 20th century, they had been abandoned and forgotten, and only a few incoherent fragments of memory persisted. When repairing the Wutong Temple in 2004, local people only remembered that the god worshipped inside "had a long pair of wings." In consequence, the present statue of Gou Mang was based completely on the speculation and research in historical documents. In addition, many aspects of the present-day revived customs for the Beginning of Spring apparently came from records in ancient books and folklore traditions from other places, instead of basing them exclusively on the villagers' memory and/or local folklore documents from people such as Wang Xiaolian.

On my way to the original site of Wutong Temple in the mountains, I had asked two accompanying villagers to recount the relocation story of "Wutong Buddha." One of them told the comparatively complete story, quite close to the version written down by Wang Xiaolian and others, so my informant had probably learned it from them or from their writings. On the other hand, the customs for beginning of Spring and the related faith in gods have largely vanished all over the country. Currently there is only one spring temple and customs related to it in Zhejiang province, and this is the one in Waichen Village. So it is understandable that it became a state-level intangible cultural heritage rather than an exclusively local one.

Being an expression of "intangible cultural heritage" also brought some fundamental changes to the sacrifice for the Beginning of Spring and the associated customs of Wutong Temple in Waichen Village. First, it has been given a newly invented name, "Sacrifice for Beginning of Spring in Jiuhua." In the process of becoming public and a heritage for the local folk culture, being "renamed" if very often a necessary step. Perhaps considering the administrative relationship of Jiuhua Township to Waichen Village, the Sacrifice for the Beginning of Spring in Wutong Temple was associated with "Jiuhua" instead of the largely unimportant and unknown "Waichen." As the saying goes, "the direct leader is better than the top officials." According to this folk wisdom, I noted that the village respected the direct leader, namely Jiuhua township government, very much while preparing their celebrations. They asked for instructions of everything, and dared not overstep the authority a little. Jiuhua Township can indeed serve the function of a go-between in the culture communication between Waichen Village and the Kecheng District.

Secondly, the official character of the sacrificial ceremony was strengthened at the same time as the religiosity of folk beliefs was rather suppressed. Because villagers were aware that officials from all levels would attend the award ceremony, in the arrangement of the celebration they imitated some forms of contemporary official ritual, such as the distribution of specially produced attendance cards, adding the etiquette of "offering the flower basket respectfully." Girls in the village also acted in the role of Miss Etiquette to lead guests, letting the children make up and collectively recite spring poems. Meanwhile, some behaviors considered as "religious superstition" were removed or covered up. In the afternoon of February 4, a piece of red paper was suddenly pasted on the door of the temple quietly. A big character "taboo" was on it. It also wrote: "Sacrifice to the stage spirits and a cleaning ritual will be held in the afternoon of January 13 according to the lunar calendar. Those who were born in the year of rat, cattle, and dog and children should stay off. Sacrificial time: 4:00-6:00 p.m., hereby announced." From the date February 1, 2012, we can infer that this announcement was prepared earlier, but could only be put in place after the end of the official ceremony.

I heard from the village secretary that he wanted to stop this ritual, but the old villagers insisted that there be a cleansing ritual and argued that the stage had not been used to perform operas for years, for which reason it should be cleaned in advance to avoid misfortune. I was very excited to hear this and hurriedly ran to the house to wait, but the secretary personally advised me to leave and have dinner with him. I wanted to argue that it did not matter to me to have a look because I was not born in a rat, cattle or dog year, and could watch without incurring into personal dangers, and I was curious to see it. The secretary still did not want to give me permission, saying that although my zodiac did not pose a problem, I had not yet reached the age to visit the performance (only the elderly can watch), so it would be better for me to leave. Out of politeness, I obeyed him.

I heard something about the sacrifice from the villagers afterwards. It seemed to have been a ceremony similar to praying for blessings. Those who will perform ghosts and spirits must dress and paint themselves at an abandoned graveyard. After returning wearing masks, they dance on the stage. Then chicken blood should be offered at the altar. After that a ceremony of chasing the ghosts took place: some villagers drive the ghosts out of the village, while those performing ghosts later removed their makeup in a hidden place, changed their shoes and disposed of the old ones, signifying that the evils had been abolished and everything would be all right. Because of the ghosts, children (including young adults) and people born in the above three zodiacal years were likely to be hurt. That was the reason for this taboo. Though I still doubt the reason for wanting to keep me away was mostly out of these concerns, the secretary had in mind that such a "superstitious" ceremony was incompatible with the awarded title of a non-material cultural heritage. It is thus clear that when a folk custom becomes public cultural heritage, even if the administration does not intervene directly, the bearers of the custom may feel it wise to adapt their program to what they understand to be state ideology and public expectations.

Besides, the public and formal character of the ceremony is strengthened. On February 3, the old villagers who brought their offerings to the altar were organized to rehearse again and again in the temple with empty baskets in their hands. They were told how to enter the temple, how to put the offerings neatly in front of the altar, and how to exit orderly. Children attending the ceremony were made up and dressed in unified clothing. The men who presented offerings and carried the deities during the procession wore unified silk garments. The deity Gou Mang, traditionally portrayed by a boy, was portrayed by a girl, probably because the girl looked beautiful and had a clear voice. Rituals were centralized around the temple, and household activities decreased significantly. Everybody was busy all day in the temple with the three meals eaten there. Customs originally held in the family, such as "inserting pine branches in the door," "eating green vegetables," and "worshipping in one's own field" were not stressed anymore since they were private, not public.

In the 1960es the German Folklorist Hans Moser had put forward the concept of "Folklorismus", to describe the process in which customs, often traditionally performed very simply, were changed to exaggerated artificial performances under the influence of mass tourism or adapted to the needs of mass media. Subsequent discussion of "Folklorismus" in German academic folklore was mainly focused on four issues: 1) the contrast between serving the expectations of the spectators of an ancient folk custom and the effects thought essential to modern performance in Folklorismus; 2) the questionable category of "real", often referred to by promoters of Folklorismus and its corollary, the inclusion of fakelore; 3) the involuntary contribution of folklore to Folklorismus; and 4) the political implementation of folklore by activists of Folklorismus, intending to present the past as a epoch without evil and problems.① Although traditional folk customs have performance characteristics, and often function to serve local politics and economy, the performing and utilitarian characteristics of "Folklorismus" behavior are more intense and

---

① Cf. Hermann Bausinger: "Folklorismus", in: *Enzyklopaedie des Märchen: Handwörterbuch zur historischen und vergleichenden Erzählforschung* Ⅳ, columns 1406-1407.

obvious, and the interference of politicians, folkloristic experts and journalists is more strongly present.

The discovery of the Wutong Temple and the development of its "Sacrifice for the Beginning of Spring in Jiuhua" was motivated by the desire to develop local tourism. Local folklorists and cultural activists as Wang Xiaolian; the later Cui Chengzhi, former President of Quzhou Folk Artist Association; and Ye Yulong, vice-chairman of Quzhou Poetry Association played a great role in promoting the recovery process of sacrifice and customs, and provided professional consulting for villagers to "reinvent" ceremonies. Nevertheless, in their collected data presented inthe official "application for world heritage" status and recognition, all information, whether historic or modern, national or local, mythic or real, was treated as "historical truth," without distinguishing truth from invention. In the end, "the Sacrifice for Beginning of Spring in Jiuhua" was chosen by the cultural department of the local government as the local event that would be recommended for provincial and national intangible cultural heritage. Hence the sacrifice got an official coloring, that made it more useful for local political purposes. For example, township government officials made use of the ceremony as a chance to showcase themselves and to attract the attention of higher level political leaders and the media. Should we call this "Folklorismus" and doubt its authenticity?

According to my personal participation and observations, I think that today's "Sacrifice for the Beginning of Spring in Jiuhua" is not in the same league with the "Folklorismus" criticized by German and other scholars. The most decisive and positive point is that the personal body carrying the inherited traditions did not change. During the whole activities, the villagers of Waichen Village still play a leading role. Nearly 200 people, including many young adults working outside at ordinary times, participated actively.① Furthermore, the central theme that villagers worship the Spring deity; "greet Spring and receive blessings;" and pray for blessings, long life, wealth, and good harvests for oneself, as well as for the family and the nation, has not changed. People prepare offerings, attend rehearsals, and sacrifice with devotion and respect. Even children who were dressed up to recite poems and cry out "Spring is coming" act sincerely without artificial stimulus. In order to make a good impression on outsiders, however, the villagers try their best to keep the ceremony decent according to their own understanding: act disciplined, cover the "dark part" of the ritual, dress up the children and let them perform in the front, and so on. While these are still in the moderate range and the result of the audience oriented ritual performing characteristic of the folk custom itself, it cannot be criticized as "fakelore."

Thus my conclusion is that as long as there exists a body of bearers of the inheritance and the

---

① The farthest one was from Qatar. He told me that he had been abroad for six years. He had heard quite in advance that the village had recovered the Sacrifice for Beginning of Spring. This time he came back home for spring festival just in time for the sacrifice, feeling very happy and proud. To contribute, he volunteered to apply, on behalf of the village committee picking up guests in private car and maintaining order during the sacrificial day.

cultural subjective consciousness of the members is not lost, the authenticity and live transmission of an intangible cultural heritage can be guaranteed. The so-called body of bearers of the inheritance refers to the persons represented by the inheritor. The relationship between them should be like that of a public group and its spokesman.

Take Waichen Village for example. The national representative inheritor only has the name of one person Wang Xiaolian. The local cultural department is also preparing to submit a proposal for approval that the local key players like Y. Gong be the inheritor. Villagers of the younger generation like H. Fu and H. Wu will be cultivated as backup talents. Likewise, the township government and village committee are preparing to form a nonreligious civil association that will be responsible for the management and promotion of operating Wutong Temple and the Sacrifice for the Beginning of Spring. On the one hand, those contemporary farmers who were born and raised here and used to wearing a suit and jeans are still rooted in rural areas; on the other, they have the insight and management capability of modern people. Once they realize the value of their own local culture, they can indeed generate vast amounts of energy in inheriting the hometown culture.

As for the inheritance body behind the individual inheritor, there are more than 600 Waichen villagers and about 20,000 inhabitants in the nearby villages of Jiuhua Township. The "Sacrifice of the Beginning of Spring in Jiuhua" is their own festival and they do enjoy it. After greeting spring in the evening, actors of the Wu-opera troupe "Nine-Nine-Red" (九九红) performed on the stage of Wutong Temple. As usual, the first program was "Warming the stage up" (闹花台) by female dancers with colorful clothes and flowers in the hand, followed by "Playing the eight immortals" (摆八仙) in which all important deities of local folk belief (including the heaven deity, the finance deity, Guan Gong, the deity of literacy, etc.) are enacted bringing blessing to the audience. The crowded audience, young and old, were sitting or standing. All the deities on the stage came one by one and got together to get the mandate from the highest heaven deity to bless and protect the people. When a village representative gave the troupe leader a red envelope with money and four boxes of cigarettes as compliment, one deity showed banners with "good weather for crops" and "peace and prosperity," meaning blessings from heaven. He also put a large plastic "gold ingot" in the hand of village representative. When I saw this scene, my worries and doubts about the authenticity of folk customs after being promoted to the status of heritage vanished completely. Because I believe, as long as the fields, the village, the old temple, and the farmers exist, the joy of life will last, and traditional folk customs can survive and develop in new circumstances in their natural, native and authentic form.

The National Cowboy Poetry Gathering:
A Case Study in Authenticity

Charlie Seemann[*]

In this paper I write about my organization, the Western Folklife Center, and the largest annual event we produce, the National Cowboy Poetry Gathering, which is now (2011) in its 28th year. Of particular interest are the issues of cultural authenticity raised by the selection and presentation of the participants: the cowboy poets, musicians, and other artists at this festival.

The Western Folklife Center is a private, not-for-profit, non-governmental organization, and its mission is to enhance the vitality of American life through the experience, understanding, and appreciation of the diverse cultural heritage of the American West. This mission is implemented through the annual *National Cowboy Poetry Gathering*, and through performances, exhibitions, educational programs, media productions (radio and television), research, documentation, and preservation projects that celebrate the wisdom, artistry, and ingenuity of western US folkways.

In pursuing our work, we are concerned with the rich, varied, multicultural identities of the peoples of the American West. Although the Center has historically focused on the stories, poetry, music, and crafts of ranching culture, our broader mission is to honor and preserve the expressive life of diverse occupational, tribal, ethnic, generational, and spiritual traditions found in the western US. Today, however, I am going to focus specifically on our work with ranching culture and cowboys.

When I talk about the American cowboy, I am not talking about the romanticized stereotype of the American cowboy perpetuated by motion pictures, that has made the image of the cowboy almost mythic and known around the world. We aren't talking about John Wayne or Clint Eastwood or nostalgic recreations of earlier times in what is called "the Old West." At the Western Folklife Center we deal with actual contemporary working cowboys, whose occupation involves working withhorses, cattle, and other livestock. The cowboy's occupation is not romantic at all; it is hard,

---

[*] Charlie Seemann, Executive Director of the Western Folklife Center.

dangerous, dirty work performed for very low wages. It is a profession chosen not for monetary reasons but for love of the work. Those who pursue it value the lifestyle: working outside, in open country, on the back of a horse. Real cowboys are very proud of their special skills and horsemanship and they resent it when others who haven't actually lived that life and done the work pose as cowboys and try to represent what they consider their culture. This makes it very important for organizations like ours to take great care that we present authentic representatives of ranching and cowboy culture, the "real deal," not costumed actors or those commonly referred to as "wannabes," "drug store cowboys" or described as "all hat and no cattle" (all style and no substance).

Cowboy poetry and music had their origins as oral traditions of cowboys driving cattle overland from the far southern United States north many miles to cities where there were railroads for shipping them. Like the intangible oral literature of many occupations, such as sailors, lumbermen, and miners, the rhyming occupational poetry and songs cowboys created reflected their daily lives and the rigors of their work. There were poems and songs about favorite horses, or bad, dangerous horses; about long days in the saddle in harsh weather; about herding cattle and terrible cattle stampedes. Some cowboy poems and songs are humorous; others tell stories of tragedy and death on the job. Today, even though much cowboy poetry and music has found its way into print, it is still almost always recited or sung from memory rather than read from a page.

Here is a working definition of cowboy poets and cowboy poetry, from former Montana State Folklorist Mike Korn: "Cowboy poetry is rhymed, metered verse written by someone who has lived a significant portion of his or her life in Western North American cattle culture. The verse reflects an intimate knowledge of that way of life, and the community from which it maintains itself in tradition. Cowboy poetry may or may not in fact be anonymous in authorship but must have qualities, content, and style that permit it to be accepted into the repertoire of the cultural community as reflecting that community's aesthetics in style, form, and content. The structural style of cowboy poetry has its antecedents in the ballad style of England and the Appalachian South. It is similar to popular works of authors such as Robert W. Service and Rudyard Kipling." Our Founding Director, Hal Cannon adds that "Many of today's poets are ranch housewives, ranch owners, auctioneers, rodeo cowboys, dude wranglers, and people that hold down eight-hour workaday jobs but raise cattle on the side."

The National Cowboy Poetry Gathering was started 28 years ago when a group of folklorists working in western US states decided it was important to document and recognize a form of intangible heritage that could be lost as the older cowboys who were bearers of the tradition died. Those folklorists conducted fieldwork in their respective states to locate and identify working cowboys who still recited or wrote traditional cowboy poetry and songs, and they organized what they called a "Cowboy Poetry Gathering" to bring some of these people together and share their poetry and music with each other and the general public. Although they only intended to do this one time, the event was extremely popular and became an annual event.

Our challenge as presenters of ranching and cowboy culture has always been how to do the best possible job of bringing "authentic" representatives to the Gathering rather than those who simply adopt cowboy costume and learn some poems songs to perform but who have little or no actual experience working with horses and cattle. We want to emphasize those who speak from experience, who embody the life they write or sing about. Real cowboys are extremely sensitive to authenticity and artificiality. In 1922, in the preface of one of the earliest collections of published cowboy poetry by poet Badger Clark, the writer said, "Cowboys are the sternest critics of those who would represent the West. No hypocrisy, no bluff, no pose can evade them." Knowing this, we decided that cowboys themselves should select the participants they most highly respected.

Those who want to perform at the Gathering are required to apply for that privilege, and must submit an audio recording of their music or recited poetry, written samples of their work, and a brief biographical statement that describes their experience with ranching culture, as ranch owners, working cowboys, ranch wives, veterinarians, or other kinds of related work. To review these applications, we created an annual peer review panel that includes a cowboy poet, a cowboy singer or musician, and a guest folklorist familiar with the tradition but not on the Western Folklife Center staff. This peer committee, which is anonymous and changes personnel every year, meets in the spring and spends two or three days listening to and discussing all the submissions. Then they vote on their recommendations. Our staff does not vote. Out of 200 to 300 applicants, 50 to 60 are invited to perform at the Gathering. This process—of allowing the cowboys themselves to select the poets and musicians they most respect and whose work they think best represents cowboy life and work—has succeeded well for us and has allowed us to continue to bring forward authentic cowboy poetry and music for 28 years. Because active tradition bearers themselves make these decisions, the results always reflect the constantly evolving aesthetic sense of this group, as well as contemporary definitions of the authentic.

The Charm of a Wildflower
—A Brief Survey Concerning "Saye'erhe"

Liu Shouhua[*]

Since 2005, 1,372 items have been accepted onto the national lists of China's ICH safeguarding project. "Saye'erhe" from Tujia people in Changyang, Hubei was included on the first list. The Saye'erhe tradition evolved from "army dancing" of the ancestors of the Tujia—the ancient Ba People. The dance has generated great interest, and is one of the brightest spots of the Chinese safeguarding of ICH project. As a member of the Committee of the Center of Safeguarding ICH of Hubei Province, I participated in the examination of the Saye'erhe application and also observed dancing in its natural context, and even participated. I will introduce Saye'erhe and briefly comment on it.

The following is the introduction to Saye'erhe provided by the Center for Safeguarding of ICH of the Ministry of Culture:

"Saye'erhe" is a kind of traditional funeral singing and dancing. Natives gather in front of the coffin, the men sing and dance, and the women surround the scene wearing traditional dress. Generally, rituals of this type are held through the whole night. Tujia people believe that the birth and death of human beings is a natural process, just like the four seasons. The old who have enjoyed their lives pass away; this reality conforms to the laws of nature and is worthy of celebration. The people express their attitudes towards birth and death through a specific kind of singing and dancing. At first, the lead singers begin to drum and sing: dancers follow, dancing to the drumming rhythms.

Saye'erhe is a systematic and harmonious art composed of singing, dancing and music. Its tunes and tones only exist in Xingshan, Hubei. Its style and structure are very similar to Songs of Chu, through which can grasp the ritual music and song in the ancient Ba and Chu

---

[*] Liu Shouhua, School of Chinese Language and Literature, CCNU.

areas. The positive attitudes towards life, birth and death of these peoples are expressed through singing and dancing.

We defined Saye'erhe as "traditional sacred singing and dancing;" actually it is "funeral dancing" or "funeral singing and dancing". In the areas where Tujia people live—on the middle of Qing River in Western Hubei and neighboring regions—natives carried out the funeral as what is termed "white happiness," when the old passed away. People gathered one entire night—even two or three. In local language, the performance is called "funeral drumming" or "funeral dancing". Saye'erhe is a word in the Tujia language, derived from a much-repeated tune in Tujia folk singing and dancing; thus natives called this kind of dancing Saye'erhe.

I

What is the unique style and touching charm of Saye'erhe? I will explain by making three points:

First, people gather to conduct a funeral as a time of happiness. Special attitudes towards birth and death allow natives to address death calmly, and then to gather singing and dancing in a funeral ceremony.

Second, singing, playing musical instruments and dancing are integrated. The ceremony is held in the hall of the house where the gong and drum are performed. One person, to the left of the coffin, drums and leads the singing; others follow to sing and dance. The whole occasion is controlled by the drummer and singer's drumbeat and singing tunes, with rhythms and tune names varying regularly. Meanwhile, the lead drummer-singer, the dancer and the spectactor could freely interchange their identities.

Third, the funeral dancing of the Tujia people is not only composed of enthusiastic singing and dancing, but also strictly abides by the rules of the funeral. Leaders select and change tunes based on lyrical content. Contents of lyrics are varied, and include such themes as the feasts of ancestors, the life story of the departed, local customs, and love and sex. Among various possibilities, long ballads of ancient people and ancient history are suitable for funeral dancing: for an instance, "The Darkness." However, love songs are most popular.

Today, the Saye'erhe tradition maintains its active social function in the Tujia area.

II

Three points explain the continuing relevance of funeral dancing for the Tujia people.

First, funeral dancing fulfills the need for traditional group activities in a rural area where population density is low, where human settlements are scattered and isolated on mountains and in valleys.

Second, assistance from all over the neighborhood is required in order to carry out the custom of in-the-ground burial. "Dancing and helping" has itself become a folk custom linking one generation with another.

Third, Tujia people express their loss and love to the departed parents. Relatives and neighbors accompany them while they overcome sorrow by singing, dancing, and laughing.

The Hubei Changyang Tujia Autonomous County achieved outstanding results in the survey, application, and safeguarding project addressing Saye'erhe as intangible cultural heritage. This process and outcome can be regarded as a successful example of ICH protection.

III

In addressing the issue of the authenticity and integrity of the safeguarding process, it should be noted that the unified tradition linking funeral dancing and crying is not suitable for commercial exploitation and development. However, Tan Xuecong isolated only the singing and dancing, formed an authentic singing team to take part in the National Youth Singers Competition, and ultimately earned a Gold Medal Award. This can be seen as a successful example of cultural development. However, Tan's group performance is the adaptation and recreation of traditional folk singing and dancing, rather than authentic funeral dancing.

Many cultural departments rushed into commercial development of ICH items, even though their projects barely touched the surface of the history, origin, contexts, cultural meanings and features of the items on the list; usually such efforts could not succeed. As Feng Jicai pointed out, "the definition of development (exploiting) can never be used connected with cultural heritage". Ideas and practices put in place to make money through the development of heritage always distorts and destroys it. When considering the Saye'erhe tradition of the Tujia people in Changyang, Hubei, although there were some setbacks and controversies during application and examination, the funeral dance project remains successful. It can be regarded as a model of safeguarding ICH in China—a model that need more serious attention from academia in and out of China.

Curating a Smithsonian Folklife Festival Program

James I. Deutsch*

Often referred to as "a museum without walls" or "a living, outdoor museum," the Smithsonian Folklife Festival was established in 1967 to honor some of the finest living practitioners and bearers of intangible cultural heritage. Long before UNESCO defined intangible cultural heritage, the Festival of American Folklife (as it was known until 1998) was sharing precisely those same forms of culture with hundreds of thousands of visitors each year: that is, "the practices, representations, expressions, knowledge, skills—as well as the instruments, objects, artifacts and cultural spaces associated therewith—that communities, groups and, in some cases, individuals recognize as part of their cultural heritage." Under the aegis of the Smithsonian Institution—the national museum of the United States, which was established in 1846—the Smithsonian Folklife Festival since its earliest years has sought to celebrate and help safeguard the traditional culture (including music, dance, performance, crafts, foodways, and much more) of roughly one hundred different countries, every US state, and a wide variety of occupational and religious groups.

The Smithsonian Folklife Festival is easily the most prominent and popular event taking place each year in Washington, D. C. , within the boundaries of the National Mall of the United States. The National Mall is administered by the US National Park Service—the same federal agency that maintains and preserves Grand Canyon National Park, Yellowstone National Park, the Statue of Liberty National Monument, and nearly 400 other special places in the United States. The National Mall is where Martin Luther King Jr. declared his dream in 1963, where large protest marches and demonstrations regularly take place, and where millions of people stood in below-freezing temperatures to watch the inauguration of President Barack Obama in January 2009. With the US Capitol on the eastern end, the Lincoln Memorialon the western end, the Washington Monument

---

* James I. Deutsch, a curator and editor at the Smithsonian Center for Folklife and Cultural Heritage.

and National World War II Memorial in the center, and several museums of the Smithsonian Institution on both north and south, the National Mall is arguably the nation's most important civic space. The Smithsonian Folklife Festival almost always lasts for ten days: during the period before, during, and after the Fourth of July—American Independence Day—which is the nation's most important civic holiday. It takes place entirely outdoors under a series of tents and temporary structures, which may range in size from 200 to 11,000 square feet (or roughly 19 to 1,000 square meters).

According to Festival legend, S. Dillon Ripley (the head of the Smithsonian Institution from 1964 to 1984) in 1966 told Ralph Rinzler (the Festival's founding director) to "take the instruments out of their cases and let them sing," meaning that the Folklife Festival should not only demonstrate the utility and vitality of the Smithsonian's extensive collections of musical instruments (most of which were locked inside museum exhibition cases and vitrines), but also present the vitality of diverse musicians and performers, and thus the vitality of their cultural heritage, both old and new. Ever since, the two primary goals of the Smithsonian Folklife Festival have been: 1) to strengthen and preserve this cultural heritage by presenting it on the National Mall in a respectful and informative way; and 2) to promote mutual understanding between Festival participants and Festival visitors through what Festival planners call a "cultural conversation": a type of cultural exchange in which Festival participants and visitors speak directly to each other in their own voices.

The range of Festival programs since 1967 has been extraordinarily diverse, including: state programs, such as Ohio (1971), New Jersey (1983), and New Mexico (1992); city programs, such as Philadelphia (1984), Washington, D. C. (2000), and New York City (2001); international programs, such as Korea (1982), Senegal (1990), and Scotland (2003); regional programs that incorporate several states or nations, such as the Mississippi Delta (1997), Río Grande (2000), and Mekong River (2007); occupational culture programs, such as American trial lawyers (1987), White House workers (1992), and masters of the building arts (2001); US national government agencies, such as the US Forest Service (2005), the National Aeronautics and Space Administration (2008), and the Peace Corps (2011); and broader themes relating to transnational cultural heritage, such as Maroon culture in the Americas (1992) and the African, British, and Native American roots of Virginia (2007). There are no precise counts of the number of participants who have represented their cultural heritage and traditions at the Folklife Festival since 1967, but a very rough estimate would place the number at 30,000.

A typical year at the Smithsonian Folklife Festival will see three different programs taking place simultaneously on the National Mall. (The one and only exception occurred in 2002, when a single program, The Silk Road: Connecting Cultures, Creating Trust, featured the living traditions of people from twenty-two different countries along the ancient Silk Road—from China, Japan, and Korea in the east, all the way to Venice, Italy, in the west.) For instance, the three programs in

2013 are: 1) Hungarian Heritage: Roots to Revival, which highlights the vitality of Hungary's cultural heritage in music, dance, costume, crafts, gastronomy, and more; 2) One World, Many Voices: Endangered Languages and Cultural Heritage, which demonstrates how language diversity is a vital part of our human heritage by bringing cultural experts from communities around the world to demonstrate their cultural knowledge, identity, values, technologies, and arts; and 3) The Will to Adorn: African American Diversity, Style, and Identity, which showcases the distinctive ways in which the diversity of African American attire and adornment communicates a variety of cultural traditions, artistry, and identity. Coming up in 2014 is a Festival program presenting the cultural heritage of China, thanks to a partnership between the Smithsonian Institution and the Ministry of Culture of the People's Republic of China. Approximately 150 Chinese bearers of tradition, representing perhaps ten categories of intangible cultural heritage, may participate in the program.

Each Smithsonian Folklife Festival program takes shape under the leadership of one or two Smithsonian curators: generally someone on the year-round staff of the Center for Folklife and Cultural Heritage, who works closely with a curatorial team of subject specialists and sometimes with a co-curator who provides additional expertise on the program's themes and topics. All Festival programs, especially ones as diverse as Hungarian heritage, endangered languages, and African American adornment, may have different concepts, goals, and curatorial visions, not to mention their own special challenges. Yet whether the participants are coming from Budapest, Bogotá, or Baltimore, all Festival programs share a common curatorial goal, which is to help Festival visitors better understand and appreciate the traditions, and especially the tradition bearers themselves who are featured on the Mall. One of the best ways to achieve this, as indicated earlier, is to facilitate "cultural conversations," in which Festival participants and visitors speak directly to each other in their own voices, without any interference or censorship from the Smithsonian.

Accordingly, almost every step along the way of this curatorial process is designed to bring participants and visitors closer together: the actual selection of participants, based on fieldwork and research; the ongoing conversations with participants to learn more about their traditions, customs, and skills; the design of the site and patterns of visitor movement; the writing and display of signs and other visual aids; the physical arrangement of interior and exterior spaces; the role of presenters and moderators; and much more.

Needless to say, curators also work very closely with other members of the Smithsonian Folklife Festival team: program coordinators, art directors and designers, technical crews (including electricians, carpenters, and plumbers), administrators and budget specialists, transportation coordinators, sales associates in the Festival Marketplace, procurers of supplies for Festival participants, participant staff members (who arrange travel and housing), and many others.

Festival curators must also consult regularly with their curatorial teams, program sponsors, community members, and potential visitor. For instance, the curatorial team for the Hungarian Heritage program in 2013 includes experts from the Balassi Institute (an organization based in Budapest that presents Hungarian culture around the world), the Association of Hungarian Folk Artists (which produces the annual Festival of Folk Arts in Budapest), György Martin Folk Dance Association, Hungarian House of Traditions, Hungarian Open Air Museum, and National Museum of Ethnography in Budapest. The aim is that the Folklife Festival itself should be highly collaborative, with Smithsonian staff members contributing their expertise, based on years of experience in producing large public programs on the National Mall, but also utilizing and benefiting from the cultural-heritage research contributed by their partners from the countries and regions that are featured at the Folklife Festival. The objective is to promote cooperative learning, rather than to rely exclusively on Smithsonian expertise; the latter process is much more the norm for the exhibitions that are curated at the Smithsonian's indoor museums.

Based on annual surveys of visitors, the Smithsonian seems to be doing some things right. The survey at the 2012 Folklife Festival found that 65 percent of visitors rated their experience as excellent or superior, and another 27 percent rated it good. Only 8 percent found it less than good. The results in 2011 were even better: 78 percent of the respondents to the visitor survey rated it excellent or superior; 29 percent rated it good; and only 3 percent found it less than good. But there is always room for improvement.

In 2016, if all goes according to plan, the fiftieth Folklife Festival will take place, and in preparation for that anniversary, Smithsonian staff members continue to reexamine the Festival's past practices and future priorities. It is clear that today's Festival visitors, especially those under the age of thirty, are relying more on digital media and less on face-to-face interaction (and "cultural conversations") for their education and entertainment. It is also clear that the temperatures on the National Mall seem to be getting warmer each year, perhaps due to global climate change. The Folklife Festival in 2012, for instance, was the hottest ever recorded: with an average high temperature of 99 degrees Fahrenheit (37 degrees Celsius) and the loss of one day due to damage from high winds. Should the Smithsonian Folklife Festival keep trying to attract as many physical visitors as possible to perspire outdoors on the National Mall for ten sweltering days in late June and early July? Or should the Festival try to engage its 21st-century audiences with many more online activities and participatory opportunities? To help Festival staff members determine the answers to these questions, all readers of this publication are encouraged to visit the National Mall, June 25-29 and July 2-6, 2014, when the cultural heritage of China will be featured at the 48th annual Smithsonian Folklife Festival.

Research on the Application of Digital Technology to Work in Chinese Intangible Cultural Heritage

Huang Yonglin, Tan Guoxin[*]

Since the 1990s, digital technology—information technology and the Internet—has produced significant achievements with wide applicability in industry, while opening up new approaches to the protection of cultural heritage. UNESCO and other entities in the larger world have already embraced various approaches to the digital protection of monuments and buildings—*tangible* cultural heritage. However, when it comes to the protection of *intangible* cultural heritage, many countries, especially China, are just getting off the ground. This is mostly because intangible cultural heritage is in motion—passing from generation to generation, advancing through years of continual transformation through word-of-mouth and hands-on teaching, providing ICH with the essential characteristics of "living" —ecology, inheritance or transmission, and variability. Thus, unlike a tangible object, it is not easily "fixed" for preservation. By assessing the significance of digital technology in protecting and inheriting Chinese intangible cultural heritage, we will discuss its development and application to the protection and transmission of Chinese ICH, providing ideas for promoting digital technology and its development and application to preservation challenges.

1. The Significance of Digital Technology in the Protection and Inheritance ofIntangible Cultural Heritage

To "Digitalize" intangible cultural heritage is to convert, reproduce, and restore an object

---

[*] Huang Yonglin, vice chairman of China Folklore Society, director of National Research Center of Cultural Industries, vice-principal, professor of Central China Normal University, with cultural resource and cultural industry as major research field. Tan Guoxin, professor of Central China Normal University.

into shareable and reproducible digital forms by employing the technology of digital acquisition, digital storage, digital processing, digital display, digital distribution, giving a new perspective to interpretation, a new approach to preservation, and new opportunities for utilization.[1] Stated simply, the development of modern digital technology has provided a wider space for the acquisition, preservation, display and distribution of intangible cultural heritage.

1.1 Digitalized Acquisition and Storage Technology Guarantee the Complete Preservation of Intangible Cultural Heritage

Approaches to the preservation of Chinese intangible cultural heritage have remained simple—taking photos, interviewing people, recording and collecting related materials—and have managed to preserve a large quantity of precious examples of ICH. However, books decay, tapes age, the colors of videos fade, and recorded sounds and images distort. Such phenomena might actually make information about ICH objects unreliable. With limited technology and limited techniques of the past, over the years objects were neither protected nor utilized. In contrast, digital technology offers many brand-new methods for the protective collection and recording of intangible cultural heritage, including scanning, stereoscanning, holography, digital photography and motion capture. The digital realm offers a number of new protections as well, including effective preservation of the resources of intangible cultural heritage through data bases, RAID, CD-ROM tower, optical fiber, network connections sustained by a series of related regulations and protocols. Through modern technologies of digital acquisition and storage, it is possible to edit and convert archival data such as manuscripts, music, photograph, video and images, then preserve them in physical formats such as digital tape and CDs. Following these procedures, a multimedia network database can store and manage items so that they are organized and easy to retrieve. Through such activities the overall level of intangible cultural heritage protection will be lifted.

Today, one of the main tenets of the Chinese Intangible Cultural Heritage Protection Project is the application of modern technology, including digital multimedia, to authentically, systematically and completely record, construct profiles, and build databases. However, intangible cultural heritage consists of both its traditional manifestation and its dependence on a specific cultural context, an aspect of ICH that simple digitalization often neglects, so it remains difficult to capture intangible cultural heritage as a complete entity. Consider digitalization of the dancing motion as an example: in the traditional recording process, the actor's motion is recorded by description, photographs and videos. Nevertheless, such techniques could not record the actual dancing performance, especially the actor's precise and complete motion. Though data could be conveniently saved in such media as video tape and hard drives, it is difficult to reproduce and re-edit. What is more, complete reproduction requires the involvement of dancing artists and actors. It is thus difficult to further exploit and utilize acquired data (for example, using it in the production of movies and television or animations). If the data is to be modified, actors are required to demonstrate the dance again, greatly increasing the project's workload.

Modern acquisition and management of digital information is better able not only to organize, collect and record intangible cultural heritage, but also to break through the limitations of old storage techniques, preserving precious intangible cultural heritage more securely over a longer time.

1.2 Digital Restoration and Reconstruction Technology Supports the Effective Inheritance of Intangible Cultural Heritage

The challenge of transmitting and inheriting intangible cultural heritage is ultimately shaped by modes of production and context, since maintaining old methods of production and old lifestyles collides with the global trend toward modernization. This is the most basic dilemma in the protection of intangible cultural heritage. To help address this challenge, maturing digital restoration and reconstruction technologies such as modern computer graphics, digital image processing and virtual reality will provide more advanced means to inherit intangible cultural heritage. After digitalization, multiple intangible traditions can be converted into visible virtualproducts from which viewers can learn, research and innovate. For example, by applying 2D or 3D digital animation, the phenomena, scenes, events and processes of intangible cultural heritage can be reproduced and interpreted. Original scenes are restored completely; by utilizing the technologies of realistic character generation, scene construction, action integration, HCI, knowledge modeling and so on, settings and movements involved in ICH performances are instantaneously generated on screen, traditional practices are accurately reproduced, enabling both observation and interpretation. Applying these technologies, more people can absorb the disappearing original features of intangible cultural heritage through observation. In addition, it is possible to upload data into the system database through the Internet or data discs, enabling an even larger audience to understand our ethnic culture. In this way, interest in art will be stimulated, enhancing the vitality of our ethnic culture.

For example, consider the world-famous Nantong Banyao Kite. The kite integrates the handcrafts of carving, calligraphy, painting and embroidery. Among these crafts, whistling kites feature carving most prominently, and carved whistles on the Banyao Kite vary in size, shape and material. The position of mouthpieces vary with the angles shaping the kite, its length and width, so that the volume, timbre and tones produced are ever-changing. Moreover, makers skillfully combine whistles with various tones allowing the composition of different "mid-air symphonies." Computer technology can capture the parameters of the size and shape of whistles, and the position, size, angle, length and width of the mouthpiece. Using this information, a digital program can be designed to refine the whistle's tone and timbre. In addition, by modeling a virtual scene, the computer aided design technology actually programs the process of carving whistles, and displays it using 3D animation enabling observers to make an especially-close examination of the creative process.

Furthermore, paintings on the Banyao Kite are rather delicate, combining exquisite scenery and larger elements that depict figures from folk stories in order to represent dreams and wishes about flying. Digital protection and exploitation can synthesize the characters, theme elements and styles of stories, with relevant software developing baseline images to form a sketch-language system which can be used in both contemporary design and transmission of the central elements of folk culture. [2]

1.3 Digital Display and Dissemination Technology Creates a "Sharing Platform" for Intangible Cultural Heritage

Digital virtual display technology integrates virtual reality with images, texts, sounds and graphics, intuitively presenting intangible cultural heritage to a mass audience in the computer virtual world in the form of flat panel displays, panoramic displays or stereo imaging that demonstrate the combined effect of sound, light and electricity from every angle. This display and dissemination of intangible cultural heritage can be applied in three distinct ways: first, animation technology such as 3D scene modeling, special effects, virtual scene coordination display are used to faithfully reproduce patterns of production, utilization, consumption, distribution and dissemination of intangible cultural heritage, especially traditional handcraft. Second, "digital museums" exhibiting intangible cultural heritage using scripts, sounds, images, videos and data can be constructed with the help of integrated media, digital photography and knowledge modeling. Third, intangible cultural heritage information stored in various media can be integrated and later disseminated using telecommunication, wireless transmission, the Internet, cable television and all kinds of digital TV networks, breaking old limitations of time and space while establishing a new ICH platform for mass communication. In this way, intangible cultural heritage will be more conveniently and completely displayed, disseminated and applied, and the greatest quantity of resources will be shared to the greatest extent possible.

For example, the digital museum is an appropriate display platform for ethnic intangible cultural heritage. Unlike an ordinary museum, offering static collections, it digitalizes and saves additional relevant information about art, including the history of a craft, its cultural context, and documentation regarding folk artists, means of dissemination, craftsmanship, raw materials and folk lifestyles. In this way, in the digital virtual museum, forms of living culture are used to show the content and essence of representative ethnic folk intangible culture. For instance, "blue all-over," a kind of traditional dyeing craft in China, is famous for its pure hand-craftsmanship, spontaneity, and harmonious blue and white beauty. When we enter the digital museum, with a mere click, we can see the tradition's entire process, including the planting of bluegrass, making dye, carving a pattern board, dyeing and drying. Clearly, in this way, the development and popularization of the digital museum is bringing the public to a deeper understanding of excellent intangible cultural heritage.

1.4 Virtual Reality Technology Provides Opportunities for Exploitation and Utilization of Intangible Cultural Heritage

In this modern era, we should be increasingly aware of the importance of intangible cultural heritage, but at the same time we must foster innovative thinking in order to explore additional ways to protect ICH. The true value of intangible cultural heritage resides in its rich cultural components, and these can be converted into brilliant cultural products that exhibit unique ethnic styles and local features through the manufacture, dissemination and sale of products. Through this kind of protection process, products allow traditions to again fit into the real world where they become part of daily life. This kind of productive protection is the best way to employ creative thinking to ensure the continuity of culture.[3] In fact, virtual reality technology offers a broad space in which to exploit and make use of intangible cultural heritage. By adopting digital technology, industrialized techniques can be applied to ICH, thereby converting tradition into cultural products that generate economic benefit; through this process popular enthusiasm for protection and development of intangible cultural heritage will be mobilized.

"Digitized virtual intangible cultural heritage" means digital reconstruction of ICH through the application of advanced virtual reality technology. In this process, human-computer interaction techniques represent key technologies, while the concept of industrialization further requires the engagement of high-performance hardware. Given the progress of technology and the development of digitalization and information management, key technological challenges will be solved while at the same time high-end equipment emerges; both trends benefit the productive protection of intangible cultural heritage. The maximum advantage of digitalizing intangible cultural heritage is that the information documenting intangible cultural heritage can not only be saved and recorded, but can also be used in digital production (digital replication, digital publication, digital reconstruction) and digital dissemination, so that the unique cultural value and economic value of ICH are integrated. Therefore, through the technology of digital virtual reality, the exploitation and utilization of intangible cultural heritage for industrial production and operations is conductive to the formation of a new industry and derivative products, in this way the industrial chain is extended and the proportion of the cultural products within the larger economy is increased. The value of cultural industries within today's economy is immeasurable. Consider the fact that, through digital technology, the industrialization of intangible cultural heritage has promoted knowledge and skills of multiple components of ethnic culture, including dress culture, craftsmanship, folk literature, folk dance, folk music, customs of consumption, social protocols, holiday celebrations, entertainments, artistic skills and food culture—each has been rendered more valuable.

2. The Further Development of Digital Technology in Protecting and Inheriting Intangible Cultural Heritage

Though digital technology has made significant contributions in protecting, inheriting and transmitting intangible cultural heritage, it is not yet fully integrated into the process. In general, as information technology has evolved, digital technology has played a much more effective role in protection, inheritance and exploitation. However, because ICH exhibits characteristics of "living" (the possibility to inherit and change), traditionality (the inner connection between specific cultural origin and its location and environment), integrality (a combination of ecology and culture), mere digital storage frequently neglects the truth that heritage derives meaning from its "cultural space." For this reason, we ought to reexamine, re-evaluate and rediscover the potential value of new technologies and study traditional culture again from the perspective of knowledge representation and visualization, by building a multilevel classification system for the resources using the perspective of knowledge engineering and grammar granularity; establishing a data-collecting technical standard; constructing a methodology and process for a technology-based system of intangible cultural heritage protection and inheritance. By analyzingthe technique of scene modeling and behavioral interaction, techniques of knowledge visualization, techniques of action binding and web technology, a set of synthesis application technologies which fit various kinds of ICH data recording, saving, preserving and inheriting can be established; simultaneously building a multimedia interactive system. In this way, the cultural industries and related industries in China are developed, the technological capacity of our cultural industries is increased, and the design and development of original products are promoted. These changes will secure the importance of digital innovation in the protection, heritage and industrial development of intangible cultural heritage.

2.1 Build a Digital Classification System for the Intangible Cultural Heritage Resources

China has numerous intangible cultural heritage assets exhibiting various forms: for example, diverse folk cultures exhibiting local conditions and customs, traditional protocols, religions and celebrations, and orally-transmitted folk literatures such as myths, epic poems, folk stories, allegories, ballads and proverbs, vivid artistic performances such as music, dancing, folk dramas, operas, and excellent handcrafts such as dough figurines, sugar sculptures, paper-cuts, knitting, embroidery, and batik. Because intangible cultural heritage is differentiated in form and creative practices, digitalization must be both general in methodology and specific to the character of individual traditions. Because it exhibits characteristics of "living" —tradition plus integrity—the features of its ICH knowledge—systematic, complicated and implicit—must be analyzed and studied carefully. Given variety in form, content, and external meaning, the components of the ICH knowledge base will be explored from the perspectives of folklore, sociology, anthropology, history, psychology, aesthetics, history and psychology so that the broad nature of traditional knowledge is recognized and summarized. In addition, the evolution, performance method, form, corresponding region and context will be approached through the questions "When, How, What, Where, Why;" the connections among these five types of knowledge will then be constructed from the perspective of grammar granularity, hence a multilevel classification system can be formed. This means that by applying digital technology, intangible cultural heritage resources can be classified academically and stored digitally in order to establish a virtual library and a material database for ICH assets.

2.2 Establishing a Standard for Data Acquisition Technology

Currently, resource databases documenting Chinese intangible cultural heritage around China vary in technical goals, and technical criteria and techniques of management are frequently inappropriate. Therefore, a series of activities and operations must be established. First, trends in the development of modern information technology should be monitored, and should be integrated with the construction of The National Digital Library, Digital Museum and National Cultural Information Resources Sharing Project. In addition, there must be a focus on the need to build, depict, organize, search, serve and store intangible cultural heritage resources in the long term; this commitment must include intensive study and development of relevant technical criteria which fit the features of Chinese intangible cultural heritage—criteria including technical criteria for digitalized resource collection, resource description (metadata), resource organization, resource management and long-term resource preservation. If these activities are pursued, regulation of the technical management of ICH assets will be established throughout the country using the same regular, scientific criteria.

2.3 Exploring the Visual Representation of Knowledge within Intangible Cultural Heritage

The visualization of intangible cultural heritage is essentially different from that of tangible cultural assets. Tangible cultural heritage can be visualized in the form of pictures, videos and 3D animations, while intangible cultural heritage visualization gives greater emphasis to making visible ideas, processes or knowledge. "Knowledge visualization" is a brand-new area which has not yet developed extensive studies, but it appears as an effective way to protect and inherit ICH. The primary attributes of the visualization of intangible cultural heritage can be positioned in four layers—knowledge sources, knowledge description, visual representation and knowledge application. There exist multiple knowledge sources documenting intangible cultural heritage, such as historical records, folk activity, folk craft, drama and dance, which are semantically heterogeneous. The knowledge description layer encompasses cultural spatial knowledge, as well as such internal classifications as region, time, expressive method, form of expression and sense of causation and influences. The visual representation layer illustrates features of traditional knowledge and its composing classifications, selecting appropriate models for present to enable multiple users to study, share and innovate in relation to traditional practices. The knowledge application layer enables users to select visual representations that fit best, allowing investigators to learn and construct cultural spatial knowledge that conforms to their own cultural background and organization of knowledge. Through learning and communication engaging cultural spatial knowledge in ICH, content, process, and the background and experience of researchers continually interact and are made current.

2.4 Constructing a Comprehensive New Technology Application System for Intangible Cultural Heritage

As an aspect of local culture, intangible cultural heritage is an asset that has been passed on through long-term practice and withstood the tests of time; it includes both multiple traditional cultural manifestations and a "cultural space" closely related to the lives of everyday people. As we have established, this cultural space possesses the special characteristics of "living"—tradition and integrity—so it is challenging to present the complicated relationships among ICH items merely by describing things like singing and dancing through the use of texts, images, videos or animations. Inevitably, simple digital storage often neglects the fact that the character of ICH is dependent on its cultural space or context; several new techniques must be utilized in combination to comprehensively engage both the protection and inheritance of intangible cultural heritage. The necessary ICH technology system combines the technique of scene modeling and behavioral control, the technique of resource management, and service and visualization technology (as shown in Figure 1).

2.4.1 The Digital Technology of Intangible Cultural Heritage.

Establish a set of data collecting methods targeting the multifaceted digitalization of intangible cultural heritage, including the capture of "moving target" 3D data by comprehensively utilizing action-capture technology, establishing the methodologies and outcomes that could be calculated and inferred from the data, thereby constructing the 3D motion of a moving object. Using 3D scanning, investigate a new, simple and reliable 3D model-building method which suits the features of heritage, incorporating the technology of a geometry and texture-integrating data model,

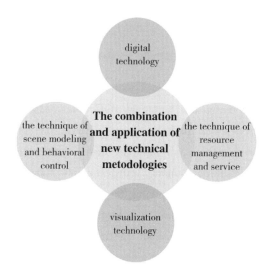

Figure 1 The combination and application of new technical metodologies

constructing both the model base and texture base of 3D body objects.

2.4.2 The Technique of Scene Modeling and Behavioral Control.

Apply the technology of realistic role generation, action-capture technology, multi-agent group-control technology, and scenario generation technology in a comprehensive manner, allowing rapid generation of 3D scenes, roles and actions within traditions of intangible cultural heritage. All of the virtual roles will be represented by "agent models," an attempt to solve difficulties with consistency in 3D representation and interactive technology in the creation of digital representations of intangible cultural heritage.

2.4.3 Resource Management and Service.

Apply the distributed database technology comprehensively, including mass data storage techniques, intangible cultural heritage ontology, semantic retrieval technology and so on in order to realize and standardize such functions as unified representation, knowledge storage, resource rights information, resource catalog service, registration service, resource retrieval and publication of intangible cultural heritage resources.

2.4.4 Visualization Technology.

Broadly apply 3D animation technology, virtual reality, semantic Web technology and knowledge visualization technology to establish an ontology-based intangible cultural heritage visual knowledge-modeling system, in order to realize multiple subjects, including queries based on the semantics of knowledge, knowledge of natural language and semantic comprehension, knowledge sharing among various ontology and knowledge-based systems. This will enable and enhance study of cultural space by illuminating the expression or comprehension of knowledge related to a specific intangible cultural heritage project through knowledge visualization technology and ontology-based

CIDOC CRM (Conceptual Reference Model).

2.5 Setting up a Multimedia Interactivity System for Intangible Cultural Heritage

Taking account of the "bottleneck problem" in the exploitation of intangible cultural heritage digital products, and acknowledging the technical difficulties inherent in 3D scene and role-animation interactive production in cultural activities, we will use model data preserved in the intangible cultural heritage resource base, introducing high-precision terrain reconstruction as well as modeling of the interactive cultural element, providing new ideas and pathways for the rapid generation of 3D scenes. Meanwhile, by applying the technology of realistic facial role-modeling, we can provide realistic human models for the development of animated projections of ICH inheritors. We can then employ this "action data" in the database to efficiently produce role action animation. Finally, we can utilize visualization technologies such as knowledge modeling, behavior modeling and interaction to visualize intangible cultural heritage resources, and disseminate the visualized products through the multimedia interactivity system. The platform frame is shown in Figure 2.

2.6 Structuring a National Technical System of Protection and Inheritance for Intangible Cultural Heritage

Intangible cultural heritage includes both traditional cultural representations and the cultural context surrounding the Chinese people. It is especially close to the lives of common people, passed on generation to generation. Compared to tangible heritage such as buildings and monuments, it exhibits unique characteristics—for instance, tradition and context are not easy to preserve, so preservation requires a multifaceted approach. Because of its unique features, and because a comprehensive national technical system to preserve ICH has not yet been established, it has been notably difficult to protect and transmit traditional culture. Thus, it is important to both study and construct such a technical system.

A national technical system addressing intangible cultural heritage should include digitalization technology (the process of documenting and labeling texts, videos and audios, pictures, actions, using digitalized models), resources storage technology (the classification system of resources, metadata standards, technical specifications regarding storage, copyright protection technology), resource management technology (resource publishing technology, retrieval technology, resource registration and catalog service technology, etc.), scene modeling technology (figures, scenes, actions generating technology, and multi-Agent group-control technology), visualization technology (3D animation, virtual reality technology, semantic Web technology and knowledge visualization technology) and finally, dissemination and service-provider technology. By building such a technical system addressing intangible cultural heritage, China's splendid ethnic culture will be secured by integral protection, meaning that materials and processes are preserved along with the "cultural soils" in which it lives. The frame for this technical system is shown in Figure 3.

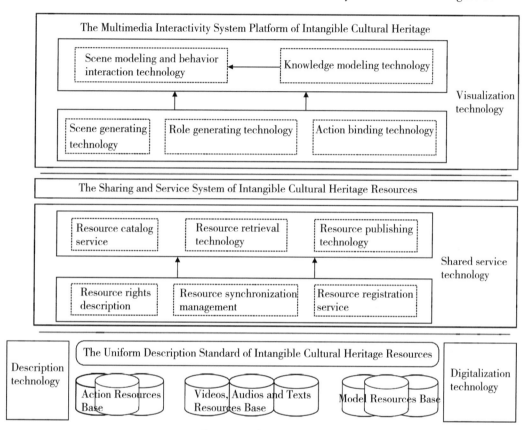

Figure 2   Platform Frame

3. Considering Questions about Digitalization Technology in Protection, and in Developing Applications to Intangible Cultural Heritage

Digitalization technology is, at present, our most-advanced information technology. In fact, it can be said that the emergence of virtual reality has made the 21st century a "Virtual Era". For the protection and development of intangible cultural heritage, applying the latest technology also means providing a deeper high-tech support system so that established methods of protection and inheritance are expanded and strengthened. However, there exist four questions that must be considered regarding digitalization technology as applied to protecting ICH.

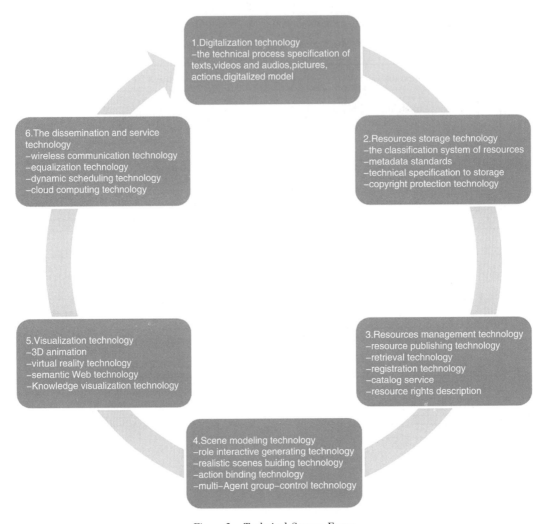

Figure 3　Technical System Frame

3.1　Digitalization Technology and a Balanced Cultural Ecology

Digitalization technology is a meaningful component of the preservation and restoration, virtual modeling, and reconstruction of intangible cultural heritage, but too much dependence on technology risks making culture merely rigid data and heritage from the past; to some extent dismantling cultural diversity and disrupting cultural ecological balance. Therefore, because intangible cultural heritage is ever-changing, dynamic and developing, the application of digital technology must shift from emphasizing "static heritage" to emphasizing both "static heritage" and "dynamic heritage." Because the material and non-material heritage reflects the same cultural elements, which are jointly-comprised and inseparable, applications must shift from focusing on "material elements" to emphasizing both "material elements" and "non-material elements." In addition, ecological features of the intangible cultural heritage must be kept in sight so that the ICH items are able to live and develop in a comfortable, suitable place. All things considered, digitalization is a new way to preserve ICH, while securing the maintenance of its diversity, vitality and ecological balance as a most-fundamental purpose.

3.2 Multidisciplinary Intersections and Digitalization Technology

Unlike traditional manifestations of culture, digitalized intangible cultural heritage presents culture in virtual space. Thus, it is not a physical entity, but instead resides in a trans-regional and transnational information space and information system which combines humanistic and social science, natural science and technical expertise; it is therefore interdisciplinary. For example, the extraction of intangible cultural heritage features and the drafting of processing regulations require joint efforts of anthropology, ethnology, sociology, film and television expertise, communication science and the arts and humanities. The study object, along with related fields and technical aspects of digitalized intangible cultural heritage, form an integrated large-span intersection and overlapping composition. Once digital technology has been applied to the protection and inheritance of ICH, we should break disciplinary boundaries and combine all sorts of discipline knowledge into a comprehensive, overlapping space. By so-doing, a new discipline of digitalized intangible cultural heritage will gradually be built. In addition, by enhancing multi-industry research, a suitable set of administrative and operational mechanisms for protecting and utilizing digitalized intangible cultural heritage will be established.

3.3 Digitalization Technology and the Cultivation of Multi-skilled Talent

The digital protection and utilization of intangible cultural heritage is systematic, persistent and technical. Unfortunately, the cultural area lacks experienced experts in digital technology, so it is hard to succeed in our efforts to combine advanced digital technology with profound cultural insight. Thus, the key to develop the digitalizationof intangible cultural heritage is to cultivate a "talent team" —one which requires not only high-quality scientific professionalism, but also strict training in interdisciplinary research. We should reinforce the study of digitalization in intangible cultural heritage and the cultivation of professionals, merging such discipline resources as ethnic studies, humanities, arts, information and engineering. What is more, the cultivation of multidisciplinary talents should be emphasized and made a part of economic development in cultural industries and in any talent-team construction plan. Therefore, a multi-talented team which has knowledge of culture, management and technology would be formed under the cultivation system by employing multi-channel training, multi-evaluation, multi-level utilization, multi-mode stimulation and comprehensive service.

3.4 Digitalization Technology and the Development of Cultural Industries

The culture and information industries are two "super industries that interact with each other." The information industry has an impact on the production, dissemination and consumption of cultural products so that original creativity is enhanced and new cultural products are developed. As a result, both the competitiveness and vitality of the cultural industries are enhanced. Nevertheless, from the perspective of industry development, information techniques are merely methods or techniques, while the core purpose is serving content. We should give greater emphasis to building content; the richer the digital culture content, the higher the degree of information sharing, the more people can enjoy new commercial opportunities. Today, information technology is flourishing, so it is best that intangible cultural heritage develop through digitalization. A special industry combining culture, media and information will emerge. As a unique "industrial intersection" of high-tech with high cultural value, the digitalized intangible cultural heritage should be effectively protected and at the same time promoted as a cultural product that is both intellectual property and capital asset. If this is accomplished, the cultural resource advantage will be transformed into economic advantage, creating financial and social value so that the economy and society are pushed forward—faster and better.

(Cooperating with Tan Guoxin, *Journal of Huazhong Normal University*, No. 2, 2012; *Xinhua Digest*, No. 11, 2012, full-text reprinted)

Comments:

[1] 王耀希主编:《民族文化遗产数字化》,北京:人民出版社,2009年版。
[2] 《非物质文化遗产的数字化保护》,来源:文化传播网,发布时间:2006年9月11日。
[3] 黄永林:《非物质文化遗产生产是最好的保护》,《光明日报》2011年10月7日。

Surviving Katrina and Rita in Houston: A Case Study of a Survivor-Centered Disaster Response

Carl Lindahl, Pat Jasper[*]

Surviving Katrina and Rita in Houston (SKRH) is a survivor-centered documentation project created by folklorists to draw upon the local knowledge of a community displaced by disaster. At the heart of the project are stories told by survivors and recorded by their fellow survivors. Through this process, survivors become active agents in their own recovery. The following discussion begins with a brief history of the project, proceeds to describe the methods used to train the survivors interviewers, and ends by assessing the project's products and effects.

In late August 2005, Hurricane Katrina bore down on the United States Gulf Coast. About 1.5 million people evacuated before the storm reached land on August 29, 2005. Hundreds of thousands failed to evacuate; most of these were poor black citizens of New Orleans, Louisiana, who were unable to leave; they were trapped in the city for as long as a week, most of them with little or no food or water. The storm killed at least 1,836 people and destroyed the homes of at least 450,000. In the early days of September 2005, with New Orleans under water, 200,000 trapped citizens were rescued from the disaster area and sent to safe locations. This was the largest overnight displacement in American history: about 1,200,000 people were forced to leave their homes, some for months or years, others permanently.

In the early days of September 2005, hundreds of buses transported hurricane survivors from New Orleans into massive shelters in Houston. Houston's population grew by as many as 250,000, while New Orleans's dwindled to a few thousand. The city government, aid agencies, church congregations, and ordinary citizens gathered massive material resources to distribute to the survivors as volunteers worked overtime to meet their needs.

---

[*] Carl Lindahl, Professor of folklore at University of Houston. Pat Jasper, Director of folklife and traditional arts at the Houston Arts Alliance.

SKRH co-director Carl Lindahl joined the response by volunteering at Houston's George R. Brown Convention Center, to help distribute necessities to the thousands of survivors sheltered there. Generous citizens had donated mountains of clothing, blankets, and personal items. The material aid offered was enormous, but something was happening in the shelters that transcended the generosity of the volunteers. The material needs of the survivors were undeniably great, and they in turn expressed great gratitude for our gifts. Yet, in listening to these men and women, Lindahl discovered immediately that they needed something far less tangible and far more valuable than their second-hand shirt or their second tube of toothpaste. They needed to tell us their stories. And the people of Houston needed to hear them. The tellers were transfigured in the act of speaking as they began to see on the faces of the volunteers that someone was finally beginning to understand something about their ordeal.

The Surviving Katrina and Rita in Houston project is, among other things, an attempt to fill the need for survivors to narrate and the need for outsiders to listen. The project was conceived by Carl Lindahl and co-directed by Pat Jasper in an effort to counter sensationalized media accounts, to document survivors' stories for the public record, and to disseminate them to the world at large. SKRH was designed for the express purpose of representing survivors in their own words and on their own terms. The project would meet its goal most effectively and innovatively by relying upon the survivors themselves: by giving them the opportunity to produce their own history and, in a time of economic need and life-altering circumstances, to create their own "jobs."

With the help of the American Folklife Center at the Library of Congress (AFC), we designed "field schools" in which survivors received training as interviewers. We developed an intensive curriculum to accommodate the participants and offered compensation for work completed. The great majority of trainees did not possess educational backgrounds related to ethnographic research, but instead of academic preparedness, we stressed common experience. Each trainee shared one crucial bond with her interviewee: both of their lives had been upended by the hurricanes. The project ultimately created an archive of 433 recorded interviews on deposit at the University of Houston. Currently, more than 100 are also available at the AFC.

Because there had been no previous project in which disaster survivors had taken the lead in documenting disaster, we had no precise model for the schools. Therefore, we began with one foundational principle: sovereignty over one's own story was the guiding precept. There are some people whose stories are their prized possessions, literally the most valuable thing that they can call their own; having lost their homes and undergone separation from friends and family members, the survivors of Katrina often clung to their stories. The right to tell their own stories was especially important for them because, to a person, those who took part in our training sessions felt profoundly misrepresented by media accounts. They wanted their stories back; they did not want us to break in and pre-empt them.

So we sought "natural narratives": stories shaped by the speaker rather than the interviewer, but also shared with a fellow survivor—in effect, within the community for which, and by which, they were created in the first place. It was our hope that the project narratives would be natural enough to allow the entire world to sit in on a survivor conversation; this kind of record would be both the most valuable for folklorists and the best for survivors themselves: it was what they most wanted for each other and what they most needed to begin to heal.

Because survivors' stories are personal statements inflected with community styles, they are far more important than information per se. We asked interviewers to record three separate but closely entwined stories centered on the concept of community.

Each interviewee was asked to describe the community where he lived before the storm hit. This part of the interview served important documentary purposes because many of these neighborhoods had been greatly changed, or completely destroyed, by the hurricane. It was also therapeutic for many of the interviewees (particularly the older survivors) to speak at length about their experiences in special places to which they could not return.

Second, interviewers asked survivors to recount their experience of the storm. In the early months of our project, the "storm story" was the overwhelmingly dominant part of the narrative, but as the years passed, the accounts of life before and after the storm became longer, and the storm became more a chapter in a long story, rather than the whole story that the teller was trying to convey.

Third, in order to record survivors' efforts to re-build social networks and create new communities, interviewers asked survivors about their life in Houston following the storm. For many people, the struggle to adjust in Houston became the main narrative focus, and it served as an opportunity to meditate upon the things that the tellers most missed about their former lives.

Field school training involved sharing technical information and instructions for administering release and consent forms, but the bulk of the training was to stress practices and precepts that privileged the interviewee. The following rules steered the training sessions:

Valorize the Survivors' Motives: As training began, we asked participants to share their reasons for signing on. Few mentioned money, inspite of the fact that even temporary employment and a modest paycheck represented a major difference in their lives. Unanimously, they spoke of the need for the survivors' voices to be heard; unanimously, they affirmed that the best person to interview a survivor was a fellow survivor. The great majority shared with us words to this effect: "We want people to know who we are. So many have been so generous, but even the most generous often do not have a clue of what we've been through. We are not criminals, fools, or deadbeats. We have honor, respect, and pride, in others and in ourselves. We don't want people to scorn or pity us—just to know who we are." This exercise reinforced the notion that the goals of the project were, in fact, exactly what the survivors wanted from it.

Recognize the Survivors' Expertise: Next we told the survivors that they were the experts: in fact, each was the world's leading expert in her (the great majority of our trainees are female) personal experience, and that in Katrina, each had had an experience that we, the teachers, could not fully share—they had told and heard hurricane stories as part of their daily lives, they knew how such stories unfolded in everyday situations, and they did not have to be reminded how deeply important these stories were to those who told them. This gesture was intended to recognize the trainees' superior knowledge and experience; their most common response was to nod knowingly and in apparent confidence. They seemed relieved to have arrived, finally, in a place where their experience was honored.

Volunteer at Every Level That You Solicit: If you are not ready to tell your own story, you are not ready to record others. In the training sessions, each participant took turns on both sides of the microphone. This practice was essential for overcoming the role of the objectifying interviewer.

Never Force a Story: In narrating freely with each other, the trainees were acting on a principle that we later articulated as a central project rule: the interviewee must be ready and willing to narrate. Never entice, cajole, or otherwise push a person to share a storm story. The need for the narrative to emerge voluntarily is crucial to its potential for healing. Some mental health specialists warned us that it could be harmful for survivors to tell their storm stories; however, the trauma specialists who advised us most closely stressed that the narrators would self-select. They would know when it was time to speak. As long as we did not push, the chances of inflicting harm by soliciting a story were minute.

Create a Kitchen Table Environment: Respect and empathy for the narrator came naturally to the trainees, but eliciting narrative proved to be their greatest challenge. Our field school proverb, "it's far easier to tell a story than to record one," was borne out again and again. The hoped-for result, fully achieved in perhaps half of the recordings, was a "kitchen table" story that privileged performance over information to record the teller's subjective truths and in the process draw upon the survivor communities' traditional verbal communicative and healing strategies. The trainees recognized instinctively and valued intrinsically what we were looking for. But because the interviews were to be recorded, there were many impediments to a natural context. We explained, with words to this effect:

> Across the kitchen table you are facing someone with whom you are sharing a profoundly life-changing experience. You feel an immediate bond with the person; that person feels an immediate bond with you. But this particular kitchen table is cluttered with things that endanger that bond. There will be an audio recorder and a microphone; you will be wearing earphones: both the storyteller and you are likely to feel at least a little bit nervous as you position the microphone, test the sound, monitor the room for ambient noises. Then, just

before you begin the interview, you have to read to your host a long "informed consent" form in legalese, and then get the storyteller to sign it. For a fellow survivors with numerous, painful, recent experiences signing government forms that seldom brought them benefit, the paperwork might be more than merely inconvenient—it might be unsettling.

And that is just the beginning, because at the same time that you are cluttering your host's table, you are trying to clear it: to turn a difficult, artificial situation into an intimate one. While you are encouraging narrators to relax and find their natural voices, you have to be monitoring the sound quality of the recording. You do everything you can to let the storyteller be herself, while you must be three people: the friend across the table, the technician tracking the sound, and the evaluator taking mental notes and thinking up questions to ask later, after the story has flowed to completion.

When the narrator and the interviewer break through the technical and legal impediments to achieve a kitchen table situation, they can tap dimensions of the survivors' experience that seldom emerge through other documentation techniques.

Practice Solicitous Listening: Training sessions focused on ways through which interviewers transformed themselves into listeners by transferring narrative control to the person on the other side of the microphone. The basic idea was, "Be eager to listen but never forcefully ask." Oral history methodology typically favors a "directed" interview, in which the interviewer sets the narrative agenda. Here, the idea is for the interviewer to signal, through intent listening, a willingness to go wherever the narrator leads. Oral history methodology also instructs interviewers to induce interviewees to explain any references that might not be clear for future listeners; in contrast, the model survivor interviewer never interrupts. While she may feel the urge to jump in to fill in missing information, she must let the storytellers go their own way. In an early field school practice interview, the narrator was vividly describing how she woke up suddenly on the morning of Katrina's landfall to feel the water rushing in on her; then she gestured with her hand, pointing to her torso and saying that the water was "up to here" by the time that rescuers arrived. The interviewer then interrupted to ask, for the benefit of an absent audience, "Up past your waist, you mean?" In this instance, the narrator charged right through the question and back into her narrative, but we cautioned her and her fellow trainees not to take the chance of ruining a story to retrieve a fact, but rather to refer to the hand gesture in written notes that would be submitted along with the recorded interview. At the end of an interview, the interviewer may ask for clarifications or to fill in missing details, but because "stories are harder to get than information" she should always yield the storyteller the floor.

Stick to the Concrete: Even once narrators have begun their stories, interviewers must allow them to select their own comfort levels. The interviewer asks for narration— "Then what happened?" —and avoids soliciting emotions and interpretations. Such questions as "How did that make you feel?", or "What does that mean to you?" are pre-emptive. The narrator is entitled to express emotion and offer interpretations in her own way, in her own time.

The Interviewee Is Always Right: This is the guiding principle behind all of the precepts we have just discussed.

The work of the survivor narrators and interviewers created both short-term and long-term responses to the devastation of Hurricane Katrina. First, participants soon discovered that they project was not merely documenting the formation of new post-Katrina communities; it was creating new communities. Simply in the process of coming together, the diasporic population of survivors quickly became mutual friends and supporters. They created a sense of community among themselves that allowed them to adjust to life in a new, strange city more quickly and easily than they otherwise would. By sharing their own stories and by helping others tell theirs, the survivors took part in a group self-healing project. As a result, SKRH began receiving funding support as a behavioral health project.

By sharing their stories with their Houston hosts, survivors were able to confront media stereotypes. Through public programming—including radio programs and live panel presentations—survivors used their stories to introduce themselves to their fellow Houstonians. Because SKRH is the world's first project in which survivors have taken the lead in recording their fellow survivors' experiences of disaster, the recorded interviews are special documents. Free from external research agendas, the SKRH interviews allow outsiders to access the survivors' perspectives directly. Carl Lindahl designed a database to identify the most common problems that the survivors experienced as well as the strategies used by survivors to overcome the hardships created by the storm. By studying this database, researchers can discover an insider's view of disaster and call upon the traditional healing strategies of the afflicted community to plan more effective responses to future disasters.

In large-scale disasters like Katrina, the greatest untapped response resource is the survivor community itself. Survivors feel a need to help their fellows, they are often available to take on new work because they have been displaced or left unemployed, and they usually know the needs of their community far better than do outsider, professional responders. Through compassionate listening and community building, effective tools fashioned by folklorists and perfected by survivors, the SKRH project has created a model for future disaster survivors to own their own stories and, through those stories, to heal. It is our hope that ethnographers in disaster areas worldwide will form similar partnerships with survivors in order to allow the survivors to become active agents in their own healing.

Bibliography:

[1] Carl Lindahl: "Storms of Memory: New Orleanians Surviving Katrina and Rita in Houston," *Callaloo*

29, 4 (2007): 1526 –1538.

[2] Carl Lindahl: "Legends of Hurricane Katrina: The Right to Be Wrong, Survivor-to-Survivor Storytelling, and Healing," *Journal of American Folklore* 125 (2012): 139 –176.

Bear or Dragon?
—The Origin of the Dragon and China's Rice-Cultivating Civilization

Jiang Mingzhi*

The "Jade-carved dragon" is the most representative artifact within the jade cluster of Hongshan. It was first designated as "Pig-Dragon" by archaeologists. Later, Lishi—a Taiwanese with roots in Liaoyang—strongly argued for the existence of a bear cult within Hongshan culture, first drawing on the evidence of some complete bear jawbones found in a Hongshan site, then connecting these findings with research indicating that bear cults had appeared in northern ethnic groups from ancient times. Lishi also supported his interpretation by citing the story, recorded in ancient history, that the Yellow Emperor used "Youxiongshi" as his alias.②

Inspired by this initial work, archaeologist Guo Dashun re-interpreted the jade group within Hongshan culture. He felt that "the C-shaped dragon was actually based on a pig or deer, while the Jue-shaped (Jue: a slotted jade piece in semi-circular form) dragon was based on the bear, so can be simply called 'Bear Dragon.' "③ Therefore, Guo Dashun sought out clues of bear images in Hongshan culture and related sites to use as circumstantial evidence, formally arguing that "the magical bear dragon carved in jade maybe one of the keys to unlock legend of the five emperors, which has long been complicated and confusing."④

Drawing on this background of academic research and interpretation, Mr. Ye Shuxian further elucidated the "dragon carved in jade" by integrating it with phenomena that once existed throughout Eurasia—that is the belief that regarded the bear as a symbol of movement from death to life. Mr. Ye wrote additional papers such as, *Are We Descendants of the Dragon or the Bear?* — *Analysis and Reflection on Chinese Ancestor Totem*, and his book *The Bear Totem—Seeking Origins of Myths of Chinese Ancestors*, published in 2009, which raised the profile of the bear totem to an

---

* Jiang Mingzhi, male, from Guilin, Guangxi, Professor, Chinese Intangible Cultural Heritage at Sun Yat-Sen University.
② 郭大顺:《龙出辽河源》, 百花文艺出版社 2001 年版, 第 117 页。
③ 郭大顺:《龙出辽河源》, 第 126 页。
④ 郭大顺:《龙出辽河源》, 第 126 页。

unprecedented level. He pointed out that, "The first totem animal in China—the dragon is directly concerned with the bear in the sense of generative theory. The discovery of a Hongshan Goddess temple in the Neolithic Age brought a brand-new situation to the study of origins of the dragon. Transformation from bear-goddess worship to bear dragon indistinctly outlined the decline of goddess myths and traditions."① Ye even deduced that the "…rediscovery of the bear totem made us realize again that profound and extensive belief in 'Descendants of the bear' lies behind the popular saying of 'Descendants of the Dragon,' through which we can gain new understanding of the roots of Chinese culture in the macro-background of Eurasia."②

However, Mr. Ye Shuxian's "Eurasian viewpoint" quickly sparked protests among Korean scholars and Internet users. His was originally just a single book that attempted to trace "the bear totem" in Chinese myths, but in Korea Ye's work was interpreted as: "The Chinese even want to take away our myths of Dangun." This response was possibly not justified, for at the same time Mr. Ye Shuxian himself admitted that his "theory of bear totem" actually was not especially popular in China.

In addition to the viewpoints mentioned above, different opinions have been advanced by other scholars. For example, Mr. Liu Qingzhu, Director of the Institute of Archaeology, Chinese Academy of Social Sciences, thought that some tribes did use the bear totem, but it still could not be regarded as the totem of the Chinese nation. It is clear that the dragon was a fictional character, so it's hard to imagine that images of the dragon would be widespread if the bear-totem cult was most-dominant in Chinese civilization, and there would not likely be any dragon-shaped artifacts among the massive quantities of preserved Chinese cultural relics. If the bear is advanced as China's totem, and if the bear is the most-noble animal, how do we explain the position and importance of the dragon?③ Mr. Liu Qingzhu didn't explain his point in detail, so drawing on his work, this paper will attempt a broad, in-depth analysis of the multiple cultural and social factors placing the dragon at the center of Chinese civilization.

1. Dragon Pattern on Painted Pottery in Hongshan Culture and Its Significance

Early dragons discovered in the archeology of the Liaohe River Basin can be divided into eight types. Arranged in roughly chronological order, we find dragons formed by arranging objects, and

---

① 叶舒宪:《熊图腾——中华祖先神话探源》,上海锦绣文章出版社 2007 年版,第 90 页。
② 叶舒宪:《熊图腾——中华祖先神话探源》,第 99 页。
③ 李健亚:《"熊图腾说"证据不充分》,《江南时报》2006 年 8 月 15 日第 8 版。

in bas-relief, wood carving, engraving, painted pottery, clay sculpture, jade-carving and color painting.① Jade-carved Dragons are among the most common ones found in sites of Hongshan culture, and they can be divided into two subtypes. Subtype I is represented by Sanxing Tala Jade Dragon, which is carved in dark green jade, with height of 26 centimeters, long mouth, smooth head and face, two noses, eyes with fusiform shape, long neck hair, featuring a raised pointed-end arm as though the dragon is flying. Of fine size and bent into a "C" shape; it was once identified as "pig dragon" because its head characteristics resemble those of a pig. Dragons of this type have been regarded as typical specimens among jade dragons in Hongshan culture, but there haven't yet been any recovered in official excavations. The only two from official excavation sites were unearthed in the northern area of Chifeng, where many sites of Zhaobaogou culture are distributed. This type of C-shaped dragon is thought to belong to Zhaobaogou culture. (Their prototype may have something to do with deer, as its head is similar to that of deer and other dragons with deer heads are common in Zhaobaogou culture.)

There are a total of 16 pieces in Subtype II, two of which were found in Niuheliang stone tombs while others are found in places within the distribution area of Hongshan culture, such as Jianping county in Liaoning province, Weichang county in Hebei province, Balin Zuoqi, Balin Youqi and Aohan Qi in Inner Mongolia. Their common features are: big head, full ring-shaped body, two short and erect ears, big round eyes, and wrinkles engraved near the mouth. When this type of dragon was first identified as Hongshan, there was an association developed through the pig shape of head. Later on, as complete bear jawbones were unearthed in Niuheliang stone tombs many times, people came to associate this type of dragon with bear, calling them the "bear dragon."

However, in addition to the jade-carved dragon, there are also dragons in clay sculpture and painted pottery; these are much earlier than jade-carved dragons. Dragons executed in a type of clay sculpture were found in the Niuheliang goddess temple. They were bear and pig-like and thought to be a clay-sculpture example of the bear-dragon type. Dragons in painted pottery were found in colored pottery works of Hongshan culture. These can be divided into two subtypes: Subtype I is the coiled dragon pattern in the center of a painted pottery urn, painted red in black-figure style, with two or three stripes, and with rows of dragon scales with alternation of black-figure and red color on the dragon. The pattern of dragon scales in Hongshan culture had come to be clearly defined by their fixed shape, regularity of lines, and equal distance between black-and-white segments—ways of representing dragon scales similar to work seen in bronze ware of the Shang dynasty. Seen on two types of painted pottery—the oval belly-shaped pot and bottomless tube-shaped devices that specific in Hongshan culture—Subtype II exhibits only amplified dragon scales with no body. There are different types of dragons even in same Hongshan cultural sites, indicating

---

① 郭大顺：《龙出辽河源》，第56页。

that diversity of dragon shapes occurred in Hongshan culture, and that Hongshan culture had a tendency toward the integration of regional culture.

Actually, jade-carved dragons appeared in the transition period from Stone Age to Bronze Age. The Hongshan custom of using jade as sacrificial funerary objects became a highlighted feature in the structure of Hongshan culture. In this period stratification of clan members and clan dignitaries had appeared. Rules for using and burying jade according to one's social class had developed and the influence of more-primitive clan communes was disintegrating. Emergence of the dragon shape in this period was relatively late.

Dragons in painted pottery are relatively important, not just because they are earlier than jade-carved dragons, but also because of characteristics of texture and shape held in common with Yangshao culture of the Central Plain. Decoration on this pottery was, "mainly geometric patterns made up of straight lines, such as triangles, the rhombus, and broad patterns of parallel lines; secondly, a kind of combination of many concentric circle patterns and triangle hooking patterns."[①] The so-called triangle pattern is actually a continuous horizontal pattern of S, which is much the same as continuous patterns of a Banpo type. This feature indicates that painted pottery in Hongshan culture had been influenced by Yangshao culture. Painted pottery of Yangshao culture was mainly distributed in Shaanxi, Henan, Hebei and Shanxi, works of which can be divided into types such as Banpo and Miaodigou. Most of the painted potteries of the Banpo type are vessels used in daily life such as pots, jars, bottles, and earthen bowls; decorative patterns are mainly found in such places as the edge of pot, the upper middle part of the jar belly, neck area of bottles, and inner wall of the pot. Decoration includes geometric patterns and also relatively-literal representations of animals, the human face, fishing nets and so on. Typical artifacts in the Miaodigou type of Yangshao culture include bowls exhibiting contracted mouths and curved belly-pots with curled edges and bellies. V-shape bottles and flat bottomed bottles are mainly in black-figure style with a few in red-figure style; white painted pottery can also be found. Again, decorative patterns of painted pottery are mostly geometric figures with a few animal patterns.

Painted pottery was a product of matriarchal society. The manufacture of painted pottery was popular in the middle of Neolithic Age. Clan society was in a Matriarchal stage but began a transition to patriarchal structure which coincided with the last phase in the decline of painted pottery. The flourishing of painted pottery memorialized the power of matriarchy; the glory of women in that age was recorded.[②] At the same time, decorative patterns of painted pottery also symbolized various kinds of human communities, serving as totems representing clans or as objects

---

① 《辽宁省喀左县东山嘴红山文化建筑群址发掘简报》,《文物》1984 年第 11 期。
② 参见郑为《中国彩陶艺术》,上海人民出版社 1985 年版,第 68 页。

of worship.① It is decorative patterns that take the most important role in symbolically distinguishing different cultures; that is, a culture is represented by a specific type of pottery pattern. Therefore, just as bowl and bottle decoration represent Yangshao culture of the Central Plain, S-shaped patterns on painted pottery of Hongshan culture are totemic symbols of its matriarchal clan.

Painted pottery was preceded by stamped pottery, which can be traced as far as the early stage of the Neolithic. Decorative patterns of stamped pottery can be classified into woven patterns, curved patterns, lattice-work patterns, round patterns, waveform patterns, streak, cloud and thunder patterns, vein-like patterns, tooth form pattern, jomon pattern and claw-shape pattern.② There are seven primary distribution areas of stamped pottery: the area of Ganjiang River and Poyang Lake, Taihu Lake, Nanjing-Zhenjiang area, Hunan, Lingnan area, Fujian, the Minnan area and the eastern part of Guangdong. "It is universally acknowledged that remaining geometric stamped pottery is closely connected to the ancient Yue ethnicity, indicating that the tradition of stamped pottery was created by ancient Yue people".③

Thus, we can legitimately ask whether these S-like patterns symbolize the bear or, in fact, anything else?

2. The S-shaped Pattern and Rainbow Worship

The Chinese character for dragon in inscriptions on bones or tortoise shells, "龙" is actually formed by adding a crown atop an S-shaped pattern, while a pair of hands are intentionally added in bronze inscription below the S-shape to represent worship. In comparison with the Chinese character for god in inscriptions on bones or tortoise shells— "神", either "龙" is just the character that developed on the basis of "神", or "龙" is created by comparison with "神". "神" was the first character created; it not only became the basis for the creation of later characters representing divinity, but also laid down standards for creating of images of gods.

On bronze-ware of the Shang and Zhou Dynasties used for ancestor worship and sacrifices to gods, dragon patterns are generally engraved and presented with the S shape. This intentional pursuit of the S shape was in fact advancing under emergent character standards set for suggesting god's image. Just as was pointed out in the book *Decoration and Human Culture* by Japanese scholar—Umino Hiroshi: "both the thunder pattern and the dragon pattern can be simplified and decomposed into the C shape or the S shape, which just shows that they share a common basic

---

① 石兴邦:《有关马家窑文化的一些问题》,《考古》1962 年第 6 期。
② 叶茂林:《陶器鉴赏》,漓江出版社 1995 年版,第 153 页。
③ 叶茂林:《陶器鉴赏》,第 151 页。

pattern that is also called a 'keynote.'"

As is memorialized in myths of countries all over the world, the force of nature is the core of primitive religious beliefs. Thus the most primordial god is neither an animal god nor a divinity of landscape, but instead is based on natural forces and natural phenomena of the vast universe and the heavens. Consider the Chinese Han nationality as an example: the Chinese character for god "神" was developed from the character "申". That is, "申" is the ancient form of "神". The character "神", the left structural part of which was added by the Zhou people, first appeared in bronze sculpture. The character "申" mostly meant "heavenly stems" and "earthly branches" in ancient books, but it was explained in the book *The Interpretation of Words* as the character for god "神" which was interpreted as "the god that created everything." All things on earth were created by the earliest god and should be later in terms of time.

I have noted that Dingshan put forward his opinion that the "Rainbow" was the prototype for the dragon in his book, *Study of Religions and Myths of Ancient China*. In addition, Mr. He Xingliang argued that, "dragon and snake were the earliest image for the rainbow god."① The Chinese character for rainbow "虹" appeared more than 3 thousand years ago in inscriptions on bones or tortoise shells, in half-arc bow shape, with heads like that of a snake (or dragon) on both ends of the bow. Patterns of rainbow on bronze-ware of the Zhou Dynasty were more lifelike, with a bow-shaped bent body and two symmetrical heads of dragons on both ends. In the book *The Interpretation of Words* it was noted that: "the rainbow ('虹'), called Didong, has a wormlike shape. Its shape emphasizes the left part of the character ('虫'), pronunciation follows the right part ('工')". Duan Yucai added an annotation that: "It means worm ('虫'). The rainbow looks like it, so "虫" becomes part of the character '虹'". The wormlike "it" here is actually a snake. The worm ("虫") said by Duan Yucai doesn't generally mean small reptiles but Hui ("虺"), the Amphisbaena.

The fact that "Rainbow" was the prototype for the dragon helps explain the relationship between the dragon and rainwater. The rainbow is associated with thunder and lightning, phenomena which bring rainwater directly to earth. Especially when a rainbow disappears, thunder and lightning begin, along with strong winds, pouring rain, and even terrible lightning, for original ancestors inspiring immense awe. It no doubt seemed that the huge rainbow hanging in the sky somehow controlled the storm, so the rainbow was deified and rainbow worship emerged.

Relevant evidence can also be found in documentary records of past dynasties. Like what was said in the book *Guangzi*, "Chapter for Water and Ground": The dragon was born in water and could swim boundlessly cloaked in five colors, so it became a god. It could become as small as a silkworm or larvae of a moth or butterfly; become large enough to cover heaven and earth; it could

---

① 何星亮:《中国自然神与自然崇拜》,上海三联书店 1992 年版,第 299 页。

rise to the clouds above; dive into deep springs below." And it says in the book *The Interpretation of Words* that: "The dragon, flies to the heaven when spring equinox comes and dives into deep waters when autumnal equinox comes." All this demonstrates that there is close relationship between the dragon and water.

The rainbow is the prototype of the dragon, and rainbows constituted totemic symbols within primitive, matriarchal clan society. Vivid representations of this function can be found in China's ancient insemination and child-bearing mythologies. It was recorded in the book *Collection of Emendation for Records of Generations of Emperors*, that the mother of Yellow Emperor, Fubao gave birth to him after "seeing the phenomenon of strong lightning winding around the big dipper." Of course, "strong lightning" means thunder and lightning.

In addition, because of their long, thin meandering shape and power, ancient people constantly and easily connected thunder and lightning with the dragon. Wangchong of the East Han dynasty, says in his book *Lunheng*, "Chapter for Fiction of the Dragon Image": "Observe that when thunder and lightning occur, the dragon springs up along with it; when trees are struck by thunder and lightning, the dragon flies up; that is to say, the dragon flies up to heaven from the trees. In fact, thunder and dragon are of the same kind, and they can respond to and call for each other through the atmosphere. It says in *the Book of Changes*, "Qian Diagram" that: 'cloud follows the dragon and wind follows the tiger.'" The birth of emperor Shaohao has been described in the book *Records of Generations of Emperors*: "Emperor Shaohao was named "Zhi", with alias Qingyang and family name Ji. Shaohao's mother was named Nvjie. It said that, in the era of the Yellow Emperor, a big shooting star streaked across the sky like a rainbow and fell down to the ancient place named Huazhu; Nvjie was inseminated by god in her dream and gave birth to Shaohao." "Rainbow", namely "Dragon," its "five-colored, large and long shape with function of communicating between heaven and earth and its close relationship with rainwater made our ancestors connect it with dragon". [①] It appears that Shaohao was born as a result of conception with a dragon. Therefore, the seventh volume of *Postscript for the book Historical Records of Chinese History and Culture* says frankly that, "Shaohao's father was named Qing and he was the fifth son of the yellow emperor."

The book *Jiangshi* compiled by Masu of the Qing dynasty quoted what is said in the book *Shi Han Shen Wu*: "...a beautiful jade-like brilliance just like neon, ran though the full moon; Nvshu felt it and gave birth to Zhuanxu. In fact, since "neon" equals "rainbow," the conception and child-bearing mythologies of Shaohao and Zhuanxu are exactly the same.

Yao, Shun and Yu were also conceived with dragons. It is recorded in the book *Chun Qiu He Cheng Tu* that: "Yao's mother was named Qingdou ... who lived in the mountain located south of the

---

① 刘志雄等:《龙与中国文化》,人民出版社 1992 年版,第 111 页。

three rivers. With thunder and lightning from heaven, blood-flow was infused into the big stone, then the stone got pregnant and gave birth to Qingdou ... mating with the red dragon, Qingdou got pregnant, then the dragon disappeared and Yao was born." It says in the book *Shi Han Shen Wu* that: "When she saw the rainbow, Shun's mother Wodeng felt herself conceive and gave birth to Shun," and it says in the book *Records of Generations of Emperors* that: "Yu's father Gun, married Xiuji, who saw the shooting star running through the star that named Maoxing and was inseminated by heaven in her dream; she then swallowed fruits of a kind of crop called Job's tears, felt uncomfortable, like vomiting, and gave birth to Yu."

Why would rainbows be said to be their own ancestors? This notion is derived from the ancient belief that life emerged from the sun. Rainbows appear when colorful sunlight shines on ever-changing clouds, which are linked to the sun. And, because the worm-like rainbow appeared similar to the male genital organ, primitive people connected the birth of their ancestors with the rainbow. More importantly, the earliest ancestor was born by insemination by heaven, which conferred divinity. Therefore, the earliest ancestors are presented in half-man half-god images in myths and legends.

Thus, as our examination of artifacts, language, literature and myth clearly indicates, it is the rainbow-dragon—not the bear-dragon—that constitutes the shared humanistic symbol as primogenitor of the Chinese nation.

3. The Origin of Dragon and Civilization of Rice Cultivating

Archaeologists Sun Shoudao and Guo Dashun argue that, "... there are many factors contributing to the emergence of civilization, such as the development of agriculture and irrigation, formation of castles and cities, the emergence of class, nation, and so on. However, the origin of the dragon—grounded in the development of primitive agriculture, associated with celestial phenomena and a product of the development of primitive religious belief, ideology and culture and art, can be said to be the outcome of all aspects of civilization".[①] This is pertinent. However, the issue they focused on is a one that focuses on only primitive agricultural civilization and origins of the dragon in the Liaohe River Basin. Thus, their interpretation makes sense within a partial perspective, but when extended to a broad view of all China the theory becomes untenable.

Today, archaeologists of agriculture have come to agree that there were two centers of origin for agriculture in ancient China. One is the rice cultivating center that developed mainly in the middle and lower reaches of the Changjiang River, gradually developing into a system of paddy-field

---

① 孙守道、郭大顺:《论辽河流域的原始文明与龙的起源》,《文物》1984 年第 11 期。

agriculture, later concentrating on rice cultivation; the other is the millet-planting center mostly in the middle reaches of the Yellow River, which gradually developed into a system of dry-land agriculture focused on millet planting. The Liaohe River Basin is only the first area in the introduction of millet-planting agriculture. Although it might also have evolved early cultivation of proso millet, it was still not a separate center of early agriculture independent of the middle reaches of the yellow river, but instead a fringe or border area of the same center.① Scholars have pointed out that, "the appearance and spread of Northeast Asian agriculture depended successively on two centers of origin of agriculture. First, the center of origin of dry-land millet planting agriculture in the middle reaches of the Yellow River that spread to the east of the Liaohe River and the Korean Peninsula through the Liaohe River Basin, and then spread to far eastern regions of Russia through Jilin and Heilongjiang provinces. The second center of origin of paddy-field rice cultivating emerged in the middle and lower reaches of the Changjiang River, joined with dry-land agriculture through the Shandong Peninsula, and then traveled to Japan through the Liaodong Peninsula and Korea.②

In ancient times when early people depended on the weather for food, water was the lifeblood of rice cultivation. Because, in primitive agriculture, the harvest was completely dependent on good weather, praying for rain became the primary sacrificial ritual linked to rice-cultivation. The dragon emerged at that moment.

The Classic of Mountains and Seas, the book that first recorded myths in China, states that the winged dragon called Yinglong was sent to the South by the Yellow Emperor to chase Chiyou and Kua Fu; but for some reason it didn't travel back to heaven to ride the clouds, bringing rain to the earth, so drought ensued. For that reason, and from that time forward, Yinglong always stays in the South, so southern regions are rainy all year. Therefore, according to the principles of homoeopathic or imitative magic, a dragon (yinglong) would be mimicked in ritual as something to be fought against by our primitive ancestors. *The Classic of Mountains and Seas* also says that, when in a drought, a dragon (yinglong) made of soil would be carried in a parade so that rain would come as requested. This is the earliest record of a dragon dance performance as an invocation to produce rain in ancient China. It established the precedent for Chinese citizens to perform the dragon dance to pray for rain, and was the origin of the long-standing convention of dragon dance performance in future generations.

The convention of praying for rain by constructing or building a dragon is also reflected in stone relief work from the Han Dynasty. An arc-shaped dragon with two heads (as we have seen, the rainbow) was carved on the top of the "drawing of praying to the dragon for rain" in stone relief, with both dragon mouths opening down as if to spray rain on people kneeling below with pots on their

---

① 严文明:《农业发生与文明起源》,科学出版社 2000 年版,第 37 页。
② 严文明:《中国稻作的起源和向日本的传播》,《文物天地》1991 年 5. 6 期。

head to collect water. Below the dragon, the carving also included the phoenix, feathered men, and wizards performing sacrificial practices, reflecting a complete picture of rain-prayer with dragon in ancient times.

The custom of praying for rain by buildinga dragon of soil was also recorded in James George Frazer's book *Golden Bough*: "The Chinese are adept in the art of taking the kingdom of heaven by storm. Thus, when rain is desired they make a huge dragon of paper or wood to represent the rain-god, and carry it about in a procession."①

In the second half of 1993, during construction of the Jingjiu Railway in Jiaodun, Huangmei county, Hubei province, 25 kilometers to the north of Yangtze River, the original dragon constructed using arranged pebbles was unearthed in the site of Daxi culture, predecessor of Qujialing culture. An impressive 4.46 meters in length, 2.28 in height and 0.3 to 0.65 meters in width, with raised head and straight body, flexed neck and curled tail, three fins on its back, three feet stretching out from its abdomen, a long, crooked and curled beard and one single raised horn, it is has the appearance of a huge flying dragon. The original dragon shaped from arranged pebbles has existed for 6000 years. Researchers have been arguing about which dragon prototype "pebble-dragon" belongs, yet they remain ignorant of its significance. I believe that this dragon was used for rain-prayer in rice cultivation, exactly like the soil-dragon discussed earlier.

Dong Zhongshu, master of Confucian classics, recorded magic rituals of Han Dynasty rain prayer in his book *Chun Qiu Fan Lu*. Dong notes that people prayed for rain during spring drought. All officials and civilians were asked to pray to the god of land and grain and the mountain god on the "water day" (a sacrificial day). A big blue and green dragon (namely Canglong) was built on the first and second days of the month, with length of 8 zhang (unit of measurement) and was centrally placed. Another 7 dragons of small size were built with a length of 4 zhang and placed in the east position, with heads facing east, each separated by a distance of 8 feet. Eight young boys, having fasted for 3 days, danced dressed in blue and green clothing. Farmers should also fast for 3 days, dress in blue and green and stand at the site.

Similarly, when praying for rain in summer, a big red dragon was built on the third and fourth days of the month, with length of 7 zhang, placed centrally; another 6 dragons of small size were also prepared each 3.5 zhang in length and placed in the southern position, with heads facing south and distance of 7 feet between every two dragons. Seven strong young men, who should fast for 3 days, danced dressed in red. Local officials in charge of water conservancy should also fast for 3 days, dress in red and stand on site.

A big yellow dragon was built on the fifth and sixth days of the month with length of 5 zhang. Four smaller dragons were also prepared with length of 2.5 zhang, placed in the southern position,

---

① 弗雷泽:《金枝》,徐育新等译,中国民间文艺出版社1987年版,第112页。

with heads facing south, each separated by 5 feet. Five men, who should fast for 3 days, danced dressed in yellow. Five elderly people should also fast for 3 days, dressing in yellow, and stand nearby.

In autumn, the witch was exposed under the blazing sun for a long time and the disabled prayed for 9 days, abstaining from making fire, cooking and smelting iron. One big white dragon was built on the seventh and eighth days of the month, 9 zhang long and centrally placed. Another 8 dragons of small size were built with length of 4.5 zhang and placed in a western position, with heads facing west and distance of 9 feet between every two dragons. Nine old bachelors, fasting for 3 days, dressed in white and danced. Officials in charge of military and administrative affairs should similarly fast, dress in white and stand in the ceremony.

In winter the dragon dance would last for 6 days and famous mountains were chosen as subjects of rain prayer. One large black dragon was built on the ninth and tenth days of the month, with length of 6 zhang, placed at the center; another 5 dragons of small size were also prepared and placed to the north, with heads facing north, and separated by a distance of 6 feet. Six elderly people, fasting for 3 days, dressed in black and danced. Officials who help dealing with matters involving violence should fast and remain at the site.

Dragons should be built with clean soil on "water days" when praying for rain in each season, and a canopy should be positioned above it and not be opened until the dragon had been completed. ①

Although primary rituals of magical prayer for rain in ancient times had been maintained in the Han Dynasty, praying for rain had also been integrated into the theoretical frame of Yin-Yang and the five elements. In this sense, colors of participant clothing should also correspond to both the 5 matched colors of the dragon and the 5 elements: blue and green, red, yellow, white and black.

The concept of praying for rain using the soil-dragon in the Han Dynasty was explained by Huantan in his book *Xin Lun*: "To pray for rain, Liuxin prepared dragons all of soil, played sacrificial music, and got all equipment and supplies for sacrifice well prepared. Huantan asked him: 'why are dragons of soil built for praying for rain?' Liuxin said: 'wind and rain come to the place where the dragon appears so as to welcome and see off the dragon, so we made dragons of soil according to its shape to pray for rain.'" Wangchong, of the Eastern Han Dynasty, also said that: "Dong Zhongshu advocated praying for rain using rituals as recorded in the book *Spring and Autumn Annals* by building dragons of soil, because soil-dragons had the same shape as the cloud dragon. And, it said in *the Book of Changes* that: 'Clouds come with the appearance of the dragon; winds come with the appearance of the tiger.' By inference from this kind of analogy, dragons were built of soil, as all things of Yin and Yang would be accompanied by the appearance of things of the same

---

① 董仲舒:《春秋繁露》,上海古籍出版社 1989 年版,第 88、89 页。

kind, then cloud and rain would come naturally." In view of this, people in Han Dynasty built dragons from soil and prayed for rain by using soil's property of water, which was the same property of cloud and rain. But it must be noted that this was qualitatively different from merchants begging for rain by using the dragon as the medium through which to communicate with god.

James George Frazer once incisively pointed out in his book *The Golden Bough* that: "Of the things which the public magician sets himself to do for the good of the tribe, a chief one is to control the weather and especially to ensure adequate rainfall."[1] Thus, magicians' control of rainwater by dragon magic became the most important magical event in ancient China.

First appearing in aboriginal tribes, magicians and magic were messengers to communicate with god, serve god, surrender to god and entertain god. The magician, an individualmagic performer, achieved a unique position in a tribe or community once he rose to be a public performer of magic. Frazer states: "When the welfare of the tribe is supposed to depend on the performance of these magical rites, the magician rises into a position of much influence and repute, and may readily acquire the rank and authority of a chief or king."[2] And, in fact, it can be seen that chiefs of aboriginal tribes often carried out the priesthood of a magician, and control of rain was the most important work of the priest.

In this sense, new explanations can be provided for stories about "riding the dragon" in Chinese mythologies. The book *Da Dai Li*, "Virtue of the Five Emperors" states that: "Zhuanxu gets to places in the whole world by riding a dragon." Gods of the four directions: the east god Goumang, the south god of fire namely Zhurong, the west god Rushou and the north god Yuqiang all rode on two dragons. Yu's son, Xia Houqi also rode on two dragons. It will be better-suited to the realities of rice civilization to explain "riding on two dragons" as praying for rain than to put forward the idea that dragons were primarily media establishing communication between heaven and earth, human and god.

On account of the long standing of agricultural civilization within the Chinese nation, the belief in praying for rain through the use of the dragon emerges as the most fundamental component of dragon culture. Only by comprehending the prototypical dragon in China, engaging its cultural context and its essential property of water, its ties to the rainbow, and its close relationship to the civilization of rice cultivation, can essence of Chinese dragon culture be grasped. Although the bear may have totemic importance in Europe and Asia, it is the dragon that is embedded in the fabric of China's history, economy, and culture.

---

[1] 弗雷泽:《金枝》,第 95 页。
[2] 弗雷泽:《金枝》,第 70 页。

The "American" Quilt
—The Intersections and Challenges of Preserving and Safeguarding a Traditional Cultural Heritage Form

Marsha MacDowell[*]

In this presentation, I will examine issues of preservation and safeguards to cultural heritage through the lens of the tangible and intangible dimensions of one expressive art form—quilts, a form of textiles also sometimes known by its type of construction (i. e. patchwork) or by its use (i. e. blanket or wall hanging). In constructing this essay I will draw on my experience as both a folklorist and an art historian, as one whose research takes place in the field and in museums, archives, and libraries, and as one who has long held a university-based museum curatorial and faculty position that demands constant engagement with both academic and public audiences. Furthermore, this presentation will be informed by my experience as the director of Michigan's traditional arts program, a statewide arts service program devoted to documenting, preserving, presenting, and advocating for the traditional artists and art forms of our state as well as my cultural heritage work in South Africa, Thailand, and now in China.[①]

---

[*] Marsha MacDowell, Professor at the Michigan State University Museum.

[①] I would like to acknowledge that many of these activities have been conducted in collaboration with my colleagues at the Michigan State University Museum whose advice and assistance have been critical to these inquiries into the history, production and meaning of quilts. I would like to especially acknowledge C. Kurt Dewhurst, Mary Worrall, Beth Donaldson, Lynne Swanson, and Pearl Yee Wong for their help in preparing for the presentation of this paper. I am also grateful to my colleagues Bill Ivey, C. Kurt Dewhurst, Zhang Juwen, and Timothy Lloyd for their dedication on behalf of the American Folklore Society in building and strengthening bridges between those in China and in the U. S. whose research and advocacy is focused on traditional tangible and intangible cultural heritage. I am also appreciative of the support and interest of Siddarth Chandra and Zhao Weijun at Michigan State University for their assistance, along with Lu Zhangshen, Director-General, National Museum of China, and Qu Shengrui, Inspector, Department of Intangible Cultural Heritage, Ministry of Culture, P. R. China. A special thank you is extended to Chen Xi for her enthusiam for learning about American quiltmaking and for advancing my understanding of the challenges of communicating across language divides the terminology associated with quiltmaking. In addition, my inquiry into Chinese quilts is related to several intertwined projects connecting Chinese and American museums with a shared interest in researching and developing exhibitions, digital resources, and publications related to quilts. One of those projects has already resulted in a touring exhibition of American quilts in China and an accompanying exhibition catalogue, *The Sum of Many Parts*: 25 *Quiltmakers in 21st Century America* (Minneapolis, Minnesota: Arts Midwest with South Arts, 2012) for which MacDowell and Worrall served as co-curators and co-authors of the catalogue essay.

The art form known as the quilt in the United States draws from textile traditions around the world. The techniques of piecing, patching, and appliquéing fabrics together and then binding layers of fabric together with stitches—the fundamental elements associated with quilts—have been known to exist for centuries in different locales and cultures. Textile items known as quilts—items typically used for bedcovers, wall hangings, and shroud covers—have also been known to exist in antiquity. For instance, decorative quilts made of silk dating back as far as 770 B. C., during the Eastern Zhou dynasty, have been discovered in China. ①

In America, the presence of quilts dates back over 200 years to colonial times. Most likely quiltmaking was first introduced to the North American continent by the waves of Western Europeans who settled the eastern American seaboard and it is within this transported Western European culture that the art form first flourished in America. Over time, these quiltmaking traditions introduced to the continent have been influenced by both the indigenous cultures already living on the continent and by the cultures of all peoples who subsequently migrated to the United States. Choices of patterns, forms, construction techniques, colors, fabrics, and functions of quilts may bear unmistakable references to the ethnicity, region, religion, occupational, and tribal affiliations of their makers or the communities in the art is made.

Today, at the beginning of the 21st century, interest in this art numbers in the millions. According to a 2010 American craft industry report, there over 21 million individuals in the U. S. engaged in some aspect of quiltmaking and millions more in countries around the world. ② This number includes not only those who make, use, collect, and sell quilts but also those who make, market, and collect the tools, patterns, and fabrics associated with making quilts, produce quilt festivals, curate and show collections, participate in real-life or on-line clubs and communities, market and communicate information regarding quilts, and document and study quilts. In 1978, Patricia Mainardi, feminist scholar and art critic, declared quilts the "great American art"③ and the history and traditions of this largely female textile art has become the focus of studies by feminists, folklorists, art historians, collectors, folklorists, museum curators, and others. Since the early 1980s, thousands of individuals, largely volunteers, have engaged in state and regional grassroots documentation efforts have recorded information on tens of thousands of quilts, a fraction

---

① See Patsy Orlofsky and Myron Orlofsky, *Quilts in America*, New York: Abbeville Press, 2005, p. 17, citing Mary Symonds (Mrs. Guy Antrobus) and Louisa Preece, *Needlework Through the Ages*, London: Hodder and Stoughton, London, 1928, p82. See also Shelagh J. Vainker, *Chinese Silk: A Cultural History*, London: British Museum Press, 2004, p. 36. For an especially good resource on Chinese textiles, including examples of quilts made by Chinese minority artists, see *Writing with Thread: Traditional Textiles of Southwest Chinese Minorities* (exhibition catalogue), Honolulu: University of Hawaii Art Gallery, 2009.

② Quilting in America. 2010. Presented by Quilters Newsletter, a Creative Crafts Group publication, in cooperation with International Quilt Market & Festival, divisions of Quilts, Inc. http://www.quilts.com/announcements/y2010/QIA2010_OneSheet.pdf

③ Patricia Mainardi, *Quilts: The Great American Art*, San Pedro, CA: Miles & Weir, Ltd., 1978, p. 2.

of the number that have been made in America. ① Slowly those records and others are being made accessible through The Quilt Index (www.quiltindex.org), an online repository of distributed digital data about quilts and related stories from and about their makers and their uses. As of July 2013, the Index already showcases more than 70,000 historical and contemporary quilts. ②

Today, quilts are often considered the quintessential American art form and, for many, a symbol of our country's values and our respect for the handmade and traditional. Accounts of quilt-related stories, customs and beliefs can be found in numerous nonfiction sources (i.e. diaries, oral histories, letters) as well as in fiction written by some of America's most well known authors. ③ The words "quilt" and "patchwork" have permeated our American language and speech, and are frequently employed as metaphors for anything in which disparate pieces form a unified whole or to represent and reflect such concepts as domesticity, patriotism, care and nurturing, and diversity and unity. ④ Some scholars have even considered quilts and quiltmaking as a cultural concept that transcends their physicality.

It is within this vast landscape of the making and use of quilts in America that one can explore some of the most fundamental and thorny issues related to traditional cultural heritage, including issues of authenticity, cultural dislocations, definitions of traditional, impact of marketplace, and, if needed, appropriate strategies and interventions to protect and safeguard intangible and tangible heritage related to quiltmaking.

Within this presentation then, I will first briefly provide a basic description of what constitutes a quilt and then I will examine, both broadly and with specific American examples, arenas in which quilts and issues of preservation of traditional tangible and intangible cultural heritage coincide.

So, first, what is a quilt? In many parts of the world, and certainly in America, the strictest definition of a quilt is that a rectangular-shaped textile made by sewing usually three—but sometimes

---

① Kathlyn F. Sullivan, *Gatherings: American's Quilt Heritage*, Paducah, Kentucky: American Quilter's Society, 1995.

② The Quilt Index is a continually expanding and searchable repository of digital photographs, texts (oral, video, and written), and documents pertaining to quilts, quiltmakers, and quilt-related activities. This research platform and laboratory of thematic material culture is built around digital collections drawn from museums, libraries, archives, research projects, and private individuals around the world. The Quilt Index is a partnership endeavor led by the Michigan State University Museum, MATRIX: Center for Humane Arts, Letters, and Social Sciences Online at MSU, and the Alliance for American Quilts in collaboration with its many contributors.

③ Among the most well known is Alice Walker's "Everyday Use" in *In Love and Trouble: Stories of Black Women*, New York: Harcourt Brace, 1973.

④ Although many scholars have recognized the use of quilt-related terms in American language, two have paid particular attention. See Judy Elsley, *Quilts as Text iles: The Semiotics of Quilting*, New York: Peter Lang Publishing, 1996 and Elaine Showalter, *Sister's Choice: Tradition and Change in American Women's Writing*, Oxford: Clarendon Press, 1991. See also Marsha MacDowell and Wolfgang Mieder. 2010. "When Life Hands Your Scraps, Make a Quilt": Quiltmakers and the Tradition of Proverbial Inscriptions, *Proverbium: Yearbook of International Proverb Scholarship* 27, 2010, pp. 113 – 172.

just two—layers of fabric together. The variations on how this basic form is constructed are, however, seemingly endless. The shape might not be a rectangle and the size of the quilt might vary from miniature—i. e. , just a few inches in width and length—to the size of The NAMES Project AIDS Memorial Quilt that is larger than a US football field (roughly 100 meters long by 50 meters wide). ① The top and backing might be made of one, two, or many types of fabrics patched, pieced, appliquéd, or otherwise put together in named patterns and with quilting stitch designs that are commercially available, created by the quiltmaker, or borrowed, adapted, or learned from another quiltmaker. The filling or middle layer—if there is one—might be made of natural fibers, manufactured cloth, recycled old quilts or other textiles. The quiltmaker might embellish the surfaces with embroidery, paint, additional fabric, and handmade or manufactured objects. All or portions of the quilt might be done by hand or by machine, including highly computerized machines. The quilt might be made by one or more persons, sometimes separating out very specific tasks, or could be made by a group of individuals who share affinities of culture, religion, occupation, and friendship. While historically the skills and knowledge about quiltmaking as well as aesthetic preferences were largely passed on informally from one person to the next, quilt knowledge has long been shared through more formal means, such as classes, workshops, guilds, how-to publications, and, more recently, webinars, workshops, YouTube videos, and blogs on the Internet.

The reasons why quilts are made and how they are used are also tremendously varied. Quilts are made and used most often for bed coverings, but they are also used for everyday purposes, such as shade awnings, infants' swing cradles, weather insulation, and soft places to sit on the ground. Quilts are made to commemorate important personal, family, community, and national occasions; as gifts; for bartering and trading; as instruments of social change and education; and as a means of earning a livelihood or supplementing income. Some quilts are made to express the maker's personal, creative ideas about color, texture, pattern, shape, and form. Other quilts are made intentionally for exhibition—be it at county fairs or art museums, for the walls of collectors, or as art in public places. Every community in which quiltmaking occurs recognizes not only when a textile is a quilt, but also the feature and standards upon which to evaluate the quilts. Depending on the characteristics of the community—family, ethnic, occupation, region, etc. —these features and standards will vary. ②

Given the myriad variations of traditions and traditionality of quiltmaking in America, it is safe

---

① The AIDS Memorial Quilt, http://www. aidsquilt. org/about/the-aids-memorial-quilt; Mickey Weems, Marsha MacDowell, and Mike Smith, "The Quilt," Qualia, posted December 2011. http://www. qualiafolk. com/2011/12/08/the-quilt/; and "Creativity and Crisis: Unfolding the AIDS Memorial Quilt," 2012 Smithsonian Folklife Festival, http://www. festival. si. edu/2012/creativity_ and_ crisis/

② This description of the elements of a quilt in adapted from Marsha MacDowell "Folk Art," in Yvonne Lockwood and Marsha MacDowell, eds. 1999 *Michigan Folklife Annual*, East Lansing: Michigan State University Museum, 1999, pp. 30 – 35.

to say that this realm of intangible cultural heritage offers many, many opportunities to examine issues related to providing protective protection. Let me offer Seven brief examples in which specific quiltmaking traditions in America have been impacted by activities both within and outside the communities from which the traditions have emanated and one additional example in which a newly created tradition is flourishing.

1) The so-called "Smithsonian quilt controversy": In 1991 the Smithsonian Institution licensed Chinese manufacturers to reproduce and market four American quilts from the Smithsonian's collections. Thousands of American quiltmakers called and wrote the Smithsonian in protest, claiming that the reproductions, produced and sold at low cost, undermined the value of the work done by American quiltmakers. One group of protestors, calling themselves the American Quilt Defense Fund (AQDF), hired a lobbyist to negotiate with the Smithsonian. The direct result of the protest was that the Smithsonian did not renew the contract to make reproductions and, instead, contracted with a domestic cooperative of American quiltmakers to produce three quilt designs for sale by the Smithsonian. The AQDF worked with the Smithsonian to establish a special quilt legacy program to exhibitions, conservation, educational activities and an ongoing display case for quilts at the National Museum of American History. ①

2) Gee's Bend quilts: African American women in a rural area called Gee's Bend in Alabama (in the southern US) have long made quilts, and in the late 20th century their work had been sold at major departments stores in New York City and had been the subject of study by journalists and folklorists. However, when a folk art collector created a highly-promoted exhibition of their work that was showcased in a major New York City museum, the artists' work was hailed by cultural critics and the establishment media as a new discovery and the exhibition was singled out by an art critic at *the New York Times* as one of the top ten art exhibitions of the year. ② Presented and critiqued as art, the traditional quiltmaking of these rural artists quickly became highly-prized commodities and spin-off items that replicated the quilts were mass produced. ③

---

① For a good overview of the controversy, see July Elsley, "The Smithsonian Quilt Controversy: Cultural Dislocation," pp. 199 – 136 in Laurel Horton, ed., *Uncoverings* 1993, Volume 14 of the *Research Papers of the American Quilt Study Group*, San Francisco: American Quilt Study Group, 1993.

② Michael Kimmelman, "Art/Architecture: The Year in Review—The Critics/10 Moments; Richter, And Cloth, Were Abundant," *The New York Times*, December 29, 2002.

③ The two books accompanying the exhibition were John Bearsley, William Arnett, Paul Arnett, and Jane Livingston, *The Quilts of Gee's Bend*, Atlanta, GA: Tinwood Books, 2002 and John Bearsley, William Arnett, Paul Arnett, and Jane Livingston, *Gee's Bend: The Women and Their Quilts*, Atlanta, GA: Tinwood Books, 2002. Patricia A. Turner examined the evolution of the attention to and the impact on Gee's Bend quilters in her *Crafted Lives: Stories and Studies of African American Quilters* (University of Mississippi Press, 2009). Andrew Dietz examined the role of an outsider in cultivatingattention to the quilters in his *The Last Folk Hero: A True Story of Race and Art, Power and Profit* (Atlanta, GA: Ellis Lane Press, 2006). Victoria P. Phillips also provides an insightful look at the commodification issues regarding the Gee's Bend quiltmakers in "Symposium: Commodification, Intellectual Property and the Quilters of Gee's Bend." *American University Journal of Gender*, Social Policy & the Law. 15, no. 2 (2007): 359 – 377.

3) Michigan Traditional Arts Apprenticeship and Michigan Heritage Awards programs: In Detroit, Michigan, African American quiltmaker Lula Williams learned early in life to make quilts and continues to make quilts and teach quiltmaking. In recognition of the excellence of her art and for her commitment to carrying on her art as well as teaching it to others, she has been honored with a Michigan Heritage Award. The Michigan Traditional Arts Program, a statewide arts partnership program of the Michigan State University Museum and the Michigan Council for Arts and Cultural Affairs, administers the awards program. Through this program and a companion program called the Michigan Traditional Arts Apprenticeship Program, traditional artists throughout the state of Michigan are directly receiving recognition and support. ①

4) Hmong/Amish quilts: The Amish, a conservative Christian religious sect in the United States, produced handmade quilts in designs and color palettes that reflect their religious beliefs and often showed distinctive styles associated with the geographic location of their religious community. They also made quilts in a variety of styles to sale to non-Amish and were effective in generating a market for their handmade work. In the late 1970s, Hmong refugees began settling in the United States and with them they brought their distinct textile skills and traditions. When they settled in regions that brought them in contact with Amish, textile artists from both cultures began to work together. Hmong artists began making bed-sized textiles, Hmong and Amish collaborated on producing work they could sell to the market for "Amish" quilts even though the quilt made have been wholly or partially made by a Hmong textile worker. ②

5) Factory-made Hawaiian quilts: In the early 19th century, Native Hawaiians were introduced by American missionaries to the art of quiltmaking but they went on to developed their own distinctive quilt style and traditions, including the practice of a creator of a new pattern owned that pattern and it could not be used by someone else unless they were gifted it. Quilts were made for various purposes within the Native Hawaiian community and for sale to outsiders, including tourists. For many years, a visitor to Hawaii could purchase a Native Hawaiian quilt, made by a Native Hawaiian artist in local craft shops. Today, however, there is a chain of Hawaiian quilt stores in which one can purchase Hawaiian quilts and a variety of other items sporting Hawaiian quilt patterns—virtually none of which is made in Hawaii or by Native Hawaiians and some of which

---

① Michigan Traditional Arts Apprenticeship Program, http://museum.msu.edu/s-program/mtap/mtaap/mtaap.html and Michigan Heritage Awards, http://museum.msu.edu/s-program/mh_awards/mha.html. Accessed July 25, 2013.

② Two of the first published studies of this cultural exchange were Marsha MacDowell, "Old Techniques of Paj Ntaub, New Patterns of Expression," in Ruth Fitzgerald and Yvonne Lockwood, eds. 1993 *Festival of Michigan Folklife*, East Lansing: Michigan State University Museum, 1993, pp. 42 – 45 and Trish Faubion, "The Amish and the Hmong: Two Cultures and One Quilt," *Piecework* 1 (1993), pp. 26 – 35. More recently, Janneken Smucker devoted deep attention to the continuation of the interaction of Hmong and Amish in producing and marketing quilts in her dissertation *From rags to riches: Amish quilts and the crafting of value* (University of Delaware, August 2010) and Amish Quilts: Crafting an American Icon (Johns Hopkins University Press, forthcoming 2013).

illegally uses patterns owned by the original Native Hawaiian designers. ①

6) The Quilt Index and QSOS: Digital images of quilts and their related stories (mostly documented through the efforts of thousands of volunteer citizen-scholars) are being collected, preserved, and presented in two online repositories: The Quilt Index and Quilters Save Our Stories (QSOS). ② The access to this material culture and related stories about the objects and their makers is unprecedented and provides multiple opportunities for research and educational uses. The individual retains ownership of the images and the stories or organization that "contributes" the information to the Index and permission to use the story or the image of the quilt—or to make a quilt identical to one in the Index—must be secured from that contributor. Originally begun with primarily data collected on American quilts, the Index has become international. As of 2013, collections from South Africa and Canada have been added and initiatives to add Australian and Chinese quilt collections are underway. ③

7) The Underground Railroad secret quilt code story: In 1999 a scholarly-appearing book, *Hidden in Plain View*, was published. The book contained one person's unverified story that during the period prior to and during the American Civil War, African American slaves living in the South used a secret code found in quilts to guide their way to freedom in the North. Many authoritative institutions were complicit in endorsing and marketing this story and today the belief in this story is widespread. Since 1999, hundreds of quilts displaying the blocks used in the Code have been made, museums have done exhibitions on Underground Railroad quilts, educators use the story to teach schoolchildren about African American history, and Code-related fabric lines and books and

---

① Marsha MacDowell and C. Kurt Dewhurst, field notes. *To Honor and Comfort: Native Quilting Traditions project*. Two businesses, in particular, each of which has several retail stores in Honolulu and also sell online are Royal Hawaiian Quilt (http://www.thehawaiianquilt.com/) and Hawaiian Quilt Collection (http://www.hawaiian-quilts.com/). Marsha MacDowell, field notes, 2012.

② See note 5 for information about the Quilt Index. The Quilters Save Our Stories project (http://www.allianceforamericanquilts.org/qsos/) is led by the Quilt Alliance. Stories can be accessed through the QSOS website or through the Quilt Index. QSOS interviews are archived at the American Folklife Center, Library of Congress.

③ The addition of Chinese quilts to the Quilt Index is being led by Michigan State University Museum and facilitated through support from several sources, including the Luce Foundation and the Asia Cultural Council which have supported museum staff exchanges. As of 2013, Chinese partners include the Yunnan Nationalities Museum (Kunming, China), Guizhou Nationalities Museum (Guiyang, China); Guangxi Museum of Nationalities (Nanning, China); and the Department of Intangible Cultural Heritage, Ministry of Culture, China. American partners include the American Folklore Society, Arts Midwest, International Quilt Study Center and Museum, University of Nebraska-Lincoln (Lincoln, Nebraska), Mather Museum of World Culture, Indiana University (Bloomington, Indiana), Museum of International Folk Art (Santa Fe, New Mexico) and a private collector.

videotapes on making a Code quilt have subsequently been produced. ①

8) Design and marketing in the "traditional" or "folk" arts style: In 1983, fashion designer Ralph Lauren introduced a line of clothing done in patchwork and home furnishings for which accompanying advertising claimed "a new tradition begins."② What Lauren and countless other well and lesser-known producers of material culture have done is to slightly tweak the design or production of traditional arts to create products, sometimes mass-produced, for the global marketplace. Many times this occurs among well-meaning leaders of economic development project aiming to assist communities or groups solve unemployment, devastation of resources impacting local traditions, displacement from homelands, etc. But any individual with an eye towards what is selling in the marketplace can imitate work that is the cultural patrimony of others.

The above snapshots of quilt-related production, preservation, and presentation reveal important issues of authenticity of tradition, the impact of the Internet as well as global and local markets on intangible cultural heritage, and the complicity, for positive and negative outcomes, of museums and other authoritative institutions in sustaining traditional culture.

National programs, like the Smithsonian Folklife Festival or the National Heritage Fellowship awards, state folklife festivals, folklife heritage award programs and traditional arts apprenticeship programs (such as those run by the Michigan Traditional Arts Program at the Michigan State University Museum), folk arts exhibitions produced by museums, and online digital repositories like the Quilt Index are all current strategies being used by folklorists and other cultural heritage workers to bring recognition to and help sustain the traditional intangible cultural heritage that make

---

① Jacqueline L. Tobin and Raymond G. Dobard, *Hidden in Plain View: The Secret Story of Quilts and the Underground Railroad*. New York, N. Y. : Doubleday, 1999 quickly became a subject for public and scholarly debate. One of the first scholarly refutes of the story was Marsha MacDowell, "Quilts and Their Stories: Revealing a Hidden History", *Uncoverings: Journal of the American Quilt Study Group*, 21, 2000, pp. 155 – 166. An analysis of the authoritative agencies that have contributed to credentialing the story has been conducted and reported by Marsha MacDowell "Quilts, Primary Sources, and Authenticity". Unpublished paper from invited Presidential Panel, American Historical Association, San Diego, California. January 9, 2010. Folklorist Laurel Horton's inquiry into the beliefs surrounding the story can be seen in an online podcast, "The Underground Railroad Quilt Controversy: Looking for the 'Truth'" at http://www.quiltstudy.org/education/public_programs.html. Patricia A. Turner has also examined the secret quilt code story in *Crafted Lives: Stories and Studies of African American Quilters* (University of Mississippi Press, 2009). Leigh Fellner, "Betsy Ross Redux: The Underground Railroad 'Quilt Code'", 2006. Downloadable at http://www.ugrrquilt.hartcottagequilts.com/. Another excellent analysis of the contestation surrounding the quilt code story can be seen in Shelley Zegart, "Myth and methodology: Shelley Zegart Unpicks African American Quilt Scholarship," Selvedge, Issue 21 (Jan/February 2008) pp. 48 – 56.

② C. Kurt Dewhurst and Marsha MacDowell, "The Marketing of Objects in the Folk Art Style", *New York Folklore*, Vol. 12, Nos. 1 – 2, 1986. , pp. 49 – 55.

both nation and community unique.① Yet, as each of the above examples of the intersections of localized quiltmaking traditions and larger influences begin to illustrate, the notion of protective production is complex and each traditional activity must carefully be examined to determine what traditions should be protected, how they should be protected, by whom, and who benefits from the protection—and then to evaluate impacts of any protective production activity. It is incumbent upon folklorists and other cultural workers to be active and critical partners in any protective production activity related to intangible cultural heritage. The issues related to preservation and safeguarding of intangible cultural heritage are deeply complex and, as folklorists, we must be engaged in not only documenting and studying these traditions but being active—and critical—voices in how traditions intersect with protective production.

---

① For more information on the Smithsonian Folklife Festival, which offers a companion marketplace for not only the work of artists presented in the festival but from other traditional artists around the world, see http://www.festival.si.edu. For more information on the Great Lakes Folk Festival, which also includes marketing opportunities for traditional artists, see www.greatlakesfolkfest.net. For more information on the National Heritage Fellowships, go to http://www.nea.gov/honors/heritage/. A special issue of *New York Folklore* Vol. 12, Nos. 1 - 2, 1986 contained a number of articles examining facets of marketing folk art. Two articles are of special interest for the ways in which folklorists could serve as advocates and activists in preserving traditions while at the same time helping them become stronger and more economically viable. See Mary Arnold Twining, "Marketing the Art of Migrant Workers", pp. 25 - 41; Rosemary O. Joyce, "To Market, To Market, to Sell Some Folk Art," pp. 43-47; Alf H. Walle, "Mitigating Marketing: A Window of Opportunity for Applied Folklorists," pp. 91 - 112; Robert T. Teske, "Crafts Assistance Programs and Traditional Crafts", pp. 75 - 85; Egle Victoria Zygas, "Who Will Market the Folk Arts?", pp. 69 - 74; Elaine Eff, "Traditions for Sale: Marketing Mechanisms for Baltimore's Screen Art, 1913 - 1983", pp. 57 - 68; Geraldine Johnson, "Commentary", p. 85, and John Michael Vlach, "Commentary", pp. 88 - 89. For engagement by a folklorist in surveying areas of folk arts in one state for which targeted efforts could assist in preserving and strengthening them, including in the marketplace and in tourism, see Marsha MacDowell and Julie Avery, *CraftWORKS! Michigan: A Report on Traditional Crafts and Economic Development in Michigan*. East Lansing, MI: Michigan State University Museum in collaboration with Office of Economic Development, Department of History, Arts, and Libraries, State of Michigan, 2006.

Multiform Practices for Safeguarding Epic Singing Tradition: A Case Study of King Gesar Epic in the Dur-bud Tribe

Chao Gejin[*]

The Dur-bud Tribe is located in kho-chu Township, in the dgav-bde County of the mgo-log Tibetan Autonomous Prefecture in south-eastern Qinghai-Tibet Plateau, adjacent to the Amye Machin Snow Mountain and near the source region of the Yellow River. Further more, the Dur-bud's growing influence extends continually to the Tibetan a'mdo and khams dialect areas between 91°59′ and 102°01′ east longitude, and between 29°48′ and 36°17′ north latitude, covering Tibetan communities in the mgo-log, yu-shul, and mtsho-lho prefectures of Qinghai Province, the ma-chu County of kan-lho Prefecture in Gansu Province, the sde-dge, gser-thar, ser-shul and other counties of dkar-mdzes Prefecture of Sichuan Province, as well as the nag-chu and chab-mdo districts of the Tibet Autonomous Region.

The oral epic of King Gesar is a paradigmatic example of humanity's accomplishment in the verbal arts. The Gesar cycle, recounting the sacred deeds of the ancient hero King Gesar has been handed down primarily among the Tibetans and Mongolians in China.

Since the 1980s, modernization, globalization, urbanization and information technologies have consecutively brought tremendous change to the native land. Even in local communities, epic singing and storytelling have suffered from shrinking interest. As the result, a self-fashioned plan of rescue has emerged. Since 2003, for example, a close collaboration with academic institutions, folk societies, and governmental organs has generated a series of safeguarding measures and a long-term self-governed plan for maintaining the epic's viability and visibility.

Thanks to the example provided by community-based practices within the Dur-dub Tribe, the project has gone through several key stages and adopted a series of measures to safeguard the Gesar

---

[*] Chao Gejin, Institute of Ethnic Literature, Chinese Academy of Social Sciences.

epic tradition.

1. Wide participation of clans, households, performers, lamas, and Buddhist monasteries.

2. Active reinstallation of epic singing within popular folk festivals.

3. Establishment of the "Dur-bud Gesar Culture and the Epic Village" and its "Villager Committee."

4. Financial remuneration to respected elders for youth training.

5. Collaboration between academic and governmental institutions to build a "Ling Gesar Performers House."

To aid in safeguarding the cultural ecosystem, the local government has conducted several supportive measures to revitalize the singing tradition: (1) "Rma-yul Gesar Culture and Art Festival"; (2) meetings to honor master singers; (3) inclusion of Gesar in pimarary and secondary school curricula; (4) "Development Plan for Safeguarding Gesar Culture in Mgo-log Prefecture"; (5) "Mgo-lo rma-yul Long Gesar Culture Corridor along the Banks of the Yellow River," now under construction; (6) Thematic museum of Gesar epic tradition and "Mgo-log Cultural Ecological Reserve for Gesar Culture," both underway.

The present case will provide an effective working model for safeguarding the Gesar epic in regions of China with similar social and cultural conditions.

It is also a working model applicable to traditions outside of China, since Gesar, as one of the world's largest oral epic traditions, is disseminated in different languages throughout neighbouring countries and regions, including Bhutan, Nepal, Pakistan, India, Mongolia, and the Buriat and Kalmuck areas of Russia.

Applied Ethnography and Indigenous Representation in the Virtual Exhibit *Dane Wajich — Dane-zaa Stories and Songs: Dreamers and the Land*

Amber Ridington*

【Note to Readers】 A visual online version of this presentation can be viewed online at http://prezi.com/rqhfb1t57jaq/?utm_campaign=share&utm_medium=copy&rc=ex0share

Click on the "play" icon at the bottom of the Prezi screen to advance the slide show.

This case study features Doig River First Nation's community directed exhibition: *Dane Wajich — Dane-zaa Stories and Songs: Dreamers and the Land* which was launched on the Virtual Museum of Canada's web portal in 2007 and can be found at: http://www.museevirtuel-virtualmuseum.ca/sgc-cms/expositions-exhibitions/danewajich/.

The Doig River First Nation is one of four Dane-zaa (previously known as Beaver Indian) indigenous communities from northeastern British Columbia, Canada. The Dane-zaa live in the Peace River region within the Arctic Ocean watershed. Before European colonization of Canada, the Dane-zaa were subarctic hunting and gathering peoples who lived in small kin-based groups. They flourished through hunting and gathering in a semi-nomadic and heterarchical manner. Their traditional language is Dane-zaa, also known as the Beaver Language, which is a member of the Athapaskan language family which is spoken by Indigenous peoples in northwestern North America.

Beginning in the late 1700s, the Dane-zaa engaged in cultural and material exchange with the first Europeans in their lands, and participated in the fur trade as suppliers, but they did not give up their semi-nomadic lifestyle, gathering plant resources in the summer months and breaking into smaller kinship groups to hunt and trap in the fall and winter, until their traditional lands were

---

* Amber Ridington, Ph.D candidate at the Folklorist and Heritage Consultant, Memorial University of Newfoundland.

opened up to significant European settlement by the building of the Alaska-Canada Highway during World War II.

It is just since the 1950s that Dane-zaa people were forced by the Canadian Government to settle on Indian Reserves and to send their children to school. Because of this intervention on traditional life, the process of colonization and policies of "cultural assimilation" with European settler culture significantly altered Dane-zaa patterns of living and learning. Only in the last 20 years has the Doig River First Nation begun heritage vitalization efforts, such as culture camps and traditional language programs, to re-engage younger generations with the traditional knowledge and language of their elders.

Beginning in the early years of the 21st Century the Doig River First Nation extended their heritage vitalization efforts into the digital realm, and began to collaborate on a series of digital media projects which have focused on:

- archival preservation
- virtual repatriation of heritage materials through online access
- collaborative and participatory ethnographic documentation, and
- web-based multimedia exhibition about Dane-zaa culture and traditions

My collaborative work with the Doig River First Nation began in 2002 as a grant writer, project facilitator and ethnographic mentor for some of these new digital media heritage projects. I have had a lifelong connection to the Dane-zaa since I was born in their territory in 1969 while my parents were doing anthropological work with them. My parents, Antonia Mills and Robin Ridington, began documenting Dane-zaa culture in 1964 as graduate students at Harvard University and their work with the Dane-zaa has continued to this day (R. Ridington, 1978, 1981, 1988, 1990; Mills, 1982, 1988, 2004; R. Ridington, J. Ridington, 2003, 2006, 2013).

My working relationship with the Doig River First Nation has built upon my connections to people in the communities, my familiarity with their Dane-zaa culture and history, and mutual trust between me and the people. While my relationship with the community has been an asset for initiating collaborative digital media projects I have been careful to maintain community trust in a reciprocal manner; In particular I work towards sustaining open dialogue pathways that are attuned with traditional Dane-zaa customs for communication so that we can work through challenging issues about their heritage stewardship and public representation as they arise.

With this brief introduction to Dane-zaa culture and to how I came to work with the Doig River First Nation set out, I now turn to the case study for this forum, the online multimedia exhibition titled: *Dane Wajich – Dane-zaa Stories and Songs: Dreamers and the Land*. In this presentation I will share the methodologies that we utilized and the effects upon the tradition that have arisen from sharing Doig River's heritage in a new digital form, and with a world-wide audience, through the online multimedia exhibition.

This exhibition draws on the principles of applied ethnography to showcase the theme of Dane-zaa stories and songs and the relationship of Dane-zaa stories and songs to Dane-zaa dreamers and Dane-zaa traditional lands. The process for creating the exhibition was designed so that it could be directed by the Doig River First Nation but also make use of the skills of professional ethnographers, linguists, educators, curators, and web-designers to help the First Nation deliver their message and to provide them with the opportunity to learn some of these professional skills. The exhibit is built around oral narratives (ICH) that have been documented with digital video by Dane-zaa youth who were trained during the course of the project. The process of documenting oral stories and songs (ICH) has created tangible heritage media, which has been supplemented with both contemporary and archival photographs and song recordings along with interpretive text to contextualize the material for an outside audience. The exhibit contains a great deal of material in the Doig River First Nation's Dane-zaa language. To make it accessible to a broader audience the Dane-zaa language material has been curated with textualinterpretation and Dane-zaa language translation in both of Canada's official languages, English and French. Because oral communication is the mode that Dane-zaa people are most comfortable with, extending their deeply rooted oral traditions (stories and songs) into the digital age has been important for the Doig River First Nation. By sharing video recordings on the Internet the Doig River First Nation has been able to literally speak for themselves to both local and world-wide audiences. This self-representation through oral communication has allowed them to transcend some of the disadvantages that they have experienced within non-Indigenous settler culture more oriented to textual communication (Brody, 1981; Roe, 2003).

While the community directed the project, the exhibit represents the work of many people over a four-year period. The project was initially conceived of and designed by the Chief of the Doig River First Nation at the time, Chief Garry Oker; a small group of elders; and myself, an independent consulting folklorist. This group was quickly expanded so that the project brought together a broad segment of the Doig River First Nation community and included elders, community leaders (a series of three different Chiefs and Councilors elected by the Doig River First Nation over the course of the project), adults, and youth, along with community members consulted periodically because of their expertise and knowledge about specific cultural practices. In addition to myself and Kate Hennessy who served as co-curators and co-coordinators for the project other collaborators included a wide range of professionals, who each brought their own specialized set of skills to share with the project team. Collaborating professionals for the Dane Wajich exhibition included folklorist and heritage consultant Amber Ridington (doctoral candidate, Memorial University of Newfoundland); media anthropologist Dr. Kate Hennessy (now a professor, Simon Fraser University); linguistic anthropologists Dr. Patrick Moore (professor, University of British

Columbia) and Dr. Julia Miller (doctoral student, University of Washington); visual anthropologist Dr. Peter Biella (professor, San Francisco State University); cultural anthropologists Dr. Robin Ridington and Jillian Ridington (Dr. Ridington is professor emeritus at the University of British Columbia. He and his colleague and wife, Jillian Ridington, have long standing connections with the community); website designers from Unlimited Digital Communication; and acurriculum development team from the North Peace School District First Nations Resource Center, along with independent curriculum consultant Angela Wheelock. Each professional helped the community realize their priorities for youth and elder engagement, language and traditional culture documentation and vitalization, heritage preservation, skill development, capacity building, and self-representation.

The Dane Wajich exhibit was made possible by grants and financial support from a number of partners who endorsed the main Virtual Museum of Canada Partnership Fund application which I prepared on behalf of the Doig River First Nation. The project's financial partners included the Virtual Museum of Canada, an initiative of the department of Canadian Heritage (main project funder, and website publisher); the Doig River First Nation (which supported administration and elders council participation); the Volkswagen Foundation's Endangered Languages Program (which funded bilingual Dane-zaa/Beaver language translation and transcription of the video narratives); the North East Native Advancing Society (which supported youth training and work for video production); and the North Peace School District #60 First Nations Education Program (which coordinated and supported the preparation of accompanying teachers' resources according to the school district's curriculum mandate). Drawing on multiple sources of financial support, each with their own mandates for sponsorship, helped expand the scope of the project and helped to integrate more of the community's goals into the process of creating their public exhibition about their community.

The project developed organically from a relatively generalized "applied" approach. In hindsight it is clear that the project is aligned with collaborative, action oriented research models with goals of empowering the community to shape the research agenda and to choose their public representation. These methodologies include 1) participatory action research (PAR), 2) participatory video, 3) collaborative ethnography, and 4) post-colonial theory and discourse. Informally, aspects of each of these methodologies were combined so that the project fulfilled some of the community priorities for: youth skill development; culture and language vitalization; documentation of traditional use of Doig River First Nation lands, documentation of industrial impacts on Doig River First Nation lands; and the assertion of the Doig River First Nation's Treaty and Aboriginal rights.

Participatory Action Research (PAR) is a model in which researchers work to help solve social problems identified by the people being studied. Sol Tax coined the term in 1948 after working in this type of collaborative process with Meskwaki (also known as Fox Indians) in the US state of Iowa. PAR has been expanded and applied within many different disciplines since this time (Ervin, 2005: 222; Kindon, Pain and Kesby, 2007). The practice of participatory video was introduced by visual anthropologist and filmmaker Jean Rouch. Beginning his work in the 1940s in Africa, Rouch coined the term "cinema verite" and was one of the first ethnographers to give the camera to the people so they could choose what to document, to introduce the notion of "shared anthropology," and to utilize reflexive media practices including the subject's "feedback" during the production process (Henley, 2009, Hennessy, 2010: 165-170). Although Rouch's work was affected by the colonial climate he worked within, he set the stage for the contemporary praxis of collaborative/participatory filmmaking and multimedia exhibition (Henley, 2009: 357-58). Since the late 1970s collaborative ethnography has grown out of reflexive approaches to ethnographic fieldwork which shift the focus from the outside researcher's agenda to that of the informant or community being studied, and acknowledges the influence of the researcher to the fieldwork. This work has been nicely represented by Luke Eric Lassiter in his writings on the practice of collaborative ethnography (2001, 2005) as well as by the contributors to Denzin, Lincoln, and Tuhiwai Smith's edited book on critical and Indigenous methodologies (2008). These post-colonial approaches and practices have also been problematized and reported on by the contributors to the journal *Collaborative Anthropologies* (2008-current issue), among others.

Drawing on the methodological influences mentioned above, the production phase of the Dane Wajich project began with a number of planning meetings and storyboarding exercises that included the entire team and were recorded on video by Dane-zaa youth and their video production mentors. While the grant application had listed stories and songs as the main content for the exhibition the actual selection of stories and songs for the exhibition was left open so that the community could choose the exhibition material and the manner in which it is contextualized. Ongoing community review and revision of the storyboard, and drafts of the exhibit, was also an integral part of the process of production. For example, during post-production excerpts of the oral history videos were chosen for inclusion in the exhibit by the curators and exhibit drafts were shared with the community for feedback. Community review of content was accomplished by presenting the draft to the community using a LCD projector so that they could see the specific video clips, images, songs, and text selected for each web page. Interpretive text was read out loud as the community preferred this oral form of text review to editing written words on paper.

To one of the first planning meetings, Chief Oker brought a drum with a dreamer's drawing on it. Chief Oker explained that he did not know much about the history of the drum but that it had been cared for by his late grandfather, Albert Askoty, who had been an important songkeeper for the Doig River First Nation. Tommy Attachie, himself a songkeeper, recognized the drum immediately. Attachie proceeded to recount oral history which connected the drum and its drawing to Dane-zaa genealogy, to Dane-zaa experiences at particular places, and to Dane-zaa world view and disposition on reality (spirituality). He recounted that the drum had been made by the late Dreamer Gaayęą who passed away in 1923 at Gat Tah Kwâ̧ (Montney). He explained that Gaayęą had painted the drum skin with a map of the trail to heaven that Gaayęą had received during a dream. He said that Gaayęą had shared his vision on the drum so that Dane-zaa people could remember it and use it to guide them on their journey to the spirit world once they have died. The drum became a central symbol that guided the storyline and content that was eventually chosen for the exhibition project. It also became a metaphor for the vitalization of Dane-zaa culture through oral histories that connect Dane-zaa youth with the long line of Dane-zaa dreamers and their history on the land.

The next day, at a follow up storyboarding meeting, Tommy Attachie spoke in Dane-zaa Záágé? (The Dane-zaa/Beaver Language) and further connected Dreamer Gaayęą's drum to Dane-zaa history, memory, land use, and spirituality. He used these principles to direct his community to "tell them the important stories" and to direct the project team to document the video material you see throughout the Dane Wajich website. A video excerpt of Tommy Attachie speaking at the planning meeting has been incorporated into the exhibition and can be watched online. The video is accompanied by a bilingual transcription which scrolls beside the video as it plays. Community and academic linguists worked together to carefully translate and to transcribe this narrative told in the Dane-zaa language, as well as other narratives included in the exhibit, using Dane-zaa orthography. Below is an excerpt from the video transcription of the planning meeting:

02:58
Guu hǫ́hch'ii ?éh kenaahjíίh dé wawajich éh.
You should tell them about the things you can remember...
03:09
E gwene lhǫlaadeh watsę́? náághazhelé,
Generation after generation, growing and raising kids,
03:13
nahhagrandma anahhéhjii dǫ́h,
our grandmother told us,
03:16
jeh haak'e ghaseda,
how to live,
03:18
gwada?uu juuhdzenéh.
long ago and today...

04:08

Eh nahę daahkene elder ahlhe ję kénaahjííh,

And you elders, you remember things from back then,

04:12

ii juu gwekéh.

[tell them about] those things.

04:14

in the bush sadejiitl gwats'ę? juu,

And as we go all over into the bush,

04:18

jǫ de je héwǫ́hch'ii de guudaadawajii.

you tell them the important stories.

(Excerpt of Tommy Attachie speaking in 2005 at a Dane Wajich storyboarding meeting. Translated by Billy Attachie, Madeline Oker, and Eddie Apsassin, July 2006. Orthographic Dane-zaa transcript by Dr. Patrick Moore, Julia Colleen Miller, Billy Attachie, and Madeline Oker, July 2006. Available at: http://www.museevirtuel-virtualmuseum.ca/sgc-cms/expositions-exhibitions/danewajich/english/stories/video.php?action=fla/tommyatcomplex.)

Developing out of the initial storyboarding meetings, and during the summer of 2005, the project team visited eight "places" in Doig River territory so that elders could share their knowledge of important stories, songs, people, and experiences that connect Doig River First Nation people to these locations. Community members took this opportunity to describe their traditional relationship to the land and their contemporary concerns about the ecological effects that oil and gas industrialization has had on these places and the plants and animals on which Dane-zaa people have depended on for centuries.

The Places main page also fulfils community priorities for Dane-zaa language vitalization and public education by using Dane-zaa place names rather than the English place names that are used on government maps of the area. In addition it has an interactive aural element: an audio file of an elder saying the place name is activated as the user's mouse rolls over the place on the map. Clicking on any of the eight place names brings the viewer to a section for that place with multimedia displays about the place (video stories, audio songs, text, images). I invite readers to explore the Places main- and sub-pages on your own. You will see how the material has been contextualized through hyperlinks to multiple web-pages within the exhibit that give the navigator the opportunity to find biographies of individual speakers in the videos; to information about the project and its process of procuction; and to information about Doig River First Nation history and their broader Dane-zaa culture, language, and dreamer chronology.

The extensive process of community selection and review of exhibit content over a three-year period led to the community's increased awareness of their opportunity to speak to both local and global audiences through the medium of the Internet. Along with this opportunity for self-representation to a global audience, they realized that the Internet also opened up risks of digital duplication and distribution of the images, stories and songs that they included in the exhibit. With these new risks associated with digital mobility and transmission they chose to protect some of their heritage materials from unscrutinized use and to keep them for their community use only; in effect, to balance the goal of cultural sharing with that of protecting their digital cultural heritage materials.

The community review process also led to an important ongoing articulation of culturally based cultural property protocols for controlling access to and distribution of various types of digital cultural heritage—more mobile than traditional forms of tangible heritage. Through dealing with culturally sensitive materials, and through dealing with IP protocols for digital cultural materials like songs and images, the community—balancing open access with closed—developed protocols that are relevant to both insider/local traditional patterns of use and control as well as outsider/Western contemporary concepts of property. For the community, the process is equally as important as the product.

During the storyboarding and community review process, the community took the authoritative role in the selection of proposed content, including community review of drafts put together by the curators and website designers. We undertook reflection, dialogue, and the mediation of issues with all stakeholders, who gave direction to curators about what to change or edit. This process continued until the community was comfortable with the web exhibit.

I found that maintaining these open dialogue pathways was integral throughout the project, and that utilizing various forms of dialogue was essential—particularly those oriented to Dane-zaa customs, which avoid direct confrontation and rely on people without a vested interest in the outcome to convey information between people and groups with different opinions. For example, my colleague Kate Hennessy (the co-curator and co-coordinator for the project) and I utilized both group and individual discussions between various stakeholders in order to help mediate differences of opinion and misunderstandings as they arose during all of the production and post production stages of the ICH documentation and exhibition project.

In all of these ways, the Doig River community has used this public digital forum, with a global reach, for self-representation and social action. Through their use of new media, they have been able to offer alternatives to Western-biased master narratives about indigenous people and have been able to document the vitality of their culture and tradition within contemporary Canadian society. This project is an example of how the Doig River First Nation, like many other indigenous peoples and under-represented communities, are using digital online media as a form of social action to provide voice and agency though storytelling on the Internet.

References by Subject Area

1. Research Methodologies

Henley, Paul. 2009. The Adventure of the Real: Jean Rouch and the Craft of Ethnographic Cinema. Chicago and London: University of Chicago Press.

Kindon, Sara, Rachel Pain and Mike Kesby. 2007. Participatory Action Research Approaches and Methods: Connecting People, Participation and Place. New York: Routledge.

Lassiter, Luke E. 2005. The Chicago Guide to Collaborative Ethnography, Chicago Guides to Writing, Editing, and Publishing. Chicago: University of Chicago Press.

Rouch, Jean. 1981. La mise en scene de la realite et le point de vue documentaire sur l'imaginaire. In P. E. Gallet (ed.) Jean Rouch, une rétrospective. Paris: Ministère de relations exterieures/Centre National de Recherches Scientifigues.

Seeger, Anthony. 2008. Theories Forged in the Crucible of Action: The Joys, Dangers, and Potentials of Advocacy and Fieldwork. In Gregory Barz and Timothy J. Cooley (eds.) Shadows in the Field: New Perspectives for Fieldwork in Ethnomusicology. Second Edition, pp. 271-288. New York: Oxford University Press.

2. The Dane-zaa

Brody, Hugh. 1981. Maps and Dreams: Indians and the British Columbia Frontier. Vancouver: Douglas and McIntyre.

Doig River First Nation. 2004. Hadaa ka naadzet: The Dane-zaa Moose Hunt [Virtual Multimedia Exhibit]. Doig River First Nation; Canada's Digital Collection/Industry Canada. Currently offline. Previously available from http://www.moosehunt.doigriverfn.com, accessed December 11, 2006.

—. 2007. Dane Wajich—Dane-zaa Stories and Songs: Dreamers and the Land [Virtual Multimedia Exhibit]. Doig River First Nation; Virtual Museum of Canada. Available from http://www.museevirtuel-virtualmuseum.ca/sgc-cms/expositions-exhibitions/danewajich/, accessed December 10, 2011.

Hennessy, Kate. 2010. Repatriation, Digital Technology, and Culture in a Northern Athapaskan Community. PhD. Thesis, Anthropology, University of British Columbia, Vancouver.

Mills, Antonia C. 1982. The Beaver Indian Prophet Dance and Related Movements Among North American Indians. PhD. Thesis, Anthropology, Harvard University.

—. 1988. A Preliminary Investigation of Cases of Reincarnation among the Beaver and Gitksan Indians. Anthropologica 30 (1): 23 –59.

—. 2004. The Ghost Dance and Prophet Dance. In Shamanism: An Encyclopedia of World Beliefs, Practices, and Culture, ed. Maria Walter and Eva Friedman, pp. 287 – 292. Santa Barbara: ABC-CLIO Press.

Ridington, Amber. 2012. Continuity and Innovation in the Dane-zaa Dreamers' Song and Dance Tradition: A Forty-Year Perspective. In Anna Hoefnagels and BeverlyDiamond (eds.) Aboriginal Music in Contemporary Canada: Echoes and Exchanges, pp. 31 –60. Kingston: McGill-Queens University Press.

—. In Press. After Digital Repatriation: Reflecting on Collaborative Projects, Processes, and Products with a Northwestern Athapascan Community. Journal of American Folklore.

Ridington, Amber, and Kate Hennessy. 2008. Building Indigenous Agency Through Web-Based Exhibition: Dane-Wajich - Dane-zaa Stories and Songs: Dreamers and the Land. In J. Trant and D. Bearman (eds.) Museums and the Web 2008: Proceedings (CD-ROM), Toronto: Archives & Museum Informatics. Published March 31,

2008. Available from: http://www. archimuse. com/mw2008/papers/ridington/ridington. html, accessed January 12, 2012.

Ridington, Robin. 1978. Swan People: A Study of the Dunne-za Prophet Dance. Vol. No. 38, Mercury Series. Ottawa: National Museum of Man.

—. 1981. Beaver Indians. In June Helm (ed.) Handbook of North American Indians, Vol. 6: 350 – 360, Washington, DC: Smithsonian Institution.

—. 1988. Trail to Heaven: Knowledge and Narrative in a Northern Native Community. Vancouver: Douglas and McIntyre.

—. 1990. Little Bit Know Something: Stories in a Language of Anthropology. Iowa City: University of Iowa Press.

Ridington, Robin, and Jillian Ridington. 2003. Archiving Actualities: Sharing Authoritywith Dane-zaa First Nations. Comma: International Journal on Archives 2003. 1: 61 – 68.

—. 2006. When You Sing It Now Just Like New: First Nations Poetics Voices and Representations. Lincoln: University of Nebraska Press.

Ridington, Robin, Jillian Ridington and Doig River First Nation. 2003. The Ridington/Dane-zaa Digital Archive - Dane-zaa Archive Catalogue [Password-Secured Online Database]. Doig River First Nation. Available from http://fishability. biz/Doig, accessed January 12, 2012.

Ridington, Robin, Jillian Ridington and Elders of the Dane-zaa First Nations. 2013. Where Happiness Dwells: A History of the Dane-zaa First Nations. Vancouver: University of British Columbia Press.

Ridington, Robin, and J. Ridington, P. Moore, K. Hennessy and A. Ridington. 2011. Ethnopoetic Translation in Relation to Audio, Video, and New Media Representations. In Brian Swann (ed.) Born in the Blood: On Native American Translation, 211 – 241. Lincoln: University of Nebraska Press.

Roe, Steve. 2003. "If The Story Could Be Heard:" Colonial Discourse and the Surrender of Indian Reserve 172. BC Studies 138/139 (Summer/Autumn): 115 – 136.

Research on the Mode of Protecting the Inheritors of Intangible Cultural Heritage
—Take the Folk Story Tellers Sun Jiaxiang, Liu Depei and Liu Defang in Yichang, Hubei, China as An Example

Huang Yonglin[*]

Through the ages, asis pointed out by Feng Jicai, standing beside the numerous strategists, philosophers, statesmen, authors and artists who have been recorded in history, there are also a great number of anonymous but eminent folk culture inheritors from all ethnic groups who mastered the subtle techniques and cultural traditions created by their ancestors. They are a symbolic and consequential component of the great Chinese civilization. As the living storehouses of folk culture serving all Chinese ethnic groups, these eminent inheritors of folk culture are carrying both a cultural essence passed on from ancestors as well as the gift of creativity which expresses their individual character. Chinese folk-cultural heritage lives in the memory and techniques of these eminent inheritors. Since transmission from generation to generation is the most crucial mechanism enabling the advancement of culture and even civilization, inheritors are not only central to folk-cultural transmission over generations, but are also the likely force that brings the culture of the nation and the age to its historical apex.[②] The key to the preservation of intangible cultural heritage is the establishment and perfection of a sustainable mechanism of transmission that caters to the needs of an era grounded in the inner characteristics of heritage itself, enabling ICH (which is traditionally passed on by oral and face-to-face teaching) to be sustained even under modern conditions. The inheritors stand in the central place of this mechanism. Therefore, protection of inheritors is the highest priority in the preservation of intangible cultural heritage.

---

[*] Huang Yonglin, Vice president of Huazhong Normal University, Chairman of National Culture Research Center, President of China Society of New Literature, Vice President of China Society of Folklore.

[②] 中国民间文艺家协会编:《中国民间文化杰出传承人调查、认定、命名工作手册》,2005年8月印行,第11页。转引自刘锡诚著:《非物质文化遗产:理论与实践》,北京:学苑出版社2009年版,第140—141页。

1. Modes of Protecting the Inheritors of ICH

The Chinese government has paid significant attention to the protection of inheritors of intangible cultural heritage. In the political/official realm, inheritors are recognized and afforded both high social status and honorable reputations. From a financial perspective, inheritors are provided with a living allowance and support to encourage their work in cultural continuity and exploitation in order to advance preservation and inheritance. The three folk storytellers, Sun Jiaxiang (from Changyang Tujia Autonomous County, Yichang, Hubei), Liu Depei (from Wufeng Tujia Autonomous County, Yichang, Hubei) and Liu Defang (from Yiling District, Yichang, Hubei) are typical examples of inheritors of Chinese folk culture. Almost the same age and living in the same area of Yichang, Hubei, they are all peasants and excellent storytellers recognized at home and abroad.

Identification as a storyteller has to some extent changed their lives. However, modes of protection adopted by governments of different districts were not exactly the same. Sun Jiaxiang was protected in the static mode, maintaining a comfortable senior-citizen life in what amounted to near cultural segregation; Liu Depei was protected in active mode that emphasized process and continuity within his cultural ecology; and Liu Defang was protected in a productive mode, combining innovation with the development of a cultural industry.

1.1 The Static Mode of Protection

The static mode of protection involves prolonging the continuity of heritage and the lifespan of inheritors using a wide variety of protective measures, first by employing the rescue strategy of maintaining a consistent, complete, authentic and systematic record of intangible cultural heritage with the help of high-tech tools and scientific methodology. Through video, record, photograph and text and by means of images, books, internet, databases and digital multimedia, complete files that maintain an authentic record of heritage are established for convenient, widely-available use. In this way, the static mode of protection facilitates the sharing of information and advances the study, research, continuation, and the development and promotion of heritage.

The static mode has the following two primary purposes:

1.1.1 Prolonging the Continuation of Heritage and Inheritor Lifespan

The most-striking feature of intangible cultural heritage—its continuation over generations through the activity of transmission — "passing on" —from individual-to-individual or within a group—will disappear once the individual or group ends transmission activities. Under the weight of modernization, much intangible cultural heritage is disappearing as time advances and traditions are not carried on after the death of inheritors. Inheritors sustain the life of intangible cultural heritage; their contributions are central to its rise or decline. Therefore, extending the lifespan of inheritors is part of the rescue-protection approach to ICH. Acting on this connection, China has paid great attention to providing special attention to eminent ICH inheritors who are advanced in years or seriously ill. Government at all levels has developed policies addressing the well-being of key inheritors, even resolving routine problems so that, freed of everyday concerns, they can focus on the transmission of intangible cultural heritage. Some governments have also established medical security systems for inheritors. Medical insurance is provided and regular physical examinations are arranged to address any disease early on, ensuring their ability to engage in heritage continuation and control, reducing risk of loss caused as a result of health factors.

1.1.2 Rescuing the Cultural Heritage of Inheritors

As important creators and carriers of intangible cultural heritage, inheritors possess knowledge and mastery of techniques that are more extensive and varied, more comprehensive, and more systematic than knowledge and skill exhibited by common people. They are not only living treasuries of intangible cultural heritage but also the bearers of its defining inter-generational transmission process.

Today, rescuing and preserving intangible cultural heritage as carried on by inheritors is the current focus of ICH efforts. *The Provisional Measure on the Identification and Administration of the Representative Inheritors of the National Intangible Cultural Heritage* (Promulgated by Decree No. 45 of the Ministry of Culture of the People's Republic of China on May 14, 2008) stipulates and specifies the protection and management of representative inheritors. Article 11 clearly states that "all institutions responsible for the protection of the national intangible cultural heritage should keep a complete record of presentation style, technique, and knowledge in the form of texts, photos, records, videos, and so on; using a plan, collect the representative works of inheritors and keep related files." In other words, the provision includes two requirements: The first is to keep a complete record of the manner of presentation, the technique, the knowledge and so on using multiple media; the second is to collect representative works of inheritors, archiving related examples together.

Measures taken to protect Sun Jiaxiang, the folktale teller in Changyang Tujia Autonomous County, were limited to the static mode. Born in Nov. 30th, 1919 (the 9th day of the tenth lunar month) in Dujiachong, Duzhenwan Town, Changyang Tujia Autonomous County, Sun Jiaxiang is a female peasant of Tujia nationality. Although she has never gone to school and literally lacks even an idea of how to write her own name she has, thanks to her outstanding intelligence, strong memory, optimistic character and her persistent resistance to what might seem to be her "fate," developed her unusual storytelling ability in the special environment of Dujiachong, Duzhenwan, Changyang.① Capable of performing more than 600 stories, Sun is the first female storyteller of Tujia who has been nationally recognized as an Eminent Inheritor of Chinese Folk Culture, and as the "representative inheritor" in the third group of national ICH. In 1998, Changjiang Literature and Art Press published her story collection, *Sun Jiaxiang Stories*; Media like *People's Daily*, *Guangming Daily* and Xinhua News Agency have given her life and storytelling special coverage.

Folk stories narrated orally by Sun are complete in structure, plain and smooth in language, intricate and catchy in plot and profound in meaning; they exhibit a fascinating artistic charm and distinctive show-and-tell style of narration, reflecting Sun's extensive interest in folk art as well as her great ability in handling folk expression. Most of her stories are fairy tales which, in the imaginary world of art, exhibit a strong local Tujia flavor, which emphasizes an optimistic and positive spirit. As is pointed out by Professor Liu Shouhua, a famous Chinese expert on folk story research, most of the stories by Sun, instead of being local, are representative of type widely popular at home and even abroad. The ability to narrate so many outstanding stories from the treasury of folk stories at home and around the world is an important indicator of Sun's eminence as a storyteller.②

Before becoming a storyteller, Sun had always lived in Duzhenwan. Whether at work or during leisure time, wherever she went Sun told stories. Unlike others, Sun was, "willing to tell stories as long as there were listeners." The more people listened attentively, the better and the more excitedly she told a story. Because of her poor living conditions, challenging economic situation, advanced years and stomach and eye disease, once Sun was certified as a master of storytelling the government took special care of her, providing good living conditions and medical care, removed all of her worries in life. Through care delivered by government at all levels, Sun was relocated from remote and poor Dujiachong to Duzhenwan Welfare House in Oct. 21st, 2003. Since then, all Sun's living expenses have been taken care of by the government; the first senior peasant in the county to be treated this way.

On March 16th, 2005, the local government moved the 86-year-old Sun for the second time, from Duzhenwan Town to the First Welfare House in the county, where Sun could be better cared for. At the same time, the local government set up a Relief Fund for the Aged Inheritors of Folk Culture, which provided financial aid. (The former Secretary of Hubei provincial Party committee Yu Zhengsheng regularly inquired about the well-being of aged inheritors of folk culture and donated money to the Fund.)③ The government of Changyang County made this effort to create a comfortable

---

① 林继富:《土家村寨盛产故事能手 都镇湾民间故事多广奇趣》,《中国文化报》2010年9月2日。
② 刘守华:《土家族故事讲述家孙家香故事集序》,《土家族故事讲述家孙家香故事集》,萧国松整理,武汉:长江文艺出版社1998年版,第7页。
③ 林继富:《宜昌民间故事家孙家香》,宁夏人民出版社2009年1月版,第77—80页。

and happy environment for Sun's remaining years so that she could carry on her storytelling inheritance.

However, having left her hometown, Sun now spent time with widows and physically-disabled aged people every day; she lost both her usual audience and its surrounding, lively, conversational storytelling scene. She told stories much less; lively and natural tales gradually disappeared. Beginning in 1997, Professor Lin Jifu, a scholar of the transmission of folk stories, conducted follow-up research on Sun's situation. For comparative purposes, Lin collected hundreds of stories told by Sun in different periods and found that after leaving her hometown setting and her neighborhood circle, stories with local flavor gradually disappeared, as did her exciting storytelling style. [1]

Because of its oral character, intangible cultural heritage relies on people for its very existence. It is an especially vulnerable part of living culture and tradition because it is presented in the form of sound, images and techniques and maintained through physical or oral mechanisms of transmission within its "cultural chain." Human transmission turns out to be especially crucial to moving-forward ICH. For this reason, the static mode of protection remains very necessary—prolonging the lives of inheritors while, at the same time, recording and indexing their manner of presentation, their techniques and knowledge of heritage, using books, disks or databases, and thoughtful organization within a library or archive.

However, this static mode of protection is also far from sufficient. Active measures should also be taken to sustain heritage and assist inheritors in transmitting it to the next generation. As the saying goes, "the fish can only live in flowing water." The transformation of Sun's storytelling process after she entered the welfare house shows us the importance of retaining "cultural ecology," supporting a relatively-stable, original cultural environment for inheritors and heritage so they can continue to present and transmit under nurturing conditions. Since much intangible cultural heritage is addressed within a group or community, emphasis should be placed on the maintenance of the community environment instead of separating inheritors from community cultural ecology. In fact, the best way to protect the inheritors is to leave them in their specific, familiar environment. Only then can intangible cultural heritage maintain its original form, carrying on tradition, avoiding extinction.

1.2 The Active Mode of Protection

"The attempt to keeping folk literature in a permanent, unchanging natural state is doomed from the start," said a famous Finnish scholar; "it is not the talking or singing performance of folk literature but the record of the performance that could be abused or should be preserved…The symbol

---

[1] 林继富:《民间叙述传统与故事传承》,北京:中国社会科学出版社2007年版,第70—128页。

of 'the second chance of life' for folk literature is that people want to make use of it…Perhaps it can be said that only folk literature saved as documents can be protected efficiently. As for living folk literature, the theme and the thought that exist in the heart of inheritors and that are presented in a wide diversity of ways cannot be directly protected since they exist, change, and wither with personal social life, with its manner of presentation uncontrollable from the outside world."① Thus, intangible cultural heritage should be protected in an active way, and protecting the ecological environment surrounding cultural transmission is critical. Special attention should be paid to the needs of cultural ecology when protecting inheritors of intangible cultural heritage, so they can carry forward heritage within a nurturing cultural environment.

Common people who are identified as craftsmen, great storytellers or great folksingers must be knowledgeable, well-respected and should spread happiness and knowledge around. They must assume leadership roles and take an active part in cultural activities of the group (an ethnic group, community or a village), promoting the transmission, the popularization and the continuation of intangible cultural heritage among the ethnic group, the community or the village. They should be active in this spare-time cultural role, enhancing their own mental health and values, contributing to the stability and harmony of the ethnic group, the community or the village. To insure these functions, the government should, when assuming the responsibility for protecting inheritors of intangible cultural heritage (apart from providing a favorable material condition for inheritors), enable inheritors to carry inheritance forward within its original cultural ecology.

Liu Depei, another storyteller, was protected in this kind of active mode by the government of Wufeng Tujia Autonomous County, Yichang. Male, born in 1912 in Pearl Mountain Village, Bailu Village, Wufeng Tujia Autonomous County, Hubei, Liu Depei enjoyed a life of rich experience. He attended an old-style private school for two years, worked as a long-term laborer, a short-term laborer, a porter, a postman, an apprentice in a vegetarian restaurant, a tile-collector, a peasant in the busy work season and an actor of shadow puppetry in a theatrical troupe. He learned fortune telling and medical diagnoses; he was invited to be the guest manager or general manager whenever there were weddings, funerals or meetings of all sizes in the village. His footprints could be traced across counties in western Hubei such as Wufeng, Songzi, Yidu, Changyang, Zhijiang, Zigui, Hefeng, he maintained extensive contact with all kinds of people from the bottom of society. Maintaining a repertory of 512 amusing stories, more than 1000 folk songs, over 2000 common sayings, over 800 riddles, Liu had told stories and jokes since childhood as his way of entertaining others as well as himself. Regularly published by Shanghai Literature and Art Press since 1989, the 480-thousand-word collection *New Funny Stories* is Liu's masterpiece. More than 400 pieces of folk art he inherited were published or quoted by over 20

---

① 刘守华:《故事村与民间故事保护》,《民间文化论坛》2006 年第 5 期。

newspapers, presses and university liberal arts textbooks. Subjects of stories by Liu Depei range from the creation of the world to modern society, and offer vivid representations of all kinds of people, skillful narration, and the use of both speaking and singing in plain, yet subtle and infectious, language. In 1982, his orally-narrated story "Du Laoyao" was selected as a story in the collection of folk stories *Du Laoyao* published by Changjiang Literature and Art Press.

In September, 1983, he was recognized as member of the Hubei provincial chapter of the China Society for the Study of Folk Literature and Art. In December of the same year, he was awarded the title "A Folk Story Narrator" by the Hubei Provincial Mass Art Gallery and Hubei Society of Nationalities. He occupied the first position on the list of China awarded Top Ten Folk Story Narrators by UNESCO. He was also the first folk story narrator in the country included on the list of candidates for the first China Shanhua Award for folk Literature and Art. In the company of literary giants Zhong Jingwen and Jia Zhi, Liu finally won the award.

The government of Wufeng Tujia Autonomous County took excellent care of the eminent local story narrator Liu Depei; a series of protective measures of protections were put in place both before and after Liu's death. Once he was named the "Hubei Folk Story Narrator" in 1984, the county government decided to take special care of him during his remaining years. It offered Liu Depei an allowance every month, and later, processed grains. Personnel representing county or village government called on him to convey greetings every holiday; the civil affairs department sent him cotton coats and quilts in winter to keep out the cold; the people's insurance company of the county offered accident and medical insurance coverage for him until he passed away. In addition, the county government allocated a special fund for the publication of Liu's story collection and his material collection, for the establishment of a Liu Depei research association and for the construction of an archive for Liu Depei, which preserved and displayed more than 10 thousand items in text, record or video form.

Although provided with an allowance, commercial sources of food, as well as care in all aspects of life from 1984 forward, Liu Depei never left his hometown, the Pearl Mountain of Bailu Village; he played an active role in the neighborhood, transmitting his inheritance of folk stories until he passed away. Beginning in 1938, the year of his initial rise to fame, until 2000, the year of his death, Liu's life as a transmitter lasted 62 years. As recalled by his widow, Mrs. Mei Zuyou, who had spent 48 years of marriage with Liu Depei, "when the villagers are doing agricultural work on the land, he told stories there. He also told stories while walking to anybody he met on the way; these people today; those people tomorrow, as long as there was audience. He told stories at weddings and funerals and when picking tiles to stop leaks for other households. His stories varied with the days and were never exhausted. If there was no one else, he told stories to his grandsons. If the grandsons were sleeping or out, he told the stories to me, no matter I was mowing grass, doing laundry or cooking. Later he was ill, but he insisted on telling funny stories as long as he was not seriously ill.① If he had not told stories for three days, that meant he was really, seriously ill."

I have observed the storytelling activities of Liu Depei several times and conducted special research tracking him, documenting on various occasions his reactions to different people and to varied responses from the audience. Through observation, it is clear in the course of folk storytelling that the interaction between the folk storyteller and the audience is very significant. Without audience participation storytelling is hard to accomplish, and even if it can be somehow carried out, the result is fragmentary and simplified, lacking embellishments added in the traditional version. The narrator will be influenced by the audience, by its gender, its size, facial expressions, by reactions and interruptions of the audience as well as by interactions and competition among narrators, all of which stimulate the emotions of the narrator, exerting influence on the choice of stories, the shaping of stories and the degree to which narrating skills are engaged.② Therefore, while we care about the life of inheritors, we should, more importantly, respect the inheritor's role in the continuity of tradition, and therefore protect the ecological environment supporting cultural continuation by enabling inheritors to live in their familiar environment, where they can interact with an audience.

Vital and people-oriented, intangible cultural heritage emphasizes the techniques, experience, and spirit that are human-centered and that exhibit a characteristic level of activity and fluidity. It is a style of production and life associated with national traits, as well as the active embodiment of national character and of China's national instinct for appreciating beauty. Therefore, for those inheritors of intangible cultural heritage in good health, instead of keeping them as if in a pen or a greenhouse, we should respect their commitment to the protection of the ecological environment surrounding cultural inheritance, allowing them to live in their home, where can interact with a familiar audience. Through an active approach to protection that returns inheritors to the natural state of cultural ecology, cultural inheritance can be carried on even in the larger, surrounding and ever-changing social/cultural environment, developing through continuation, continuing through development.

1.3　The Productive Mode of Protection

The productive mode of protection refers to protection that transforms intangible cultural heritage into cultural products by means of manufacture, distribution, and sale, while retaining authenticity, integrity and tradition at its core, while honoring the efficient transmission of intangible culture heritage as its priority.③ To inheritors, their most fundamental mission is to

---

① 王作栋：《他是一座珍珠山——追忆五峰民间故事家刘德培》,《湖北日报》2003 年 12 月 5 日。
② 黄永林：《从信息论看民间故事的讲述活动》,《中国民间文化》1991 年第 4 集。
③ 黄永林：《非物质文化遗产　生产是最好的保护》,《光明日报》2011 年 10 月 7 日。

continue tradition, preserve household disciplines, and inherit cultural property from previous generations. However, even if it is especially protected, a cultural phenomenon that loses vitality has poor prospects for the future. Produced and embraced in a specific natural or socio-cultural environment, intangible cultural heritage is either inherited or extinguished as a result of environmental change. Much intangible cultural heritage is endangered or has died out either because of its failure to adapt to changes in the natural or socio-cultural environment, or because of the disappearance of certain socio-cultural environment on which it has depended.

Objectively speaking, intangible cultural heritage is always changing and developing even as it is passed forward. Since we are neither able to turn back modern life nor preserve in great scale the original context for intangible cultural heritage, the "original state" we seek for most intangible cultural heritage is not necessarily an original state in a literal sense. Instead, it is what we recognize to be original from the perspective of an historical overview.

It is important to observe that it is not the socio-cultural environment that must adapt itself to our inheritance of intangible cultural heritage, but intangible cultural heritage that should, if it is to continue, adapt to the ever-changing social cultural environment. A rigid state of protection—unrealistic and not in accord with basic rules of evolution and culture—is merely an ideal; instead, cultural innovation can represent a realistic and comprehensive approach to protecting intangible cultural heritage. Truly eminent intangible cultural inheritors are those who are able to make cultural choices and accept cultural innovation while inheriting a tradition. Such individuals make extraordinary contributions to inheritance, protection, continuation and the development of intangible cultural heritage.

Taking account of the characteristics defining any era (including those related to working conditions and psychological needs of the public), while maintaining respect for the value and meaning of the traditional culture, inheritors should actively promote development within the pathway of traditional culture in order to demonstrate the underlying spiritual vitality of intangible cultural heritage and its ability to grow in modern society. In addition to salvage, support and protection provided endangered items, serious effort should be made to encourage productive protection—the reasonable utilization of representative items and the exploitation of those cultural products and cultural items that possess both distinctive local and national features and market potential. Such a productive mode of protection appears as a promising direction, because if intangible cultural heritage is transformed into products through production, traditions can exert a positive social influence and bring considerable economic benefit, both of which gives heritage a vital relevance that leads to further development.

Born and raised in rural areas, folk artists deeply rooted in the countryside have directly absorbed artistic nutrition from rural life; they maintain a natural bond with peasants and play a central connecting role in the inheritance of folk culture. In the cultural construction of a "new countryside," it is important that folk artists exert positive, active influence in rural cultural life and in the process of carrying on and communicating national folk culture in order to stimulate the cultural vitality of the countryside itself. ①

Protection provided to famous folk story narrator Liu Defang by the government of Yiling District, Yichang, Hubei, illustrates the productive mode of protection. Born in 1938 to a landowning family in Tanjiaping Village, Xiabaoping Township, Yiling District, Yichang, Liu Defang became obsessed with storytelling after only two years of schooling. As an adult, when he left his hometown to work in the construction of river embankments and railways, Liu connected with people from diverse places and listened to their stories. Thanks to his extraordinary memory and expressive talents, Liu can vividly retell all these stories—even those he heard only one time. In total he can recount 400 stories and sing dozens of folksongs; he has memorized about 10 million words of folk stories, lyrics of folksongs, libretti of shadow plays, and messages of condolence. In recent years, related agencies in Yichang have synthesized and published for Liu Defang, in succession, the folk story collection *Yeshan Xiaolin*, the folksong collection *Lang A Jie*, the long biography *Adventure Life*, and the DVD *The Joke House of Liu Defang*. Utilizing a great number of ancient and modern folk stories combined with his unique creativity, Liu Defang tells funny and vivid tales exhibiting both rich content and fascinating artistry, —presentations worthy of academic research from the perspective of folk literature, linguistics, sociology, ethics, folklore, and aesthetics that have drawn significant attention from both the academic field and media. Liu Defang was awarded the title "China Folk Art Narrator" by the China Society of Folk Literature and Art on December 8th, 2004 and, "China Eminent Inheritor of Folk Art" by the China Association of Literature and Art and China Society of Folk Artists in June, 2007.

Under the care of local government and armed with a great reputation, Liu Defang then began to actively expand his activities. He was relocated from the forested area in Xiabaoping to Yiling urban district, offered a job in the cultural center, housed in a suite with three living rooms financed by a local private entrepreneur, with his living and medical expense and a special allocation for the publication of his monographs and tapes covered by the district budget. To fully develop his potential, the local government established the "Liu Defang Folk Art Troupe," which carries out commercial performances of folk literature for tourists visiting the Three Gorges area. Currently, the Liu Defang group is engaged in diverse performances, which includes telling stories for tourists in such scenic spots as Chexi and Xiaofeng Ancient Soldiers Villages.

Liu is also dedicated to the cultivation and maintenance of peasant culture; more than 20 apprentices from Xiabaoping Township ranging from 56 to less than 30 years of age enrolled to constitute a new generation of inheritors. Apart from the narration of traditional folk stories, Liu

---

① 黄永林《充分发挥传统民间文化在新农村文化建设中的作用》,《光明日报》2006 年 5 月 15 日。

also composes many new stories based on the essential elements he absorbs from folk stories from diverse places. It is for the great contribution he has made to the preservation and development of folk literature by receiving, storing, transmitting and developing the narrated works of predecessors that he is recognized by experts as "the most vital folk story narrator and folk artist in the Three Gorges area". ①

Liu Defang, recognized as a representative inheritor of intangible cultural heritage by the government, treated with special material and spiritual support, relocated from his home town, Xiabaoping Township, the rural area where his stories are transmitted and inherited for the urban area, experienced a transition from an oppressed and painfully-struggling class to the spotlight glare of government and the public. Through such change he is being directly influenced, and his storytelling altered, by this reconfiguration of personal identity, of his life context, his lifestyle, and his thoughts and values. ② As a result of the peculiar local environment in Xiabaoping Township, Yiling District, Yichang, Hubei, in Liu's former home—a typical mountain area of complicated topography, featuring numerous mountains, inconvenient transportation and spotty communication—storytelling was the primary source of cultural entertainment for local people during leisure time. It was in such a village with this tradition of storytelling that Liu Defang grew to be a distinguished narrator. After he was relocated by the concerned government of Yiling District to Xiaoxita, —a newly-developed little town and close suburb of Yichang—great changes took place in Liu Defang's environment, performance style, and the content of narration. Reconfiguring the village atmosphere surrounding narration into an environment in which people seated in a circle take an active role in amusing interactions, new circumstances for the most part required presentation that is entertaining as an artistic performance, suitable for the critical scrutiny of leaders and scholars, and sometimes catering to tourists visiting scenic spots. In such a place Liu is more engaged in promoting folk stories to the market through commercial operations—narration for some kind of benefit or reward.

I appears that, while a focus on tradition is a priority for inheritors of intangible cultural heritage, efforts can be made to promote logical and gradual development; productive exploitation and utilization can be implemented in accord with specific situations. However, if we blindly push intangible cultural heritage to the market regardless of its characteristics, we will likely at the same time be tearing asunder our original tradition. Such action will undoubtedly degrade its essence, actually accelerating the extinction of valuable heritage.

Consider the protection of heritage by exploiting it as a component of tourism that, in recent

---

① 刘守华:《长江三峡民间故事家刘德方传讲故事集野山笑林序》,《长江三峡民间故事家刘德方传讲故事集野山笑林》,余贵富采录,黄世堂整理,北京:大众文艺出版社1999年版,第4页。
② 王丹:《从乡村到城市的文化转型——刘德方进城前后故事讲述变化研究》,《民族文学研究》2009年第2期。

years, has become common in many parts of China. This transformation of numerous forms of national folk art performance into tourist attractions or products brings about both significant social effects and economic benefits. However, because the true nature of intangible cultural heritage is rather complicated, only certain specific heritage items are suitable for this kind of productive protection. The situation demands clear delineation of appropriate traditions and, in addition, careful monitoring to avoid commercialization or industrialization that "changes the original flavor" in an attempt to satisfy markets.

Consider folksong artists as an example. All the good folksingers who had been found with great effort by culture workers and whose original representation of songs and vocal styles had been recorded eventually began to perform in tourist areas. Over the years, as these artistic forms were widely disbursed, they became alienated from their real origins. But blind projection of insufficiently-protected heritage into market conditions for exploitation is no different than breaking tradition into pieces, an outcome that contradicts the original intent of protection. Therefore, intangible cultural heritage should be securely protected in a "right direction," exploited only in accordance with principles of *Law of the People's Republic of China on Intangible Cultural Heritage*, engaged on the basis of authenticity, integrity and continuity, actively promoted to contribute to society and serve the citizens of today.

2. Thinking about the Protection of the Inheritors of Intangible Cultural Heritage

Through an analysis of the three modes of protection as applied to three folk story narrators, we have acquired fundamental experience that enable the development of rules for strengthening the protection of the inheritors of intangible cultural heritage.

2.1 The key to the protection of inheritors—nurture the active functioning of different types of protectors

The various sectors that provide protection for cultural inheritance are primarily government at all levels, the academic community, news media, social groups, and businessmen. In protecting our three folk story narrators in Yichang, both governmental and non-governmental actors have played important roles. Attention by the government and the application of its executive power has brought folk story narrators into the spotlight, transforming them from common peasants into well-respected, subsidized cultural celebrities. Intervention by experts and scholars recognizing storytellers as inheritors has changed their lives; publicity by news media has accelerated their ascent as story narrators while enhancing their influence; major support from social groups and businessmen have elevated their social status and improved the care they receive in financial matters. This complex pattern indicates that protection for inheritors of intangible cultural heritage can be implemented effectively only when government at all levels, the academic sphere, news media, social groups and businessmen all play an attentive role, providing active support, warm encouragement and sincere promotion applying their multiple strengths in administration, scholarship, finance and public opinion.

2.2 The foundation of inheritor protection—caring for the health and life of the inheritors

As to the protection of intangible cultural heritage, it is critical to protect the inheritor, especially the key inheritors, who are not only the "objects of action" of protectors, but are themselves also key actors in protecting intangible cultural heritage. Government, business, scholarship, and media bring power and influence to preservation, but none of them can substitute for the inheritor as the one entity that actually carries inheritance forward. Therefore protectors, when offering protection, should give priority to the protection of inheritors themselves, taking active care of their life and health to ensure their wellbeing, prolong their lifespan and thereby extend the lifespan of cultural continuity.

Significant government attention at all levels to the life of inheritors is embodied in the case of Sun Jiaxiang, for whom the government of Changyang County provides overall support, sending her to the No. 1 Welfare House of the county, providing favorable living and health-care situations. The case of Liu Depei is similar; the government of Wufeng County provided special care by subsidizing him every month, offering commercially-produced food and purchasing his accident and medical insurance. In the case of Liu Defang, the government of Yiling District adopted special measures such as bringing him from a remote mountain village to the city, offering a culture-center job and accommodations, while including his living and medical expenses as part of an overall subsidy. Through these strategies, the primary and fundamental effort in protecting key inheritors that emerges is an effort to provide care and support for life and health, enabling them to leave life worries behind.

2.3 The key to the protection of inheritors—adapting different modes based on the situations of the inheritors

In the analysis of protection measures affecting Sun Jiaxiang, Liu Depei and Liu Defang—the folk story narrators in Yichang, Hubei—I have described three modes of protection of key inheritors of intangible cultural heritage against a backdrop of a modern society and economy: the static mode, the active mode and the productive mode of protection, each of which may be suitable for the protection of different types of inheritors in different situations.

First, the static mode of protection helps prolong the cultural lifespan of inheritors who are aged and weak.

For those inheritors who are solitary in old age, living in poverty and poor in health, it is good to prolong their physical and cultural lifespan by providing comfortable senior years, improving their living situation and medical condition, offering subsidies and sending them to a welfare house. However, the resulting static mode that keeps inheritors as if in a pen or greenhouse is likely to induce a withering of artistic life, because isolation separates cultural tradition from the natural home of intangible cultural heritage and from the cultural ecology that sustains inheritance, a situation that is likely to drain cultural life of future inheritors. Despite its well-intended effort to take better care of an inheritor, what the Changyang government has actually done by relocating Sun Jiaxiang from a remote mountain village to the welfare house in an urban area is to deprive Sun of situations in which villagers seated in a circle told stories one after another. Instead, she now tells shorter and shorter stories that no longer include scenes of passionate narration. Therefore, such an "encircled" application of the static mode may be suitable and effective in the protecting inheritors as aged and weak as Sun Jiaxiang, but is not applicable to the situation of hundreds of healthy, active inheritors.

Second, the active mode of protection helps protect cultural ecology for the inheritors that are healthy.

As is pointed out by Thompson, we relate the actions of a person to his life history and the history of social situations with which he is engaged. The narration of personal life is part of a group of related narratives that together constitute the story of a group of people who derive their status within their community.① The talent and creativity of each inheritor of intangible cultural heritage are closely related to the social situations and the community in which they live, thus representing a certain synthesizing and generalizing of mass wisdom and aesthetic value. Transmitted through face-to-face interaction, intangible cultural heritage can only be completely preserved and carried on when it is protected in an active mode. Actions taken by Wufeng County for Liu Depei stand in contrast to the experience of Sun Jiaxiang. Instead of taking him away from his original country life, he was kept in a specific, familiar environment, where he could carry on his inheritance within its original cultural ecology.

In addition, when carried forward and preserved by inheritors, community culture in the form of daily life activities provides an important source of story material. Also, traditional ethics, values and moral principles of the community energize the aesthetic principle within the story world of inheritors even as the folk-custom and natural environment of the community form the cultural

---

① [英] 保尔·汤普逊：《过去的声音——口述史》. 沈阳：辽宁教育出版社 2000 年 3 月版.

background for narrating performance.① Therefore, the active mode of protection is the most appropriate and beneficial way of protecting those inheritors who are physically healthy.

Third, the productive mode of protection helps develop the cultural brand of inheritors who are healthy and active.

As stated in Article Two of *the Convention for the Safeguarding of the Intangible Cultural Heritage*, " this intangible cultural heritage, transmitted from generation to generation, is constantly recreated by communities and groups in response to their environment, their interaction with nature and their history, and provides them with a sense of identity and continuity, thus promoting respect for cultural diversity and human creativity." Currently, as we improve the living conditions and the social status of inheritors of intangible cultural heritage, it becomes more important to develop both their spirit of innovation and their innovative impact and, through productive measures of protection, turn intangible cultural heritage into resources of production that exhibit economic impact. Unlike Liu Depei and Sun Jiaxiang, Liu Defang was enabled to take on additional activities after he became famous. To fully develop the potential of this folk artist, the "Liu Defang Folk Art Troupe" was established to offer commercial performances of folk art in the Three Gorges tourist area. Such a productive mode of protection provides an opportunity for social expression by inheritors, expanding their societal influence and enlarging the social space for cultural inheritance so that the transmission and preservation of intangible cultural heritage can be integrated into the larger society and into priorities of the current age. Whether through public performance or storytelling, participation in large-scale cultural events integrates inherited cultural art into traditional festival activities, public cultural activities, and tourism, conveying both social standing and economic impact.

Fourth, the emerging emphasis in protection of inheritors is from the static mode toward the active mode and to the productive mode.

Putting great emphasis on the protection, transmission and development of intangible cultural heritage, the Chinese government has given significant support to activities advancing the continuation and transmission of representative intangible cultural heritage sustained by representative inheritors. Article 30 of *Law of the People's Republic of China on Intangible Cultural Heritage* stipulates that departments in charge of culture within people's governments above the county level shall, based specific needs, adopt the following measures to support the representative inheritors of representative items of intangible cultural heritage in carrying out the inheritance and spread of intangible cultural heritage. (1) Provide requisite inheritance premises; (2) Provide necessary funding to support the representative inheritors to carry out activities such as teaching,

---

① 林继富:《传承人保护策略研究——以湖北省民间故事传承人保护为例》,载文化部民族民间文艺发展中心编《中国非物质文化遗产保护研究》(下),北京师范大学出版社2007年版。

imparting skills or exchanges; (3) Sponsor representative inheritors to participate in charitable activities in the society; and (4) Support representative inheritors to carry out other measures on behalf of inheritance and dissemination of intangible cultural heritage.

Inheritors of intangible cultural heritage shoulder the sacred responsibility of statically storing the content of heritage, actively imparting oral technique, and productively pursuing some form of commercial exploitation and development. In the present situation, in order to protect endangered intangible cultural heritage, efforts should be made to locate and create markets for heritage items as the basis of rescue so that traditions themselves can recover the cost of their continual existence through market exploitation. This approach demands that we proceed along the road from static protection through active protection to productive production—an approach that means we no longer care *only* for the health and life of inheritors, but also nurture the cultural ecology of inheritors and, more importantly, make good use of the cultural brand of inheritors on behalf of the transmission and development of cultural industries. Of course, productive protection starts us down the road to marketization, a direction which suggests pursuit of maximum economic impact and certainly has its disadvantages. To counteract an excessive marketization of the protection of intangible cultural heritage that tends to push all heritage items onto the market, producing an arbitrary mischievous distortion of heritage items, we should both monitor and properly supervise markets in a timely fashion.

In a word, we should discuss the protection of inheritors of intangible cultural heritage on the basis of both the reality of China today and on the conclusions drawn from our experience in order to work out a new way to properly and effectively carry out truly meaningful and effective protection to inheritors of intangible cultural heritage.

(This paper is a themed report at the international academic seminar, "the Second Sino-American Intangible Cultural Heritage Forum: Case Study" held in Nashville, USA from 29th Apr. to 1st May, 2012.)

The Role of Archives in the Preservation of and Access to Intangible Cultural Heritage

Nicole Saylor[*]

When Jesse Walter Fewkes made the first field documentary recordings in 1890, he recognized that the newly invented Edison wax cylinder recording machine would allow ethnographers to bring people's songs and their stories back to the laboratory for study. That strong link between the study of intangible cultural heritage and the need for preservation and access to the resulting documentation continues more than a century later.

While intangible cultural heritage documentation can take many forms, this paper will focus on the preservation of and access to ethnographic documentation captured in real time. It is that kind of documentation that provides the foundation of the American Folklife Center (AFC) Archive at the Library of Congress (the national library of the US), home to more than three million photographs, manuscripts, audio recordings, and moving images. It consists of documentation of traditional culture from all around the world including the earliest field recordings made in the 1890s on wax cylinder through recordings made using digital technology. It is America's first national archive of traditional life, and one of the oldest and largest of such repositories in the world.

Today, archives devoted to intangible cultural heritage face enormous preservation challenges as formats deteriorate and a deluge of born-digital documentation is generated. At the same time, funding to pay for large-scale documentation projects becomes increasingly scarce. To meet today's challenges, intangible cultural heritage archives are working across disciplines and leveraging technology to find innovative solutions.

I would like to begin by discussing the origins of the AFC archives—the largest ICH archives in the country—and its placement within the Library of Congress—the largest library in the world—are worth brief explanation for what they reveal about the archive's values, resources, and specific challenges. The archives begin as the vision of Robert W. Gordon, who in 1928 was hired by the

---

[*] Nicole Saylor, Head of the American Folklife Center Archive.

Librarian of Congress to create a large collection of American folk music. It was the beginning of the Library's decades-long efforts to document and preserve American folksong, and it marks the first time the Library embarked on a mission to develop its own collection, in addition to the traditional work of acquiring published materials and archival collections created by others.

Jumping ahead to 1976, with the archive's origins firmly in folksong, the archive became part of the American Folklife Center. Congress established the American Folklife Center to recognize the importance of regional and ethnic cultures. It is not a coincidence that the center was established the same year as the American Revolution Bicentennial, which marked a shift away from the pluralism of American life and the beginning of an emphasis on the nation's diverse cultures. The mission is both preserving and presenting folklife, which means that along with the archives is a public programs arm of the center that creates concerts & lectures featuring traditional artists and ICH scholars, hosts field schools to teach ethnographic documentation techniques, and partners with tradition-bearers and scholars on a number of initiatives. The Center's focus on working directly with tradition-bearers to present & perpetuate traditional cultures is a collaborative approach also reflected in the archives.

Preservation: As intangible cultural heritage archives struggle to meet the preservation challenge, the AFC Archive is fortunate to be situated within the Library of Congress, a leader in digital preservation and audio-video conservation storage. The Library has made significant investments in facilities and systems to support a scalable and sustainable preservation program.

The Packard Campus for Audio-Visual Conservation is 75 miles west of Washington, DC. It's a state-of-the-art storage facility built into a large hillside. It holds 6.3 million collection items, among them many of our audio & video holdings. It also has a digital archive to preserve digital content at the petabyte (1 million gigabyte) level. Beyond basic preservation activities, the Archive is also partnering with the Library's Recorded Sound Section to experiment with emerging preservation techniques. A project planned for the coming year involves capturing sound from unplayable wax cylinders using digital technology that captures images of grooves and uses the images to reconstruct the sound.

On the Library's main campus we administer a digital archives of roughly a quarter of a million digital objects, including audio recordings from StoryCorps. To give you a sense of scale, from March 1, 2012 to April 1, 2013 we acquired 60,720 unique born-digital original objects. To give you a sense of some of our challenges, I will briefly discuss StoryCorps. StoryCorps provides people of all backgrounds and beliefs with the opportunity to record, share, and preserve their stories. Since 2003, StoryCorps has collected and archived more than 45,000 interviews with nearly 90,000 participants. Each conversation is recorded and is preserved at the American Folklife Center. In terms of digital item type, we receive largely manuscripts—202,274 so far, compared to 139,480 still images, 47,173 sound recordings, and a single moving image. Yet, when you look at the collection by size, it's the audio—16TB—that takes up the most space. Managing the manuscripts (10.48 GB), still images (397.74 GB) and the video (0.35 GB) is fairly inconsequential.

Documentation: Central to the AFC's mission is the initiation, encouragement, support, organization, and promotion of research, scholarship, and training in American intangible cultural heritage. AFC works with community members and fieldworkers across the United States to provide training and encourage documentation activities, creating a dialog between AFC and communities. Numerous documentation projects have been coordinated or supported by the Library dating back to the founding of the Archive of American Folk-Song in the Library's Music Division in 1928, the origins of what would become the AFC's archives.

The most recent effort, launched in 2010, provides a new approach to AFC's traditional documentation projects. The Occupational Folklore Project aims to capture a portrait of America's workforce at a time of economic transition through interviews with workers across the United States. (After obtaining a signed release, interviewers upload digital recorded oral history interviews to AFC's web-based storage and simultaneously submit information about the interview through an online cataloging tool.) This has allowed AFC to coordinate a national collecting project that is both cost-effective and labor-efficient. In turn, geographically dispersed fieldworkers are able to gain experience with oral history techniques and twenty-first-century digital archiving skills.

(Access: Whether providing in-person or digital access, balancing the need for access with necessary protections of indigenous cultural production and traditional knowledge require thoughtful, nuanced approaches. This creates interesting tensions when trying to meet the demands of digital scale. Still, some intangible cultural heritage archives are experimenting with the development of software and systems for the annotation, playback, and other functions associated with letting users more readily access and personalize ethnographic documentation.)

(With more than 75 years of combined experience, AFC reference staff's knowledge of the collections runs deep. The members of our reference staff have professional academic training in everything from ethnomusicology and American studies to library science, which makes them well positioned to provide in-depth assistance for those seeking information about the collections. [Finally, a responsibility to the communities documented informs our staff's approach to providing access to the materials in our collections.] If the fieldworker is the first archivist, perhaps the reference archivist is the last. Access is where the true value of an archives is on full display.)

Chinese "Kazakh Aqin Aytis" in Germany: The Intercultural Communication of an ICH Item

Xiaobing Wang-Riese[*]

During the "Deutsch-Chinesisches Jahr der Wissenschaft und Bildung" in 2009 to 2010, I participated in planning and organizing a research project entitled "Kazakh Aqin Aytis: Text, Performance and Ritual." Apart from several Central Asian ethnologists, most of the German scholars involved had neither an academic background in Kazakh literature, nor did they speak the Kazakh language. Our motivation for participating in this research project was twofold: one was to fill up a gap in German ethnology, since only very few institutions and scholars in Germany are concerned with Kazakh nomadic culture in Xinjiang Province, China. The other was to observe the cultural shock that would happen when the aytis, the treasure of the Kazakh culture which comes from the depth of Mount Tianshan, encounters scholars and ordinary people without any Kazakh cultural background who live in a German cultural environment. The activity consisted in two parts, in the first part two Kazakh aqin singers and several Chinese Kazakh scholars visited Germany in May, 2010 for 10 days, and the aqins performed aytis on different occasions. In the second part a group of German scholars visited Xinjiang in June, 2010 for 12 days and made an investigation on the aytis culture and the situation of its inheritance. The following research report is based on the first part of our activities and the data we collected at that time.

1. Aqin Aytis as Verbal Art

Aqin aytis is a form of folk performing art that originated in the Kazakh nation between the 15th

---

[*] Xiaobing Wang-Riese, Professor at the Institute of Chinese Intangible Cultural Heritage at Sun Yat-sen University.

and the 18th century. It is deeply rooted in the traditions of singing in varieties of folk rituals, for instance, the wedding and the funeral. In the Kazakh language, "aytis" has many meanings, including "search," "competition," "argument," "contest," "singing a round," and "antiphonal singing." Later its meaning was extended to included "the competition of wisdom by poetry." Aqin is the specific name for the aytis poets and singers. They are poets, rappers, singers, and musicians who can perform improvised songs and play accompanying music by themselves. Most of their melodies come from folk tunes, with a certain regional and tribal style and characteristics. When singing aytis, aqins usually appear in pairs, and compete with each other in verbal performance. ①

The difficulty of aqin aytis lies in improvisation. An outstanding aqin not only has an appealing singing voice and can play Dombra long-necked lute skillfully, but his most important ability is to improvise poetry. In order to stay on a high level, aqin singers pay much attention to accumulating their knowledge. As talented folk poets, they have an extraordinary ability to absorb and digest everything they see and hear. Later on, they convert this into poetry and sing it instantly. According to Nagman (b. 1979), one of the aqin singers who visited Germany, aqins must prepare in advance for months before participating in the "Competition Conference of Aytis" in the autonomous prefecture or in the autonomous region Xinjiang. Nagman was sometimes lost in thinking about the lyrics and had a strong feeling that he was growing old quickly for his hair was becoming thinner although he was still young. This shows that the improvisatory singing is very hard mental work, which demands an intensive concentration.

We can also say that aqin aytis is a typical performative verbal art which is called "situated behavior" following Richard Bauman. ② The situationality that is rooted in the traditional form of aytis is very obvious, especially in the folk aytis, which is often presented in weddings, funerals, births, and other festive occasions, and sometimes as a collective performance (i.e., a group of young men versus a group of young women). Among them, the wedding songs are classified under the category "sarən", a kind of song containing philosophical meanings and advices. Such wedding songs are also classified as "aw-ʤar". For the reason that every sentence ends with a clause "ʤar-ʤar," it is also called "ʤar-ʤar." The singers are in two groups: a group of girls who are friends of the bride and a group of boys who are friends of the groom. The melody is blue and soothing in which the girls express the bride's sadness of leaving her home while the boys are trying to comfort the bride. After the wedding ceremony, the farewell aytis is antiphonally sung by the bride sitting in the tent, accompanied by her sister-in-law, and girlfriends, while the young men sing outside the tent before the girl is about to come out. The girls continue to express the

---

① 新疆维吾尔自治区文化厅编《哈萨克族阿依特斯论文集》, 乌鲁木齐: 新疆人民出版社2010年版。
② Df. Richard Bauman, *Verbal Art as Performance*, Waveland Press, 1984.

feeling of regret to the farewell while the boys remind the bride that she is now married and will become a good housewife.

The essence of the situational performance, as Richard Bauman pointed out, is a mode of communication at the scene. It first occurs in the antiphonal singing between two singers, both of which ritually "attack" each other by a verbal competition back and forth. On the other hand, they will not forget the audience irrespective of how fierce the competition is. When the aytis starts, aqins are used to convert the "situation" and the "events" directly into verse. I will take the first antiphonal singing of Nagman and Jamyga (b. 1987) at the Humboldt University of Berlin as an example. It started with the male aqin singer, Nagman, who is eight years older than the female singer Jamyga. He sings,

> If a man does not support his nation, he should be ashamed
> If he does not fulfill the expectations of his nation, that is wrong
> Oh, white horse, bring me the muse
> I will be like rain falling over Berlin
> With my poems I have marched to Europe
> Like Grandpa Attyla
> The nation has raised scholars like Abay, Xohan and Khilx
> It is my nation called Kazakh
> It extends over wide regions such as the Altai, Tarbaghat and Yili
> I brought its greetings here
> Oh my friends, may holy light shine over you
> May all of us be embraced by happiness
> Let us go ahead in Berlin
> Like the golden steed of the Edigen tribe

Here he expresses the mood in which Jamyga and he came to Europe and staged their performance. They were burdened by the expectation of their nation, just as their ancestor "Grandpa Attyla" confronting Europeans in the past, hoping to live up to the expectations and turning their songs into "nourishing rain in Berlin." He also introduces the different tribes to which he and his partner belong and the common Kazakh nationality. He sends greetings to the foreign audience who sits in front of him and he encourages his companion to work hard. Then begins the first round of ridicule, teasing Jamyga for being sturdy and not able to wait to perform. This serves to introduce her to her stage appearance.

Certainly, the beginning of each performance would not be repetitive, and it would change in each situation to come. A few days later, we left Berlin and traveled to Bonn on the Rhine, where we held a colloquium on "Kazakh aqin aytis and Central Asian Verbal Traditions." In the evening, we invited the two aqins from Xinjiang to give a performance for the attending scholars. As with the previous performance, it started with the elder male singer Nagman. This time, he sang,

> In the name of Allah I begin to order my words
> We are young people who explore the future with poems
> My special thanks go to all of you
> Since you propagate our Kazakh aytis
> To begin with our history:
> We are descendents of Xiongnu and Turk people
> Following Oyrat we have been fighting for more than two hundred years
> Sometimes we were scared like wild deer fleeing from the hunter
> During the reign of Abilay Khan we recovered
> Flags fluttered in front of white tents
> Heroes like Kabanbay and Bogenbay led the army
> Who struck the Junggars
> Today we bring you greetings from this nation
> We are brave young people
> Repeating the words of elder generations
> Jamyga, may you have a successful aytis
> Allah lets us meet again
> For poetry I will do my best
> Be patient as usual
> Sing well on the Rhine River
> Perhaps we will never again have such a chance
> Now it's your turn Jamyga
> The beautiful girl who looks like a grandma's black soap
> hey yeah yeah yeah

The introductory sentence "to start combing the words in the name of Allah", and the concluding exclamation "hey yeah yeah yeah" are formulas which help the singer to organize his thinking and words. Other words are improvised and sung in versified form taking as their subject the specific situations. When facing scholars from different countries who attended the meeting and listened to his singing, he showed his gratefulness first and then narrated Kazakh history briefly in eight sentences without pause. Next, he introduced Jamyga and himself as descendants and representatives of their nation, and he encouraged his partner to sing well, reminding her of being patient since this might be the only opportunity to stand on that stage. In his last sentence he ridicules Jamyga again, turning the topic and drawing the audience's attention to her.

What would Jamyga respond? In Berlin, she sings,

> Oh my friend, we will enjoy whatever you say,
> May aytis stay with us forever
> What are our Kirgiz friends discussing?
> Perhaps they have reached a conclusion
> Since ancient times Kirgiz and Kazakh are one family
> How happy we are in our family!
> Look, this is Mambat,① a relative of Kazakh
> May he find a girl marrying into his family next summer
> Ah, we will take the kind people as our example
> And show them our culture
> Which motivates us to travel abroad
> Lucky circumstances arranged our meeting here all together
> Following your command I will sing.
> An aqin will never hesitate when challenged in a competition
> Since our blood is Kazakh and its origins are Turkish
> As I heard and read in history books
> We have owned aytis for several hundred years
> Due to many holy Kazakh sages of ancient times.
> To study our Kazakh aytis
> Foreign scholars joined us.
> I admire this country for its diligent mentality,
> And now my heart is filled with joy.
> After having taken a look at the history
> And having recited epics of other nations
> My poem will flow out like colorful silk
> I will dance beside the goddess of silk
> The girl's poem can make you drunk, like the wine from a mare's milk.
> Ah, all Berliners come now to listen.
> The lovely little girl will begin to sing.
> My hometown educated me to be a smart and capable girl,

---

① Mambat was a group member who teaches Kirgiz literature at the Xinjiang Normal University, Urumqi.

And I will not be defeated by your mocking words!
Your mother has cultivated you to be an honest man
Your mockery can only make me stronger
Like the badgers: the more you beat them, the stronger they get
People have let the two of us compete many times
We should go ahead to achieve our dreams
We are renowned aqins in Xinjiang
We have inherited the wonderful blood of the heroes

Ah, how happy we are!
The people are astonished by the wonderful aytis
Let our songs whirl over the heaven above the German capital
What more can we wish after having presented aytis in Berlin?

In her lyrics, Jamyga expressed her excitement and joy in the first place. In order to answer Nagman's words, she further describes the setting of the performance: "To study our Kazakh aytis/ Foreign scholars joined us." Since scholars from the Humboldt University, who are experts in Kirgiz language and culture, made up a large part of the audience, she praises the friendship between Kazakh and Kirgiz in her lyrics. She also played jokes on the people who talked with each other (for simultaneous translation) during the performance. Responding to Nagman's encouragement she sang, "Ah, all Berliners come now to listen...Let our songs whirl over the heaven above the German capital." She humorously boasts that she is a "lovely little girl," while actually she is a rather corpulent person, so as to make an interesting atmosphere, and claims that her "poem will flow out like colorful silk," "The girl's poem can make you drunk, like the wine from a mare's milk."

Improvisation does not only exist in the prologue, but continues through the entire performance. Aqins constantly incorporate events around them into their lyrics. For instance, Jamyga deliberately criticizes some listeners in asking, "What are they talking about?" In the antiphonal singing in the University of Bonn, she uses a similar rhetoric,

Ah, I am willing to sing until sunrise
The silent night, the silent world is awakened.
We are so satisfied with our relatives here
They have friendly and polite manners
But why are those elder brothers and sisters who accompany us
Whispering to each other all the time?
On such an occasion you should listen concentratedly

If no one takes care of the horse, how can it gallop for thousands of kilometers?
Hey yeah yeah yeah

When compared with Nagman, who is a genius at using allusions and has a excellent poetic style, Jamyga seems to be using plain words cast into ironic speech. For example, when Nagman likened her to a hunted badger, she replied with wit and humor:

Jamyga praises you, my kind brother!
You bear the expectation of our nation
You said that the badger can be caught in creeks
So as to show off your own talent
But a land like Germany has its strict and precise laws
Even if you do not grasp any of these rules
They not only protect badgers but also ants!
You have not yet learned the laws of this country
Anyway, Jamyga will be protected here.
If somebody wants to touch me, he must be careful so as not to be caught

The glamour of aytis as a performance of verbal art lies in constantly considering the partner and the audience, singing out the situation, and compiling witty words to mock the partner in order to amuse to audience. Since the communication is instantaneous, random, rather than programmed and prepared in advance, achieving positive interaction and communication between aqins and the audience are particularly needed. Otherwise, when aqins get no response, they may fall into a low mood that leads them to a great reduction of creativity and ability to improvise. Their art then becomes what Jamyga expresses thus, "If no one takes care of the horse, how can it gallop for thousands of kilometers?"

2. The Dilemma of Interaction

Interaction is the best condition when the audience and the performers come from the same language environment and are familiar with each other. While visiting Xinjiang, I was told by several aqins that some people try to arrange Xinjiang Kazakh aqins and aqins from Kazakhstan to join in singing contests which resulted in a relatively poor communication due to their different cultural backgrounds. We encountered the same situation in the county of Tekesi, Xinjiang

Province. When we visited a folklore park, the local public officials casually invited a few pairs of aqins to give a concert for us. Possibly the leading members of the county administration had made some requirements for them in advance, and since we were strangers to them, the aqins were quite reserved and performed routinely. The content was courtesy and failed to demonstrate the ability to improvise and to interact with the audience.

For aqins in the performance, a simple response by the audience such as cheers, applause and laughter is crucial. During the visit in Germany, two aqins performed four times respectively in Berlin (twice), Bonn, and Munich. The first was held at the Institute of Central Asia of the Humboldt University, Berlin. Occasional applause and laughter were a great inspiration for the two young singers because some scholars did understand the Kazakh language. However on the next day in the Chinese Culture Center, more than 20 Germans and German citizens of Chinese origin were present, most of who did not understand Kazakh. The audience listened seriously and silently out of respect towards the singers just as they appreciated classical European music with neither applause nor acclaim during the performance. That frustrated the singers who always need interaction with the audience to encourage themselves. We can see how Jamyga was complaining about the situation in her following words,

> Ah, with the support of the audience, aqins can be more creative
> We will never be tired while flying towards our dream kingdom
> Kazakh's wonderful aytis
> Was inherited for coming generations
> Five days have passed in Germany
> We are happy as flowers in full blossom.
> On the first day we had a big audience and they were happy,
> They knew to value aqin aytis
> On the second day there were about twenty Germans
> They did not understand and only shook their heads
> On the third day about ten scholars are here
> They want to examine our talent
> How will it be if it goes on like this?
> The number of people in the audience will be fewer than the aqins!
> Hey yeah yeah yeah

When communication begins to get difficult, aqins have to cheer up each other. The elder singer Nagman tries to comfort Jamyga while at the same time he thinks about how to please the strangers sitting and listening in the audience,

What kind of songs can match your favor?
With your presence my poems will be better
Look, Grandma Johansen is here
To enjoy the conference
With an inherited dombra in our hands
Poems will give us courage
We also have Dilmurat, Mambat, and Professor Wang
And someone called Bagdat, our true friend.
So many experts visit our concert
Don't worry that nobody listens to you
In my eyes the presence of this audience
Is more valuable than that of a thousand people
Hey yeah yeah yeah

This seems to convince Jamyga and she responds,

Ah, your younger sister will follow your advice
To sing humorous poems about you
Whoever has an elder brother need not worry
She need not worry about the future if her brother is present.
Those are true scholars listening to our songs
Where Kazakhs are present, aytis will never disappear
If the scholars study our aytis
The entire world will get to know the Kazakh nation

Ah, let the birds of ideas fly toward the sky
May my dear brother go ahead smoothly
Give a good example to the coming generation
It is said that you should do what you can
Kazakhs can bring humor into life
Nothing can be compared with the flying bird of inspiration
My brother, your brilliant achievements
Have begun to spread all over the world
German men are all bald-headed
Their DNA is different from that of Moslems

Ah, among young people in Xinjiang only you are bald-headed
Please give me a reasonable answer
If you say that you have thought too much for the people
That is only an excuse to hide your embarrassment
The reason why you have so few hairs
Probably lies in chemical materials
Probably because the few original hairs
Have disappeared under the touch of my sister-in-law

Hence, they started a quarrel on "baldness" to demonstrate their poetic creativity:

Nagman:
I am not an aqin who just wants to be famous
One with a good tongue will have competition
You have not yet yielded to me
In contrast you are quite interested in my head
You always say that my hair has disappeared under the touch of your sister-in-law
How absurd does such a gossip sound
If the touch of a woman can remove men's hair
Someday you will get your chance too
Jamyga, if you are like your sister-in-law
You will also make your husband bald-headed
Thinking about the world
There are many different heads
Some with big ears, some with fat noses, and some intelligent heads
And those nobody wants to see
Both hands being chained
Criminal heads
But my head
With few hairs
Has been used to make poetry for the people
It is an intelligent and valuable head!
Do you understand this
Jamyga, you little fool?

Jamyga:
Ah, don't talk such unreasonable things before foreigners
These seem not to be the words of my elder brother
To be able to overcome you
I have to find a bald head too
We belong to the Turkish alliance
The life of our nation is filled up with songs.
Hey yeah yeah yeah

Nagman:
Jamyga, may god bless you
You pretty and lovely girl!
I hope that you will be always besides me
Yet I still have not gotten rid of the troubles you caused me
We are children of the great Kazakh
Our mother has granted us the essence of songs
If you are a true aqin
Please pass on this tradition
We have a lot to learn in our lives
Make a good impression upon the people!
Let them experience Kazakh's colorful world.
Hey yeah yeah yeah

The two aqins amused themselves by improvising a sequence of verses that completed this wonderful duel. On the one hand, the success was due to their extraordinary performance; on the other hand, they were very outspoken that such difficulties were temporary. When they would return home, everything would be normal again. Therefore, they could not help filling the emotional void with memories and imaginations of their home while they were singing in Bonn,

Nagman:
You should play like a lively pony
Then your elder brother will be happy
To propagate Kazakh aytis
I got many blessings from my hometown
I know your temperament
You will continue to work hard for aytis

But I will not be angry because of your words
And will remain quiet as usual
Whatever you say
My heart remains open

Jamyga:
Ah, why should only you respect me?
It will be better if we respect each other
I enjoy the tender affection of my elder brother
A smile shines on your face.
We came to Europe
Due to Allah's blessing
Thus we work hard together
Calling Abilay's name when we climb onto a horse
Ah, elder brother you carry the expectation of our nation
May your great deeds will be spread and praised among Kazakhs
If you really get the relatives to be guest at our home
Sure, we can host them well
I am a generous girl of the Kerey tribe
I will never confess to being tired when hosting guests
There you will never find anything like pizza
Lambs and ponies are to be killed for you
You will see the kind faces of Kazakhs
Welcome, we will await you all

The two aqins, who visited Europe for the first time, had not only to face the plight of a totally foreign language, but also to deal with all sorts of "culture shock." Jamyga incorporated these into the poetry in a ridiculous tone. For example, in her eyes, Germans always have earnest faces and are not joyful at all. They always treat them with pizza, hamburgers and raw vegetables (salad). What's more, they are always made to walk without the courtesy of a car. This, she argued, is completely different from the customs in her home country: When a distinguished guest is welcomed to the Kazakh yurt, the lord will kill a horse or a sheep to feed him. Consequently, a sharp cultural contrast appears in her lyrics:

Walking on the streets of the German capital
We cannot find any milk tea and dry bread

Looking into every restaurant
Only the beer is famous around the world
But to have a taste will make you drunk
Besides this, only vegetables and hamburgers are provided
If you refuse them your stomach will protest[①]

Ah, my honorable brother
The autumn wind disperses my dreams of memory
Thanks to our leader Dilmurat
The journey has gone smoothly
In the future we may visit more continents
I hope that you will reach more achievements
Now I want to make a joke with our relatives
Could you please show a warm smile on your face?
Everyday we have to walk on foot
Although everywhere there are vehicles
Going by foot on the street all day
Our shoes are worn out
Fearing Dilmurat, our leader, we did not dare to complain
Both legs can not move any more
Although Allah has not yet pronounced our judgment (in heaven)
We have received punishment on earth!
Hey yeah yeah yeah[②]

These words, which were translated by other experts at the scene, were brought to our understanding immediately, and from then onward we dared not to let them walk and tried to organize public transportation or a taxi whenever we went out. From this detail, we could fully understand that the Kazakh aqins are smart and good at communication due to their cultural tradition. It is said that in ancient times, Kazakh aqins could convince the rulers to do something in the interest of people by a silver tongue. Even today, they are always mocking at government leaders and criticizing current affairs in a relaxed atmosphere by playing good jokes. For instance, Dilmurat, the leader of the visiting group, for fearing that the two aqins might get lost, asked them to follow him narrowly all the time. Hence, when they performed in Berlin, Jamyga mocked

---

① From the presentation on May 7th 2011 at the Humboldt University of Berlin.
② From the presentation on May 11th 2011 at the University of Bonn.

at him,

> We have been in Berlin for two days now
> All our behavior is legal
> Strolling on the street we will get lost
> Wandering here and there without orientation
> Our leader just wants to bring us back safely
> He can't even sleep during the night
> Always counting the number of us
> As if we were in danger of getting lost
> In Xinjiang he counts the number of teaching hours every day
> In Berlin he gets tired of counting persons
> Hey yeah yeah yeah[①]

3. How can national become global?

The plight of communication that the Kazakh aqins Nagman and Jamyga encountered in the intercultural environment was an accidental situation for them, which could be overcome by personal efforts. However, there can be no doubt that even an aqin with extraordinary wisdom and bravery fails to overcome the difficulties when the accidental turn to be the inevitable. The modern Chinese writer Lu Xun once said, "Things with strong local features can easily become known in the world."[②] This statement refers to the worldwide distribution of literature and art and only indicates possibility instead of necessity. In fact, there is a long way to go transforming the national into the global.

International and intercultural communication of national literature and art is no easy task. The Chinese classic novel "Dream of the Red Chamber" (*Hongloumeng*), was not really appreciated by the majority of intellectuals and literates in Germany. When it was first translated and published in 1932, the most sophisticated parts in which Chinese classic poetries and social relations play a major role were omitted.[③] The first complete German version was published only in 2007.[④] What is more, Chinese literary lovers find it unacceptable that in 2000 Gao Xingjian (b. 1940) won the

---

[①] From the presentation on May 7th 2011 at the Humboldt University of Berlin.
[②] 《致陈烟桥》,1934 年 4 月 19 日,见《鲁迅全集》第 13 卷,第 81 页,人民文学出版社 2005 年版。
[③] *Der Traum der Roten Kammer*, translated by Frank Kuhn, Insel Verlag, 1932.
[④] *Der Traum der Roten Kammer oder Die Geschichte vom Stein*, translated by Rainer Schwarz & Martin Wösler, Bochum: Europäischer Universitätsverlag, 2007-2009.

first Nobel Prize for Literature awarded to a Chinese author, since most Chinese readers would have preferred other authors whose writing represent Chinese literary culture much better than Gao's western writing style and values. Similarly other internationally celebrated Chinese artists as the renown film director Zhang Yimou (b. 1950) are sometimes criticized to have promoted pseudo traditional Chinese culture intend to appeal to western taste. This criticism is not primarily targeted towards the artists mentioned but intends to focus on the neglect of promoting authentic Chinese culture and values represented by other internationally less known figures in the Chinese literary and art scene.

Some people might suggest that such kind of problems of intercultural communication could be resolved by providing qualified translation and interpretations. But, whoever has an experience in translating knows that the conversion of language is extremely hard and unreliable. Even a translator with professional language skills and a strong sense of responsibility might misunderstand the literary works for one or the other reason. The aesthetic tastes and the cultural connotation in a good literary work would certainly be lost to a great extend in a translation. Different cultural backgrounds cause deviations in the comprehension. In our case, it was impossible to understand the poetic texts sung by the aqins even after a verbal translation into Chinese had been provided. A second "cultural" translation was needed. This had to be done in cooperation of the aqin singer and researcher with Kazakh language skills.

How much cultural content, values and aesthetics can be preserved through the multi-stage translation? Therefore a paradox appears: the more national, the more likely it would become the global, at the same time, the less it becomes globally appreciated. Though it is in an era of cultural globalization nowadays, intercultural communication becomes more frequent than ever. Folk arts are better promoted worldwide. However, if you look on the traditional arts that first entered the international market, you will find more superficial items than culturally profound specimens. The dramatist Fu Jin pinpointed the reason for this phenomenon when he wrote, "When it seemed as if we had gained a global perspective, and our horizon of appreciation of art and aesthetic taste had rapidly surpassed the boundaries of state and nation, the trend of this development is nevertheless surprisingly monotonous. We will realize the disappointing impression that despite of the ever more colorful surface what we see is far removed from our ideal. The extreme monotony is hiding behind the celebrated diversity of culture and entertainment of our time, because the aesthetic taste of the world is controlled and shaped by a handful of multinational corporations with shrewd methods."①

Due to the above reasons, many countries are nowadays resisting universalization and globalization. Some countries tried to join UNESCO's *Convention for the Safeguarding of Intangible*

---

① 傅谨:《全球化时代的中国戏剧》,第7页,《艺术百家》2008年第6期.

Cultural Heritage (2003), in order to ensure the diversity of human culture, making their own national culture escape the fate of globalized simplification. While facing this kind of psychological status, Chinese folklorist Liu Kuili has made the following statement: "In the wave of globalization, economic integration and modern social life, our national culture is suffering greatly from the strong impact of foreign culture. Imported culture is considered powerful and fashionable by some people, and hence the fashionable will turn out to be the valued. When facing this monotonous cultural model, people find it necessary to discover and foster the outstanding traditions of Chinese culture."① Does protecting the intangible cultural heritage really help to resist the negative effects of globalization? In fact, not all nations have a positive view on this.

For instance, some European countries (including Germany) have, by the end of 2012, not yet joined the UNESCO's ICH convention. When I interviewed Martin Wölzmüller, president of the Bayerischer Landesverein für Heimatpfleger E. V. in Germany, I learned that the German government was then considering to join the convention, since it might be useful for the development of local culture. But many culture representatives including Wölzmüller were worrying whether the original intention of this convention will be left intact when only selected culture items can be nominated as intangible cultural heritage. He responded humorously, UNESCO probably would select the "Oktoberfest" (a beer festival organized for tourists and local people held in Autumn) in Munich as the representative of German ICH, while a large amount of folk art would be ignored.

All governments and academia can do is to investigate and check the history and current state of their national or local Intangible Cultural Heritage, to nominate selected items for different listings and to give attention and support to the bearers of these items. The goal of transforming national into global heritage can probably be achieved only by international cooperation or by a few famous global stars as Zhang Yimou. Can the profound national heritage survive this situation of cultural globalization? This is a question that I want to raise. To answer it will require further study.

---

① 刘魁立:《论全球化背景下的中国非物质文化遗产保护》,第27—28页,《河南社会科学》2007年第1期。

Themes for Ongoing Consideration

Redefine the Concept of Intangible Cultural Heritage

Yuan Li, Gu Jun[*]

  Can Huxian peasant paintings and Jingshan peasant paintings be regarded as intangible cultural heritage? Consider whether the historical ceremony of "offering sacrifices to heaven and earth on Mount Tai" can be regarded as intangible cultural heritage. How about "Impression · Liu Sanjie", the large-scale public memorial ceremony and live-action performance organized by the government, written and directed by Zhang Yimou? What about foot-binding, wife-pledging, or traditional handicrafts that everybody possesses? And how about the courtyard house and ancient villages, as well as spirit of Lei Feng and Mao Zedong thought? At this point, I'd like to explicitly point out that all the cases mentioned above are not really intangible cultural heritage. But, why do similar problematic questions appear in reality, even during the intangible cultural heritage application process? Quite simply, it is our concept of intangible cultural heritage that has gone wrong; to be more specific, there is problem with our understanding of intangible cultural heritage.

  Just as material science has to make clear "what is the material" and history has to make clear "what is history," the field of intangible cultural heritage should also make clear "what is intangible cultural heritage" before beginning academic debate. After all, it is the logical starting point for the subject. If we go wrong in solving the problem of "what is intangible cultural heritage" —the logical starting point of the subject—there will be various deviations in our future process of identification of intangible cultural heritage. Just as when we buttoned up our clothes by ourselves in childhood, all buttons would go wrong if the first one was incorrect. So we must ask, why are the above-mentioned "intangible cultural heritage" examples not really intangible cultural heritage? Comments below will focus on and "talk-through" this problem.

---

[*] Yuan Li, Researcher at the Chinese National Academy of Arts. Gu Jun, Professor at Beijing Union University.

1. Why is it said that peasant paintings in Huxian and Jingshan are not intangible cultural heritage?

In terms of a time period linked to inheritance, intangible cultural heritage should possess a long history (a history of at least 100 years). Therefore, Huxian peasant paintings and Jingshan peasant paintings that were generated, respectively, in the 1950s and 1970s cannot be designated as intangible cultural heritage at present, as the practice is less than one hundred years old.

Living inheritance is an important characteristic of intangible cultural heritage, but this doesn't mean that all culture authentically handed down to the present day in active form can become intangible cultural heritage. Once again, the frequently discussed Huxian peasant paintings (generated in 1950s) and Jingshan peasant paintings (generated in 1970s), are living traditions, but neither has reached the access-threshold time period for inheritance of intangible cultural heritage—a history of at least one hundred years, and thus cannot be designated as intangible cultural heritage.

The access threshold for intangible cultural heritage in China is limited to a period of one hundredyears, because, first, it is desirable to carry on the approach to designation of intangible cultural heritage already adopted by many countries around the world; second, the late Qing dynasty and the early Republic of China represent the last peak period for Chinese traditional manual technology and traditional development processes in performing arts, festivals, and ceremony. Exploration of excellent intangible cultural heritage generated in this period (including traditions that originated before the late Qing/Early-Republic period) and handed down to us will no doubt play a multiplier role in protection of intangible cultural heritage. Of course, the one hundred year age limit is merely the most basic access threshold we set for intangible cultural heritage. In fact, in an ancient civilization like China, with 5000 years of history, items of intangible cultural heritage are frequently hundreds or even thousands of years old. Performing arts like Kunqu opera and Beking opera have a history of at least several hundred years, wood-block new-year paintings almost a thousand years, kite-making nearly two thousand years; ancient techniques like drilling wood to make fire may be hundreds of thousands of years old. Therefore, the established lower limit of at least one hundred years should primarily be understood as an access threshold for the intangible cultural heritage application process. This is because designated "heritage" should be a kind of cultural wealth left to us by the wealth creator after his death. If the wealth creator is still alive, how could the cultural wealth given to us be called "cultural heritage"?

In fact, each country has set its own limitations on the age of intangible cultural heritage entered in their selection process. Take Japan and Korea as examples: there has never been any established time limit as an access threshold for intangible cultural heritage in these two countries, but time frames for accepting intangible cultural heritage with the shortest histories are usually set, at a minimum, at more than one hundred years. Thus it is obvious that this standard is appropriate for most countries.

It is important to note that the one hundred year period mentioned here does not refer to one thing in particular, but refers to a certain category or class of things, and the project will have the qualification to be selected as intangible cultural heritage provided that the certain kind of things have had a history of more than one hundred years while also meeting certain other conditions.

2. Why is it said that the ceremony of "offering sacrifices to heaven and earth on Mount Tai" in the past does not constitute intangible cultural heritage?

When it comes to the form of inheritance, intangible cultural heritage items should all be handed down to the present day in an active form. Therefore, items similar to the ceremony of "offering sacrifices to heaven and earth on Mount Tai," which in fact existed in history but have now disappeared, cannot apply for intangible cultural heritage recognition.

It has been argued that intangible cultural heritage is not always in an active state and if the example has historical significance or if it can be restored through the use of literature and material objects, the item can be considered for intangible cultural heritage recognition even if it has disappeared. We do not agree with this statement.

In fact, the biggest difference between intangible and tangible cultural heritage is the former's "active" state. That is to say, intangible cultural heritage has to be authentically handed down to the present in an active form. Those traditional cultural items that did exist in history but later disappeared cannot be eligible for intangible cultural heritage status even if they possess important historical conceptual value, cultural value, artistic value, social value and scientific value. For example, the ceremony of "offering sacrifices to heaven and earth on Mount Tai" began in the Qin dynasty in a manner typical of traditional cultural practice. From the time that the first emperor of Qin climbed Mount Tai to offer a sacrifice to heaven, emperors of many later dynasties, as a way of demonstrating their great power once ascended to the throne, led all officials to climb Mount Tai, offering a sacrifice to heaven with grand ceremonies. Despite this fact, such items still cannot be eligible for consideration as intangible cultural heritage. This is because although the ceremony of "offering sacrifices to heaven and earth on Mount Tai" did exist in history, it disappeared early in the Song dynasty (the ceremony was held for the last time in A. D. 1008—the first year of Dazhong Xiangfu during the reign of emperor Song Zhenzong Zhao Heng), and traditional cultural items that similarly disappeared more than one thousand years ago cannot apply for intangible cultural heritage no matter how remarkable or outstanding these cultural features might be.

3. Why is it said that large-scale public memorial ceremonies organized by the government are not intangible cultural heritage?

Considering the character of its "living state," intangible cultural heritage should be handed down to the present retaining its "authentic" look. Therefore, various large-scale public memorial ceremonies that reconstruct and artificially re-create traditions do not constitute intangible cultural heritage.

To carry forward local culture and create a menu of activities for local visits, many communities and districts are trying to exhume local people famous in history, holding ambitious public memorial ceremonies (referring to various large-scale public memorial ceremonies held by the local government) for them. Although these large-scale public memorial ceremonies do not lack positive community significance, they have nothing to do with intangible cultural heritage.

A public memorial ceremony can be evaluated as intangible cultural heritage depending on, first, whether the activities did actually exist in history, and second, whether they have been authentically handed down to the present day in active form. Public memorial ceremonies are likely to be intangible cultural heritage if they did exist in history and have been authentically transmitted in active form. In case there were no such ceremonies in the past and they are "created" by local governments themselves, or even if there were such ceremonies in history, but they've been currently restored after having disappeared for a long time for various causes, they generally cannot be regarded as intangible cultural heritage.

The easiest way to judge the authenticity of a public memorial ceremony is to evaluate or assess the inheritor. In a situation in which the priest who performed the ceremony (theoretically the inheritor of this intangible cultural heritage) cannot be found, it will be empty talk to say that the ceremony is handed down in an active form. It can be seen from field investigation that most public memorial ceremonies in the history of the Central Plains have been interrupted, and there has been no inheritor who has handed down all the procedures of ancient public memorial ceremonies in an authentic manner. The "public memorial ceremonies" we see today, despite their "famous titles," almost have nothing to do with public memorial ceremonies in history—they use "ancient dance" imagined by today's stage directors, "ancient music" that written by today's musicians, "ancient costume" designed by today's costume designers, and "ancient sacrificial offerings" which are for the most part plagiarized by today's planners drawing on ancient books. What historical conceptual value would such public memorial recognition ceremonies have? They have no qualifications to participate in the selection of intangible cultural heritage. We are not blindly opposed to participation in public memorial ceremonies but must emphasize that the eligible item has to be like a "living fossil" in history that has remained to this day, so as to preserve as much ancient information as possible. The reasons why we repeatedly emphasize the "authenticity" of application items are clear: only by authentically preserving the dance of that time can we know what sacrificial dance looked like in memorial ceremonies thousands of years ago; only by authentically preserving the music of that time can we know how sacrificial music was used in memorial ceremonies thousands of years ago; only by authentically preserving sacrificial costumes of that time can we know how the sacrificial costume appeared in memorial ceremonies thousands of years ago; only by authentically preserving sacrificial offerings in that time can we know how the sacrificial offerings were used in memorial ceremonies thousands of years ago. Only these kinds of public memorial ceremonies are of historic value to human consciousness. If all of these memorial ceremonies are false and are fakes "created" by contemporary people, it is of course unnecessary for us to either regard them as heritage that our ancestors left to us or to carry them forward.

Certainly, in consideration of the unique historical conceptual value these public memorial ceremonies possess, it is not impossible for us to make some concessions when it comes to selection criteria. For example, if certain public memorial ceremonies were merely interrupted for short periods by political movements like "the Cultural Revolution", if priests who performed the ceremonies or people who attended the ceremonies are still alive and if those who experienced the ceremonies can authentically present these ceremonies today, then I think these items can still apply for recognition as intangible cultural heritage. However, if those who experienced the ceremonies have died, if the so-called memorial ceremonies are restored only through the use of written records of the time, such items cannot apply to the intangible cultural heritage process.

4. Why is it said that foot-binding and wife-pledging are not intangible cultural heritage items?

When we consider the quality or character of inheritance, intangible cultural heritage should be of significant, unique value while at the same time exhibiting achievement and even excellence. For this reason, both evil practices and corrupt customs like foot-binding and wife-pledging and traditional handicrafts common to all cannot apply for recognition in the intangible cultural heritage process.

In the eyes of many people, so-called "intangible cultural heritage" is the same as "traditional culture," what we also usually call "folk-custom." Because of this confusion, some people think that all "traditional culture" such as opium smoking, foot-binding, wife-pledging and keeping concubines can be considered as "intangible cultural heritage." In fact, statements like this are all wrong; they fundamentally misread the original intention of intangible cultural heritage protection.

There is no denying that there are similarities between "intangible cultural heritage" and "traditional culture." For example, both are products of history, both have been created in the past and transmitted to the present in different forms by human action, both are part of history and of historical consciousness. But there are indeed distinct differences between the two, the biggest of which is the fact that intangible cultural heritage is not ordinary traditional culture but cultural elements elevated through a process of valuation. That is to say, intangible cultural heritage traditions are the ones selected from multiple national traditional cultural elements because they can embody the most excellent traditions of the nation. They are essentially different from traditional cultural elements that have not undergone a valuation process.

What are the standards of evaluation that separate intangible cultural heritage from traditional culture? There are five benchmarks: first, whether the traditional element is of important historical value; second, whether it is of important cultural value; third, whether it is of important artistic value; fourth, whether it possesses important scientific value; fifth, whether it is of important social value. Traditional cultural practices or products in which these five values are very prominent are defined as intangible cultural heritage, while those lacking these five characteristics, or in which these five values are not particularly prominent, are not intangible cultural heritage. For example, braised pork with vermicelli cooked by old granny, loach through bean-curd, shredded pork with garlic sauce, fried pancake and deep-fried dough sticks are not entirely without historical and scientific value, but it is certain that different degrees of significance can be seen when such a meal is compared with the way the Manchu Han Imperial Feast and Luoyang's Water Banquet enable an understanding of the development of Chinese culinary arts. Intangible cultural heritage is the essence of a nation's traditional culture and important representation of a nation's excellent national traditions. For example, the Honghe and Longji rice terraces represent the highest level of terrace development technique in Chinese history, and Rongbaozhai new-year images using wood-block printing represent the highest level of Chinese wood-block new-year art. The first example is far more meaningful than ordinary or everyday terraces that lack high technological content, and the second is greater than ordinary new-year paintings that don't exhibit high artistic value. This sense of being special, unique, and of high quality is the difference between intangible cultural heritage and traditional culture in general. However, many people do not realize the difference between intangible cultural heritage and the traditional culture in everyday life and accept many ordinary traditional cultural elements that lack heritage value, even going so far as to accept evil practices and corrupt customs as intangible cultural heritage. This kind of indiscriminate protection will ultimately bring unnecessary harm to the work of protecting legitimate intangible cultural heritage.

If we have to use one sentence to distinguish intangible cultural heritage from traditional culture, whether we can say this: what we called "intangible cultural heritage" is traditional culture selected through a process of valuation.

5. Why is it said that "props," "material objects," "finished products" and "relevant places" are not intangible cultural heritage?

From perspective of the essence of inheritance, the biggest feature of intangible cultural heritage is its "being intangible." Therefore, however important they are for protection of intangible cultural heritage, "props," "material objects," "finished products" and "relevant places" do not fit the proper definition of intangible cultural heritage.

There is a sentence to this effect in *The Convention for the Safeguarding of the Intangible Cultural Heritage* passed by UNESCO in 2003: "what we called intangible cultural heritage refers to various kinds of social activities, narrating arts, performing arts, production & life experience and various handicraft techniques." There may not be too many problems with this definition if we stop here. However, to emphasize the environment from which intangible cultural heritage is derived or for other reasons, the definition adds that apart from the elements mentioned above, intangible cultural heritage also includes, "various tools, material objects, finished products and relevant places used in narration, performance and implementation of these techniques and skills." As interpreted in the *Convention*, it seems that we can do deduce the following—for example, "construction skills of traditional architecture in Huizhou" are intangible cultural heritage, then, those closely related traditional construction tools—the huge crane and the winch, those closely related material objects—the bricks and the woods, those closely related finished products—the magnificent ancient dwellings with white walls and dark tiles in Huizhou, and even those various closely related places—the ancient Xidi Village and the Hong village, are all intangible cultural heritage. If all these "visible" and "touchable" material elements of tradition turn out to be "intangible" heritage, what else is there to separate out *tangible* cultural heritage? Extending and applying this logic, *the Intangible Cultural Heritage List* in China will in the near future easily turn to be *List of Chinese Famous Villages*, *List of Chinese Famous Residences*, *List of Chinese Famous Wine*, *List of Chinese Famous Paintings* and *List of Chinese Famous Products*.

Let's repeat: what we call intangible cultural heritage refers to knowledge and experience, techniques and skills that lie deep within the minds of inheritors. Although some tools, material objects, finished products and even some of places are helpful to our understanding of both inheritance and protection of intangible cultural heritage (and in fact should be collected by museums), these tools, material objects, finished products and relevant places are not themselves intangible cultural heritage.

6. Why is it said that literary works, moral ideas and political views are not intangible cultural heritage?

Within the broad category of inheritance, intangible cultural heritage items are mainly distributed in the three fields of performing arts (folk literature and performing arts), traditional craft skills (traditional arts and crafts, traditional production knowledge and traditional life knowledge) as well as traditional festivals & rituals (traditional festivals and traditional rituals). Those literary works, moral ideas and political views that are not included in these categories cannot be regarded as intangible cultural heritage.

In addition to considering definitional limitations based on time period, form, contemporary vitality, quality or excellence and essential character, limits on included categories should also be considered in establishing the overall concept of intangible cultural heritage. Unlike many elements of traditional culture, intangible cultural heritage items are usually distributed across only the three fields of traditional performing arts, traditional craft skills, and traditional festivals & rituals. Traditional culture outside of these three fields is generally not intangible cultural heritage. For example, although "intangible cultural heritage" items prepared for the application process in recent years—like the four great classical novels of China, genealogies of famous persons, traditional notions of filial piety and even the ideological essence and political views of some famous politicians (Marxism, Sun Yat-sen thought and Mao Zedong thought, etc.), are all products of history and of important historical value, cultural value, artistic value, social value and even scientific value, they can't apply for intangible cultural heritage status, nor can they enter *The Intangible Cultural Heritage List* because they are not included in the three key fields of intangible cultural heritage.

In conclusion, the correct definition of intangible cultural heritage should include restrictions as follows:

First, as to the time period of inheritance, intangible cultural heritage must be created in human history. Activities or elements without a history of at least one hundred years cannot be identified as intangible cultural heritage.

Second, as to the form of inheritance, intangible cultural heritage items should all be handed down to the present in an active form. Those which actually existed in history but have disappeared today, or which have been retained to this day only as writings and material remains, cannot be regarded as intangible cultural heritage.

Third, from the living state of inheritance, intangible cultural heritage must have been authentically handed down or transmitted to the present. Those "traditional cultural items" that have been artificially reconstructed, especially the ones that have been deliberately reconstructed by the government, academia, the commercial sector or even by inheritors, cannot be regarded as intangible cultural heritage.

Fourth, as to the quality or character of inheritance, intangible cultural heritage must be of important historical value, cultural value, artistic value, scientific value and social value, and cultural items lacking these above-mentioned values cannot be regarded as intangible cultural heritage.

Fifth, regarding the essential character of inheritance, intangible cultural heritage refers in particular to traditional knowledge and experience, traditional techniques and skills created in human history and handed down to the present in active form. Therefore, even material objects, tools, and finished products created with this knowledge and experience, as well as techniques and skills or closely-related cultural sites or locales, which are of great significance for protection of intangible cultural heritage, also cannot in themselves be regarded as intangible cultural heritage, simply because they are "tangible."

Finally, within the overall category of inheritance, intangible cultural heritage refers in particular to kinds of traditional cultural items like performing arts, craft skills, festivals and ceremonies among traditional cultures of a nation. Other cultural activities—such as literary works by outstanding writers, political views of famous politicians and even some fine traditional moral ideologies, do not fit the definition of intangible cultural heritages and are thus excluded from protection.

Recognizing the Practice of Tradition in Community Well-Being

—Towards A Model of Sustainable Intangible Cultural Heritage

Amy Kitchener[*]

In this paper I will offer an alternative to the "productive protection" model of safeguarding ICH. People who engage in the traditional art forms of their cultures develop a sense of community, cultural pride, and personal achievement that improves their sense of well-being and may ultimately benefit their health, as individuals and as members of a community. Practitioners from diverse traditions are well aware of the meanings and effects of cultural maintenance and often articulate these impacts in terms of health and well-being when asked about their motivations for participation. Instead of potentially interrupting community-based processes and aesthetics by introducing external markets driven by outsiders, we can recognize and offer support to bolster the deep dimensions of community health that are maintained by cultural leaders engaging the practice and active preservation in ICH.

Identifying cultural leadership and offering direct support, in the forms of small grants, opportunities to convene, and individualized assistance are effective manners of building alliances in helping communities maintain their ICH. This approach, in which we employ an active, practitioner-centered and community-driven process towards maintaining cultural values and practices, defines the work of the Alliance for California Traditional Arts (ACTA), the non-governmental organization I co-founded

---

[*] Amy Kitchener, Executive Director at Alliance for California Traditional Arts.

and lead, which serves as the state-designated support organization for all folk and traditional arts and artists in California.

Of California's diverse population of over 37 million people, 37% are Latino, 13% are Asian, 6.2% are African American, and another 17% belong to races other than Caucasian. Over 25% of the total population originates from outside the US. Our efforts have already helped to ensure that the state's future retains cultural elements from the past, and more, that these traditional expressions flourish and adapt in a dynamic process. ACTA identifies and communicates directly with tradition bearers, is responsive to their needs, and provides resources for practitioners and participants alike to, practice, share, engage and document in these traditional art forms.

ACTA's programs are designed to align with community processes. We have learned through observation that in order for ICH to be maintained and thrive, the principal driver needs to be based in the community of practice. We make efforts to celebrate the different ways of knowing, recognizing different forms of practice, aesthetics, and communication. While we feel there is much value in the efforts to document, classify and categorize traditional forms, our efforts are focused on recognizing processes of transmission, manners of preservation (more along lines of lineage rather than form), and the effects on community. This leads us is to a closer engagement with people, rather than the genre or form of ICH. As folklorists, we recognize the myriad of continuous transformations of traditional forms due to the movement of people, the cross-cultural interaction of people and communities and the continual recontextualizing of practices through space and time—processes which are reflective of the American experience over the relatively short history of the US which has shaped the unique ICH of the diverse population of California.

ACTA's two signature programs—the Apprenticeship Program and Living Cultures Grants Program—provide small grants to individuals, informal groups, and non-governmental organizations to further the continuance of traditional arts practice in the array of California cultural communities. Through the Apprenticeship Program, following a model that parallels those used in over 30 other states, ACTA offers a contract of $3,000 dollars (about RMB 19,000) to a master-level traditional artist to work intensively with an experienced apprentice over the course of six months to a year. The artists are selected in a competitive application process judged by a review committee that includes academics and practitioners. Once the awards are made, ACTA's staff works closely with each of the 17-20 annual teams to establish a supportive relationship and to monitor and document each pair's progress.

In the Living Cultures Grants Program, we invest a larger grant of up to $7,500 dollars (about RMB 47,000) in small non-governmental or community-based organizations to undertake a wide range of activities that they select to support the practice, engagement, and ultimately, the preservation of California's unique mosaic of cultural patrimonies. Even though the funding is relatively small, in each of

these programs this support provides significant tangible resources and financial rewards, as well as validation, to participants. We consider these participants as "investment partners" rather than "grantees," in a relationship similar to micro-lending (but without a required financial repayment). These relatively small investments yield significant results in community-driven preservation projects involving five principal support strategies.

1. The transmission of expressive culture is at the heart of our work and a large portion of our programs is dedicated to this process. Staying connected or becoming connected to one's cultural heritage is a strong motivation for many learners to engage in a traditional art form, and can also provide an important sense of identity and well-being. Connection to cultural heritage is often based upon the reconnection or maintenance of identity and the establishment of well-being and a knowledge base that is fortified

through participation and engagement in traditional art practices. For some, this could involve reclaiming an identity that may have become dormant during their own or their parents' processes of migration and assimilation into US cultures, or as a result of other forms of cultural dislocation, such as colonization, or (in the case of California Native Americans) cultural genocide.

Learning traditional arts—whether in the more intensive setting of a one-on-one apprenticeship, or in a group learning setting—does not only involve training in the skills and techniques of an art form: it also requires experience in deeper cultural aspects of knowledge, values, protocol, and spirituality. Those who learn in a traditional mode can begin to understand how their art form intersects with other cultural values and practices. The eminent folklorist Barre Toelken wrote about hosting a residency in Native California Hupa basket-making with master artist Mrs. Elvira Matt. She first taught her students to sing a number of Native songs, which were sung during the gathering of native plant materials and the arduous preparation of weaving materials. When she finally began teaching the weaving, one of her students asked why so much time was spent on learning songs, rather than on making baskets. She replied: "Well, after all, you know, a basket is a song that's become visible." There is a much deeper significance in an expressive form when it is understood and experienced at the intersection of other cultural concepts, practices and traditions.

2. A second strategy for sustaining ICH involves presenting through festivals, concerts, and exhibitions. This work takes many forms and may involve "bonding" among those who share a common tradition, such as these participants in a Yiddish cultural festival celebrating Jewish music and dance traditions, or it may involve "bridging" to audiences outside the group of ICH inheritors, or sometimes both bonding and bridging occur in the

3. A third strand of work involves gatherings and convenings among ICH practitioners, which has proven to be a highly productive strategy giving inheritors the opportunity to meet, learn, discuss critical issues, network and organize.

4. Another important type of support facilitates the creation of spaces or the acquisition of materials that are necessary to the practice of folklore or ICH. ACTA made a grant to the Native Yorok of Blue Creek Ah Pah to build a redwood ceremonial dance pit.

5. Our last support strategy focuses on documentation, research and archiving that encompasses a wide array of activities. For example, Native Ohlone basketmaker Linda Yamane has been re-introducing her ancestral basketweaving traditions by learning from neighboring tribes and researching baskets in museums—here she is recording data about a Rumsien Ohlone feather and shell basket in the British Museum in London.

These five support strategies constitute the core categories of community requests for grants we receive, and each has proven effective in the work to sustain the living ICH in California cultural communities. In thinking about the interventions or circumstances that nurture successful preservation strategies—community health effects provide a compelling motivation for folklore and ICH inheritors.

Recognizing the frequency and consistency with which practitioners mentioned the connections between engagement in their traditions and personal and community health and well-being, in 2006 ACTA launched a multi-year study with health researchers at the University of California, Davis, to formally evaluate the health effects and other outcomes experienced by participants in ACTA's

Apprenticeship Program and the Living Cultures Grants Program. This research study revealed recurring themes of growth, health, and holistic well-being at the individual, family, community, and wider social levels.

The themes were remarkable, both for the deeply personal insights shared and for the consistency of the responses across domains of artistic undertaking, diverse cultures, array of languages, and disparate age and generational groups. Participants also vividly described the multi-directional benefits of participation in folk traditions, whether as a teacher, a learner, or a performer of a traditional art. Participants reported personally meaningful individual-level benefits, including increased self-esteem, a closer connection to tradition and community, and interconnected mind-body awareness and wellness, along with the healing qualities of the traditional art.

At the family level, participants shared the joy and benefit of intergenerational activities, a sense of respect for elders and traditions, the transmission of cultural heritage and practices, and the mitigation of historical trauma.

At the community or neighborhood level, participants touted the benefit of a gathering space in which all generations could commune and communicate, leading naturally to several wider impacts, including the perception of artists as community leaders and organizers, and of folk arts activity as a means to bridge gaps between communities, and between generations in a single cultural or ethnic group.

Perpetuating knowledge about the powerful effects of individual and community well-being can be a pathway to stimulating the preservation of folklore and ICH within communities and with external policy-makers, government funding agencies, and private philanthropy. Since the release of our health-study report in October 2011, there has been heightened interest in this subject, and new funding initiatives calling for  research at the intersection of culture and health at the federal arts and health agencies. A broader understanding about the powerful productive health-related effects of folklore and ICH engagement could bring greater recognition, value, and ultimately resources, to communities maintaining their culture. I believe this is a healthy alternative to "productive protection" efforts, in which external markets may potentially disrupt the processes, aesthetic systems, and community contexts of folklore and ICH.

Pomo Native basketmaker Luwana Quitiquit's words provide a fitting reflection with which to close. She said, "...storytelling is wellness, and the reason it's wellness for my family is because it puts my kids back in touch with my grandmother, with people that they never got to see. It inspires them to carry on their culture. That's wellness."

ICH Protection and Bridging Ethnic Conflicts[①]

Song Junhua[*]

1. Introduction

The two challenges to society represented by ICH protection and the bridging ethnic conflicts are connected.[②]

Driven by clashing cultural difference, ethnic conflict has become more and more prominent, becoming one of the most important problems emerging from the process of social development, particularly in countries undergoing high-speed urbanization and globalization like China.

In recent years, conflicts between different ethnic groups have broken out in several parts of China. Among the examples: conflict between a Sichuan migrant worker and local people over setting up a booth in Daguo Village, Xintang Town, Zengcheng City, Guangzhou, that took place from June 10 to 14, 2011. Conflict between unpaid Sichuan migrant workers and local people in Guxiang Town, Chaozhou City, from June 1 to 6, 2011. A protest assembly of migrant workers triggered by conflict between two teenagers in Shaxi Town, Zhongshan City, Guangdong Province, from June 25 to 26, 2012. Migrant workers' confrontation with the police in Longgang District, Shenzhen City on June 28, 2012, and so on. Despite different specific causes, all of these conflicts reflected problems of ethnic relations. Ethnic conflicts have become an important factor affecting the stability of the state.

Like ethnic conflict, ICH protection is also a problem brought to light and shaped by human

---

[*] Song Junhua, Professor at the key research institute of humanities and social science-Intangible Cultural Heritage Research Center of Sun Yat-Sen University and the Collaborative Innovation Center for Inheritance and Digital Protection of Intangible Cultural Heritage.

[①] This article is one of the achievements of the major Program— "Study on Intangible Cultural Heritage and Social Management Innovation" that set up for "Study on the Spirit of the Eighteenth Congress of Chinese Communist Party and Practices in Guangdong" by Guangdong Provincial Publicity Department (2013SBDZB09).

[②] For brevity, "intangible cultural heritage" is referred to as "ICH" in this article.

and social development. First, intangible cultural heritage—based on tradition, native style and the lives of ethnic groups—is rapidlybeing eroded or pushed aside by urbanization and globalization: many types of ICH face the risk of being forgotten, destroyed or changed. Second, ideas and solutions derived from ICH protection can actually help settle problems encountered through social development, such as the squandering of resources, ecological damage, the decline in innovation, and so on. In fact, intangible cultural heritage can be a kind of "guarantor" of "sustainable development," a "consensus concept" for much of mankind. Third, it has been more than ten years since the first batch of ICH masterpieces of oral and intangible ICH assets in China have been protected under the 2001 UNESCO *Convention for the Safeguarding of the Intangible Cultural Heritage*; during this time ICH recognition and protection has been initiated by many countries. Through this process we have obtained valuable experience and positive examples of preservation projects.

Of course, intangible cultural heritage is closely related to a specific ethnic group. Every ethnic group has its own ICH, which serves as both the cultural foundation for ethnic self-identity and self-development, and as an important symbol distinguishing one group from all others. Therefore, the very process of ICH protection has an inevitable effect on two aspects of interactions between ethnic groups—ethnic *conflict* and ethnic *integration*. At times, the nomination and review of ICH masterpieces and the designation of representative successors have actually caused cultural controversies between countries or regions. For example, at one time conflicting claims of cultural ownership of the dragon boat festival, Chinese characters, and Chinese medicine caused disagreement between China and Korea. Domestically, there were also conflicts between Xiamen and Quanzhou over the recognition of Nanyin music. Such ICH controversies or conflicts between countries or regions are essentially a manifestation of smaller cultural conflicts between ethnic groups.

Thus, we must consider a number of problems: how do we observe and explain the relationship between ICH protection and ethnic conflict? Can solutions that bridge ethnic rifts be discovered within the process of ICH protection? Can alternative approaches to ICH protection be identified in the process of settling ethnic relationships? How do we deal with the contradiction between individualized demands of ethnic groups and the shared objectives of ICH protection, whiles similarly balancing the relationship between ethnic identity and the needs of modern society, including development?

2. Intangible Cultural Heritage and Ethnic Identity

Intangible cultural heritage was defined in *Convention for the Safeguarding of the Intangible*

Cultural Heritage by the UNESCO this way: "the practices, representations, expressions, knowledge, skills as well as the instruments, objects, artefacts and cultural spaces associated therewith—that communities, groups and, in some cases, individuals recognize as part of their cultaral heritago. This intangible cultural heritage, transmitted from generation to generation, is constantly recreated by communities and groups in their history, and provides them with a sense of identity and continuity, thus promoting respect for cultural diversity and human creativity. For the purposes of this Convention, consideration will be given solely to such intangible cultural heritage as is computible with existing international human rights instruments, as well as with the requirements of mutual respect among communities, groups and individuals, and of sustainable developments."[①] In short, intangible cultural heritage assets are cultural treasures created by human communities, groups or individuals that are recognized and inherited by later generations through mechanisms of communication such as oral instruction and rote memory. Intangible cultural heritage has the characteristics of continuity, of an active state of being, of utility, collective meaning, and spirituality.

The word "ethnic group" comes from the Greek *ethnos*, which originally referenced tribes and races. From ancient times forward, the meaning of "ethnic group" has continually changed. According to information assembled by Ma Rong, there are more than 20 different definitions of "ethnic group" in English scholarship[②]; of these the definition advanced by Max Weber has had an especially-strong influence in China. He defined a group as *ethnic*, "when it has a subjective belief in its common lineage due to their similarity in constitutional type and culture, or their collective memory of migration, and in which this kind of belief is very important to the continuation of relationships of non-contiguous communities."[③] Generally speaking, an ethnic group is a group of people subjectively self-identified and separated from other groups because of their shared or similar objective origins (hereditary inheritance, descent and constitution) and culture (language, religion, belief and custom) within a larger social and cultural system[④]. Ethnic groups can be distinguished by birthplace, place of residence and ancestral home, for example, groups like emigrated Chinese, Shanxi people, or Taiwanese. They can also be divided according to religious beliefs, such as Muslims who follow the Islamic faith; can be defined by shared lifestyle, such as dating groups, the SOHOs and the DINKs in modern times.

---

① The definition is of significance but also defectiveness, please refer to my article:《非物质文化遗产概念的诠释与重构》,《学术研究》2006 年第 9 期。

② 马戎《民族关系的社会学研究》,周星、王铭铭主编《社会文化人类学讲演集》,天津人民出版社 1996 年,第 501 页。

③ Max Weber, *The Ethnic Group*, In: Parsons and shills, et al (eds.). *Theories of Society*, Vol. 1 Gleercol Illinois, The Free Press, 1961, p. 306.

④ 孙九霞:《试论族群与族群认同》,《中山大学学报》1998 年第 2 期,第 25 页。

Conceptually, there is a correlation between intangible cultural heritage and ethnic group. Characteristics of ICH—continuity, contemporary vitality, practicality, collective meaning and spirituality—are also characteristics of ethnic groups themselves. Thus, intangible cultural heritage can be understood as the collective manifestation of the internal validation of the group to which it belongs, and also to external verification by others, a phenomenon very similar to the processes of self-identification and other-validation that define ethnic groups. Moreover, intangible cultural heritage assets frequently are closely correlated with specific ethnic groups, becoming both the foundation for and symbol of self-identification. For these reasons, ethnic groups can be studied to understand both ICH creation and inheritance and significance of traditional culture.

The word "identity" derives from psychology, its original meaning conveying the notion of acceptance or recognition given to one individual by another. More recently, through its use in philosophy, sociology and anthropology, the term has come to indicate the sense of belonging connecting individual and group, or even relationships between groups.① Today ethnic identity means the "social members' awareness of and emotional attachment to their own ethnic belonging"②. Common or similar origins (hereditary inheritance, descent and constitution) and culture (language, religion, belief and custom) undergird the formation of ethnic groups and provide the basic elements of ethnic identity. Common ancestry, origin and environmental context help secure a consistent ethnic identity. Identical or similar dialects, beliefs, customs, art and lifestyle serve as symbols of distinction for ethnic groups and can also intensify differences between their inner-group and others in communication among ethnic groups.

Intangible cultural heritage is not only reflected in indigenous elements such as the lineage, descent and constitution of ethnic groups, but is also reflected in cultural factors like language, beliefs, customs, art and lifestyle. Intangible cultural heritage materials are important symbols of ethnic identity, among which self-referential epics, legends, beliefs, language, customs, and arts are self-defined symbols that also provide markers distinguishing one group from others. More importantly, intangible cultural heritage traditions are "practices" of ethnic identity, reaching a kind of tacit understanding and identity within ethnic groups while simultaneously achieving spiritual communication with the past through the recreation and reenactment of cultures created and practiced by ancestors. Grounded in both external symbols and internal practices of intangible cultural heritage, this tradition-based ethnic identity is both profound and lasting.

---

① 孙九霞:《试论族群与族群认同》,《中山大学学报》1998 年第 2 期, 第 27 页。
② 王希恩:《民族认同与民族意识》,《民族研究》1995 年第 6 期, 第 17 页。

3. Intangible Cultural Heritage and Ethnic Conflicts

Ethnic identity proceeds on the basis of ethnic difference; only in comparison and distinction with another group can internal identification appear. The reverse is also true; ethnic difference is formed and intensified on the basis of self-identification by each ethnic group; this kind of difference often becomes the basis for ethnic antagonism and conflict.

As UNESCO made clear in *Convention for the Safeguarding of the Intangible Cultural Heritage*, ICH protection is based on *the UNESCO Universal Declaration on Cultural Diversity*, which emphasizes "the importance of the intangible cultural heritage as a mainspring of cultural diversity and a guarantee of sustainable development."[①]. For UNESCO, ICH is a reflection of cultural diversity, thus to protect intangible cultural heritage is to guarantee the existence of cultural diversity, including ethnic diversity. However, this concept of protection takes as a basic principle equality, respect and mutual understanding between cultures and ethnic groups. If this principle can be both well understood and implemented, conflicts between ethnic groups can be avoided.

Obviously, the very existence of cultural diversity is premised on an affirmation of difference between cultures and ethnic groups. Difference framed this way can provide genetic resources for human cultural ecology and for the sustainable development of culture. However, certain obstacles will arise as communication and understanding between ethnic groups is actually formulated. Far from being celebrated, differences in language, folk-custom, religion and lifestyle may cause misunderstanding and prejudice, leading to antagonism and conflicts. Especially when one ethnic group tries to impose its own language, folk-custom, religion and lifestyle on other groups—even replacing established cultural practices—serious ethnic conflict is inevitable. "Social division utilizing 'ethnic group' as its basic dividing line exists in regard to the social status and economic income of each ethnic group within multi-ethnic countries. Ethnic identity determines one's privilege or susceptibility to discrimination in the allocation of social benefits and economic opportunity: a situation in which the bigger the ethnic difference, the more serious will be discrimination, and the stronger the drive for advantaged countries or groups to guard their own privilege and for the disadvantaged to attempt to change reality."[②]

In the overall process of maintaining cultural diversity, intangible cultural heritage intensifies the distinctiveness of region, religion, language and the culture of ethnic groups, leading to antagonism and conflict. Take "region" for example: "ethnic groups who define themselves as

---

① The UNESCO, Convention for the Safeguarding of the Intangible Cultural Heritage.
② 罗惠翾:《族群认同与国家认同:和谐何以可能》,《理论视野》2009 年第 8 期,第 45 页。

'nations' long for their own territory and national structure (consider the Kurds, Palestinians, Tamils, the Quebecois and Basques). Even when designated territory and national organization don't exist, a certain locale will be identified as their own, a phenomenon which becomes very important in judgments about ethnic identification and the expansion of ethnic groups."① Therefore, conflicts between Indigenous Fijians and Indo-Fijians, Kosovo's Serbs and Albanians, U. S. Native Americans and Mexican Americans as well as black Americans all emerged from regional conflicts. In the situation in which publicity campaigns and protection programs are conducted on behalf of different regional ICH forms specific to ethnic groups, such as music, dance, drama, or folk-custom, inherent regional differences will certainly be intensified, thus increasing the probability of ethnic conflicts.

Generally speaking, the stronger the "identification effect" of specific intangible cultural heritage assets within a group, the more the differences between ethnic groups will be highlighted, producing greater difficulties in understanding between ethnic groups and a greater likelihood that antagonism and conflict will develop. Of course, there exist complex and multiple causes of ethnic antagonism and conflict, but cultural difference between ethnic groups may be the deepest one.

4. Significance of ICH Protection on Bridging Ethnic Conflicts

As an active cultural practice that honors intergenerational succession, intangible cultural heritage plays an important role, and has generated valuable experience, in addressing relationships between generations as well as between members within a group, an attribute distinct from its role distinguishing group members from "outsiders."

First, intangible cultural heritage is an important *mechanism* for bridging internal conflicts between generations and between members of the same generation within ethnic groups. For example, repetition of intangible cultural heritage practices such as ritual, folk-custom, song and dance that originated from common ancestors, totems, religions, beliefs and values, can help practitioners achieve conceptual unity and identification between generations and among members of the same generation, contributing to the elimination of divergence and antagonism. This mechanism for bridging internal divergence or antagonism within ethnic groups through shared cultural awareness and practice has played an important role in maintaining cohesive traditional ethnic groups. This bridging concept, of course, may be extended to the development of relationships between different ethnic groups.

The river-crossing legend is both intangible cultural heritage of the Yao nationality and an

---

① 王剑峰：《族群性的陷阱与族群冲突》，《思想战线》2004 年第 4 期，第 61 页。

important practice through which the Yao maintain cohesion by worshiping common ancestors. A story found in both Yao literature *Guo Shan Bang* and legend of Pan Yao villages states that the Yao people migrated across the sea to avoid disaster. During this journey they encountered a storm and knelt down, pleading to Pan Wang, who employed magic to save them. As a result, the Yao people promised that, "It was nobody else but Pan Wang who saved the Yao people; nobody knelt down and offer sacrifices to Pan Wang, but future generations of the Yao people would always piously worship and serve Pan Wang, blessing for flourishing population and wealth, and prosperity of all the future generations."① Through the use of this legend, the Yao established a kind of "contract" with Pan Wang. This contract or understanding became the foundation of various rituals and intangible cultural heritages across the entire Yao nationality; family names, worship practices and marriage ceremonies of the Yao were all developed on this foundation.

The Yao people's fulfillment of their promise to Pan Wang through a form of religious activity developed after they crossed the sea. Every three to five years a small-scale sacrifice was held, a great sacrifice every ten years. People dressed in traditional costumes, sang songs of Pan Wang and danced the tambourine dance to broadcast the merits and virtues of both Pan Wang and their ancestors. By speaking the same language, dressing in the same costumes and worshiping common deities, people participating reinforced a clear "Yao ethnic identity of Yao" from this ceremony—a set of practices which, even as they emphasize identity, also bring the legends of ancestors closer to contemporary life, achieving cohesion within the ethnic group.②

The custom of "the bodhisattva goes across the neighborhoods" in Dabu village, Ma Chong Town, Dongguan City, provides the cultural underpinning for seven small ethnic groups (Zhang, Guo, Wang, Ning, Zhao, Cai, Peng), encouraging the elimination of differences and the achievement of harmonious coexistence. The seven groups take turns holding the bodhisattva parade on the eighteenth and nineteenth day of the first lunar month each year, in order to protect their region, encourage people to live in peace, driving out evil spirits while welcoming good things. These seven groups in Dabu village evolved from armies dispatched for military reclamation during the Ming dynasty, and are descendants of seven leaders with seven different family names. These military settlers opened up the wasteland in Dabu village, developed the ethnic groups represented by specific family names and, at the same time, achieved integration among these small ethnic groups through worship practices similar to "the bodhisattva goes across the neighborhoods," held annually to build common faith, including worship ceremony, song and dance, and parades. It is

---

① The river crossing legend is a myth that commonly existed in the Yao ethnic minorities over the country with different versions and similar content. The article here is based on records in Guo Shan Bang, folk literature of the Yao people, which is also called as Ping Huang Quan Die, Ping Wang Quan Die and Pan Wang Quan Die.

② 罗宗志、陈桂:《神话传说与族群认同——立足于盘瑶渡海神话的考察》,《贵州民族学院学报》2009 年第 6 期,第 43—46 页。

very common to observe similar examples in which the sharing of identical or similar folk-belief activity promotes harmonious coexistence between different ethnic groups. ①

Like the custom of "the bodhisattva goes across the neighborhoods" in Dabu village, "god-parade" activities are held on a selected day before the lantern festival each year in multiple villages of Qianshan Town, Xu Wen County, Guangdong Province. On that day, parades from each village invoke their own god, gathering by prearrangement in front of a specific temple, and after a series of greeting rituals of drinking tea and offering sacrifices, all come together in a single large group, parading to all the villages to drive out evil spirits and welcome good things. Every family in the multiple villages conducting god-parade activities provides a lavish feast and invites relatives and friends from neighboring villages to dinner. There are communication between village gods and interaction between villagers during the entire ceremony; both play an important role in communication and integration among different ethnic groups. ②

Second, intangible cultural heritage grounded in the existence of human cultural diversity and requirements for sustainable development have created *ideological circumstances* encouraging mutual understanding and the elimination of differences between ethnic groups. Respect for and protection of differences defining each group is necessary for sustainable development; it is the fundamental requirement of ICH protection and is for this reason a shared aspiration of multiple ethnic groups. Seeking and achieving shared interests while preserving difference and harmonious coexistence requires this kind of fundamental understanding at every level.

The UNESCO's concept of ICH protection reflects the human desire for both development and respect for human rights and cultural rights. The concept emphasizes that all people from different countries, regions, ethnic groups or social classes have the right to possess and inherit their own cultural heritage, and that cultures of different ethnic groups are essentially equal. The UNESCO formulation provides strong support to cultural inheritance and development of countries, regions, and ethnic groups disadvantaged in economic and social development, while acting as a kind of on the instinctive cultural colonization of powerful nations. Such provisions and concepts at the level of international law and regulation helps promote cultural interaction and understanding between ethnic groups all over the world, and helps eliminate antagonism and conflict caused by cultural differences and misunderstandings.

Finally, intangible cultural heritage is a kind of *practical process* based on self-knowledge and evaluation-by-others. The self-knowledge of ethnic groups about intangible cultural heritage and

---

① The author went to investigate the custom of "the bodhisattva goes across the neighborhoods" in Dabu village, Ma Chong Town, Dongguan City during the spring festival, 2012 and have personally experienced its function in coordinated development of different ethnic groups.

② The author went to investigate the parade activities in Qianshan Town, Xu Wen County during the spring festival, 2000. Please refer to my article: Song Junhua,《广东省徐闻县前山镇元宵节游神仪式》,《民俗曲艺》(台北) 2001 年总第 134 辑。

"other-evaluation" are interconnected processes. For this reason, the very work of ICH protection is conductive to internal and external cultural communication among ethnic groups, promoting interaction advancing both self-knowledge and the evaluation of others in regard to the same object. This kind of interaction has important significance in advancing mutual understanding among different ethnic groups.

Although ICH protection advocated by the UNESCO and actively promoted by the contracting states is conducted in a top-down and outside-in manner, each part in the process of ICH protection, from application of masterpieces to development and implementation of protection measures, has to be established on the basis of combination of self-knowledge, or autonomy, and on outsider-evaluation, including external aid. Establishing this kind of internal and external combined protection mechanism not only reflects a legal understanding of the special and universal values of intangible cultural heritage, but also requires cooperation of different people and ethnic groups on general matters of IHC protection. This kind of understanding and cooperation is embedded in the policy and practice of ICH work, and is of great importance to bridging ethnic conflicts and establishing harmonious ethnic relations.

Of course, immigration and ethnic interaction brought on by urbanization and globalization have had an impact on both intangible cultural heritage and on maintenance of the unique character of the ethnic group to which it belongs. However, if urbanization and globalization can be reconsidered and reformulated using the perspective of ICH protection, these negative impacts will not only be slowed, but also be of great significance in the construction of a new and sustainable kind of ethnic relationship actually based on intangible cultural heritage and uniqueness of the ethnic group it belongs to.

5. Conclusion

ICH protection and bridging ethnic groups represent the two problems—two challenges—our modern society must face.

Difficulty in ICH protection is not only about the difficulty of protecting a kind of invisible, active and evanescent cultural tradition, nor is it only about overcoming the big differences between intergenerational concepts, demands and practices, but it also involves facing the problem of how to coordinate the conflicts between intangible cultural heritage and unique identity of the ethnic group to which it belongs, while advancing the sense of cultural universality required by urbanization, modernization and globalization.

Difficulties in bridging ethnic groups, on the one hand, lies in immigration and ethnic interaction brought about by urbanization and globalization, which continuously intensify the self-consciousness of ethnic groups, highlighting difference between the "self-group" and "other-group", advancing this kind of difference as a symbol of cohesion within the group and symbol of striving for external resources and rights. But on the other hand, difficulties lie in the development of the nation-state, in urbanization and globalization that requires that the self-interest of ethnic groups be put aside or eliminated in order to construct a new kind of ethnic relations that take account of both tradition and the interests of different, outside ethnic groups. These two mutually contradictory demands coexist within the ethnic group's interaction with the modern society, constituting problems that each ethnic group must face.

The use of experience in dealing with internal relationships within intangible cultural heritage, cultural equality and with modern concepts of social development advocated by ICH protection and management of the relationship between self-knowledge and outsider evaluation, autonomy and external aid in ICH protection within ethnic groups are each important factors in both ICH protection itself and the process of bridging ethnic groups. These ideas not only provide the basis for ethnic groups' harmonious coexistence at the conceptual and legal level, but also provide referential experience for practical, harmonious coexistence within ethnic groups and between different ethnic groups. Therefore, to understand intangible cultural heritage and ICH protection from the perspective of both ethnic groups and ethnic relations, and to understand ethnic groups and inter-ethnic relations from the perspective of ICH protection, is to engage the most important inspiration and contribution ICH study can offer two contemporary social challenges—ICH protection and the bridging of ethnic conflicts.

Working with Immigrant Communities: Best Ethnographic Practices

Debra Lattanzi Shutika*

Ethnography is a curious research practice. It offers the promise of first-hand knowledge of a community or group, yet the method for obtaining that knowledge is largely dependent on the individual researcher and the relationships that he/she will develop in the field. While ethnographic variation, the inability to effectively replicate an ethnographic collection, is oft-cited critique of ethnography (Massey, 2000), but it is also its strength. The ethnographic process unfolds as progressive relationships; it intimately documents the day-to-day lives of subjects, providing nuance that is impossible to collect with quantitative methodologies. Despite its limitations, ethnographic research is particularly useful approach to study immigrant communities.

My earliest work with Latinos began in 1991, long before I ever considered becoming a folklorist. At that time I was a registered nurse working at Columbia Hospital for Women in Washington DC, and noticed the increasing numbers of Latinas giving birth in our facility. I would sneak in to visit with them during coffee and lunch breaks, ostensibly to practice my Spanish, which I hadn't actually studied since I was a sophomore in high school. True, I would have liked to become a more proficient Spanish speaker, but in truth I was curious. Why did these families, the majority from El Salvador, come to Washington? How had they managed to figure out how to live in the US? And what connections did the have to their home community?

From the hospital I started to volunteer a wellness clinic in the nearby Adams Morgan neighborhood. Later, when I went to Philadelphia to study folklore at the University of Pennsylvania, I found myself volunteering as a nurse in a immigrant health clinic as a way to enter the community, gain trust and eventually begin an ethnographic project that would become my book, *Beyond the Borderlands: Migration and Belonging in the United States and Mexico* (2011). Since then I've worked with Latinos from Nicaragua, Guatemala, and Honduras in the distant

---

* Debra Lattanzi Shutika, Associate Professor at George Mason University.

suburbs of Northern Virginia, and more recently with Bolivians in Arlington County, Virginia.

The time that I spent working with immigrants as a non-academic allowed me to develop a working list of best practices that I use regularly in my ethnographic methods classes at George Mason University. What I outline below emerged in the exploration phase of my ethnographic work with immigrant communities, well before I was officially conducting research.

If I were to identify one consistent problem with ethnographic practice, it would be that most graduate programs lack a consistent structure to teach ethnographic methods. All programs offer methods courses, certainly, but rarely do these courses require students to complete a full-scale ethnographic project under faculty supervision. Graduate students will read ethnographic accounts, do small-scale ethnographic projects and will discuss fieldwork projects with their professors and peers. While offering students the basics of ethnography, these practices often fall short for students who will complete long-term ethnographic research. Most importantly, they will not learn how to manage the hundreds of pages of fieldnotes, digitally recorded interviews, photographs, video footage and ephemera that are the basis of an ethnographic collection.

Following these best practices, ethnographic researchers are more likely to collect data that is comprehensive and accurately represents the immigrant community under study.

Know the community: This is the one aspect of my research is distinct from other ethnographers is the attention I paid to the immigrants' receiving community. In most book-length accounts of Latino migration, researchers focus almost exclusively on the Latino population. When I say "know the community," I am specifically referencing the long-term residents—those people whose lives in the community pre-dates the immigrants' arrival. This is important because the local long-term residents are the people who are most likely to shape the lives and experiences of immigrants. Including them in a study of migration is essential to a nuanced understanding of the community you're documenting (Lattanzi Shutika, 2011).

When looking at the long-term community, you should identify stakeholders and their perceptions of their new neighbors. How do they feel about immigrants and the ways immigration are changing the community? Are they willing to help develop support systems for newcomers? Are they prepared to share the community? (How invested are long-term residents in their ideas of cultural heritage and does their community "story" allow for newcomers, adaptation and change?) These local variations are essential to understanding immigrant experiences: long-term residents often shape the daily experiences of the immigrant community, including neighbors, local business owners, and politicians.

Know the immigrant population: Once you understand the local context, your next step is to thoroughly examine what you know about the immigrant population. Starting with demographic data, assess the people who make up the immigrant population. Where are they from? Does the community consist of families or unattached workers? What are their occupations, and their reasons for migrating to this particular place (e. g. , a local industry or a robust economy)?

While most folklorists understand that "Latino" is a broad term that encompasses people from Mexico, Central and South America, it is important when working with a specific populations to acknowledge their distinct cultural heritage and their homeland. Most Bolivians prefer to be identified as Bolivian as opposed to "Latino," for instance.

Know the homeland (and community members' connection to it): The reasons why a group of people migrates are often complex and variable, and those reasons are usually evident on both sides of the border. Once you know where the immigrant population is from, it is important to consider the history of their homeland and what events might have precipitated their migration. In many cases, immigrants move for economic and educational opportunities, but not always to escape poverty. In other instances, migration is precipitated by political instability (Massey, et al. , 1987; Massey, 2008).

(Most immigrants maintain some connection to their birth community, and it is important to consider how significant theses connections important is it to maintain connections to the homeland, and what strategies do they employ to accomplish this?) Do immigrants return to visit the homeland for holidays and family events like weddings and baptisms? How is technology (cell phones, e-mail, Face Time, Skype) used to maintain connections with family and friends? (Smith, 2006).

Know the scholarly context: When working with immigrant communities one should never presume that you can do so without being intimately familiar with the extensive body of scholarly literature on migration. Although a folklorist might want to document the occupational folk culture of an immigrant community, it is important that the project is grounded in the literature of immigration and migration. Folk traditions do not exist in a vacuum, (and the socio-political context of immigrant traditions are not only "larger than local,") (Shuman, 1993) they are shaped by global economic processes, all of which have been studied in depth by sociologists, demographers, political scientists, among others.

I point this out not because knowing this context and applying it our particular approach to the study of migration greatly expands the pool of readers who will be interested in the work we do. As a profession, we have much to offer scholars who study migration, especially those who focus on quantitative analyses. While their work provides a broad picture of the immigrant experience, (it does so at the expense of the human story.) Situating our work as folklorists within this scholarly tradition deepens the ethnographic process and produces work that is useful and accessible to a larger community of scholars.

Know the community's cultural practices, but don't assume they all come from the homeland: Too often scholars often assume that immigrant groups come from the Robert Redfield's (1947) idea of a folk society, a small face-to-face community, or that immigrants will have special talents (folk crafts, folk music) that they bring with them from the homeland. In many cases, Latino immigrants come to the US from urban areas, as immigrants from rural areas often move into cities before making the journey to the US. Once in the US they may live for long periods of time in one part of the country before they settle permanently else where. These multiple migrations will influence cultural practices and foster the creation of new traditions.

The Bolivian community in Northern Virginia is an example of this. Bolivian immigrants to the US are more likely to be urban and well educated; many held professional positions before coming to the US. The Northern Virginia Bolivian population, the largest outside of La Paz, is known for its vibrant folk dancing tradition. But this iconic cultural practice is one that the majority of Bolivians in the US did not engage in when they lived in Bolivia. Instead, the dance community emerged in the 1970s as a means to preserve a sense of Bolivian identity in a new context.

Know their faith: The default assumption is that the majority of Latinos are Roman Catholic, and while many are, it is important to recognize that many protestant evangelical faiths are popular in Central and South America, as are a number of syncretic religious traditions, such as Santería and Candomblé.

Latino immigrants who are Roman Catholic may not have strong associations with the institutional church, but are very likely to have a strong connection to their local parish, particularly the patron saint of their village. Understanding the connection to their faith is important because it is one of the few cultural traditions that can be transported to the US. In many instances, the church community becomes the foundation of immigrant support networks (Lattanzi Shutika, 2011).

Know the relevant language (s): While it is true that most immigrants from Latin America speak Spanish, it is not always the case, particularly among indigenous groups. In those instances, indigenous immigrants will speak a native language and Spanish is often the second language. Similarly, immigrants from Brazil will speak Portuguese.

Know the law: While national immigration laws will influence large trends in immigration, the effects of federal laws on day-to-day life may be overshadowed by local and state ordinances. An undocumented immigrant, for instance, may be able to find employment, purchase a home and raise a family if the local community accepts immigrant families as part of the community.

Immigration laws vary from state to state and in some cases, will differ at the county or city level. Immigrants working in Manassas, Virginia, in 2007-2008 were singled out by a number of countywide ordinances that were designed to drive Latinos out. The results were amazingly effective: within a twelve-month period the immigrant population dropped significantly. Many of the Latino families resettled in nearby communities in Fairfax and Arlington Counties, jurisdictions that were more tolerant of immigrant residents. Latino families that stayed behind noted that living in Manassas was extremely stressful. Many reported feeling afraid to let their children play outside and simple day-to-day acts like driving children to school or going to the grocery store were cause for anxiety, as they could not be certain that local authorities would apprehend them (Cleaveland and Pierson, 2009; Singer, Wilson and DeRenzis, 2009).

Most immigrant communities are a mix of documented (i.e., legal) immigrants and the undocumented. In many cases, immigrant communities provide support and assistance to family and friends regardless of their documentation status. Local ordinances will determine how immigrants will create their communities and to what degree they will engage with others in their community.

Have a plan for organizing and archiving your collection: When most ethnographers think about their research plan, they consider human subjects approval, grant writing, and purchasing field equipment, all of which is important to the outcome of the project. But the long-term success of any ethnographic collection should include project planning, organizing the materials collected, and a submitting the materials to an archive so they will be available for future researchers. Remember, the field ethnographer is the first archivist.

In this regard there are multiple resources available to organize and archive even the most complex ethnographic collections. The American Folklife Center at the Library of Congress provides a number of free resources on project planning (http://www.loc.gov/folklife/edresources/ed-trainingdocuments.html). Each item collected should be documented in a spread sheet with appropriate metadata using the Dublin Core standards to identify metadata in the collection (http://dublincore.org/).

Although archiving ethnographic field materials is a common practice, many researchers see this as an end of career activity. In practice, I insist that my students consider submitting their research materials when they have completed their projects, theses or dissertations. Donating materials to a local archive effectively returns the materials to the immigrant community and to future researchers. At George Mason University, students archive their projects through the National Folklife Archives Initiative (http://folklorecollections.org/) or a local library archive in the communities where they conduct fieldwork.

Ethnographic research methods offer a comprehensive approach to the study of immigrant communities. By adopting a best practices approach, researchers are more likely to complete collections that accurate and thoroughly represent the immigrant communities. Researchers should draw on the many available resources to plan and implement their projects with the goal of donating their ethnographic materials to an archive at the end of the collection.

Works Cited

Cleaveland, Carol, and Leo Pierson. 2009. "Parking Lots and Police: Undocumented Latinos' Tactics for Finding Day Labor Jobs." Ethnography 10 (4) (December 1): 515–533. doi: 10.1177/1466138109346987.

Lattanzi Shutika, Debra. 2011. Beyond the Borderlands: Migration and Belonging in the United States and

Mexico. Berkeley: University of California Press.

Massey, D. S. 2000. "A Validation of the Ethnosurvey: The Case of Mexico-US Migration." International Migration Review 34 (3): 766 – 793.

Massey, Douglas S, Rafael Alarcon, Jorge Durand, and González Huberto. 1987. Return to Aztlan: The Social Process of International Migration from Western Mexico. Berkeley: University of California Press.

Redfield, Robert. 1947. "The Folk Society." American Journal of Sociology 52 (4) (January 1): 293 – 308.

Shuman, Amy. 1993. "Dismantling Local Culture." Western Folklore 52 (2/4) (April 1): 345 – 364. doi: 10. 2307/1500094.

Singer, Audrey, Jill H. Wilson, and Brooke DeRenzis. 2009. "Immigrants, Politics, and Local Response in Suburban Washington". Metropolitan Policy Program. Brookings Institution.

Smith, Robert C. 2006. Mexican New York: Transnational Lives of New Immigrants. Berkeley: University of California Press.

Considering the Concept, Principle, and Questions Related to the Productive Protection of Intangible Cultural Heritage

Xiao Fang[*]

The ephemeral and spiritual character of intangible cultural heritage distinguishes it from tangible cultural heritage such as buildings and monuments. ICH emphasizes subjective cognition, emotional experience, spiritual creation and representations of wisdom and knowledge. Therefore, to protect intangible cultural heritage is to protect the diverse cultural traditions that carry on human feeling, spirit and wisdom. In today's globalized world, we have many different choices and practices directed at safeguarding intangible cultural heritage, including such effective measures as the three-level system of Lists of Intangible Cultural Heritage, the delineation of cultural ecological preservation districts and the establishing an "Inheritor" system. For most intangible cultural heritage these measures are very important. However, when carried forward by forces outside governments, these measures are inevitably to some extent passive. Thus, it is worth considering how to activate cultural energy within intangible cultural heritage to insure that it continues and develops in good health by working within the supportive environment provided by governments. It is clear that advancing the concept of "productive protection" opens up a broad space for safeguarding intangible cultural heritage. In fact, productive protection holds special advantages as a beneficial practice for safeguarding ICH within the current social environment.

---

[*] Xiao Fang, Professor at Beijing Normal University.

1. The concept, scope, and the object of productive protection of intangible cultural heritage

Engagement with intangible cultural heritage constitutes a recognition of a spiritual heritage that possesses valuable knowledge applicable to life, along with the activities, objects and physical environments associated with ICH. According to UNESCO, intangible cultural heritage is manifest within the following five domains: oral traditions and expressions, including language as a vehicle of the ICH; performing arts; social practices, rituals and festive events; knowledge and practices concerning nature and the universe; and traditional craftsmanship. These five domains cover almost every aspect of intangible cultural heritage, an arena of human behavior so rich in content and complicated in form that we must adopt different methods of protection to match the characteristics of different ICH objects. One technique is "productive protection."

Productive protection refers to "transforming intangible cultural as well as its resources into cultural products as part of the process of protective practice by means of the production, circulation and sale of goods and services, while insisting on authenticity, integrity and inheritance at its core, giving priority to the effective transmission of intangible cultural techniques."[①] Emphasizing the protection of material production primarily defined by traditional techniques or skills, the definition of productive protection provided by the Department of Culture states that, "at present, this method of protection is primarily applied to intangible cultural heritage in the domains of traditional techniques, traditional arts and traditional medical procedure." In other words, most intangible cultural heritage cannot be protected in a productive way because the method is limited to such common domains as craft techniques, arts and medicine. This definition of productive protection in a narrow sense reveals the cautious attitude of this government department toward the safeguarding intangible cultural heritage.

However, as scholars, we can engage in wide discussions about policy, expressing our opinions about the protection of intangible cultural heritage with reference to other related domains. In my opinion, productive protection should be seen as the primary approach to safeguarding intangible cultural heritage—an approach that can be combined with existing rescue techniques. When dealing with the concept of productive protection, our understanding should expand the range of productive protection from a narrow sense of material-based craftsmanship into a broad perspective that encompasses the reproduction of all of culture.

It must be emphasized that when it comes to taking a broad view of productive protection in

---

① 《文化部关于加强非物质文化遗产生产性保护的指导意见》，文非遗发〔2012〕4号。

safeguarding such intangible cultural heritage as oral traditions, performing arts, social practices, festive events and rituals, instead of having these items participate as products in markets in a normal sense, our aim should be to bring these traditional cultural patterns back into everyday life through the mechanism of cultural reproduction.

Consider epics, stories, ballads and proverbs in oral tradition as examples. Today these are not only circulated within their primary environment but also via diverse new media. However, unlike oral tradition, transmission of this kind exhibits social influence greater, not smaller, than in the past. Traditions spread broadly via media will have greater impact if we reduce distortion and loss as much as is possible by paying sufficient attention to the cultural meaning of heritage items. As another example, traditional operas can also be productively safeguarded in a broad sense when we create performance environments that attract audiences while simultaneously informing the audience by conveying knowledge of opera's history and charm.

The concept of productive protection is also applicable to urban festival events. Through the historical study of urban traditions, appropriate scheduling, and the collaborative planning and cooperation of cultural, municipal and charitable sectors, urban festivals can be revived and held regularly. The festival process in turn provides opportunities for additional items of urban intangible cultural heritage such as performances, urban memory, urban industrial and commercial traditions, urban craftsmanship, and so on.

This active approach to productive protection provides access and allows us to actually experience and enjoy ICH, a process which, by establishing an intimate connection to intangible cultural heritage, awakens the consciousness of the whole society about the importance of safeguarding intangible cultural heritage. Because this process enhances the social influence of ICH, the vitality of traditional cultural in general is also advanced. This is the most effective way to carry on intangible cultural heritage in an active way, and it is also consistent with the stipulation of Article 37 in Chapter Four of *Law of The People's Republic of China on Intangible Cultural Heritage*, "the State encourages and supports the leveraging of the special advantages of intangible cultural heritage resources and the reasonable utilization of the representative items of intangible cultural heritage to develop cultural products and cultural services with local and ethnical features and market potential on the basis of effective protection of those items."

2. The Basic Principle of Safeguarding Intangible Cultural Heritage

Since the promulgation of *Law of The People's Republic of China on Intangible Cultural Heritage* on June 1st, 2011, safeguarding intangible cultural heritage has become the legal obligation of every citizen. The principle shaping this effort is clearly stated in Article 4 of Chapter One, that "when protecting intangible cultural heritage, focus shall be on its authenticity, integrity and inheritance and such protection shall be conducive to strengthening the recognition of the culture of Chinese nation, maintaining the unification of the country and the unity of the nation and promoting social harmony and sustainable development. " Authenticity, integrity and inheritance constitute the basic principle underlying the safeguarding intangible cultural heritage. Because productive protection has emerged as a new direction and a new technique in the safeguarding intangible cultural heritage in contemporary China, it is important that we insist on the maintenance of these three principles, especially authenticity.

As we have seen, as we assemble items that are suitable for material production or cultural events onto lists of objects to be protected, it is natural to raise the question of whether such activities might influence the authenticity of ICH. In many situations, both material production and the cultural production of intangible cultural heritage take place naturally in traditional society, what we call productive protection refers to restoration and reproduction generated artificially after the natural process of production became recognized as heritage. In this situation the Principle of Authenticity must be stressed. In my view, it is necessary to give emphasis to the primary role of authenticity in the process of safeguarding intangible cultural heritage. This requires that every product exhibit complete faithfulness to its cultural meaning, its core techniques, and that it conform to the essential character of the tradition.

However, culture evolves. Intangible cultural heritage responds to ever-changing times, undergoing natural change by adapting to the social environment and to the generational and creative differences that distinguish specific inheritors during their work in safeguarding heritage. For instance, in ICH involving folk craftsmanship it is important to inherit and advance traditional themes through completely authentic and traditional work. However, at the same time, since craft work involves more than simply replicating cultural relics or antiques, the ICH craft process can also produce art works combining new themes with traditional techniques, catering to the public's changing tastes and social needs. It is a two-pronged process; authenticity in craftsmanship should be maintained strictly, yet with an element of ease.

The situation is similar but more difficult when we insist on authenticity in carrying out group festival events as intangible cultural heritage. Unlike artwork, which maintains core techniques and comparatively-fixed forms that enable people to objectify intangible traditional characteristics through an object, intangible cultural heritage events require interaction among a group of people in an activity that inevitably generates emotion, spirits, longings and rewards. In such a setting, maintaining authenticity means attending to the event's basic form—the time, the venue, the manner of participation and, above all, to an understanding of the activity's cultural meaning. In productively protecting festive events or temple fairs, special attention should be paid to their core cultural significance, including their function in accommodating the pace of living and work to the spiritual needs of local citizens. Despite the often-diverse character of festival performances and ceremonies, the central, interior significance of the event must be maintained. Maintaining core cultural meaning is the key application of the principle of authenticity to the productive protection of intangible cultural heritage. It is important to keep in mind that the principle of authenticity is not limited to history, but adapts in accordance with the needs of society and public psychology, it is this flexible understanding of the principle of authenticity that may lead us to an essential scientific truth.

Integrity is another important principle in safeguard ingintangible cultural heritage. Intangible cultural heritage is not simply an organism onto itself, complete in form and meaning, but is closely connected to the larger world. It is difficult to retain the integrity of heritage in modern society, an environment in which enormous changes in the social environment make it especially difficult for people to carry out basic protection of heritage, especially the maintenance of environments that sustain the organism of the heritage. Therefore, when we consider the principle of integrity, we should bring a flexible attitude that can adjust to specific situations and objects. Generally speaking, integrity should be rigorously pursued for intangible cultural heritage history and objects, and maintained as much as possible when engaging the environment surrounding ICH, which must be considered in relation to the characteristics and situation of specific items. In particular, integrity must be honored in folk arts, handwork, the collection of medicine, the technical process of drug production and the cultural ideology behind it. In addition, integrity should be of special importance in oral traditions, performances, festive events in their scenes of presentation, major plot elements, procedures, types and patterns, auxiliary stage property, and so on. No arbitrary adaptation of major parts or key elements can be allowed. As for the productive protection of group activities, attention should be paid to the integrity of staging, addressing such key elements as traditional timing, space, organization, props and costumes, and execution of events. It should be noted that requirements affecting the external environment of festivals are just reference points to guide us in carrying out productive protection in today's social situation. Rather than stick to rules, we focus on the integrity of the intangible cultural heritage itself, while at the same time paying attention to the relationship between intangible cultural heritage and the current social environment. The process by which the former is integrated with the mechanics of modern society constitutes a new question regarding the role and nature of integrity in ICH work.

Inheritance is a fundamental principle in safeguarding intangible cultural heritage. Sincethe protection of intangible cultural heritage requires the transmission of culture by specific means, "inheritance" is a central attribute of intangible cultural heritage. Unlike tangible property inherited as concrete objects, ICH stresses the continuation of such intangible elements as spiritual meaning and traditional technique, a characteristic that places special demands on both recipients and their environment. So when implementing productive protection, we should be clear about the purpose of carrying on intangible cultural heritage: the purpose of such production is to provide access to heritage for the public, which in turn enriches of daily life. Although not our primary purpose, as a natural consequence of productive protection, sales, consumption and profits will accrue; such revenue generation can assist the self-maintenance and development of ICH.

Undoubtedly, we should always be mindful of the productive protection methods we employ to aid the inheritance of ICH, making certain that traditional resources are neither abused nor over-exploited in the name of productive protection. Take festivals as an example: attending to their cultural inheritance, we design events for the public and arrange timing and staging so both organizations and individuals are able to take part in the representation and the protection of ICH. Through this approach, a social effect is embedded within the form and meaning of the festival, making the active inheritance of intangible cultural heritage "real" in social life. In contrast, activities produced for public consumption with only commercial benefits as the goal stand in opposition to the essential purpose of intangible cultural heritage protection. No matter how successful such commercial operations are, no matter how great their social impact, they fail to nurture cultural inheritance.

3. Some Noteworthy Questions in the Protection of Intangible Cultural Heritage

As a new approach to safeguarding cultural heritage, productive protection is different from traditional protection in that it shifts passive preservation and protection into active production. Once such a process is underway, predictable problems will arise if we are determined to insure that heritage put into production will retain its cultural properties. Discretion and meticulous care are required if we are to avoid turning productive protection into "productive damage." The following questions are noteworthy:

First, productive protection only works with certain objects, and is not applicable to all kinds of ICH.

We should decide which intangible cultural heritage should be made available for productive protection according to specific characteristics. According to the Ministry of Culture, such protection is limited to traditional craftsmanship, traditional arts and traditional medical practice. This narrow restriction has clear application to the initial efforts at productive protection. Such limits have a positive role, discouraging the over-exploitation of heritage resources by swarms of people, but it is too limiting. But we can also carrying out productive protection of heritage in group cultural domains like festivals and temple fairs. While cultural reproduction of festive events and material reproduction of heritage techniques are different in form, both can be approached with the goal of cultural protection and cultural inheritance.

Second, different strategies of productive protection for intangible cultural heritage should be adopted, tailored to specific objects.

Distinct approaches and practices are suitable for productive protection activities, in contrast to those that address the productive protection of cultures. The former is mainly about the inheritance of techniques and the sale of material products, while the latter focuses on group activities, social participation, and recognition. Each category must have its own criteria for evaluation and/or assessing the applicability of a productive protection approach to a specific object, tradition, or event.

Third, productive protection should be both appropriate and restrained.

Unlike the production of ordinary products, economic benefit is not the main priority in the production of intangible cultural heritage. Instead, the purpose of production is to facilitate active inheritance transmission while enriching the social life of the public. Naturally, if it exists, a significant market can be properly engaged on behalf of specific ICH products, which can generate considerable profit. Since the market for most intangible cultural heritage is confined to specific subgroups of consumers, productive protection must take into consideration realistic possibilities for sales and heritage circulation. During the process of product development and sales, the original material, techniques and style should be diligently retained. Some innovation is permitted, but it should be modest and in no way harm the basic character of heritage. For example, the staging of *the Peony Pavilion*, a Kunju Opera, has had its pace moderately accelerated, the color of costumes slightly adjusted, and lighting and stage effects enhanced in conformance with traditional singing, but plots and the appearance of actors remained unchanged. Limited innovation of this kind is appropriate.

In contrast, it would in fact be destructive production to just carelessly increase the popularity of intangible cultural heritage items and activities that have been considered worth of productive protection without taking true protective measures, or taking the step of arbitrarily changing its technical procedures. To insure appropriate engagement between ICH and protective measures, productive protection of intangible cultural heritage should be included within the range of ICH work supervised by a department of government.

Productive protection for intangible cultural heritage is so new that we have little practical experience and only limited theoretical discussion on the subject; many practical problems are awaiting solutions. This essay represents a humble attempt to lay the groundwork for future research and intellectual exploration as we begin an exciting new phase in China's engagement with traditional heritage.

(The essay has been published in the 1st edition, 2013 of *Study and Research*)

Postscript

To spur the academic communication of intangible cultural heritage studies between China and the US, China Folklore Society, American Folklore Society, the Institute of Chinese Intangible Cultural Heritage at Sun Yat-sen University, the Curb Center for Art, Enterprise & Public Policy at Vanderbilt University, the National Research Center of Cultural Industries at Central China Normal University, Smithsonian Institution mutually hold four China-US forums of intangible cultural heritage (hereinafter referred to as ICH) and, greatly promote the discourse and collaboration among researches of theICH safeguarding on policies, cases, productive safeguarding, fieldwork, archiving and so on.

This book is one achievement of the above-mentioned discourse and collaboration between Chinese and American scholars and experts.

This book is co-edited by Director and Professor Song Junhua from the Institute of Chinese Intangible Cultural Heritage at Sun Yat-sen University, the former president of American Folklore Society Bill Ivey, Director and Professor Huang Yonglin from the National Research Center of Cultural Industries at Central China Normal University and, is proofread by Tim Lloyd, the Executive Director of American Folklore Society, by He Yan and Huang Hao, the PHD students of Sun Yat-sen University. The translation is mutually done by Chen Xi from the institute and the graduate students from the School of Foreign Languages at Sun Yat-sen University. Because of various condition limits, the translation may hardly achieve a perfect result of "Faithfulness, Expressiveness and Elegance" and asks for the authors and the readers' understanding.